Salt of the Earth,

Conscience of the Court

Salt of the Earth, Conscience of the Court

The Story of Justice Wiley Rutledge

John M. Ferren

The University of North Carolina Press

Chapel Hill and London

Publication of this book was supported in part
by a generous grant from the Supreme Court Historical Society.

Designed by Charles Ellertson
Set in Ruzicka with Melior display
by Tseng Information Systems, Inc.
Manufactured in the United States of America

Portions of the introduction and Chapter 19 have been published as
"General Yamashita and Justice Rutledge," 28 *J. Sup. Ct. Hist.* 54 (2003).
Portions of Chapter 15 appeared as "Military Curfew, Race-Based
Internment, and Mr. Justice Rutledge," 28 *J. Sup. Ct. Hist.* 252 (2003).

⊗ The paper in this book meets the guidelines
for permanence and durability of the Committee
on Production Guidelines for Book Longevity of the
Council on Library Resources.

Library of Congress Cataloging-in-Publication Data
Ferren, John M.
Salt of the earth, conscience of the court: the story of Justice Wiley Rutledge /
John M. Ferren.
p. cm.
Includes bibliographical references and index.
ISBN 0-8078-2866-1 (cloth: alk. paper)
1. Rutledge, Wiley, 1894–1949. 2. Judges—United States—Biography. 3. United
States. Supreme Court—Biography. I. Rutledge, Wiley, 1894–1949. II. Title.
KF8745.R87F47 2004
347.73'2634—dc22   2003027752

08 07 06 05 04   5 4 3 2 1

Frontispiece: Justice Wiley Rutledge upon joining the Supreme Court. (Photograph by
Harris and Ewing; Collection of the Supreme Court of the United States, 1943.8.2)

For Linda,
   who makes all the difference

Ye are the salt of the earth. . . .
—Matthew 5:13 (King James)

In reflecting over a lifetime in the law, a former clerk
of Justice Douglas remarked not long ago: "If I were a
defendant being tried by a single judge, I'd rather have
Justice Rutledge than any judge I have known."
—Lucile Lomen, March 28, 1996

Wiley Rutledge truly liked people. Regardless of station.
And that led to everything.

Contents

Illustrations

Salt of the Earth,
Conscience of the Court

Yamashita

At 2:30 in the morning on February 23, 1946, in a small country village south of Manila in the Philippines, Lieutenant General Tomoyuki Yamashita of Japan was told, "It's time." Not three weeks after the U.S. Supreme Court had denied his request for review—with Justices Wiley Rutledge and Frank Murphy dissenting—General Yamashita, the "Tiger of Malaya," was hanged.[1]

Yamashita had earned his title by taking Singapore from the British in January 1942 with but 30,000 men to Britain's 100,000. Yamashita, clearly, was a brilliant strategist. But no "tiger." Although he was "a heavily muscled bear of a man," he was a calm soul, a lover of nature. He outspokenly had opposed war with the United States and Great Britain, and thus the Tojo faction rising in Japan had despised him. The Japanese high command had needed Yamashita in Malaya, but straightaway thereafter Hideki Tojo assigned him to an outpost in Manchukuo for the next two and a half years. When Saipan fell in July 1944, and Tojo and his cabinet resigned, the successors in power recalled Yamashita to defend the Philippines—a hopeless proposition, he discovered. Also named the Philippines' military governor, Yamashita took control of Japan's 14th Area Army on October 9, 1944, when American invasion was imminent.[2]

Less than two weeks later, General MacArthur landed on Leyte Island midway along the Philippine archipelago while the Pacific Fleet was crippling the Japanese navy in Leyte Gulf. General Yamashita devised a plan to defend the Japanese occupation on the large northern island of Luzon in the mountains around Manila. He then had but 100,000 troops, the Americans more than 400,000. On January 9, 1945, MacArthur reached Luzon and advanced toward Manila. Yamashita had not declared Manila an "open city," outside the battle zone, because he depended on supplies stashed there. He left a skeleton force in Manila to inhibit the American advance while his main forces withdrew. Although Yamashita had gained effective control over the air force and ordered it out of the capital city, he had not been able to assume authority over the navy, which left a force of 20,000 in Manila after informing Yamashita—now in mountain headquarters—that 4,000 would remain. Contrary to Yamashita's orders, moreover, his subordinates, in discussions with the Japanese naval commander, Rear Admiral Sanji Iwabuchi, did not negotiate a timely naval retreat from Manila. Although on paper Iwabuchi was under Yamashita, he complied instead with Vice-Admiral Desuchi Okuchi's order to remain in Manila, destroy all naval facilities, and "fight MacArthur 'to the death.'" As a result, MacArthur—arriving on February 3—trapped the imperial navy.[3]

In his headquarters 125 miles north of Manila, Yamashita had not been able to learn how rapidly the Americans were advancing, but by mid-February he realized the situation and, for the second time, ordered the Japanese navy out of Manila. It was too late. By March 3, Japan's naval and residual army forces there, including Admiral Iwabuchi, were dead. In holding out as long as they could before the Americans wiped them out, however, Iwabuchi's navy—filled with liquor and ordered to take enemy lives—had spread out as a drunken mob to rape, torture, shoot, and burn. "Young girls and old women were raped and then beheaded; men's bodies were hung in the air and mutilated; babies' eyeballs were ripped out and smeared across walls; patients were tied down to their beds and then the hospital burned to the ground"—until MacArthur's forces, fighting Japanese sailors hand to hand, ended the atrocities.[4]

To this day it is unknown whether Yamashita at the time had any idea of the carnage. He had divided his forces into three groups: one under his direct command in the mountains well north of Manila, another under Lieutenant General Shizuo Yokoyama to the east, and the third under Major General Rikichi Tsukada to the west. Yamashita's communications within his own group, as well as with the other two, ranged from limited to impossible. General Yokayama's troops, in the meantime, were harassed by Filipino guerillas making way for MacArthur's advancing forces, and, in a fateful decision, Yokoyama left guerilla control—without issuing guidelines—to his field commanders. As a result, one of his colonels, Masatoshi Fujishige, leading his "Fuji Force," deemed as enemy guerillas all civilians in Fuji's way, including women. "[K]ill all of them," Fujishige ordered. By the time the Americans liberated the area east of Manila, the Fuji Force had massacred 25,000 of the estimated 30,000 to 40,000 civilians slain by the retreating Japanese in Manila and southern Luzon. Isolated from both Yokoyama's and Tsukada's forces, General Yamashita retreated with his own troops northward, resisting American attacks until September 3, 1945, when he surrendered all Japan's forces remaining on Luzon.[5]

General Tomoyuki Yamashita surrendering to Allied forces, September 3, 1945.
(U.S. Army photograph; National Archives, III-SC-662462)

ON AUGUST 8, 1945, when the Allies signed a war crimes agreement in
London, it covered only atrocities in Europe; at the time not even our own
War Department was prepared to offer a policy for the Pacific. By the end
of August, however, the department forwarded to General MacArthur a list
of suspected war criminals and put the burden on him not only to round
them up and to identify and capture others but also to initiate a plan for
bringing them all to trial. Eventually, the secretary of war and the attorney
general, as well as the Joint Chiefs of Staff, concluded that military commanders had authority to try suspected war criminals before military com-

missions established under regulations that the commanders themselves had promulgated. This left matters up to MacArthur.[6]

Immediately after Japan's surrender on September 2, President Truman pressed MacArthur to get on with war crimes prosecutions. Those prosecuted, however, would not include major war politicians such as Hideki Tojo, who were to face charges of crimes against the peace, as well as against the law of war, before an international tribunal in Tokyo similar to the trial of the German high command in Nuremberg. As to crimes suitable for trial before a military commission, the U.S. War Crimes Office in the Department of the Judge Advocate General offered suggestions to MacArthur, whose deputy chief of staff, Major General R. J. Marshall, convened a conference in Manila on September 14 to work out the details. Marshall informed the gathering that the first trial would deal with charges, largely developed already, against General Yamashita, then in custody. Essentially, Marshall reported—acknowledging that there was no legal precedent for the charge—Yamashita would be tried criminally for "'negligence in allowing his subordinates to commit atrocities.'" MacArthur also decided to try forthwith Lieutenant General Masaharu Homma, whose campaign on Luzon, resulting in the Bataan "Death March," had forced MacArthur's flight from the Philippines in 1942. These first Japanese war crimes trials from the Second World War would deal—virtually without precedent—with a commander's responsibility for atrocities by his troops in violation of the law of war established by international conventions.[7]

After drafting charges against Yamashita, MacArthur's headquarters authorized Lieutenant General Wilhelm Styer, who commanded U.S. Army forces in the Western Pacific, to form a military commission based on procedures supplied by MacArthur. Next, after requesting a brief from Washington on the theory of command responsibility for use against Yamashita, headquarters referred to General Styer a team of five experienced prosecutors from the Judge Advocate's Department, later supplemented by a sixth, Filipino member. Defense lawyers were not named until just before arraignment, and none had much criminal or trial experience. The chief of the defense team was director of the army's prison in the Philippines, three members came from the staff that processed Philippine civilian claims against the U.S. Army, another was a tax lawyer, and the sixth was legal advisor to the military police.[8]

Three major generals and two brigadier generals composed the commission. None was a lawyer. Although each had had some combat experience against the Japanese, all came more recently from desk jobs. The commission called the arraignment proceeding to order in the ballroom of the Philippine High Commissioner's residence in Manila on October 8, 1945, and read the following charge:

[B]etween 9 October 1944 and 2 September 1945, at Manila and at other places in the Philippine Islands, while commander of armed forces of Japan at war with the United States of America and its allies, [General Tomoyuki Yamashita] unlawfully disregarded and failed to discharge his duty as commander to control the operations of the members of his command, permitting them to commit brutal atrocities and other high crimes against people of the United States and of its allies and dependencies, particularly the Philippines; and he, General Tomoyuki Yamashita, thereby violated the law of war.

There were, in addition, sixty-four individual charges specifying atrocities. Not one mentioned a direct link to Yamashita. He pleaded not guilty. Trial was scheduled for October 29.[9]

Three days before trial, the prosecution—which had reserved the right to file additional charges—served defense counsel with fifty-nine more. The defense moved for a continuance. It was denied. The senior defense counsel, Colonel Harry Clarke, then moved to dismiss all charges for lack of specificity:

The Bill of Particulars . . . sets forth no instance of neglect of duty by the Accused. Nor does it set forth any acts of commission or omission by the Accused as amounting to a "permitting" of the crimes in question.

The Accused is not charged with having done something or having failed to do something, but solely with having been something. For the gravamen of the charge is that the Accused was the commander of the Japanese forces, and by virtue of that fact alone, is guilty of every crime committed by every soldier assigned to his command.

American jurisprudence recognizes no such principle so far as its own military personnel is concerned. The Articles of War denounce and punish improper conduct by military personnel, but they do not hold a commanding officer [responsible] for the crimes committed by his subordinates. No one would even suggest that the Commanding General of an American occupation force becomes a criminal every time an American soldier violates the law. . . .

Clarke accordingly was suggesting—to use a more recent example to emphasize the point—that under the prosecution's theory (as a number of scholars later argued), Generals Westmoreland and Abrams could be found criminally responsible for the massacre directed by Lieutenant Calley at My Lai in South Vietnam. In response, the chief prosecutor, Major Robert Kerr, stressed that the atrocities were so "notorious" and "flagrant" and "enormous" that Yamashita must have known about them "if he were making any effort whatever" to meet his responsibilities, and that if he did not know "it was simply because he took affirmative action not to know."[10] Motion to dismiss denied.

The trial, open to the public, lasted for nineteen days of testimony by 286 witnesses—including not only eyewitness testimony but also hearsay upon hearsay, and even uncross-examined affidavits—spelling out the gruesome details. Only two witnesses offered testimony directly connecting General Yamashita to the brutality. The defense so discredited this testimony that Major Kerr did not mention it in his final argument to the commission. In his defense, General Yamashita testified, without contradiction during cross-examination, that he neither had directed nor even known about the atrocities committed in Manila, and that he had turned evacuation of the city entirely over to General Yokoyama while Yamashita had taken his own army north into the mountains. Yokoyama himself testified, confirming his superior's story. Even the butcher Fujishige was there to testify to the same effect, admitting his own personal responsibility.[11]

In closing argument, Major Kerr offered as legal precedent a recent Connecticut case in which the officers and employees of a circus company were found criminally responsible for the deaths of spectators in a circus tent that caught fire because of the defendants' failure to take the steps necessary to prevent it. The commission retired on December 5 to review the evidence, announcing that it would issue its findings in open court two days later. The reporters who had covered the entire trial—twelve American, British, and Australian journalists—took a secret poll and voted 12–0 for acquittal.[12]

On December 7, 1945, the fourth anniversary of the Japanese attack on Pearl Harbor, the commission reconvened. Its presiding officer, Major General Russell B. Reynolds, summarized the evidence presented by each side and announced the commission's findings (in part):

> The Prosecution presented evidence to show that the crimes were so extensive and widespread, both as to time and area, that they must have been wilfully permitted by the Accused or secretly ordered by the Accused. . . .

> It is absurd . . . to consider a commander a murderer or rapist because one of his soldiers commits a murder or a rape. Nonetheless, where murder and rape and vicious, revengeful actions are widespread offenses and there is not effective attempt by a commander to discover and control the criminal acts, such a commander may be held responsible, even criminally liable, for the lawless acts of his troops, depending upon their nature and the circumstances surrounding them. . . .

Courtroom during the military commission trial of General Tomoyuki Yamashita, seated with counsel at far left. (U.S. Army photograph; National Archives, III-SC-324846)

Then, after hearing a final claim of innocence from General Yamashita personally, General Reynolds announced the commission's ruling. Based on "a series of atrocities and other high crimes . . . committed by members of the Japanese armed forces under your command," and given the failure "to provide effective control of your troops as was required by the circumstances," the commission—"upon secret written ballot, two-thirds or more of the members concurring"—"finds you guilty as charged and sentences you to death by hanging."[13]

WHILE THE TRIAL was in progress, Yamashita's defense team filed an appeal with the Philippine Supreme Court challenging the commission's jurisdiction to try the general and contending that he had not violated the law of war. The appeal was denied—one justice dissenting—on November 27, whereupon defense counsel petitioned the U.S. Supreme Court for review. In the meantime, the day after the commission's decision, an angry MacArthur notified the War Department that he did not recognize any right of appeal to civilian courts and that he planned, accordingly, to go forward under his own announced procedures, which allowed for review of Yamashita's conviction only by General Styer, then by MacArthur himself. This notification telegraphed an intention to approve the commission's ruling and hang the general forthwith. The next day, an alarmed secretary of war, Robert Patterson, ordered MacArthur to stop immediately. On December 17, the U.S. Supreme Court stayed all further proceedings.[14]

After three contentious conferences on December 18, 19, and 20, a Supreme Court majority was tending toward agreement not to hear the case, and Chief Justice Harlan Fiske Stone prepared a draft denial of the petitions. Justice Wiley Rutledge—President Roosevelt's last appointee to the Court three years earlier—penned a dissent. The votes of only four justices are required to grant review, and after a final conference on December 20 four of the brethren—Hugo Black, Frank Murphy, Rutledge, and probably Harold Burton, who recently had replaced Justice Owen J. Roberts—voted to hear the case. (Because Justice Robert Jackson was chief prosecutor at the war crimes trial in Nuremberg, only four other justices were participating—Stone, Stanley Reed, Felix Frankfurter, and William O. Douglas.) Argument was scheduled for an extraordinary six hours on January 7 and 8, 1946. To a former law clerk, Victor Brudney, Rutledge later wrote: "[T]here was a three-day battle in conference over whether we would hear the thing at all. From then on the pressure was on full force."[15]

Pressed hard in the barrage of questions from the bench, the government acknowledged "the lack of direct proof of Yamashita's guilt" but argued that by failing to carry out his duty to control his troops, he was culpable on grounds of "criminal negligence" tantamount to "manslaughter"—under the circumstances a hanging offense. Four days later at the Saturday conference, Chief Justice Stone proposed to deny all writs sought, making way for Yamashita's execution upon approval by General MacArthur unless the sentence was commuted by President Truman. Strongly supported by Reed, Frankfurter, and Douglas—while opposed by Murphy and Rutledge—the Chief assigned the opinion to himself, presumably in the belief that he could attract either Black or Burton, if not both. Stone soon circulated a draft, on January 22, expressing a desire for the Court's opinion to come down less than a week later, on January 28—which placed unusual pressure on the two colleagues who had announced their intentions to dissent.[16]

It was no small matter to dissent from anticipated majority approval of the war crimes conviction of the Japanese general found responsible for the civilian massacre in the Philippines at the end of World War II. Unwavering principle had to be at work. A good deal is known about one of the two dissenters, Justice Frank Murphy, the Irish-American politician from Michigan—eventually attorney general and then Supreme Court justice—

who became the subject of two comprehensive biographies.[17] Much less is known about the other justice, Wiley Rutledge. Who was he? What was his judicial philosophy, and where did it come from? Why did FDR choose Rutledge for the high Court? And what, in addition to a dissent in *Yamashita*, did he contribute there?

PART ONE

Preparation, 1894–1926

ONE

Kentucky and Tennessee

Cloverport, Kentucky, southwest of Louisville on the Ohio River, was the birthplace of a Supreme Court justice, Wiley Blount Rutledge Jr., who never became more pretentious than the community of 1,600 he called his first home. When he was born on July 20, 1894, the town was a lively place. It served as the shipping hub for a surrounding farm population; as the center of a coal region named the "finest in the world" at the Columbian Centennial in Chicago; and as the docking point for Ohio River showboats—the *Cotton Blossom* and *Emerson's Grand Floating Palace*—featuring "Uncle Tom's Cabin" and "Ten Nights in a Bar Room."[1]

Actually, Mary Lou Wigginton Rutledge gave birth to her first child at a cottage outside Cloverport, in a resort area called Tar Springs, because the parsonage of the Cloverport church her husband was serving had burned.[2] The senior Rutledge, a Southern Baptist minister, came from a Scotch-Irish farming family which had lived for generations in the Sequatchie Valley of eastern Tennessee near Chattanooga[3] (and was not traceable to South Carolina's John Rutledge, a signer of the Constitution and an original justice of the U.S. Supreme Court).[4] Commonly called "Brother Rutledge," Wiley Blount Rutledge Sr.—the Blount came from an admired Tennessee governor of that name—had come to Cloverport with the "bride he had freshly married in Mt. Washington," the small town of his first pastorate, near Louisville.[5]

Depression hit the nation a year before Wiley Jr. was born, and living was modest for a minister's family in any event. So parishioners would help the Rutledges through annual "donation parties" providing coal, food, dry goods, kitchenware, and—for "Baby Rutledge" one year—"a nice suit of warm clothes" and "a pretty little red chair." In 1897 a daughter, Margaret, was born to the Rutledges after they had lost an infant son. Three years later, the family decided to leave Cloverport. The young mother had

*Mary Lou and the Reverend Wiley Blount Rutledge Sr. with Margaret and
Wiley Jr. (Courtesy of the Rutledge family)*

incipient tuberculosis, so her husband accepted a pastorate in the "better
climate" of Asheville, North Carolina. There, Wiley Jr., now six, continued
the public schooling he had begun in Cloverport.[6]

On August 3, 1903, two weeks after Wiley Jr.'s ninth birthday, Mary Lou
Rutledge died, just thirty-three years old. Not much is recorded about her.
We know that she studied with her future husband during his last year at

Southern Baptist Theological Seminary in Louisville, that she taught Sunday school in Cloverport, and that after her death friends and family spoke to the young boy of his "angel mother," a "lovely Christian woman," a "favorite" among them.[7] The only detailed recollection that her son mentioned in a lifetime of correspondence was in reference to "the saloon" that his "mother used to picket in WCTU campaigns" in Cloverport.[8] But Wiley grew to manhood with a profound awareness of his mother's love during the years she nurtured him. To his wife, Annabel, soon after they were married, Wiley wrote with a curious mixture of tenses: "I want us to know that our love is true, just as I know my mother's love is true without having to have her tell me about it and keep me confident, because of what she says — it's because of what she is and was, what she did and does that I know she loves me, and even if she should never speak to me again, I would *know* she loves me and be glad."[9]

Immediately upon the death of Mrs. Rutledge, her mother, Georgia Lovell Wigginton, came to the reverend's home in North Carolina to care for Wiley and Margaret, although soon she took them back with her to Mt. Washington.[10] Their uncle Ernest recalled that when the young Rutledge family had lived in Cloverport, "Grandma Wigginton" used to drive there from Mt. Washington "in a horse-drawn buggy to see her grandchildren" — more than eighty miles over difficult terrain. Ernest Wigginton also confirmed that their grandmother had "stuck with them" in her own home or theirs "to the day of her death in 1911."[11] From her actions and a surviving photograph, we can be sure that Grandma Wigginton was a strong woman in physique, character, and spirit. Her grandson remembered her as "full of vigor and health," and a boyhood friend of Wiley's recalled her "wit and humor."[12] Most importantly, as we observe the boy's developing warmth and emotional security, it seems certain that Grandma Wigginton embraced her young grandson with deep love and affection.

The Wigintons are traceable to a Welshman who arrived in Virginia in the mid-1650s. Generations later, Wiley Jr.'s great-grandfather migrated from Virginia to Kentucky, where he acquired land and slaves. But the family's substantial wealth eventually dissipated because of property divisions required by inheritance. On her mother's side, Georgia Wigginton was a Lovell, a family of whom little is known beyond their appearance in Virginia in the mid-1700s, moving later to Kentucky.[13] Grandma had two sisters and three brothers, and in later years Wiley would mention with great fondness his two Lovell great-aunts. "I always liked Aunt Mary next to Grandma," Wiley once wrote to Annabel, and in the same letter he indicated obvious affection for his other "great-aunt 'Sal.'" Wiley also expressed affection for "poor old Uncle Jim," his great-uncle — the unex-

Grandma Wigginton and grandson Wiley Jr. (Courtesy of the Rutledge family)

plained "black sheep" of the Lovell family—with whom he used to share a room at Mt. Washington. Of his mother's immediate family, Wiley was fond of her brother, Uncle Ernest, as well as her other brother, Uncle "Lud," who gave Wiley the first money he ever earned, acting as a conductor on the wagon full of children that his uncle drove to the county fair. But he felt an especially deep love for his mother's only sister, Cora—to Wiley, always just plain "Auntie"—who had been "almost a mother" to him, he once wrote.[14]

Grandma Wigginton, Aunt Mary, Aunt Sal, and "Auntie": not a complete substitute for the loss of a boy's loving mother at the age of nine. But probably as close as it comes.

The future justice lived with his grandmother from the fall of 1903 to the summer of 1905 at Mt. Washington, where he attended "a one-room private school." Wiley also remembered happily the several weeks that he, Margaret, and his grandmother lived during the summer of 1904 with his Uncle Ernest and Aunt Bess in Waterford, Kentucky, where he spent most of his time, at the age of ten, "listening to the men talking politics" before the election won by Theodore Roosevelt. "As I recall it," he once wrote, "most of them were good Democrats, standing up for [Alton B.] Parker . . . , and naturally I joined in with them."[15]

It is not clear how often young Wiley and his sister saw their father during the first two years after their mother died. The Reverend Rutledge did not—probably could not—follow his children back to Kentucky. He apparently left Asheville for a brief pastorate in Cleveland, Tennessee, northeast of Chattanooga, a hearty distance from Mt. Washington even by train. The reverend was often described as a circuit-riding preacher, and he apparently rode more during the two years after his wife died than before or after. But there can be little, if any, doubt that Wiley Rutledge "tramped around a lot" with his father during the summer of 1904, with his grandmother along to help care for the boy and his sister.[16]

The Reverend Rutledge was a loving father, with whom his son developed a close relationship. Some have said that the reverend came to treat the boy "more like a younger brother," although on the way to such parity young Wiley literally would be taken to the woodshed when his father saw the need for a switching. The senior Rutledge taught family and parishioners alike a religion that reflected literal acceptance of the Christian Bible and an abhorrence of Roman Catholicism. A strong Democrat, he was once quoted as saying, nonetheless, that "he would vote for the blackest man in Africa before voting for Al Smith."[17] Other than this comment, we have no indication of the father's attitudes on race. We do know that the neighborhoods where the boy grew up, as well as the church congregations his father served, were racially segregated, as were other social relations. We also know that as a child, Wiley once befriended "a little Negro boy," who, according to southern custom, "was supposed to do things for him," act as a servant of sorts. According to Wiley's daughter Mary Lou, "they were very good friends," but the social distinction was intrinsic to the relationship and reinforced in Wiley a perception of racial hierarchy that in due course required undoing.[18]

As a minister, Wiley's father was known for his long sermons and his compassion—and for his church's steady attendance. Reportedly, he wrote out his sermons, never repeating one; but in going on and on "he'd come close to trying the patience of even the most devout worshipers." He conscientiously visited the members of his flock and received the affection and respect of those in his spiritual care. Fondly, his parishioners recalled his "kindness" and "wise counsel." One in particular remembered the pastor as "a broad minded lovable character"; another observed that the senior Rutledge "was one preacher who did not know which side of the railroad track a member lived on." The reverend loved "a good conversation"; he enjoyed "stopping to talk with people." Indeed, he "liked," even "loved," people generally. Those acquainted with him also recognized "a good sense of humor." And, as one friend recalled, Brother Rutledge loved a good "coon hunt."[19]

In 1905 the Reverend Rutledge accepted a pastorate in Pikeville, Tennessee—a farming community of fewer than 500 souls near his birthplace in Sequatchie Valley—where almost all the residents were native-born, white Americans, and where Protestant community "singings" and church revivals "were the greatest social events of the year." Living near his own father and relatives, the reverend helped "with the farming and logging when he had spare time," and his son Wiley "enjoyed the family there" while earning top grades at the Pikeville Training School (92s to 99s, with straight 100s in "Deportment"). These were, Wiley once recalled, his "Mark Twain years"— years of the "old swimming hole." And fights. "About the worst fight I ever had in my life," he later wrote, "was with Tom Swafford," whose father had "ambushed and killed" another boy's father in a feud. "Tom was a bully and before I had known him very long we had tied into each other," Rutledge recalled, but the fight ended in a draw followed by "mutual respect." Wiley, it is clear, was no sissy. Beyond that, he had the knack for good peer relations in these early years, even with boys, he once recalled, "who were older than" he. Pikeville also gave Wiley a foretaste of his future. "[A]s I look back," he once revealed, "I got my first interest in the law . . . by attending trials at the Bledsoe County courthouse."[20]

In 1908 Wiley's father took another pastorate, in Maryville, Tennessee, population 2,400, a community twelve miles south of Knoxville at the gateway of the Great Smoky Mountains. Like Pikeville, Maryville was surrounded by farms in a county where almost all the residents were native white Americans. Because of Maryville's small Presbyterian preparatory school and college—together called Maryville College—the town offered considerably more educational and cultural opportunity than Pikeville. The boy thus moved to a more sophisticated community that he called home for five years, a period of powerful influences on his life. Wiley's interest in a legal career received "added impetus at Maryville." He recalled, in particular, "the trial of John Mitchell for the murder of his father-in-law. . . . We all wondered whether John really cut in self-defense, because he was much taller, younger and stronger than the old man and was sober when he did the deed. Nevertheless, Mose Gambell and one or two associates success- fully defended Mitchell, and I think I shall never again hear oratory like that which Gambell used in his defense before the jury."[21]

Also during his Maryville years, Wiley's fascination with politics received major reinforcement, especially in the summer of 1910 when he was six- teen. His father, "always very much interested in political affairs," had often brought him along to hear noted political, religious, and other speakers. When the reverend learned that William Jennings Bryan was coming to Knoxville, he took his son over to hear the Great Commoner. Wiley was particularly excited, because when Bryan had run for president two years earlier, the family "had been his enthusiastic supporters" but had not been able to hear him in person. Wiley listened spellbound with "some five or six thousand people . . . for more than two hours." When Bryan then waited to shake hands with the hundreds who filed by, Rutledge and his father stood in line. "Just to touch his hand was a thrill for me," Rutledge later reminisced. So he stood in line again and shook hands with Bryan a second time.[22]

In the fall of 1910, Wiley Rutledge began his college career at Mary- ville, a coeducational school with a student body of 190 or so.[23] Founded in 1819 as the Southern and Western Theological Seminary and renamed Maryville College in 1842, the college was "New School Presbyterian." That is to say, it adhered to "Hopkinsianism," a doctrine named after the New England theologian Dr. Samuel Hopkins, who regarded "self-love" as sinful and preached "disinterested benevolence" that focused on helping others. As a New School institution, moreover, Maryville welcomed women, as well as a few African Americans and Cherokee and Choctaw Indians, as early as the 1820s. Maryville closed during the Civil War but reopened as a liberal arts college in 1866. Soon women were on the faculty, as well as in class, and by the late 1880s, largely as a result of Christian missionary graduates, Maryville began to welcome foreign students from the world around. In the meantime, a group on the board of directors committed to educating young African Americans prevailed against those who opposed it, and by the 1880s African American graduates of Maryville were working, teach- ing, and preaching in eight states. Others followed until 1901, when the Tennessee legislature barred racial integration of private, as well as public, institutions. Wiley Rutledge thus entered a racially segregated Maryville College, but he could not have been entirely oblivious to its history of racial tolerance, if not equality.[24]

Wiley Rutledge at Maryville College. (Courtesy of the Rutledge family)

No thought had been given about universities for Wiley outside Tennes-see; the educational universe simply did not extend further. Consideration had been given to the state university at Knoxville, but Wiley feared its size. There would be greater comfort at home near his father and Grandma Wigginton. And, it appears, Maryville gave a tuition break to preachers' children.[25]

Wiley flourished at Maryville and made lifelong friends there. He had an outstanding academic record, with most grades in the 90s or high 80s. He majored in Latin and Greek while taking courses in mathematics, English, philosophy, and the sciences (which brought his lowest grades). Among his activities were the Law Club and the Political Science Club, and as a sopho-more he played center on the football team, once making a legendary mid-field flying tackle. His most significant extracurricular activity at Maryville, however, was public speaking—debate and oratory.[26] In the spring of 1912, Wiley took the negative on the proposition that Tennessee should amend

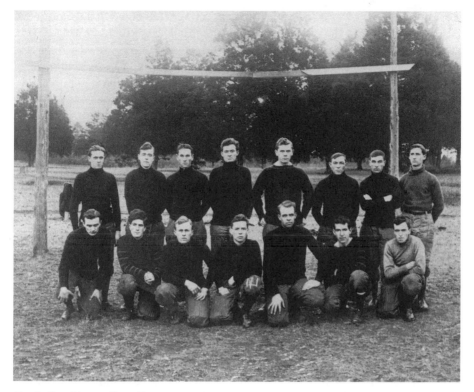

Football at Maryville College, 1911. Wiley Rutledge Jr. is front row center.
(Courtesy of Maryville College)

its Constitution "to provide for an Initiative and Referendum," as in Oregon.[27] The following fall, he was the windup speaker supporting Woodrow Wilson in a debate with backers of Theodore Roosevelt in the presidential election (Taft was not represented).[28] And in early 1913, he affirmed the proposition "that the United States should adopt a form of responsible cabinet government modeled on the English system."[29] Wiley also offered an oration at the commencement exercises for a local high school, attacking the Payne-Aldrich Tariff (1909) with an economic analysis showing why the protective tariff was the principal cause of "our present-day trusts and monopolies."[30] From the notes and texts of these presentations, it is apparent that young Rutledge offered well-researched, cogent, and clearly expressed arguments.

The political debate revealed Wiley's fundamental reason for rejecting Roosevelt progressivism: its virtual deification of majorities. He blasted "the extremely radical wing of the Republican party which holds that the 'voice of the people is the voice of God,' that a majority cannot be mistaken, that would take away from the minority and the individual those God-given and, let us pray, God-protected rights and privileges, which are guaranteed to them under the provisions of our present constitution, and which are the inalienable rights of every citizen of any well-governed nation." Then, after a story about an "old darky preacher" (which he told extemporaneously, leaving no notes), Wiley summed up: "And so the third great party seeking power, is the old party of Jefferson, still steadfast in those fundamental principles of justice and right upon which the government was founded," without promoting "such radical and socialistic theories as the recall of judges and of judicial decision."[31]

An earlier debate is especially interesting for what it reveals about Rutledge's social outlook in these early years. In the spring of 1910, he was winding up high school in the preparatory department at Maryville College, but even then he was a member of the Athenian society, participating in a debate with its Maryville rival, Alpha Sigma, on an emotional topic: "Resolved, that foreign immigration is advantageous to the South." He was the second speaker for the negative. It is not known whether the teams negotiated who would support the resolution, and who would oppose it; or whether the sides were assigned before the topic itself was selected; or in any event whether any particular speaker agreed with the proposition he advocated. But whatever Wiley's personal position was on the issue, he did not appear uncomfortable with a shrill, xenophobic approach emphasizing the racial inferiority and criminal propensities of "south" European immigrants.[32]

Wiley's debate partner, the first speaker for the negative, explained why foreign immigration was financially and morally disadvantageous; Wiley then elaborated on why politically and socially it was a disaster. As to politics, he claimed—citing Milwaukee—that "foreigners are the ones who constitute the Socialist party in this country"; that they are unfit for citizenship because of their "poverty, illiteracy, and criminality" (citing illiteracy statistics for particular immigrant groups and for immigrants overall); that "they furnish a fertile field for bossism," willing to sell their votes; and that they disproportionately support anarchy, urging "their comrades to use explosives." Wiley exclaimed: "If anarchy had done nothing else for America than to kill William McKinley, the honored friend of the South, that alone would justify us in shutting our gates to aliens forever. Tell me the death of that great and good man was of advantage to the South! No! And now I come to my second point in the debate."[33]

Socially, Rutledge argued, the "60 different nationalities" in the United States "cannot be molded into one race without lowering the standard of society"—citing, for example, "the South Italian," who has intermingled his blood with that of the Arabian, the Saracen and many races of other portions of Asia and Northern Africa, until they are not the same race as the North Italian, who has kept his Roman blood pure and untainted from the gore of foreign peoples. . . .

Honorable judges, . . . [p]ut your children on the bench beside the children of the dirty Italian, who my colleague has shown you, are of the most immoral character. . . . Will you allow your children and even yourselves to be brought into contact with these undesirables, with these slum dwellers and these plotting anarchists? No! [34]

Furthermore, Rutledge contended, immigration to the South would "cause trouble with the Negro." Why? Because "[t]hese foreigners know nothing of the differences between the Negro and the white man," and thus will treat the Negro as an equal. But "[e]very Southerner knows," Rutledge claimed, "that the negro considers everyone who associates with him on terms of equality as his inferior." The Negro thus will put down "the Greek, the Syrian, or the 'Dago' as he calls the Italian," and the South will have a second race problem. One such problem is enough, Rutledge stressed.

The South from its very birth, has had a race problem which our best intellect has tried to solve, and still it remains unsettled. One entire race, the Negro, came for the profit of the slave-traders and ship-owners. It almost ruined the South and it is still a problem whether in the face of race hatred the Southern Caucasians will be able to maintain a racial separation. . . . Now, Honorable Judges, a race problem in which only two races are involved is bad enough, but when we add another to these, not one knows what will be the result. [35]

Finally, Rutledge announced, came "the most dangerous and most dreaded phase of this question[:] . . . foreign immigration is to-day forcing suicide upon the purest, noblest, and most upright race in existence." Why? "The recent immigration . . . from Southern and Eastern Europe is . . . decreasing the average stature of the American. It is said that the skull is growing shorter and broader." This ominous development, according to Wiley—citing the 1900 census—was attributable to a "birth-rate of the foreigners [that] exceeded the death rate by 44.5% per thousand," whereas "the native death-rate exceeded the birth rate by 1.5%." He pounded his point home: "Do you think that a mixture of the Negro and the Italian with the Caucasian would produce a race superior to the Caucasian? It is impossible to believe it." Wiley closed by quoting an unnamed author "whose heart is overflowing with a love for the South[:] . . . 'I delight in watching the lurid glare of her furnaces as it lights the very heavens . . . ; but, Gentlemen,

I would rather see her fires banked and her smoke dissipated to the four winds than to see that prosperity erected upon the graves of our Caucasian civilization.'"[36]

Wiley Rutledge had done his homework, seeking information even from the National Liberal Immigration League. And, as indicated, he used data to support many of his generalizations. But his viewpoint was largely subjective, in crucial respects undocumented, and offered without expressed reluctance or regret that the land of freedom and opportunity should close its ports to many who would enter. That said, one probably should not have expected more of a boy, not yet sixteen, debating this topic in the South in 1910. For all its blatant nativism, or worse, Wiley's presentation was well organized, with nicely crafted sentences and—under the circumstances—felicitous phrases. This high school senior, especially given his audience, packaged an impressive presentation. And, to complete the story, Wiley and his partner won the debate.[37]

Wiley's memberships in debating societies were valuable not only for the formal presentations he had to prepare and deliver but also, and perhaps even more so, for the intellectual growth stimulated by regular discussions with his colleagues. Meeting "Friday evenings of each week," he once wrote, the debaters "had great times talking about all sorts of things. . . . These would run from international affairs to all types of philosophical and religious matters."[38] This activity accordingly forced Wiley, in a disciplined but most congenial way, to think deeply about public and personal issues—and to come to coherent conclusions about them, however tentatively. Simply put, debate helped him learn to think critically, and to enjoy doing so, as a life-enhancing responsibility.

That Wiley Rutledge was an intense debater at Maryville does not mean he was super-serious, however. Quite the contrary. As for most young men, Wiley's college days were laced with frivolity. A description under a college photo from 1912 called him "Content to live, but not to work." He chewed and smoked tobacco. And he loved a good time. According to the *Maryville College Annual* the same year, Rutledge belonged to a small social club called "The Band of Bucks." Conducting itself under the motto "'Fratrus Simus,' Let Us Be Brothers," the club reported: "'right jolly times so we have—yea, verily, profitable times. Many are the ephemeral fowls of the air consumed by us, purloined in the cause of suffering humanity.'" Rutledge held the office of "'Forager.'" By shotgun or thievery? We are not told.[39]

Rutledge was respected as a leader, even on lighthearted occasions. Foreshadowing his eventual vocation, Maryville's *Junior Daily Chronicle* once reported that "Victor Detty was arraigned before Judge Rutledge today for assault and battery yesterday while eating dinner at the same restaurant

"The Band of Bucks," 1912. Wiley Rutledge Jr. stands at far left.
(Courtesy of Maryville College)

with D. F. Gaston[;] the latter accused Detty of moonshin[in]g. Hot words followed."[40] Rutledge also—as his son, Neal, has put it—"loved to play practical jokes" and could engage in a "Tennessee brand of humor" with an "edge of cruelty to it." Once during college, according to Neal Rutledge, his father was more than a little irritated with an increasingly uppity friend for putting on "airs." Years later, a newspaper reported that Wiley had invited his victim to join in a train ride to Knoxville for a visit to the purported Rutledge home there. Upon their arrival, Wiley led his friend "to the palatial home of Gen. Cary Spence," then "told him to go right in and . . . upstairs to the first room on the right" while Wiley "went to get some sandwiches." Wiley "was standing just around the corner when the embarrassed visitor was ushered out by Gen. Spence's servants."[41]

Of greatest importance, during his sophomore year Rutledge met his future wife, Annabel Person, Maryville's new Greek teacher—and five years older than Wiley. Annabel's forebears on both sides—the Persons (originally Pearsons) and the Howes—came from England to Massachusetts in the 1630s and migrated to Michigan. Annabel lived midway between Detroit and Lansing in Howell, Michigan, where her father, who died when she was

Maryville's Greek teacher, Annabel Person. (Courtesy of the Rutledge family)

eighteen or nineteen, taught high school and operated a family vineyard. Annabel was the offspring of a Methodist mother and a Unitarian father, favoring the Unitarian church herself. And she was a 1911 graduate of Olivet College in Michigan.[42]

When Wiley met Annabel, she had just begun to teach. It "was not 'Greek' altogether that took you to her classroom," recalled a friend from Maryville, who remembered Annabel as a "beautiful" young woman. Another agreed, recalling Annabel as "that gracious lady, the lady with the smile." Wiley fell for her virtually on sight. He called Annabel for a date, and she said no, perhaps feeling it would be inappropriate for a teacher to date a student. But he persisted, insisting that he could not hear her over the phone and replying that he would be over to pick her up. She did not turn him away; a lifelong love for both of them began. And Annabel gave Wiley two 95s and a 90 for his three quarters of sophomore Greek! That he would pursue a woman years older than he, and his teacher at that, suggests a considerable sense of personal security in relating to women along with his male peers and elders.[43]

There is no evidence that college authorities ever told Wiley and Annabel they could not date, and so their relationship continued at Maryville. Sometime in his junior year, however, Wiley decided that he should obtain a degree at a better-known institution and that science offered the best prospects for secure employment. Any more specific reason that Wiley may have had for seeking a better academic credential, and for turning away from his anticipated study of law, is not known. Neal Rutledge has observed that Annabel was employed, and that Wiley—hoping for marriage as soon as possible—was concerned most of all about becoming at least an equally reliable breadwinner, presumably sooner than he could by taking the additional years required for law school. And so young Wiley Rutledge, whose lowest college grades were in science, elected to try a major shift of emphasis: the study of chemistry.[44]

Hearing of Wiley's plans, the president of Maryville College, alarmed at the prospect of losing one of Maryville's top students, offered him a scholarship for his senior year covering "full tuition and room rent." But Wiley declined. In 1913, on recommendation of his Maryville chemistry professor, he enrolled for his senior year at the University of Wisconsin at Madison. Annabel, too, decided to leave Maryville to join her former Greek instructor and mentor on the faculty of Grove City College in Pennsylvania. Wiley and Annabel had an understanding, however, that someday they would marry.[45]

Wiley Rutledge once wrote, "I, of course, owe more to Maryville College than I do perhaps to any of the other educational institutions which I attended." He remembered Maryville for his "fundamental education." It had provided a "foundation for educational growth"—for learning, most importantly, the "forms of thinking" rather than mere "substance of thought." But he also came "in real touch with ideas," particularly through his experiences in formal debates. Rutledge later realized that from those Maryville days he had also gained "an appreciation of the earth and its beauty," and "especially a foundation for idealism & service to others." Significantly, moreover, he had come to recognize that "a rigid fundamentalism of reli-

gious belief" leads to a "closed mind & intolerance toward others." Maryville College days, therefore, led him to deplore "sectarian behavior." Being
a Baptist was "not quite right." [46]

In the fall of 1913, Wiley completed a summer mathematics course at
the University of Tennessee and headed to Madison for his senior year.
And his father remarried. The reverend's bride was Tamsey Cate (always
"Miss Tamsey" to Wiley), who was twenty years younger than her husband.
Brother Rutledge and his bride left Maryville for a pastorate east of Knoxville at White Pine, Tennessee, where his son established residence and
recalled "living briefly." There, Wiley Rutledge "used to stand on the hill
across the river and look down upon the Swann estate with envy." But he
never dwelt on such thoughts. He was interested more in completing his
education and finding a future with Annabel. [47]

Wisconsin, Indiana, North Carolina, New Mexico

When Wiley Rutledge arrived in Madison, Wisconsin, in 1913, he entered a city of 30,000, over a dozen times larger than Maryville. Like everywhere Wiley had lived, Madison was almost entirely white, but unlike the overwhelmingly native-born populations of his homes in Kentucky and Tennessee, Madison had substantial numbers of Germans and Norwegians, Irish, English, and Italians.[1] The state university, chartered in 1848, was at the center of the city's cultural life. Wisconsin's founders had been political "Barnburners"—originally upstate New York reform Democrats who reputedly were willing to burn their barns to kill rats, and thus willing to destroy the Democratic party for high principle. Barnburners had vigorously opposed slavery while promoting free expression of religion, expanded suffrage, women's rights, and prison reform.[2]

Motivated by this egalitarian philosophy, the university's first chancellors sought to build a great research institution that not only would benefit Wisconsin's farmers and laborers but also would employ the social sciences to reform the state's schools, hospitals, courts, prisons, and public welfare programs, and even the professions. Inherent in this pursuit of applied research and law reform, moreover, was a moral responsibility of the faculty to offer technical assistance to farm, labor, and community organizations. Among the students powerfully influenced by the call for public service was Robert M. La Follette, a progressive Republican who gained political prominence in Wisconsin after a period of agrarian and labor unrest throughout the nation. Elected Wisconsin's governor in 1900, La Follette thwarted the "Stalwarts" of his own party by implementing political reform—including a direct primary and civil service legislation—as well as railroad regulation. In 1905 La Follette entered the U.S. Senate, where he served until 1921 as the dominant political force in Wisconsin.[3]

While still governor, La Follette prevailed on the Board of Regents to select as university president Charles R. Van Hise, who furthered the philosophy—eventually known as the "Wisconsin idea"—that teaching, research, and public service were "fundamental and interrelated missions." By 1911 forty-six professors, including Van Hise himself, were serving in state agencies and gathering statistics, drafting legislation, teaching agriculture, or advising on economic policy. When Wiley Rutledge arrived in Madison in the fall of 1913, the Wisconsin idea was at its peak. Wiley thus entered a state energized by the most progressive politics and educational policies in the nation. La Follette and Van Hise represented the kind of "government-can-do" outlook, reinforced by an ethic of public service, that surely must have impressed the new Wisconsin senior from Tennessee. Indeed, Wiley's senior year was a watershed year for progressive government throughout the nation. Woodrow Wilson, who had won the presidency in 1912 over President Taft and the "Bull Moose" candidacy of former President Roosevelt, had begun to launch the "New Freedom," his anti-monopoly program of regulated competition. The autumn of 1913 also brought ratification of the Sixteenth Amendment to the Constitution, authorizing the federal income tax, and the Seventeenth, providing for direct election of U.S. senators. And in late 1913, pressed by Wilson, Congress itself made major statements, creating the Federal Reserve System and adopting the Underwood Tariff, the first downward revision of tariffs since the Civil War. In January 1914, moreover, perhaps the most significant breakthrough of all occurred—at least for the national economy and international prestige—when the United States completed the Panama Canal. It was a time of national pride and exhilaration, especially for a young man with Wiley Rutledge's progressive outlook.[4]

The nation was moving in new directions, but the Wisconsin chemistry department was not an answer for the young southerner. In one chemistry course he received a "fair," in the other a "conditional," which meant that he could not graduate without a makeup course in the summer session of 1914. There is virtually no record of the future justice's year in Madison, only a grade report showing that he took two courses in chemistry, as well as two others in Latin and one in German (a new language to him, presumably essential to further work in the sciences). It would appear that Wiley Rutledge—spending hours in the chemistry laboratory, performing poorly in his course work, and missing Annabel—did not engage much with others at Wisconsin in the ways he did during every other year of his life. None of his correspondence with Annabel during his year in Wisconsin has been preserved, so we lack the obvious avenue to his thoughts and experiences at the time. But given their commitment to each other and their subsequent letter-writing patterns when apart, Wiley more than likely wrote to Annabel every day, further withdrawing himself into a personal, and to a substantial extent lonely, world. Years later, each time his name surfaced in connection with Supreme Court speculation, a flood of letters would pour in to him from friends at Maryville and every other place he had lived — except Madison. Rutledge's Wisconsin year was one of difficult, unpleasant study and of uncharacteristic withdrawal. Later he recalled it as one of the "hardest," most "painful" years of his life, for which he was "grateful" nonetheless because he "learned how to work."[5]

Wiley could not have been oblivious, however, to the progressive politics of Robert La Follette or to the "Wisconsin idea" implemented by President Van Hise—a subject that Rutledge the justice later wrote about. A newspaper once reported, "Dean Rutledge's friends say that he acquired many of his sociological views from the elder La Follette, while a student at Wisconsin." Wiley never confirmed this in correspondence, but there has to be some truth to it. He may have turned inward for a year, but given his political views, sharpened at Maryville, he surely absorbed the progressive thinking that he encountered in Madison.[6]

In view of his unhappy experience with chemistry, Wiley easily decided that his earlier ambition to become a lawyer was the correct one, but he could not afford to stay at Wisconsin. His father, anticipating a new family with Miss Tamsey, was no longer in a position to help, as he had done by paying for Wiley's senior year. The young man thus needed a job. Because of "one factor or another," however—including most notably his need to repeat course work in the summer of 1914—he had not found employment. So he went to live with his "Auntie" Cora in Kentucky while he took a refresher shorthand course at Bowling Green Business University. He did so, he later wrote, with a view to preparing for civil service examinations, "thinking that by securing such an appointment" he "might be able to enter a law school . . . in Washington[, D.C.]." Why Washington? We do not know. As it turned out, however, the head of the commercial department of the Bloomington, Indiana, high school sought a part-time teacher through Bowling Green, and Wiley accepted, for $37.50 per month from January through June 1915.[7]

Also beginning in January 1915, Wiley enrolled in the first-year law class at Indiana University. Attending classes in the mornings while teaching high school in the afternoons, he plunged into his studies within months after the "guns of August" had signaled the outbreak of eventual world war in Europe. The strain of his course work and teaching obligations was considerable. After winter, spring, and summer terms at Indiana, during which he earned two A's and five B's, Rutledge concluded that he could no longer do both at the levels he demanded of himself. Thus in the spring of 1915—in order to put away money for full-time, undivided attention to his legal studies—he began to seek full-time high school teaching positions in the Midwest.[8]

After receiving a firm offer of $1,120 per year from St. Louis, Missouri, he found an almost equally lucrative position at the high school in Connersville, Indiana, northeast of Indianapolis, a community new to him and one far smaller and closer than St. Louis. He signed on there to teach business subjects, beginning in the fall of 1915, and he agreed, for more money, to coach basketball. "I made the most miserable failure of that task of any which I have ever undertaken," he wrote years later. "In the first place, I didn't know anything about basketball; in the second place, I'd never played it except casually; and third, the boys on our team were real experts." In all other respects Wiley enjoyed his new position, and his students enjoyed him.[9]

Wiley missed Annabel terribly. Their correspondence not only reflects their feelings but also reveals an interesting mode of expression: they referred to themselves in the third person, using nicknames. Annabel called Wiley "Boy Dear," almost always "B. D." for short. And Wiley had a nickname for Annabel, "D. T.," which both of them used, but which no correspondence spells out. (Nor did their children pursue or learn the answer.)[10] The appellation "Dear Teacher" seems plausible, but there is no proof. In any event, by December 1915 Wiley was anticipating the Christmas holidays in Michigan with Annabel. "Sweetheart," he wrote, "Your B.D. . . . will be [so] glad when this whole week is over & he & his D.T. can have a few days again of what they have found to be worth everything else—togetherness."

Soon after he arrived at Annabel's home, however, Wiley became ill with chills and a fever, followed by a cold, then la grippe and a cough that would not go away. By February 1916, a doctor had diagnosed the malady as tuberculosis but prescribed exactly the wrong cure: a serum, coupled with a regimen of long walks and (ironically) hours in the gym playing basketball. In the meantime, assuming he would get better, Wiley began to look for an even higher-paying job. In an application indicating that his specialties were bookkeeping, Pittman shorthand, typewriting, and commercial law, and that he was willing to teach arithmetic and penmanship (his own, mercifully for the biographer, was excellent), Wiley—twenty-two years old and reportedly in "good health," standing 5'10" tall and weighing 145 pounds—sought a minimum salary of $1,500 per year. He collected outstanding recommendations from former teachers and employers and eventually received an offer from the Champaign, Illinois, public schools meeting his terms.[11]

By May 1916, as the Illinois superintendent's letter was arriving, Wiley was spitting up blood. He consulted with the doctor in Asheville who had treated his mother, and by July he had entered the state sanatorium, located near Aberdeen in North Carolina's Piedmont section. While the nation was preparing to reelect President Wilson—very narrowly—over Supreme Court Justice Charles Evans Hughes for keeping the country out of the war overrunning Europe, young Rutledge's focus was entirely personal. According to an autobiographical essay, "Adventures in the Land of T.B.," which he penned years later, Wiley learned at the time that his disease, contracted in early childhood though dormant while he grew, had become "moderately advanced," and that he would have to change his habits—"to learn to live over again." In "Adventures," Wiley wrote his story in detail, in part in dialogue form, meticulously incorporating dialect when, for example, he asked a "negro boy" who had "sluffed around the corner of the infirmary" how to find the doctor. The "darky replied," according to Wiley: "'Dis am rest houah, an' Docta Dane am gone away. Docta Morrow is up to de big house takin' his rest houah, but he'll be heah in 'bout 'notha houah.'"[12]

Rutledge was confined, initially, to the infirmary and not permitted out of bed. After five days he was allowed into the dining hall and, after another five, was transferred to the "Men's Shack," where he was allowed walks of fifteen minutes, twice a day. Soon thereafter he moved to David Hall, where patients "on exercise" were quartered, and his twice-daily walks were increased over time to one and a half hours. From September through November, Wiley and his friend "Jake," a "railroad man"—a "princely fellow" who had "lost his wife by T. B."—hiked almost every day to rest at a clearing in the woods on a "foot-deep" bed of pine needles, breathing in the "sweetness of that pine-scented air." By March 1917, after eight months, Rutledge was ready to leave.[13]

While recuperating at the "San" and characterizing his stay as "a course in the University of Health," Wiley Rutledge took stock of his situation and wrote to himself: "How much do I need to make me happy? . . . I have more obstacles in my way than most young men of my age and yet I could be perfectly happy on $800 per year now. And that is a liberal estimate. I am not a miser nor am I lacking in ambition—yet $75 per month would give me everything I want for myself & for those I want to help." He then reviewed his life in terms of "the things that seem to make up happiness: health, friends, home, education, religion, recreation and freedom from abnormal cares & harmful vices."[14] Having learned from the doctors that he could die, as his mother had, from TB, Wiley was immediately aware that his health—not some long-term ambition—had priority, and he was concerned about finding the means to pay for his care. As to the other criteria, he recognized that he had "friends, religion to some extent, partial education & freedom from harmful vices." And as to a home (he included family), Wiley looked forward to leaving the San and getting married; he wanted the money to help meet his sister's hospital expenses after a recent operation; and he worried about his "Auntie, who had been deserted by a "conscienceless husband." He wanted to "send a little" to her "on the side." Wiley's incomplete education was a major concern. "[D]on't you hate to see a house, built to the roof, the rafters laid, and left to stand in the weather without a cover? That's just how I feel—the foundation's there, the framework & all, but there's *no top*." Wiley concluded: "I haven't got it—$800 per year. I may not have it soon. But it's been fun to think about it, & if He should let me have my health again, what fun it will be when the luck turns and things start coming my way! Won't you envy me?" Basically he was at peace, close to optimistic.[15]

Central to Wiley's survival at the San had been the indispensability of other people. By his own accounting, as he wrote in "Adventures," he had come together there with "lawyers, doctors, preachers, students, teachers, mountaineers, steel workers, farmers, sheriffs, bankers, bookkeepers, clerks, railroad men, insurance men, scions of wealthy families, merchants, dependent children, nurses, and many, many others." He met a man who looked like "a living skeleton," never spent an hour out of bed, was aware that death was certain, and yet never uttered a "cheerless or discouraged" word. Others had collapsed lungs; still others were diseased so pervasively that their only utterances were whispers. And yet most showed fighting spirits. There was, accordingly, a togetherness at the San, attributable to a common affliction, that was not unlike what a platoon of soldiers under fire must feel. And that togetherness was reinforced by the character—the "pure grit," as Wiley put it—that so many members of the San community exhibited. If, in the sanatorium, there was not a physical dependency on one another as in the military, there was still an emotional dependency, resulting in a caring born of empathy, that was palpable. And Wiley Rutledge felt those emotional connections deeply.[16]

Immune on medical grounds from joining the recent entry of the United States into world war, Wiley continued his rest during the summer of 1917 in the mountains of western North Carolina at Swannanoa near his sister, who was recovering at a sanatorium in Asheville. On this sojourn he decided, following conventional wisdom, to continue his recuperation by "chasing the cure," if possible, in the West. After an unproductive, and unidentified, flirtation with a job possibility in Reno, Nevada, Wiley's luck turned. When Annabel was visiting him in late August, he received word that he had been "elected" a "commercial teacher in the Albuquerque High School" at a salary of $1,500 per year. "Expect you Monday morning Sept. 3," the wire said. School authorities hoped that Wiley could build up the shorthand department.[17]

Wiley and Annabel wanted to go west together, but in those days that kind of joint venture presupposed marriage. So they decided to tie the knot immediately—on August 28, 1917—at a ceremony in Margaret's room at the Asheville sanatorium. Wiley's father performed the service, with only a doctor and two nurses present as witnesses since none of Annabel's family could come on so little notice. Annabel elaborated for her mother: "Mr. R.'s father was a little fussed marrying his own son and . . . got a little balled up in his ceremony. . . . Margaret burst out laughing in her bed—and that made us all smile." The Reverend Rutledge had planned to "baptize[] us that night *as I* intended joining the Baptist church." But he couldn't stay, "so he arranged with the pastor here and we were both baptized about ten o'clock that night before about a half dozen church officials. It was a very sweet and beautiful service."[18]

Annabel could not have been serious in writing that she wanted to join the Baptist church, or even that the baptism—indeed, her total immersion!—was "very sweet and beautiful." She was doing Wiley a favor by accommodating the strong feelings of his father, and she never actually joined a Baptist congregation. Nor could either of the newlyweds have been happy about a baptism at ten o'clock on their wedding night, especially when Wiley was leaving the next day for months away from his bride. In any event, "at about noon" on August 29, Wiley left for New Mexico while Annabel stayed in Asheville to look after Margaret, hoping to head west by late November.[19]

SINCE JUNE 1917, American soldiers had been joining the war raging abroad. Two months later, as the young Rutledges were preparing to begin their lives together in Albuquerque, Wiley was thrilled to be joined, finally, with Annabel. But he felt more than a little ashamed about avoiding the war. On his way west through Knoxville in late August, Wiley had seen a Maryville friend from debating days, Robert "Wood" Wright, who soon would be headed for Europe. Years later, Wright reminded Wiley: "I'll never forget the last time I saw you in Knoxville. . . . There was a look on your face. . . . Dave Brittain and I were going. You wanted to go but couldn't. I still choke when I realize how you felt then."[20]

ALBUQUERQUE, NEW MEXICO, by 1917 a community exceeding 20,000 situated on a high mesa in view of snow-capped mountain peaks, referred to itself as the "Heart of the Health Country." On the recommendation of eastern doctors, "health seekers by the thousands came to Albuquerque to fill sanatoriums, rooming houses, and even to live in tents." In fact, when Wiley Rutledge headed west, "the dollars imported by health seekers and the payroll of the Santa Fe Railroad" were sustaining the city's economy. Albuquerque had been settled over a period of two and a half centuries by gold seekers, farmers, and soldiers, "mostly Spanish and Mexican," followed generations later by adventurers reflecting "a veritable melting pot" of settlers. English, German, and Italian pioneers, as well as Spanish and Mexican newcomers and "even a few Chinese and blacks," settled there, bringing an "entrepreneurial vigor" to the community. By 1912 the factories, mills, and agriculture of Albuquerque, as well as its mines—gold, lead, zinc, copper, and coal—dominated trade over a 200,000-square-mile territory served by railways radiating in all directions. And intellectual and cultural activities emanated from the University of New Mexico, founded in 1892.[21]

Wiley met his first classes in Albuquerque—bookkeeping, shorthand, typewriting—on September 4. Classes went well, but at the first teachers' meeting, he later wrote, the superintendent threw "a bombshell into my camp, wholly unexpected—'No salary checks will be issued until you have filed your health certificate with the superintendent's office.'" The "blank form of certificate . . . required by the Board of Education" called for a doctor "to certify that he could find no trace of tuberculosis in the person examined!" After flirting with the idea of looking either for a "crooked" doctor or for a "very, very kind-hearted one," Wiley "decided to go to the best lung specialist in town, make full disclosure of the situation, and frankly ask his aid." The doctor told Wiley that his TB was inactive and he "wouldn't be dangerous in the school-room," but the doctor said he could not certify that Wiley was "sound in health." Wiley, after all, had come to New Mexico "with a spit cup in his hand" and requiring considerable bed rest. The doctor offered, nonetheless, to consult with the superintendent, who as a result informed the young teacher: "'Your work has been satisfactory, and we could hardly get another man now. . . . If you make it, all right; if not,—,' and he smiled." "That," recorded Wiley, "was the last word we had" on the matter.[22]

By the third week of November, Annabel's move to Albuquerque was near at hand. "How does it make you feel to know that two weeks from today we'll be together?," she wrote her husband. "It makes little thrills creep up Mrs. D. T. 'cause it will be our very first housekeeping and honeymoon." Wiley, too, was excited, replying:

[W]hen you read this I hope You will be with me, and I can watch You, and hold You, and love You as You ought to be, with my arms and hands and eyes and mouth and everything else about me that can love and be loved! I can say more heart-talk with my eyes and hands in ten minutes than I can with a pen or typewriter in an hour or forty of them. It takes so much energy to make love by writing, but when one has his Love with him he just radiates it, and She knows he loves Her without his having to put It into horrible, old awkward words.

Annabel joined Wiley in Albuquerque sometime before Christmas. Upon disembarking from the train and seeing the dry, barren country she burst into tears. But surely her emotions were overwhelmed, even more, by seeing her husband—finally. Wiley happily recalled: "[W]e had our honey-moon fixing up our three-room flat to suit our tastes and pocketbook." He added as to his health: "Of course during the winter I had ups and downs with Old Man T. B., but more ups than downs. Several times I taught thru the day, when the morning had started with 'streaks,' traces of blood in the sputum."[23]

The Rutledges' years in Albuquerque were largely uneventful. They worked hard, attended church, and made friends. Wiley never enjoyed teaching more than he did that first year in Albuquerque, and he believed his efforts started the commercial department on "an upward trend." Eager to contribute to the family income in a way that furthered a worthy purpose, Annabel taught English to Native American students for two years in the local high school. The young couple wanted to move into a house as soon as possible, as well as find a way to save money. To these ends, the two ventured creatively into real estate. They sold Annabel's piano for use as a down payment on two lots, then assigned Wiley's summer salary to the bank as security on a cash loan they used "as first payment on a little bungalow." Soon they converted their lots into a down payment on residential rental property that would net them approximately $500 per year. They now had a comfortable home near the center of town and a virtually failsafe investment.[24]

In the spring of 1918, the superintendent of schools approached Wiley about leaving the classroom to become the board's business manager and to stand in for the superintendent or the principal, as needed. He accepted, receiving a nice raise to $1,800, then $2,000, while undertaking "the most strenuous" year of his life to date, burdened by lingering illness. After two years, unsatisfied with his salary for duties "too heavy for one person to carry efficiently," Wiley decided to resign effective July 15, 1920. He had been eager to reenter law school. Fortunately, the real estate investments freed the young couple to move on. By selling their home and rental property for a $3,000 profit, added to another $3,000 they had saved during their three years in Albuquerque, the Rutledges were able to pay most of the debt for Wiley's sickness while holding some funds in reserve for his legal education. So, with money in the bank and "a fair assurance" that Wiley's "health was steadily improving," they decided to move to Boulder, Colorado, the venue closest to Albuquerque with both a law school and an acceptable climate. They anticipated returning to Albuquerque to establish Wiley's eventual law practice and were looking forward to a bright future as the country, after the armistice of 1918, was preparing to return to "normalcy" by electing Warren G. Harding president two years later. In the meantime, to cover law school and living expenses, Wiley got busy in May 1920 seeking a teaching position in Boulder for the fall. He obtained part-time employment teaching afternoon commercial classes at the State Preparatory School, and thus would be free for law school classes each morning.[25]

WITH THE EXCEPTION of a visit by Annabel's sister, Myrtie, the Rutledges had not seen their families for almost three years. A visit east was long overdue. Wiley, moreover, had learned that his father—as Mary Lou Wigginton's heir—had joined a lawsuit with other Wiggintons to quiet (settle) title to the family farm at Mt. Washington, Kentucky, against a squatter's claim. So the young couple traveled in late July to Annabel's family home in Michigan, from which Wiley soon headed to Kentucky for the trial. After all the testimony, the judge ruled for the Wiggintons: no reasonable jury, he concluded, could find that the squatters had gained title through "adverse possession." Thus ended Wiley's first personal experience with a lawsuit.[26]

Wiley moved on to Maryville for a few days with friends, then to Chattanooga to visit his father and sister. On the Chattanooga trip, a "deaf and dumb fellow canvassed the train selling mending tape for clothes. I didn't have any [money]," Wiley wrote Annabel, "but just before we reached Chatt. he sat down behind me & I heard the old bug cough. I wrote on a slip of paper & asked him if he had any trouble in his chest. Said he had—and it was getting worse. . . . I told him about myself, my T. B., history. . . . He was very grateful." But Wiley did not stop there. "I wrote to him for an hour in [the] station after I left [the] train."[27] Just as the Reverend Rutledge would have done.

Wiley was especially concerned about his father's financial situation, stressing to Annabel the importance of paying him "in full" for his contributions to Wiley's education. Wiley was worried, ultimately, about Margaret's future, recognizing how frail, emotionally and physically, she continued to be and believing that Miss Tamsey would feel no obligation to her. Wiley assured his father that he would deed his own eventual share of the Mt. Washington farm over to Margaret, and while still in Tennessee Wiley proposed to Annabel—and she agreed wholeheartedly—that they would invite

Margaret to live with them in Boulder. Where she was staying, Margaret was getting "no milk, practically no meat or eggs, and half the time only leftovers," he wrote to Annabel. Wiley speculated, however, that Margaret would not be willing to leave her father, endure the hardship of the long trip west, and take a chance on finding a suitable "denominational" school for her unfinished education. ("D. T.," Wiley wrote, "Margaret is . . . actually half crazy on religion.") Wiley was prophetic. Margaret mooted the discussion by revealing that she had found a new place to stay with a woman on Signal Mountain outside Chattanooga, where Wiley found the home "very pleasant" and agreed to pay half the monthly expense of $50.[28]

On August 28, the young Rutledges' third anniversary, Wiley left by train for Colorado, arriving in Boulder on September 1. The two had been apart almost five weeks. Without doubt, Wiley and Annabel truly missed each other (Wiley: "I guess we're terribly in love, my dear"; Annabel: "I don't feel really happy without *you too*."). They wrote to each other virtually every day, and they whimpered and chided each other if a day passed without a letter (Annabel: "I've been Tuesday, Wednesday, and today without a word from my Boy Dear"; Wiley: "Had had no mail from Mich. for two days, so made up my mind to mob the postman if he didn't do me square today."). Feelings were assuaged when the post office sometimes offered more than one letter (Wiley: "I found two letters from my D. T."; Annabel: "Had a fine bunch of mail today—two letters from you."). Wiley would typically end a letter, "I do love you, D. T., & I *want* you. *Your* B. D." And their favorite supplementary sign-off was "Idlytfeaa"—"I do love you truly for ever and always."[29]

THREE

Colorado

Wiley arrived in Boulder during the week before Labor Day 1920, while Annabel remained in Michigan to help her mother and care for her sister Myrtie. The young couple had contracted to buy a house in Boulder before they left Albuquerque, and Wiley closed the deal, left with $20 in the bank and $10 in his pocket. In his first letter to Annabel, Wiley acknowledged: "I'm glad you're not going to teach. You've done enough of it—now for a little home-life." His objection to Annabel's teaching seemed driven by his desire to have her with him, not by an objection to his wife's working. Because Annabel would arrive after the school year had begun, Wiley assumed that any last-minute job opportunity would lie outside Boulder, not only taking her away from him but also generating expenses that would swallow her income. Annabel was not convinced, especially because she wanted to be in a financial position to start a family as soon as possible. "I don't want to be away from you," she wrote to her husband, although "I'd rather sacrifice a year together than to put off and put off the other." "But Mr. B. D. scolded me," Annabel added, "and I feel quite *subdued*!" Annabel's teaching career was at an end.[1]

Before Annabel joined him, Wiley's teaching got off to a good start. He felt accepted at Boulder Prep, and the school's values impressed him. "First we had a rousing chapel—faculty on the stage (!) And every seat filled with about 20 standing—*lots of pep*," he wrote to Annabel. "They have two hymns, a scripture passage and announcements, with occasionally special music and a lecture for chapel. It really does seem as if this school is one of the old type which stood for ideals & principles rather than a commercialized, Godless educ. Institution. I am glad it is so." Wiley also found a congenial Baptist church, although he was "not dippy" about the young minister's preaching.[2]

Wiley's course load covered commercial arithmetic, commercial law, shorthand, and bookkeeping. "Things are running smoothly," he wrote to Annabel. "Had to fire a youngster yesterday for back-talk. But he came up after school and fixed it up. Has been out of school for a time, and needed taking down. Attitude today very humble!" Wiley almost immediately was beginning to feel at home in Colorado. "Can't walk a block now without someone speaking to me," he informed Annabel. "Makes me feel like I'm in the South." Annabel, on the other hand, worried about leaving her mother and sister; they "seem so unprotected," she wrote. But "I am trying to re-member, B. D., that I don't have to work it all out—that He is working too and it will all come out right." Before September's end she was with her husband as he resumed the study of law.[3]

RESPONDING TO the pioneers' clamor for an institution offering higher edu-cation, Colorado's territorial legislature established the University of Colo-rado at Boulder in 1861, although it did not open until 1877. The law school followed fifteen years later, "with 25 freshmen and one full-time faculty member" embarking on a two-year curriculum that expanded to three years in 1898. Admission depended on only a high school education until 1912, when two years of college were required. By the time Wiley Rutledge was a student beginning in 1920, the full-time faculty numbered five, supple-mented by several part-time lecturers from private practice, and the school enrolled approximately ninety students.[4]

According to the law school catalogue, Colorado students received in-struction under the "Case-system," an approach typically in place around the country by the time Rutledge attended law school.[5] Colorado thus taught primarily the "common law" derived from the opinions of judges. So what were the "common law" and the "case" method of teaching it?

The common law began to take root systematically in twelfth-century England, as judges decided cases by purporting to apply immutable prin-ciples of God's "higher," "natural" law, as revealed through custom. Begin-ning with Magna Carta in 1215, the Crown itself came under the law in some respects, and by 1611 Sir Edward Coke, chief justice of the Court of Common Pleas, was opining that "the King hath no prerogative but that which the law of the land," as interpreted by judges, "allows." Furthermore, Coke declared, even the actions of Parliament—an assemblage of barons, knights, and townsfolk who, by the end of the fifteenth century, were enact-ing "bills" that occasionally overrode judicially pronounced common law rules—would be "void" if "against common right and reason." Finally, Coke stressed, only trained judges exercising "*judicial* right reason" derived from "long study and experience" could serve as final arbiters of the common law. Coke thus contributed to Western thought the powerful idea of judicial review of the nation's chief executive and its legislature, although the realm's highest court, the "law" lords of the House of Lords, remained in Parliament itself.[6] Coke left it for another Englishman, John Locke (1632–1704), and especially a French theorist, the Baron de Montesquieu (1689–1755), to offer the idea that our founders called the "separation of powers," lodging judicial review in a branch of government, headed by a supreme court, wholly apart from the legislature.

Then came Sir William Blackstone (1723–80), whose *Commentaries on the Laws of England*, first published in 1765, focused on Parliament, assigning it two roles. Parliament was both a *law finder*, identifying and prescribing "divine and natural duties," and a *law maker*, legislating as to "things in themselves indifferent," meaning matters that God apparently did not wish to control. In either instance, Parliament was supreme and infallible, limited only by judicial review exercised by its own high court. The lower courts still had their role as law finders, scrutinizing custom, but always subject to Parliamentary veto, either by legislation or by law lords' adjudication. And clearly, the courts had no role in law making.[7]

As in England, the day-to-day adjudication of disputes in this country continued in the hands of judges who, according to traditional understanding, first found, then applied, the common law. But where was that law to be found? Well before the federal Constitution was finally ratified in 1789, all but two states had adopted constitutional or statutory "receiving" provisions. These incorporated the entire body of English common law (as well as parliamentary acts effective on the date of colonization) until "altered by a future act of the legislature." As a result, given the 150-year span between the first and last settled colonies—each of which received a unique mix of English decisional and statutory law and had added its own enactments by the colonial legislature—the law, state to state, was far from uniform in America.[8]

In annotating Blackstone for use in America and explicating the states' common law differences, St. George Tucker, a Jeffersonian scholar from Virginia writing in 1803, acknowledged that judges were capable of finding the common law in custom, but he insisted that only legislators had authority to make and thus redirect the law. Perceiving a bright line between adjudication and legislation, Tucker warned that judges had no authority to change the law they found.[9] Here, then, was the first American exposition of the doctrine of judicial restraint.

Tucker also believed, however, that all duties and rights found in the customary, common law came ultimately not from God but from the people's "tacit consent."[10] If God's moral dictates were to become law, therefore, an exercise of popular will—implicit in custom—was necessary to accomplish that result. But this new, popular-sovereignty basis for the common law brought conceptual difficulty. Once Tucker acknowledged that the unwritten common law depended for legitimacy on some discernible manner of popular acceptance, the possibility that judges could discover law, without in any way making it themselves, seemed problematic, since judicially discoverable common law rules were no longer immutable. Interpretation of a collective human will—custom—which could differ from time to time, state to state, left far more room for a creative judicial response than mere identification of a timeless, inflexible law-of-God would allow. And in any event, was it not inevitable that judges, in applying custom, would reach forks in the road where two or more customs arguably would apply, and thus force the judge to make a choice that could hardly be called passive law finding? By declaring that only legislatures had authority to change the law, Tucker ignored the fact that judges routinely had to do so.

Lecturing a decade before Tucker's exposition, one of the most prominent architects of the Constitution, Justice James Wilson of the Supreme Court of Pennsylvania, had anticipated Tucker's reliance on popular acceptance to legitimate the common law. Wilson, too, opined that the law, premised on custom, was attributable to "'nothing else'" than "'free and voluntary consent.'" But Wilson was not reticent about having judges advance the law. To him, judicially declared custom was tantamount to an exercise of democracy, since judges acted as "'trustees' or 'agents' of the sovereign people."[11] James Wilson, one might say, was America's first judicial activist.

By 1813 Judge Tapping Reeve and Judge James Gould, teaching at Litchfield Law School in Connecticut, found a way to reinterpret Wilson's acceptance of judicial lawmaking so that it would seem less blatant. They forthrightly acknowledged that common law judging was not an act of mere discovery. "'Theoretical[ly],'" they proclaimed, the "courts make no law, but in point of fact they are legislators.'" These Litchfield professors, however, lay responsibility for judicial lawmaking ultimately on the legislature itself, by deeming every legislative failure to amend or reject a judicial decision an implied act of "'acquiescence,'" as effective as affirmative legislative approval.[12]

Tucker's view of the role of common law judges, limited to implementation of long-used customary law, surely represented the conventional understanding coming out of eighteenth-century America. But the belief of Wilson, Reeve, and Gould that judges had appreciable lawmaking authority received increasing acceptance in the new nation. Professor Morton J. Horwitz has written that by 1820, law in America was no longer "conceived of as an eternal set of principles expressed in custom and derived from natural law." Judges instead had come "to think of the common law as equally responsible with legislation for governing society and promoting socially desirable conduct."[13]

Much happened during the next half-century. Students continued to read Blackstone while apprenticing in lawyers' offices. Private law schools such as Reeve's and Gould's in Litchfield emerged. And universities added law professors (William and Mary, 1779; the College of Philadelphia, 1790; and Columbia, 1793) or took over private law schools (Harvard, 1817; and Yale, 1825).[14] Moreover, judges such as James Kent in New York (professor at Columbia) and Supreme Court Justice Joseph Story from Massachusetts (dean at Harvard) further updated Blackstone's *Commentaries* and published other legal treatises that Americanized the common law.[15]

By 1850, according to Professor Horwitz, activist lawyers and judges had manipulated the law to favor commercial and industrial interests, by ruling for creditors, insurers, mill owners, bridge operators, and especially the railroads and other common carriers "at the expense of farmers, workers, consumers, and other less powerful groups."[16] A political backlash against judge-made law had resulted along the way, however, as Andrew Jackson's election to the presidency in 1828 signaled a growing divide between those who identified with the common people and those who lined up with the élite. Jackson's triumph did not shut down judicial action favoring the wealthy, but in the years ahead his followers democratized the law profoundly in other ways by forcing changes in the education of lawyers, their admission to practice, and the selection of judges.

Disdaining "undemocratic elitism," Jacksonians virtually eliminated state requirements for admission to the bar, and they engineered the popular election, and thus scrutiny, of state judges. With the abolition of admission requirements, therefore, a law school credential, never more than a voluntary supplement to apprenticeship, lost even more value. And the law schools declined, leaving but eighteen with a total enrollment of five to six hundred students by the late 1850s. The years immediately before the Civil War, however, brought a rebirth of legal education at Columbia under Theodore William Dwight and a new law school at Michigan led by Thomas McIntyre Cooley. These giants of the profession—law reformers as well as academics—launched a resurgence of legal education in the schools that began to overtake apprenticeship as the indispensable teacher of lawyers in America. Dwight and Cooley were pioneering educators, teaching through lectures supplemented by textbooks, class discussion, and moot courts.[17] But the greatest leap forward came from Harvard.

In 1870 Harvard's president Charles W. Eliot appointed Christopher Columbus Langdell as dean of the law school, which he led for the next twenty-five years. Born in rural New Hampshire, Langdell attended Philips

Exeter Academy, Harvard College, and Harvard Law School; could be described, politically, as a Hamiltonian Federalist if not a royalist; and reportedly had no interest in legal developments after 1850. Langdell's impact was colossal. There appears to be a consensus among legal historians that at least until 1920 Harvard Law School "intellectually, socially, and numerically overwhelmed all the others." Langdell's contributions were massive in both legal doctrine and teaching methodology. As to doctrine, Langdell began from the premise that "law was a science"—meaning a natural science—dealing with fundamental principles identifiable in the common law and universally applicable across state lines. The principles were fair irrespective of context. And they were applied easily once the facts were sorted out. Langdell thus postulated a virtually static, closed system of fixed principles applicable to all cases with little regard for social change. They were to be discerned from written judicial decisions. To Langdell, therefore—reflecting Coke, Blackstone, and Tucker—judges merely found, never made, the law. Langdell's source of law, however, was not God but rather—closer to Tucker's view—the "historically produced legal system itself." The cases themselves, when properly selected, thus *were* the law, a surprisingly small, "logically coherent system of technical rules," ready for application without further refinement.[18]

Langdell acknowledged a role for the legislature, namely as a political route to changing the law. But he viewed the study of law as wholly separate from the appraisal of legislation. The science of law, said Langdell, focused on the law "as it is," not as it "ought to be."[19] The latter, in Langdell's mind, was the stuff of jurisprudence for graduate work in the liberal arts, not a concern of law schools training lawyers for private practice.

Langdell's premise that cases *are* the law led ineluctably to the conclusion that meaningful legal education required the intensive study of cases. This realization brought his most lasting contribution. Langdell rejected Dwight's and Cooley's textbook, lecture, and sporadic recitation method for the classroom. Instead of spoon-feeding legal principles from treatises to a passive student audience stirred by occasional questions, Langdell forced his students to discover the law themselves, over a three-year course of study, by experiencing the "case" method of instruction imparted through "Socratic" dialogue. To this end he collected illustrative opinions from appellate courts in "casebooks" for students to read before classes in, for example, contracts, torts, real property, criminal law, corporations, domestic relations, evidence, and wills. Then, creating an intense, interactive experience, Langdell would call on a student to recite a case, and answer question after question about it, until the student under fire—or another—came up with the rule of law that the case embodied.[20]

The new instructional method eventually came to serve well even those

Professor Herbert S. Hadley.
(Courtesy of University of Colorado
School of Law)

professors who did not share Langdell's doctrinal rigidity but found judicial decisions, explored through Socratic dialogue, the most effective way to teach the law—and what it ought to be. Spearheaded by élite institutions in the East (Harvard and Columbia) and Midwest (Northwestern, Chicago, and Michigan), the case method eventually experienced by Wiley Rutledge became standard in most American university law schools by 1910.[21]

IN CONTRAST with his Indiana experience, Wiley's teaching at Boulder Prep while carrying a full load at the law school did not affect his academic performance. Most of his grades were in the high 90s, and he earned a reputation as a serious student, perceived by many as the brightest in the class. Consistent with that reputation, during his third year, in the spring of 1922, Wiley "practically taught" the first-year criminal law class because its professor, Herbert S. Hadley, was sick or away much of the time. In addition to criminal law, Wiley took three courses—private corporations, municipal corporations, and legal ethics—from Professor Hadley, who quickly became a hero to him. A progressive Republican, Hadley had been attorney general of Missouri at thirty-two, governor of the state when he was thirty-six, and Theodore Roosevelt's floor leader at the 1912 Republican Convention. The press began to speculate about Hadley as a Republican presidential candidate in 1916, but Hadley had succumbed to tuberculosis and his health was too poor to allow a run for high office. In 1917 Hadley left his practice as a railroad lawyer in Kansas City to restore his health in the mountain air at Boulder as a professor of law. In 1894, the year Rutledge was born, Hadley had graduated at the top of his class from the law school at Northwestern, where he felt the influence of John Henry Wigmore, eventually Northwestern's legendary dean, a prolific scholar, and an energetic law reformer.[22]

Wiley Rutledge once wrote that he "owe[d] more professionally to Governor Hadley than to any other person. . . . As a teacher he stands out in my mind as the instructor who had the greatest influence upon my thinking, not only in law school but throughout the period of my own education." Hadley, explained Rutledge, would "consider[] the problem not merely in light of precedent but in relation to the social significance of the solution and its effect upon the law as an instrument of forward-looking social action. . . . No one could sit at his feet as a student and escape the fact that he was dealing with law not merely as a science but also as an art in the process of living." Law, wrote Rutledge citing Hadley's view, "was an instrumentality for justice and social progress." Rutledge recalled that from Hadley's course on private corporations he derived an insight "into law as a functioning of the social order for social purposes." Hadley pierced "through the formulations of legal language to the real social and economic issues they so often conceal." Wiley Rutledge may have learned through Langdell's Socratic case method, and yet, as his own words reveal, he was absorbing not Langdell's system of fixed legal principles but Hadley's presentation of a more recent Harvard contribution: the "sociological jurisprudence" of Dean Roscoe Pound. Pound rejected the idea that case law could be applied mechanically in new contexts; in the absence of a statute or persuasive precedent, Pound wrote, judges could not avoid making choices that inevitably meant deciding public policy. The progressive Hadley drove that lesson home. Reportedly telling others that "Rutledge was the ablest man he had ever taught,"[23] Hadley was to become a major player in Wiley's future.

AT ABOUT THE TIME Rutledge graduated from law school in the summer of 1922, he had come to have "serious intentions of going to California to practice." Wiley and Annabel had never seen California, and, given their circumstances, California represented more a daydream than an intended home. The two did not pursue the idea because financially it would have been impractical for them to do so and especially because, since early February, Annabel had been pregnant. Despite a plea from Wiley's pastor in Albuquerque to "come home! Come Home!"—"we all love and believe in you and your good wife"[24]—Colorado seemed the place to stay.

Before finishing his classes, Wiley left for Denver in June to take (and

*Wiley Rutledge,
University of
Colorado School
of Law graduate.
(Courtesy of the
Rutledge family)*

pass) the Colorado bar examination. He then contacted law firms all over the state and even considered hanging out his own shingle. In the fall, however, he took the most secure opportunity available and joined a Boulder law firm, Goss, Kimbrough, and Hutchinson. Two months later, on November 5, 1922, speaking for two ecstatic parents, Wiley fired off a telegram to Annabel's sister: "Mary Lou Rutledge arrived six tonight[.] Annabel doing well." [25]

IN 1858 the first permanent settlers arrived in the Boulder valley, long a lush, green hunting ground for the Arapaho at the base of dramatic formations of red rock. Within months the gold seekers made their first strike in the mountains not far to the west. By mid-February 1859, 2,000 residents had swarmed into the area, and the new Coloradans had organized Boulder City. Boasting a population of just over 11,000 after the First World War, Boulder, like Albuquerque, was a culturally diverse community of Native Americans, Hispanics, and Asians in addition to English-speaking Americans. Also as in Albuquerque, mining, agriculture, and tourism brought Boulder a sound economy. But by adopting the initiative, referendum, and recall of judges, plus municipal home rule, Colorado was more progressive politically than its neighbor.[26]

Cultural diversity and progressive politics did not bring open-minded-ness, however. During the years from the outbreak of world war through the 1920s, the University of Colorado, like other comparable institutions, was vulnerable to major assaults on academic freedom. In 1915, for example, responding to hysteria over "labor radicalism," the law school declined to renew an instructor who had testified before a congressional committee on behalf of the United Mine Workers. Later, during the war, the university dropped two members of the faculty who had "'expressed pro-German sympathies.'"[27] After the war, as Wiley and Annabel Rutledge were settling in Boulder, a new threat to freedom and decency arrived: the Ku Klux Klan. Within a few years the Klansmen—"puffing big CYANA (Catholics, You Are Not Americans) cigars"—"claimed to have signed up thirty thousand" ad-herents. In 1924 the Klan helped elect one of its own as Colorado's governor and achieved control over both houses of the legislature. The new governor promised the university its desired appropriation only if it "would dismiss from its staff all Catholics and all Jews." The university president, George Norlin, rebuffed him, resulting in severe financial loss for the university over the next two years. The Klan's power ran its course by 1926, how-ever, leaving Norlin's principled stand as an established warning against undue political interference with higher education in Colorado. This firm-ness must have impressed the young Boulder lawyer mightily, for in later years Rutledge kept Norlin's photograph on his office wall and would ac-knowledge that Norlin "had especially influenced his professional life and thinking."[28]

In the meantime, as Wiley was beginning to practice law in 1922, he took up public speaking. In December he addressed the local Lions Club on "The Evolution of the Law," warning that a state of barbarism was preventing the settlement of industrial disputes, and endorsing the establishment of industrial courts for enforced submission of disputes between capital and labor.[29] Wiley also engaged in politics "in a small way," as he once put it.[30] By mid-1923 he was president of the Democratic League of Boulder, a speedy accomplishment. He engineered an appearance at a league dinner by the former secretary of the navy under President Wilson, Josephus Daniels, then president of the Raleigh *News and Observer*.[31] There is no evidence, however, that Wiley took a principled enough interest in state politics to speak out against the Klan-dominated governor's office. Indeed, after this brief foray into organized party politics, Rutledge never made one again.

DURING THE TWO YEARS after he passed the bar examination, Wiley Rutledge poured out in poetry his emotional outlook on life, reflecting not only
his experiences at the "San" but also his awareness of a loving God. Beginning in Maryville, Wiley's Christian faith—while still expressed through
traditional worship—had been evolving toward faith in a God who revealed
Himself, fundamentally, through nature. "[T]he hills," Wiley wrote, "are
the habitation of God." The beauty, as well as the power, of the Creation was
a sign that God could be trusted, and Wiley felt a personal connection with
this God. He had written to Annabel in the summer of 1920: "God *is* good
to those who trust and wait." Regular church attendance in Albuquerque
and in Boulder confirmed his continued belief in that theme. Wiley, in fact,
related to God through prayer in those years, routinely on his knees, much
as he had in the days when he was learning the more literal religion of his
father, revealed through scripture. Prayer, however, was not a way to ma-
nipulate God; it was a way of turning oneself over—of asking God to reveal
His plan for one's life, and of asking for readiness and peace should death
present itself. There was, essentially, a fatalism, but nonetheless a freedom,
and corresponding responsibility, to respond with courage and a positive
attitude to what is given.[32]

Wiley expressed this theology indirectly in poems that focused on the
seasons or "cycles" of life; on human "impotence" compared to God's
power; on the glory of nature—"beauty," "summer," "western autumn evening"—that reveals God, not man or woman, as the source of all individuality. He also wrote on "fortitude," coupled with a cheerful attitude ("What's
the Use o' Frownin'?" and "When Your Plans Don't Pan"); and on the inevitable call, at any time, of death as one's "friend."[33] In February 1924, in
a reflection on human vulnerability—including, perhaps, a recollection of
his own infant brother's death—he wrote:

> It is the broken thing we love the best—
> The helpless sparrow with the broken wing
> That flutters on the ground beneath its nest,
> The broken doll, an empty, loveless thing
> Of rags and tatters to the stranger's eye,
> But our dear token of the startled cry
> It brought from baby lips on swift-caught breath
> Long, long ago—now hushed and still in death.[34]

Wiley seemed focused on connecting with loved ones lost to death—including his mother.

> Let in the night.
> For shadows sometimes bear

Within their folds thru evening air
The images of those we love—
As if, escaping from the land we know not of,
They steal back to us from the sight
Of God to bid us love them still—
And then our hearts with comfort shadows fill.[35]

He also wrote poetry to Annabel, referring in one instance to "Perfect love."[36]

The San had confronted Wiley Rutledge with his mortality; with the need to get straight what counted most in life day to day; with the suffering and courage of ordinary people; and with the healing connection—the need to care for one another—that a terrible, but common, human experience can generate among human beings. Ultimately, he had a trust in God's handling of suffering that left him emotionally secure and at peace, reflected, poignantly, in his own rewriting of three Psalms of David: the 23rd, 121st, and 130th.[37] And that trust in one's own well-being from God reflected a gratitude that called forth a reciprocal, personal obligation to help God take care of others.

HERBERT HADLEY left Colorado in 1923, returning to Missouri as chancellor of Washington University in St. Louis and as a criminal justice reformer. Also, with others—lawyers, professors, and judges from around the country—he helped incorporate the American Law Institute, with a mission to restate the common law in clear language. Hadley took with him to Missouri a young professor from Colorado, Bryant Smith, and Wiley Rutledge was invited to fill the Colorado vacancy in the fall of 1924. He accepted.[38]

There is no direct evidence indicating why Wiley made the career change, although the reasons are not difficult to discern. In the first place, law practice at the time, while stable at Wiley's firm in Boulder, was cyclical enough to cause worry; it was not a sure thing for the most junior lawyer. Furthermore, the offer of a professorship at the state university law school was a tremendous honor—a recognition of Wiley's superior ability. Finally, Wiley loved, and had been good at, teaching. The opportunity to engage in it in his chosen profession, therefore, must have felt to him like a good fit, or at least a challenge worth accepting. And at some level of consciousness, Wiley Rutledge must have heard the call to become, if at all possible, another Professor Herbert Hadley.

In his first year on the Colorado faculty, Rutledge "taught around the curriculum" (as new professors would put it), offering torts, criminal law, bills and notes, damages, suretyship and guarantee, conflict of laws, and partnership. In his second year, he shifted some of his hours to agency, insurance, and private corporations. Within two years his colleagues were reporting to Hadley that Wiley enjoyed "very considerable success" as a teacher. Beyond this general approbation—and a very large file of Colorado law school examinations in the Rutledge papers at the Library of Congress—we know nothing more specific about his teaching career in Boulder.[39]

On June 28, 1925, while Wiley was grading final exams, Annabel gave birth to their second daughter, Jean Ann. The young parents again were thrilled. And just as Mary Lou's arrival had signaled a rethinking of Wiley's career, the addition of Jean Ann paralleled, and perhaps triggered, further introspection. Wiley began to wonder whether he was sufficiently credentialed. Law professors commonly sought advancement to faculties of the better schools by earning doctoral degrees, so midway through his second year of teaching Wiley contacted Professor Manly O. Hudson, director of the international law program at Harvard Law School. Hudson confirmed that Wiley could probably obtain a graduate fellowship at Harvard but that first he should learn French, preferably during "a summer in France." It would appear that Wiley was thinking of the international field as a way of maximizing his professional attractiveness where the supply of professors was limited. The requirements that Hudson prescribed must have felt out of the question for the Rutledges, however, and there is no indication that Wiley pursued graduate education any further.[40]

In April 1926, Herbert Hadley extended a feeler: "[I]f at any time you should decide that you would like to make a change, you let me know." Wiley replied that he had been "very happy" in his work but would welcome an opportunity to consider any vacancy that Hadley thought he could fill, not only because of the "usual considerations of advancement" but also because of a desire to locate nearer his father and Annabel's mother. Soon thereafter, Professor Bryant Smith decided to leave St. Louis for the University of Texas and Hadley offered Rutledge his second opportunity to take Smith's place. Wiley said he could not consider the offer without the blessings of President Norlin and the law school's dean, John D. Fleming. The two would not stand in the young professor's way but tried to retain him with "a small increase in salary." Hadley trumped that offer by proposing an annual salary of $4,250. That sealed the deal. Wiley and Annabel may have had family reasons for relocating further east, but perhaps even more importantly Wiley was coming to the university presided over by one of the men he admired most.[41]

PART TWO

Law Professor and Dean,
1926–1939

FOUR

St. Louis

High Standards and a "Big Heart"

Founded by fur traders of French descent in 1764 after the French and Indian War, and named for Louis IX, the Crusader King of France, the city of St. Louis—on the Mississippi River ten miles below the mouth of the Missouri—became the crossroads of western expansion after the Louisiana Purchase in 1803. By the outbreak of Civil War, St. Louis had become a "uniquely American mix of raucous frontier and European sophistication." French, German, Italian, and Polish were spoken on the street, with a large German population dominating much of the city's life. When the war cut off the river trade, "Chicago took up the slack, and more," but by 1874 St. Louis's economic future was assured when the great engineer James Eads completed his magnificent arched bridge over the Mississippi River, inviting the railroads to head west through this gateway city. As business grew and diversified, St. Louis became one of the nation's principal grain markets, as well as a major manufacturing center, bringing the city's population to nearly 800,000 by the time the Rutledge family moved there.[1]

Washington University had become a major institution in St. Louis. In February 1853, a prominent local businessman had obtained a charter for "Eliot Seminary," named for the pastor of a local Unitarian church, William Greenleaf Eliot. Originally from Massachusetts and Harvard Divinity School, Eliot was willing to head the new school but declined to lend his name. The school accordingly took the name of the nation's first president, in order to put its heterodox, Unitarian beginnings outside the sight of malcontents—especially "Know Nothing" nativists—who in the 1850s were attacking all but the most traditional of American institutions.[2]

The university's law department opened after the Civil War in 1867 when a class of twelve embarked on a two-year curriculum, covering six months a year, designed to supplement the standard law office apprenticeship. Served by unsalaried, part-time faculty drawn from practitioners in St. Louis, the school lacked a full-time dean until 1881, when William Gardiner Hammond was recruited from the University of Iowa. Hammond was a real catch. The son of a Barnburner Democratic leader from Rhode Island, Hammond had graduated from Amherst College, served as an apprentice in a law office in Brooklyn, and later studied legal history at Heidelberg. Of particular importance, Hammond was an acquaintance and adherent of the renowned Columbia University professor Francis Lieber, a Prussian-born scholar who had become the nation's first full-time law professor, in 1835, at the College of South Carolina. Lieber had published several major works, most prominently his *Legal and Political Hermeneutics* (the study of principles of interpretation), which Hammond edited and republished the year before he came to St. Louis.[3]

In Francis Lieber, one finds some roots of the eventual judicial philosophy of Wiley Rutledge. Lieber looked for the ultimate source of the common law not in God, or in God-created Nature, but in human culture as it evolved over time. Although Lieber was convinced that for every judicial decision cultural values at the time would yield only one correct answer, he recognized that common law decision making was dynamic; judicial discovery of the law would inevitably bring change in the law as first-time cases pushed the limits of established rules. And Lieber also understood that political bias could cloud a judge's detection of the right result. Lieber thus recognized that the judge's task was inherently political, not simply logical, though more constrained than the wide-open kinds of choices concededly available to legislators. Lieber accordingly stressed a judge's moral obligation to make every effort to interpret the law as consistently as possible with the cultural values of the day, objectively observed. And he believed that such consistency was substantially achievable—in some instances by reference to the empirical study of social problems, an approach that he pioneered through the American Social Science Association.[4]

In editing Lieber's work and publishing his own, similar views, William Gardiner Hammond joined Washington University as one of the nation's premier legal scholars. He remained dean until his death in 1894. By then he had led the school to qualify as one of the twenty-five charter members of the Association of American Law Schools, organized in 1900, and had added an optional third year to the curriculum, which by 1904 the university required for a degree.[5] In one important respect, however, Washington University had been a leader even before Dean Hammond's intellectual contribution. Although the first woman lawyer in America appeared in colonial Maryland in 1638, no woman was formally admitted to the bar in this country until 1869 in Iowa. Within three more years, however, six women had been admitted in five states and the District of Columbia, including two trained at Washington University.[6]

The two deans after Hammond did not keep the school in the vanguard of legal education. Indeed, after Hammond there were no full-time faculty members until 1912, and although most law schools had adopted the case method by 1910, the first to use it at Washington University joined the faculty only in 1917. When Chancellor Hadley named Tyrrell Williams acting dean in 1926, the year Wiley Rutledge joined the faculty, Hadley sent Williams a list of "rules" that Hadley considered "imperative," emphasizing "Application of the case system."[7]

A FEW DAYS after Labor Day 1926, Wiley, Annabel, Mary Lou (age four), and Jean Ann (age two) — and their fox terrier, Bow-wow — left Colorado by train for Kansas City. From there, Wiley departed for St. Louis while the others headed for Michigan to visit family.[8] Wiley began quickly to get acclimated at the university, reporting to Annabel: "The university plant is wonderful — set high on a hill," with buildings "all in a Gothic style of stone, & modern inside." He was to have "the nicest office in the bldg. — why I do not know," adding, "it's a beauty & so nicely furnished. . . . I feel like a millionaire." In fact, he reported, the "whole school has an atmosphere of wealth about it."[9] That atmosphere had to leave Wiley feeling more than a tad nervous, for money was hardly his long suit. Within a few days of his arrival he wrote to Annabel, "My cash is running short"; he had only $19. Not long thereafter he was "down to $3.50." He asked Annabel to send him $10 in cash, rather than a check: "I don't want to be cashing $10.00 checks every few days — it looks small & appearances count for something at the start." Soon he found a cheaper room at "$6.00 a week."[10]

The atmosphere at Washington University also had social implications that worried Wiley. Hadley "took particular pains" to point out to his protégé that another faculty member whom Hadley had brought on board "had not made a great hit," largely because "he let it be known as soon as he came here that he didn't intend to do anything socially himself, nor did he care to accept invitations." This led Wiley to think, he wrote Annabel, that Hadley "would like to have us do what we could" socially. Wiley reported having told Hadley that his family "would have to be careful about finances for a while," but that they "would be glad to do" what was possible. Wiley held back that a new dimension in their lives — "little Mr. (or Miss?!) X" — would soon "explain itself." Annabel was pregnant, expecting in February.[11]

Wiley's obvious anxiety over Hadley's comments about socializing was not merely financial. He wrote to Annabel a few weeks later about a reception at Hadley's home: "Had a very nice time, met lots of folks, got thru it without any great blunders, I think, left about quarter to six, and glad to be thru with it." Wiley added: "Don't notice it while it's going on, but these social affairs leave me all sapped of nervous energy — just like a class when it is over."[12] Superficial chatter — small talk — was hard work for Wiley. It seemed inherently shallow, inviting insincerity and self-promotion, and thus to him it felt, for the most part, pointless. The hard work involved, therefore, was in sustaining honest, though inoffensive, discourse in an environment that begs one to be disingenuous. One of Wiley's greatest joys was in relating — at an honest and deep level — to other people. Understandably, therefore, one of his least favorite, and most difficult, experiences occurred when relating to others in a guarded and superficial way.

Classes began on September 23, and Wiley was "most glad" to be teaching torts to the freshmen, as well as bills and notes to the second-year students. He was particularly busy, for he had decided to reconstruct his torts course by using a casebook he had not tried before, in addition to spending untold hours looking for affordable housing for his family. And there were sundry faculty invitations to a football game, a reception, or a dinner. Wiley eventually found two suitable rentals in suburban Kirkwood, each with the same "questionable feature": they were "near the darkies." To Annabel he wrote, "I'm afraid you might not like that." (Could he have been projecting onto Annabel his own reluctance?) Wiley then found in suburban Clayton, bordering St. Louis not far from the university, just the right "new brick bungalow."[13]

Wiley was happy. In his very first letter to Annabel, he exclaimed: "I think I'm going to like things fine, & I'm sure the change will work out for the best, as we planned it." Two days later he was writing that all the faculty treated him "splendidly." Wiley's mood was brightened by enjoyment of his classes. After the first week he observed to Annabel: "I think I am getting them lined up in shape," although two weeks later he admitted that the second-year students in bills and notes were "still loafing on the job, tho improving." All possible doubts he may have had about his classroom reception, however, were allayed by positive student reactions. A month into his classes, he wrote Annabel, Acting Dean Williams had told him twice that he had "heard good reports from the students." The ever-upbeat Rutledge added in the days that followed: "I feel sure we're going to enjoy living here more than we did out west." Wiley was, of course, missing his family and wrote to Annabel almost daily, typically ending, "I do love you, My Sweetheart, & want you now" and signing off, "B.D. Daddy," followed by "xxxx (D.T) xxx (M.L.) xxx (J.A.)." By mid-November, the other three Rutledges arrived in St. Louis, accompanied by Annabel's mother and sister Myrtie.[14]

Time began to pass swiftly. On February 23, 1927, Wiley and Annabel Rutledge welcomed their third child, a son, Neal, named after Annabel's deceased brother, Cornelius. In the meantime, Dean Fleming at Colorado had begun to pursue Wiley for a teaching position at two summer sessions in Boulder in 1927, which Wiley accepted—and renewed regularly for years thereafter.[15]

FROM THE BEGINNING a full professor of law, Wiley Rutledge became a popular teacher at Washington University and, eventually, a respected dean. He was to stay in St. Louis for nine years. As in Colorado, he was expected to teach around the curriculum, with courses including, after torts and bills and notes, agency, conflict of laws, legal ethics, domestic relations, and—his eventual specialties—partnership and private corporations. Teaching law at Washington University was a real challenge. The new dean, William Green Hale, who came from Oregon the year after Rutledge joined the faculty, inherited a very young, not particularly well qualified, and often rowdy student body—in Wiley's words, "where the athletes congregated." Only two years of college, with minimal academic achievement, were required for admission, and Wiley found the standards of work far less stringent than at Colorado. Students had not even been required to "brief their cases" in preparation for discussion and felt perfectly free to answer "unprepared." The student body, in short, was largely a bunch of undisciplined kids.[16]

Chancellor Hadley had warned the young professor about the "serious disciplinary problem" at the school. Early on, a rowdy element in the class of 1928 tested the new teacher. A student ventriloquist, reputedly Clark Clifford, several times sent a loud "moan" across the classroom. This was the "school yell, a sort of moan without words." One observer recalls that Rutledge took off his coat, walked down the aisle, and exclaimed: "'If there's a joker here big enough to acknowledge it, I'm ready to meet him outside.'" Nobody spoke up, and the moan was never heard again. Years later, when Rutledge was on the Supreme Court and spied Clifford in the courtroom, he sent his former student a note from the bench: "Don't you dare give a B___rrr___p in here . . . Wiley."[17]

Clifford, who became President Truman's intimate advisor and President Lyndon Johnson's secretary of defense, was the ringleader of pranksters who sometimes went overboard. For some reason displeased with the university's administrator of buildings and grounds, Clifford supplied a false obituary for him, and its publication almost resulted in dismissal of the university newspaper employees who had accepted it. At another time, Clifford had learned somehow that cows can walk up stairs, but not down, and reportedly led one up to the top of the chapel tower—to the outrage of the administration. Clifford never lacked for self-confidence. Not long after Clifford graduated, Rutledge encountered him walking along the street, dressed immaculately. The dean reportedly inquired, "Don't you

think a jury would be prejudiced against someone who dressed as beautifully as you?"—to which Clifford was said to have replied, "No, everybody
knows I dress this beautifully, so if I didn't the jury would think I'm playing
down to them." Rutledge later wrote that he became "very fond" of Clifford,
whom he called a "big devil," largely because the "pranks created a bond"
between them.[18]

Others in later classes found their own pranks to play, most notably in
flare-ups with engineering students. One year when Rutledge was dean,
a law student lent his dad's Packard to the engineers so that they could
bring their queen and her court to the engineers' ball in style. The "laws"
then waylaid the young women and their driver and abandoned them far up
river. The engineers arranged an "all points bulletin," whereupon the police
intercepted the kidnappers and locked them up. Rutledge bailed them out,
trying to appear "very serious," but the students saw the sides of his mouth
"wrinkling up." Matters could get worse, however. After the engineers held
their annual dance honoring their patron saint, St. Patrick, in March 1931,
the editor of the university's newspaper *Student Life*, a law student, wrote
a pejorative article about the engineers that led to a fracas lasting several
days. It culminated with the engineers storming the law building to seize
the offending editor, lassoing the wrong law student, and almost pulling him
outside a first-floor window by his neck, "his nose bleeding and the skin of
his neck torn"—at which point Rutledge and the engineers' dean arrived
and the boy was let go. Just before a hundred or so law students were about
to pour into the engineers' building in retaliation, a committee of engineers
came out and negotiated a peace; hostilities subsided, followed by a letter
of apology directed to Dean Rutledge.[19]

THE LAW SCHOOL FACULTY during the Rutledge years at Washington University was not, over all, outstanding. The faculty produced little if any significant scholarship, and in teaching it received mixed reviews from the
students. The initial employer of the case method, Ernest Conant, an "old
timer" who reportedly taught torts from his student notes at Harvard, "did
not have much control of the class," was not taken seriously, and was routinely the butt of Clark Clifford's jokes.[20] Another senior faculty member,
the real-property professor Charles Cullen—a tall, mustachioed man called
"Firpo" because he resembled the heavyweight prizefighter[21]—was generally well liked, but he was a weak taskmaster who overall did not rank
highly as a teacher.[22] In contrast, some students called the constitutional
law teacher, Isidor Loeb, "brilliant," "remarkable." A "little fellow," he lectured with such vigor that it appeared he had to "hold onto the lectern to
keep it from flying away."[23]

Washington University School of Law faculty members, 1930. From left: Ralph Fuchs, Dean William Hale, Tyrrell Williams, Charles Cullen, Wiley Rutledge, and Ernest Conant. (Courtesy of Washington University School of Law)

In addition to Rutledge, three younger members of the faculty showed real promise, especially in the eyes of the better students. One reported that Ralph Fuchs, who joined the faculty in 1927 and became Wiley's closest friend for the rest of his life, "talked over the heads of nearly everybody." But that same student, who had attended two summer sessions at Michigan, acknowledged that Fuchs would have been well received in the more intellectual environment of Ann Arbor. Others saw Fuchs, who taught criminal law, personal property, domestic relations, administrative law, trade regulation, and municipal corporations—and was known to be a socialist who "always believed in the underdog—as "a brilliant man if there ever was one," as "one of the best professors," or simply as "my favorite." Philip Mechem, Wiley's law school classmate at Colorado, was also a well "respected," "good teacher" of torts, equity, and wills—remembered, too, for regularly "scratching his neck against the edge of the blackboard." The third young teacher was Israel Treiman, a Rhodes Scholar who taught trusts and took over torts and equity in 1930 when Mechem departed for Iowa. A student from the class of 1933, reflecting the sentiments of many, rated Treiman "one of the best professors" he "ever had for anything." [24]

The law school's senior member, Tyrrell Williams, was considered the "grand old man of the faculty"—"the most prominent professor we had," one student recalled. "Old Ty" Williams, a professor of contracts and pleading, had been a student of Woodrow Wilson at Princeton and was almost universally "revered and respected," both as a teacher and as a person.

Williams was avuncular. When Clark Clifford and his cronies were in serious trouble with the chancellor for walking the cow up the tower, "Old Ty" reportedly asked the culprits, indignantly, "Who brings these unjust charges?" and got the chancellor to calm down.[25]

Then there was Wiley Rutledge. He was remembered as one of the top three teachers, along with Williams and Treiman—a consensus verified in 1931, it would appear, when the seniors chose the three as banquet speakers at the annual spring Lawyers' Day. Wiley's former students at Washington University report that he was "low key" in class, but "all business," "no-nonsense," and sometimes "pretty stern," yet always "polite," "never rude." He was a "hard taskmaster." When several students were unprepared he was known to slam his book shut, dismiss the class, and walk out. The students considered him "fair" nonetheless, even while definitely the "hardest grader."[26] According to Jerome Gross of the class of 1931, the students wrote a song about Rutledge to the tune of "Finiculi, Finicula":

> Rutledge, Rutledge, he's the man for me,
> Rutledge, Rutledge, fair as he can be,
> He gives a C, a C, a D, a D, a C, a C, a D;
> Or if he is feeling well he sometimes gives a B.[27]

Typically, Wiley taught while sitting at a desk, dressed almost invariably in a rumpled, blue serge suit, occasionally getting up to emphasize a point or to open a window. Despite sitting, he had "an animated teaching style" combining lecture with intensive, highly fact-oriented class discussion while the students—each clothed in white shirt, coat, and tie—stood to recite. The emphasis was not on absorbing legal rules but on learning to think—beginning, Rutledge made clear, by asking, " 'What *is* the *question*?' " He taught students to "weigh both sides" and to "challenge everything."[28]

Students almost invariably recalled Rutledge as "highly intelligent," a "great thinker," even "brilliant," with "a very lively mind."[29] For most students he was "the best" or "near the top" as a teacher, "well prepared" and not only commanding attention but inspiring "respect." One graduate referred to Rutledge as the most "outstanding law professor" with whom he had "ever been associated."[30] Students remember that he was "great at explaining the background of cases that had social significance," without being overtly political in class. "He was very insistent on recognizing basic considerations of public policy involved in nearly every aspect of law" and saw the law as "an instrument for affirmative social action," especially for reining in corporations.[31] Students also "sensed his earnestness about legal ethics and decent behavior both professionally and socially." One wrote that "so often in his lectures, he emphasized 'Character,' 'Integrity,' 'Honesty.' "

Students recognized that they "were in the presence of an unusual, high minded man." One student remarked that "as a man of great character" Rutledge "may have influenced his students to a greater extent" than if he had been a more distinguished legal scholar. Another called Rutledge his "hero"—a "'Man For All Seasons'": he "has been my inspiration and in many ways has had more influence on my intellectual life than any other person."[32]

Remembered as a "warm," even "radiant," personality, Rutledge "was very well liked," indeed seen as a "wonderful human being." He "had no favorites" and "bore no grudges." He "was equally interested in the best and the worst students." Many thought Rutledge "had the greatest interest in students of any professor." He was "very approachable," ready for lunch with students on the quadrangle and always available through an open office door. He once trusted a student who overslept after a late-night job during the Depression to take a final exam on his own time. He helped students to find jobs and loans. Students recognized in Wiley Rutledge "a big heart" and—out of class—a "good sense of humor." The few women in the class felt especially well treated.[33]

Wiley Rutledge was seen as "honest through and through." Indeed, he was a "simple person"; there was "nothing high flown about him." One student called him "a little more friendly; a little more human; a little less stiff-necked than the other Professors." Rutledge noticeably "loved people," and thus was concerned about the "well-being of people." "Students were like his children," one reported. And students were inspired because they "could just feel his love for the law and for what he was doing."[34]

WHEN HERBERT HADLEY returned to St. Louis in 1923 as the university's new chancellor, he became concerned immediately about the inadequacy of the law school. He attacked the fundamental problem, weak finances, by collaborating with the president of the university corporation, the St. Louis entrepreneur and philanthropist Robert S. Brookings, in building a university endowment. Brookings, who headed the corporation between 1895 and 1928, had become wealthy as a partner in a massive warehouse complex in downtown St. Louis near the railroads. In addition to his work for the university, Brookings spent significant time on the boards of the Institute of Economics and the Institute of Government Research, both in Washington, D.C., which later were reorganized as today's Brookings Institution. A bachelor until the age of seventy-seven, "he lavished on the University affections that others reserved for home and family."[35]

At the university's commencement in 1927, Brookings gave an address, "Education for Political Leadership," that reflected Hadley's as well as Brookings's own views. The university's historian, Professor Ralph E. Morrow, summarized Brookings's message: "because the commonwealth functioned through laws and because lawyers manned many offices in government, law students ought to receive training for public service." Accordingly, Brookings maintained, law schools should stress "not only cases and texts" but also " 'the underlying principles of law [as] embodied in the social, economic, and political sciences.' " Later, according to Morrow, Brookings told Ralph Fuchs that the law school must aim to " 'turn out *statesmen* as well as *technical practitioners*' " — a theme traceable to Governor Thomas Jefferson's creation of the law department at William and Mary and one that contrasted sharply with the narrow education for private practice that characterized Langdell's mission at Harvard. Brookings's clarion call in mid-1927 thus set the tone for the law school as the first year of teaching ended for Wiley Rutledge in his new, St. Louis venue. Within six months, however, Wiley felt a severe personal blow. His dear friend and mentor, Herbert Hadley, died of heart failure on the 1st of December.[36]

BY 1926, despite admission standards that conformed to the policies of the Association of American Law Schools, the administration's application of those standards had been so lax at Washington University — and the acceptance of poor student performance so routine — that AALS placed the School of Law on a two-year probation: improve or give up association membership. Beginning with his arrival in 1927, Dean Hale raised admission and performance standards; substantial numbers failed, in no small measure because of Wiley Rutledge, and the dean's standing with the students plummeted despite his recognition as an outstanding teacher. Hale was "not well liked," and he "had too much starch in him" even to generate students' respect for conducting a rigorous institution. "The dean's a butt" would be heard as Hale passed by. Black Tuesday came on October 29, 1929. As the Great Depression unfolded, resources for the law school were cut despite a faculty protest joined by Rutledge. Fed up, Hale resigned in 1930 after three years at the helm.[37]

When Chancellor Hadley died in 1927, the university had appointed as his successor Hadley's assistant, a former professor of Greek, George R. Throop (pronounced "Troop"). Chancellor Throop named Rutledge acting dean as of July 1, 1930, upon Hale's resignation and, a year later, designated Rutledge — age thirty-seven — as the dean. Rutledge had not been Throop's first choice, however. Virtually no resources were available for the school of law aside from tuition fees; the endowment fund totaled a mere $3,905 of the $1 million Brookings had sought before the Depression hit; and so the chancellor had hoped to go outside the faculty for a dean of considerable

Washington University chancellor George R. Throop.
(Courtesy of Washington University Archives)

stature who would enhance the possibilities for raising money. As early as February 1931, Throop offered the position to Armistead M. Dobie, a highly published professor at the University of Virginia (and later dean there), who had turned down Hadley for the deanship in 1927 before the chancellor settled on Hale. Not even an extraordinary annual salary of $10,000, plus a promised campaign for an endowment of $1.25 million, could lure Dobie. Throop concluded that he could not find another outsider who was likely to generate big money, and because funds were so tight he decided not to fill even Hale's faculty position. The new dean, therefore, would have to come from within the law school faculty and be content with one less colleague to cover courses and committees.[38]

Tyrrell Williams, who had served as acting dean twice, was not interested himself, and he strongly supported Rutledge. A month before Throop appointed Wiley acting dean, Williams had informed the chancellor that Wiley had recently "declined an offer to become a regular member of the faculty of the Law School at the University of Missouri" (an offer about which we have no other information). By the end of the year, therefore, Williams was obviously concerned that unless Throop moved quickly, Wiley might leave. Wiley was willing, perhaps even eager, to become dean, but there is no indication that he might have moved on had Throop not offered him the post. Years later, Wiley wrote a friend that during his first few years at Washington University he had come to "question the value" of his work, feeling that his "function in life was to educate legal racketeers in the niceties of their game." But this feeling disappeared with the "crash of '29," which, paradoxically, generated a wave of idealism that changed the school's atmosphere to Wiley's liking. His only real worry, therefore, was that the chancellor might keep the permanent post open for another year, imposing caretaking duties that would further impede his scholarship—in particular the preparation of a casebook on private corporations for which he had a commitment to the Lawyers Co-operative Publishing Company.[39]

Perhaps of some significance, in April 1931 over 80 percent of the senior class signed a petition to the university's board of directors recommending Rutledge for the deanship. In any event, no one else on the faculty was a likely candidate. Professors Conant and Cullen were not much respected by the students; Ralph Fuchs, who had joined the faculty a year after Rutledge, was five years Wiley's junior; and Philip Mechem, with experience as acting dean for a year at Kansas, had left for Iowa.[40] Finally, and most importantly, Rutledge had been an assertive, creative, and effective acting dean. He had sought to improve student writing, and to foster equal opportunity, by offering every student with a B average the option of joining the law review, with faculty supervision and, for the first time, with academic credit—an experience previously available only to students selected by the faculty. Furthermore, believing that the study of law was too one-dimensional, Wiley had organized in the fall of 1930 a full year's series of twenty-two "Law School Assemblies" featuring an amazing variety of lectures that explored Robert Brookings's favorite theme: relationships between law and the social sciences. Wiley Rutledge deserved appointment as dean, and Chancellor Throop clearly saw that. Thus, in July 1931 Rutledge took full charge of a school of 131 students, with seven full-time faculty members and several part-time instructors from downtown law firms. He received an annual salary of $7,000, certainly not the $10,000 that Throop had been willing to gamble on the outsider, Dobie, or even the $7,500 that Hale had received upon joining the school, but surely fair in light of Wiley's experience and the school's salary scale in hard times.[41]

Wiley's year as acting dean had been eventful, though often difficult, for his family. In November 1930, Annabel's brother Seymour, a lawyer, had been elected to Congress from the Lansing, Michigan, area as a "wet" Republican. But the following March, Annabel's sister, Myrtie, died. After the funeral, Annabel's mother joined the Rutledges in St. Louis, where she lived with them until her own death four years later.[42] Wiley's sister, in the meantime, had been persuaded to enter a sanitarium in Battle Creek, Michigan, where a variety of treatments failed to help her physically or emotionally. She never recovered and died there in 1936.[43]

As DEAN, Rutledge further raised admission standards, eventually leading the faculty to recommend a required three years of college for admission. He also worked hard to strengthen the curriculum. When he joined the faculty, Wiley recalled, "the curriculum was a hodgepodge of abbreviated courses, established apparently in the effort to give the student's a bird's-eye view of every legal subject and intensive consideration of none." He established a standing committee to make major recommendations for the curriculum, with the dean as chair;[44] but in the meantime, given a Depression-reduced faculty, he looked for unusual ways to enhance the student's learning experience. He revived and expanded the classwork in legal ethics, beginning by offering a required first-year course himself.[45] He strengthened the thesis requirement, while providing greater faculty supervision. He supported the faculty's adoption of a required "practice court" in the third year for academic credit. With the aid of a St. Louis attorney he established a legal aid clinic in which students would help the poor. And he initiated a program of graduate study leading to a master of laws degree. Rutledge also sought ways to increase collaboration between lawyers and social workers and thus expanded the commitment to broadening legal horizons that he had initiated through the assembly lectures while serving as acting dean. Rutledge, in short, became an academic leader.[46]

FIVE

St. Louis

A Public Liberal

During Rutledge's years in St. Louis he was active in a variety of civic organizations, but none interested him more, or affected him more profoundly, than the Public Question Club. This dinner and discussion group for men only, which he joined in 1928, was founded in 1904 to offer members from "a wide range of human endeavor—doctors, lawyers, teachers, business men, newspaper men, Republicans, Democrats, Socialists, Labor"—an opportunity to "air their reasons, faiths or points of view" informally, and "'off the record,'" on domestic and international issues of the day. Governed by a motto, "Unexpressed Is Only Half Thought," and self-characterized as "a discussion group, not a debating society"—the only rule was that "no one ever speaks twice"—the approximately one hundred members chosen by invitation took "no stands" and espoused "no principles but the principle of free speech."[1]

The club each year covered twenty or so timely topics, such as "The German Crisis," "Eugenics," "Racketeering," "Is Philosophy a Substitute for Religion?" "The Decline of the Home," "The Nature of Economic Depressions," "The Lawyer Today," and "Intercollegiate Football" (Rutledge spoke for the view that it was "inimical to higher education and should be abolished"). Topics during Wiley's year as club president, 1932–33, included: "How Shall I Vote (Hoover, Roosevelt, Thomas)?" "The Plight of the Farmer," "The Manchurian Issue," "The Trend in Drama," "Huey Long," "Sex Policy," and "The Golden Rule." One speaker would present an overview, then two others would advocate positions pro and con. Everyone else present would respond for a minute or two each. These meetings broadly informed the members and sharpened their speaking skills. For Wiley Rutledge, they tended to reinforce his domestic liberalism and foster a strong internationalism, unusual in the Midwest.[2]

Topics at the Public Question Club often confronted Wiley with religion.

He still regularly attended church although he did not formally affiliate with a congregation in St. Louis until November 1928, when he joined Delmar Baptist and occasionally taught the men's fellowship class. (Although she attended with Wiley, Annabel—still of Unitarian persuasion—never joined the Baptists beyond the immersion she had tolerated on her wedding day.)[3] Despite his church-going, Wiley continued to wrestle with God. His interest in science, first evident in his shift to chemistry at Wisconsin, collided with his Baptist upbringing. He clipped and collected articles on science and religion, made notes on them, and tested his own views at the Public Question Club and elsewhere.[4] Although the club assured that all sides of a question were presented, it is most unlikely that it would have had to conscript someone to speak a line antithetical to his own religious outlook; and from all indications Wiley was comfortable, not merely accommodating, in standing before his peers as a religious skeptic.

While a member of the club, Wiley experienced no fewer than eleven discussions of religious topics.[5] In January 1930 he spoke on why "Science Offers No Evidence of Immortality or God," in answer to Branch Rickey, owner of the St. Louis Cardinals, who defended the "Faith of Our Fathers."[6] A year later, Rutledge explained "Modern Scientific Theory" to club members, calling it "A Triumph of Rationalism."[7] Probably the most comprehensive outline of his religious views at this time, however, is reflected in notes of a speech entitled "Religion and Social Progress,"[8] which are undated and unidentified as to forum but appear to come from his St. Louis years during the Great Depression. Acknowledging the "modern spirit of lassitude"— the "hopelessness" leading one to wonder, "Is life worth living?"—Wiley focused on "the paradox of too much to eat and too many who are hungry." He cited the "failure of the old religious motivations." Specifically, he said, living for the "glory of God," as the old catechism demanded, honored a "figment of imagination." Pursuing "immortality," he warned, reinforced a "delusion." Seeking to avoid "Hell," he added, focused on a "nightmare"— "horrible but unreal." Thus, Wiley concluded, it would appear that human "life only," not an afterlife, "is real." And life is "hopeless"—unless one can find in religion a "renewal" of "ideals for modern life" that solve human problems. Wiley found that renewal. Does not religion, he asked, embrace a spirit to seek "peace"? To help others find "work" and "security"? To distribute equitably the "goods of life" in a manner consistent with the fundamentals of our "democracy"?[9]

Wiley Rutledge, here, was premising religion purely on the imperatives of humanity, meaning the dignity and worth of every human being—espousing, in other words, an outlook best characterized either as classic secular humanism or as a strain of Midwestern Unitarianism[10] of the sort that Annabel's father had brought to her. And yet Wiley's personal behavior—his allegiance to the Baptist church—betrayed roots in a more fundamental Christian faith that he could not altogether let go. Was there necessarily inconsistency? Not really. The Christian story—its teaching for the *individual* life—provided the basis for the very renewal of *community* life that Wiley sought. How so? The capacity to serve any humanistic goal requires subordination of self—love of one's neighbor. And who better to remind one of that truth than Jesus of Nazareth? Moreover, even if prayer has no personal Hearer—and thus no responsive Actor in a Heavenly Mansion—the very Christian-inspired acts of confessing one's sins, acknowledging the need for forgiveness, cleansing a scornful heart, seeking a strengthened spirit, and turning about-face in repentance might well be a way of finding the personal renewal necessary before one can truly treat others, both as individuals and in society, as one would wish to be treated by others.

Certainly in Wiley's view the Christian's language and approach would not be the exclusive route to self-renewal; he would quickly acknowledge that other faiths, or perhaps even tough-minded self-reliance, might well fuel a similar readiness to care for others. But in Wiley's case, the few humanistic elements of the traditional Baptist faith that were found in intercessory prayer, preaching, and old-fashioned hymn-singing understandably offered the best way to help him feel, express, and renew his own responsibilities to others. And this theology of a life-for-others, drawn from Midwestern Unitarianism[11] (and even from the Hopkinsianism that launched Maryville College), satisfied Rutledge wholly apart from any need for assurance of personal salvation beyond this life. Put another way, Wiley arrived, intellectually, at a blend—Christian humanism—rejecting dependency on a loving, saving God while hanging, emotionally, onto a Social Gospel that he could find even in a church emphasizing, far more often, the kind of personal salvation he found far-fetched. The spiritual reward available from the very act of giving oneself to others was real, available on earth, and surely enough for Wiley Rutledge.

Eventually, Wiley outgrew his need to attend church regularly. He would take the family to Delmar Baptist on the few occasions when his father visited St. Louis, but when Annabel's mother came to live with them—and expected to attend the Methodist church—Annabel took her while Wiley stayed home. After the family moved to Iowa in 1935, Annabel (her mother no longer living) attended the Congregational church, usually without Wiley—apparently the closest that Annabel could come to a Unitarian congregation. Not until the Rutledges moved to Washington did Wiley himself find a church home: the All Souls Unitarian Church. There a power-

ful, intellectually stimulating preacher, A. Powell Davies, who had joined
in founding Americans for Democratic Action, preached against political
witch hunting and worked for civilian control of atomic energy[12]—surely
this was someone whom Wiley Rutledge enjoyed hearing.

One would think that Wiley's religious orientation, as it grew from his
early Southern Baptist faith to Christian humanism, influenced his attitudes on race, and surely this transition must have helped take him beyond
his upbringing in a lawfully segregated society. But Wiley Rutledge is not
known to have invoked religion as a basis for any liberalization of his outlook on race or indeed as the reason for any expression of his humanitarian
views. He tended not to express his personal beliefs about religion, apart
from those indicated during formal presentations at a church Bible class
or at the Public Question Club; and the reason for that omission may have
been, very simply, that despite the Christian roots of his humanism, he
came emotionally, as well as intellectually, to abandon any theistic rationale or vocabulary for treating others with dignity and fairness, or for asking
society at large to do the same. And, as more an intellectual person than a
self-conscious preacher's son—or perhaps because he *was* a self-conscious
preacher's son—he emphasized reason, not revelation, for urging others to
follow their better natures. But back to the question: how did Wiley's attitudes on race evolve beyond those of the college debater who denigrated
"the Negro" for tainted blood, and the law school graduate who reminisced
in black dialect?

Wiley's children believe that on social issues, Annabel initially was more
liberal than Wiley, and they all credit her with opening his eyes to racism.
Coming from the North, Annabel virtually had no experience with African Americans as she was growing up; there was only one black family in
Howell, Michigan. But she came from a socially liberal family and attended
a college which had been racially "integrated since the mid-nineteenth century—a pathsetter in race relations." (Maryville, too, had of course been
such a path setter, but we have noted that by the time Wiley was in college, Tennessee law forbade racial integration even of private institutions.)
One lesson from Annabel particularly caught Wiley's attention. Contrary
to Southern tradition, she insisted that African American women, like all
women, be addressed as "Mrs." or "Miss," not by their first names. While
growing up, Wiley had never heard a black woman addressed as Annabel
demanded (in fact, as a high school teacher in Indiana he had distinguished
racially between males as well by applying the reverse tradition, calling
white boys by their first names, blacks by their last). Upon confrontation
by Annabel, however, Wiley readily agreed with her position. The Public
Question Club also helped to liberalize Wiley's views on race, according to

his son Neal, when Rutledge and his colleagues addressed questions such as, "Have Minorities Any Rights?"[13]

Several other incidents demonstrate that Wiley's racial views mellowed with his years in St. Louis. Neal recalls his father's showing him the Dred Scott monument on the St. Louis waterfront. Rutledge explained to his young son why that Supreme Court decision—holding that Scott, as slave property, was not a citizen entitled to sue in a Missouri court—was a national disgrace. So were the waterfront "Hoovervilles"—Neal's father pointed them out—built of cardboard and orange crates, where African Americans lived in Depression days. Also one day in St. Louis, Neal recalls, white kids pushed a black boy off a ledge high above a quarry filled with water where youngsters of both races swam regularly—at opposite ends. The boy drowned. The community's only response was to pour oil on the water so that nobody could swim there—a heartless response that distressed Neal's father greatly. He was "moved by it," Neal added. Neal accordingly was aware at an early age that his father "had an attitude more friendly to blacks than I was accustomed to seeing around St. Louis."[14]

As Neal Rutledge has also noted, his mother as well once observed that Wiley had undergone a major change in his attitude toward blacks while in St. Louis. But that change reflected far more empathy than action. Wiley had to be aware that during his tenure African Americans would not be admitted to Washington University, including the School of Law. Between 1881 and 1896, nine African Americans had entered Washington University, of whom four graduated from the law school. Thereafter, however, the university became racially segregated until the late 1940s, when change began at the medical school. In contrast, in 1947 the School of Law refused a $15,000 grant to its scholarship fund because the donor required a color-blind admissions policy. A former student from the class of 1930 filed a vigorous protest with the chancellor and sent a copy to the "Hon. Wiley Rutledge," by that time on the Supreme Court. The justice replied: "I am really glad I am not on the campus now, although I suppose we had the same problem when I was there, but not so dramatically posed. It is quite a commentary on both our so-called civilization and our so-called educational processes."[15] Three years before writing this letter, however, the justice was still repeating stories about an "old darky" or a "culud gentleman," but to some extent his personal writing style had changed. After the 1930s he would refer episodically to the proverbial "fly in the ointment," no longer to a "nigger in the woodpile."[16]

IN ST. LOUIS, Wiley began to involve himself in major professional issues, national as well as state and local. He joined the American Bar Association; worked actively in the Association of American Law Schools; became, as dean, an ex officio member of the American Law Institute; and worked assiduously as one of Missouri's three commissioners, appointed by the governor, to the National Conference of Commissioners on Uniform State Laws. His most visible contributions, however, occurred at the state level. He spoke out in favor of reforming the Missouri Criminal Code; making women eligible for jury duty; creating a voluntary defender plan while rooting out the "unconscionable criminal lawyer"; and shifting from the legislature to the organized bar the authority to admit and supervise lawyers. Rutledge also sought to bring racial and religious groups closer together by serving actively on the Social Justice Commission of St. Louis. And he joined the board of directors of the St. Louis Civil Liberties Committee.[17]

In 1930 Rutledge addressed gangsterism, in particular the "Scorfina" case in Kansas City, opining that the criminal justice system was not up to the task of suppressing it. He proposed an extraordinary change. Noting the racketeers' ability to conceal evidence of specific acts, to terrorize witnesses and jurors, and to move about freely, the dean proposed enactment of laws that would "recognize and define as public enemies men who are known to participate in gang activities and thus make it possible for society to remove them without conviction of specific acts." That is to say, he urged creation of a public enemy status. He further proposed creation of a special commission or court of "able lawyers or judges" to "find both the facts and the law in a given case," as well as authority to prescribe the "penalty" or "treatment," including "permanent removal from society." If the evidence was insufficient for guilt but enough for "a strong suspicion of guilt," the public enemy could be put under a peace bond and ordered to report his whereabouts daily to the police, he said.[18] Rutledge recognized that his proposals would probably require constitutional amendment, although he believed that the Sherman Antitrust Act, with its very general outline of punishable offenses, might serve by analogy to justify a rather general definition of unlawful gangsterism. He also suggested "defin[ing] gangsterism as a form of insanity or mental abnormality" in order to "avoid most of the troublesome constitutional questions." In short, he proposed that because gangsters in most cases "are definitely known but cannot be convicted," the special "commission could deal with them simply by proving them gangsters," thereafter putting "the burden of proof on the suspected individual[s]" to keep in touch with the police when not immediately incarcerated.[19] (Incredible!)

Wiley's main cause during his years in St. Louis was the protection of children forced to work. He noticed that by 1933, exploitation of children during the Depression was intensifying, with a corresponding increase in tuberculosis and accidental injury, not to mention illiteracy and lost child-hood.[20] For two years he doggedly pursued that concern.[21] He began with a speech before the St. Louis Conference of Social Work in May 1933, criticizing the president of the American Bar Association, Charles Martin,[22] for attacking the Child Labor Amendment that Congress had sent to the states for ratification in 1924. Twice the Supreme Court had struck down, as outside the commerce and taxing powers, federal legislation to limit children in the workforce by imposing minimum age and maximum hours requirements.[23] The amendment accordingly would have empowered Congress "to limit, regulate and prohibit the labor of persons under eighteen years of age," while leaving "unimpaired" the "power of the several states" themselves to protect child labor unless preempted by Congress.[24]

Only six states had ratified the amendment by 1932, most before the Depression.[25] But in 1933 increasing unemployment, exacerbated by "sweatshop" operators who employed children to replace adults at lower and lower wages—which led to a children's strike in Pennsylvania—triggered renewed interest in the amendment.[26] In that year alone nine states,[27] some of which had rejected the amendment earlier,[28] joined in ratification, leaving twenty-one more required before the amendment would become law.[29] In the meantime, Congress had added to the National Recovery Administration (NRA) industrial codes new provisions barring child labor under the age of sixteen.[30] But as Wiley emphasized in an article for the *St. Louis Post-Dispatch*, those code provisions would expire in two years; and in any event, he added, the entire national recovery program of which they were a part was vulnerable to a legal attack (which eventually succeeded).[31] Child labor opponents, therefore, including Wiley Rutledge, remained energized.

Wiley was particularly galled by the "violent attack" on the amendment by President Martin of the ABA, because Martin was implying strongly that the legal profession itself, not just the ABA, monolithically opposed the amendment. To the contrary, Wiley perceived "a large and growing element among lawyers" that dissented from Martin's position, "not only with reference to the merits of the Child Labor Amendment, but also in relation to the fundamental political philosophy" that Martin was espousing.[32] And Wiley was bent on conveying that dissenting view. Rutledge thus undertook a personal full-court press on the Missouri legislature, writing to state senators, spelling out the reasons for the amendment, and rebutting opposing arguments.[33] He also supplied the legislature with a nineteen-page memorandum answering legal questions concerning state ratification.[34] And he wrote a signed editorial for the *Post-Dispatch*, spoke to the League of Women Voters, and keynoted a major hearing in St. Louis to generate local support.[35]

In his address to the St. Louis Conference of Social Work in 1933, Wiley vilified not only Martin but everyone who over the years had advocated a similar philosophy:

Social progress in the form of national legislation is faced constantly with the three hurdles of so-called "natural rights," "state rights," and "republican institutions." Behind these legal and political dogma of the eighteenth century all forms of commercialized greed have sought to establish their interests beyond the reach of government control. They are the sheep's wool in which the institution of human slavery was legally clothed; the guise under which railway combinations and other forms of trusts sought freedom from national restraint in order to establish monopoly; the shield behind which vast power combinations seek similar freedom today; the basis upon which workmen's compensation acts, minimum wage laws, laws regulating hours of labor, and all other forms of legislation in the public interest have been resisted. Nowhere have these hoary philosophies been more effectively employed than in tying the hands of the federal government in the protection of children.[36]

Rutledge then blasted Martin's arguments. Martin had contended that the amendment was too broad because it would "nationalize" not merely a child's employment in the workplace but also a child's labor in the home, which parents alone, he said, had a natural right to control. Wiley showed that Martin had proved too much. If parents had a natural right to control a child's health and morals, then how could that right not extend to boycotting "compulsory education" and "compulsory vaccination," as well as to ignoring "all state legislation affecting child labor" in the workplace?—all of which Martin himself, a states rights advocate, considered legitimate.[37]

Wiley also cited "vicious" forms of "child labor" that technically might not constitute "child employment" but surely invited government scrutiny. Under a "so-called family agreement," for example, such as the typical arrangement negotiated with a sharecropper, an employer contracted with one parent for "the labor of the entire family for a lump sum." As a result, a child who labored at the parent's direction would not necessarily be the other contractor's "employee." But whatever the arrangement, Wiley argued, parents and guardians should not be privileged to abuse their children any more than employers were. "The power of Congress," he insisted, "should be plenary in the protection of the health, education, and morals of the child."[38]

Martin's inconsistent fallback argument, that child labor regulation should be limited to the states, would be entirely ineffective, Wiley added. The competitive advantage of businesses in states with the weakest child labor protections would lead the other states, he predicted, to drop their protections to the lowest standards in the land. The governor of Massachusetts, he noted, had threatened to do just that unless the southern states raised their standards. But even if this would not happen everywhere, he stressed, the accomplishment of adequate remedies "in forty-eight states" would require "not less than a quarter of a century."[39]

Rutledge concluded his rebuttal with devastating critiques of the Supreme Court's decisions striking down child labor legislation as exceeding Congress's commerce power (1918) and taxing power (1922), and he predicted that the Court "as now constituted"—with Chief Justice Hughes and Justices Roberts, Cardozo, Stone, and Brandeis—would uphold that same legislation if it were renewed by Congress. Still, if the commerce and taxing powers "be thought insufficient," he emphasized, there was still another constitutional basis for upholding federal child labor protections. The "time has come to give full force" to the general welfare clause, which surely could be read to protect children, Rutledge claimed.[40]

In addition to Martin's railing, Wiley encountered still other objections to the amendment. Some opponents cited the unhappy experience with Prohibition—with the Eighteenth Amendment—that was repealed by the Twenty-First Amendment as of December 5, 1933, while the child labor debate was intensifying. Rutledge pointed out, in response, that unlike the Eighteenth, "the Child Labor Amendment would not introduce regulatory provisions into the Constitution" itself. It would merely empower Congress to legislate, and thus could not lead "to more regulation than Congress was willing to authorize."[41] Wiley also answered concerns that the amendment would "interfere with religious education," assuring a radio audience, as well as individual legislators, that leading Roman Catholic authorities "declare unhesitatingly that the amendment confers no power over education." To those who opposed the amendment out of fear that the federal government was "something in the nature of an alien power," he pointed out that early opponents, such as the "manufacturing" and other "big business" interests, no longer stood in the way. And, finally, to those who simply rejected the amendment as "un-American," he stressed that in offering the amendment in 1924, both political parties—supported by the conservative President Coolidge—had acted on party platforms dating back to 1916.[42]

The push for the amendment during 1933 failed in Missouri but was renewed in 1935 with the dean's help—and with the same result.[43] When the national effort ended in 1937, the amendment had fallen eight states short of the thirty-six required for ratification. In mid-1938, however, Congress enacted the Fair Labor Standards Act, which not only created the forty-hour work week and a minimum wage, but also banned from interstate commerce all goods produced by anyone who had hired an employee under the age of sixteen, or under eighteen in particularly hazardous occupations such as mining. Then in 1941, in *United States v. Darby*, a reconstituted Supreme Court unanimously upheld the act, expressly overruling *Hammer v. Dagenhart*, the first decision to strike down child labor legislation. Justice Stone's analysis of *Dagenhart*, rather than track the elliptical dissent of Justice Holmes, paralleled the commerce clause arguments that Wiley Rutledge had proffered eight years earlier in his public refutation of the ABA's Martin.[44]

Wiley had cited legal principles, but his presentations had been laced with sharp rhetoric. Beginning in 1933 he had been unreservedly critical of the "pirates of industry and finance who have brought the country to the point of 'dying by inches.'" He accused Charles Martin of "'red baiting.'" And he criticized the U.S. Supreme Court with restrained derision. Rutledge cited Court-approved bans on interstate commerce in "lottery tickets, obscene matter, diseased cattle and persons, and intoxicating liquor, even before prohibition." The Court, he observed, had approved "assistance to farmers in producing better hogs." So, the dean lamented to a radio audience, "Congress can improve and protect hogs and cattle, but not children." He continued: "The Senate and the House are composed largely of able constitutional lawyers, and they have four times declared their belief in Federal power to place children upon an equality with pigs. But all this is nullified by the views of five men" on the Supreme Court. Because, he concluded, these men "have been invested with this power under our constitutional system, we have acquiesced in their decision. But the time for acquiescence has passed. The Amendment offers the constitutional method for correcting what we believe to be their mistake." Wiley Rutledge never turned back from this broad view of federal power that he expressed forcefully in 1933 while dean in St. Louis.[45]

RUTLEDGE UNDOUBTEDLY would have been as strongly committed to the child labor movement if Martin had come from an organization other than the ABA. But some element of his emotion surely was attributable to his profound aversion to the ABA's social and political conservatism at the time. Early on, the ABA seemed progressive enough. Founded in 1878 "to fight low standards and corruption in the profession," the ABA by 1897 was seeking to protect the public by recommending three years of law school education, including a diploma, for admission to practice. By 1908, joined by the Association of American Law Schools, the ABA was pressing the states to require two years of college before admission to law school. Harvard and Columbia, followed by Pennsylvania, Stanford, Western Reserve, and Yale, had begun to require a college degree for admission by the 1920s, and thus the élite schools—supported by the ABA and AALS leaders from their ranks—came to see legal education no longer as an alternative to college but as a program of graduate study.[46]

While many understood these developments as efforts to protect the public, others saw them as evidence of discrimination. The proprietary, or "night," law schools damned the graduate study model as perniciously bigoted and anti-democratic, and between 1913 and 1921 two Carnegie Foundation studies of legal education and the profession reflected sympathy for that concern, documenting the need for at least two kinds of law schools—university-affiliated and proprietary—to satisfy two discrete markets for legal services: the well-to-do, and those in the lower social classes. The ABA balked. Many candidates for proprietary schools were Jews, Catholics, and other immigrants whom one future ABA president, in 1915, found "'gifted with a marvelous intellectual ability'" but, sadly, "'without the incalculable advantage of having been brought up in the American family life.'" Accordingly, he said, they "'can hardly be taught the ethics of the profession as adequately as we would desire.'" This ABA leader unfortunately spoke for many others at the top of the profession and in the university law schools.[47] Open warfare developed between those who saw lawyers exclusively as bearers of advanced degrees, and those who saw room for trade school graduates as members of the bar. The drive for improving lawyers' competence through increased formal education had turned ugly.

During the early 1920s, while Wiley Rutledge was in law school and beginning practice, a resolution of the conflict emerged, one that seemed to be a compromise only in the sense that it forestalled efforts by the AALS to drive the proprietary schools out of business. A committee of the ABA chaired by Senator Elihu Root of New York—former secretary of state, winner of the Nobel Peace Prize, and former president of the ABA—issued a report, endorsed by Chief Justice Taft and by a national conference of bar and law school leaders in 1922, prescribing standards for law school accreditation.[48] These included at least two years of college for law school admission, a minimum ratio of full-time faculty to students, a library of at least 7,500 volumes, and three years of full-time law school study—or, for the proprietary schools, at least four years of part-time study. The war between the ABA and the proprietary schools continued nonetheless. Even by 1928 "not an evening law school in the country" was on the ABA-approved list, a situation that continued over the next decade as proprietary schools failed to meet ABA requirements for full-time faculty and library. The establishment—the ABA and the AALS—had cemented its control. By 1938 "only eight states did not require two years of college before law studies," and in-

creasingly the states were requiring candidates for admission to the bar to
have been educated at ABA-approved law schools.[49]

Wiley Rutledge's efforts to strengthen admission standards at Washington University manifested a strong belief not only in improving his own
school's student body but also in raising admission standards generally to
protect the public. While not an opponent of the proprietary schools, he
was not their advocate either. But ABA élitism and related political conservatism upset him deeply, and from time to time he would threaten to resign
from the ABA[50]—although he never did.

INHERENT IN Rutledge's concerns about child labor was a profound aversion to predatory business corporations. In 1935 he wrote a long article for
the *St. Louis Post-Dispatch* describing the power of interstate holding companies and advocating adoption of the Wheeler Rayburn bill to bring public
utility holding companies, in particular, under federal regulation. Indeed
he went further, advocating national incorporation (and regulation) of all
corporations engaged in interstate commerce.[51]

In addition to writing newspaper articles on public policy, Wiley loved to
make speeches. That love, more than any sense of obligation, drove him to
speak virtually to any local group that invited him to do so. Often elaborating on topics aired at the Public Question Club, he spoke during his years in
St. Louis to, among others, the United Hebrew Temple Men's Club on "The
Ancient Case of Stalin v. Hoover,"[52] to the Social Justice Commission of St.
Louis on "The Cultural Lag in the Law,"[53] to the Downtown Y.M.C.A. on
reforming the criminal law,[54] to the local chapter of the American Society
of Mechanical Engineers on workers' compensation laws,[55] to a chapter of
Phi Delta Kappa on whether the schools were "preparing for intelligent,
dynamic citizenship,"[56] to the Tuesday Club on "Present Foreign Policy and
Peace,"[57] and to the Missouri Society for Mental Hygiene on "Legal Aspects
of Delinquency and Crime."[58]

Wiley Rutledge was always eager to propose solutions, not merely to
identify a problem. On occasion he could go overboard, as he had in 1930
in recommending criminal sanctions for "gangsterism." Five years later,
he proffered some other provocative thoughts, this time about the international situation. To the Webster Groves (Missouri) Peace Council, he declared that war in Europe was inevitable and urged formation of a war policy
immediately. Specifically, he endorsed a national resolve against protecting
U.S. citizens who chose to visit foreign territories, legislation nationalizing
the manufacture of arms, and a new mechanism for declaring war by requiring an affirmative majority in a national referendum. In later years, he
would explain away this brief flirtation with isolationism, much as he would

minimize his plan for isolating gangsters. But however unusual his proposals were, one must credit Rutledge with facing up to virtually every major problem of the day and committing himself publicly with his best answer, even if far-fetched, until he found a better one.[59]

BY LATE 1932, the university's financial condition was grim, a situation attributable to the Depression-induced decline of its endowment. Effective November 1, the university's board of directors imposed a 5 percent salary reduction on all officers and employees, followed by an additional 5 percent the next July. By 1935 Wiley's own salary was still at $6,300. He could accept the reality of retrenchment, but he chafed under his relationship with Chancellor Throop, who in Wiley's view—though he was "more than good" to him personally—shared too little of his authority with university faculties, discriminated against the law school by cutting its budget every year without leaving even a "very small contingent fund" for the dean's use, and engaged in continuing conflict with a university trustee over law school affairs, bringing about a detrimental "stalemate."[60] Thus, President Eugene Gilmore of the State University of Iowa caught Rutledge's attention when Gilmore wrote to him in May 1935 to say, "Your name, along with many others, has been suggested" for "the deanship here" in the College of Law. "[C]ome up and spend the day with us," Gilmore invited, and Wiley agreed. Wiley cautioned, however, that "in no event" would he "care to enter a situation which would be greatly complicated by faculty jealousy or disappointment." He was concerned that he not get involved in a contest with a candidate from within Iowa's own faculty.[61]

There was, in fact, an inside candidate, Mason Ladd, but Gilmore—despite support for Ladd from Dean Roscoe Pound at Harvard—was not disposed to look at home. And he was in a hurry. Gilmore had become Iowa's president in 1934 while serving as its law school dean, had continued in that dual capacity, and was eager to avoid handling the dean's duties for another year. Twice he had offered the job to others who had turned him down: Dean Herschel Arant of Ohio State and Professor E. Blythe Stason of Michigan. Gilmore had also been pursuing Professor Charles T. McCormick of Northwestern, who eventually withdrew from consideration, as did another candidate recommended by Pound, Harold M. Stephens, a former trial judge and professor from Utah, then an assistant attorney general with the U.S. Department of Justice.[62]

It is not clear why Gilmore turned to Wiley Rutledge. Although his name appeared on Gilmore's list of thirty-four potential candidates, no letter suggesting him can be found in the dean's file. Undoubtedly the two knew each other from the two years they served together on the National Confer-

State University of Iowa
president Eugene A. Gilmore.
(Courtesy of University of Iowa
Archives, Department of Special
Collections, University of Iowa
Libraries)

ence of Commissioners on Uniform State Laws, when Gilmore had represented Iowa and Rutledge Missouri. But their acquaintanceship must have
been slight, given the formality of their correspondence. Possibly Wiley's
Colorado classmate, former Washington University colleague—and good
friend—Philip Mechem, then of the Iowa faculty, urged Gilmore to turn
to Rutledge. But if so, one may wonder why Gilmore waited for two weeks
after he had written to Wiley to ask Mechem, then in New York, to wire his
estimate of Wiley's "teaching ability" and of how he was "regarded in this
respect by students and faculty [at] Washington University." In any event,
Mechem replied: "I have sat in Rutledge[']s class and thought him first rate
teacher. . . . Believe this to be universal opinion Washington. . . . This is
further attested by his repeated summer teaching at Colorado." Wiley thus
had a strong internal advocate. And, at forty-one, Wiley was four years older
than the insider, Ladd. Gilmore's file shows no other check on Rutledge.[63]

Events moved swiftly. Wiley visited Iowa City on June 4, and Gilmore
telephoned an offer on June 10. Wiley immediately replied that his "inclination" was "to accept," but that Chancellor Throop had asked him to "withhold decision" until the two of them could "discuss the matter thoroughly."
Wiley accepted on June 22. Throop took the resignation "with regret" and
wished his departing dean "success."[64]

In explaining his decision to Throop, Wiley wrote, "I wavered back and forth until the very last. My own personal preference, I still believe, was to remain." He added: "One doesn't live and work in an institution for nine years—nor in a community—without creating ties which to sever is like cutting arteries. That's just how I feel about it—with a sort of sickness in the stomach-pit. You have been good to me, the faculty of the law school are like blood brothers, and there are dear friends in the other faculties and the community." Wiley then told Throop that his "primary reason" for leaving was consideration of his children's education. He was concerned about the quality of the public schools in and around "the large city" and could not afford three private school tuitions. He then emphasized that Throop had done "everything which it was humanly possible to do" to persuade him to stay; that the decision was not about "self-advancement"; that he was apprehensive about the "bigger job" to be done at Iowa; and that if he found he had made a mistake he might apply "for the new professorship" he hoped would be endowed at Washington University.[65]

Wiley told others, in addition to Throop, that the "controlling consideration" in accepting the Iowa deanship had been his children's education, but while that was a concern, the schools in Webster Groves surely were more than a cut above those in the "large city" next door. Other factors had to be at work.[66] An important, if not compelling, reason for the move, of course, was the Iowa College of Law itself: a larger school in a major state university with a more distinguished faculty headed by a nationally renowned president, Eugene Gilmore—earlier a Harvard-trained law professor at Wisconsin who had drafted regulatory legislation for the state, engaged in criminal law reform, and promoted the progressive "Wisconsin idea" that involved the faculty in public service. Perhaps Gilmore's most enduring legacy was a proposal that led in 1923 to the creation of the American Law Institute, which ever since has published "Restatements" of the common law cited often by the courts as useful precedent. Gilmore had a socially conservative streak, but he also had a national reputation in legal education that must have led Wiley Rutledge to believe that he would receive the kind of support from the president's office that a dean needs.[67]

Although Wiley's letter to Throop sugar-coated his feelings about the law school's treatment at Washington University, his comment that the move did not reflect a desire for "self-advancement" was substantially true. His ambition, at most, had been to serve as a professor and dean at a good law school in a community where he liked to live. Washington University generally satisfied those criteria, and there was reason to hope that the Depression would lift soon enough to permit improvement of the School of Law's finances—and thus its quality. But Wiley saw an impediment that would not go away in the foreseeable future. All things considered, the "controlling consideration," really, was Wiley's disenchantment with the Washington

University administration, meaning Chancellor Throop and Throop's on-going dispute with the university's board member Charles Nagel (earlier secretary of commerce and labor under President Taft).[68]

When pressed by Throop, Wiley had offered two conditions for remaining: sufficient endowment for "at least two more" full-time faculty members and immediate board approval of "a three-year" college entrance requirement. Throop and Nagel had been willing to change the entrance requirement without delay and to assure one more full-time professor, with "every effort" to add a second. As further inducement, Rutledge was offered a salary "within $500" of the $8,050 that Iowa had proposed. But all this was not enough. "Had there been nothing else in the picture," Wiley later wrote to a friend, "their assurances would have come so close to my conditions that I would have remained." But, he concluded, the conflict between Throop and Nagel gave him little hope of further progress. "Consequently," Wiley wrote to William Green Hale, his former dean, "with every misgiving, I decided to leave."[69]

Letters poured in from colleagues and the community expressing profound appreciation for Wiley's service and genuine sadness at his leaving. One from an official at the St. Louis office of the National Recovery Administration was typical: "Your leaving Washington University is a real loss, not only to the school, but the community at large, and I am appalled to think of what it may mean. This stuffy, conservative old city needs men like you for clear exposition and support of the liberal causes. How could you bear to leave them in the lurch?"[70] A former young instructor whom Rutledge had brought onto the faculty, Sam Elson, wrote:

Perhaps, despite your acuteness and awareness of the surrounding scene, you do not realize how important and inspiring a part you had in the University and in the Law School. Personally I know that I owe you a tremendous debt for the stimulus you gave me and for whatever habits of scholastic integrity and persistence I may now have. All the alumni who have talked to me after hearing the news are deeply regretful at your departure, and all seem to feel a sense of personal loss, as well as the aching void that will be left at the Law School.[71]

Ralph Fuchs added his blessings: "There is not a shadow of a doubt in my mind about the wisdom of your decision, and I hope you and Annabel may soon reach the stage of exuberant happiness about it. . . . It is a tribute to Gilmore's capacity that, despite his conservatism, he recognized your quality and pursued you. Now you are in the main stream of advance in the law school and educational world; and I place no limit in my own mind upon the distance you are likely to go. Congratulations!"[72]

SIX

Legal Philosophy

In 1928, while settling into a new home deep on a lot lined with oaks and maples in suburban Webster Groves, Wiley Rutledge challenged an eminent member of the academy, Professor Joseph H. Beale of Harvard. The young professor had received from the American Law Institute a set of "Tentative Drafts" of ALI "Restatements" of the common law. He wrote to the ALI director criticizing the *Restatement of Contracts*, in particular its single rule for determining the validity of every contract. The letter was forwarded to Beale, the Restatement's "Reporter" and principal author, who wrote to Wiley in reply that, yes, at present "there is no one generally accepted rule on this point." But that is exactly the idea, stressed Beale; there must be one. The authors of the Restatement had "chosen among the rules accepted by courts" the one that appeared "best fitted practically for the administration of law." Beale concluded: "I think you would agree that [in] dealing with law as a practical science it is much more important to have a fixed rule applicable to all cases than to leave counsel, clients and courts uncertain in the matter."[1]

Wiley replied: "I agree with you fully as to the practical importance of certainty in the law. . . . However, there are situations in which certainty should be avoided as poison. Nothing is so deadly to growth in the law as artificial finality either of judicial decision or of legislative fiat." Areas of rapid legal development in particular, he stressed, such as contractual efforts to modify labor law, strict liability, and legal cause, were much too fluid for application of a single rule. The Restatement proposal was undesirable, therefore, because it could lead very easily to an unsatisfactory decision on the extreme facts of a particular case, "leaving both the courts and the bar dissatisfied . . . and dubious as to its future application." As a result, Wiley concluded, "constant and repeated attack" on the rule would occur, bringing increased uncertainty, not the settled law intended.[2]

84

The young professor from Washington University, taking a realistic look, thus disagreed forcefully but tactfully with an unyielding disciple of Langdell who had insisted on an explicit rule regardless of context or consequence. However progressive some members of the ALI and their Restatements may have been, it was not at all irrational for Wiley to fear recognition of "black letter" rules by an organization of the establishment, dominated by lawyers who typically represented management and tort defendants. Years later, as a federal appellate judge, he still did "not place much value" on ALI Restatements.[3]

IN 1929, during his fifth year as a law professor, Wiley Rutledge published his first scholarly article, attacking another Harvard professor. He critiqued a treatise, *Corporate Advantages without Incorporation*, published earlier in the year by Edward H. ("Bull") Warren, Harvard's distinguished Weld Professor of Law, known for his tendency to "gore" his students with questions. Warren's treatise addressed three related questions: (1) When does the law consider a group of individuals conducting business together as "merged into a composite unit," such as a corporation, with power to do business as an entity? (2) Who should answer that question: the legislature, the judiciary, or either one? (3) If the law characterizes the group as no more than an aggregation of individuals, such as a partnership, vulnerable to individual liability for collective action, can the group nonetheless enter into contractual arrangements that will achieve for its members the various personal protections and other advantages of a corporate entity?[4]

In answering the second question, "Who should decide?"—the question of particular interest to Rutledge—Warren observed that at the time of the American Revolution, the law according to Blackstone recognized a group of human beings "as merged in a composite unit" only if deemed so by the sovereign. Because the legislature had replaced the king as the sovereign in this country, Warren concluded, "the legislature's consent is necessary" for recognition of "a legal unit which is not a natural person."[5]

Wiley Rutledge had long been familiar with "Bull" Warren, whose casebook on private corporations he had used while a student in Herbert Hadley's class and as a teacher himself in Colorado and St. Louis. When the young professor came across Warren's new treatise, he reacted with an intensity that showed he felt let down by a scholar he undoubtedly admired. Believing strongly that common law judges had the power to grant legal entity status to a group of individuals with attendant protections when fairness required, Rutledge attacked Warren with an uncharacteristic, and inappropriate, outburst remarkable as the only example of arrogance that Rutledge ever exhibited in writing. Rutledge charged that Warren's analysis "would appear to be absurd did it not proceed from so eminent an authority." He concluded that Warren's "thesis must be supported, if at all, by more potent consideration than the outworn legal philosophy"—Blackstone—"which he so naively assumes." This verbal bravado not only was unbecoming but surely reflected an unconscious intellectual insecurity that, it must be emphasized, he soon outgrew.[6]

Rutledge had a respectable theoretical basis for questioning Warren's unwillingness to grant to the courts common law power equal to the legislature's authority to confer legal status on groups—at least when the legislature had not preempted the field. But if Rutledge ever reread his article years later, he surely must have found it an embarrassment. He addressed three quarters of it to defining a group "unit" or "person" capable of legal relations—an interminable prelude to discussing his quarrel with Warren. Furthermore, the issue that concerned Rutledge was largely moot, for by the time he was writing, the legislature had substantially preempted the inquiry. With the advent of general incorporation laws beginning in the 1850s, virtually the only room left for a court to confer legal status on a group was in the area of labor unions and other unincorporated associations—examples that Warren addressed but Rutledge did not even mention.[7] Even as to defectively created corporations, Rutledge failed to pose realistic hypotheticals that would have tested Warren's absolutist position.

Furthermore, in berating Warren for subscribing to Blackstone's "Legislative Absolute," Rutledge himself went overboard, touting an absolute of his own, judicial supremacy, as the "new Ultimate." In doing so, Rutledge blurred the differences among judicial review for constitutional violations, where courts are unquestionably empowered to constrain the legislature; judicial construction of statutes, where courts are required to honor legislative intent but allowed to fill in the gaps; and judicial discernment of the common law, when courts on occasion find themselves at doctrinal crossroads and the decision, in a case of first impression, will inevitably make new law. By not clearly delimiting his advocacy of judicial supremacy, Rutledge could be understood to have favored an imperial judiciary, constrained only, if at all, by external, political reaction. Rutledge wrote, for example, of reining in the judiciary, when necessary, through "selection of judges by popular vote, . . . the recall of judges and their decisions, [and] . . . requiring more than a bare majority of the court to set aside an act of Congress."[8] This collage of remedies evidenced a failure to distinguish between state law remedies and constitutional adjudication, or between state and federal courts, or even to acknowledge the judge's responsibility to honor principled self-limitations on the exercise of judicial power.[9]

Finally, in chastising Professor Warren for placing lawmaking authority exclusively in the legislature, Rutledge did not effectively teach us why judges as well should have that authority. He cited—without discussing—the views of Dean Roscoe Pound to show that common law judges inevitably make, not merely find, the law.[10] But he never explained why it is necessary, even desirable, for judges to engage in lawmaking. That failure virtually undermined Rutledge's thesis that Professor Warren should have recognized the judicial prerogative to confer group "personality." The critique of Warren's treatise is noteworthy, therefore, not for contributing to legal scholarship but for revealing Rutledge's early acceptance of the judge as lawmaker.

Two legal giants who had written on the common law, Thomas McIntyre Cooley and Oliver Wendell Holmes Jr., accepted James Wilson's reality that judicial rulings inevitably made law. Cooley and Holmes further acknowledged Francis Lieber's concern that human biases pressure a judge's ruling. In furtherance of the democratic principle, therefore, both advocated judicial restraint. Cooley in particular—as a significant treatise writer, as dean of the law school at Michigan in the late nineteenth century, and concurrently as a Michigan Supreme Court justice—called upon judges, in their common law rulings, to follow popular expectations by reference to the state's social history and constitutional values. And when addressing legislation, he said, judges should sustain the law unless it was unconstitutional beyond a reasonable doubt.[11] Holmes, too, after long endorsing judge-made law, had concluded by 1897 that legislatures, not courts, were the preferred policymakers, since customary rules too often were unavailable for deciding novel cases, and thus the law, absent a legislative decision, could have no more legitimacy than what an inevitably biased judge proclaimed.[12]

Wiley Rutledge's luminary, however, Dean Roscoe Pound, instead took the activist view. If one understands Pound on the common law, one understands Rutledge. Born in Nebraska, where he earned a doctorate in botany at the state university, Pound studied law for a year at Harvard and eventually became Nebraska's law dean before teaching at Northwestern, then Chicago followed by Harvard, becoming dean there in 1916. Influenced by Harvard's John Chipman Gray, who had developed a "historical jurisprudence" that accepted judge-made law with the enthusiasm of a James Wilson, Pound attacked not only Langdell's legal science but also Cooley's and Holmes's judicial caution. As elaborated in *The Spirit of the Common Law* (1921), published while Rutledge was a student in Colorado, Pound saw the common law not as a "fixed body of definite rules" but as a "mode of treating legal problems"—a dynamic process. The outcome of that process, Pound acknowledged, is influenced by the judge's upbringing and education, associations, and class interest. The common law, therefore, is admit-

Harvard Law School dean Roscoe Pound. (Courtesy of Art and Visual Materials, Special Collections Department, Harvard Law School Library)

tedly shaped by judicial personality, but Pound, unlike Cooley and Holmes, was left untroubled. The people could rely on the legislature, he said, to correct the results of common law adjudication that overly favored particular rights and related interests—the solution to excessive judicial activism offered a century earlier by Judge Reeve and Judge Gould at Litchfield. Absent legislative override, therefore, the courts legitimately will reign "supreme" in announcing common law rules.[13]

Pound applauded the courts' progressive common law initiatives—using the very judicial power exercised a half-century earlier to benefit the entrepreneurial class—to prevent antisocial uses of private property, impose public duties on public utilities, prevent the perpetuation of monopolies, limit abuses by creditors, impose liability without fault for certain injuries, impose municipal liability for injuries, and limit private appropriation of public resources such as running water. Pound stressed that in contrast with the relatively homogeneous frontier, social and economic classes did "in fact exist in our industrial society," with an "inequality . . . in bargainings between them." He noted, accordingly, that the demands from the cities "to regulate housing, to enforce sanitation, to inspect the supply of milk, to prevent imposition upon ignorant and credulous immigrants, to protect the small investor of savings from get-rich-quick enterprises, [and] to regulate conditions of labor and provide a minimum wage" were based on realities that could not be satisfied by the "rules and principles," alien to government intervention, "developed for rural communities and small towns." Obviously referring to Langdell, Pound condemned judicial use of "mechanical jurisprudence" in addressing such matters. He favored instead a "sociological" jurisprudence that adjusts "principles and doctrines to the human conditions they are to govern." Pound was thus pleased by the shift that he perceived in judicial policy from "individualistic justice" in the nineteenth century to "social justice" in the twentieth. He championed a jurisprudence requiring judges "to keep in touch with life." He envisioned a "socialization of the law" by which he meant that the object of law had become a "great series of tasks of social engineering."[14]

These views of Pound were the source of "the new Ultimate, the judiciary," that Wiley Rutledge touted in his castigation of "Bull" Warren.[15] There was an unaddressed problem here, however. In relying on legislative overrides of runaway common law judges, Pound did not go further in his *Common Law* to address the limits, if any (short of impeachment), that would restrain a judge from using the Constitution, not merely the common law, to impose personal values that the legislature would be powerless to overturn. Wiley Rutledge would have to resolve that issue for himself in the years ahead.

AT FIRST it seems odd that Wiley Rutledge should have chosen to become primarily a professor of business organizations. Neither he nor any close family member had ever owned, or even worked in, a private business (other than Annabel's father's orchard). Wiley took no business or economics courses in college. And his several months at the Kentucky commercial college where he prepared for teaching high school offered no meaningful insights into the business world. There is evidence, however, that Wiley's brief law practice included work for a public utility that caused him to question "the holding company set-up." And that experience appears to have reinforced Professor Hadley's preaching at Colorado about the social responsibility, and the related political accountability, of corporate wealth.[16]

Undoubtedly, more than any other influence, Hadley had a defining impact on Wiley's teaching career, especially because Hadley's approach was so much in harmony with the young professor's instincts. Educated during the trust-busting years of Presidents Theodore Roosevelt, Taft, and Wilson, Rutledge had shown since his days at Maryville College his commitment to progressive politics. The Hadley teaching model, therefore, suggested that the course on business organizations—including large, merger-hunting, union-bashing corporations—would address the central economic, social, and political questions of the day. In fact, when Rutledge studied and taught at Colorado, any instruction in antitrust law would have come in the private corporations course.[17] A business organizations professor, therefore, could challenge students to ascertain the best possible blend of commercial opportunity and social responsibility, monitored as needed by government regulation. The teaching mission could transcend mere explication of corporate law; it could focus, more broadly, on the business entity as a force for good—or for ill.

For perspective it is important to ask: When Wiley Rutledge began teaching, what were prevalent notions of the American business corporation that the new professor would explore? Unlike a partnership, the private business corporation was a separate legal entity, not a mere aggregation of individual owners. It had continuing existence through transferable shares; conducted business exclusively in its own name; and had, figuratively, a "corporate veil" that substantially shielded the shareholders from personal liability to third parties.[18] These characteristics facilitated business expansion far more readily than a partnership could usually do. In 1819 in the *Dartmouth College* case, Chief Justice John Marshall, reflecting Blackstone, called the corporation an "artificial being, invisible and intangible," a "mere creature of law." This characterization had legal significance. In *Bank of Augusta v. Earle*, for example, the Supreme Court acknowledged a state's power to bar transactions by "foreign" corporations because a corporation, as an "artificial person" existing only "by force of the law," lost existence at the border of its own state unless the next state, with no constitutional obligation to do so, chose as a matter of comity to recognize it.[19]

Business corporations in the United States were originally created as concessions by the state to private interests that would serve public purposes: banks, turnpikes, railroads, fire insurance companies. But Jacksonian democracy in the 1830s and 1840s denounced the common bribery of legislators to obtain exclusive corporate grants. Popular outrage led to the enactment of general incorporation statutes between 1850 and 1870, permitting any local business to elect the corporate form. The business corporation thus came to be understood as a special kind of contract among the state, the corporation, and its shareholders—more a private arrangement than a state-controlled instrument.[20]

After the Civil War, however, corporate lawyers manipulated the law to achieve various business combinations, not recognized by statute, through so-called business trusts that owned a controlling block of shares—in effect, separate holding companies.[21] But just as state courts began striking down these arrangements as unauthorized by statute and forbidden at common law, state legislatures started to respond to pressures from big business and to the ideology of free enterprise.[22] Beginning in 1888 with New Jersey, for example, states amended their laws to permit a corporation to acquire the stock, and thus ultimately the control, of another corporation.[23] As states yielded to entrepreneurs' desires, however, the federal government—reacting to monopoly and other anticompetitive practices—imposed restrictions on the expansion of corporate power. In 1890, two years after New Jersey legitimated the holding company, Congress enacted the Sherman Antitrust Act, declaring illegal all combinations "in the form of trust or otherwise" in restraint of interstate or foreign commerce. Years later, Wiley Rutledge wrote that the "brief period from 1888 to 1890" had presented "one of the strangest and most profound paradoxes in American legal and industrial history. Just at the time," he noted, "when the Federal Government was coming to the aid of the states' historic policy toward corporations and was adopting strong measures to make that policy effective, the states themselves began to turn in the opposite direction."[24]

Soon after the turn of the century, when corporate mergers were becoming commonplace, Theodore Roosevelt's Justice Department launched a program of "trust busting" that was intensified under his successors, Taft and Wilson. And by the middle of President Wilson's first term, in 1914, Congress had enacted legislation creating a new Federal Trade Commission to address "unfair methods of competition," and had adopted the Clayton Act, prohibiting a corporation from, among other things, acquiring stock in another if the result would lessen competition or create a monopoly.[25] Because federal antitrust law could supersede increasingly permissive state corporation laws, therefore, entrepreneurs sought a more sympathetic understanding of the corporation. Was there a way to reconceptualize it, as an entity separate enough from the state to justify greater insulation from government control than the "artificial person" protected by *Dartmouth College* against impairment of its charter, but vulnerable nonetheless to reserved state power?

The Supreme Court appeared to say yes. In 1886 the Court issued a cryptic, one-paragraph decision in *Santa Clara v. Southern Pacific Railroad*, holding that the equal protection clause entitled a "private" railroad corporation—a "person" under the Fourteenth Amendment—to nondiscriminatory taxation under state law.[26] Two decades later, the Court extended to private business corporations the Fourth Amendment protection of the "people" against unreasonable searches and seizures.[27] The Court's rulings accordingly helped change the common understanding of a corporation from that of an artificial creature of the state to that of an intrinsically independent organism much like a human being. According to this "natural person" theory, more commonly called the "natural entity" theory, the collective minds, emotions, and voices of corporate shareholders, directors, and officers reflected a unique "common spirit," and exercised a unique corporate "will," that led to inspired transactions which the owners and managers could have accomplished in no other way. The corporation, it was said, had a life truly of its own.[28] What was the basis, then, on which the government could step in to regulate a "person" no longer dependent umbilically on the state?

Progressive writers after the turn of the century, as legal positivists, believed that *all* rights, "both corporate and personal, were entirely the creatures of the state." They rejected any idea of "natural" rights that would inherently immunize individuals, let alone entities, from state regulation. This belief accordingly freed progressives to reject the notion that protections available to "persons" under the Constitution necessarily had to extend beyond humans to corporations. To progressives, therefore, the corporation—left only with private "interests," not inherent rights—was legally susceptible under the state's police power to reasonable legislative restraints designed to prevent and punish corporate abuse. The law applicable to corporations would thus be dictated by reference not to human personality but to the realities of corporate operations in society.[29]

In 1910 Woodrow Wilson elaborated this view. He argued that reference to the corporation as a "legal person" implied a level of inherent personal rights unsuitable to the "complex organization"—he called it "an economic society, a little economic state"—that the modern business corporation had become. Speaking before the American Bar Association when a candidate for governor of New Jersey, Wilson berated the corporation-as-person notion as a "fatuous, antiquated, and quite unnecessary fiction"; this fiction, he asserted, stood in the way of perceiving corporations, realistically, as institutions that "span society" and, as a result, had become "the responsibilities of society itself." Wilson conceded, however, that the fiction had been "innocent and convenient enough so long as corporations were comparatively small and only one of many quite as important instrumentalities used in business."[30]

As Wilson's address made clear, the politics of the early twentieth century, when Wiley Rutledge came of age and began to teach law, still entertained two conflicting visions of an economic America. Supporters of federal antitrust legislation and state laws protecting the rights of shareholders and the public—like Louis D. Brandeis—envisioned vigorous competition among enterprises, not shockingly large ones, whose corporate form was justified primarily as a convenience for the owners in managing and perpetuating their own businesses. Holders of this view still tended to understand the corporation, fundamentally, as a partnership among shareholders who controlled the business (while shielded substantially from personal liability). In contrast, major entrepreneurs were convinced that dynamic economic growth depended on large corporations whose economies of scale would achieve better and cheaper products than smaller, competing enterprises could, and whose large numbers of shareholders—little more than investors in no position to oversee corporate affairs—necessarily yielded corporate control to the directors and officers.[31] Wiley Rutledge had to wrestle intellectually, as well as emotionally, with both visions, and theories, as he began to teach in 1924.

AFTER HIS FIRST YEAR at Colorado, Wiley taught private corporations, or business organizations—a mix of agency, partnership, and corporation law —over fourteen straight years, at three law schools, before he left teaching for the bench. During that entire period, moreover, his principal research was in the corporate field. As a professor at schools west of the Mississippi that were not feeding large law firms—firms he once disparagingly called "urban professional 'factories'"—Wiley targeted his teaching toward students who would "become general practitioners, not specialists in some phase of so-called 'corporate practice.'" He focused on students, with special concern for those of average ability, who would typically represent small businesses and would "have as many problems of partnership as corporate ones." Thus, he put together a two-semester introductory course that embraced a full range of business operations from simple to complex.[32]

During his tenure at Washington University, Rutledge compiled part of a casebook—he never fulfilled his contract to publish—on *Private Corporations*, comprising 258 single-spaced typewritten pages issued to students in mimeographed form, enough to serve for almost a full semester.[33] The casebook began with a thirteen-page "Introductory" on the "Social Significance of the Corporation." It featured, first, selections that alternately praised and condemned the growth of the large corporation but, on balance, left the impression—according to quoted testimony from a Senate hearing—that the "growth of corporate enterprise has been drying up individual independence and initiative, drying up the life of the big town and the small town, and the hamlet. We are becoming a nation of hired men, hired by great aggregations of capital." Rutledge next included a selection from a book lamenting the failure of large corporations to realize their "'ethical opportunity of shortening labor hours and increasing labor compensation.'" Finally, as in other case books, he quoted almost entirely Justice Brandeis's dissenting opinion in *Louis K. Liggett Co. v. Lee*, in which Brandeis forcefully condemned the Supreme Court's nullification of a Florida taxing statute designed to protect independently owned retail stores against the larger chains. Brandeis's dissent was a broadside, in the nature of his earlier "Brandeis briefs," warning about the dangers of concentrated corporate wealth. Brandeis called concentration a "Frankenstein monster," admonishing that "the true prosperity of our past came not from big business, but through the courage, the energy, and the resourcefulness of small men," whose release "from corporate control" was necessary for "confidence in our future" and "the maintenance of liberty." This selection from Brandeis, covering all but three pages of the introduction—and repeated two thirds of the way into the casebook!—could not have made clearer where Wiley Rutledge himself was coming from.[34]

After giving his students an introductory lecture on the history of the corporation, Rutledge announced that the course fundamentally was about the creation and enforceability of business relationships. "To have an effective legal transaction," he advised, there must be two or more parties "capable of entering into legal relations," meaning relations that create enforceable rights and duties.[35] All parties that qualified for "legal" relations, therefore, whether individuals or entities, were to be thought of, in the legal terminology of the day, as "legal persons."[36] Absent "legal personality," an entity or individual could not be party to a legal relationship and thus not to an enforceable business transaction. Rutledge, accordingly, entitled the balance (part II) of his casebook "Legal Personality," which he subdivided into categories introduced by his own essays followed by cases illustrating each topic.[37] The recurring question, then, reflecting the inquiry underlying "Bull" Warren's treatise that Rutledge had vilified, was whether a particular business—owned by an individual or by a group—had a separate legal personality that supplanted the members' individual personalities. The answer would allocate liability. If the entity legally supplanted the individual member, a third party doing business with it could have no claim against the member. Otherwise it would.

Rutledge proceeded from relatively simple legal relations involving individual trustees, executors, business trusts, and the "one man" corporation—each of which could have legal personality that immunized the individual clothed with title—to more complex relationships between group entities. Methodically, he explored the variety of rights and remedies available against the entities and the individuals associated with them, depending on where the common law or state statutes had assigned, or withheld, legal personality. As a concept, therefore, legal personality furthered two teaching objectives. First, Rutledge believed that students could understand contemporary business arrangements, as well as possible alternatives, only if they knew the origins of those arrangements—their simpler forms from simpler days when the form itself unquestionably dictated the legal result. "Legal personality" was the tool that helped him trace the development from individual to group legal relations and to understand the legal rules normally applicable to different types of business entities. Second, this approach helped students to understand how the corporation had come increasingly to differ from a trust or a partnership, often taking on a life of its own divorced from meaningful shareholder control. Students thus learned how the corporation had come more and more to mean a social, not just a business, institution. The corporation had public responsibilities, not just private prerogatives.[38]

After the first semester's historical survey, Rutledge moved on for the balance of the year to another author's published casebook to treat partnership in depth, followed by concrete issues of corporate management; the corporation's express and implied powers; acts beyond those powers ("ultra vires" acts); corporate ownership of stock in another corporation; rules governing the declaration of dividends; and issues arising from dissolution and distribution of assets, comparing corporations with partnerships.[39] As Rutledge shifted to these specific issues, reliance on legal personality to define rights and obligations virtually disappeared. Now it was time to inquire whether the personality traditionally assigned to an entity was a *hindrance* to a just result and, for principled reasons, should be scrapped in a particular case. As a consequence, the student experienced classes liberally sprinkled with Rutledge's questions about what the result *should* have been. Students were occasionally confronted, too, with his editorial comments about the "evils of holding companies" and the respective views of "'progressive[s]'" and "thinking 'conservatives'" on "federal incorporation of all corporations doing business in interstate commerce."[40]

Rutledge's unusual contribution as a casebook writer—in contrast to his rather traditional organization by reference to legal personality—was his liberal inclusion of explanatory essays, approximately thirty in all, ranging in length from less than a page to as many as four or five pages (and once eight). Other casebooks at the time rarely supplied much text. Typically, to supplement the appellate opinions printed to illustrate legal rules and consequences, a casebook provided no more than a series of "notes," string-citing judicial decisions with brief descriptions of their holdings, in order to reinforce—or question—the principal cases presented for class discussion. Wiley's essays provided much more. Some were highly conceptual, others more practical, and all were obviously first drafts.[41] Most attempted to integrate information from the other social sciences, especially psychology and political science,[42] although there were frequent references as well to legal history and jurisprudence, and especially to the writings of the corporate theorist Ernst Freund, the philosopher John Dewey, and, of course, Roscoe Pound.[43]

Rutledge's invocation of legal personality—a reliance on "conceptualism"—ran headlong into the new "legal realism" predominating at Columbia, then Yale, in the 1920s and 1930s. Realists represented not a "single school of thought," but a "general outlook" derived from the "skepticism of Holmes and the social engineering of Pound." Rejecting Langdell's conceptualist jurisprudence while retaining his case method, the realists, such as Karl Llewellyn at Columbia and Arthur Corbin and Underhill Moore at Yale, took what they called a "functional" approach, stressing that law was not an exact science, was not value free, and thus essentially was political.[44] In the business field, none took teaching materials further toward "realism" than William O. Douglas, who had come to Yale in 1928 with other realists from Columbia after resigning to protest the selection of a new Columbia dean unsympathetic, they said, to the realists' legal research.[45] With his co-author Carrol M. Shanks of the New York Bar, Douglas published "Cases and Materials" on "Business Units" in three volumes,[46] noting in the preface that their approach represented "a shift from an historical emphasis"—such as the one used by Rutledge—"to the problems of law and business today." Douglas and Shanks wanted students to arrive at principled solutions dictated not by a particular "legal classification" or personality—corporation or whatnot—but by the most enlightened possible consideration of all interests affected, public as well as private.[47]

Douglas would have preferred to banish all mention of "legal personality" as a barrier to sound analysis.[48] His approach reflected the views of John Dewey of Columbia, who in an article in 1926 attacked "legal personality" analysis so convincingly that by 1930, according to Professor Horwitz, the concept had virtually disappeared as a subject of scholarship.[49] The class notes of a Rutledge student suggest, however, that despite using legal personality as a first-semester teaching tool, Rutledge sided fundamentally with Dewey—whose article he cited—and with Douglas. "We shouldn't say that there is no legal action because there is no legal person," the student wrote; "that merely states the result or the conclusion & not how we reached it, which is the important thing."[50] Legal personality, as Rutledge made explicit in his casebook as well as in class, did not drive a particular outcome. To the contrary, Rutledge used legal personality, or the lack of it, as the way of describing a legal result: of identifying who did, and did not, enter into a legal relationship, as determined not by form of organization but by public policy. Rutledge agreed that context—the "real" relationships of the contestants—should determine in a particular case whether an entity, incorporated or not, should be treated as a group or as a mere aggregation of individuals for purposes of legal consequence.[51]

Rutledge was indeed a confirmed realist as to the corporate form itself. Unlike theorists of "the" corporation as a unified concept, Rutledge perceived three types of corporations, which he believed the law should recognize separately rather than characterize all in the same way under a single state incorporation statute. In an article on "Significant Trends in Modern Incorporation Statutes" (1937), Rutledge proffered three paradigm corporations that he believed differed in kind rather than degree: the "corner peanut wagon" having a single shareholder and called "John Doe, Incorporated"; a "small local concern," "The Acme Grocery Corporation," capitalized at around $100,000 and "having from twenty to a hundred shareholders"; and finally, the "gigantic corporation[]" he named "Steel Corporation."[52]

First, reflecting his support for John Doe, Rutledge criticized state statutes that required all corporations to elect a minimum of three directors, thus permitting outside, "'dummy'" directors to frustrate the wishes and "decide the future" of an incorporated sole proprietor. Next, Rutledge saw no reason why directors should have virtually plenary authority to dominate Acme Grocery "over the protest of a considerable minority" of the shareholders; implicitly, he still saw room for a fairly large incorporated partnership safely under the shareholders' control. Finally, as to larger, national corporations engaged in "mass production," he accepted the reality of directors' hegemony over the many dispersed, passively investing shareholders. To watch over these "extensive business" concerns, however, he looked not to the states but to federal regulation, predicting that a "national incorporation act" would probably be the "ultimate resort" necessary to serve "an impatient, if not angry, public." Basically, therefore, Wiley Rutledge saw incorporated proprietorships and partnerships as arrangements reflecting predominantly a contractual relationship among the participants, in which control should remain with the owners, whereas the large manager-dominated corporation was more a natural entity, realistically manageable only by its directors and officers—and regulated by the national government.[53]

There is no reason to suppose that law teachers, in the days of legal realism, would have flocked to Rutledge's draft casebook had it been available. He himself recognized that judging from other teaching materials on the market, business organization professors were not drawn to a conceptual or historical approach. Indeed, by the time he left St. Louis for Iowa City in 1935, Rutledge was beginning to question his own reliance on legal personality, if only because most of the "younger" casebook writers, he realized, were ignoring it entirely. Rutledge, accordingly, needed a fresh opinion about his approach and asked Clarence Morris, a former student of his at Colorado who was then teaching at the University of Wyoming, to critique his casebook. He admonished Morris that he did not "want any taffy" in his response. "If I am on the wrong track I don't want to waste more time."[54]

Morris, later an eminent scholar at Texas and Pennsylvania, encouraged his mentor: "[T]here are certain advantages which are quite obvious in your organization. The student is sure to get a broader picture of the whole problem when your technique is followed."[55] Rutledge retained his approach, especially because materials published by the realists did not address small business in particular, and thus there was little if any help on the market for systematizing that area. Although he never completed his casebook or even came close to matching Douglas's productivity, Rutledge was committed to developing a semester's worth of materials uniquely tailored to preparing students for their anticipated vocations counseling business enterprises, partnerships as well as corporations, in the smaller communities of the Midwest.[56] The conceptualism of his first semester, therefore, was consistent with Woodrow Wilson's acknowledgment that legal personality was "innocent and convenient enough" in dealing with small business. And Rutledge's insistence that the realities of large corporate behavior, not the "personality" of corporations, should dictate their legal treatment brought him close to the realists if not entirely within their fold.

WILEY RUTLEDGE was not a productive scholar during his academic life. His duties as dean, his love of people more than the library, and his difficulty in writing analytic prose all kept him from legal writing. Of these, probably the last was the main reason he wrote so little. Rutledge could lecture extemporaneously on a current issue,[57] or even write a prepared address for a bar association[58] or a high school commencement,[59] with obvious ease. Each speech would be well organized, and his language would often be eloquent. It could soar. In short, he was an outstanding public speaker, and he thrived on being one. He believed deeply in what he said, and he loved having an audience. But that ability and enthusiasm did not translate easily into legal scholarship.

Probably there was little carryover from public speaking to legal writing because the tightly reasoned, almost mathematical approach required for legal analysis—the heavy emphasis on deductive skill—came less easily to Rutledge than marshaling the facts of history or politics and proceeding, inductively, to isolate and articulate a soundly documented point of view. He must have been enthusiastic about putting together his casebook because of his dedication to teaching and love for his students. But other scholarship efforts would have been akin to hand churning butter or lifting heavy weights. This is not to say that Rutledge was unable to analyze legal problems; he could—soundly, at times brilliantly. But he preferred analyzing

problems in the classroom—on his feet, while interacting with students—
not writing about them.

Law review editors, in organizing a symposium of articles honoring Justice Rutledge after his death, published an appendix of his publications. In
addition to a series of three lectures on the commerce clause in book form,
prepared after he had joined the Supreme Court, this appendix listed eight
articles and essays, five book reviews, and twenty-one addresses.[60] Of the
articles, only two could be called legal scholarship. And of these, "Significant Trends in Modern Incorporation Statutes" (1937), a useful survey of
the evolution of state corporation statutes nationwide, was more a collation
of sources than an analysis of ideas and cannot be said to have real scholarly significance. As we have seen, moreover, Rutledge's attack on Professor
Warren's treatise was a flawed effort. His contributions as a scholar were to
await his move from the classroom to the bench.

SEVEN

Iowa City

Innovation and Influence

In the late summer of 1935, when the Rutledges left St. Louis, they came to a community of around 15,000 described by a student at the time as "a dreamy, sleepy town."[1] Located on the Iowa River forty miles east of Des Moines, Iowa City was a college community primarily. The state university had opened a law department there in 1868 (renamed the College of Law in 1900), the first public university law school west of the Mississippi River. While disapproving Langdell's closed system of fixed common law principles, Iowa's first resident professor and dean, William Gardiner Hammond, had anticipated Langdell's teaching method. As early as 1868, two years before Langdell took hold in Cambridge, Hammond was assigning appellate opinions for study in addition to textbooks and treatises; and although Iowa did not predominantly employ the case method until 1889, that was early enough for a Carnegie Corporation study to confirm that Iowa was the first law school after Harvard to adopt it officially. After Hammond left for Washington University in 1881, the College of Law had but one noteworthy leader (Emlin McClain, a recognized scholar and president of the AALS) until 1930, when Iowa attracted Eugene Alan Gilmore, the "Wisconsin idea" reformer then serving as vice-governor general of the Philippines.[2]

Five years later, when Rutledge arrived, approximately 250 students were enrolled in the College of Law. About 100 were freshmen, of whom 65 to 70 would eventually graduate, reflecting "woefully low" admission requirements in Rutledge's view.[3] The students came mostly from Iowa's farms and small towns, including sons of judges, lawyers, bankers, and insurance agents.[4] Many had entered the law school after three years of college on the "six-year plan."[5] Unlike at Washington University, each class may have had one black student—typically from a state which did not admit African Americans to a state law school but paid for their education elsewhere.[6]

Also, in a university that first conferred a law degree on a woman in 1873, there may have been as many as three women in a class, but usually no more than one or two, and in some years none.[7]

This, of course, was Depression time, and students had difficulty financing their education. Many had to work at several jobs, and because times were hard only a handful of the students were married.[8] One recalled: "I didn't have any money; I had to work 40 hours a week for room and board. I slept my freshman year an average of 4½ hours per night. In Rutledge's [8:00 A.M.] course, I propped my index finger up under my face to feel pain in order to keep awake."[9] Another student reported: "My father sent me $1 a week. . . . I asked a classmate if he could lend me 10 cents. He couldn't believe it."[10] It was the rare student—the son of a lawyer—who could say, "I didn't have to work; dad paid."[11]

Most of the men lived and took meals in a new Law Commons. The women had to live wherever they could find a room and were limited at the law school to "one toilet and a hand basin," along with an anteroom furnished with "a long library table, an assortment of castoff chairs and a chaise lounge" that they could use for "brown bag" lunches.[12] In these years, the students were not much concerned about ominous developments abroad—the rise of Hitler, the reach of Stalin, or the progress of the Spanish Civil War. They were focused almost entirely on getting through school, though vulnerable to the usual diversions that helped eclipse concern about the larger world: "dating, attending athletic events, having a good time," perhaps at a local pub where the "only drink" was "near beer spiked with alcohol" purchased from a local bootlegger.[13] According to one faculty member, however, student indifference to world affairs had political, not just personal, roots. There was a "strong, strong, strong isolationist feeling" in Iowa; the "students were almost subliminally, intuitively, and perhaps congenitally isolationist."[14]

Wiley Rutledge found himself "cordially received" in Iowa. He wrote to a friend: "the University here is much more alive" than Washington University and "has a considerably larger number of first rate men working in it."[15] His new Iowa colleagues had distinct, some even theatrical, styles. Odis Knight ("O.K.") Patton terrified students with his Socratic bludgeoning in first-year contracts, asking questions but never confirming answers. Rollin Perkins would enter the classroom in criminal law saying, "Suppose A hits B on the nose,"[16] and then lay out the law by reconciling hypotheticals. Percy Bordwell, the scholarly "Mr. Chips of the faculty," loved the St. Louis Cardinals almost as much as real property and future interests, and could always be counted on to recite "Casey at the Bat" at law school gatherings.[17] To some students, Mason Ladd, Wiley's would-be competitor for the dean-

Mason Ladd. (Courtesy of the Rutledge family)

ship, "was the character of the bunch." In his high, "squeaky tenor" voice, he routinely illustrated a point in evidence or trial practice by exclaiming, "Hell, gentlemen, when I was a County Attorney in Polk County. . . ."[18]

Everyone called Philip Mechem, the professor of agency, equity, wills, trusts, and jurisprudence, "Fidgety Phil." Apparently no longer scratching his neck on the blackboard's edge as at Washington University, Mechem now "would jerk his arms and elbows—every part of his body—while lecturing," like "a puppet on a string."[19] Paul Sayre, who taught courses ranging from civil procedure to family law to business organizations, was well remembered for his long walks to Cedar Rapids and for reading children's stories on Sunday morning radio.[20] Like Professor Conant in St. Louis, Clarence Updegraff, commonly referred to as "Upde," reportedly taught torts year after year from the same notes, believed to be from his student days at Harvard.[21]

The junior member of the faculty, responsible for constitutional law, taxation, trade regulation, and the law review, was Frank Strong, who left in 1937 to teach at Ohio State.[22] Although Rutledge regarded Strong highly, he saw the departure as an opportunity. He wrote to the dean of Northwestern, Leon Green: "I am anxious to have someone who has something of the new deal philosophy on constitutional matters. As you know, this faculty is pretty well loaded with men of the opposite point of view." He added that with the possible exception of Paul Sayre, "Phil Mechem and I are the only ones who definitely accept the broader conception of legislative power. . . . Mason Ladd is what might be called a liberal conservative, but even with these exceptions and qualifications I think our faculty is overbalanced on the side of the older point of view." Rutledge stressed, "I have no intention of packing the faculty, but I do want it to be representative."[23]

Rutledge found what he was looking for in Willard Wirtz, who came to Iowa directly from his senior year at Harvard Law School. The new dean soon noted that Wirtz, "a middle-westerner," had "the practical common-sense of that genus" without "the idiosyncrasies commonly attributed to a Harvard man."[24] The students regarded Wirtz highly—and not only as a teacher.[25] According to Rutledge, in the fall of 1937 on the Friday afternoon before homecoming, the "Liberal Arts and Engineering students decided that they would declare a holiday." Some marched over to demand that the law school close to honor the team, and headed for Wirtz's trade regulation class. When the leader informed Wirtz "in a semi-threatening manner" that class was over, Wirtz "hauled off with a good right" and—Wiley used an East Tennessee expression—he "laid the invaders' leader low."[26]

OF THE MIDWEST'S "Big Nine" universities offering legal education, Michigan's student body was the largest, numbering around 600, while Indiana with approximately 160 students and Ohio State with 200 were the smallest. Michigan had twenty full-time faculty members while Indiana and Ohio State each had eleven. In contrast, Iowa's College of Law, third from the bottom in size with 250 students, had only nine full-time faculty, the poorest student-faculty ratio of the group. Other schools—Illinois, Wisconsin, Minnesota, and Chicago—had thirteen to twenty or more faculty members,

W. Willard Wirtz. (Courtesy of W. Willard Wirtz)

including interdisciplinary professors of psychology, philosophy, political science, and economics. And Northwestern, with 275 students—many enrolled in a four-year program that included legal clinics and internships, as well as supervised independent study—had a faculty of twenty-five, plus twenty-two Illinois lawyers instructing in local law and practice.[27]

Rutledge believed that even if additional law professorships were not possible, innovations at other law schools dictated "considerable overhauling" of the Iowa curriculum. But he encountered "strong resistance" from his faculty. In reflecting on his first year at Iowa, he wrote to Green at Northwestern (whose program Rutledge coveted): "I was rather discouraged. I found a . . . much more definitely crystallized old deal attitude in the faculty, both as to politics and as to legal education, than I had expected to find."[28]

During his initial year, however, Rutledge managed to achieve agreement that first-year students deserved a more effective orientation to the study of law. He undertook that effort himself, beginning in 1936, by offering a required first-year course in the "judicial process." He sought to introduce students to the process of judicial decision making—coupled with exposure to "the broad field of public law"—through the study of cases in constitutional law. The new dean was also committed to restoring administrative law to the curriculum and elected to teach that, too, himself.[29]

Rutledge was out in front of men fixed in their ways, but he had an ability to keep disagreements professional, never personal, and a willingness to proceed slowly if necessary, by consensus rather than by risking fractures that could debilitate or even destroy the teaching mission.[30] This approach was possible for Rutledge because he fundamentally respected everyone with whom he worked—and the right of each to an honestly held viewpoint—more than he believed that his own ideas, however passionately held, should ever be force-fed. Emotionally, he could accept this gradualist approach because of his profound belief that good-faith debate, which he always took the other fellow to be engaged in, would lead to the best answer at the time. This style was more, therefore, than careful politicking; it reflected a conviction about the fundamental loyalty of people and how they behave in a common enterprise.

The dean's course in judicial process addressed a threshold question: What kind of case or controversy belongs in court? It then plunged the freshmen into a constitutional law thicket comprising the commerce clause, the taxing power, substantive due process, the privileges and immunities clause, the doctrine forbidding delegation of legislative power to the executive or to private entities, and the respective powers of federal and state courts.[31] Rutledge took the students all the way from Chief Justice Marshall's opinion in *Marbury v. Madison* (1803),[32] establishing the Court's power to declare laws unconstitutional, to the Supreme Court's decisions in 1935 and 1936 striking down New Deal legislation.

Rutledge relied on the case method of instruction.[33] Also, one of his students recalled, "he lectured quite a bit."[34] The student complained that Rutledge didn't "come to a conclusion. No golden words of summary or pearls of wisdom. . . . What he tried to teach was just the opposite of what I was trying to learn. You wanted rules, and he wanted reasons."[35] Another former student, later a law professor and dean himself, concurred that Rutledge "was always asking questions"; "he wouldn't answer questions"; "he'd make you think."[36] Still another of his students, who also became a professor of law, has suggested that the course "may have been too advanced for first-year law students. . . . Much of what he said went over our heads."[37]

Other students, though not all, agreed with that assessment.[38] (After giving the course twice, Rutledge himself concluded that the materials were "not too difficult for first year students.")[39]

Despite the perplexities of judicial process, many students found the course "very instructive."[40] According to one student,

> We could not help but be impressed by his obvious mastery of the subject and his enthusiasm for it. In this course, to a greater extent than in our other courses, we gained an understanding of law as a process rather than a static body of rules. This was exciting. We began to see how we could participate in this process. There were many roles we could play. We not only could represent clients, but we also could do something about social and economic problems.[41]

The student who had hoped for rules came to agree with this assessment:

> My respect for him grew and grew and grew as I realized what he was trying to teach me. . . . At the time, my feeling was he just couldn't teach, but he was very intelligent, highly motivated. As I matured and look back, I think he taught me more than anybody else. . . . I realize I don't remember anything specific about the rules I learned from [Perkins], but I remember concepts I learned from the Dean.[42]

Similarly, the future law dean who received "questions," but never "answers"—and who "didn't think of [Rutledge] as a particularly good teacher" at that time—"in retrospect learned a lot about how decisions were made and how the process worked."[43] One student spoke for many when he said:

> Dean Rutledge's analytical skills were impressive. Time after time, he would present an analysis of a problem that seemed to be solid, and then proceed to show its shortcomings. He then would set forth an alternative or extended analysis as a superior to the first. But as we began to relax in our seats, he came forth with still another even more persuasive analysis, and so on. At the time, this technique suggested to me a mining operation, in which we were drilling even more deeply in search of still more valuable ore. The analogy of peeling layers off an artichoke is also apt.[44]

As at Washington University, therefore, students saw in Rutledge a "most impressive intellect."[45] No one questioned that he thoroughly knew each subject he taught, and most believed that he communicated effectively.[46] Because of the dean's emphasis on learning how to think, rather than on how to assimilate information, he was not concerned about covering all the case materials. This caused consternation in his more traditional, upper-level course in business organizations. Of, say, a thousand pages, he might get through no more than three hundred over an entire year.[47] Although some students acknowledged that they had "learned quite a bit from him" in that class, others—concerned about passing the bar—were frustrated by not receiving a large enough body of knowledge.[48] One complained: "I do not recall any emphasis on practical details such as shareholders rights, strike suits, directors liability, etc. His approach to teaching was more philosophical than practical." But, like the judicial process students looking back, this business organizations student recognized that it had been the dean's goal "to get us to think . . . for ourselves and reach our own conclusions. Thus, . . . his teaching style was somewhat different than the other professors[,] most of whom expected us to learn exactly what the law was and report it back to them in the examinations."[49] Rutledge would have smiled on hearing that comment, for it captured precisely his desire: to counterbalance a faculty that in focusing on rules of law for the bar exam may have failed to take the students deeply enough into the problems presented.

Whether the dean was offering judicial process, or upper-level business organizations or administrative law, he would ask his students not merely what the court itself had decided, but what the result of a case *should* have been.[50] He would not supply "answers" or "rules of law" because every source of law—Constitution, common law, statute, or regulation—was subject to change. He wanted students always to explore what the law might be, far more than to understand what the law at the time was. To this end, unlike his faculty colleagues, he lectured extensively on the "human interest side" of each case, the "story behind the story"—its political background and social context, the personal consequences for the parties, even the personalities and predilections of the judge.[51] One former student exclaimed that the dean's approach "was fantastic! . . . You had this experience of looking at a really live law, knowing what was going on in Washington: assault by the Supreme Court."[52] And not only the recent cases were alive. Another student, recalling Rutledge's treatment of *Marbury v. Madison*, confirmed that the dean "went into the economic, political, and sociological factors present in the country at the time." That "gave it life," he said, and this student put Rutledge "right at the very top" of the faculty as a teacher.[53]

But not all students were so positive. In addition to those who were frustrated because the course in judicial process seemed over their heads, or did not provide clear legal rules, there were others who were turned off by their dean's known allegiance to President Roosevelt. Anyone in the 1930s who taught judicial process and administrative law—premised heavily on constitutional law—inevitably focused on the Supreme Court's destruction of New Deal legislation in 1935 and 1936. Although some students were liberals,[54] and a few were even socialists,[55] most at the time were politically conservative,[56] and some of them took offense when the dean questioned the conservative justices' analyses of New Deal legislation. One student reported: "Many of us were Republicans. He was strictly a New Dealer, and that didn't meet with our approval. . . . [There was] too much discussion of the New Deal. . . . I had an intense dislike of Roosevelt."[57] Another student recalled that Rutledge "tried to lecture the class on his labor and constitutional views,"[58] while still another added that judicial process basically "was a legal defense of the New Deal legislation. . . . He was very methodical and earnest in this endeavor."[59] According to one student: "We perceived Professor Rutledge as part of the New Deal process. . . . We thought that he was trying to mold or to indoctrinate us with the New Deal philosophy of big, intrusive government. We had another professor, a W. W. Wirtz, who was of similar leanings—at the time we called them 'pinks.'"[60] Less emphatically, other students also remember the dean's classes as, in part, expressions of his political views.[61]

More students, however, appear to have recognized the dean's questions and comments about the Supreme Court's handling of New Deal legislation as the standard pedagogy required for analyzing controversial decisions—many of which had been accompanied by powerful dissents and, beginning in 1937, were on their way to being overruled. Rutledge was known in the community to be a Democrat, indeed a strong supporter of the President, but a number of former students have emphasized that his partisanship, as such, did not "show in the classroom."[62] These students perceived no effort by the dean to "carry the banner for any particular purpose"; they did not "think of him as one who got up and really preached."[63] Significantly, in fact, there were conservative students who did not experience an effort by the dean to push the New Deal. "I wasn't in sympathy with the liberal side and he didn't irritate me," said one.[64] Another added: "He was more or less apolitical in class. We all knew where he stood, but he didn't seem to overdo it in class as far as I was concerned. I was rather conservative. I would have noticed that, and I didn't notice it."[65]

Although most students probably would have said that Rutledge "gave away his political leanings in discussing the Supreme Court,"[66] most also probably would not have experienced this as sermonizing. Rutledge always pressed his students to think for themselves, and did not berate those who may have disagreed with him. Thus, even a Republican student who lamented that his classes "always lost the arguments" with the dean over New Deal legislation could say that Rutledge taught "one of the best classes" he had in law school.[67]

State University of Iowa dean Wiley Rutledge. (Courtesy of the Rutledge family)

Rutledge did not "speak harshly" of Republicans as such or take shots at individual justices.[68] He dealt with all sides respectfully, trying to keep the discussion at a high, intellectual level. Even at the beginning of his written examination in judicial process, he carefully explained: "The issues are legal issues, but you need not fear discredit from the expression of any political opinion or consideration which is pertinent."[69] Given how passionately he felt about the New Deal and the Supreme Court's actions against it, his students overall gave him high marks for fairness of presentation. Most probably would have subscribed to the view that for the most part, the dean's politics—while discernible—did not come through in class "explicitly."[70]

WILEY RUTLEDGE would arrive at class promptly at 8:00 A.M., typically dressed in a three-piece brown suit (his Washington University blue serge garb was apparently gone). He was a good-looking man in a rough-hewn way, although not handsome. He had a large, rectangular face, large brown eyes with noticeable eyebrows, brown—slightly graying—wavy hair, and a dark, ruddy complexion prone to a five o'clock shadow. ("When I think of Dean Rutledge, I think of the color brown," one former student recalled.) He was about 5′10″ tall and "on the portly side."[71]

As at Washington University, Wiley Rutledge was "all business" in class, speaking in a "deep, good voice," "every syllable" of which "you could hear . . . in a big classroom." In contrast to his teaching posture in St. Louis, he would typically stand to conduct class, moving slowly from side to side. Often he would use the blackboard to outline his points, then continue— without using notes—while sitting on the edge of the desk in front of the room. In contrast with Patton and Ladd, he showed "no flamboyance"; he was "not a performer," "not a story teller." But Rutledge would enjoy humorous situations, and when confronted by one he "could laugh like everybody else." Occasionally, he would take the initiative, exhibiting a dry sense of humor typically based on irony. One day, a top student, sitting in the back row, did not give a useful answer. Rutledge retorted: " 'If you'd read the cases once in awhile . . .' and that brought down the house. He was a bookworm. And Rutledge knew it."[72] The dean presided in class with "quiet dignity, students recalled." His serious demeanor was not "overly harsh"; despite his resonant voice he had a "softly spoken" manner, even-tempered and polite. He was "friendly" and "obviously enjoyed the students." And "they enjoyed him."[73]

There was, nonetheless, a "firmness" about Rutledge, one student recalled, that "let you know he was not to be taken for granted."[74] He would get upset when students were not prepared, and would walk out of class— according to an Iowa tradition—if three students in a row had not read the assigned material. But Rutledge was not an intimidating teacher. Students did not fear him as they did others, for he rarely put students down.[75] On one occasion, however, he seemed out of character in reprimanding a student for his failure to ready himself for class. When Rutledge called on him—a co-editor-in-chief of the law review who had won the moot court competition the night before—the student apologized but said he was unprepared. "I expected a gentle admonition along with some congratulations," he reported. Instead, Rutledge insisted, " 'there is no excuse for non-

preparation. I will not meet with the class in this state. Class dismissed.'"
The student has written: "He made his point and I never forgot it." Nor was
it lost on the class, he said. "Rutledge may be a gentle person, but he has
standards which he expects to be met without deviation."[76] The dean was
regarded, in sum, as "tough, but very, very fair."[77] One student spoke for
many: "I would have hated to inform him I was not prepared. . . . I would
have had the feeling that I was letting down a very, very fine man."[78]

Most Rutledge students at Iowa believed he was a good teacher. Some
complained that he "droned on in a monotone," or found him "a little on
the boring side," or said that he "didn't leave a sense of accomplishment."[79]
But just as many characterized Rutledge as "at the very top" or "near the
top,"[80] while others put him in the top third.[81] Probably the largest group
would have put the dean "about in the middle."[82]

EVEN STUDENTS who gave Wiley Rutledge only mixed reviews as a classroom teacher both liked and respected him, and were inspired by his example. In dealing with their dean outside class, students found not the
intensely serious persona from the classroom but a "friendly," "modest"
man who could "laugh very easily" and "had a delightful sense of humor."
Students emphasized he was "never aloof;" he "didn't carry [a superior]
attitude." Many remember him as "unfailingly kind and considerate" and
recalled they "always felt at ease in his presence."[83] One student noted:
Dean Rutledge "always could find something good to say about everybody,
[and] I never heard him say a mean word about anybody."[84] His former colleague Willard Wirtz remembers Rutledge as a "very warm human being,"
who genuinely was "more interested in the person he was talking to than in
himself." As a result, according to Wirtz, "personal ambition played a very
small part in that man's life."[85]

Wirtz himself had significant personal experiences with Rutledge. Near
the end of Wirtz's third year at Harvard Law School, when he was days away
from graduating and joining a law firm in Chicago, Iowa's dean came to
Harvard to recruit a replacement for Frank Strong. Someone in authority
at Harvard asked Wirtz, who had never thought about teaching, to meet
with Rutledge. Wirtz received a gentle reminder that Harvard had given
him a scholarship, implying that Wirtz should return the favor by meeting
with the Iowa dean whether he wanted to or not. Wirtz "went determined
to get it over as soon as possible." To that end, he told Rutledge that he had
approved of Roosevelt's Court-packing plan, which to his amazement the
dean also endorsed. In any event, in the period of a brief interview, Wirtz decided that "in terms of human qualities, this was the man I wanted to work
for." Wirtz went home to tell his wife that he now wanted to teach for Wiley

Rutledge in Iowa City. And that happened. Later, as a new teacher eager to get all the assistance he could with his new courses in constitutional law and trade regulation, Wirtz sought help from the dean. "I sure got it from him. I went in to ask him a question, and I'd be there an hour. . . . I would welcome the experience greatly. He was so generous with . . . everything he had."[86]

One who is liked is not always respected, but Rutledge was. One of his former students observed that some individuals gain respect, "but respect came with Rutledge; he didn't have to work that hard at it." Why not? "Personality." In the army, the student said, "some people have a command presence," and "some don't." Rutledge had it—and, of equal importance, he did not flaunt it. "His humility was probably more impressive than anything else. . . . [H]e could say hard things with great humility—make decisions so they seemed okay. [He was] honest and direct."[87] And inspirational. A student reflected: "I don't remember he was that great of a teacher, but he sure was a great leader. . . . How much I learned from him! . . . Judge Rutledge is the model on which I have tried . . . to guide my life." Later, as a member of the Iowa legislature, this student remembered Rutledge saying, "Don't ever vote what your conscience tells you not to. Don't let other people influence you." So the young man voted against the wishes of the chamber of commerce on a tax bill, despite great pressures from its representatives in the gallery.[88] In conversation, Rutledge would also help students expand their worlds. He encouraged one student to read the *New York Times*, which the young man had never heard of. "I'm sure I joined the NAACP and the ACLU because of his influence," the student added, although Rutledge had never suggested he do so.[89] Another student, who made a career of legal aid, said, "I got into legal aid because of Rutledge."[90]

Students perceived that fundamentally, compassion for people animated Rutledge's personal actions, as well as his political views. The dean was worried, for example, about students who did not get enough to eat. Rutledge expressed this concern to the father of an Iowa City law student, who, as a result, invited classmates home for meals.[91] Other students also experienced Rutledge's compassion. One reported: "He counseled with me after a difficult freshman year. He was understanding and seemed to feel my problems. He gave me the desire to continue."[92] Although Rutledge's interactions with students outside the classroom commonly fell within his duties as dean, his actions reflected his character—his concerns as a human being. He would invite a student who was working long hours at outside jobs into his office for a chat, to be sure the student was not taking on too much.[93] He would give "pointers" to help a student get through classes, including his own.[94] He went out of his way to help a student with an alcohol problem stay in school and keep a job in the law library.[95]

The dean was willing to reveal his own missteps in the hope of offering useful perspective. In counseling a student who was depressed about failing a course and was thinking of dropping out, Rutledge advised that this "should not be a fatal blow to his career plans" because Rutledge himself "had failed a course."[96] He made allowances even for those who made serious mistakes. One year a scholarship student gambled away a tuition check from the treasurer's office in a poker game at Racine's Cigar Store. Rutledge allowed him to take a year off to earn money to repay the university and then return to school.[97]

Dean Rutledge did not limit his interactions with students outside class to problem solving. He was easily accessible for any reason, simply because he liked people. According to a member of the class of 1939, the future justice "went out of his way to establish a friendship with the students in law school. . . . His relationship with the students at Iowa at that time was unique as far as I was concerned. I recall having coffee with Justice Rutledge on many occasions at Racines['] . . . lunch counter. . . . We'd talk about questions of the day; and, he was a sports fan—liked baseball."[98] The dean especially enjoyed "talking politics and international relations," warning students that "our country had better prepare because Hitler was bent upon aggression."[99] And Rutledge could be just plain thoughtful. One student reported an occasion when the dean "went down to Clinton, 40 to 60 miles from Iowa City, to talk to the bar," and invited a student to drive with him simply because the young man's "brother was in Clinton." This, the first student added, was "a nice gesture . . . , a real nice thing."[100]

What distinguished Rutledge as a dean, teacher, and friend was the fact that he gave a part of himself to each student; he did not act merely as a broker of information or analysis. Rutledge related to his students individually; all came to recognize that he cared for them "as persons"—not only by treating them with respect but by giving them time for the smallest of problems. He would drop everything to give a student, or for that matter a faculty colleague or other friend, undivided attention. This created a bond, an intimate connection from the simple acts of giving that left the student with a reminder—an image or an echo—of the giver and the values he represented. Wiley Rutledge may have helped students learn about the law, but more importantly, he helped them learn what it means to be a compassionate, ethical person.[101]

Iowa City

Support for Minorities, Legal Aid,
and Court-Packing

Around St. Patrick's Day every year the engineering students at Iowa celebrated "Mecca" week, which ended with a fancy ball. As at Washington University, the "Engineers" and the "Laws" had a rivalry characterized by pranks, which could be more funny than destructive, such as "throwing a skunk in the ventilating system in the memorial union at the time of the [Engineers'] big dance there."[1] In 1937, however, Mecca Week got out of hand. The engineers stole the "Law" sign from the Commons and—outlining the sign with light bulbs shining the Engineers' color green—hoisted it atop the engineering building. In retaliation, a throng of enraged law students stormed and sacked the building, causing considerable damage, and threw the Engineers' own electrically lighted "Mecca" sign from the roof three stories down to the street.[2] One student remembered that Dean Rutledge was "terribly angry, so angry that he was shaking . . . on the lecture stand" the next morning. The dean exclaimed, "I thought you were men who could reason with your minds and act accordingly." But you "went over there and relied on your bodies not your minds."[3] "Man, was he mad," recalled another student.[4] No one was expelled, but the law students association had to surrender its entire treasury to pay for the damage.[5]

Two years later, after a fracas between the Laws and Engineers that brought enough "serious pushing" for the police to release tear gas, the dean went "from class to class" angrily reminding students that the state legislature and the *Des Moines Register* were not happy with the university at the time. He warned that if there were any further "'fight' or commotion between the Laws and the Engineers," everyone involved would "be removed from this Law School and never allowed to re-enter." He also personally would "see to it" that the offender was "not allowed to enroll in any other Law School in this country!" The reporter of this incident recalled that the students were "scared" but not "upset" by what they had heard, because the dean had come across "like a stern father lecturing his children on Halloween: 'if you get in trouble and the police arrest you, I'll not bail you out!' But dad would have."[6]

There were, of course, high points during the law school year. The most notable was Supreme Court Day in April, when high-ranking students would be inducted into the Order of the Coif, a national honor society, followed by the final round of the moot court competition argued before the Iowa Supreme Court. The day culminated in a banquet where a student skit, which Rutledge always enjoyed thoroughly, would portray faculty members with little mercy. The dean, called "Mr. Wilcy Asafox" one year, was not immune. His one notorious fault as a teacher was his unconscionable delay in grading exams. That year, the skit portrayed the dean as a judge, grading papers on the bench. A white-bearded old man in a wheelchair looked up at the judge and asked, "Did my pappy pass Business Organizations?"[7]

IN THE FALL of 1935, a few months after Rutledge arrived in Iowa City, he received a letter from a friend, Rabbi Ferdinand M. Isserman of the Social Justice Commission of St. Louis, alerting him to possible anti-Semitism on campus. The director of the School of Religion at Iowa, the rabbi wrote, had given a speech saying that Iowa students treated Jews "worse than Negroes are treated in the south." The rabbi acknowledged that this information, "received from a second-hand source," was "quite garbled," but if it was true, he added, he knew that with Rutledge now at Iowa, "the situation will be speedily remedied." Three days later, Rutledge wrote Isserman that he had not learned whether the statement had been made, but that "[s]o far as I am able to discern, Jewish students here are treated with the same courtesy and consideration on the whole as others receive. . . . I know, for instance, that Jewish students occupy quarters in the Law Commons, in some instances rooming with Gentile students." Curiously, however, in his next sentence Rutledge wrote: "There is, of course, the fraternity discrimination but that is not peculiar to Iowa." He concluded by assuring his friend that "if there are conditions of unjust discrimination here I will do all in my power to alleviate them. Necessarily, any influence I may have in this, as in all other directions, will come as a matter of growth."[8]

Many students from these years have not been able to recall acts, or even sentiments, reflecting anti-Semitism.[9] One Jewish student, originally from the state of Iowa, agreed: "Six years at Iowa and I never encountered anything like that."[10] But others have reported that anti-Semitism was pervasive.[11] While it may have been true, as the dean assured the rabbi, that some Jewish students roomed with those who were not, that was exceptional. One Jewish student recalled that in his first year, two years before Rutledge came to Iowa, "the guy assigning rooms made it clear he'd have to find a Jewish person to share a room with me." The same Jewish student was approached for membership in one of the legal fraternities and was told the "Christian oath" could be changed to accommodate him. Because of this persistence he agreed and paid his initiation fee. "Three months later, they returned my $15. . . . This experience I had as a freshman turned me off, ... I never ha[ve] gone to a reunion at the law school."[12]

According to one student, there "were very strong feelings" about Jews "in the dining hall in the Law Commons, where they were seated separately." Rutledge "took a strong stand on this problem" by encouraging one of the fraternities—the one he had joined years before—to accept Jewish members and thus include them at the table.[13] But national policies served as the excuse for turning Rutledge down.[14] His effort "had limited effect on the general student attitudes," recalled one observer, and the "Jewish students . . . were never fully accepted as part of the social life at the Commons."[15]

Some former students have suggested that to the extent anti-Semitism manifested itself at the College of Law, it was directed at Jewish students from Chicago and farther east, not at those from Iowa.[16] When asked about that distinction, a student who was not Jewish reacted, "Absolutely not!" She said that pervasively, "the student body at the Law School was anti-Semitic. . . . The discrimination was so palpable that for the first time in my life I tried to pick out the Jews, and figure out in what ways they were different from the rest of us." She elaborated:

> It was safe for the worst of [the students] to put their pens down and stare out of the window when a [J]ewish student recited, or to put a pained expression on their faces when one of them volunteered. Or when, called upon to critique [a Jewish student's comments in class], to use such phrases as "Well, considering his bent of mind . . ." or "Some people are more interested in money than anything else . . ." and the like. This may not sound like much, but it certainly struck me as being terribly wrong, especially when accompanied by asides [whispered, but loud enough for me to hear]: "What would you expect from the Kike?" or, "Wasn't that just like a Sheenie?"[17]

The one or two African American students in a class appear to have experienced less, if any, overt discrimination. "Quite honestly," said a Caucasian student, "if there had been more [black students] there might have been a problem." He went on: the "one black in our class . . . probably wasn't accepted socially as well as the other students," although, added another, "[e]veryone liked him."[18] This particular student, Myron Bush, went on to be a successful politician in Ohio, and, according to one student, "but for an untimely death, he probably would have become the first black Mayor of Cincinnati."[19] Another African American student has had only praise for Iowa—and for Dean Rutledge. Subsidized by West Virginia, which would not admit him to the state law school, he said he had picked Iowa because "schools in the east were very expensive" and in any event, "in the Midwest —farming country—I wouldn't be known [and] no special clothes" would be required. He liked the College of Law and was treated "exceptionally fine," better than he thought he would be. "They didn't know anything about discriminating too much in Iowa," he recalled appreciatively. He added that West Virginia once missed a tuition payment, and that the billing office notified him that he was to be dropped from school. Rutledge intervened to prevent that until the matter could be straightened out. The dean's action was routine, but the student still considered it tantamount to divine intervention. "He's responsible for my being here now" practicing law in West Virginia; "if he hadn't helped me, I'd have never gone back" to law school.[20]

Iowa students from the 1930s have also commented on the treatment of the few women in each class. Years later, many of the men did not recall any harassment.[21] One said that the women were "treated just like everybody else."[22] Indeed, recalled another, they were "treated like the men."[23] Then, interestingly, one man put it another way: "We didn't have any trouble with them."[24] But other men—and certainly the women—saw the situation differently. A male member of the class of 1939, which included two women, recalled: "When one of the girls would recite, the law students would shuffle their feet and make noise" to distract her. Rutledge stood in the well of the classroom and said: "I can see every foot in this room, and the first one that moves when (I believe it was) Ms. Schwilck continues her recitation, will flunk this course. That took care of that." In the other classes, he added, the "men did whatever they could get away with." Only Rutledge "got mad about it."[25] Other students reported that "some of the professors enjoyed embarrassing the women, describing rape in great detail," for example.[26] One white male remembers that by the end of the semester, his professor in one class "had called on everybody except the girl and the Chinese fellow and the Black fellow and me."[27]

Women also received shoddy treatment outside the classroom. A brilliant female student who graduated with "high distinction" recalled: "one of the students . . . sent his sister, a former law student, to tell me it was inadvisable to talk in class and I should desist at once. At the end of the year we met in a Law School classroom to write the bar examination for three

days on legal pads furnished to us. In one examination, I filled my pad before finishing the examination. . . . I approached the Proctor and asked for
a new pad. As he handed one to me and I turned to return to my seat, a
loud chorus of hisses flooded the room and I slunk to my seat."[28] Another
woman had a demeaning experience with the law review. "My only contact,"
she said, "was a dismal failure. By my third year I figured that I had some
thoughts which should be published. . . . I told [the editor] I wanted to write
a note on the effect of the lack of precedent on the rights of consumers. He
started laughing and laughed me right outside of the law review office."[29]

A woman from the class of 1939 recalled that of the faculty, only Rutledge and Professor Bordwell seemed to enjoy having women in the school,
and that Rutledge had helped her obtain a scholarship at the University
of Chicago for her second year so that she could join her husband there.
Remembering Rutledge, she recalled: "I shall always be grateful for his
ability to empathize with the unorthodox needs of a woman law student
and willingly help her."[30] By today's standards, it is difficult to understand
Rutledge's treatment of women as anything particularly special. But in the
perspective of the times, his support of female students' individual needs—
and, perhaps even more significantly, his refusal to participate with faculty and students alike in deprecating women and Jews—set him apart. On
the other hand, Rutledge was no zealot in such matters. In making recommendations for employment, for example, he would identify religious or
racial background ("a Jewish boy" with "unusual abilities" and a "very fine
record,"[31] or "a man of unusual promise [who] happens to be a Catholic").[32]
While at Iowa he explained to a correspondent:

> You know, of course, that it is distasteful for me to mention either
> religious or racial considerations in connection with recommenda-
> tions. I have found, however, from long experience that it is better
> to state all the facts, even those bearing upon such angles. However
> much I may dislike discriminations on these bases, I know that men
> do take such factors into account. In order to prevent waste of time
> and energy it has seemed to me, therefore, better policy to state these
> factors frankly.[33]

Rutledge would make known his own positions opposing religious, racial,
and gender discrimination, as he did in criticizing fraternity admission and
dining practices and classroom harassment at Iowa; but in the absence of
restrictive legislation, the dean did not combat discrimination in ways he
believed would be fruitless, perhaps even counterproductive. He was willing to act on his passions to eliminate sweatshops employing child labor
and to regulate predatory holding companies. But, like many if not most

liberals of the day, he did not feel moved—even within his own faculty—
to take on the more explosive social issues surrounding race, religion, and
gender much beyond the impact of his own personal example.

RUTLEDGE DID NOT assume responsibilities outside Iowa during his first
year and a half there. He planted university and community roots, offering,
for example, "a series of eight lectures to students in the Department of
Social Work on the general topic of 'Law and Social Work,'"[34] as well as a
wide range of speeches at the local Rotary Club (where he became a member)[35] and at other luncheon gatherings on topics such as "the future of
local self-government,"[36] and the national economic power of corporations
under inadequate state controls.[37]

By mid-1936, the Supreme Court had cast most of its stones killing New
Deal legislation, and Wiley Rutledge was profoundly worried. He spoke in
June to the state District Judges' Association, proclaiming: "I am one of
those who believe that the court has gone too far in its delimitation of the
legislative power." But he reminded the judges that the nation had always
found some way out other than adopting one measure or another for "emas-
culating the court." He warned against the "profound temptation" to con-
strict the role of judicial review, and concluded that "[i]f the court has gone
contrary to the preponderant" sentiment of the community in its recent
decisions, correction was available by amendment.[38]

By the end of the year, Rutledge was ready to branch out. He was invited
to present a paper to the AALS Business Associations Round Table survey-
ing the corporation statutes recently adopted by various states, with special emphasis on significant innovations, trends, and problems. He agreed
and eventually converted the presentation into his law review article "Significant Trends."[39] In 1937 the dean accepted appointment as chairman
of the Round Table itself, ultimately convening a panel discussion on the
pros and cons of requiring federal incorporation or licensing of interstate
businesses.[40]

A month after accepting the Round Table chairmanship, Rutledge agreed
to chair another AALS effort, its Committee on Co-operation with the Bench
and Bar, an assignment reflecting high esteem for Rutledge among his
peers. The AALS president, Lloyd K. Garrison, dean at Wisconsin, had called
for the expansion of legal aid to the poor, and Iowa's dean, energized by
the appointment, quickly made legal aid his own priority. Garrison gave
Rutledge a strong, supportive committee: Deans Charles E. Clark of Yale,
Wayne Morse of Oregon, Albert J. Harno of Illinois, Everett Fraser of Minnesota, and M. T. Van Hecke of North Carolina, as well as Professors Karl
Llewellyn of Columbia and Joseph A. Wickes of Texas.[41] Rutledge circu-

lated a twenty-two-page draft report in early November. In it, he criticized a report issued in 1936 by the Committee on Professional Economics of the New York County Lawyers' Association, which had complained that an "idle population" of at least 30 million people required, but did not use, legal services "they can pay for," while many lawyers were "at or near the starvation point." The dean wrote that the New York committee had maligned "nearly one-third of our population" for unwillingness to pay legal fees, rather than face up to the likelihood that fees were unaffordable by many. "No legal system can survive" in a democracy, Rutledge wrote, when "so large a proportion of the general population" is ignored. Rutledge contrasted the refusal of the New York County committee "to face squarely the problem of legal aid" with the commendable efforts of the American Bar Association to foster state and local bar committees on legal aid. But he was skeptical about the ABA's recommendation that bar associations assume control of the needed expansion, given widespread resistance among lawyers to legal aid as a misperceived threat to their pocketbooks.[42]

The draft then minced no words. "It is the opinion of your committee, despite some notable exceptions to the contrary, that the general attitude of the organized legal profession has been one of almost appalling apathy and indifference, occasionally of active hostility, toward any effective general program of legal aid extension." He acknowledged the possibility that government might have to become involved.

> Suggestions for governmental assumption of the functions of legal aid encounter opposition to the "socialization of the legal profession." . . . Your committee is not ready as yet to take the position that governmental assumption of legal aid functions offers the only or the best method of general expansion. But it believes such expansion would be better than little or none, if the choice were to be made, and further it does not believe such a program, properly established and administered, would involve any real conflict of interest with the private practitioner. On the contrary, it would seem to us to afford opportunity for utilizing the services of many lawyers who cannot now find decently remunerative employment.[43]

Referring to a concern that had long troubled Rutledge himself, the draft report also warned that attacks against "unauthorized practice of the law" — often targeting banks, title companies, automobile associations, and other institutions — should not be leveled so generally that nonprofit legal aid societies, commonly organized as corporations, would fall within a prohibition. And Rutledge ended with praise for a proposal by Karl Llewellyn for the creation of legal clinics where clients of "modest means" could obtain service "on a fair and moderate but not charity basis."[44]

Reaction to Rutledge's draft was swift. Most committee members praised it, but Dean Harno called it "too contentious," and Dean Clark said it would "probably offend not merely the lawyers, but also the law teachers. . . . [Y]ou would be well advised to change the tone of the report quite considerably." Dean Van Hecke, on the other hand, replied, "[T]he provocative character of your report is splendid." Dean Fraser agreed: "I enjoy the crack that you take at the Bar Associations and their activities in respect to unauthorized practice," and Dean Morse, calling the draft "excellent," was "willing to sign it as written." Rutledge accepted almost all specific suggestions for revision, toning down his broadside against the New York County Committee and removing other offending references to the bar and its lawyers. But he rejected several recommendations for shortening the portion on legal aid.[45]

In the final report, the basic message came through powerfully, including the committee's willingness to condemn the profession's "almost appalling apathy and indifference," and even its occasional "active hostility" to legal aid. And the draft's prophetic anticipation of government involvement in providing legal services to the poor stayed in as drafted.[46] Wiley Rutledge once remarked that he sometimes wished he had made as much money as he could practicing law "honestly" for "ten or twenty years," then devoted himself entirely to offering legal services to people dependent on charity.[47] He cared deeply about equal access to justice, and he used his initiative as chair of the AALS committee to bring the teaching profession along with him, if at all possible.

IN JULY 1937 the governor of Iowa named Rutledge a state commissioner for the National Conference of Commissioners on Uniform State Laws, the group he had served for five years while representing Missouri.[48] In contrast with the reverence for judge-made common law that animated creation of the American Law Institute in 1923, a nineteenth-century movement to codify the common law had inspired organization of the National Conference even earlier, in 1892.[49] With roots back to Jefferson but especially to Jackson, whose followers wanted to see the common law in plain English and to thwart judges who would change it, the codification movement achieved only mixed results by the 1880s.[50] Rather than continue the effort for wholesale codification, therefore, the commissioners—with considerable success over the years—elected to deal individually with legal fields believed especially suitable for uniform statutory treatment.

Wiley relished rejoining the commissioners, and by year's end he had assumed responsibility for drafting—in a field new to him—a Uniform Resale Price Maintenance Act.[51] The dean, as we have seen, was skeptical about ALI Restatement efforts to freeze the common law into "black letter" formulations prematurely, but he was enthusiastic about efforts of the

National Conference in areas where legislative and judicial experimentation had revealed that the time was right for uniformity. We should add, too, that although Rutledge attended ALI meetings he never became part of its upper echelon, drawn at the time from the "cream of the American legal establishment."[52] He enjoyed far more the give and take among lawyers from around the country, including those from small firms, who gathered as commissioners of the National Conference.

ALSO IN 1937, Rutledge joined an effort to persuade the Iowa Supreme Court to "integrate"—meaning unify—the bar by adopting a court rule that would bring all the lawyers of the state together into one association financed by dues. Bar unification, it was hoped, would produce "modern standards of legal education and admission," keep out "the definitely unfit," and protect the public through canons of ethics prescribed and enforced by the court.[53] The dean represented the rule's supporters before the Supreme Court of Iowa. Afterwards, an assistant state attorney general wrote to him: "I haven't heard a more masterly presentation of a legal principle than was contained in your argument to the supreme court."[54] Wrote another: "I do not recall having heard a more clear, logical and convincing argument in that room at any time, and I have been listening to them there for over a quarter of a century."[55] One lawyer opposed to the plan, however, was infuriated that the "schemers" who were promoting bar integration had used Rutledge "as a stalking horse."[56] The Iowa Supreme Court decided not to act without a referendum on the issue conducted by the voluntary state bar association. In August 1938, the proposal for bar integration failed by a vote of 1,295 to 1,255.[57]

In the meantime, the dean had been invited to address the June meeting of the Iowa State Bar Association in Des Moines. He wrote to Ralph Fuchs: "I probably will throw a bombshell into the camp of the lawyers in a short discussion of unauthorized practice."[58] He did. He told the Association: "The lawyers should not have and claim a monopoly of any service which can be rendered as well or better by laymen or other experts," even when "times are hard and the lawyer needs the business. To take this attitude smacks of the worst features of trade unionism and even racketeering."[59]

NONE OF THESE activities was as controversial as the dean's involvement with President Roosevelt's Court-packing plan. On February 5, FDR sent to Congress a plan for the addition of up to fifty federal judges—including as many as six on the Supreme Court—to augment the federal benches where judges with at least ten years of service had reached age seventy. Roosevelt purported to justify such legislation on the questionable ground that the federal courts were behind in their work, and that the large number of active judges over seventy could not carry a full load.[60] The president's camouflage fooled no one. He was launching an obvious, frontal attack on the Supreme Court. During the seventeen months between January 1935 and May 1936, the Court had killed a collage of economic reforms at the heart of the New Deal—often by 5-4 or 6-3 votes. Indeed, the Court had struck down statutes in their entirety, entombing, for example, the National Industrial Recovery Act,[61] the Railroad Retirement Act,[62] the Agricultural Adjustment Act,[63] the Guffey Coal Act,[64] the Municipal Bankruptcy Act,[65] and an act to protect farmers against foreclosures, the Frazier-Lemke Act.[66]

In justifying its resistance to Roosevelt's concededly novel measures, the Court majority held fast to legal doctrines without much sympathetic reference to the imperiled economy. As a result, by invoking substantive due process, the nondelegation doctrine, and the constitutional powers reserved to the states, the Court effectively circumscribed the authority of Congress to regulate the economy under the commerce clause and to tax and spend for the general welfare. The justices accordingly created impenetrable barriers to legislative innovation. No middle ground appeared to be left.

Despite Roosevelt's huge victory the previous November, his Court proposal caused a firestorm of controversy and brought far more opposition than the president had anticipated, even among his supporters.[67] Wiley Rutledge was not "wildly excited" about the plan, but he supported it as "perhaps the least harmful method of change" the president could have proposed.[68] But what kind of "change," according to Rutledge, was so urgent that restructuring the Supreme Court was called for? And why would Court-packing be the "least harmful" way to achieve it? These questions forced the dean to make the deepest inquiry he had ever made into his own legal and political philosophy.

A draft document in the Rutledge papers—without known authorship—undoubtedly reflects the dean's thinking. It supports FDR's bill in polemical language of the sort Rutledge regularly used in speeches, and a speech is the purpose for which the document was probably prepared, since it would have been wholly inappropriate for use as testimony, for example, at a Senate hearing. There is a rub, however. The draft contains language—without attribution—directly quoting, though sometimes paraphrasing, selected passages from *Storm over the Constitution*, a recent book by Irving Brant, editorial writer for the *St. Louis Star-Times*, which Rutledge had reviewed with great praise for the *Iowa City Press Citizen*. The best guess would be that the dean, not one to pirate another's prose, either gave a student research assistant a copy of *Storm* and asked for a speech draft supporting the Court bill, or accepted a draft from Brant himself. Because there can be no doubt that Rutledge would have been comfortable delivering the substance of the manuscript to a bar association audience, with attribution to Brant as appropriate, we may consider it Rutledge's.[69]

The document began from the factual premise that "[t]oday no community has local problems[;] . . . all are national in scope."[70] The "interdependence of all our people, rural and urban, employer and employee, fisherman and lumberjack, farmer and manufacturer,"[71] means that only the federal government can effectively "attack problems of overproduction, underconsumption, technological unemployment, budget balancing by decades, land-planning and conservation in terms of half-century projects, and social security."[72] The states are not "powerful enough to cope" with the contending forces, and, in any event, these complex problems do not permit resolution "in forty-eight different ways." Rutledge worried that the economic situation was serious enough to lead to the dismantling of our democracy, either "by a dictatorship of wealth, which will perpetuate concentrated property holdings by force," or "by a mass movement seeking to destroy the existing economic system of capitalism."[73] In the days of accelerating fascism and communism abroad, Rutledge was not sanguine about our own nation's future unless the Supreme Court could be made "an agency of social and economic reform," rather than a "refuge for industrial and financial malefactors."[74] He believed "that the basic principles of national democracy were at stake."[75] He had "no doubt" that if the Court's "trend of decisions" continued, the country would confront "another Dred Scott situation."[76]

He then moved to a second—this time legal—premise: that the founders had "put the power in the Constitution to deal with national issues in a national way."[77] Rutledge saw the Constitution "as a living document, endowing the federal government with implied powers of sweeping extent."[78] His adherence to this broad construction rested on the assumption that the framers could not possibly have anticipated all the problems that would plague future generations, and thus had employed general enough language—such as "necessary and proper" and "due process"—to allow for a variety of government responses. As a result, he said, although the Supreme Court purports to "proclaim the Constitution as it is," the justices often decide "what the law ought to be."[79] In applying the Constitution's general, and thus flexible, language, he stressed, the justices do so according to their own personal "theories, prejudices, and preconceptions"[80]—in effect, they enact "judicial legislation."[81] He recalled the words of Charles Evans Hughes when governor of New York: "'the Constitution is what the judges say it is.'"[82]

From the perspective of someone, like Rutledge, who perceived a broad role for the federal government under the Constitution, but also recognized that judges had enormous power to legislate their own predispositions, it followed easily that the Supreme Court should not lag appreciably behind the "will of the people" expressed through national legislation to address national needs.[83] Although Rutledge accepted judicial legislation by common law judges, he had always been quick to acknowledge that all judicial rulings were subject to modification, even rejection, by the legislature (absent a constitutional prohibition). It followed, therefore—he was reflecting Cooley and Holmes—that as long as there were principled, articulable bases under the Constitution for sustaining congressional legislation, the Court should affirm what the people's representatives had enacted. Thus, the "real issue," as Rutledge saw it, was "whether or not the political philosophy of the Supreme Court can be brought into substantial agreement with the will of the people as expressed in legislative action."[84]

The Supreme Court's *Tipaldo* decision in 1936, which had nullified the New York minimum wage law for women and children,[85] was in Rutledge's words "a perfect example of judges interpreting the Constitution to deny lawful power. . . . Five justices said this law took away the liberty of citizens 'without due process of law.' It violated their 'freedom of contract.' Whose freedom to contract for what? The freedom of hungry women and children to contract to work for starvation wages."[86] Rutledge noted that the Constitution itself "throws no light on" the question of whether a minimum wage "deprived workers and employers of 'the due process of law'"; indeed, he wrote, "the fathers of the Constitution . . . had never heard of minimum wages."[87] And yet the Court majority imported a substantive contractual right for the benefit of employers into the due process clause to nullify even a state—not a federal—law to protect the general welfare. Clearly, to Rutledge, these justices had imposed "their own political philosophy."[88] He called this decision, as well as those that invalidated New Deal legislation, "constitutional wreckage" attributable to "the abuse of judicial power rather than to the inadequacy of the Constitution to modern needs."[89] The country, he said, was stalemated by justices who—although appointed by the president and confirmed by the Senate—are "responsible to nobody" but "hold dominion over everybody."[90] He emphasized that "[w]hen any small group of men has ultimate political power we have an autocracy."[91]

Although Wiley Rutledge clearly understood the seriousness of a political move to change the Supreme Court—an effort ostensibly intended to undermine the separation of powers—he noted that the Constitution did not specify the number of justices.[92] Presidents, including Lincoln, as well as Congress itself, he said, had successfully initiated changes in the number of justices, for political reasons, on six occasions.[93] He wrote to a friend:

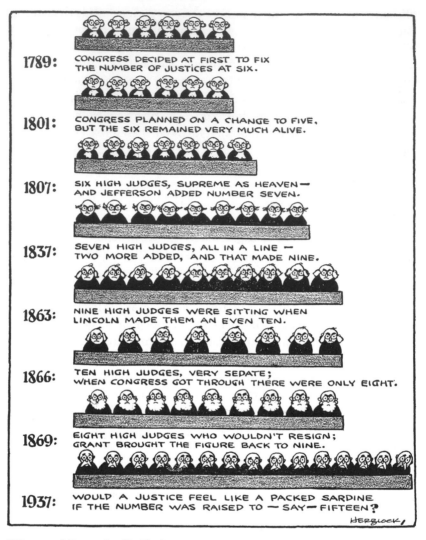

"Historical Figures"—Herblock cartoon on court-packing. (From Herblock:
A Cartoonist's Life *[Times Books, 1998]; reprinted with permission of The Herb
Block Foundation)*

"While I do not like the idea of political control of the court, still it is my
belief that the constitution left the organization of the court specifically to
congress as one of the controls upon overreaching judicial action. I do not
know why else power should have been conferred on congress to fix the
court's apparent jurisdiction." James Monroe, Rutledge noted, had said that
the power of Congress to organize the Supreme Court had been intended

"as a means of enabling congress to bring the court into line with popular views when once it gets too far out of line with them."[94] Thus, the Court-packing proposal was best characterized, in Rutledge's mind, as an unfortunate but under the circumstances proper political response to a pattern of judicial vetoes which had gotten out of hand.[95]

But why did Rutledge consider Roosevelt's Court-packing plan the "least harmful" response? Many liberals were arguing, as Rutledge himself had said to Iowa's district judges a year earlier, that constitutional amendment was the proper response to a Supreme Court interpretation that the country found unacceptable. Still others proposed legislation that would have required a super-majority of the Court to declare a law unconstitutional, or permitted Congress "to reenact laws over the judicial veto by a two-thirds vote." Rutledge rejected these ideas. He believed that legislation limiting the power of the Court to declare statutes unconstitutional would itself be held unconstitutional.[96]

Most importantly, he did not want to limit the power of judicial review, because that could result in the contraction of civil liberties. In March 1937 he wrote to a friend: "Because of my feeling that judicial protection for the fundamental liberties is a valuable one, and by these I mean such liberties as freedom of speech and thought, freedom of the press and freedom of religion, I do not want to see the institutions of judicial legislation disappear entirely." He noted that Dean Clark of Yale, Dean Garrison of Wisconsin, and others had "tried to draft an amendment which would give necessary economic controls [to Congress] and at the same time preserve civil liberties." These efforts, he said, had been "successful in creating the controls but highly questionable in preserving the protection of civil liberty." Because he thus believed it "impossible to draft an amendment," he had come to "favor the direct attack."[97]

Significantly, therefore, the easy deference that Wiley Rutledge would have the Supreme Court accord to the legislature—the will of the people— was limited to regulation of property rights. He was not willing to fetter in any way the Supreme Court's review of a legislative majority's actions affecting civil liberties guaranteed by the Constitution. This higher value that Rutledge placed on personal liberties than on property rights—stated unequivocally in 1937 (and traceable to class discussion during his years in St. Louis)[98]—foreshadowed the famous footnote in Chief Justice Stone's *Carolene Products* opinion a year later, in which Stone suggested that the Court might appropriately impose a "more exacting judicial scrutiny" of a claimed violation of a "specific prohibition of the Constitution, such as those found in the first ten amendments," or of statutes directed, prejudicially, at "discrete and insular minorities."[99] Not all justices agreed with Stone's proposition. Rutledge accordingly anticipated the divide between the liberal and conservative wings of the Court in the 1940s, in which Rutledge himself eventually came to play a major role.[100]

Senate hearings on the president's proposal began on March 10, 1937, and continued for six weeks. In early April, the *Des Moines Register* carried a story that "the supporters of the President's program may draw upon Dean Rutledge of the University of Iowa Law school for legal support of its program to counteract the recent testimony of the dean of the University of Michigan Law School."[101] Although he did not want to be seen as "agitating on the subject" or "seeking publicity" for his "personal views,"[102] Rutledge had already satisfied requests to make public his position on the plan in various informal appearances before local groups[103] and in a question-and-answer interview with the *Cedar Rapids Gazette*.[104] The possibility of his testifying before the Senate, however, was another matter.

State Representative Leo Hoegh of Lucas County, later governor of Iowa, immediately wrote to inquire whether the dean would purport to speak on behalf of the University or the state of Iowa. Rutledge replied that if asked to testify, he would do so "exclusively in a personal capacity and not as a representative of the University or of the College of Law." He added: "If there is one constitutional principle that is sacred above all others, it is the principle of free but responsible speech, and if there is any institution in the national community which should exemplify this principle at its highest, it is our universities, where the business of the institution is thinking."[105]

The dean faced a more serious challenge from the university president, Gilmore. Once the word was out that he might testify, Rutledge later wrote, Gilmore had called him "on the presidential carpet" and warned him to "watch [his] step." Rutledge concluded, "[T]he issue was too clear for me to dodge, and the ultimatum too degrading for me to accept." He recognized that the state legislature was in session considering the university's efforts to restore faculty salaries to pre-Depression levels. Thus, in order not to prejudice these efforts, Rutledge told Gilmore that he would testify if summoned, but would submit his resignation "on the day [he] left for Washington" and give a copy of his letter to the press.[106] Rutledge did not consider this a courageous move, however, for he was sure that he had support from the university's board of trustees, the legislature, and the governor.[107] In any event, Rutledge was not called to testify, and he was relieved. Strong as his feelings about the matter were, he neither believed his own appearance important nor liked the idea of causing a local stir.

The story of what happened thereafter is well known. On March 29, while the Senate hearings were in progress, the Supreme Court upheld the state of Washington's minimum wage law, overruling the *Tipaldo* de-

Justice Owen J. Roberts at work on his sixty-third birthday, May 2, 1938, a year after his "switch in time" began saving New Deal legislation. (Photograph by Harris and Ewing; Collection of the Supreme Court of the United States, 1930.10.1)

cision issued less than a year earlier.[108] In April, the Court sustained the National Labor Relations Act[109] and in May, the Social Security Act.[110] Justice Roberts had switched sides. The Court's reversal of its course obviously deflated Roosevelt's effort; the controversial bill now seemed unnecessary. Furthermore, on May 18, not long after Congress authorized Supreme Court justices with ten years' service to retire at full salary for life, Justice Van Devanter announced his retirement.[111] Of significance in halting whatever momentum remained, moreover, was the sudden death in mid-July of the Senate majority leader, Joseph Robinson of Arkansas. Whatever senators Robinson held in tow were thus released. And the bill failed.[112]

Once Justice Roberts changed his position, Wiley Rutledge knew that "the President had substantially won everything that he was really fighting for" and, as Rutledge saw it, should have called off the fight. But Rutledge had "no doubt whatever" that Roosevelt's "fight up to that time" had been "necessary" and had "saved the constitution from so narrow an interpretation that it could not have functioned in the future."[113]

NINE

Roosevelt's First Court Vacancies

Van Devanter, Sutherland, Cardozo

A Supreme Court vacancy triggers a number of predictable events. White House insiders, promised that they will be identified only as "informed persons,"[1] feed the press the names of their own preferred candidates under "serious consideration." Elected officials—especially senators responsible for confirming the nominee—publicly back their own choices, often reflecting support for a home state or regional favorite. Still others interested in particular hopefuls launch letter-writing and telephone campaigns to convince the president. Usually they approach the attorney general, who traditionally assumes principal responsibility for investigating suggested candidates and formally recommending a nominee to the president. Rarely will the president give solid indication of a preferred nominee early on, although the president is not likely to be altogether passive. The president may prescribe criteria, or offhandedly stress a particular quality, or even ask to have a name checked out.

The press reports on all who are talked about, usually leading with the names of those who were in the running for the previous vacancy. Before a decision is reached, therefore, the press will have reported snippets of information, with varying degrees of reliability depending not only on how close the source is to the president or the attorney general—and on how current the information is in a fast-moving, often changing situation—but also on whether the source is reflecting the president's views, or is merely trying to influence them by creating the impression of a groundswell. These nomination rituals occurred eight times during the presidency of Franklin Roosevelt.

The day after Justice Van Devanter announced his retirement, the press, without a vacancy to report since President Hoover had named Justice Cardozo in 1932,[2] published a long list of likely contenders gleaned from government service, the bench, and academia. The cast from the *New York*

Times included Senate Majority Leader Joseph T. Robinson of Arkansas and Senator Robert F. Wagner of New York; Representative Hatton Sumners of Texas; two federal appellate judges, Judge Florence Allen of the U.S. Court of Appeals for the Sixth Circuit, and Judge Learned Hand from the Second Circuit; Attorney General Homer Cummings; Solicitor General Stanley Reed; Assistant Attorney General Robert H. Jackson; Professor Felix Frankfurter of Harvard Law School; James M. Landis, chairman of the Securities and Exchange Commission (and recently designated Harvard's law dean); John P. Devaney, former chief justice of Minnesota and subsequently president of the National Lawyers Guild; Frank Murphy, governor of Michigan (and formerly high commissioner of the Philippines); two New York Supreme Court (trial) judges—Samuel Rosenman, who had been a counselor to Roosevelt when he was governor of New York, and Ferdinand Pecora who as an SEC commissioner had investigated Wall Street; two Roosevelt intimates, Benjamin V. Cohen, from the Public Works Administration, and Thomas G. Corcoran, with the Reconstruction Finance Corporation, both of whom had drafted New Deal legislation; Judge Justin Miller, former law dean at Duke and a member of the U.S. Board of Tax Appeals from California; and Donald R. Richberg, former director of the National Recovery Administration.[3] The *Washington Post* added Sam G. Bratton, a federal circuit court judge and former senator from New Mexico.[4] Senator Hugo Black of Alabama did not make the cut.

Despite the shopping list the press had created for the president, it was common knowledge that Roosevelt had promised the first vacancy to Majority Leader Robinson, who was leading the Court-packing fight.[5] Immediately upon Justice Van Devanter's announced retirement, four Democratic senators, taking Robinson's nomination for granted, announced their candidacy to succeed him as majority leader.[6] According to a headline in the *Washington Post* referring to Robinson: "Appointment Sure, Say Advisers Close to Roosevelt."[7]

Roosevelt initially told the press that he "would not give an indication of when the appointment would be made."[8] Indeed, as long as the Court bill was alive in the Senate, the President did not know whether he would have only one Court nomination or several, so he was in no hurry to make a difficult, single choice, especially because the Court would not convene to hear argument again until October.[9] When Senator Robinson died unexpectedly on July 14, however, everything changed.[10] The Court-packing fight was over—except for Roosevelt's fury.

The press, in the meantime, had added two southern candidates from the U.S. Court of Appeals for the Fifth Circuit: Judge Samuel H. Sibley of Georgia and Judge Joseph C. Hutcheson Jr. of Texas.[11] Reporters also began to play up the Senate's new favorite, Judge Sam Bratton.[12] Roosevelt, however, was not about to appease the Senate. Indeed, according to one historian, on July 27 FDR telegraphed the possibility of a choice "particularly offensive" to the Senate by announcing that "he was exploring the possibility of filling the vacancy" with a recess appointment "after the Senate had adjourned."[13] The president had been conducting virtually a covert operation, leaving the press in the dark as Attorney General Homer Cummings and the solicitor general, Stanley Reed, sifted over fifty[14]—some say up to seventy-five[15]—names. But the number quickly became nine, including five appellate judges.[16] At that point, Roosevelt himself removed as "not liberal enough" the judges on the list—Bratton, Sibley, Hutcheson, and two others who had initially impressed the president and Cummings: North Carolina's chief justice, Walter P. Stacy, and the federal circuit judge John J. Parker, also of North Carolina. (The Senate had rejected Parker in 1930 when Hoover had nominated him to the Court despite opposition by organized labor and the National Association for the Advancement of Colored People, which was showing political muscle for the first time.)[17] The remaining four—Senator Black, Solicitor General Reed, Senator Sherman Minton of Indiana (himself a Black promoter), and Dean Lloyd Garrison of Wisconsin—became two, and the president chose the more liberal Black over Reed.[18]

As early as January 1937, two progressive Republican senators, George Norris of Nebraska and Robert La Follette of Wisconsin, had urged Roosevelt to appoint Black when a Court vacancy occurred. So had Minton, who, believing himself a potential political liability, withdrew his own name from consideration because of his unsparing personal attacks on the justices during the Court-packing fight. Cummings accordingly asked Minton to sound out Black. Initially reluctant—Black hoped eventually to become Senate majority leader and then seek the presidency—Black acceded to his wife's desire for a "refuge from political life" and told Minton he would take the appointment if offered. Black himself was a personal favorite of the president, who liked Black's "aggressive leadership of the liberal bloc" in the Senate. The senator had been a Court-packing lieutenant of Majority Leader Robinson on the Senate floor and, unlike some supporters of the Court bill, unquestionably believed in the proposal. Indeed, Black had given a powerful radio address in its defense.[19]

The president had wanted to force onto the high bench the strongest possible administration supporter. His preoccupation with New Deal economic policy was palpable, indeed determinative, in deciding upon a justice. He was looking for "a true believer in expanding governmental power." Attorney General Homer Cummings, Senator Alben Barkley of Kentucky,

Senator Hugo L. Black, 1937. (Photograph by Harris and Ewing; Collection of the Supreme Court of the United States, 1937.11)

and the president's principal legal advisor from academia, Professor Felix Frankfurter of Harvard, had all strongly recommended Solicitor General Stanley Reed as more experienced with the Court than Black. Nomination of the solid, highly regarded solicitor general, moreover, would have been well received as a conciliatory gesture to the Senate. But Roosevelt would not be moved. He was embittered over the Court fight and not of a mind to use the nomination to heal the recent breach within his own party by paying attention to the conservatives. Nor did he fear losing a floor fight. Creating a "neat and cruel irony," the "rather vengeful President" offered the South the appointment but chose "one of the two or three left-wingers in the Senate." He would defy the senators to reject one of their own. On August 12, he sent Black's name to the upper chamber.[20]

Although Black was confirmed four days later by a vote of 63 to 16, the ensuing revelation that Black had been affiliated with the Ku Klux Klan in the early 1920s (resigning in 1925) brought controversy that reached the level of political convulsion. On October 1, three days before the Court convened for the fall term, Black sought to salvage his reputation and quiet the furor by addressing the nation over the radio. He acknowledged his earlier Klan membership, and—without naming the Klan—expressed disdain for organizations that would interfere with "complete religious freedom." He added that many of his best friends were Catholics, Jews, and "members of the colored race." On balance, he probably achieved his objective; after the address the Gallup Poll indicated that 56 percent of the respondents answered that Black should stay on the Court, whereas 59 percent had called for his resignation before he spoke. Nonetheless, his failure to denounce the Klan by name, or to offer any apology, or to condemn Klan atrocities, or even to reveal his earlier Klan affiliation during Senate discussion of that rumor in the confirmation hearing, continued to leave many unsatisfied. The "KKK angle" troubled Wiley Rutledge greatly, causing him to wonder "what kind of a judge he will make."[21]

Barely three months after Justice Black took his seat on the Court, Justice Sutherland announced his intention to retire effective January 18, 1938. The president implicitly acknowledged the need for a smoothly acceptable choice by settling quickly on his solicitor general, Stanley Reed of Kentucky, and sending his name to the Senate ten days after Sutherland's announcement. As usual, the press had assembled the list of frontrunners remaining from the last vacancy, beginning with Reed and Minton. A few new names had emerged—Judge Harold M. Stephens of the U.S. Court of Appeals for the District of Columbia; Dean Acheson, former undersecretary of the treasury; and John J. Burns, former counsel to the SEC.[22] But under the circumstances Reed had been a shoo-in. One Reed biographer quoted

Solicitor General Stanley F. Reed leaving the Supreme Court for the last time, January 17, 1938, before becoming Justice Reed. (Photograph by Acme Newspictures, Inc.; Collection of the Supreme Court of the United States, 1977.15.19.16.1)

another: the new justice "'was certainly a nominee as circumspect and unobtrusive as Black was bellicose.'"[23] Rutledge wrote to a former student, Louise Larrabee, wondering, "when everybody is so nearly unanimous in expressing approval," whether "the man can stand for anything or not." But he realized that his comment perhaps was "unfair" because the unanimity was "simply an expression of relief resulting from the contrast between this appointment and the Black one."[24]

IN THE SAME MONTH, January 1938, Justice Benjamin Cardozo, the scholar-successor to Justice Holmes, suffered a paralyzing stroke; he died six months later on July 9.[25] With the "switch" by Justice Roberts and the retirements of Justices Van Devanter and Sutherland, only two unreconstructed conservative justices remained on the Court, McReynolds and Butler. With the disability of Justice Cardozo, however—and thus with only an eight-judge Court—there was no assuredly cohesive, pro–New Deal majority among Chief Justice Hughes and his moderate-to-liberal associates: Roberts, Stone, Brandeis, Reed, and Black. In the view of some New Deal supporters, therefore, the president's next pick—indeed, his next two picks, keeping in mind that Justice Brandeis was nearing eighty-two—would be crucial in forming a coherent economic philosophy on the Court that would protect administration initiatives and give organized labor its due.[26]

The early betting on the Cardozo vacancy, based on strong support from the legal and academic communities—and early endorsement by the progressive Republican senator George Norris of Nebraska[27]—favored Felix Frankfurter, an expert on administrative law and a Roosevelt confidant for over a decade. Editorial writers and columnists pointed out that "the vacant seat on the Supreme Court was the scholar's seat; it had been filled by Story, Holmes, Cardozo."[28] And, of major significance, Frankfurter had the unqualified support of the White House insiders Tommy Corcoran, Ben Cohen, Harry Hopkins, Harold Ickes, Robert Jackson, and William O. Douglas.[29] By September 1938, a poll by the American Bar Association of its membership asking who should succeed Justice Cardozo revealed that Frankfurter had received more than five times the vote given to each of his nearest competitors, John W. Davis, the Democratic presidential nominee in 1924, and Judge Learned Hand.[30]

There were substantial impediments to naming Frankfurter, however, and FDR did not move to fill the seat quickly. First, there was strong pressure from the Senate to name a westerner. With Van Devanter, from Wyoming, and Sutherland, of Utah, off the Court, Justice Pierce Butler—a Minnesota resident from "the east bank of the Mississippi at St. Paul"—was the westernmost member of the Court. Soon after Cardozo's death, therefore, the president himself, "nervous and embarrassed," told Frankfurter at Hyde Park that (in Frankfurter's words) he had given "'definite promises to Senators and party people that the next appointment to the Court would be someone west of the Mississippi.'" Jim Farley, Roosevelt's postmaster general, had the same recollection. He wrote that Roosevelt had told him in December 1938 that Frankfurter wanted the appointment "'in the worst

Harvard law professor Felix Frankfurter. (Courtesy of Art and Visual Materials, Special Collections Department, Harvard Law School Library)

way,'" but that "'some months ago . . . at Hyde Park'" the President had told Frankfurter he "'just couldn't appoint him for many reasons. In the first place the appointment has to go west.'" Farley then quoted Roosevelt's next reason: "'I told Felix that I could not appoint another Jew.'"[31]

This, then, was the second barrier. Both Cardozo and Justice Brandeis, like Frankfurter, were Jewish. In those days anti-Semitism was a factor influencing Supreme Court appointments, and in this case more than one seat was involved. As Rutledge himself put the issue indirectly in letters to friends, President Hoover had done the "right and courageous thing" in appointing Cardozo when Brandeis was on the Court.[32] In late 1938, however, not even the Jewish community itself was united behind Frankfurter. According to the editor of the Roosevelt-Frankfurter correspondence, "a group of wealthy and important Jews called on Roosevelt to beg him to make no effort at all to get Frankfurter appointed," fearing "a dangerous growth of anti-Semitism." One of Frankfurter's biographers confirmed that Secretary of the Treasury Henry Morgenthau Jr. "kept up a steady drumfire of anti-Frankfurter criticism, as did a group of other prominent Jews headed by Arthur Hays Sulzberger of the *New York Times*, who warned Roosevelt that putting a second Jew on the Court could play into the hands of anti-Semites at home and abroad."[33]

There was a third barrier. The man primarily responsible for recommending a nominee, Attorney General Homer Cummings, as well as Jim Farley and even General Hugh Johnson, head of the NRA, opposed Frankfurter. Joining those who were urging appointment of a westerner, Cummings and Farley expressed concern that Senate confirmation would not go smoothly for the Harvard professor. For a time Roosevelt, too, apparently had the same worry. A year earlier, when Justice Cardozo was still active and the president was discussing with Morgenthau who should join the Court when the elderly Brandeis stepped down—Frankfurter or Dean James Landis Jr. of Harvard—the president himself reportedly favored Frankfurter. But he told Morgenthau, "I think I would have a terrible time getting Frankfurter confirmed." The references to confirmation worries invoked geography and even Frankfurter's reputation as a radical supporter of "reds" and Sacco and Vanzetti. But they were also veiled words of caution against appointment of a Jew.[34]

There was still another dynamic at work. Irving Brant, the editorial writer for the *St. Louis Star-Times* who had recently published *Storm over the Constitution*, and who was supporting Frankfurter, began to promote Wiley Rutledge as the most suitable alternative in the event the president had to look west. Described by others as "tall, sandy-haired, likeable"—indeed, "very down to earth" and "straight-shooting"—Irving Newton Brant was nine years older than Rutledge, a graduate of the State University of Iowa, and eventually best known for his six-volume biography of James Madison.[35] But Brant was an activist as much as a scholar. He worked ardently for public housing,[36] for conservation of natural resources,[37] and especially for civil rights and civil liberties.[38] A dedicated Democrat, Brant had begun

Irving Brant.
(St. Louis
Star-Times)

to watch Franklin Roosevelt as early as 1920, when Roosevelt was running
for vice president on the Cox ticket.[39] Later, when Roosevelt was governor
of New York, Brant regularly sent copies of his editorials to Roosevelt and
wrote him letters, pro and con, about his conduct in office.[40] Brant's candid,
yet supportive, approach to Roosevelt paid off for Brant; a mutually respectful personal relationship developed between them. And upon Roosevelt's
election as president in 1932, that relationship became important to Roosevelt, as well as to the persistent editorial writer himself, for Brant was one
of the few major newspaper editors in the country who generally supported
the administration day by day.[41] Brant, in short, was a man the president
could not afford to ignore.

Irving Brant saw Attorney General Cummings pushing Judge Harold
Stephens of the District of Columbia's federal court of appeals for the Car-

dozo seat. Originally from Nebraska, Stephens had served as a state trial judge in Utah and, more recently, had been Cummings's antitrust chief at the Justice Department until appointed to the appellate bench in 1935. Although Brant strongly favored Frankfurter, he was concerned that Cummings might prevail in supporting Stephens, a westerner who in Brant's view did "not rate high" with the more liberal justices on the Supreme Court. Brant was especially worried that Stephens might get the nod because of speculation that Brandeis would soon step down. On that assumption, Roosevelt presumably could soon name Frankfurter, his favorite, to the seat of the other Jewish justice with relative ease—helped along, of course, by naming a westerner in the meantime to replace Cardozo. So Brant devised a plan: push Frankfurter but also offer Wiley Rutledge, as the westerner most likely to further New Deal principles on the Court. In this way Brant urged two names on the president for the next two appointments.[42]

Brant, in fact, had been touting Rutledge to FDR for almost three years. As an editor in St. Louis, Brant was well aware of Rutledge as the outspoken liberal law dean at Washington University. As a member of the Social Justice Commission of St. Louis, Dean Rutledge, in Brant's eyes, "went to the front in practically every case of injustice that came to public notice." Brant also saw Rutledge as particularly "influential in maintaining civil liberties for the faculty and students of Washington University, in the face of a very conservative Board of Trustees." And Brant was especially impressed when, in 1933, Rutledge publicly chastised the president of the American Bar Association for defending the Supreme Court's decisions striking down limitations on child labor. After Rutledge accepted the Iowa deanship, Brant wrote an editorial praising his accomplishments at Washington University, and Rutledge responded graciously, without a hint that the two were even acquaintances (Brant, for example, was not a member of the Public Question Club).[43]

Six months later, in January 1936, the Supreme Court handed down its *Butler* decision, declaring unconstitutional the processing taxes used under the Agricultural Adjustment Act to support federal aid to agriculture.[44] Brant's recollection of Rutledge's attack on that decision evidenced a profound impact on the editor:

> Rutledge was in St. Louis when news came [of the *Butler* decision]. Newspapers came out just before noon with long extracts from Justice Roberts' majority opinion in the *AAA* case, followed by a bare statement that three justices dissented. Dean Rutledge picked up a paper as he went to speak before the Cathedral Luncheon Club, a non-sectarian group of business and professional men. Putting aside his intended remarks, he talked for an hour on the case, analyzing the

constitutional issues and challenging the soundness of the Court's position. Offhand, with no preliminary study and no time for reflection, he presented the same arguments against it that were published [the] next day in the dissenting opinion of Justice Stone.[45]

Soon thereafter, Brant advised the president that Wiley Rutledge was Supreme Court material, and Roosevelt asked Brant to provide him with more detail.[46] So Brant, purportedly conducting a survey of law deans on constitutional issues, wrote the Iowa dean asking for "citations of articles you have written on the Constitution, or the work of the courts, or any addresses you have delivered on the subject." Rutledge, in reply, referenced his article on child labor from 1933 and a speech on social changes and the law given in 1934, but he cautioned that he had never taught constitutional law, made "no special pretensions to any competence in that vast field," and had never engaged in "productive scholarship." Rutledge ended the letter with a diatribe against the *Butler* decision: "when the verbiage is pared down to the real issue the court does nothing more than *assert* the invalidity of the act. . . . If the people of the country do not let the Liberty League et al. pull the wool over their eyes and have sense enough to return Roosevelt for another term, I feel sure that he will have the opportunity to make a sufficient number of liberal appointments to undo the major harm."[47] A few months later, in agreeing to read and comment on Brant's manuscript of *Storm over the Constitution*, Rutledge again poured out his anger at the Supreme Court's most recent decisions: "My head is not so bloody as yet . . . that I can endow these edicts with the respect which their authoritative source should evoke. . . . But I'm as confident as that I breathe that these perversions of and abstractions from the Federal power will be corrected and restored eventually. But what a struggle lies ahead."[48]

Reelected overwhelmingly in November, Roosevelt carried forty-six states. Rutledge wrote Brant "congratulations," calling him "one of the few distinguished editorial writers outside the South[] who saw the campaign whole and true." Then venting still again his feelings about the Supreme Court, Rutledge observed: "The old four-square block remains intact—as the Social Security (N.Y.) decision demonstrates. . . . Roberts and Hughes may have squinted sideways at the returns, but the Four Horsemen do not know that we had an election."[49]

Two years later, on November 12, 1938, Brant wrote Roosevelt to remind the president that "early in 1936" Brant had mentioned Rutledge "for the Supreme Court." Brant added that at the president's request, he had "assembled some information" from Rutledge about his constitutional views, "[w]ithout giving any hint" of the reason. Brant explained that he had not presented the material when the first two Court vacancies occurred because "political conditions" at that time did not dictate consideration of Rutledge. Brant then stressed: "As I told you a few weeks ago, . . . many circumstances combine to make Felix Frankfurter the only possible nominee," and "the balancing of the court geographically ought to be held back till the next vacancy occurs"—when Rutledge should be the choice.[50]

Brant stressed the dean's Colorado and Missouri, as well as Iowa, connections; reminded the president that Rutledge was known as a "strong progressive and defender of civil liberties," citing instances at Washington University and Iowa; and added that his candidate was "vigorous physically, and 'doesn't look like a professor.'" Brant then got to the heart of the man: "Among Rutledge's traits are extreme modesty and simplicity combined with an aggressive fighting instinct and fighting power. (The enclosed photograph, clipped from a newspaper, suggests that quality of ruggedness.) He has met what I regard as the one and only absolute test of liberalism— he has been a liberal in conservative communities and against all counterpressures, when all logical prospect of gain to himself, and all social factors, ran in the other direction."[51] Brant acknowledged that "outside the legal profession, Rutledge [was] not well known," but he emphasized to Roosevelt that this adverse factor was far outweighed by Rutledge's western connections, his "right age and physical equipment," his "technical" skills and "energy," his "personal traits," and his "exceptional understanding of economic realities"—which Brant illustrated with enclosures of Rutledge's writings on "child labor" and on the importance of controlling "corporate power." Brant concluded by telling the president that Rutledge was "the only technically qualified man living west of the Mississippi who [could] be absolutely relied on for continuing life-long liberalism."[52]

The same day, Brant wrote Rutledge that it looked "very much as if Felix Frankfurter"—whom he had "strongly" recommended to the president— would be named, although Brant wished "there were more of a western call" for him. Wiley Rutledge, who had used Frankfurter's casebook in his own course on administrative law and had a high regard for the Harvard professor, replied that Frankfurter "would be an ideal selection, notwithstanding the geographical qualification." Rutledge believed this was a situation in which geography "should be disregarded as Hoover did with Cardozo's appointment." "Nor," added Rutledge, "is there anyone west of the Mississippi that I know who would be even within close distance to Frankfurter on the basis of qualifications, with the possible exception of Joseph C. Hutcheson of Texas." Brant soon asked him about Hutcheson, and Rutledge quickly replied that he considered the judge "a real liberal in the sense that his judgment is balanced and . . . his philosophy of life as well as of law is the golden mean." Furthermore, because Hutcheson had intellectual firepower commanding the respect of the Association of American Law Schools and the American Law Institute, Rutledge "deem[ed] him to be probably the one man west of the Mississippi who measure[d] up somewhat closely to the Brandeis-Cardozo-Frankfurter standard."[53]

Brant's November initiative with the president had an intended effect. On December 2, Attorney General Cummings personally sought the views of an Iowa federal court of appeals judge about Rutledge. At the same time, Cummings asked his assistant to "make a quick check-up" on Rutledge. Within two weeks Cummings had received several brief reports. Soon the newspapers began to carry Rutledge's name as a possible nominee to succeed Cardozo, and Wiley's friends began to write to him. Then, terminating a "mild dissimulation," Brant acknowledged to Rutledge his own role in the contest, adding that because FDR saw demand for a westerner as a powerful deterrent to Frankfurter's candidacy, the president had arranged for typewritten copies to be made of everything Rutledge had written to Brant and "sent them to a number of advisers for comment." As a result, the enthusiasm of the White House for Rutledge had led an insider to ask Brant for a "good endorsement" of Rutledge from Colorado, whereupon Brant had enlisted enthusiastic support from the University of Colorado president, George Norlin. Brant added that another presidential adviser, in learning from Brant what Rutledge had "said in praise of Judge Hutcheson," replied: "'That's a good argument for Rutledge. I like men who talk about the merits of other men rather than their own.'"[54] Brant concluded that "the situation is very confused." He expected Frankfurter to be "nominated next week," but still he worried that pressure from the west could not only derail Frankfurter but also result in somebody "who will make up in political strength what he may lack in judicial qualifications"—a clear concern that more conservative Democrats might prevail.[55]

The next day, December 28, Brant wrote to the president, alarmed by two recent Supreme Court decisions in which, he said, only the two Roosevelt appointees, Justices Black and Reed, had reflected, in dissent, a realistic "economic outlook." Brant told the president that the administration's economic program would not be safe until his Court appointees could win over enough of the middle group—meaning the most likely candidate, Justice Stone—to form a reliable majority. According to Brant, therefore, the next two appointments should be "akin to Reed and Black in their economic outlook, and to Justice Stone in his attitude toward judicial processes." But this could "not be achieved merely by appointing men who [would] be likely to vote with Black and Reed." The "cementing power" now necessary within the Court, Brant wrote, required men of established "legal learning" such as

"Frankfurter and Rutledge." Brant believed it "highly significant that both Justices Stone and Black" had said to him during the past year—"in connection with cases in which they had differed"—that "they wished Frankfurter was on the court," and Brant ended by saying that he wished the president and Justice Stone "could find occasion to talk together. . . . If you care to have such a talk, and will give me the word at the next press conference, I will talk to him about it."[56]

In the meantime, near the end of December, the president of the St. Louis Bar Association, Roscoe Anderson, wrote to Rutledge to say that according to the morning paper, Judge Hutcheson and Rutledge had been "the candidates most commonly mentioned," in addition to Frankfurter, for the vacancy. By January 4, 1939, Anderson had sent to the president a resolution of the Bar Association's Executive Committee "earnestly" urging Rutledge's appointment to the Court. And there were other outpourings for Wiley Rutledge. In the first days of January, one of his closest friends, his Colorado schoolmate Clay Apple, asked a mutual friend to try to reach the president on Rutledge's behalf through Thurman Arnold. Other St. Louis friends from the legal community, including an "irreconcilable" Republican lawyer, sent the president strong personal endorsements; and still another prominent St. Louis lawyer agreed to write to Stone and Reed in an effort to reach the White House. Endorsements from the Washington University law faculty also were sent. Ralph Fuchs wrote to Rutledge: "Under the circumstances, it is up to those who feel so inclined to bestir themselves, and in this part of the world they jolly well are. I won't go into details about that unless you write back wanting to know who is doing what; but I think it is fair to say that all of the worth-while backing that this community can produce is being furnished. And it's all in good taste, so that neither you nor anyone else need feel embarrassment if nothing results—as I suppose the odds still are that nothing will." In addition to the full-court press from Missouri, two letters came to the White House from Iowa. But these were fortuitous; Iowa had no Irving Brant organizing for Rutledge, and Wiley himself did not encourage an effort on his behalf in Iowa (or anywhere).[57]

Meanwhile, Frankfurter's White House supporters had been urging the president to take Brant up on his offer to broker a meeting between the president and Stone. Roosevelt sent for the justice, who advised the president "to waive the geographical considerations usually brought to bear on Supreme Court appointments and appoint Frankfurter." According to Harold Ickes, the president's many references to "what Justice Stone had said to him" indicated that "Stone had made a great impression on his mind."[58] Nonetheless, at year's end the president was still shaky on Frankfurter. Just after Christmas 1938, Roosevelt gave him a negative signal. According to Frankfurter himself, "[Roosevelt] asked me to give him my views on Wiley Rutledge's qualifications for the Supreme Court, and I sent him a memorandum—after I had adequately informed myself—saying he was entirely qualified for this bench." This presidential request reflected the White House insiders' view that Roosevelt was going to choose from the west, even though the president acknowledged to Harold Ickes on December 27 that "[t]here isn't anyone in that section who is of sufficient stature." When Ickes pressed Roosevelt to appoint Frankfurter—who, the president agreed (in Ickes's words), "stood head and shoulders above every other possible appointee"—the president said he would appoint Frankfurter when Brandeis resigned. Ickes protested that Roosevelt could not be sure Brandeis would leave the Court in time for Roosevelt to make that appointment.[59] Ickes might have been thinking, moreover, that a third term controversy could foreshorten the period in 1939 when the president could count on confirmation of any nominee should Brandeis resign.

The next day, the newspapers predicted that Judge Stephens—who in Ickes's view was "inclined to be stupid"—would succeed Cardozo. By that time, however, Stephens's chief supporter, Attorney General Cummings, had announced his resignation as of the end of the year and thus ceased being a player. An important barrier to Frankfurter had been removed. Cummings was replaced by Frank Murphy, recently defeated for reelection as governor of Michigan, whom the president named attorney general on New Year's day 1939.[60]

According to Ickes, on January 2 Harry Hopkins, then secretary of commerce and FDR's confidant, called Ickes to suggest that Senator Norris be asked to urge the president to appoint Frankfurter, but Ickes countered by suggesting that Murphy instead should approach Roosevelt. Hopkins concurred and "undertook to talk to Murphy," who weighed in for Frankfurter. Hopkins advised Ickes, however, that the president had a new liberal candidate, Senator Lewis B. Schwellenbach of Washington, as well as Rutledge, in mind, because "[j]ust now he is very much of the opinion that the appointment ought to come from west of the Mississippi." Hopkins also informed Ickes that he had talked with Solicitor General Robert Jackson, who concurred with Ickes, Hopkins, and other White House insiders that "if the liberal position of the Supreme Court is to be held, Frankfurter must go in. He is the only one in sight who can sit down at the council table and hold his own with Chief Justice Hughes." Finally, Hopkins, reflecting Ickes's own view, reported to Ickes that he had told the president it was "wishful thinking" to believe that Justice Brandeis was "likely to resign during this administration," and thus that he had advised the president "to go on the theory that this will be the last appointment to the Supreme Court that he will have the opportunity to make."[61]

Wiley Rutledge and Senator Schwellenbach, as the so-called western finalists, had impeccable New Deal credentials. Schwellenbach in particular, a strong supporter of the Court-packing plan, had substantial labor support, especially from the CIO. The other most talked-about westerners, Judges Stephens and Bratton, were more conservative. The president had nixed Bratton because, in Roosevelt's words (as reported by Ickes), Bratton had the type of judicial mind "'able to find a justification in the Constitution (and this can always be done) for declaring unconstitutional a law which does not comport with his social and economic views.'" The president was looking for the other type of judicial mind, one that Ickes summarized as inclined to "follow[] the Constitution, even if that means sustaining laws which are unwise or even threaten the economic security of the country." According to Ickes, the president believed "that if Congress has the constitutional right to ruin the country," the Supreme Court should not restrain it from doing so.[62] In short, the president was looking for a justice who would defer to congressional authority to enact the president's economic program.

In addition to the shift in the attorney general's office from Stephens (through Cummings) to Frankfurter (through Murphy), those who were insisting on a westerner received a blow when the progressive Republican senator George Norris of Nebraska, described by some as "the most respected liberal leader in the Senate," wrote a strong letter to the president recommending Frankfurter and made his endorsement public. On January 4, 1939, two days after Ickes recorded his concerns, the president called Frankfurter and offered him the Supreme Court. The next day, Wiley Rutledge—expressing relief—wrote to Brant: "Word has just come of Frankfurter's nomination. The President has done the right & courageous thing. No other designation would have been fitting for the successor to Holmes & Cardozo; and any other person would have had upon his shoulders the double burden, and the impossible one, of carrying on their tradition . . . and of taking the onus for displacing the man who has been named. Believe me, it is a relief to escape that, if in fact there was a possibility that I might be asked to assume it." The relieved (or, probably more accurately, the conflicted) dean wrote Frankfurter an enthusiastic "letter of congratulations."[63]

Because Roosevelt was often inscrutable, it is not clear how close he came to naming a westerner rather than his personal favorite, Frankfurter. There can be no doubt, however, that Wiley Rutledge was a westerner the president seriously considered, although we do not know how Rutledge compared in the president's mind with Senator Schwellenbach or Judge Stephens. Brant told Rutledge that "hardly a week before Frankfurter was appointed," the president had told Frankfurter that he must await the Brandeis vacancy. If true, this explains Roosevelt's deputizing Frankfurter to inquire about Rutledge right after Christmas. Presumably because of the late-December insiders' push for Frankfurter, however, Brant had gained the impression by year's end that Frankfurter would succeed Cardozo, with the next vacancy going west. Brant accordingly concluded that White House intimates had "secured publicity for Rutledge to build him up for the future" and to neutralize conservative western pressure for Stephens. Then, according to Brant, the attorney general nominee, Frank Murphy, "swung the influence of his office to Frankfurter. Senator Norris of Nebraska added his endorsement and the appointment was made." The Senate confirmed Frankfurter without a dissenting vote.[64]

In the aftermath Rutledge's friends looked forward to the next vacancy. The securities and exchange commissioner Edward Eicher of Iowa wrote to Wiley that the impression made on his "behalf might very possibly bear fruit later on." He continued: "I expect to take advantage of the first opportunity that may come to me for again discussing your availability with the President in person." Rutledge replied: "The more I think about the matter the more I am astonished at my own connection with the situation. Even more pleasing and unexpected than that were the reactions of my friends toward the suggestion. Ever since the nomination of Professor Frankfurter they have been more than kind. I, however, know that these things begin, crystallize, and then are dissipated. Consequently, I am building my plans on the continuance of my work in the great job I have to do here rather than some other kind of preferment."[65]

Brant, of course, was ready for the next round. He wrote Frankfurter a congratulatory letter, concluding with an effort to line up the new justice's support for Rutledge the next time by quoting from Rutledge's letters steadfastly supporting Frankfurter's nomination when FDR "was almost committed" to naming a westerner.[66] The president himself, moreover, had been impressed by the movement that Brant had inspired for Rutledge. Two weeks after nominating Frankfurter, Roosevelt sent a confidential memorandum to Frankfurter asking him to "read and return" Brant's letter of "12/28/38 to the President . . . [s]uggest[ing] the appt. of 'Frankfurter and Dean Wiley Rutledge' to the Supreme Court."[67] Roosevelt, too, was apparently anticipating the next Court vacancy and, quite obviously, was signaling his interest in having Frankfurter help him to evaluate likely candidates.

In reporting favorably about Rutledge to the president in late December, Frankfurter had called for help from his Harvard colleague, the constitutional scholar Thomas Reed Powell, who was attending the annual meeting of the Association of American Law Schools in Chicago. Powell had found Rutledge dining with a friend and joined them for an hour.[68] Years later,

Powell reminded Rutledge that he had prepared a memorandum of his "impressions" after their "Chicago conversation" and sent it to Frankfurter—"from an intellectual snob to an intellectual snob, both of whom like to use such measuring rods as Oliver Wendell Holmes and John Dewey, and both of whom also think that Gus Hand as a judge is superior to his much more intellectually brilliant cousin, Learned Hand."[69] According to Powell, Frankfurter had been "sincerely helping the President to find a Western man." Powell continued: "I got to Felix a memorandum on that Thursday, and he was greatly impressed in favor of the Mr. X. [in the] memorandum. Later he told me that the memorandum was to find its way to where it should go. Still later he showed me a letter from Irving Brant with references to you and quotations from you which also greatly enhanced the already high opinion he had formed from my memorandum."[70]

Upon Rutledge's appointment to the Supreme Court four years later, Powell sent him a copy of the memorandum to Frankfurter:

Of Mr. X's human qualities, solid judgment and discernment I have the highest opinion. In our talk about various deans and law teachers, he seemed to me to be most perspicacious. He talks slowly and quietly, but directly and without hesitation. When told by me of a Dean who seemed unwilling to grant a teacher a leave of absence for fear that he might get an offer elsewhere, he was shocked and pained, and the expression on his face was a more severe rebuke than any diatribe could be. I should regard him as free from any temperamental instabilities as any person I know. . . . His membership in any group would add a leaven from the point of view of the inter-relations of the people in the group to an extent not equaled by many. His poise and wisdom seem to me a certain guarantee against any blunders of practical judgment or in human relations. There is a standfast quality about him that is superb. It would help to make a good team out of any but the wildest horses. . . . I would bet completely that Mr. X would never have the current of his thought and outlook swerved by self interest or assume a role from any thought of self advancement.

On the intellectual side, there is nothing outstanding. His is pretty clearly not a quick cutting mind. It is a judgmatical mind, rather like Gus Hand's. Abstract thinking would seem not to be natural to it. . . .

Powell compared Rutledge with various lawyers whom he and Frankfurter knew in common, opining that Rutledge, like others he named, might have been a solid B student at Harvard "but so much superior to most men" deemed "more brilliant" because they scored higher. Powell continued:

As I compare him with Stanley Reed, I should think him deeper than Reed and more really reflective. I think that there would be a bigger and more lasting deposit from a three-hour talk with X than from one with Stanley Reed. Yet I doubt if Mr. X would be as smooth a performer as Reed. Some of Reed's associates in the Department of Justice say that he found it hard to write and anticipated that writing opinions would be laborious and difficult for him. I find no evidence that it has so turned out in Reed's case, but I suspect that it might so turn out in Mr. X's case. . . .

Mr. X is solid, stable and wise. He is far ahead of Ste[ph]ens or Schwellenbach. . . . I should think his mind quite as good as Lloyd Garrison's, though expression would not flow from him as easily. He hasn't Lloyd's polish, but he has in a different more uncut way a great charm. He has to my mind a most discerning and trustworthy insight into the intellectual and moral qualities of others. We talked about both youngsters and oldsters whom we both know, and I was impressed by every comment that he made.[71]

A week after Frankfurter's nomination, Senator Guy Gillette of Iowa wrote to Rutledge that he was "still of the opinion that there ought to be a member of the Supreme Court from the western half of the United States. . . . In the event another vacancy occurs, I hope you will permit your friends to suggest your name."[72] Wiley Rutledge indeed gave that permission.

TEN

The Brandeis Vacancy

On February 13, 1939, five weeks after Frankfurter's nomination, Justice Louis Brandeis retired. The next day, administration officials informed the press that Roosevelt would select "from among candidates from the West if a suitable person could be found," although the same sources agreed that but for the commitment to look west, Solicitor General Jackson from New York—the home state of Chief Justice Hughes and Justice Stone—"would be the most likely choice of Mr. Roosevelt."[1] To remove further speculation, Jackson issued a statement on February 17 that "he was not, under any circumstances, a candidate for the Brandeis vacancy."[2]

The press began to feature those who had been named recently in connection with the Cardozo vacancy. On February 14, the *New York Times* reported in a headline that Senator "Schwellenbach is in line," ahead of Judge Stephens. The *Times* added that a group of western senators, led by Senator Adams of Colorado, continued to recommend Sam Bratton, the federal circuit judge from New Mexico, and the article concluded by mentioning Dean Wiley Blount Rutledge of Iowa.[3] Other newspapers featured Charles Fahy, the NLRB general counsel, also from New Mexico;[4] Joseph C. Hutcheson Jr., federal circuit judge from Texas; and, stretching the definition of westerner, Senator Sherman Minton of Indiana.[5]

Immediately after the Brandeis announcement, the White House insiders who had supported Frankfurter—Jerome Frank, Ben Cohen, Tommy Corcoran, Harold Ickes, and Robert Jackson—got behind the SEC chairman, William O. Douglas.[6] The son of an evangelical Presbyterian minister, Douglas was born in Minnesota and educated at Whitman College in Washington state before heading east to attend Columbia Law School in New York.[7] He thus had western roots that his supporters hoped would be sufficient, despite his nomination "from Connecticut" to chair the SEC.[8] By February 15, newspapers from coast to coast had installed Douglas as a "prominent" candidate who had "hitherto not been mentioned." It was reported, in fact, that the day after Brandeis retired, Douglas "spent nearly half an hour in the private quarters of Mr. Roosevelt."[9]

Although the *Times* reported on February 18 that Douglas's name kept "coming to the fore,"[10] the same article further reported that Vice President Garner and several senators had "clustered around Senator Schwellenbach's chair," calling him "'Mr. Justice'" amid reports that he had been "definitely assured of the nomination."[11] Also, the *Times* noted, Joseph B. Keenan, holdover assistant to former Attorney General Cummings, had "been making definite inquiries concerning the views of Wiley Blount Rutledge, Jr."[12] Keenan told the press that "four persons" were in the "center of the picture." Actually, on February 15, Keenan had forwarded to Murphy "all of the information available" on three candidates: Rutledge, Schwellenbach, and Douglas.[13] The material on Rutledge (as well as information about Judge Stephens and two others) had been left with Keenan by Cummings as he left office.[14]

The FBI report of December 13, 1938, which Keenan sent to Murphy as part of the package, summarized comments from teaching colleagues and others in part as follows: "Mr. Rutledge is regarded as a man of character and probity, . . . he is a highly successful Dean, competent teacher, excellent speaker, and . . . is regarded as having the ability to meet and get along with people. . . . Although he is not regarded as a brilliant legal scholar, he is considered to have a knowledge of law above that of the average lawyer."[15] The attorney general himself reached Dean Henry Bates of Michigan the same day. Murphy learned that Rutledge was "a good man—there isn't any doubt about that. Excellent character, nice personality and a pretty good lawyer"; but "[t]here isn't much chance that he would ever be thought of as a great judge. Isn't distinguished. He would be a respectable judge." On the same memo Murphy noted in pen several comments he had received from Irving Brant stressing Rutledge's "courage," "sense of indignation," and support of Frankfurter when Rutledge himself was under discussion.[16] In contrast with the Rutledge file, the information about Douglas at the time contained merely a professional résumé reflecting that Douglas had written thirteen law review articles, all but three in the journals at Harvard, Yale, Columbia, or Chicago, and was a co-author of four law school casebooks.[17]

On the evening of Brandeis's announcement, Annabel called her brother, Seymour, to elicit his help (as a former Republican congressman) in promoting Wiley for the Court. Seymour immediately wired the Democratic committeeman from Michigan and wrote to, among others, the state's Democratic senator, Prentiss Brown, and to Attorney General Murphy, both of whom he knew "rather well."[18] Spontaneously, moreover, Wiley's friends from around the country began to act. During the week immediately following Brandeis's retirement, a lawyer from St. Louis reported to Rutledge that he would reactivate the resolution supporting him passed by the executive committee of the St. Louis Bar Association; would write to the president of the Iowa Bar Association to urge the same; and had sent an FBI agent to retrieve an editorial published in the *Post Dispatch* in 1935 praising Rutledge's support for federal holding company legislation. An Iowa member of the Commissioners on Uniform State Laws advised Rutledge that he had referred a "G-man"—whose report was due by telephone "at once"—to a Republican lawyer who was "an enthusiastic supporter" of Rutledge. Others, such as the chief justice of Colorado, a former teaching colleague then in Ohio, and an associate on the Social Justice Commission in St. Louis, wrote to the president or the attorney general directly—as did former students organized by Mrs. Agnes Haskell, Governor Hadley's widow.[19]

Some friends sought Wiley's help in his own cause. Commissioner Eicher of the SEC asked for a copy of the St. Louis speech attacking the opposition of the ABA's president Charles Martin to the child labor amendment, which Eicher could use "with a close adviser to the President." A friend from St. Louis called on Wiley for damage control: he had become concerned when an FBI agent learned of a Rutledge speech favoring trials of some criminals without affording them "proper consideration by the courts" of their "fundamental rights." (Rutledge replied defensively, if not disingenuously—and avoiding particulars—that "someone may have twisted or misconstrued" the talk he had given about the Scorfina case a decade earlier, making "tentative suggestions" for dealing with gangsterism before the FBI "got busy and cleaned up the gang situation throughout the country.") Still other letters from well wishers arrived daily. While some were merely congratulatory—"I am happy that geography and fitness coincide"—most of them added reminiscent praise: Rutledge "was a little more friendly; a little more human; a little less stiff necked than the other professors"; he was an "uncommon common man."[20]

Rutledge himself joined in the effort. In thanking a friend in St. Louis for his support, he wrote: "My attitude in this situation is exactly what it was in the former one, although I am frank to say that there is no one in the picture now whom I consider so outstanding in qualifications as Frankfurter was." In replying to his Colorado friend Clay Apple, who had written to Senator Norris, Wiley counseled Apple not to bother pursuing the two Colorado senators; they would support Judge Bratton.[21] Wiley also rejected Annabel's suggestion that she contact Senator Brown of Michigan, who had a personal connection with her family and, presumably, a relationship with Attorney General Murphy. He did not, he said, "want to put any of my relatives or Annabel's who do not know me as well on the spot." Nor would he authorize efforts to obtain a supportive resolution from the state bar of Michigan. "Certainly it would be helpful," he informed his brother-in-law, "but I wonder whether they ought to be asked to endorse a man with whom they are so little acquainted and who has not either practiced or taught in the state." But Wiley was not unmindful of the critical role that Attorney General Murphy would play. He advised Seymour: "I think the principal thing you can do . . . may be to prevent Murphy from crystallizing his attitudes in favor of someone else. I have seen some reports indicating that he favors Stephens." Wiley added that he had received a letter from Senator Gillette indicating that Senator Norris—who, in Wiley's view, "had a bit to do with finally persuading the President to appoint Frankfurter"—had "expressed particular interest" in Rutledge for the Brandeis seat.[22]

In the meantime, on February 16, the president had left for Florida on his way to a Caribbean cruise to relax, watch naval maneuvers,[23] and consider dossiers on seven Court prospects: Rutledge, Schwellenbach, Douglas, Dean Garrison, and the federal circuit judges Hutcheson, Stephens, and Bratton.[24] The next day, the columnists Joseph Alsop and Robert Kintner discussed various candidates and called the appointment "a trial of Frank Murphy's powers." They noted that "[i]n nominations like that of Francis Biddle to the Federal Circuit in Philadelphia, Murphy has already shown his willingness to do battle for learned, well qualified men." If "he will do battle again in the more important instance of the high bench vacancy[,] . . . a man of the type of Dean Wiley B. Rutledge, Jr. of the Iowa Law School, of whose scholarship and broad views excellent reports have come to Washington, will be the best bet." The column indicated that if Roosevelt "were wholly free to consult his own inclinations" he would probably choose his trusted advisor, Benjamin V. Cohen, but that the president was more likely to "incline strongly" to Schwellenbach, who was "a 200 percent New Dealer." Although "infuriating to orthodox Democrats," Schwellenbach surely would be confirmable, they said. "Overcoming Schwellenbach may be the biggest part of Murphy's trial," Alsop and Kintner concluded. Finally, they said: "If sectional considerations are to be disregarded, other candidates to remember are Solicitor General Robert H. Jackson, former Dean Charles Clark of the Yale Law School, Dean G. Acheson, and Chairman William O. Douglas of the SEC." But "[i]f sectional considerations predominate," other candidates would include Judges Hutcheson, Bratton, and Stephens, as well as Assistant Attorney General Thurman W. Arnold (of Wyoming) and the NLRB general counsel Charles Fahy (of New Mexico).[25]

Alsop's and Kintner's view that Douglas was not a true westerner was widely shared. By February 18, according to the *New York Times*, Sena-

President Franklin D. Roosevelt and Senator Lewis B. Schwellenbach.
(The Spokesman-Review, *Spokane, Washington*)

tor William H. King of Utah, supporting Judge Stephens, was "certainly not for Douglas. . . . He is not a Westerner." Senator David W. Clark of Idaho, also supporting Stephens, said it had "'never occurred'" to him "that Mr. Douglas might be from the West." Several other western senators reportedly agreed with that view. The *Times* indicated that Senator Norris was not certain about Douglas's residency. On the other hand, it continued, "'the geographical aspect of an appointment'" did not impress Norris very much; he was "'open minded'" in favor of finding "'the best man.'"[26] As the president headed for the Caribbean, therefore, the choice appeared to be wide open.

On February 19, Irving Brant, in Washington, wrote to Rutledge for the first time since Brandeis had stepped down. "The indication at the moment is that Senator Schwellenbach will be named, but that your name is so near the top of the list that it is almost a toss-up." Brant added that Schwellenbach had earned the president's gratitude for supporting the New Deal to the point that the senator's reelection in 1940 was in jeopardy. Brant then reported that he and Ralph Fuchs had visited with Justice Black, Justice Frankfurter, and Benjamin Cohen, all of whom regarded Rutledge highly, although Brant surmised that Black might prefer Schwellenbach because of their close relationship in the Senate. Brant then revealed his meeting with Murphy on the day after Brandeis's retirement was announced. "I am quite sure that Murphy's first inclination was toward Schwellenbach; whether it is now I have no way of knowing." Also, according to Brant, Raymond Clapper's column had caused a "great deal of embarrassment" at the White House by reporting that some members of the inner circle had proposed the name of W. O. Douglas to head off Schwellenbach. Brant believed that "Douglas would make a fine member of the court" but considered his nomination unlikely because "his western residence terminated shortly after he left college."[27]

While letters from all across the country to the White House and the attorney general may have marginal value as evidence of the broad acceptability of a candidate, that is not how potential nominees are evaluated. Whether or not Roosevelt was thinking of a third term—with the first primary election but a year away[28]—there was a White House consensus that for political reasons, especially after had selected Frankfurter less than two months earlier, Brandeis must be succeeded by a westerner. And that meant a nominee supported by western senators. In his three and a half years in Iowa, Wiley Rutledge had not become acquainted with the senators from Iowa, Guy M. Gillette and Clyde L. Herring.[29] But both were Democrats, knew of Rutledge's favorable reputation in the state, his strong support for the New Deal, and his high place on the list for the Court when Frankfurter was selected. They accordingly stood ready to push for this recent, now favorite, son of Iowa—a state which had yielded, to date, only one Supreme Court justice, Lincoln's appointee Samuel F. Miller (1862-1890).[30] Gillette became, in effect, Rutledge's campaign manager from the Senate, although this role amounted to an unspoken one. Reelected in 1938, Senator Gillette had survived not only the president's effort to prevent his renomination (a result of Gillette's opposition to the Court-packing bill), but also a Republican electoral surge in that year that took eighty-one House and eight

Senate seats away from the Democrats, though leaving the president's party in comfortable control nonetheless.[31]

After learning that Senator Norris and other senators had "expressed particular interest" in Rutledge, Gillette wrote to Rutledge with a question prompted by a report from the columnist Drew Pearson. Was it true that Rutledge "had advised the President, when Dr. Frankfurter's name was under consideration," that his own name "not be further considered at the time?" If so, the senator wrote, the action was "exceptionally commendable," and the senators "would be moved to strong support" of Rutledge "in connection with the appointment."[32] Before Gillette's letter, Rutledge had answered a similar query from a reporter for the *Des Moines Register*. In both instances he replied that he had not contacted the president, either before or after he had learned that his own name was under consideration, since it would have been "presumptuous" to do so in either case absent a "specific request." But he told the reporter that his "views sympathetic to Frankfurter" had been "expressed . . . privately" and "probably were quoted to the President," but without his knowledge. Then, to Gillette, Rutledge elaborated on his correspondence with Irving Brant, explaining that before he knew his own name had been suggested he had written to Brant that "Frankfurter was predominantly qualified for the place above all others," and that the president "should disregard geographical considerations and appoint Frankfurter." Rutledge added that he had expected Brant to pass that word on to the president. Rutledge then told the senator that upon learning that his own name was being considered, he wrote to Brant to emphasize that he "still felt that Frankfurter was the outstanding man for the place and should have the nomination." Rutledge suggested that Senator Gillette communicate with Brant himself for verification (which Gillette did). Three days later, on February 21, Senator Gillette wrote to Rutledge that his "full and frank" response had given "added reason for admiring" Rutledge's "position and attitude," and that after learning the contents of Rutledge's letter, Senator Norris had "evinced a great interest" in him for the Brandeis vacancy.[33]

Soon thereafter, Gillette wrote to Rutledge again to say that two or three senators favored the selection of someone who had "experience in the practice of the law." He asked for relevant information. Wiley reported on his two-year "general practice" in Boulder, describing the "volume and variety of experience" and adding that some matters "required attention during the entire period" of his teaching at Colorado. To another inquiry from Arkansas, Rutledge responded—with exaggeration—that in his two years of practice he had garnered "a variety and volume of experience . . . which many young men don't get in five or ten."[34]

Senator George Norris of Nebraska. (Library of Congress, USZ262-98135)

On February 21, Senator Norris registered his views with Murphy in writing. "I have made quite an investigation in regard to Dean Rutledge, of Iowa. I have reached the conclusion that he is an especially fine man, and if the President should see fit to fill this vacancy by the appointment of Dean Rutledge, I believe such an appointment would be satisfactory to every Progressive in the country." Although Norris was "not laying down the rule that the appointment must be a western man," he understood that the president had decided to appoint a candidate "from west of the Mississippi River."

Norris was aware as well that William O. Douglas—"who also would be a fine appointment"—was under consideration along with Rutledge. Because Douglas had been nominated "from Connecticut" to head the SEC, wrote the senator, the president—if he were to select Douglas—should acknowledge Douglas's eastern residence and not say that he was from the state of Washington.[35]

On February 22, Wiley and Annabel attended a small luncheon for Harry Hopkins at the home of the executive secretary of Grinnell College, a contact very likely arranged by Commissioner Eicher. That day, the *St. Louis Post-Dispatch* reported the view of three senators that the White House had narrowed the president's canvass of "possible Supreme Court appointees" to Rutledge and Schwellenbach. The article quoted Senator Norris as calling Rutledge a "'high class liberal who would make a very good judge,'" although he added that there were several "'equally desirable appointees.'" The article noted several reports continuing to suggest that the president might appoint Douglas, even though a number of senators were arguing that Douglas "would not qualify as a Westerner."[36]

At this point, Rutledge's prospects looked good; according to Irving Brant, Senator Schwellenbach appeared to be the only other serious contender. But Brant, for all his access to inside information, was profoundly wrong about Schwellenbach. White House insiders reportedly were pushing hard for Douglas, who had been running nonstop for the Court with the help of family and friends, including Arthur Krock of the *New York Times*.[37] According to the *Nashville Banner* on February 24: "[W]iley B. Rutledge, Jr. of Iowa and William O. Douglas of 'Connecticut' were installed as favorites today in the Supreme Court handicap. . . . Senator Louis [*sic*] B. Schwellenbach of Washington and District of Columbia Appeals Court Justice Harold M. Stephens of Utah appear to be eliminated from the race." The article noted that Stephens had "lost his position as a favorite" with the retirement of Attorney General Cummings. And "Senator Schwellenbach, an early favorite for the post, lost his advantage by voting against confirmation of Floyd H. Roberts as Federal Judge for the Western District of Virginia," whom the members of the Senate—acceding to the wishes of their Virginia colleague, Senator Carter Glass—rejected 72 to 9. An informant said that the president regarded that vote as a test of loyalty. When Schwellenbach sided with Glass, the *Banner* reported, "it is said he lost out at the White House."[38]

The newspaper's substitution of Douglas for Schwellenbach as Rutledge's chief competitor was attributable to the efforts of a trio consisting of Jerome Frank, an SEC commissioner close to Douglas, and two White house insiders lodged at the National Power Policy Committee, Thomas Corcoran

Jerome Frank after taking his oath as judge of the U.S. Court of Appeals for the Second Circuit in May 1941, two years after Frank led the White House insiders' drive for the Supreme Court nomination of William O. Douglas. (AP/Wide World Photos)

FIFTEEN CENTS   September 12, 1938

TIME
The Weekly Newsmagazine

Volume XXXII   COHEN & CORCORAN   Number 11
                      They call themselves catalysts.
                         (See NATIONAL AFFAIRS)

"They Call Themselves Catalysts"—Benjamin V. Cohen and Thomas G. Corcoran on the cover of Time magazine, September 12, 1938. (Reprinted with permission of Getty Images) and Benjamin Cohen. According to David Ginsburg, then an SEC staffer on loan to the same Power Policy Committee and later Douglas's first law clerk, "Jerry Frank took the initiative and was a marvelous leader—intense, outgoing, enthusiastic, a born leader for intellectuals, and an independent thinker." Frank was "devoted to Douglas"; they had been "very close" during their years teaching law together at Yale; there was a camaraderie between them, "almost a union." Corcoran and Cohen, too, were quite close personally to Douglas. Frank, Corcoran, and Cohen commenced a labor of love.[39]

"The big problem," Ginsburg recalled, was this: "how can you convert a man from Connecticut to a man from the state of Washington?" "It was Jerry's idea," Ginsburg said; "let's get Borah," the progressive Republican senator from Idaho.[40] William E. Borah knew Douglas—they had served together in 1938 on the Temporary National Economic Committee, organized to investigate monopolies[41]—and a meeting was arranged between them. Thereafter, according to Ginsburg, "we had to draft a speech for Borah" blessing Douglas. Tommy Corcoran initiated the first draft, Ben Cohen made it "even more literate," and finally Jerry Frank "got his innings in." Then Borah's office made changes. Douglas "certainly wanted the Court appointment; there was no doubt about that." Ginsburg sensed that Douglas "felt it would be the next step up; he saw beyond it to the [Charles Evans] Hughes experience"—running for president—"but we never discussed that."[42]

Curiously, the speech itself was never given,[43] but Borah came out strongly for Douglas and generated Senate support for him conveyed through notes and phone calls to the White House.[44] By February 20, Joseph Alsop and Robert Kintner reported that FDR was ready to consider Douglas if he could be "called a true Westerner."[45] Borah had begun forwarding endorsement letters to Attorney General Murphy,[46] and by March 6 Drew Pearson and Robert S. Allen were recognizing Borah as one of Douglas's "most active backers." Their column continued: Borah was "drumming up support for Douglas all over the country—particularly on the Pacific Coast," piling up "an impressive list, particularly from business men and lawyers." Borah, according to Pearson and Allen, was urging Douglas's appointment because, he argued, Douglas was a "brilliant young New Dealer" who was the "ablest" in the running, and because he was a "corporation and financial expert" like Brandeis, whose seat he would fill. The column ended by noting that "[s]ome of the most prominent West Coast newspapers [were] urging Douglas' selection."[47] Senator Borah's laying on of hands, therefore, ostensibly made Douglas western enough to meet the test.

In the meantime, on February 23, Brant had written to Murphy report-

*Senator
William E. Borah
of Idaho.
(Photograph by
Harris and
Ewing; Library
of Congress,
USZ262-72232)*

ing the details of Rutledge's support of Frankfurter and of Gillette's inquiry about whether Rutledge had withdrawn in favor of Frankfurter. He
added, incorrectly, that after learning that Senator Gillette had recommended Rutledge to the president for the Cardozo vacancy, Rutledge had
"asked the Senator to see the President again and withdraw his name"
(although Frankfurter's nomination had mooted the request).[48]

On February 26, not yet informed that Douglas was his most serious
competitor, Rutledge wrote to Brant: "I can understand well the President's
sense of obligation to Schwellenbach," but "[o]n the basis of personal acquaintance, my preferences would be for Garrison, Douglas, and Hutcheson, in that order." (Interestingly, on February 18, Garrison had written a
letter to the president endorsing Douglas.) By March 1, however, Rutledge
knew about Douglas. He wrote to Clay Apple, "Douglas is a fine and able
young man, a member of the Yale faculty of course, and prominently men-

tioned for the Deanship there. . . . Douglas would make an excellent appointment."[49] Although Wiley Rutledge was unquestionably caught up in the race in the absence of a superior consensus candidate—he told Apple, "it's been a lot of fun every minute"—he was realistic enough about his own limitations, as well as his (or anyone's) chances for the Supreme Court, that he never allowed himself to believe that his nomination would happen. Perhaps, in an early response to Senator Gillette, he was politicking with self-effacement when he wrote: "I know that there are many others better qualified than myself." But he was essentially humble and straight enough not to make that a dishonest statement. Practically from the beginning, moreover, he told friends that his chances were "not more than one in ten." "Consequently," he would say, "we are not making any plans for a change in scene or status. If we should be lucky it will be an honor which has been beyond the utmost reach of our imagination. If not, we shall be happy that the incident has occurred because it has brought us back in touch with many old friends like yourself and has shown how far those loyalties actually go. That is a priceless possession, one which no honor or dignity could confer."[50]

The emergence of Douglas, a candidate whom Rutledge personally liked and respected, injected a quality that gave Rutledge pause. Douglas was both a highly regarded academic and, quite literally, a card-playing crony of the president. By March 1, therefore, Rutledge was emphasizing in some correspondence a basic philosophy: "I long ago gave up the idea of achieving any particular station or place and don't intend to begin doing so now."[51] To intimates, moreover, Rutledge expressed doubt whether he really wanted to be on the Supreme Court—an implicit rationalization of expected rejection but, again, not clearly dishonest given his ambivalence about giving up being a teacher and dean.

On March 4, "in response to a tip from Irving Brant that the time was propitious," Ralph Fuchs sent messages to several law teachers—friends of Rutledge—from Arkansas, Texas, Minnesota, Nebraska, and Wyoming, "asking them to secure editorials and to get messages to the President and the Attorney General." The response, he later wrote to Wiley, had "been grand," including strong editorial support from Laramie and Omaha and a faculty endorsement from the state law school in Little Rock.[52]

Roosevelt returned from the Caribbean in early March. The next day, the column by Pearson and Allen reported that the White House inner circle which had supported Frankfurter was now divided, with "Tommy Corcoran, Ben Cohen and most of the other 'downtown' militants . . . beating the drum for Douglas," while "Secretary Henry Wallace and Midwestern New Dealers [were] pulling wires" for Rutledge, and "various administrationites in the Senate [were] rooting for" Schwellenbach. The same day, presumably expecting a White House announcement very soon, Rutledge wrote to a relative in Kentucky: "[M]y hunch at the moment is that the man who probably will be selected is William O. Douglas. . . . He is entirely worthy of the position in every way." Also that day, Thomas Reed Powell reinforced Rutledge's belief: "The President is trying hard to make a Westerner out of Bill Douglas." By March 9, Rutledge seemed convinced: "The indications now seem to point in the direction of Douglas for the Court," he wrote to a friend in Nevada, and, to another the same day, he wrote, referring to Douglas: "I have known him for many years and have a very high regard for him, both as a lawyer and as a man"; he would "make a creditable addition to the Court and render valuable service there."[53]

Harold Ickes was not so sure that Douglas would make it, however. On March 8, a day after he had dined with Douglas and the president of the University of Chicago, Robert Hutchins, who had come to Washington to try to persuade Douglas to take the law school deanship at Chicago, Ickes met with the president and brought up the Brandeis vacancy. Ickes recorded: "it was perfectly clear that the President was again leaning strongly in the direction of Schwellenbach." Ickes opposed the senator for his failure to be "a good enough lawyer" and for lacking "an intellectual grasp on the principles of liberalism." Ickes also learned that Rutledge was "under serious consideration," and that what the president had to say about him was "quite convincing." When Ickes then realized that the president "was not particularly inclined to appoint Douglas," he urged him to consider Hutchins, stressing that Chicago was western enough, that it ranked second only to New York in population and business activity, and that no justice from there had served since the time of Chief Justice Fuller.[54]

The day before, the president had heard from Senator Norris, who had sent along an editorial in the *Lincoln* (Nebraska) *Star* endorsing Rutledge. Norris told Roosevelt: "I think it might be well for you to give consideration to this, as coming from the West. . . ." In paying compliments to Rutledge publicly, Norris always acknowledged that there were other acceptable candidates, but in dealing with the administration he made clear that he favored Rutledge. Indeed, the next day, he wrote to Murphy to make sure he had received Norris's letter of February 21 praising Rutledge.[55] In the meantime, however, Murphy, who (contrary to Brant's understanding) did not like Schwellenbach and did not know Rutledge, had come to support Douglas upon Corcoran's urging — especially after Douglas dulled some labor opposition by taking a swipe at Wall Street.[56]

At week's end, on Friday, March 10, Ralph Fuchs wrote to Rutledge: "According to the radio this morning, the President will make his decision this week-end. Yesterday the *Post-Dispatch* had Douglas as good as 'in.'" After mailing this letter, Fuchs received the same prediction in a letter from Rutledge.[57] Also that day, Irving Brant wrote his final pitch to the president. It was an essay on how to address the "double added burden" imposed by the "loss of Justices Cardozo and Brandeis." First, he said, both appointments must hold the liberal wing together numerically and coherently (implicitly, of course, Frankfurter had been a good start). The Court's "new liberalism . . . must be carried to the country, and approval won," without benefit of the prestige counted on from the "masterful minds and pens" of Cardozo and Brandeis. To achieve these objectives, Brant wrote, the first task was "to win back Justice Stone to the liberal wing." If that does not happen, "Hughes and McReynolds will stick to the court to their last breath . . . hoping that their successors will be chosen by a conservative President." The second task "is to bottle up the conservative lawyers in the country . . . by naming somebody . . . whose legal scholarship, integrity and aloofness from politics will force them to silence when they contemplate his liberalism." Brant then stressed that Rutledge not only was "the one who would perfectly reinforce Frankfurter in winning Stone back," but also had gained enough broad support to be acceptable, while being far more liberal than generally perceived—a wolf in sheep's clothing. Brant added that "a lot of people have learned just enough about Rutledge to be receptive toward him on the basis of general attainments, character and scholarship, who would not be for him if they realized the depth and intensity of his liberalism." He summarized: "If, Mr. President, you can gain at this particular moment what you want on the Supreme Court with the acquiescence of those who don't know what you are getting, they will have to 'forever hold their peace.'"[58]

The president made no announcement on the weekend of March 11–12. On March 13, Jerome Frank informed Senator Borah that according to Ben Cohen, Harold Ickes had urged the president to appoint Douglas. Frank was worried nonetheless. Referring, we must surmise, either to Rutledge or to Schwellenbach, Frank wrote to Borah: "It is difficult to discover just how seriously we must regard the possible appointment of the person you and I discussed this morning." Frank asked Borah to write to FDR, emphasizing Douglas's western heritage and asking to visit the president personally.[59]

Rutledge continued to write that he expected Douglas, "now of Connecticut but in his youth" from Washington, to be nominated. He told a friend: "I hope you won't think it's sour grapes, at all, but the longer this thing drags on, the more I wonder whether I want to become one of the 'nine old men.' . . . I'd say 'yes,' if a remote contingency should bring the thing my way, but I'm not so in love with the idea that life would be spoiled for me if the contingency doesn't become anything but remote."[60] Apparently by the first of the week, the president had decided upon Douglas. On Tuesday, March 14, Joseph R. Hayden, a confidant of Attorney General Murphy who taught in the political science department at the University of Michigan, sent Murphy some favorable information about Rutledge, even though Hayden "judge[d] that Dean Rutledge is not now being seriously considered for the position that we discussed over the telephone."[61] Possibly Hayden was relying on newspaper talk, but more likely his letter reflected a recent conversation with Murphy.

The very day that Hayden wrote, something happened that Rutledge did not expect. As he described it to Brant a few days later, Attorney General Murphy called in the afternoon and, after pleasantries, said that Rutledge's "name . . . was still in the picture." But Murphy "ask[ed] whether, in case the nomination should go to another," Rutledge "would accept a place on the D.C. Court of Appeals" (an idea that Tommy Corcoran claims to have suggested as a way of honoring but deferring Rutledge).[62] Rutledge replied, "I always consult with my wife," but he agreed to Murphy's request to call him in the White House at midnight.[63] Interestingly, the president had tried to conscript Dean Acheson, once a clerk to Brandeis and later Roosevelt's undersecretary of the treasury, for this new seat on the federal court of appeals in the District of Columbia that Congress had created in mid-1938. The president explained to Acheson that he was in a dispute with the Senate about a federal judicial nomination in Virginia that he had submitted without consulting Senators Glass and Byrd, and that to make the point he wanted to submit to the Senate without consultation three unassailable nominees for circuit court judgeships—Robert Patterson, Francis Biddle, and Acheson—whom the Senate would have to confirm. But Acheson declined.[64]

Rutledge later wrote to Clay Apple that he had consulted Ralph Fuchs, two faculty colleagues—Willard Wirtz and Philip Mechem—and his brother-in-law. (He did not mention Annabel; presumably, she demurred.) On the assumption that Murphy's call meant an end to Rutledge's prospects for the Supreme Court, Wirtz and Mechem advised, he should "unhesitatingly, 'accept'" the alternative, not only because of the national significance of the Court of Appeals but also because of "the rather discouraging prospects here—tightwad legislature, no real prospects for expansion, etc." Fuchs, Rutledge reported, also "said 'yes, unless you want to be a university president,' which most emphatically I do not." Seymour Person thought that the answer "'Supreme Court or nothing'" might generate appointment to the high court but "admitted it was a gamble." Rutledge had also wanted to consult Brant and Clay Apple. He found out, however, that Brant had an unlisted number in Washington, and because Wiley "felt fairly clear" that the "nearly unanimous[]" recommendation of the others was sound, he decided, without calling Apple, to tell Murphy he would accept the Court of Appeals.[65]

Murphy was not at the White House at midnight when Rutledge telephoned. Murphy called Thursday morning before Rutledge had finished shaving, however, and Rutledge gave Murphy an affirmative answer, "but with some misgivings, not controlling, on the score of personal or family interest." Rutledge elaborated that there was some question "whether there would be any financial advantage for us, living in Washington and facing the stringent educational period ahead" for the children; but the next day, apparently out of embarrassment at mentioning a financial issue, he wrote to Murphy to assure him that on balance, finances were "secondary in our major vocational choices to other considerations, including the opportunity to render some constructive service in stations we may be equipped modestly to fill and to causes we believe in."[66]

The White House publicly was silent until March 20. That day, Rutledge wrote to Brant: "Word came over the radio this morning of Douglas' nomination, and I have a suspicion that you are feeling worse about the matter than I am." He then said: "My only regret is the disappointment which will come, undoubtedly, to some of the many friends who have supported the suggestion of my name so loyally. If only there were some way by which I could communicate to each of them that the outcome really does not make me downhearted, I'd not feel badly at all. . . . I was fully prepared for Douglas' appointment ten days ago."[67] Wiley immediately wrote to the nominee: "Dear Douglas: Congratulations, and best wishes for a speedy confirmation and to a fine career on the Court."[68]

Rutledge had no doubt about Douglas's confirmation, "probably without any real opposition," he advised Brant. He added: "The attempt to make him appear a 'westerner' was a little ludicrous, despite his youthful background in the west, and I hope this is not carried further. The case should be placed simply on the ground that he was the best man for the place." To another friend, referring to a recent news photo of Douglas in Mexican headgear, Wiley wrote: "between you and me I thought his 'sombrero' trick last week was in pretty bad taste. It is the first thing I have known him to do which has lowered him even slightly in my estimation. However, it was done under obvious stress, and perhaps such things so done should not be taken too seriously." Finally, to Brant the next day Wiley wrote: "I know you will not expect me to put into words my gratitude to you. That I could not do, if I had the eloquence of a Bryan. I'll not attempt it, but rely on your capacity for understanding."[69]

SEC chairman William O. Douglas on the day after his nomination to the Supreme Court. (Photograph by Harris & Ewing; Collection of the Supreme Court of the United States, 1939.19.1)

Unlike Brant, Rutledge perceived that he was as likely as Douglas to be considered too "liberal" by western senators. At the same time, he believed that if the western senators had thought they could head off Douglas, they would "have concentrated on someone like Bratton. . . . I suspect they were not too enthusiastic concerning the choice between Douglas and myself." And "[w]hen it appeared to the boys from the wild & woolly that it was Douglas or me, they kn[e]w & liked him better, & and quite justifiably so." Rutledge then revealed that after he had talked with Murphy early in the morning on March 16, "[t]here was no further word from anyone, except press reports of Douglas' nomination, until this morning [March 21] when an A-P reporter appeared suddenly in my office and asked what I would do about the nomination. I sparred around until I found out what he knew, then declined to make any public statement—for lack of any official notification. An hour later, Murphy called." Murphy had sent a letter to Roosevelt: "My dear Mr. President: I have the honor to enclose herewith a nomination in favor of Wiley Blount Rutledge, Jr., of Iowa, to be an Associate Justice of the U.S. Court of Appeals for the District of Columbia, to fill a position

"A Winning Daily Double"—cartoon by Eugene Elderman,
1939 (© 1939 Washington Post; *reprinted with permission)*

created by the Act of Congress of May 31, 1938. . . ." The president sent the
nomination to the Senate. That day Brant wrote to Ralph Fuchs, observing
that "the appointment to the D.C. court puts Rutledge in a far better position than he was before, in connection with any future vacancy. Roosevelt
could not name a third law school man in succession to the Supreme Court,
but if Rutledge should be considered in connection with such a vacancy, it
will be on the basis of whatever he proves to be as a federal judge."[70]

In many ways the appointment of Douglas was like that of Frankfurter.
The president settled on a man he knew well, liked, and trusted. Although
he allowed himself to overlook the political pressure for a westerner when
the Cardozo vacancy occurred, he could not do so when Brandeis retired.
But Senator Borah of Idaho solved his problem there. The *Washington Post*
reported on March 21 that Borah's support for Douglas had "tempered"
western opposition.[71] Furthermore, although Senator Norris of Nebraska
had supported Rutledge, he was on record as saying that geographical considerations were secondary to finding the best-qualified nominee, and had

made clear his high regard for Douglas. (Rutledge may have wondered what the president would have done if Norris had been as rigidly sectional as Borah about the nomination.) Even if Rutledge had been known personally to Frank, Corcoran, Cohen, Ickes, and their crowd, moreover, he simply did not have the required intellectual standing with men who were stressing Douglas's brilliance as a prerequisite to filling the Brandeis chair. And the attorney general, Murphy, had joined their team. Finally, Roosevelt was not friendly to the many senators who had opposed his Court-packing plan — including Rutledge's sponsor, Guy Gillette of Iowa, and the far westerners who had been promoting Judge Bratton. And although Senator Schwellenbach had been a New Deal stalwart, he had joined — unpardonably — in defeating overwhelmingly FDR's judicial nominee from Virginia.[72]

It would be unproductive to speculate whether, in the end, Rutledge or Schwellenbach was the runner-up in the president's mind (although the evidence tends to favor Rutledge here). The president named to the high court the man he wanted — at forty, the second-youngest nominee in the Court's history.[73] And the president sent Wiley Rutledge — at forty-four, a young man now in FDR's sights — to the proving ground.

PART THREE

Judge, 1939–1949

ELEVEN

Court of Appeals Years

Adjustment and Impending World War

Jurisdiction over appeals of decisions by federal trial courts (or "district" courts) was originally lodged by Congress in ad hoc panels, composed of U.S. Supreme Court justices and federal district judges who "rode circuit." There was a brief period in 1801-1802 when the infamous "midnight judges" appointed by President John Adams on the eve of Thomas Jefferson's inauguration made up a separate appellate bench. Otherwise, the circuit riding system prevailed until 1891, when Congress established standalone federal courts of appeals grouped by states geographically into ten (now eleven) numbered "circuits." The District of Columbia was a special case, however. Judges of the district's principal trial court—called its "supreme" court—reviewed the decisions of their own colleagues, allowing even the judge under review to participate. To correct that anomaly, Congress created a three-judge "Court of Appeals of the District of Columbia" in 1893 to review decisions of the district's supreme court and, eventually, of other, inferior trial courts—the Police Court, Municipal Court, and Juvenile Court—that Congress had created to adjudicate local D.C. affairs.[1]

Before Wiley Rutledge came to Washington, the U.S. Supreme Court had ruled that the Court of Appeals of the District of Columbia had the same constitutional authority, and its judges were entitled to the same protections—life tenure without reduction of salary—that Article III of the Constitution conferred on the other federal appellate courts. The D.C. court, accordingly, was on par with those of the numbered federal circuits and was renamed, near the end of Rutledge's service there, the U.S. Court of Appeals for the District of Columbia Circuit. By the time Franklin Roosevelt became president, the appellate court had grown to five "justices" (eventually renamed "judges"), and in 1938 Congress added the sixth seat, filled a year later by Rutledge.[2]

With federal jurisdiction identical to that of all the federal circuits, the court on which Rutledge served had the authority to review decisions not only of the federal trial court (by then called "district" court) but also of most federal administrative agencies. And D.C.'s federal appellate court retained a unique responsibility: jurisdiction over the local courts, applying to them a body of law that Congress enacted exclusively for the District of Columbia. In this respect, therefore, the U.S. Court of Appeals functioned for the District of Columbia just like a state supreme court. To ease that burden, Congress eventually created a District of Columbia Municipal Court of Appeals to review local trial court decisions in the first instance, although the U.S. Court of Appeals retained discretionary jurisdiction over all decisions of the local appellate court until home rule legislation cut that cord in 1971.[3]

In Rutledge's time, therefore, the appeals court had a dual function not granted to any other court in the United States: appellate jurisdiction over U.S. district courts and federal agencies; and "state supreme court" jurisdiction over the District of Columbia's own court system, which applied both congressionally enacted statutes and the common law to local affairs. This dual jurisdiction accordingly explains the mixture of federal and local issues that Rutledge addressed as an appellate judge.

Because of deaths and resignations, Franklin Roosevelt reconstituted the U.S. Court of Appeals for the District of Columbia almost completely. He appointed four justices before Rutledge, all several years older than he. The first, in 1935, was Harold M. Stephens, a Nebraska native. Considered, as we have seen, for the Cardozo and Brandeis vacancies, as well as earlier for the deanship of the Iowa College of Law, this former Utah trial judge and Justice Department official had one of the most conservative judicial minds of anyone whom FDR appointed to a federal appeals court. Stephens sided with Roscoe Pound in resisting the increasing use of administrative tribunals subject to looser rules of evidence than those traditionally applied at common law, and subject as well to lesser standards of judicial review that those applied to the lower courts. This put Stephens at odds with the contrary views of New Deal enthusiasts such as Felix Frankfurter and Wiley Rutledge. Stephens and Rutledge were to become friends, but more than any two other judges on the court, they were judicial antagonists.[4]

The president named Justin Miller, originally a Californian, in 1937. Like Rutledge an academic, Miller had taught at Oregon, Minnesota, and Berkeley before becoming dean of the law school first at the University of Southern California and then at Duke. From there, he became a special assistant to the attorney general, then a member of the U.S. Board of Tax Appeals, before joining the court. The president's third nominee, also in 1937, was Fred Vinson of Kentucky. Eventually named Chief Justice of the United

U.S. Court of Appeals for the District of Columbia, ca. 1939.
Back row (l. to r.): Henry W. Edgerton, Fred M. Vinson, Wiley Rutledge.
Front row (l. to r.): Harold M. Stephens, D. Lawrence Groner, Justin Miller.
(Courtesy of U.S. Court of Appeals for the District of Columbia Circuit)

States, Vinson was a former congressman who had supported Roosevelt's "Court-packing" bill, became an expert on taxation, and assumed major roles in the passage of New Deal legislation. The last judge nominated in 1937 was Henry W. Edgerton, originally from Kansas. Edgerton too was an academic who, after a stint in private practice, had taught law at George Washington and Cornell before serving as a special assistant to the attorney general in the Antitrust Division. The other justice of the six, D. Lawrence Groner—a Virginian whom President Harding had appointed to the federal trial bench—joined the court in 1930 as a Hoover appointee. Elevated to Chief Justice by Roosevelt in 1937, Groner was a conservative jurist recognized as a most capable administrator. He chaired a committee of the federal Judicial Conference to recommend reforms in judicial administration in light of revelations during the "Court-packing" fight.[5]

Given the court's federal and local jurisdiction, as well as its almost new cast of judges highly qualified to deal with the increase in complex appeals from decisions by federal administrative agencies, one can understand the brief note that Rutledge received from Arthur T. Vanderbilt of New Jersey, former president of the ABA and judicial reformer: "My heartiest con-

*U.S. Court of Appeals nominee Dean Wiley Rutledge with Senator William H.
King of Utah on March 28, 1939, after the Senate Judiciary Subcommittee had
approved the nomination. (AP/Wide World Photos)*

gratulations on your nomination to the most interesting court in the United
States."[6]

Within days of his nomination, Rutledge attended a hearing before a
Senate judiciary subcommittee, which immediately approved his nomination, although Senator William H. King, a conservative Democrat from
Utah, reserved the right—which he never explained or exercised—to oppose the nomination later. The full Senate confirmed by a voice vote on
April 4.[7] The new judge's wind-up of affairs in Iowa was frantic. He decided to keep a commitment in early April to address the Missouri League
of Women Voters, traveled to Omaha for a luncheon in his honor with
Nebraska judges, academics, and lawyers, and at Clark Clifford's invitation
returned to Missouri to speak on "Reflections of a Retiring Dean" at a dinner in his honor at the St. Louis bar association. The other April weekend
he remained in Iowa City for the College of Law's annual Supreme Court
Day banquet, at which the graduating class offered a tribute affirming the
dean's "sincerity, kindness and unfailing regard for the personal equation,"
which had "endeared him to all." Professor Percy Bordwell added his own
words of praise: "Few men could have come into a strange state and have it

adopt him as its own within the short space of less than four years. . . . No doubt many factors contributed to this reception but two are outstanding, his transparent honesty and his liking for people. These are simple qualities but they are not so common as they should be. Wiley Rutledge possesses them to a remarkable degree."[8]

Rutledge had informed President Roosevelt that he would assume his new duties around the 1st of May. He arrived in Washington in time for a swearing-in ceremony on May 2—he insisted that there be "little in the way of fuss and feathers"—attended by almost two dozen friends and official guests, including Irving Brant, Attorney General Murphy, and Senators Gillette, Herring, and Norris. For financial reasons, Annabel and the children could not join the occasion. Referring not only to his swearing-in but also to his upcoming first day in court, Annabel wrote to her husband with great pride:

> I do wish we could have been with you Tuesday noon and could be next Monday! We *are* in spirit and we're very proud of this honor & position that's come even if we didn't charter a plane & be with you and say to Washington—"We belong to this man—he's ours!" I think we have a right to be a bit thrilled about it when we think of our first years in Albuquerque and the uncertainty of the future then—But you do not seem any different to me than then except fatter[,] and it all seems such a short time.
>
> Love from us all. XXXXX Ilyfeae. D.T.

Annabel's crack about Rutledge's girth was on target; he had acknowledged to a judicial robe maker that his 5'10½" frame now carried 180 pounds.[9]

After a brief public installation ceremony on May 8, Justice Rutledge began his judicial career sitting over the next two weeks on three-judge panels with different combinations of colleagues hearing twelve cases, of which Rutledge eventually wrote the opinions in five.[10] He sat on another twelve cases in June, explaining later to a friend that his chief had dealt him a "double dose of work at the beginning." Rutledge hoped to complete the term of court and return to Iowa by the 1st of July for a few weeks' respite before driving his family to Indiana University at Bloomington, where he had agreed to teach corporation law in the summer session. But he did not get back to Iowa. He did not even issue his first signed opinion until July 10 (upholding, in a touch of irony, the district court's dismissal of a part-time law professor's claim for reinstatement and tenure).[11]

Part of this delay was due to the obligation that Rutledge felt to accept various traditional requests that came his way, such as a moot court at

Georgetown in May followed by a luncheon of young lawyers gathered in his honor in June. There, he told his young listeners that they were experiencing a creative period in the law demanding "recognition of new social rights and interests"—derived from "unemployment," "old age," and "illness"—that would enlarge the needs for representation. He called on his audience to perform legal work that was "*not* being done" and to help "develop new forms of organization for professional service," achieving "mass production" where possible consistent with due care.[12]

WILEY RUTLEDGE met President Roosevelt for the first time on May 23 and memorialized the meeting by handwritten memorandum. According to Rutledge, FDR exclaimed, "'Well, it's about time! I've been looking forward to this, and I'm mighty glad you are here.'" The president then commented on the "'most interesting variety of subject matter in that court'" and on the "'most interesting bunch of men to work with.'" Roosevelt offered "'one word of counsel. . . . [I]n view of the fine fellows you have in that court, you guard against its becoming a country club. . . . There's always a host or hostess who wants members of the judiciary in attendance. Every night something is going on!'" Rutledge assured the president: "'I think I can control that. It's not and never has been my style of living. If I thought surrender inevitable, I'd beat it back to the cornfields as fast as I could go.'" The president then told an anecdote about Justices Frankfurter, Douglas, and Black; discussed the progressive "'tax situation'" with the new justice; and, finally, after Rutledge suggested that it was time for him to leave, replied, "'I'm glad you came, and I'll be seeing you.'"[13]

THE NEW JUDGE continued to show his common touch, offering advice and a reference to a former student, reminding Annabel to give another student the $35-40 he had promised to pay for the boy's way home, and inviting his law clerk, Glen Harlan (from Iowa)—who was staying with Rutledge at the house the judge had rented for his family—to join him for Memorial Day ceremonies at Arlington Cemetery. A week or so later, apparently at his own initiative, Rutledge visited the two members of the Supreme Court whom he had come to admire most, Justice Stone and Justice Black. "I expected to spend about ten minutes with each," he wrote to Clay Apple, but "actually spent one and a half hours with Stone and better than two hours with Black." Both, he added, had "plenty on the ball."[14]

Ever resourceful, Annabel managed to find someone eager to rent the Rutledge residence in Iowa, a great relief because, as always, money was tight. Within three weeks of arriving in Washington Wiley had only $288.87 in the bank and had to apply for a $300 loan on his insurance policy to

cover initial expenses. Once on salary, however, the family was able to afford (in Wiley's words) a part-time, "very excellent maid": "a very quiet
colored girl," who was "an excellent cook" and "pleasant to have around
the house."[15]

From the beginning, Wiley found his new role "extremely interesting"
and believed he was "going to like judging." But he was so seriously behind
by the time the family arrived in Bloomington in late July that he brought
Glen Harlan along to help him satisfy his judicial commitments by working
"night and day." (Iowa's new dean, Mason Ladd, was not as fortunate. Rutledge owed the College of Law the grades for his course in the judicial process from the *first* semester of 1938 — an obligation that he continued to defer, despite gentle nagging by Ladd, until almost mid-November, 1939, when
Ladd finally received from his predecessor the "surprise of surprises.")[16]

Upon the family's return to Washington, the Rutledges enrolled Mary
Lou, Jean Ann, and Neal at the Sidwell Friends school, as Wiley readied
himself for his first full term of court. He was especially pleased that his
secretary at Iowa, Edna Lingreen, had agreed to join him in Washington
and, at the judge's urging, had decided to attend law school in the night
session at George Washington University (eventually becoming a government antitrust lawyer). Bright, well-spoken, and extremely capable, Edna
Lingreen served Rutledge on both courts until his death. As one can discern from this book, the judge was a prolific letter writer; indeed, he was a
long letter writer — commonly three to four, even up to seven single-spaced,
typewritten pages. According to Ms. Lingreen, Rutledge dictated each letter
to her "flawlessly" in person — which she would transcribe just as flawlessly,
it would appear.[17]

Again at work, Rutledge lamented to friends how "awfully slow" he was —
a reality he had not anticipated even though he recognized that he typically had difficulty in "getting things down on paper." The problem was
exacerbated by his unusually long opinions. Chief Judge Groner "strenuously objected to the length" of one opinion, Rutledge acknowledged, and
Clay Apple candidly wrote that another opinion "would have been better
if it had not been so long." The new judge appreciated this honesty. The
"truest friends" offer constructive criticism, he replied to Apple.[18]

In acknowledging his tendency to write overly long opinions, Wiley attributed it to his "academic experience" in which the cases discussed in
class often did not give sufficient attention "either to basic theory or to important though perhaps collateral points." Whether one "should attempt to
reduce the treatment to the lowest possible minimum, so as to conserve
space in the Reports, or should extend it considerably in order to serve as
a guidepost for future legal action, is always a question of rather difficult

decision," he observed. "I hope I can learn to make a sensible compromise between the two extremes." Both on the Court of Appeals and later on the Supreme Court, however, Wiley Rutledge was unsuccessful in finding that compromise. Throughout his judicial career he tended, as they say in the trade, to "write long." He never denied this. And rather than make any real effort to shorten his prose, this son of a long-winded preacher would offer reason after reason why he felt obliged to supply so much detail. He might say that he "considered the case of sufficient importance and novelty to justify full treatment," or that "the issue presented is so close and unique that it would not be wise to reduce the opinion to the minimum possible proportions," or he might apologize for the length but insist that his "theory of the case and the evidence seem[ed] to require it." There were even occasions when Rutledge would elaborate such a statement with several paragraphs of supporting reasons![19]

Not all comments on the length of his writing were condemnatory, however. A highly regarded professor of administrative law, Louis Jaffe of Buffalo and later Harvard, wrote to the new judge: "I enjoy your decisions generally" because of their "law school–law review flavor." The judge on the receiving end of that compliment—especially a judge like Rutledge who believed that courts too readily avoided the legal frontiers revealed in law review thinking—would not feel motivated to shorten the writing effort. There were occasions, moreover, when Rutledge's detailed, carefully crafted dissents brought one of his colleagues around to his view, creating a new majority and outcome. That, too, was a disincentive to brevity, especially when a friend, such as Walter Gellhorn of the Columbia law faculty, would express "enthusiasm" for Rutledge's elaborate majority opinion in an NLRB case—where initially he was in dissent—"as an outstandingly good example of a 'realistic jurisprudence.'"[20]

Rutledge's uncompromising commitment to finding the most cogent answer—not only for the sake of the litigants but also for consumption by lawyers, judges, and the law schools—virtually doomed him to write long. He surely believed, as appellate judges often say, that if he had more time he could write shorter opinions. But given the caseload, as well as the effort he expended in fashioning each product, he never found time to hone his opinions further. And despite the thoroughness of his work, Rutledge forever was discouraged by his failure from time to time to discover and scrutinize all relevant law review articles, whether cited by the parties or not.[21] Most observers would conclude that Rutledge set the bar too high for himself, beginning with a view of legal opinions that was unrealistically grandiose.

DURING THE SPRING of 1939, even as Rutledge was preparing to move to Washington, members of the Board of Regents at the University of Colorado were trying to persuade him to consider its presidency as the successor to George Norlin. Rutledge gracefully declined the overture. In early 1940, he rejected similar suggestions that he succeed Eugene Gilmore. To his Iowa friends, however, he began to acknowledge that he was "not sure" he had "an ideal temperament for the confinements of judicial activity," but that if he eventually returned to a university he would do so to teach, not to serve as a president. Already he was missing the "young, vigorous minds" of the students and the formation of new friendships with them.[22]

As 1940 unfolded, Rutledge increasingly questioned his newly chosen vocation. He felt satisfaction in having his opinions "count," an assurance not available to law review writers, but by March 1940 he still had eight opinions to write for cases heard as far back as the previous October. He was experiencing "perhaps the most strenuous year" of his life, keeping his "nose grinding on the stone all day and all night week days and Sundays." In addition to his difficulties with opinion writing, he bemoaned the "considerable element of conflict" among judicial colleagues in trying to "secure an adjustment of our sometimes widely differing points of view." To a friend in St. Louis he reported, "I find judging even harder than deaning." To Dean Ladd, he exclaimed: "Believe me, Mason, you've got a snap!"[23]

By October 1940, early in his second full term of court, Judge Rutledge could "say very confidently that of the three major activities in law" — practicing, teaching, and judging — "teaching is without any question the most enjoyable." Two months later, he was telling Ladd, "I find this damn job means that I have to give up a great many things I like best to do." He wondered "whether the sacrifice of personal relations and associations" which judging involves "is not too much to make." By January 1941, he was repeating the same refrain to Clay Apple: his temperament was "active," not "judicial."[24]

In part, Rutledge was referring to his disappointment that the crush of work, and to some extent the personalities at the court, allowed little opportunity for social, let alone intimate, relationships with his colleagues. He got along well with all members of the court, but even his growing friendship with Henry Edgerton, with whom he came to feel the closest, did not ease his concern. "While we have a hard-working and able group of men in this court, and some of them are real liberals," Wiley confided to an Ohio friend, Joseph O'Meara, "I can tell you in complete confidence that there is no one who quite fills my bill for full companionship in the way you and a few others of my friends do."[25]

Rutledge came to believe that seclusion, especially by appellate judges, had a negative effect not only on the judge's sense of well-being (or at least Rutledge's own), but also on society and the law itself. Judges stay so absorbed with the caseload, he observed to Clarence Updegraff, that they "fail to keep reasonably current with events" of professional importance they should participate in personally. Furthermore, he noted, there is an unfortunate distance between bench and bar because some judges have an inflated "sense of self-importance" that keeps them from associating with lawyers, while lawyers for their part tend to feel "a sort of distant respect" that feeds a sense of impropriety in getting to know judges well personally. "I find that the only way to get through this wall is to pick out certain people who will not take advantage of you and simply make it perfectly evident to them that outside the courtroom and within legitimate bounds the official position is to be forgotten and association is to be placed on the basis of man to man"—a job even harder for a judge than "getting the boys in Rotary to first-name me when I first went into the organization" as the "'Dean.'"[26]

Nor did appellate judges, as Rutledge observed them, try to broaden their understanding by reading outside the law. "Here," he wrote friends, "we talk, eat, drink and sleep law! It's too narrow for my taste, without leavening from other areas." "After one has wrestled with dry legal bones all day he is more apt to flop into a chair and listen to the radio than to put his mind on a really tough bit of intellectual diet, and yet it is deadly for him to do this." To a librarian in St. Louis who had sent him the results of a study entitled "Who Reads What?" Rutledge really let fly: "The very fact that stenographers, sales people, auto mechanics, policemen, taxi drivers and pipe fitters, rather than lawyers, doctors, dentists and even teachers, are reading Thomas Hardy and William James knocks into a cocked hat the idea that it is the privileged and successful people in the country who are its real thinkers and the only persons entitled really to have a say in what the country ought to do." He wanted to "take this information and ram it through the thick skulls" of his "conservative friends who still believe in the trickle philosophy and, underlying that, in the basic premise that the financially successful and fortunate few are the persons of real ability, intellectual or otherwise." Rutledge then singled out Justice Black as an exception: "[I]t is Hugo Black's life-long habit of reading outside the law which has marked him out, in my mind at least, as the outstanding man on the Supreme Court."[27]

Despite his concerns about the grind and his sense of isolation—and occasionally some "dull" cases—Rutledge found plenty that was interesting. Enthusiastically, he noted that some cases were "on the outposts of the law" where the "turn of the tale is like the toss of a coin." He had not realized, in joining the court, "how close some of the decisions would have to be," even though the court would speak "its judgment with the confidence of verity and finality." He thus especially enjoyed substantive comments on his opinions as a way of improving his own legal understanding. To a Yale

professor who had forwarded a critique, he replied that the judicial experience was "magnified" by the "opportunity for post mortems with people
who know more about the subject" than the judges do.[28]

All this said, Wiley Rutledge never escaped the feeling of intense pressure from the "hard grinding" docket. Even near the end of his tenure on
the Court of Appeals he characterized himself as "one of the slow-working
fellows who always seems to be under pressure to get out the case that was
heard six months ago." To Clay Apple during the week before Christmas
1942, he wrote: "I worked like a slave all fall, often four or five nights a
week to two or three o'clock. Through this semiherculean effort we have
succeeded finally in breaking the log jam in about a dozen cases which has
been holding up our work since last spring. I feel like Ajax with the world
off his shoulders to have these old cases out of the way." Rutledge's observations were not intended as sour grapes; he felt free to react emotionally
to his friends without being misunderstood as a bellyacher. His service on
the court from beginning to end, however, was as much a labor of duty as
of love—indeed, probably more one of duty.[29]

ON SEPTEMBER 1, 1939, as Rutledge and his family were winding up their
summer in Bloomington, Hitler invaded Poland. Anticipating the threat
to France and Great Britain, President Roosevelt successfully battled the
isolationists in Congress to obtain repeal of the nation's long-standing embargo on the sale of arms abroad, supplanting it with permission to sell to
all who would pay cash and carry arms away in their own ships. Among
Wiley's closest friends, Mason Ladd was one of the few willing to take risks
right away to support the European allies, though "without getting into it
ourselves." Rutledge agreed with aiding the allies, while doubting that the
country could keep out of war once assistance of any kind was offered.
Although "something of an internationalist" all his life, Rutledge had flirted
briefly with isolationism in the mid-1930s after losing "all hope for the
League of Nations," he wrote to a former student, Bill Bartley. But he came
to believe by late 1937, when Roosevelt called for "quarantining" the aggres-
sors, that even if the nation could survive with a "self-contained economy"
surrounded by dictatorships, the result would be "regimentation" at home
akin to that in Germany, Russia, and Italy. He thus abandoned all sympathy
with isolationism.[30]

France fell in June 1940, leaving Great Britain, soon under sustained
bombing from German aircraft, as the only Western European power in the
Fuehrer's way. In September, increasingly doubtful that Britain—and thus
the Western world—could survive without American aid, Roosevelt successfully pushed through Congress the first peacetime selective service act

in the nation's history and began to transfer old-model destroyers to Churchill's navy. By October, Rutledge was among the minority—the interventionists—convinced that the United States should enter the war by "sending over pilots" to help the British. Three months later he was writing that the United States must be prepared "to help England to any extent necessary" to save her, including all-out war.[31]

At this time Mason Ladd reflected the dominant national view—aid the allies, but stay out of the war—while other close friends of Rutledge in the Midwest, such as Ralph Fuchs and an engineering professor in Iowa City, Huber Croft, were unwavering isolationists. They believed that the British, with their aristocratic society and imperialist government, were not sufficiently preferable to the Germans, even under Hitler, to risk American lives. They were convinced that the war, without American participation, was likely to result in a stalemate that would leave the United States in a position to help broker a peace that preserved its interests. And they were confident that even if Hitler won in Europe and elsewhere, he would not unleash a war on the United States, which could survive in a world dominated by dictatorships. Finally, they believed that entry by the United States into the war would bring about domestic pressures, including an eventual depression, that would lead to fascism at home—specifically, a government dominated by large corporations, the destruction of organized labor, and the obliteration of civil liberties. Ralph Fuchs in particular expressed a genuine fear—shared by domestic radicals like him who supported the Socialist ticket headed by Norman Thomas—that war mobilization would invite the persecution of dissidents, much like the "raids" led by Attorney General A. Mitchell Palmer during the "red scare" after the First World War.[32]

Rutledge answered his friends in detail. He agreed that the United States should not enter the war "merely to save the hide of British imperialism," but he believed that with "the advent of Churchill . . . the ruling group in England ha[d] become more conscious of their paramount obligations to the nation as a whole . . . than to their class." As to the isolationists' second premise, Rutledge saw no diplomatic role for the United States in the event of a stalemate or German victory. To Croft he admonished: "Frankly, I think you are quite 'all wet' about the idea that if we should remain entirely aloof" the United States would have a say. In any event, "I don't think this thing is going to end in a stalemate. It is a death struggle." Nor did Rutledge believe that the United States would be safe from a victorious Hitler. As the president had observed, noted Rutledge, "Hitler has declared war not only on the whole of Europe but on democracy wherever it may exist." Rutledge could hardly imagine that having attained supremacy elsewhere, Hitler "would be tolerant enough to allow us to go our own way." And the threat was real.

Rutledge anticipated Hitler's "development of air machines of such range and power as to make military consequences not now conceivable entirely possible, even probable."[33]

Finally, in thinking about the domestic impact of the nation's involvement in all-out war, Rutledge sympathized with his friends' concerns about fascism at home, but he was concerned only in the event that Roosevelt lost his bid for a third term in November. Rutledge had worried that FDR "would not accept another nomination" and that the second-best ticket Rutledge could think of, Secretary of State Cordell Hull and Attorney General Robert Jackson, could not be nominated or elected. Even with the president heading the ticket again, however, Democrats including Rutledge were concerned that the Republican nominee, Wendell Willkie of Indiana—with manifest "energy and folksy charm" uncommon to the Wall Street lawyer that he was—might carry the day in a campaign reflecting minimal differences with Roosevelt. With his like-minded friend Clay Apple, Rutledge feared that a victory by Willkie would be "a long step toward fascism" because of Willkie's alliance with the power companies. Rutledge worried that Willkie's election would bring amendment of the Wheeler-Rayburn Act and of the Securities Act, permitting, once again, the "holding-company system" as well as "widespread speculation in corporate securities." He was concerned, too, about likely enactment of the Walter-Logan Bill—legislation that FDR, he believed, would veto—to impose on federal administrative agencies adjudicative procedures "so cumbersome" that the agencies, transmuted into "subordinate trial courts," could no longer operate effectively. Rutledge was particularly concerned about hamstringing the National Labor Relations Board with the "rigid" rules of evidence required in judicial proceedings. In his view, the strength of organized labor, protected by an effective NLRB, was crucial to the strength of the nation itself. "It was only the very strong hold of the labor unions in England," including "a very real voice in her government," that prevented the growth of fascism there, he believed. Rutledge worried that a victory by Willkie might trigger an outbreak of "labor strife" that would seriously weaken the nation as it moved closer to war.[34]

Rutledge also agreed with Ralph Fuchs and other friends that "bigbusiness domination of government" under Willkie, when coupled "with a war spirit," would tend to stir up "racial jealousies and hatreds" as well as "intolerance toward minorities" who opposed high business profits, and thus were deemed unpatriotic, whether "sincere and honest or of the fifth column character." Rutledge was confident, however, that a victory by Roosevelt would permit preparation for war without fomenting intolerance and canceling civil liberties. But after the election, Rutledge was shaken.

The president himself in early 1941 "linked up patriotic isolationists with appeasers," an alarming development that caused Rutledge to fear for his outspoken friend Fuchs. In mid-1941, however, the president changed his approach, to Rutledge's relief, by distinguishing "for the first time publicly" between sincere isolationism and appeasement.[35]

Rutledge's interventionist point of view was unusual, especially for the Midwest, where domestic progressives were among the nation's most vocal isolationists. FDR had become his polestar. In the president, Wiley Rutledge placed near total faith.

SOON AFTER Roosevelt's reelection, with 449 electoral votes to Willkie's 82, Congress voted nearly $18 billion for the nation's rearmament, and by the end of 1940 the United States was beginning to move, fast, toward war. Also after the election, the president made half the nation's production of military hardware available to its British ally. Because Great Britain was running out of funds to buy American military equipment, moreover, Roosevelt proposed a "lend-lease" program to make war materials available to any country that the president deemed vital to defense of the United States. Charles Lindbergh appeared before Congress in January 1941 to oppose the bill, advocating efforts instead for a negotiated peace. Ralph Fuchs found Lindbergh's testimony "eminently sensible and wise," a view Rutledge emphatically rejected. "[T]here can be no such thing as a negotiated peace," the judge replied to his friend. (After a speech in Des Moines in September, Lindbergh revealed himself. To another friend, Rutledge observed that when "any man can make the insidious kind of charges against the Jews which he made there, I can't help feeling he is a fascist at heart." He added: "At last it discloses exactly what sort of a fellow the great hero is.")[36]

Despite their views at "opposite pole[s]" on the war, the most emotional of topics, Rutledge was confident of Ralph Fuchs's continuing friendship, and of Fuchs's own confidence in the same from him. But Rutledge wanted to give reassurance, especially because Fuchs was receiving a good deal of grief from others for his outspoken isolationist views. Wrote Rutledge to his friend:

> You know without my telling you that no difference of opinion between us could ever affect our personal understanding. I feel the same necessity as you express for talking with you, not only now and then but almost every day. It takes years to build what we have together, and for my part it is indestructible, as I know it is with you. We always have been able to fight and I hope we always will, but that has been because of the other thing. I realize of course the risks which you take

in following your conscience as you do now, and I admire you all the more for it.[37]

Lend-Lease passed Congress in March 1941. Three months later, Hitler turned on his ally and attacked Russia. Roosevelt froze all German and Italian assets, closed the consulates, and deported all personnel. Rutledge was convinced more than ever that "we should go in fully, with both men and materials." He wrote to Clay Apple, "[N]ow is our big chance. If we were in, the additional help we could give to England with air and naval forces might make [Hitler's] Russian campaign a debacle. Going in a month or two months later might not have nearly so much effect." By mid-July, Rutledge had become "pretty thoroughly discouraged with American unwillingness to face the facts." A Gallup poll in June had shown that "only about twenty-one per cent of the people" favored the nation's "active military participation."[38]

By mid-1941, the European war was not this country's only serious international concern. Embroiled in a military campaign in China since 1937, Japan had announced in June 1940 its own "Monroe Doctrine" for East Asia and the South Seas—called Japan's "stabilizing power" over the region—threatening especially the Dutch East Indies, the principal supplier to the United States of rubber and tin. In September 1940, Japan had marched into French Indo-China; Roosevelt had announced an embargo on all sales of scrap iron and steel to Japan, theretofore dependent on the United States for 90 percent of its needs for these critical materials; and Japan had entered into a military alliance with Germany and Italy, forming the "Axis" powers. Relations between the United States and Japan deteriorated. Secretary of State Cordell Hull warned Americans in Japan to leave. And in July 1941, the president froze all Japanese assets in the United States.

Rutledge had all but ignored Japan but now began to worry about it. Events of course accelerated until the day of "infamy," December 7, 1941, when Japan attacked Pearl Harbor. The next day Rutledge wrote to Willard Wirtz, acknowledging that he "felt better since yesterday" than he had before. "Maybe," he added, "it's just relief at having the thing settled or at least the long stage of suspense ended. . . . It's hell to have to settle things this way, but it's worse hell to have to live indefinitely in a state of semi-armed expectancy of attack." To Mason Ladd, Wiley elaborated: "I am, frankly, glad now that it happened as it did because of its effect on national unity and in showing up how wrong the isolationists were, and I am almost glad too that Pearl Harbor got hit hard at the beginning. That will take a little bit of our cocksureness out of us, as well as our disunity, and probably we need to have both these things done."[39]

THROUGHOUT HIS YEARS on the Court of Appeals, Wiley Rutledge not only expressed his views freely in correspondence with his friends but also continued to speak out publicly when invited to do so. He repeatedly stressed the wonderful diversity of our people and their points of view; he made the protection of civil liberties of central importance—particularly in time of war, when pressures against dissent are severe. In accepting an honorary Doctor of Laws degree at the University of Colorado in June 1940—and in an extraordinary departure from the restraint off the bench expected of a federal appellate judge—Rutledge publicly criticized a recent decision by the U.S. Supreme Court upholding the constitutionality of a Pennsylvania law requiring schoolchildren, in that case objecting Jehovah's Witnesses, to salute the flag. "We forget," he stressed, "that it is [in] the regimentation of children in the Fascist and Communist salutes that the very freedom for which Jehovah's Witnesses strive has been destroyed."[40]

The following October, Wiley addressed again the related themes of national diversity and tolerance. Speaking at the Federal Bar Association's annual dinner, he used as his text Walt Whitman's poem "I hear America singing, the varied carols I hear." Observed the judge: "Our kinship is a kinship of the spirit, our brotherhood one of the soul. Black or white, Nordic or Latin, Catholic or Protestant, Jew or Gentile, rich or poor, whatever our race, creed or color, we came to seek and have tried to create a way of life which gives man comradeship with his fellow man in the conception that all men are created free and equal, that all stand equal before the law." If, he said, we forget while the nation is rearming that "the carols of democracy are varied carols," we shall destroy "what we set out to preserve." Of course, he added, "[w]e cannot tolerate the overt act of sabotage or the activities of the spy or the traitor within our gates." But in preparing for war, he stressed, "we must distinguish carefully . . . between him and the honest objector to measures we must take." Two years later, Rutledge was pounding the same theme. In July 1942 at a gathering of the American Bar Association in Cincinnati, he emphasized: "[I]t is the part of the lawyers' associations in this period not only actively to defend minority groups, but also to see that those who are guilty of violations of laws, including our defense laws, receive fair treatment. We shall not gain if, in helping to preserve democracy elsewhere, in the process we destroy it entirely here."[41]

All this said, Rutledge was not absolute in his defense of civil liberties during wartime. In response to a letter from Willard Wirtz in July 1941 asking the judge's views on "recently passed" state statutes "barring from the ballot parties advocating force or violence," Rutledge replied:

> Normally, the democratic principle comprehends freedom of expression for almost everything, including overthrow of its own institutions

by force. So long as the minority party does not present a real, present and impending danger of accomplishing this, I think the freedoms should be extended to it as well as to others. But the time does come when the danger becomes too great if the democratic institution is to survive. When that time comes I see no alternative to adoption of essentially undemocratic controls until the danger is past. . . . The danger with conceding this is that those who are fascist at heart or inclined that way will fix the point of action for instituting the controls too early.[42]

Later that year, after Pearl Harbor, Rutledge wrote that a stable world order would require an "international organization" consisting at least of a "union of the democracies of the world, particularly the British Empire and the United States." Short of that larger union, he thought, at least a "British-American Commonwealth of Nations" would be required. By late 1942, however, his ideas were becoming more grandiose. At a summer assembly at the University of Colorado, Judge Rutledge proposed a comprehensive "world organization" resembling the League of Nations but with real "power" and "sanctions"—indeed, an "international police force"—open to all nations. It must include the defeated ones in order to prevent the level of economic inequalities that resulted from the suppression of Germany after the First World War and that contributed, in his view, to the rise of Hitler and the ensuing conflagration. Crucial to the success of the organization, he added, would be its formation before the end of the war, when nations under pressure of hostilities would still be of a mind to focus on "international justice" rather than their own "selfish ends." In reiterating this proposal two months later before the Ohio Bar Association in Akron, Rutledge emphasized the need for governance of all nations under law, international as well as domestic. "There is not room in the world's society for two camps of nations, one dedicated to law, liberty and the obligation of contracts, the other constructed upon the principle of force, internally and externally. The old separation of domestic and foreign affairs is valid no longer. The world cannot be half law and half force."[43]

TWELVE

Court of Appeals Years

Judicial Approach and Outside Interests

When Wiley Rutledge served on the U.S. Court of Appeals for the District of Columbia, it was not as much a federal court as its name implied. Of the 101 opinions that Rutledge published there (85 for the court, 6 concurring, and 10 in dissent), only 30 presented federal issues.[1] Thus, 71 originated under local, not federal, law. Primarily, therefore, the court heard appeals concerning personal injuries, crime and habeas corpus, domestic relations, contracts and sales, wills and trusts, property and mortgages, corporations, insurance, local taxes, and insolvency. Rutledge and his colleagues accordingly spent most of their time sitting as a state supreme court for the District of Columbia.[2]

During his nearly four years of service, Rutledge participated in 311 (or 49 percent) of the court's 637 published decisions.[3] The caseload overall did not generate much dissent—in part, perhaps, because judicial ethics at the time discouraged dissent,[4] but mostly, one can surmise, because aside from the handful of discretionary appeals taken from the D.C. Municipal Court of Appeals, the court adjudicated appeals of right, which did not yield the high proportion of close cases that an entirely discretionary appellate system tends to do. Rutledge's results were typical; his 85 published opinions for the court provoked only 14 dissents—9 by Justice Harold Stephens. And no majority opinion by Rutledge brought reversal by the U.S. Supreme Court.

Only eleven of Rutledge's opinions addressed constitutional issues of any significance, and of these nine came from local, not federal, appeals. Furthermore, of the judge's dozen most significant opinions, local and federal combined, only three presented constitutional questions. Each of these had major impact, however. In the first, a dissent in *Busey v. District of Columbia,* Rutledge wrote a broadside against Justice Edgerton's opinion that sustained the conviction of a Jehovah's Witness for selling literature on the street without paying a license tax. Rutledge found interference with the right to free exercise of religion under the First Amendment, concluding:

> This is no time to wear away further the freedoms of conscience and mind. . . . Everywhere they are fighting for life. War now has added its censorships. They, with other liberties, give ground in the struggle. They can be lost in time also by steady legal erosion, wearing down broad principle into thin right. Jehovah's Witnesses have had to choose between their consciences and public education for their children. In my judgment, they should not have to give up also the right to disseminate their religious views in an orderly manner on the public street, exercise it at the whim of public officials, or be taxed for doing so without their license.[5]

Supreme Court Justices Stone, Black, Douglas, and Murphy would take the same position two months later, dissenting in a nearly identical case, *Jones v. City of Opelika*, with Murphy citing Rutledge.[6] Indeed, it was a position that Rutledge himself would help vindicate for the nation when the Supreme Court reheard *Opelika* soon after he joined its ranks.

In *Wood v. United States*, a superbly crafted opinion for a unanimous panel, Rutledge broke new ground in reversing the robbery conviction of an indigent, uncounseled defendant who had pleaded guilty at a preliminary hearing without having been informed of his Fifth Amendment privilege against self-incrimination and his Sixth Amendment right to a lawyer. By the time of trial, the defendant had been assigned an attorney, who arranged for withdrawal of the plea. But at trial the court admitted the plea in evidence nonetheless, on the ground that the defendant had offered it voluntarily. Rutledge noted that the court had found the initial plea voluntary without considering whether the defendant knew of rights that would have helped him decide how to plead. Not only fairness to the defendant but also concern for the trial court's own integrity required exclusion of the plea evidence, Rutledge concluded. A preliminary hearing should not become "a trap for luring the unwary into confession or admission which is fatal or prejudicial. So to use it would pervert its function and make of the court, not an arbiter, but an arm of the prosecution" (a position he took years later on the Supreme Court in dissent).[7]

In another case concerning the right to counsel, *Boykin v. Huff*, a federal district judge had turned down a convicted felon's written request for a lawyer to pursue an appeal. The judge, after conferring with trial counsel, had informed the indigent prisoner, Boykin, that he would have no chance for success on appeal, and that the judge would neither appoint counsel nor even note a pro se appeal for him on the court's docket. Boykin filed a pro se petition for writ of habeas corpus challenging the court's order. It was denied. On appeal, Rutledge avoided a constitutional decision by deeming Boykin's letter to the trial judge to be, functionally, a timely appeal and remanding for appointment of counsel. But Rutledge left no doubt where he stood on the constitutional implications. He cited statistics showing that in a recent year, the federal appellate courts had reversed 24 percent of all criminal convictions appealed. Rutledge concluded, for a unanimous panel: "[W]hen the life or the liberty of the citizen is at stake on a serious criminal charge, and appeals are given as a matter of right to those who are able to pay for them, it may be doubted (though as to this we express no opinion) whether they can be withheld from indigent persons solely on the ground of their poverty or otherwise than so as to give them substantially equal protection with more fortunate citizens."[8]

Rutledge also wrote two especially significant opinions in appeals construing federal statutes. In *National Broadcasting Co. v. FCC*, he expanded the meaning of a "person aggrieved" under the Communications Act of 1934. When a radio station in Boston sought FCC permission to increase the power of its signal, the Court of Appeals sitting en banc reversed, 4 to 2, the commission's refusal to allow a station in Denver—affected by "electrical interference" from the signal emanating from Boston—to intervene in the commission proceeding. Recent Supreme Court dictum had suggested that the aggrievement required for intervention was financial injury, a claim that the station in Denver could not make. Rutledge observed that this standard, in addition to prejudicing the Denver station, might preclude noncommercial broadcasters—"churches, universities, colleges, charitable foundations, and others"—from intervening in the public interest when commercial license applications were pending. He would not bow prematurely to the Supreme Court; there were "strong reasons why the dictum should not be accepted as either stating or forecasting the law." In ruling for the Denver station, Rutledge concluded that the ambiguously written statute must be construed to permit intervention, in order to avoid a violation of procedural due process under the Fifth Amendment. He correctly anticipated the Supreme Court, which affirmed, 4 to 2, though strictly on statutory grounds.[9]

The other statutory appeal, *Washington Terminal Co. v. Boswell*, upheld (over a dissent by Stephens) a provision of the Railway Labor Act severely limiting the right of a terminal company to contest the ruling of an adjustment board that awarded a group of unionized employees various jobs performed at the time by others whom the company employed. Because the adjustment board had no enforcement authority, the act empowered successful employees to seek district court enforcement of a board award at any time within two years. The act provided no way for an *employer* to challenge the award, however, other than by defending an employee enforcement action. In an analysis of unusual complexity, Rutledge rejected the employer's effort to get around the act by going to court immediately for declaratory relief to determine which group of employees should have the work. He found no substantial prejudice, let alone a violation of due process, in a congressional scheme that potentially could hold up an employer's challenge for two years, even though the employer in the meantime, whether electing to comply with the award or not, could remain caught between two groups of employees. (The Supreme Court affirmed.)[10]

Rutledge also wrote three pathbreaking common law decisions. In the case of a nurse who accidentally slammed a door on a visitor to Georgetown University Hospital, the court overturned the hospital's traditional charitable immunity from liability for personal injury caused by a negligent employee, recognizing that insurance could protect the charitable assets.[11] And in an automobile collision case, Rutledge abandoned the venerable common law rule that barred a plaintiff who settled with one defendant from pursuing other defendants jointly responsible for the injuries.[12] Finally, a third opinion by Rutledge extended the common law tort of malicious prosecution to misuse of administrative proceedings, paralleling its traditional application to misuse of judicial proceedings.[13]

Judge Rutledge also extended the reach of the District of Columbia "long-arm" statute. That law conferred personal jurisdiction on the federal district courts in the District of Columbia over defendants from elsewhere that were "doing business" in the District. Previously, the courts had held that "mere solicitation" of business was not a sufficient basis for jurisdiction. Joined by Edgerton (with Stephens dissenting), Rutledge found jurisdiction over a Kentucky cement company, which had no office in D.C. but used a single salesman on a "regular, continuous, and sustained" basis to solicit orders there, subject to acceptance of the orders in Louisville. Because the salesman also visited D.C. job sites in order to offer advice to customers that were using his company's products, Rutledge opined that the salesman's activities amounted to the "solicitation-plus" that had traditionally justified "long-arm" jurisdiction. As a realist, however, Rutledge noted that solicitation, more than the formality of completing a contract, was "the foundation of sales." "No business man," he said, "would regard 'selling,' the 'taking of orders,' 'solicitation' as not 'doing business.'" He thus left no doubt that in his view, a regular course of "mere solicitation," without more, would be enough for "long-arm" jurisdiction—implicitly satisfying the requirements of due process (a position that the Supreme Court took in another case after Rutledge joined the Court).[14]

Rutledge wrote two lawmaking opinions of particular help to women. One concerned an action for maintenance and counsel fees pending resolution of a divorce proceeding. He held that the statutory prerequisite, "living separate and apart," was satisfied when the spouses had lived separately in the same house, and that a trial court had little if any discretion to withhold maintenance, given the typical economic inequality between husband and wife.[15] In the other case, a former husband argued that a claim for alimony, including arrearages, could not reach his disability payments, because of a District of Columbia statute exempting disability insurance proceeds from creditors' claims.[16] Rutledge concluded that alimony was not a "debt" or "liability" entitled to statutory protection, because a legislative purpose in shielding disability payments from creditors was to protect the insured family's principal means of support. That purpose, Rutledge concluded, would be frustrated by permitting an estranged husband to withhold disability payments initially intended for the entire family.

Several of Rutledge's nine dissents in addition to his Jehovah's Witness dissent in *Busey* deserve special mention because they highlight his standards for reviewing the actions of federal agencies.[17] Finding evidence sufficient to support an NLRB ruling that the Gannett newspaper organization had committed an unfair labor practice by firing employees for union activity, Rutledge dissented from a decision modifying the order for the employer's benefit.[18] In this case, as in his administrative law opinions for a court majority—including opinions in three labor appeals (not discussed here) that sustained NLRB rulings[19]—Rutledge applied a standard of review giving great deference to agency factfinding and discretionary relief. On the other hand, in the case of a jurisdictional dispute between two unions, Rutledge dissented from an opinion affirming a decision of the National Mediation Board that under the Railway Labor Act, all yardmen working for the New York Central must make up a single bargaining unit. Rutledge found no such statutory mandate and warned that the ruling would throw "the whole weight of the legislation in favor of[] the big unions as against the smaller ones." In construing "the terms, purposes and policies of the statute," therefore, Rutledge did not defer to the agency's interpretation of the statute it administered in the same way that he deferred to agency factfinding and discretionary relief.[20]

Rutledge's other interesting dissents were in local law appeals. In a landlord and tenant case, *Geracy, Inc. v. Hoover*, he refused to allow the hybrid structure of the local-federal court system to prevent a tenant's appeal. The landlord had sued in Municipal Court for possession of the premises and overdue rent. The tenant defended on the ground that the premises were not in the condition promised because of rain leaks. The jury found for the landlord. The tenant then filed a civil action in federal district court, alleging $2,859 in damages to personal property inside the premises from the leaks. The suit was dismissed on the ground that the Municipal Court jury had already resolved the leaks issue against the tenant. Although Rutledge agreed that ordinarily the doctrine of *res judicata* (claim preclusion) would have barred the tenant's district court lawsuit, he noted that the tenant had used the leakage claim only as a defense in the local Municipal Court, not also as a counterclaim for affirmative relief (since that local court's jurisdiction limited claims for damages to $1,000, and thus could not have afforded complete relief to the tenant). There was no statutory provision for removing the entire case from the Municipal Court to the district court, which had no limit on damages. Without a district court lawsuit, said Rutledge, the Municipal Court effectively decided a damages claim "in excess of its jurisdictional limit," a result that Congress could not have intended. Under these peculiar circumstances, he concluded, the tenant should have had an opportunity to make a complete case. Writing for the majority, Judge Miller implicitly chided his dissenting colleague. Because the U.S. Court of Appeals did not have "the judicial powers of an oriental caliph," the court was "bound by the rule of *res judicata*" to permit the harsh result that the court structure imposed. Rutledge was unmoved: he would not, he replied, support "a landlord's paradise."[21]

In another provocative dissent, Rutledge would have found the Evening Star Newspaper Company liable for injuries caused by the negligence of a delivery truck driver who, at the command of a police officer hanging on the running board, had chased a traffic violator at high speed and, instead of capturing the suspect, collided with the plaintiff. According to Rutledge, who cited substantial case law, the truck driver had a public duty to respond to the officer's summons for help; the newspaper, whose agent the driver was, had a like duty as a corporate citizen; and thus liability should flow as usual from negligence in performance of duty.[22]

Finally, in an unusual twist, Rutledge dissented from a decision by Stephens and Vinson ordering a hearing and appointment of counsel to review the mental state of a convicted felon who challenged his continuing confinement at St. Elizabeth's hospital after a finding of insanity. Rutledge would not permit such prisoners to languish without regular review of their situations, but in this case the petitioner had received two reviews since confinement, one nine months before the current petition, the other four months before. Rutledge stressed that the orderly administration of justice required "some limit to the number and frequency of hearings a petitioner may have upon the same issues, even in habeas corpus." In the absence of statutory guidance, he argued that "the courts may impose reasonable restrictions," reviewable for abuse of discretion. He suggested "a conclusive period of six months"—the period that Congress eventually enacted.[23]

Rutledge found writing dissents to be "more fun" than opinions for the majority because "one is more free to say what he wants to say," without need for compromise. A dissent, moreover, had an important purpose. Citing Justice Brandeis, he explained to a friend how a dissent often gives a truer "picture of the facts" and is "more valuable" than the majority opinion, because the dissent may "point the way" toward resolving "fundamental problems of social policy" that cannot be determined, finally, in one case. Often, Rutledge believed, the difficult questions before the courts "offer so much room for difference of opinion" that a unanimous decision—attempting "to confine history in the making within the covers of a calf-bound book"—very likely will generate less confidence in the courts than a split decision that reflects the complexity of an issue and thus gives hope for change if the majority view proves unworkable.[24]

IN ARRIVING at judicial decisions, Judge Rutledge felt free to consult with friends on law faculties[25]—a practice, he acknowledged, that several of his colleagues disapproved of.[26] Today, federal judicial ethics forbid a judge to communicate with an outside expert pending decision unless counsel for all parties are notified and have an opportunity for rebuttal. Absent formal prohibition at the time, however, Rutledge invited professional comment before finalizing his opinions in a handful of cases that he found especially difficult. He believed that the most perceptive and creative legal thinking came from the schools, and he was convinced, presumably, that his academic friends had no axes to grind. These considerations trumped any awareness that a party might feel prejudiced by the perceived dogmatism (or even possible financial ties) of an undisclosed academic commentator not officially before the court.[27]

In using this approach to achieve the most cogent result, Rutledge was naïve in ignoring the serious problem of appearances, if not undue influence, that he allowed into the process. In *Evening Star Newspaper*,[28] where the court rejected the newspaper's liability for injuries by its runaway truck driver, Rutledge shifted to a dissent after his correspondent had weighed in—arguably no harm, no foul. But in *Washington Terminal*,[29] upholding the Railway Labor Act, Rutledge's opinion—initially a dissent—eventually spoke for a majority after his friends had contributed their views. Later, the Supreme Court affirmed 4 to 4, with its newest member, Wiley Rutledge, not participating.[30] As a matter of appearances, therefore, one could argue that several academic friends of Rutledge had helped shape his opinion to the point that it persuaded a colleague to switch sides and thus achieve a result that otherwise never would have occurred, even after Supreme Court review. All this said, however, Rutledge felt free to consult academics during opinion writing on only a few occasions during his early years on the Court of Appeals. No evidence suggests that he ever took a case outside the Marble Palace while he served as a justice of the Supreme Court.

Washington Terminal and *Evening Star Newspaper* were also the kinds of first-time cases that brought the judge to a better understanding of his approach to doctrinal resolution of the issues before him. Rutledge had long believed that "courts make more law perhaps than legislatures do," and that it "belittle[d] the judicial function to refer to what they do as being always mere interpretation or application of established principles." We have also seen Rutledge's belief—reflecting the views of Roscoe Pound—that judges must be open to revising the law especially in times of rapid social and economic change, when prevailing common law rules reflect "doubtful social policy." Rutledge thus hoped for the selection of judges with vision—judges "not only familiar with past traditions but possessed of a sense of direction for the future," coupled with "the ability to recognize when a particular tradition conflicts with that new direction so much that the tradition must be thrown overboard or modified." Perception of required change, he knew, was not an entirely rational process, especially if several relevant rules of law or canons of interpretation collide when applied to a novel set of facts, or to ambiguous legislative language, in emotionally charged cases. Rutledge acknowledged that in such difficult cases "all law" becomes "personal," meaning (as Holmes had emphasized) that law "cannot escape the impress of the personalities of those who administer it." The "judge's slant on social and economic problems" thus forms a major part in judicial decision making, Rutledge believed.[31] But how?

In correspondence with Irving Brant, Rutledge had touted the federal circuit judge Joseph C. Hutcheson Jr. of Texas as second only to Felix Frankfurter in qualifications for the Supreme Court.[32] Supported by farmers and labor unions for the Butler vacancy that went to Justice Murphy in 1940, the liberal Hutcheson had written an influential article in 1929 arguing that "good judges . . . 'feel' their way to a decision of a close and difficult case." Hutcheson thus acknowledged that he decided many of his own cases by "hunch," meaning "intuition" nurtured by a "brooding mind," followed by the "apologia" or "rationalization" in a written legal opinion. Rutledge must have read the article, for his own views reflected not only Hutcheson's thinking (traceable, Hutcheson said, to Holmes, Cardozo, and Brandeis) but also Hutcheson's very language.[33] Rutledge conceded that because value judgments are involved, he ultimately decided hard cases by "hunch," a "subconscious process" that "gives a clear signal" after several days of

Judge Joseph C. Hutcheson Jr. of the U.S. Court of Appeals for the Fifth Circuit, who wrote about the function of the "hunch" in judicial decision making. (Courtesy of the U.S. Court of Appeals for the Fifth Circuit)

"mulling." "Feeling does have something to do with law and liability after all," he observed.[34]

So what, then, constrains a judge, as Rutledge put it, against "arbitrary and tyrannical action"? First, he said, a judge is duty-bound to respect "tradition," honoring the rebuttable presumption that *stare decisis*—precedent—applies. A mere inarticulate "hunch for justice" must not be allowed to supersede a well-reasoned, established rule. But that is unlikely to happen, according to Rutledge. Even if a particular judicial hunch is more visceral than reasoned, he noted, the possibility that one judge's arbitrary approach might control will be tempered by interaction with the hunches proffered by other judges on the appellate panel, checked further by the hunches of judges from previous days whose decisions in comparable situations "have crystallized into accepted tradition." Second, observed Rutledge, the very freedom to reject an earlier decision when circumstances suggest change also provides an opportunity to correct any mischief caused by an initial departure from tradition. Like Brandeis, Rutledge believed that any movement away from the past must be considered tentative until enough applications prove that the change is sound.[35] Finally, Rutledge demonstrated that the ultimate check on imposition of arbitrary judicial hunches must come from the explanation of decision, the judicial opinion itself—the only real way to test whether the judge is true to the judicial calling. We thus turn to that process.

The word best describing a typical Rutledge opinion is "comprehensive." We have seen that this often meant "long," and that in part that length was attributable to the twin goals of explaining the result thoroughly to the parties and setting forth the law clearly to guide others. Whatever drawbacks there may have been to Rutledge's encyclopedic offerings, their advantage was a completeness of analysis that would force even those who disagreed with the outcome to acknowledge that the opinion had integrity.

After tipping the reader off to the nature of the case, Wiley Rutledge— like virtually all appellate judges would begin with a presentation of the facts, followed by sequential discussion of the issues in a logical order, typically beginning with jurisdictional and procedural matters before addressing the merits. But his factual statement, sometimes augmented in footnotes, was usually more comprehensive than what most judges would offer.[36] This served the purpose of putting the court clearly on the line, offering the loser a target for seeking a rehearing before the full court if the three-judge panel demonstrably had misconstrued the record. To nonparties, however, the extended factual presentation often caused reader fatigue from nonessentials, allowing the trees to hide the forest.

Rutledge's discussion of the issues often brought similar comprehensiveness, even repetition. On the positive side, however, any lawmaking decision, common law or constitutional, would offer the benefit of a historical approach that catalogued the authorities, pro and con, by groups of states or federal circuits. In major decisions, literally scores of legal citations would fill a single footnote. And sometimes narrative footnotes would explain why a particular case was, or was not, authoritative. Similarly, in cases of statutory interpretation that resulted in lawmaking when ambiguity forced a choice among plausible alternatives that Congress had never foreseen, Rutledge would make available, by a combination of text and footnote, all the legislative language germane to the decision, and would quote pertinent legislative history from committee reports and floor debates. Thus, the opinion became a self-contained guide to the law.[37]

This comprehensive approach was not limited to judicial lawmaking. Rutledge could be as detailed in cases that turned on evaluation of the evidence, whether involving a major labor dispute,[38] a medical malpractice case,[39] an estate administration,[40] a family corporation's stock redemption fight,[41] or especially a sentence to life imprisonment.[42] He believed that when a case turned on the evidence, it was especially important to demonstrate that the court was not according the case merely summary treatment. If, moreover, in taking the side of one family member against another, he could explain the result without casting moral blame, Rutledge would go out of his way to say that the law, not venality, dictated the result.[43]

A Rutledge opinion, therefore, had the features not of a narrowly focused, accelerating argument toward an irresistible conclusion, but of a law review article that painstakingly explored the alternatives before eventually yielding a result. This does not mean that Rutledge's scholarly approach lacked force, however diverting his lengthy factual and legal background discussions might have been. Once he announced a rule, he would apply it convincingly to the facts. His power lay, ultimately, in demonstrating how the facts virtually dictated the statutory interpretation or common law rule selected and thus favored one party, not the other. Commonly, Rutledge would announce a conclusion, only to say that if it were unsound, the losing party would fail for still another reason—or even a third or fourth one. His academic exploration would end with nail-pounding intensity, well written and occasionally eloquent.[44]

Perhaps the judge felt a personal need, if only unconsciously, to demonstrate at long last an impressive legal scholarship. But there can be no doubt that at the same time, he felt obliged to lay his thinking out completely—he would deal even with the loser's marginal arguments before saying "no"—so that any vulnerability in analysis, like the comprehensive statement of facts, could be challenged on petition for rehearing by reference to what Rutledge said, not to what, allegedly, he had swept under the rug. In the process of presenting its answer, therefore, the opinion would come to grips with its weakest element. It had to answer with total candor.

IN ADDITION to his speeches on civil liberties, the war, and the eventual world order, Judge Rutledge called for reform of the justice system. From the day he addressed the young lawyers in June 1939, he trumpeted the professional responsibility of lawyers to perform public service. In July 1940 he admonished District of Columbia lawyers to be less "tool-minded" for their "personal benefit" and to use their skills for the broader public good. In the following year he was pressing Ohio lawyers to serve the "low income group." And in September 1942, in a speech before the ABA Committee on Legal Aid at Indianapolis, he made specific proposals more varied than his AALS presentation had called for three years earlier.[45] Nothing in the Constitution, Rutledge reminded his ABA audience, "says that no person *except the poor person* shall be deprived of his life, liberty or property without due process of law." But the "general operation of our system," he declared, excluded the poor—indeed, even "the average citizen"—from the benefits of the justice system. Specifically, he attacked the "barbarous system" of assigning inexperienced attorneys to represent indigent criminal defendants, and he deplored the inability of so many to afford the costs of transcripts and witness fees, and especially attorney's fees, in civil as well as criminal cases. "*[J]ustice*," declared Rutledge—including access to lawyers and other expenses of litigation—must be given as a matter of "right," not charity.[46]

The judge recognized, however, that there would never be enough lawyers to serve all in need if society limited dispute resolution to traditional forums. So he used his speech to encourage innovation—in particular, group legal services (a form of legal insurance); alternative forums such as small claims courts (perhaps without lawyers) for simpler, more expedited proceedings at less cost; and specialized administrative tribunals for high-volume caseloads of "workmen's compensation" claims or even "automobile litigation." For situations where a lawyer's assistance was necessary, however, Rutledge never let go of his support for legal aid, civil or criminal, as a government-guaranteed right. And in speech after speech he laid out that challenge in language prophetic of the federal Legal Services Program in the U.S. Office of Economic Opportunity, launched a quarter-century later under President Lyndon Johnson's War on Poverty.[47]

Rutledge also pressed for reform of the criminal law. Addressing a council of social agencies in June 1941, he characterized the criminal trial judge as an "'absolute monarch'" when imposing sentences; noted the unacceptable "variation of sentences" for similar crimes; and recommended transferring criminal sentencing to specially created boards that "would investigate the prisoner's whole life" and justify all sentences by careful, detailed reference to "the individual's need for treatment and reformation." Indeed, the judge's imagination continued to produce amazing ideas. In the same speech, he also advocated a plan to reduce traffic accidents by appointing a group of citizens who would report to the police "any careless driving they observed," and who would appear later "as witnesses in prosecuting the driver." Rutledge explained: "Instead of waiting until a person has an accident and then throwing the book at him, a better way would be to fine him a dollar every time he violated a traffic regulation, regardless of the fact no accident resulted."[48]

DESPITE THE PRESSURE to turn out legal opinions, Rutledge did not deprive himself of opportunities to make other professional contributions. He continued to represent Iowa on the National Conference of Commissioners on Uniform State Laws, chairing two committees.[49] And in 1941 he accepted appointment to the Board of Trustees of the Washington College of Law, an independent school founded by women and for women until it yielded to a male student majority in 1914, as women were gaining admittance to other law schools in the Washington area.[50] The judge agreed to chair the committee charged with advancing the school's provisional ABA accreditation to full approval, which he doggedly pursued and accomplished.[51] He also chaired another committee on cooperation with the American University in Washington that eventually resulted in merger.[52] And beginning in January 1942 he agreed to teach corporation law three nights a week, even undertaking "to work up a new casebook."[53]

Rutledge also devoted time to still another major project. In October 1941, Herbert Wechsler—a young professor on leave from the Columbia law faculty as a special assistant to Attorney General Francis Biddle—asked Rutledge for help in developing a "new legal personnel system for the Federal Government." Wechsler had become acquainted with Rutledge through Ralph Fuchs and AALS gatherings, and asked the judge to comment on a proposal for the new system. Rutledge, in reply, emphasized that "qualified older attorneys" should be "fit into the scheme" along with younger ones. He also warned against the "very considerable discrimination" in favor of eastern law graduates attributable, at least in part, to the prohibitive costs of traveling east for the required personal interview. Rutledge accordingly proposed "setting up regional offices throughout the country for interviewing and examining applicants" for federal service.[54]

Wechsler worked quickly. Effective December 24, 1941, Rutledge received an appointment—crafted to implement his own ideas—as an "Expert Examiner for the Board of Legal Examiners, to serve without compensation." Whereupon the judge took charge of putting together regional boards comprising "a federal judge, a law teacher, and a practicing lawyer" to conduct the examinations. By September 1942, Rutledge and his colleagues had recruited sixty-nine examiners from thirty-two states. He reported to a former student in the army that congressmen could no longer "foist off on governmental agencies their political henchmen."[55]

While helping Wechsler, Rutledge also received a presidential appointment to a newly created National Railway Labor Panel. He was to be one of nine members available to serve on emergency factfinding boards established to advise the president when mediation failed to settle a railway labor dispute that might interfere with the war effort if unresolved. Rutledge replied to Roosevelt that he felt "very much honored," had been eager to serve "more directly in the war effort," and was "willing to make any sacrifice" to help solve "problems arising from the war."[56]

RUTLEDGE HAD BEEN distressed at the possibility of losing his suffrage upon moving to Washington. He thus took the position that the Court of Appeals was "purely a constitutional" court, clothed with authority under Article III alone, and thus in no way was a local court that might imply the judges were District of Columbia residents. He regularly took steps to maintain his voting (and taxing) residence in Iowa. And he was responsible, even, for writing an opinion, *Sweeney v. District of Columbia*, confirming that federal employees presumptively retained the domiciles of the states from which they came, and thus were subject to state—not District of Columbia—taxation.[57]

Rutledge was troubled in that case, as were local editorial writers, by Sweeney's escape from District taxation, since Sweeney had apparently not paid taxes to Massachusetts, where he had come from twenty years earlier to serve in the military. A handwritten draft opinion shows that initially, the judge was prepared to hold that Sweeney, by failing to pay Massachusetts taxes, had been insufficiently "meticulous" in preserving his "*bona fide*" residence elsewhere and thus was "liable" to the District for "the tax assessed." Concluding, however, that placement of the burden on the individual to prove domicile elsewhere would be too heavy—and concerned, apparently, that too many would lose their state voting rights in the end— Rutledge changed the opinion to announce a "presumption of continuity of state domiciliation during the Federal employment" requiring "strong evidence" in the District of Columbia's hands "to overcome it." The "state domicile," he wrote, "could not be overthrown by mere proof of long residence during performance or ambiguous showing of intention to change."[58]

The tax case, as well as a lingering concern about "carpet-bagging" in the designation of judges for the District of Columbia, caused Rutledge to think pointedly about the District's political status. To Clay Apple he expressed sympathy with those who regarded the national capital "as a local community having many of the characteristics of a state."[59] And to the Massachusetts commissioner of corporations and taxation, who had written to praise *Sweeney*, Rutledge replied expressing concern for problems of the District, and particularly for the fact that permanent residents had "no semblance of suffrage" and bore "an undue proportion of the burden" of the costs of local government without a "voice in matters of their own taxation."[60]

Inevitably, it seemed, Rutledge eventually communicated with advocates of home rule for the District. In June 1942 he submitted to a local political committee a three-point proposal: a constitutional amendment to give District citizens the right to vote for president, vice president, and membership in the House of Representatives; a "revamped" District government of five commissioners, two elected by local residents; and recognition by Congress of its responsibility to make a larger financial contribution to the District government. He did not suggest including a senator or two for the District, because the "Senatorial prerogative would introduce too much local politics in too many national matters and interests connected with the District government." And he believed that an inevitable "conflict between national and local interests" should limit District residents to minority membership on the board of commissioners.[61] A month later, activists on a District Delegate Committee led by a local lawyer, E. Barrett Prettyman—later to become chief judge of the U.S. Court of Appeals for the District of Columbia Circuit—proposed a bill for a nonvoting "delegate" to the U.S. House of Representatives, to be elected by District citizens. Prettyman asked Rutledge to join the committee, but Rutledge, while affirming that the District's "second, third or fourth class of citizenship" was "one of the gravest injustices existing in our governmental structure," declined "with regret" on grounds of "possible impropriety."[62] One can wonder, however, why the judge had found no impropriety in submitting his three-part proposal to a political committee.

BEGINNING AS EARLY as March 1940, Attorney General Robert Jackson tried intermittently to move Wiley Rutledge to the U.S. Court of Appeals for the Eighth Circuit, which included Iowa and Missouri, or even to the Tenth Circuit, which included New Mexico and Colorado. Apparently, Jackson favored individuals for various federal circuit court appointments whom he could not easily clear with senators who had their own favorites for the circuits comprising the states they served. He reasoned that Rutledge's credentials within the Eighth Circuit, especially, would make his appointment there impossible to oppose, with Jackson then free to appoint his own favorite from the Eighth Circuit to the appellate vacancy in the District of Columbia.[63]

Wiley acknowledged the attraction of the lighter workload in the Tenth Circuit and the benefits from getting "back into the normal surroundings of a state again" in the Eighth, but he decided to stay put despite Jackson's approaching him three times. After Jackson had taken his seat on the Supreme Court, either his successor, Francis Biddle, or someone else in the meantime ratcheted up the transfer proposal from an "offer" to a "request." Apparently finding the request soft enough that refusal would not be considered an act of disloyalty to the president, Rutledge remained unmoved. Even without regard to the important issues coming before him in the District of Columbia, he was wise enough to recognize, as he wrote to a friend, that "there is always danger in returning to old associations after one has left them."[64]

WILEY RUTLEDGE was conflicted over his own responsibilities as America took steps in aid of the Allied war effort. In advising former students, after enactment of the draft, about seeking alternative defense jobs or other government positions in Washington, he would typically say that he wanted "to get in the thick of things and do his bit," even "join up somewhere to get ready to carry a gun." To George Haskell, Rutledge wrote in early 1941, "It makes me feel like piddling around with jack straws to be deciding little family fusses, scraps between businessmen or even between business and labor." And yet the judge reminded himself and Haskell, "I know that these things are the very essence of the democratic process"—the "things which the defense program and even the war itself are to conserve and defend." Rutledge thus intellectually could accept the importance of what he was doing during the war, and he even publicly questioned the government's failure to grant deferments for lawyers whom he believed essential to war mobilization at home. But he always felt it was "just rotten," once America itself was at war, that the "younger generation ha[d] to be loaded" with the burden of "the real fighting." He was credible in exclaiming that he would "rather be potshotting at Japs" than "sitting in the overstuffed chair upstairs," and in telling a former student, "I envy you the opportunity to see active service and wish that I might be in an outfit with you."[65]

Former students were not the only ones who sought Rutledge's advice as America was moving toward war. By the fall of 1941, the law schools were closing down for lack of faculty, as well as students, and former colleagues asked their friend for help. Wrote Edward Stimson, dean at Toledo, "Will you keep your eye open for opportunities which my training and experience fit me?" More poignantly, Willard Wirtz at Northwestern disclosed: "I have some pretty serious problems of readjustment coming up and I'm hungry for advice. We have practically been given our walking papers here (for the duration) and I am not sure which way to turn." Just before Pearl Harbor, Wirtz was particularly low, groping for something to believe in. "I know your answer," he wrote to Rutledge, "American democracy." But, Wirtz added, "I must confess that I no longer know what that means—and it's too big a project anyway, for definite action, I mean, by a mere pawn." Rutledge replied, the day after the Japanese attack: "[A]bove all things, don't let go of your grip. There are things worth living for even in a hellish world like this. And I would go further and say there are things worth fighting for. I know you would say that[,] too, though you would prefer fighting in another way. The times are dark but there's not a total absence of light."[66]

As to the approaching war, Wiley Rutledge had been a realist: "[M]y philosophy," he wrote to George Haskell early in 1941, with particular reference to those who were proclaiming that America could keep out of the war, "has always been that it doesn't help any to shut one's eyes and say that something which stands in his way just doesn't exist." Rutledge acknowledged to Bill Bartley that he would rather have his son, Neal, "take his chances in a front line with the possibility of surviving and living in something which offers at least a hope of democracy than to have him make no resistance and live the life of a slave in a totalitarian state." But Rutledge's realism, rather than despairing, was somehow motivating. "I can see the possibility of a better world in the long run," he wrote to Haskell, "even if the immediate future should bring Hitler victory." However the war turned out, there was "at least a ray of hope" that the world would see the need for an international "political organization," embracing a rational economic order based on free trade, and that such an organization would thus be achieved.[67]

THERE WERE A FEW brief respites. After receiving an honorary doctorate at Colorado in early June 1940, Wiley joined Clay Apple for a brief fishing trip to Wyoming.[68] A month later, the Rutledges acquired a home in the Spring Valley section of northwest D.C. While settling in, Rutledge was tackling his opinion backlog, finishing enough to allow the family nearly a month's vacation in upper Mackinac County, Michigan, followed by a trip in early September to Iowa City, then to St. Louis, before putting Mary Lou on the train to Bloomington for her freshman year at Indiana University and returning to Washington.[69]

On February 1, 1941, Justice James C. McReynolds—the last of the "Four Horsemen" who had been anathema to President Roosevelt—stepped down from the Supreme Court. The most talked-about candidate to succeed him was Attorney General Robert Jackson, although the initial list in the newspapers included the usual suspects, such as the federal circuit judge Sam Bratton of New Mexico, Dean James M. Landis of Harvard, and Robert M. Hutchins, president of the University of Chicago, as well as Wiley's colleague Justin Miller and a few first-timers. Soon Senator James F. Byrnes of South Carolina also became a visible possibility. To Clay Apple, Wiley confided that Jackson would be a "much greater addition to the court," but that Byrnes was "well qualified, highly regarded and . . . reasonably liberal." Although either choice would suit Rutledge, he believed that Byrnes was "needed in the Senate."[70]

Roosevelt announced that he had selected McReynolds's successor but would not make it public for awhile. His reason for withholding the name became clear in June, when Chief Justice Hughes announced that he would retire effective July 1. The president then moved quickly, on June 12. He nominated Justice Stone to succeed Hughes as chief justice; Byrnes to replace McReynolds—an action the Senate confirmed without a hearing the same day by voice vote; and, to fill the Stone vacancy, Jackson, whom the Senate confirmed on July 7.[71]

Earlier, in January, Joseph O'Meara had written to Rutledge of his sincere hope that Rutledge "would be put on the Supreme Court." Rutledge answered that he would have none of it. First, the battle to "prevent the national power from becoming so restricted" that the federal government could not deal with the "big problems" of the day was "over." Second, he said, "I have come to question seriously whether the work is of a character suited to my own temperament." Furthermore, appointment to the high court would create "a sense of obligation to remain which would amount practically to perpetual discomfort." And, he concluded: "should an attractive opportunity arise for return to educational work or something of that sort I should consider it very seriously."[72]

In the meantime, life with the Rutledges had proceeded apace. Wiley and Annabel had attended an inaugural dinner in honor of the new vice president, Henry Wallace—a fellow Iowan whom Wiley had come to know slightly though never addressed informally, and whose views on the international order Wiley would come to applaud.[73] Later in the year, Clay Apple wrote of rumors about Wiley's imminent appointment to the National Labor Relations Board, which apparently was news to Rutledge and led to nothing.[74] In the summer, the Rutledges took their usual trips to St. Louis and Iowa City, where Wiley traveled his regular luncheon circuit, taking in Rotary and Kiwanis clubs.[75] By the beginning of the fall term in 1941, the judge was in better shape at work than at any time during his two and a half years in Washington; only two opinions as yet were unwritten.

The ensuing year, of course, brought war to America as Rutledge continued to decide cases, teach law, organize federal legal examiners, and speak out on public issues, including the need for postwar international organization. The summer of 1942 found him in the classroom in Boulder, then in "the wilds" again fishing with Clay Apple, followed by September in Michigan with Annabel's brother.[76] Soon thereafter, before Judge Rutledge had settled on the bench for the 1942 term, Justice James F. Byrnes dropped a bombshell.

THIRTEEN

The Byrnes Vacancy

Justice Byrnes, while on the bench, had been covertly advising the president on the war for several months. Roosevelt decided he wanted Byrnes to direct the new Office of Economic Stabilization, and the justice resigned from the Court on October 3, 1942. During the month before the midterm elections of 1942, there was no visible activity to arrive at Byrnes's successor. As Attorney General Francis Biddle put it, Roosevelt "took his time about appointing judges." The vacancy hurt the Court all the more because Byrnes had effectively been gone for ten months. Roosevelt even considered keeping the seat "open for Jimmy," but Biddle conveyed Chief Justice Stone's request for the president to act and convinced Roosevelt that he should do so. In Biddle's words, FDR rejoined: "Well then, could we not appoint some old boy for two or three years who would agree to retire when he had reached seventy, so that Jimmy could be brought back?" Biddle replied that this would not fit with Roosevelt's oft-expressed intention to nominate younger men; so the president "acquiesced without enthusiasm" and enjoined Biddle: "'See if you can't get me a nice, solid Republican . . . to balance things a bit, preferably west of the Mississippi, and not a professor.'"[1] Realistically, no confirmation could occur until Congress reconvened in early 1943, and presumably the White House, in any event, wanted to see what the new Senate looked like before sending a nomination for "advice and consent."

While interested, as always, in how the vacancy would be filled, Wiley Rutledge was not interested in joining the list of aspirants. A few days after Byrnes resigned, Carl Pryor, a friend of Rutledge's from Iowa, asked him to "report any developments which may have any bearing on the possibility" of his "appointment to the Supreme Court" so that Pryor could help. Rutledge asked him to stop: "Frankly, I do not think there is any possibility of such an eventuality as your letter mentions and, again frankly, I hope that

nothing will be done by my friends or others in an effort to bring it about."
Rutledge added that he was not "sufficiently committed" to appellate work
"to want to spend the remainder" of his life in it, and that the need to foster
"national unity" required nomination of a Republican.[2]

Pryor took his friend at his word, agreeing that a Republican should be
appointed and touting Judge Orrie Phillips of the Tenth Circuit, "who is
quite liberal minded." Rutledge answered, "I too have a high regard for
Orrie Phillips," but he favored Judge John J. Parker, who "was done an injustice when the Senate refused to confirm him in the Hoover administration." (It would be interesting to know how much Rutledge knew about
Parker's race baiting when he ran for governor of North Carolina two decades earlier.) Rutledge added that Senator Charles L. McNary of Oregon,
a Republican whose name had been mentioned—and who had run for vice
president on the Willkie ticket in 1940—"would make a fine judge and a
liberal one."[3]

Soon after the election, the Supreme Court sweepstakes appeared in the
press. In a newspaper column and on the radio, Drew Pearson identified
Rutledge as "the candidate of Chief Justice Stone." Friends began, once
again, to write to the president and the attorney general, while Rutledge
immediately tried to end the effort. To several friends he wrote letters similar to the one he had sent Carl Pryor a month earlier. Although in 1939 he
apparently had not considered it unseemly for Irving Brant and others to
campaign on his behalf, by this third time his name had been mentioned
publicly he was embarrassed by any appearance of being "a perpetual candidate" for the Court, especially given his belief that in light of his experience, he was not likely to receive the nomination. Given the enjoyment of
his pursuit of the Brandeis vacancy in 1939, however, such embarrassment
presumably would not have been enough for Rutledge to call off a campaign
in 1942 if he had not had more fundamental reasons for holding back. In
several letters, emphasizing that he did not desire a promotion to a position
he would not feel free to leave, he also stressed the personal hardships to
be anticipated: "While I enjoy judging, I have had enough of it to know one
has to make great sacrifices. . . . This includes giving up time with friends
and family, foregoing many of the most pleasant associations in life, and
grinding away at all hours of the day and night on hard, tough, legal knots.
For some men that would be unalloyed pleasure. For me it is about half and
half, or maybe forty-sixty, because I like people and immediate touch with
them." Rutledge also emphasized his aversion to life "like a gold fish" living
under a "spotlight." The judge made clear to a few friends that he would not
necessarily turn down the seat if offered; he felt a strong sense of obligation
to Roosevelt. But he did not want his friends to pursue the Court for him.

Attorney General
Francis Biddle.
(Photograph by
Maurice Constant;
Library of Congress,
LC-US 262-87188)

In exasperation, he wrote to one: "For God's sake, don't do anything about stirring up the matter! I am uncomfortable enough as it is."[4]

Wiley Rutledge did not stop there. He wrote to Attorney General Biddle the day after Drew Pearson's prediction, disavowing all efforts in his behalf "notwithstanding the obviously friendly intention of those concerned." He continued: "I hope you will believe me when I say that I do not have Supreme Courtitis. My own feeling, until the election, was that the President should appoint a Republican to this vacancy and I am still inclined to feel that would be the wiser thing both for the Court and for the country." Then, relying on Biddle's willingness to take him "exactly" at his word, Rutledge wrote: "I have said that I am not ambitious and that means that I have not built any expectations on these rumors or reports. I must recognize, however, that there may be a remote chance of there being some basis in fact. If that should prove to be true I merely want to request that before any action is taken I be given an opportunity to talk with you." Finally, recognizing that "even the making of this request might be regarded by some as presumptuous," Rutledge closed by saying that he knew Biddle would not take his comments that way, and that it was "of course entirely unnecessary" for the attorney general to reply.[5]

Irving Brant had other ideas. Before the election, on October 31, 1942, he had written to Luther Ely Smith in St. Louis that Rutledge had a "better chance" for the Supreme Court than ever before. He "has made a splendid record as a judge, jumping in two years' time to the very top in the estimation of leading members of the bar." Brant suggested that Smith write to the attorney general and obtain bar and faculty endorsements from St. Louis, emphasizing the importance of appointing a justice from west of the Mississippi, as well as endorsing Rutledge personally. A few days later, Roscoe Anderson of the St. Louis bar wrote a letter to the *Post-Dispatch*—which others sent to the president and the attorney general—summarizing Rutledge's qualifications and stressing, once again, the importance of selecting a "justice from west of the Mississippi."[6]

On November 7, Brant wrote to Virgil Hancher, president of the University of Iowa, to ask for endorsements of Rutledge from Hancher himself and the faculty—which, two days later, Hancher wrote to say had already been sent, according to Dean Ladd. Brant also told Hancher that he had recently met with Attorney General Biddle, who "came very close" to saying that the two men with the best prospects were Rutledge and Senator Alben Barkley of Kentucky, a Roosevelt supporter down the line. As Drew Pearson had pointed out on November 6, however, Barkley's chances, objectively, were limited by his age, sixty-five, and home state, Kentucky, which was also Justice Reed's home state. Furthermore, there was another southerner on the Court: Justice Black. On November 10, Brant wrote to Biddle, enclosing Anderson's letter to the *Post-Dispatch*, emphasizing why Barkley would be a bad choice, and expressing hope that the rumored idea of offering the appointment to the elderly Senator George Norris—defeated for reelection in 1942 after thirty years in the Senate—was untrue. By November 18 Brant was seeking support for Rutledge from Henry Wallace, expressing at the time Brant's disillusionment with Justice Frankfurter.[7]

Especially after the election reflecting Republican gains, Rutledge himself continued to favor a Republican for the Court, first Judge John Parker to "have that old wrong rectified," then Senator McNary. But in writing this to a friend he added: "The most graceful thing, but for his age, probably would be to appoint George Norris," a sentiment he repeated to Clay Apple a week later. Norris himself, on the other hand, had spoken out again in favor of Rutledge.[8]

A week before Christmas, Irving Brant wrote to Luther Ely Smith to report that the choice appeared to be among Rutledge, Fahy, and Acheson. "That is, as Barkley faded, Frankfurter pushed harder for his two favor-

Chief Justice Harlan Fiske Stone. (Photograph by Harris and Ewing; Collection of the Supreme Court of the United States, 90-9-01394)

ites." Added Brant: "Apparently the nomination was put over until the new Congress convened to avoid the possibility of a Senate failure to vote on confirmation." Not long after Byrnes resigned in October, Biddle had met with Brant, who told Biddle that Chief Justice Stone had suggested Rutledge and Judge John Parker for the vacancy and had "spoke[n] of Wiley Rutledge's work with praise." Brant also reported that Justices Black and Douglas had expressed enthusiasm for Rutledge. Biddle had already asked his assistant, Herbert Wechsler, to analyze Rutledge's opinions. Biddle noted in his diary that Harold Ickes wanted the job and "would make an excellent Judge," but Biddle added that Ickes, then sixty-eight, was "more important where he is." Other possible nominees in Biddle's view were Robert Hutchins, James

Landis, Judge Parker, Senator Schwellenbach, Dean Acheson, and Charles Fahy. Biddle strongly opposed rewarding Senator Norris with a seat on the Court.[9]

Two weeks after his meeting with Brant, Biddle recorded that he had met with Stone. The Chief Justice wanted, in Biddle's words, "a man of real legal training or great experience" who would "'stick,'" meaning someone who would not take off as Byrnes had after brief service on the Court. Stone thought that a judge from one of the federal circuit courts "would fit in admirably." Biddle initially was skeptical, believing as a former federal appellate judge himself that "the Circuit Courts had little material of first-rate caliber." Stone pulled a volume of federal case reports listing judges in the front and, to his own surprise, agreed. But then Stone thought of the right material from the circuits: first, Learned Hand—at seventy-one "obviously too old," according to Biddle. (Stone wrote to a Hand supporter the same day that the appointment of Hand "would greatly strengthen the Court": "I should be made very happy about it. I suspect, however, that the age question stands in the way.")[10]

After mentioning Hand, Stone spoke to Biddle about Judge Parker, in whom Stone "had a good deal of confidence," and Judges Bratton, Phillips, and Rutledge. In Biddle's words, Stone described Rutledge as "having real ability, but being a bit pedestrian and having perhaps not served long enough to make his experience valuable." Biddle understood that Stone, nonetheless, "would not be displeased with Rutledge," although Stone's resentment at Drew Pearson's reference to Rutledge as Stone's candidate made him "a little cautious in discussing Rutledge." Stone negatived two others. Although he thought Dean Acheson was "highly intelligent," he "would not have enough courage when it came to the final test," said Stone (not making clear what he meant), and the Chief dismissed Fahy because, as a Catholic, Fahy might lead the church to "think it was entitled to two." Biddle then visited Black and Douglas, both of whom were "enthusiastic about Rutledge," as Brant had reported. As a result of his inquiries, Biddle concluded that "[o]utside of Hand, who was far more distinguished than any of the others, Rutledge seemed the most promising."[11]

Wechsler had delivered his memorandum to Biddle on November 12. It convinced the attorney general that Rutledge's opinions on the D.C. Circuit, while (in Biddle's words) "a little pedestrian," were "sound." This brief characterization of Wechsler's analysis was understated and undeserved. In accepting the assignment to scrutinize Wiley's opinions, Herbert Wechsler had cautioned Biddle that he was "prejudiced in Rutledge's favor." But Biddle had to know that his young assistant—later to become one of the academy's premier scholars of constitutional law and the role of the fed-

Herbert Wechsler. (Courtesy of Doris Wechsler)

eral courts—would make an objective enough report. Wechsler's memorandum actually covered three judges: Rutledge, John J. Parker (1885–
1958) from the Fourth Circuit, and Roger John Traynor (1900–1983) of the
Supreme Court of California. Evidently Biddle had seen no basis for considering Judges Hutcheson and Phillips, despite substantial letter-writing
campaigns for each. Nor were Messrs. Hutchins, Landis, and Acheson
serious candidates; according to Wechsler in an interview, Biddle would
have heard from them if they were. There was no movement on Senator
Schwellenbach's behalf, Wechsler added, and although "in the nature of
things" the solicitor general would be under consideration, "Biddle was no
great admirer of Fahy." This left, in addition to Rutledge, the perennially
available Judge Parker and a first-time western candidate, Justice Traynor,

for whom a massive letter-writing campaign from California was going on. Although Biddle had been skeptical at the beginning that a suitable candidate from the judiciary could be found, Stone had disabused him of that worry in citing Rutledge and Parker. And Justice Traynor, well respected in both judicial and academic circles—he had been a law professor at Berkeley for years—rounded out a trio of finalists.[12]

Beginning with Rutledge, Wechsler said he had read most of the opinions the judge had written on the Court of Appeals and concluded that they indicated "soundness of judgment, a searching mind, a properly progressive approach to legal issues, some mastery of phrase and style—especially after the first year—and a dominating effort to answer all the problems in terms that will satisfy the litigant and his lawyer that their points have not been ignored." As a consequence of this last tendency, Wechsler said, Rutledge's opinions were "frequently too long," but this added to the overall impression that was, for Wechsler, "Rutledge's most striking trait—his warm sense for real people as the ultimate concern of law and his awareness of what real people are like throughout this broad land." Wechsler added that there was "constant evidence of the quality—so treasured in Holmes—of pointing [out] the implications of small things, if only by defining an underlying reason for a rule or a concealed principle of its growth." Then came an important substantive comment: "Civil liberty problems and review of administrative agencies, especially in the labor field, have been the major issues. His work leaves no room for doubt that these values are safe in his hands. More than this, however, I think it shows independence of mind within that framework. There is none of the easy factionalism to which so many liberals succumb." Wechsler then cited eight opinions by Rutledge that "will make the basis for my judgment clear," and concluded by reminding Biddle of "Rutledge's stand in favor of the Court Plan."[13]

Wechsler then summarized Judge Parker's rejection by the Senate, acknowledging that "[h]e is undoubtedly a highly competent judge," but that at the age of fifty-seven he had "reached his full development." Wechsler concluded, "Younger men, who can still grow with the times, will bring more to the Court in the difficult period that lies ahead." Justice Traynor, at forty-two, six years younger than Wiley Rutledge, had been a highly regarded tax lawyer and teacher, but of Traynor's forty or so opinions since he had been an appellate judge, Wechsler found only one "to be distinguished." Wechsler said: "the great majority are competent and nothing more. They reveal none of the philosophical groping of Rutledge, not even the keen analytical insight that one expects of men from the schools. Stylistically there is for me," Wechsler said, "an undue preponderance of the 'It is well settled' cliche."[14]

Wechsler's memorandum eliminated any concern about Rutledge's

Judge John J. Parker. (Courtesy of the Charlotte Observer)

scholarly ability that some interviews had suggested in 1939 when he was contesting Douglas. Wechsler may have seen those reports—a file of law deans' comments was available, although not the FBI files—but more to the point, scholarship as such was not a major concern. According to Wechsler, Rutledge's supporters were proposing him because "he'd been a good judge and the kind of judge you need on the Supreme Court to prevent the appointment of the kind of judge who might otherwise be appointed." There could not be "any second thought about whether Wiley was a trusty liberal; that was the most important consideration, particularly in connection with that appointment; at least it was in Biddle's mind."[15]

In the meantime, Justice Frankfurter and his friend C. C. Burlingham had begun a full-court press for the nomination of Learned Hand, venerable judge of the U.S. Court of Appeals for the Second Circuit in New York, whom Rutledge himself considered perhaps the "ablest" federal district judge and "abler than some on the Supreme Court." At seventy-one, however, Hand was well along in years—indeed, one year older than the age Roosevelt had used to justify augmentation of the Court under his failed Court-packing plan of 1937. Both Biddle and Wechsler believed that the president would have appointed Hand to succeed Byrnes if Hand had been a few years younger; but despite his emotional desire to appoint someone who would resign in favor of Byrnes's eventual return to the Court, Roosevelt was not about to invite accusations of hypocrisy by appointing even a consensus first choice whose very readiness to serve contradicted the presi-

Justice Roger J. Traynor. (Courtesy of the Supreme Court of California)

dent's strong view in 1937 for which he had fought a divisive battle. Frankfurter and Burlingham importuned the president orally and in writing to the point of Roosevelt's great annoyance. They even involved Learned Hand's cousin, Judge Augustus ("Gus") Hand, also on the Second Circuit and a lifelong Democrat, to seek the nomination for his progressive Republican relative. And in Frankfurter's enthusiasm, he even drafted for the president—he thought with FDR's blessing—a press release announcing Hand's nomination.[16]

But the efforts were in vain. On December 4, 1942, Roosevelt wrote to Frankfurter definitively: "Sometimes a fellow gets stopped by his own words and his own deeds"—the Court-packing fight—"and it is no fun for the fellow himself when that happens." Years later, Justice Douglas wrote in his autobiography that during a poker party in January 1943 he had asked the president who was "not going to be appointed" to the Byrnes vacancy. The president replied: "Learned Hand is *not* going to be appointed. . . . [T]his time Felix overplayed his hand. . . . Do you know how many people asked me today to name Learned Hand? . . . Twenty, and every one a messenger from Felix Frankfurter. . . . And by golly, I won't do it.'"[17]

On November 17, Biddle took up with Roosevelt the various possibilities

*Judge Learned
Hand. (Courtesy
of Art and Visual
Materials, Special
Collections
Department,
Harvard Law
School Library)*

for the Supreme Court, "telling him what the Chief Justice had said about
the Circuit Judges." In the words of Biddle's diary, Roosevelt thought that
"on the whole, Wiley Rutledge would be the best appointment" and said he
would decide after the cabinet meeting three days later. The president was
still concerned about Senator Norris, however, and asked Biddle to arrange
for the head of the Tennessee Valley Authority to take a federal judgeship
in Idaho so that Roosevelt could appoint Norris to chair the TVA. According
to Biddle, Norris "was moved, but not tempted." Roosevelt also mentioned
Fahy "favorably" and said he would appoint him to the Court if Murphy, a
Catholic, ever resigned.[18]

Distracted by war worries, Roosevelt let another six weeks go by. Then
word came from the White House on January 10, 1943, that the president
would submit Wiley Rutledge's name to the Senate the next day. Years later,
in his autobiography, Justice Douglas reported that he had asked the president "why he had chosen Wiley." Roosevelt replied that "Missy LeHand
had come in and said that Irving Brant of the St. Louis *Post Dispatch* [sic]
wanted to see him for a minute. Brant—whom FDR greatly admired—stayed

five minutes and convinced him that Rutledge was his man. The President was in the mood to be convinced because of the Frankfurter barrage."[19] Brant's influence, of course, had been pervasive, not last minute. But Douglas's theme was correct: more than any other person, Irving Newton Brant was responsible for the nomination of Wiley Rutledge as a federal appellate judge and, ultimately, a Supreme Court justice—helped along by the political factor that the president himself identified when he next greeted his nominee: "Wiley, you have a lot of geography."[20]

Felix Frankfurter wrote to Wiley immediately: "To the fellowship of Justices Holmes, Brandeis and Cardozo I welcome you. And no one can possibly do so more warmly than I do." All the other justices sent their congratulations and best wishes, as did Judge Parker, Benjamin Cohen, Thomas Reed Powell, and countless others.[21] Powell's letter was notable because he enclosed the memorandum he had sent about Rutledge to Felix Frankfurter in the last week of December 1938. Rutledge's reply was a gem:

It's the first time in my life I've had the chance to see myself as pictured in the mind of another with what I know to be absolute honesty and no trimming. . . . I'm essentially a dean. Mind you, I say dean, not professor, or scholar or jurist or judge. . . . I didn't know how much I liked it. Drudgery and detail, no time for research or writing or study—but every day some kid had a problem, and once in a while you could help. For purely personal satisfaction, I'd head back to Iowa Law School tomorrow—if there were one and they'd have me. It's something like once a dean always a dean. . . .

I'm getting lots of letters. I've had them before. Many just substitute me for God. That's either taffy or blindness. Others are more sensible. A few are honest. You are one of the latter. And theirs are the words that count most. When I wrote you before I knew enough of myself to realize—and to mean exactly what I said—that some mysterious leaven works up a very small amount of real merit into a big return. The leaven isn't brains, or knowledge, or grandeur of character, or any such unusual thing. So far as I can guess what it is—it's that I like people, have some sort of way of letting them know it, and in turn they like me regardless of all the other deficiencies. If that comes down to anything, it is that most folks are hungry to be liked, and return that feeling in kind when they receive it. . . .

I'll always be glad you butted in that day in Chicago. And I hope there will be many other days ahead when you'll do likewise—by letter or in person whenever I'm near you.[22]

The Rutledge family in Washington: Mary Lou, Wiley, Neal, Annabel, Jean Ann, and Laddie. (Courtesy of the Rutledge family)

On February 1, the Senate Judiciary Committee voted favorably on Rutledge's nomination with four senators withholding their vote: Langer of North Dakota, Revercomb of West Virginia, Wheeler of Montana, and Ferguson of Michigan. These four apparently were concerned about the nominee's reported backing of the president's Court-packing bill, although he received no questions about that when he appeared before the committee. On February 2, Senator Ferguson wrote to Rutledge asking about his stand at the time. After a "nice little chat" in Rutledge's chambers, Ferguson was noncommittal but later told reporters that he was satisfied. In the end, although Senator Wheeler—an arch-opponent of the Court-packing plan— had told the press he would vote against confirmation without making a speech, only Senator Langer indicated opposition on the Senate floor. He said, "I do not know Mr. Rutledge. I have no reason to believe him to be other than a man of uprightness, of honor, and of integrity. . . . These times are too solemn to permit . . . a man who, so far as I can ascertain, never practiced law inside a courtroom or, so far as I know, seldom even visited one until he came to take a seat on the United States Circuit Court of Appeals for the District of Columbia. . . . The Court is not without a professor or two already." The nomination was confirmed on a voice vote.[23]

Wiley Rutledge took his seat on the Supreme Court as its eighty-fourth justice a week later, on February 15, 1943. That day he wrote to President Roosevelt: "On my first day here, I want you to know you have been very much in my thoughts. I shall not try to put them down. But please know I shall try to serve, giving to the large task you have assigned me the best effort of which I am capable. If, in some way, they may help to establish more firmly the democratic institutions which you fight to keep, and to create through out the world, it will make me glad. May God bless and keep you."[24]

FOURTEEN

The New Justice

On February 15, 1943, the newspapers reported that American troops had captured Guadalcanal Island from the Japanese, the German defensive line had begun to crumble in southern Russia, and Justice Wiley Rutledge was to take his seat on the Supreme Court of the United States. Wiley enjoyed his first day on the bench, spying friends and particularly appreciating the "sly wink" from Jean Ann, which he "tried equally slyly to return."[1]

As he looked down the bench, the new justice saw in center chair Harlan Fiske Stone, a friendly, informal, professorial man in his early seventies. New Hampshire born, later dean of the law school at Columbia, eventually attorney general and associate justice appointed by President Coolidge, Stone had become known increasingly as a supporter of civil liberties. On Stone's immediate right was Owen J. Roberts, characterized by some as a Pennsylvania country squire. Dignified, sometimes cutting, often remote, but respected intellectually within the Court, Roberts had been a banking and railroad lawyer, then prosecutor in the Teapot Dome oil scandal, associate justice appointed by Hoover, and the "switch in time" during the Court-packing controversy.[2]

To Stone's immediate left sat Justice Black—a brilliant, dominating personality. Very much a Southerner, he was charming, never haughty, with an easy informality and winning sense of humor. But there was a toughness, even a "ferocity," about Hugo Black that when combined with his intellect and indefatigable work habits, made him a powerful leader of the liberal wing of the Court. Black operated like the politician he had always been, knowing at any moment whom to lobby—and whom to avoid. By far the Court's most skillful politician, he always knew exactly what he wanted, and thus always what he could give up to achieve a particular end. As a result, he could win a majority on occasion that one would have thought he could not accomplish.[3]

The Stone Court. Standing (l. to r.): Robert H. Jackson, William O. Douglas, Frank Murphy, Wiley Rutledge. Seated (l. to r.): Stanley F. Reed, Owen J. Roberts, Harlan Fiske Stone, Hugo L. Black, Felix Frankfurter. (Photograph by Acme Newspapers; Collection of the Supreme Court of the United States, 1943.81.4)

Justices Reed, Frankfurter, and Douglas flanked the center three. Stanley Reed, a mild-mannered Kentuckian, was friendly, very much the gentleman, even courtly—perhaps more formal than all save Roberts. Intelligent though not scholarly, Reed was a conscientious, hard-working jurist, conservative by temperament and respectful of precedent. He lacked a developed judicial philosophy, however, and thus was perceived within the Court as a "swing voter" vulnerable to switching sides under friendly persuasion.[4]

Unlike the solemn Reed, the bespectacled, fastidiously dressed Felix Frankfurter was ebullient. His coherent judicial outlook made Frankfurter the intellectual leader of the Court's conservative wing. And he exhibited a brilliance that extended well beyond the law to literature and philosophy. As one of Black's clerks proclaimed, Frankfurter "could talk about anything." Recalling the justice's questions about every kind of subject imaginable, one of his former clerks, mixing huge metaphors, likened his experience to "sitting on top of a volcano. . . . You were riding a wave and did not know where it was going to go." Clerks from every chambers—courted regularly by the gregarious Frankfurter in the office or over dinner—would chuckle appreciatively at the very mention of his name, a reaction that many of his judicial colleagues did not share because of his patronizing, didactic behavior. According to a thoughtful contemporary observer, Frankfurter's "terrific capacity to make people love to disagree with him" may have meant that Frankfurter achieved "less mileage per erg of intelligence than almost anybody on the Court," yielding ground that his colleague Black might not otherwise have taken.[5]

William O. Douglas, with perhaps the quickest mind of the group, displayed a strange mixture of attention to the Court and engagement elsewhere—many believed him to be interested in the presidency. A prodigiously fast worker, he regularly received responsibility for opinions in complicated antitrust and utility regulation cases with huge records—all areas of his expertise—that others would have taken months longer to write (except perhaps for Justice Jackson). Using overstatement to make the point, one of Black's clerks remarked that Douglas "could write an opinion and a book at the same time, one with one hand, the other with the other," and would do so on the bench while asking questions. Critics, on the other hand, would say that Douglas's opinions were often "slap dash affairs" reflecting "snap judgments" by a "result-oriented" liberal. And most of the law clerks, whether his own or the other justices', found him cold and aloof—indeed, the most unpleasant man on the Court. He treated his clerks miserably, except at an annual dinner at his home on Thanksgiving or Christmas, and he would growl or look away when any clerk on the Court walked by.[6]

Next to the left end—and thus next to Rutledge—was Justice William Francis ("Frank") Murphy, a pleasant, outgoing man with "all the Irish charm you could want," who joined the Court in 1940 after the death of Justice Pierce Butler. Murphy had served as a criminal trial judge, mayor of Detroit, governor general and then high commissioner of the Philippines, and finally governor of Michigan before Roosevelt named him attorney general and then associate justice. In short order, Murphy had emerged as the Court's leading judicial humanitarian, devoted to preserving individual rights and protecting minorities, including Native Americans. Neither brilliant nor scholarly—he had been a "terribly marginal" law student—Murphy was more "ideologue" than jurist and never pretended to be otherwise. Reportedly he once said, "There are eight good intellects" on the Court, "and they have my heart." Nor was he particularly hard-working. Unlike all the other justices (until Fred Vinson became chief in 1946), Murphy delegated all opinion writing entirely to his law clerks, one of whom—Eugene

*Justice Frank Murphy. (Photograph by Barrett Gallagher;
Collection of the Supreme Court of the United States, 1941.34.1)*

Gressman—served for five years, 1943–48, and was addressed by the other
clerks as "Mr. Justice." This is not to say that Murphy delegated his decision
making. His clerk would write up what the justice himself had decided,
sometimes reworking parts at Murphy's direction. And an early Murphy
clerk insists that the justice would add a little "Irish poetry" to the drafts.[7]
That said, Murphy was an approver, not a writer, of the opinions carry-

Justice Robert H. Jackson. (Photograph by Harris and Ewing;
Collection of the Supreme Court of the United States, 1941.173)

ing his name—opinions that overall were well composed and, on occasion, outstanding.[8]

On the far right end was Justice Robert H. Jackson, a corporation lawyer from upstate New York whom FDR had appointed solicitor general after Stanley Reed, and attorney general after Frank Murphy. Had national political considerations not dictated appointment of an esteemed Republican jurist to center chair, FDR would have appointed Jackson, not Stone, as chief to succeed Hughes. Joining Frankfurter and Roberts to make up the three most conservative members of the Court, with an approach tending to be more ad hoc and pragmatic than Frankfurter's, Jackson was a powerful intellect and a formidable personality. An outdoorsman who enjoyed riding, he exuded vitality. He was an "imperial individual" who could be courtly, debonair, witty, indeed a good story teller—very approachable and enjoyable. But he could suddenly show a mean streak, lashing out in anger even on the bench and putting colleagues and others down with a cutting sense of humor. Jackson was proud of his success as a lawyer and was bothered that most on the Court, including Rutledge, had little experience practicing law. He was extraordinarily self-confident, with little patience for those he regarded as intellectual inferiors. Jackson's self-assuredness was reinforced by his awareness that others considered him a brilliant writer—many said the most felicitous on the Court. And Jackson himself reportedly once told his clerk: "You know, I write so well that I have to be very careful, once I've written a first draft, that I'll find it so convincing I won't be adequately critical of my own stuff."[9]

This traditional seating arrangement—by seniority, surrounding the Chief in center chair—was particularly congenial for Justice Rutledge, for with his placement next to Murphy he was in easy note-passing distance of the man who was to become his closest friend on the Court.[10]

RUTLEDGE SPENT the rest of his first day writing to the president, Attorney General Biddle, Senator Norris, and others to whom he felt special gratitude. But the new justice was burdened with a difficult letter to write. He had offered a court of appeals clerkship to a young Washington University graduate, Virginia Morsey, who had "stood at the head of her class scholastically," was the "first woman editor" of the law review, and reportedly was "one of the most capable students" the law school had produced. Once confirmed by the Senate, Rutledge still felt an obligation to Morsey, but Ralph Fuchs, whose position at the solicitor general's office acquainted him with a menu of young government lawyers, urged his friend to consider instead a fresh member of the SG's staff, Victor Brudney. A law review graduate of Columbia, Brudney had served at the SEC upon graduation and then clerked briefly for Justice Byrnes until Byrnes's resignation. Rutledge found Brudney irresistible and brought him on board in February, writing Morsey an elaborate letter of explanation and apology.[11]

Brudney became the benchmark against whom every clerk thereafter was measured.[12] And he became the justice's dear friend. Probably as secure, personally, as any middle-aged man could be, Wiley Rutledge invited critical intellectual attack on his own ideas as a way of testing whether his views were coherent and persuasive. In honestly accepting his own limitations, he knew he could not do the best job of which he was capable without the aid of considerable intellectual firepower from an assertive law clerk. Thus, Rutledge and Brudney were made for each other. Years later, the justice would refer fondly to the "Vic Brudney type who will fight you to 11:59 on Monday morning before the decision comes down to get you[,] and sometimes make you[,] change your vote"—and make you "darn glad he wouldn't take 'No.'" Rutledge surely smiled when he dictated to Edna Lingreen: "I have never had a clerk who fought with me so hard when we differed as Vic

Victor Brudney. (Courtesy of Rutgers School of Law–Newark)

did. More than once I threw him out of my office only to have him come back and reopen the argument."[13]

For Brudney, the respect—and affection—became mutual. In looking back, he acknowledged, "I was brazenly arrogant; some of us [clerks] thought of ourselves as 'anointed.'" Indeed, "the judge and I often discussed—argued about—cases intensely; our voices occasionally rose." Brudney emphasized, however, that the arguments were always "on the merits, not personal." And yet the young clerk offered to quit, citing to Rutledge all the disagreement. "Imagine the impudence," Brudney recalled. Rutledge, however, made clear to his clerk how important their arguments were. He "made it impossible" for Brudney "to quit."[14]

Brudney came to think of Rutledge not only as a "wise" justice but as an unusual, very special human being. He was "an immensely friendly man"; there was "nothing fake about it"; he "simply liked people, with great gusto and pleasure." And even more important for a Supreme Court justice, Wiley Rutledge, according to Brudney, was honest and direct—indeed honest with himself. "He understood his often-conflicting values and was self-conscious about his ideological preferences and personal biases, and tried to rein them in."[15] He "had absolutely no side or cant," and "no image of himself as a great man." Said Brudney, "He came out of middle-America, and I was a New York City kid and something of a wise ass. . . . He showed me there are more complicated, richer dimensions to law and to people than I had ever thought about." And "in our relationship he was really open in ways that I feel certain few of his colleagues were with their clerks."[16]

The two worked as a team. Like the clerks who succeeded him, Victor

Brudney spent most of his time preparing memoranda on the "cert" (for *certiorari*) petitions seeking Supreme Court review. Even though the number of petitions each year was staggering for a justice with one clerk—in those days it could reach over 1,300—Rutledge did not limit his own review to the clerk's memos. He would read the petitions as well, according to Brudney, who emphasized that the justice "worked like hell; there was no question about that."[17]

Rutledge was particularly concerned about petitions filed by unrepresented indigent prisoners, because the Chief Justice, who had an extra clerk, routinely assumed responsibility for screening those petitions for all chambers and commonly sent a one-sentence memo recommending denial. Rutledge would have his clerk double-check that work and, as a result, sometimes recommended that the Court take the case. Another of Rutledge's clerks, Harry Shniderman, noted that the justice was so "anxious to be careful" that he was reluctant to send these handwritten petitions back to the court clerk's office after deciding how he would vote, because so often he would want "to rethink them." Shniderman added, "Edna [Lingreen] and I had to sneak them out."[18]

Before oral argument in cases that the Court had accepted, Rutledge would read all the briefs and confer with his clerk informally about the cases they had not discussed during cert review. After argument—which Rutledge clerks, because of time pressures, rarely attended—justice and clerk might confer briefly. But the significant chambers discussion took place every Friday night, before the weekly Saturday conference when the full Court met all day and often into the evening. There the justices decided the cases, received writing assignments from the chief or senior justice in majority, and approved the announcement of opinions, concurrences, and dissents for Monday, the Court's regular "decision day."[19]

Rutledge, not his clerk, would typically write the first draft of an opinion, although sometimes the justice would leave the Saturday conference with more than one opinion to write for the Court. In that case, he might say to his clerk, "You pick one, and I'll pick one." Each would then prepare a draft, "swap them," critique each other's work, and as a result usually generate more research. Rutledge then would complete the final draft of each, writing out the entire opinion longhand on lined, yellow foolscap for Edna Lingreen to type—and often retype with further corrections—for the Court printer. Rutledge would circulate the galleys to his colleagues for comment and eventual approval after revisions necessary to hold a majority. Nothing that his clerk wrote "emerged full blown," although Brudney did report—as later clerks would also—that occasionally he would recognize some of his prose in places, shifted around.[20]

Rutledge followed the same approach in later years, drawing for the substance of his opinions on his clerks' drafts (when available), on cert memos—sometimes augmented by "bench" memos prepared for use at argument—and on the parties' briefs. He would also scrutinize the trial court record. Justice John Paul Stevens, who clerked for Rutledge in the 1948 Term, remembered seeing his boss regularly taking home "chunks of the record." Stevens recalled, in particular, that in a First Amendment obscenity case Rutledge had not relied only on the cert petition, clerk's memorandum, and briefs. "He read the book." [21]

Because clerk-written sentences, or occasional paragraphs, would appear only here and there in the final product, everyone who worked for Wiley Rutledge would confirm that the justice's opinions were truly his own. After almost four years on the Court, Rutledge wrote to Judge Henry Edgerton that opinion writing, as on the Court of Appeals, was still "extremely hard" for him—an observation that most of his clerks would endorse. But he kept working doggedly at it. [22] Wiley Rutledge was probably alone among the justices in believing that virtually every argument, even frivolous ones, deserved attention in the Court's opinion. Most if not all his colleagues believed that the Court's opinions did not entail consideration of all the arguments proffered; their function, rather, was to address large legal questions. Rutledge would emphatically disagree. "By the time the lawyer and litigant get to the Supreme Court," he told Brudney, "they have lived years with the case, and the lawyer has put a big piece of himself into it." So "however foolish or trivial his arguments, I want them to know that I heard him" by responding to each point raised. Rutledge was fond of saying that a losing litigant never complained that the opinion was too long. Perhaps the justice had merely found a new rationalization for his propensity to "write long." After all, unlike a first-level court of appeals that granted direct review as a matter of right, the Supreme Court exercised only discretionary review, which meant that no one had a right to ask the high court to answer every question counsel put before it. But whatever Rutledge may have been doing subconsciously, he was a bulldog on the point. If colleagues believed his opinions were too long, so be it. [23]

WHETHER THE COURT was scheduled to sit for argument or not, Rutledge tended to push his most productive work toward the end of the day. He once told a reporter that he would arrive in chambers at around 9:00 A.M.— Edna Lingreen remembered it as closer to 10:00—and "'spend the morning reading and answering the day's mail'" and receiving visitors. With any time left before the Court convened at noon, he would read briefs or work on opinions, typically garbed in a black, loose-fitting alpaca coat over his

shirt and tie—a standard uniform for the justices. Fortified by cigarettes—
"regular 70 millimeter Old Golds"—and by a thermos of coffee, he smoked
"voracious[ly]" and drank coffee "incessantly." (Rutledge knew he smoked
too much but would finesse the point by saying, like Mark Twain, that he
quit "about every twenty minutes.") Court would adjourn at 2:00 for lunch
in the justices' private dining room, followed at 2:30 by more oral arguments until 4:30. Rutledge would then work on opinions for an hour, arriving home around 6:00 to walk the dog, eat dinner, and spend "'a half hour
of relaxation'" before working "'as late as 11 P.M.'"[24]

AFTER TWO MONTHS of service, on April 19, 1943, Rutledge was ready to
announce his first opinion for the Court in two companion cases styled
Aguilar v. Standard Oil Co. of New Jersey, overruling a per curiam decision
by an illustrious panel consisting of the Hand cousins and Judge Charles
Clark. Rutledge wrote for a 7 to 1 majority that under maritime law—which
imposed liability on a shipowner for injuries to a seaman only when acting
"in the service of a ship"—the shipowner could be found liable even when a
seaman was injured while on authorized shore leave, which Rutledge characterized as "an elemental necessity in the sailing of ships, a part of the
business as old as the art, not merely a personal diversion." A writer for the
St. Louis Post-Dispatch, Irving Dilliard, complimented Rutledge's "lucid
style," as well as his "sociological understanding" that reminded Dilliard of
Justice Cardozo.[25]

During the half-term that Rutledge served in 1943, he wrote three other
opinions for the Court,[26] three opinions specially concurring with the majority,[27] and one dissent.[28] Two deserve mention if only because they reflect
Rutledge's independence from day one, taking on two senior justices, Black
and Stone. In *Galloway v. United States*, an army veteran had sought recovery under the War Risk Insurance Act for total and permanent disability
by reason of insanity. Rutledge wrote for a majority sustaining the district
judge, who had directed a verdict for the government on the ground that
the evidence was insufficient for the jury to grant the veteran's claim. Justice Black dissented, however, supported by Douglas and Murphy, primarily
because Black found the directed verdict procedure itself unconstitutional.
Black opined that if the trial judge's instructions could lead the jury to only
one reasonable result on the evidence presented, the Seventh Amendment
allowed the trial judge at most to order a new trial—apparently over and
over again until a jury got it right.[29]

Black's dissent, expressed in a theory not even presented by the army
veteran, was largely a rejection of the trial judge's long-established responsibility in civil cases to take the case away from a renegade jury when the

evidence would support only one reasonable outcome. Justice Frankfurter advised Rutledge not even to dignify Black's argument by discussing it. "[C]ertain attacks," wrote "FF" to Rutledge, "call for intelligent neglect." Rutledge drafted a note (which he withheld but expressed orally) rejecting his colleague's advice, calling the issue "an old ghost with more than feline capacity for returning to life" and Black's dissent "forceful—and plausible in some respects."[30] The majority deferred to their new colleague. "I think you have used more ammunition than Black's opinion deserves," wrote Chief Justice Stone, "but I do not object to 'killing him dead.' " Justice Jackson, with the flair evident so often in his own opinions, wrote to Rutledge: "I agree. Done in a grand style—force without sacrifice of accuracy, precision without being dull. Worthy of a more important cause."[31] Rutledge thus proceeded to give the directed verdict full historical and theoretical treatment, effectively putting to rest Black's constitutional contention.

In a letter sending copies of *Aguilar* and *Galloway* to the former senator George Norris, Rutledge volunteered a glimpse into how judges' own personal lives affect their decision making. He told Norris that "perhaps the difference" between Black's and his own "slants on the question" in *Galloway* came "partly from difference" in their "experiences." Justice Black "courageously fought corporations and secured judgments against them on behalf of laboring people while practicing in Alabama[,] and one of the great obstacles he met undoubtedly was the tendency of judges to withdraw cases from juries when there was evidence which should have required submission." In contrast, wrote Rutledge, "when I first went to St. Louis I found a condition of ambulance chasing there which, to say the least, was worse than anything which I had believed might be possible in any respectable community in this country." The justice was suspicious about marginal personal injury lawsuits that asked a jury to speculate with all its "sympathies" and "prejudices" when little if any proof was offered.[32]

THE OTHER noteworthy opinion that Rutledge wrote during his first term was a dissent in *Marconi Wireless Telegraph Co. of America v. United States*, where the Chief Justice, writing for a 5 to 3 majority, upheld a judgment against the Marconi Company in a patent infringement suit. Frankfurter, joined by Roberts, dissented. Noting (in his view) the "scientific incompetence of judges," Frankfurter found the Court presumptuous in overturning the decision of patent office experts by reconstructing, in hindsight, how Marconi must have relied on someone else in creating an apparatus that concededly no other inventor had yet assembled. In an obvious slap at the Chief Justice, Frankfurter found no excuse for reversal simply "because a judge of unusual capacity for understanding scientific matters is able to demonstrate by a process of intricate ratiocination that any one could have drawn precisely the inferences that Marconi drew."[33]

Rutledge agreed with Frankfurter but was not comfortable with Frankfurter's response. Stone was the only patent law expert on the Court, and Rutledge must have sensed, as Frankfurter's remark implied, that a majority was simply deferring to the chief's analysis. But the newest justice— who had experience in writing patent cases on the Court of Appeals and was not simply going to yield to Stone—would not be party to a cheap shot. "I cannot quite swallow the manner of Frankfurter's opinion," he wrote to the chief. The junior justice wrote his own comprehensive rebuttal of Stone's opinion, explaining with considerable eloquence the evolution of wireless telegraphy in a way that showed Marconi's contribution to have been truly "inventive."[34]

WILEY RUTLEDGE knew that he had not written very much in comparison with his colleagues during his first half-term, so as the Court adjourned for the summer he wrote to Chief Justice Stone: "I do not want to allow the end of my first term here to pass without expressing to you my deep and sincere appreciation for the very great kindness and courtesy which you have shown to me in my period as a novitiate. . . . I have something of a feeling that I have not done my full share here this spring. . . . I hope to be able to function more efficiently and effectively in the fall than I have up to now."[35]

The apology had a basis in fact. Rutledge had not been willing to jump entirely into a swamp of court work. He spent hours writing to friends and enjoying visitors, especially former students in the military who were passing through Washington. From his clerk's perspective, "everybody who ever lived in Iowa came through those chambers." Edna Lingreen became so concerned that she would sometimes protect her boss by telling a friend of his who simply dropped by, even someone from out of town, that the justice was in conference—when he was not. "He will be *so* sorry to miss you," she would add. Lingreen explained her intervention by noting that Rutledge had so much work to do, and that he simply did not know how to terminate a conversation, believing that doing so would be rude. She acknowledged that visits from friends were the justice's favorite recreation—clearly his principal "refreshment"—but she justified her actions by her belief that Rutledge must have known what was going on and "never reprimanded" her. And many callers, she would add, did get through the Lingreen gate.[36]

The new justice gave prime time not only to visitors but to a whirlwind of public appearances. There were dinners—even small ones, such as those for Kappa Beta Pi and the Palaver Club—as well as law school moot courts. The president invited Wiley and Annabel to a church service. The Librarian of Congress invited them to a concert. And sundry organizations competed to honor the new justice at breakfasts, lunches, and receptions. But the real killer was speaking engagements: more than twenty during the justice's first eight months, ten of which occurred before the Court adjourned in June. His clerk recalls being "a pest badgering him about accepting" so many. "How," Brudney would ask his boss, "can you possibly take on another obligation?" To which the justice would reply, "These are my friends, to whom I owe such things." By this Rutledge meant "a moral kind of thing"—an obligation of friendship that added speech after speech to those he would have believed were institutionally required of any new justice. And of course, Wiley Rutledge loved making speeches.[37]

Beginning in late February 1943, Rutledge addressed the New York City chapter of the State University of Iowa Alumni Association and the federal judicial conference for the District of Columbia, followed in March by an appearance before a joint gathering of the Women's Bar and the National Association of Women Lawyers in Washington. In early April, Rutledge spoke to a Washington gathering of his legal fraternity, Phi Alpha Delta; and later that month he traveled to St. Louis for speeches to the local Bar Association, the League of Women Voters, and the Campus Y.M.C.A., returning to Washington for a luncheon address the next day to the Federal Bar Association. In May he spoke at the banquet for the law review at George Washington University and prepared extensive remarks for the annual meeting of the American Law Institute in Philadelphia, which Circuit Judge Herbert F. Goodrich had to present because Court business kept Rutledge in Washington.[38]

Once the Court adjourned in June and Jean Ann graduated from high school, the family—minus the father—left for Boulder, where Rutledge would join them a month later after what he called his "Chautauqua tour." From Minneapolis, where the Minnesota State Bar was honoring the judges of the Eighth Circuit, he traveled to the annual meeting of the Chicago Bar Association, where the lawyers toasted him with original verses about "Rutledge J." set to the tune of "There Is a Tavern in the Town." Next he visited the State Bar of Texas in Houston, then went through St. Louis to Iowa City, where he participated in the university's summer lecture series, spoke to his old friends at Rotary, and addressed Professor Rollin Perkins's Peace Officers Short Course. Even before he began this trek, the justice seemed "punch drunk" with fatigue, his secretary wrote to a former student of Rutledge. "I was . . . probably as tired as I have ever been in my life," Rutledge later admitted.[39]

Rutledge came, finally, to Denver for a speech to a conference of U.S. attorneys, after which he joined Annabel and the children for a rest—just enough to ready himself for the trip a month later to Chicago for his promised address to the annual meeting of the American Bar Association. That done, Rutledge interrupted his final weeks in Colorado with speeches to the Kiwanis Club of Denver and to the State Bar Association in Colorado Springs before returning to Washington by way of Iowa City in time for a late September lunch with the Federal Bar Association—this time, it appears, without having to speak. In the meantime, Mary Lou remained in Boulder to spend her junior year at the University of Colorado, while Annabel traveled to Bloomington with Jean Ann, who was entering Indiana University as a freshman. Rutledge and his family would continue this pattern for the next several years.[40]

To some audiences, such as the peace officers meeting in Iowa City and the U.S. attorneys gathered in Denver, the justice limited his remarks to the particular vocations at hand. He urged the prosecutors, for example, to put themselves "in the position of the judge who has to pass sentence," remembering always in seeking the death penalty that "once executed it is irrevocable."[41] On most occasions after joining the Court, however, Rutledge's public speeches addressed the war, the structure of the eventual peace, and ultimately the nation's postwar foreign policy—themes, as we shall see later, that he preached about relentlessly.

FIFTEEN

Denaturalized Citizenship, West Coast Curfew, and Japanese-American Internment

By the time Justice Byrnes resigned, the Court had substantially come together in sustaining congressional authority, under the commerce clause, to enact the New Deal economic program. So-called substantive due process, crafted to protect property against government regulation, was dead.[1] Justice Rutledge thus came to the Court at a time when its jurisprudential focus had largely shifted from property rights to individual rights—including the rights of enemies in wartime—for which the New Deal offered no particular policy.

Indeed, the war itself forced resolution of many new issues: denaturalization and deportation of sundry communists and Nazi sympathizers; the curfew, then internment, of West Coast Japanese aliens and Japanese-Americans; the prosecution of war crimes and other offenses before military tribunals; and a variety of cases on the selective service, price controls, and labor disputes. First Amendment issues were another significant chapter in the Supreme Court's work. And other amendments in the Bill of Rights shaped federal criminal procedure—and the Supreme Court docket —day by day. There was an additional, related concern: the Court battled frequently over whether criminal defendants in state courts were entitled to the protection of the federal Bill of Rights, or instead some lesser standard. On the flip side, in both civil and criminal cases the justices considered demands for access to federal courts and federal law in lieu of state proceedings. The Court also had to evaluate in many contexts the standards for judicial review of federal agency decision making. There were major issues under the commerce clause, especially the authority of states to tax transactions in interstate commerce. Finally, significant equal protection concerns arose—race, gender, voting—that presaged developments in the Warren Court a few years later.

The Court thus struggled with eight major areas overall, and in each year on the Court Justice Rutledge dealt with several of these. To make the presentation here more coherent than a sequential—and thus disjointed—treatment of the issues would offer, the remaining chapters are organized primarily by reference to these areas, not to the calendar, beginning with an update on the justice's judicial philosophy.

WE HAVE SEEN that from his Court of Appeals days Wiley Rutledge followed his "hunches" when deciding novel issues loaded with difficult value judg-ments. But what, more specifically, were the judicial values that informed those hunches, showing him the directions, in his words, toward which the "great landmarks" of the law "point ahead"?[2] In a lecture at the University of Kansas in December 1946, Rutledge elaborated on the "legal faith" that guided him. Although written almost five years after Rutledge joined the Supreme Court, it reflected his career-long beliefs and thus can serve as a backdrop for understanding his work from the beginning as FDR's last-appointed justice.

Fundamentally, Rutledge began, the universe had "moral meaning," discernible ultimately not "by philosophy or by reason or by science" but by "faith." Faith brings understanding "more felt than thought," he noted. Thus, a person who employs faith (here, he paraphrased St. Paul) will use "the evidence of things unseen, the assurance of things as yet unrealized" to make primarily "intuitive" choices among the many "irreconcilables" that confront us when we decide what "to live by and to die by." Reason, he acknowledged, will add "in some measure its supporting brace," but at bottom intuition informed by faith will identify the moral order.[3]

Faith led Rutledge to perceive, and to feel, the human "soul" that brings both aspiration for freedom—for the mastery of one's fate—and a yearning for the company and approval of others. This very aspiring for freedom, Rutledge believed, refuted any suggestion that a person is a "wholly electrical being" in a "mechanical" universe; and the very yearning for community, he observed, belied any notion that one could live among others without yielding a measure of one's treasured freedom "as the price of social living."[4] Fortunately, according to Rutledge, the conflicting "instincts for freedom and for social living" combined to generate a third, "accommodating instinct" not only powerful enough to sustain a desired community but also equitable enough to demand a *just* community. Over time, moreover, the "ideas of justice" continually "grow and change," he stressed, such that "justice too is a part of life, of evolution, of man's spiritual growth." Indeed, "justice is a matter of religion, of outlook upon the universe as a whole." Operationally, therefore, abstract ideas of justice, drawn from "a variety of creeds" in the community, become "concrete" norms folded into enforceable laws—never "eternally fixed and immutable, perfect and complete," but "ever-changing, imperfect and incomplete."[5]

The laws in our society change, noted Rutledge, not through imposition by the "state"—not by destroying "the freedoms to think and to believe as one's lights and conscience" give direction—but through desires of the "community" itself pressing ideas of justice "at odds" with the prevailing law. To be "worthy" of one's legal responsibility, therefore, a legislator or judge—each a lawmaker—must "catch the vision of what has come or will come and sense the moment of its common acceptance, from out the realm of abstract justice into the area of realizable application." How is this accomplished? In words applicable to constitutional as well as statutory and common law decision making, Rutledge suggested that legislator and judge alike have "instruments for objective measurement." Each "has great and concrete traditions to guide him. He has the experience of his fathers." On the other hand, "so far as the circumstances of his time may differ from theirs, calling for different action, he has the prevailing sense of his community to go by."[6] This movement

> is a thing not always easy, but neither impossible, to measure. Not his own will or desire, therefore, but his measurement made to the best of his whole ability of the balance between long-accepted tradition and prevailing demand, must determine his course. Thus and only thus may we have a government of the living law and not a government of the personal whims of men or of law archaic and outworn.[7]

The "prevailing sense" of the community is never monolithic, let alone static, however. Because legislators typically respond to political majorities and judges are commonly left to protect individuals, their respective choices between "long-accepted tradition" and "prevailing demand" are likely to differ at crucial moments, depending on whose demand, it is thought, should be honored. Ultimately, therefore, the last word must go to one decider or the other, and the Constitution gives it to the judges. Theirs, ultimately, is the responsibility to protect society against outworn laws and whimsical legislation, using the "great landmarks" of that document to constrain as well as to free government action.

Despite final constitutional authority in the judiciary, it is important to recall that Justice Rutledge since his early days as an academic (and visibly during his support of the Court-packing bill) expected federal judges to defer to democratic, legislative judgments on the rights of property—a view he would assert consistently as a justice—while standing firm against majoritarian overreaching of the individual. Concurring separately when the Court upheld government authority to issue rent control orders under the Emergency Price Control Act of 1942, Rutledge went out of his way to make the point clearly:

> Since in these cases the rights involved are rights of property, not of personal liberty or life as in criminal proceedings, the consequences, though serious, are not of the same moment under our system. . . . It is in this respect perhaps that our basic [constitutional] law, following the common law, most clearly places the rights to life and to liberty above those of property.[8]

In declaring his legal faith, Wiley Rutledge never mentioned "God," but his very use of the word "faith," his allusion to a Christian scripture, and his emphasis on the human "soul" reflected belief in an ultimate, creative force in the universe. And that force, in his view, was benevolent, inspiring human aspiration and yearning which at their most fundamental embraced freedom, community, justice. He was, still, the Christian humanist. ∠

AMERICANS HAVE FEARED European leftist radicals—anarchists, socialists, communists—since the 1870s. More recently, during the "Red Scare" of 1918–20 after the First World War, the Supreme Court endorsed that concern, sustaining convictions under newly adopted Espionage and Sedition Acts that criminalized not only "support or favor" of a wartime enemy but also virtually any utterance reflecting disloyalty to the United States. The Court of the 1940s, however, became far more protective of individual rights. Twice—over the dissents of Stone, Roberts, and Frankfurter—the justices rejected the government's efforts to hold in contempt of court, and then to deport, the Australian-born labor leader Harry Bridges, an alleged communist.[9] And in 1943 the Court, with the same dissenters, struck down a court order revoking the naturalized citizenship of an avowed communist, William Schneiderman.

In *Schneiderman v. United States*, a federal district judge in California, sustained by the U.S. Court of Appeals for the Ninth Circuit, revoked the citizenship of a naturalized American—an admitted member of the Communist Party—twelve years after naturalization. The judge held that Schneiderman had "illegally procured" his citizenship, because at the time of naturalization and during the five years preceding it, he had not, in the words of the governing statute, "behaved as a man of good moral character, attached to the principles of the Constitution of the United States, and well disposed to the good order and happiness of the same."[10]

Writing for a 6 to 3 majority after an argument featuring Wendell Willkie as Schneiderman's counsel, Justice Murphy reversed. Assuming, without deciding, that Congress could authorize the courts to reexamine a final judgment of naturalized citizenship, or at least could do so upon a finding of fraud, the majority held that the government had not met the statutory burden of proof limiting revocation to "'clear, unequivocal, and convincing evidence'" that citizenship had been illegally procured, fraudulently or otherwise. More specifically, Murphy opined, the issue was "behavior" not belief, and the "behavior requirement" must be construed in accord with "'the theory and practice of our Government'" that grants substantial leeway to "'freedom of conscience.'" One's adherence to a political party, Murphy observed, did not necessarily imply adherence "unqualifiedly to all of its platforms or asserted principles." And in any event, the trial record supported Schneiderman's denial that "he or the Party advocated the overthrow of the Government of the United States by force and violence." Nothing in the record indicated that he had ever been "connected with any overt illegal or violent action or with any disturbance of any sort." Moreover, the record indicated that in 1927, when Schneiderman had been naturalized, the Communist Party of the United States "desired to achieve its purpose by peaceful and democratic means," and justified the use of force and violence only in two extreme situations: "as a method of preventing an attempted forcible counter-overthrow once the Party had obtained control in a peaceful manner," and "as a method of last resort to enforce the majority will if at some indefinite future time because of peculiar circumstances constitutional or peaceful channels were no longer open." The government, accordingly, had not proved illegal procurement of citizenship with evidence of the required high quality.[11]

Justice Douglas, however, was unwilling to assume the validity of the Nationality Act as a way of allowing reversal on the facts. Concurring separately, he pointed out that the statute provided a number of conditions precedent to naturalization; that the statute did not expressly exclude communists from consideration (as it did anarchists and polygamists); and that the court's naturalization order presumably incorporated a finding that the conditions of "good moral character," attachment to "the principles of the Constitution," and disposition to the "good order and happiness" of the United States had been met. The naturalization order accordingly was valid, wrote Douglas, absent a finding of "fraud," the only lawful basis for setting aside a judgment. There was no need, therefore, to probe "the weight of the evidence underlying the finding."[12]

Concurring separately, Justice Rutledge went further than Douglas, emphasizing that Congress had intruded upon the courts' judicial power under

Article III of the Constitution by purporting to authorize reopening a naturalization judgment. His attack on the statute was powerful:

> An applicant might be admitted today upon evidence satisfying the court he had complied with all requirements. That judgment might be affirmed on appeal and again on certiorari here. Yet the day after, or ten years later, any district judge could overthrow it, on the same evidence, if it was conflicting or gave room for contrary inferences, or on different evidence all of which might have been presented to the first court.

> If this is the law and the right the naturalized citizen acquires, his admission creates nothing more than citizenship in attenuated, if not suspended, animation. He acquires but prima facie status, if that. . . .

> No citizen with such a threat hanging over his head could be free. If he belonged to "off-color" organizations or held too radical or, perhaps, too reactionary views, for some segment of the judicial palate, when his admission took place, he could not open his mouth without fear his words would be held against him. For whatever he might say or whatever any such organization might advocate could be hauled forth at any time to show "continuity" of belief from the day of his admission, or "concealment" at that time. Such a citizen would not be admitted to liberty. His best course would be silence or hypocrisy. This is not citizenship. Nor is it adjudication.[13]

Three terms later, having rejected other efforts to revoke the naturalized citizenship of German-Americans who actively supported the Third Reich,[14] the Court came across a revocation it could approve in the case of Paul Knauer, a "leading voice" of the German-American Bund. The evidence showed that Knauer had sworn falsely in renouncing Hitler and taking an oath of allegiance to the United States, a fraud that would vitiate the judgment conferring naturalized citizenship even under Justice Douglas's concurring theory in *Schneiderman*. Joined by Murphy, Rutledge dissented on the ground that naturalized citizenship could never be revoked, except for actions "taking place afterward." In concluding that even a fraudulent judgment conferring citizenship could not be opened, Rutledge cited the plain language of the Constitution itself. Apart from eligibility for the presidency, which is limited to native-born Americans, he stressed, there are not "two classes of citizens, one superior, the other inferior." According to Rutledge, "the power to naturalize is not the power to denaturalize. The act of admission must be taken as final, for any cause which may have existed at that time." There is no room under the Constitution for a class of citizens that is "conditional, timorous and insecure because blanketed with the threat that some act or conduct, not amounting to forfeiture for others, will be taken retroactively to show that some prescribed condition had not been fulfilled." The justice concluded: "If this means that some or even many disloyal foreign-born citizens cannot be deported, it is better so than to place so many loyal ones in inferior status. And there are other effective methods for dealing with those who are disloyal, just as there are for such citizens by birth." Three terms later Justice Rutledge, again joined only by Murphy, was concurring on the same ground—the Constitution does not countenance denaturalization "under any circumstances"—when a fractured majority joined to overturn a default judgment which had revoked the naturalized citizenship of another leader of the German-American Bund.[15]

THE COURT'S protective concern for citizenship did not transfer easily to Japanese-Americans in the years after Pearl Harbor. In June 1943, in *Hirabayashi v. United States*, the Court resolved criminal charges against Gordon Hirabayashi, an American citizen and university student born to Japanese immigrants in Seattle. He had been convicted of violating two orders issued in the spring of 1942 by Lieutenant General John L. DeWitt, the Pacific Coast military commander, in furtherance of a presidential executive order approved by Congress. One DeWitt order imposed a curfew on every person of Japanese ancestry who lived within large coastal sections of California, Oregon, and Washington which the general designated as "military areas." A second series of orders, called "exclusion orders," required all such persons to leave their homes and report to an assembly center as a "preliminary step" to relocation and internment by the government.[16]

Hirabayashi contended that Congress had unconstitutionally delegated to the military commander its legislative authority to impose the curfew, and that in any event the Fifth Amendment prohibited discrimination "between citizens of Japanese descent and those of other ancestry." In rejecting the first argument, Chief Justice Stone wrote for a unanimous Court that Congress itself had "contemplated and authorized" DeWitt's curfew order as a means of enforcing the president's executive order; and thus that "no unlawful delegation of legislative power" had occurred.[17] As to the discrimination issue, Stone again spoke for all the justices. Congress and the president, he wrote, had a "wide scope" for exercising their "judgment and discretion" over the "choice of means" for implementing the war power, and thus, "at a time of threatened air raids and invasion by the Japanese forces," the court should evaluate Hirabayashi's Fifth Amendment rights under a highly deferential test, namely:

whether in the light of all the facts and circumstances there was any substantial basis for the conclusion . . . that the curfew as applied was a protective measure necessary to meet the threat of sabotage and espionage which would substantially affect the war effort and which might reasonably be expected to aid a threatened enemy invasion.[18]

Even though the Fifth Amendment contained no equal protection clause, Stone conceded that legislative discrimination based on race alone might be serious enough to violate due process. But given the "facts and circumstances" in this "particular war setting," he concluded, "[w]e cannot close our eyes to the fact, demonstrated by experience, that in time of war residents having ethnic affiliations with an invading enemy may be a greater source of danger than those of a different ancestry." Stone wrote that espionage by persons sympathetic to the Japanese government had been "particularly effective in the surprise attack on Pearl Harbor"; that of the "126,000 persons of Japanese descent in the United States," approximately 112,000 were concentrated around Seattle, Portland, and Los Angeles; and that "social, economic and political conditions"—code words for legalized racial discrimination of various sorts—had "intensified their solidarity" and "in large measure prevented their assimilation." This solidarity, Stone observed, was evidenced by the attendance of many children of Japanese parents at "Japanese language schools" in addition to the public schools, and by the attendance of as many as 10,000 of these children at schools in Japan "for all or part of their education." Accordingly, the chief concluded, "we cannot reject as unfounded the judgment of the military authorities and of Congress that there were disloyal members of that population, whose number and strength could not be precisely and quickly ascertained" and "separately dealt with." Indeed, "it is not for any court to sit in review of the wisdom" of legislative and executive action or to "substitute its judgment" for those charged with implementing the war power. The deferential test was met. The curfew order must be sustained.[19]

Finally, the Chief Justice concluded, because Hirabayashi received concurrent three-month sentences for violating the curfew and the exclusion orders, the Court, in sustaining the curfew, had "no occasion" to consider the redundant conviction and sentence for violating the potentially more intrusive exclusion order.[20] He thus ignored the fact that Hirabayashi would be left with a criminal record showing two convictions, not one.[21]

Justice Douglas concurred separately. He was untroubled by imposing a curfew, or even temporary detention, on all Japanese-Americans. "[W]here the peril is great and the time is short," he wrote, "temporary treatment on a group basis may be the only practicable expedient. . . . [S]peed and dispatch may be of the essence." Then, extending his discussion to evacuation and detention, Douglas suggested that after compliance with the exclusion order, but only after compliance, Hirabayashi and others might have an administrative or a habeas corpus remedy that would allow them to gain freedom by proving their loyalty—an imperfect remedy, he recognized, but one not foreclosed by the Court's ruling.[22]

Initially, Justice Wiley Rutledge—and no other—joined Douglas, who in his first draft had included language even more deferential to the military, at least in tone, than the chief's. Douglas emphasized that a country, in waging war "to win," cannot second-guess "the decisions of its generals," and that a "nation which can require the individual to give up his freedom and lay down his life . . . certainly can demand these lesser sacrifices from its other citizens."[23]

Justice Murphy, alone among the justices, had reserved decision at the conference and soon circulated a dissent based primarily on the lack of evidence that Japanese-Americans were generally disloyal. But as Peter Irons has documented in his brilliant study, *Justice at War*, Justice Murphy began to have second thoughts about speaking as a lone dissenter. He may have responded more to gentle nudges from Justice Reed stressing judicial precedent than to Justice Frankfurter's accusation that Murphy was portraying his colleagues as "behaving like the enemy." In any event, Murphy eventually turned his dissent into a concurrence. He retained paragraphs emphasizing that "[d]istinctions based on color and ancestry are utterly inconsistent with our traditions and ideals"; that the treatment of Japanese-Americans bore "a melancholy resemblance to the treatment accorded to members of the Jewish race in Germany and other parts of Europe"; and that the curfew order was at "the very brink of constitutional power." But Murphy concluded, finally, that the "provisions of the Constitution protecting essential liberties" must yield to the military's reasonable conclusion that individual determinations of disloyalty, before imposition of a curfew, could not have been made "without delay that might have had tragic consequences."[24]

Murphy's law clerk at the time reportedly believed that if any other justice had signed on to Murphy's dissent, he would not have changed.[25] And Rutledge seemed tempted to do so.[26] Ultimately, however, Rutledge went out on his own, removing his name from Douglas's concurrence and writing a brief concurrence, emphasizing disagreement with an implication in Stone's opinion that neither Douglas nor Murphy expressly addressed. Stone had left room for due process review of a military commander's exercise of discretion in wartime. But other language in his opinion supplied by Justice Black—stating that it was "not for any court to sit in review of the wisdom" of a military judgment—seemed inconsistent with any enforce-able protection of civil liberties in a wartime case, unless the military itself decided to offer the protection.[27] That was an absolutist proposition Rutledge could not accept, so he wrote one paragraph, in part, as follows:

> I concur in the Court's opinion, except for the suggestion . . . that the courts have no power to review any action a military officer may "in his discretion" find it necessary to take with respect to civilian citizens in military areas or zones, once it is found that an emergency has created the conditions requiring . . . some degree of military control short of suspending habeas corpus. . . . The officer of course must have wide discretion and room for [his] operation. But it does not follow there may not be bounds beyond which he cannot go and, if he oversteps them, that the courts may not have power to protect the civilian citizen.[28]

It is interesting to note that Rutledge initially drafted a longer concurrence expressing " 'strong sympathy with Mr. Justice Murphy's views' " and calling General DeWitt's order " 'a racial discrimination only war's highest emergency could sustain' " and " 'something which approaches the ultimate stain on democratic institutions constitutionally established.' "[29] But Rutledge receded in favor of the one point he published, confined as narrowly as possible to the legal question presented.

Rutledge truly had been torn. Before the Court announced *Hirabayashi* and a companion curfew case, *Yasui v. United States*, he wrote to the chief: "I have had more anguish over this case than any I have decided, save possibly one death case in the Ct. of Appeals.' " Several months before the surprise attack on Pearl Harbor, as noted earlier, Rutledge had acknowledged to Willard Wirtz, with respect to those who advocated violent overthrow of the government, that "undemocratic controls" might become necessary when the danger appeared to have become so great that our democracy otherwise might not survive. He worried that the "danger with conceding this" would be a tendency to take such action too early.[30] But on the trial record in *Hirabayashi*—informed more by "judicial notice" than fact—Rutledge was willing to accept at least one undemocratic control. As a way of protecting against espionage and sabotage, a racially discriminatory curfew could be imposed in wartime on a population that consisted mostly of loyal Japanese-Americans.

Insight into the justice's thought process is available from remarks at the time to his law clerk, Victor Brudney, in later years a distinguished professor of law at Rutgers and then Harvard. While at the solicitor general's office before his clerkship, Brudney had been assigned to examine the constitutionality of a particular aspect of the president's executive order that did not involve the problems suggested by General DeWitt's directives. In the course of his inquiry, Brudney learned that the FBI, like Attorney General Biddle, had expressed serious doubts about the necessity for imposing sweeping restrictions that applied, without differentiation, to all persons of Japanese ancestry. Brudney suggested to the justice that the Court might benefit from receiving that FBI analysis. More in astonishment than anger, Rutledge confronted his clerk (as Brudney recalled the words):

> What do you think you are doing? Don't you understand that there are only nine of us sitting here, and that the generals have said this [curfew] is necessary for the preservation and security of the country? Pearl Harbor was attacked and more may happen! Who are we to question this? What makes you think any of us will question this? Too much is at stake, and we are too far removed from the realities. Cut it out!

Rutledge's anguish about the discrimination against mostly loyal Japanese-Americans was real, but his inclination to trust military judgment during wartime—while clinging, theoretically, to the Court's right of judicial review—controlled his judgment in *Hirabayashi*. Rutledge wrote from his head in concurring separately to provide assurance that the courts had the power and responsibility to protect against overreaching by generals; but he emoted to Brudney from the heart, revealing fear of further attack on the mainland and judicial incompetence to second-guess military necessity. "This was well before the tides had turned in the war," recalled Brudney, "and the pressure in these matters was simply unbelievable."[31]

SIXTEEN MONTHS after *Hirabayashi*, on October 11, 1944, a day when the *Washington Post* printed an eight-column headline, "Americans Blast 38 Ships off Japan," the Supreme Court began hearing argument in *Korematsu v. United States*. This was the infamous case in which a 6-to-3 majority upheld the evacuation and exclusion from their homes, and implicitly the indefinite internment, of 112,000 West Coast residents of Japanese ancestry—including 70,000 native-born American citizens—without regard to their loyalty to the United States. *Korematsu* resolved the issue left open in *Hirabayashi*, and upheld the constitutionality of the portions of General DeWitt's exclusion orders requiring persons of Japanese ancestry to leave the designated "Military Areas" and gather at "assembly centers."[32] Although the Court's ruling went no further, it was apparent that almost all those "assembled" would leave under military control for indefinite detention at ten "relocation centers" (commonly called "internment"

Newspaper headlines announcing Japanese-American relocation.
(Franklin D. Roosevelt Library, Hyde Park, New York, ID 7420 [393])

camps) spread from California to Arkansas.[33] The only limitation came in a companion case, *Ex Parte Endo*, where the Court unanimously granted a Japanese-American woman's demand for release from a relocation center largely because the Justice Department conceded she was "a loyal and law-abiding citizen."[34]

Here, then, is the Korematsu story. On May 30, 1942, a police officer in San Leandro, California, stopped a young man who claimed to be of Spanish-Hawaiian origin and who produced an obviously altered draft registration card in the name of "Clyde Sarah." He soon acknowledged that he was Fred Korematsu, age twenty-three, occupation welder, born of Japanese parents in Oakland. He was arrested and jailed for violating Exclusion Order No. 34, one of a series that required everyone of Japanese ancestry in the prescribed military area to leave as a "protection against espionage and sabotage." No one ever questioned Korematsu's loyalty to the United States. In September, the district court found Korematsu guilty of a misdemeanor and entered an order placing him on probation for five years. Despite granting bail, the judge watched helplessly while military police seized Korematsu as he left the courtroom and escorted the young man to an assembly or relocation center (it is not clear which) pending his appeal.[35]

At the end of March 1943, the U.S. Court of Appeals for the Ninth Circuit certified Korematsu's case (along with *Hirabayashi* and *Yasui*) to the Supreme Court. While the two curfew cases were ready for review on the merits, the Court of Appeals posed only a procedural question in *Korematsu*: whether the district judge's probation order, in which he had failed to impose either a fine or a prison sentence, amounted to a "final decision" ripe for appeal. The Supreme Court answered yes and returned *Korematsu* to the Court of Appeals for consideration on the merits. Relying exclusively on *Hirabayashi*, the appellate court affirmed the district court's order.[36]

The government's war power rationale for sustaining the exclusion order was the same as its justification for the curfew, but to those who suffered the consequences, the real-world sequence of events—compulsory evacuation from one's home, temporary detention at an assembly center, then indefinite confinement at a relocation center, without any finding of individual wrongdoing—felt exponentially more outrageous than a curfew. When *Korematsu* reached the Supreme Court again, the solicitor general, Charles Fahy, tried to duck the reality of confinement by emphasizing during oral argument that the only issue was evacuation—that is, Korematsu's conviction solely for refusing to leave the military area. Questions of detention, he stressed, were not before the Court. Korematsu's counsel Charles Horsky, a volunteer ACLU attorney formerly with the solicitor general's office, took the opposite tack: compelled evacuation inescapably embraced an order to report for temporary detention, followed by indefinite confinement; realistically, Horsky emphasized, there was but one, nonseverable order at issue.[37]

Because the Supreme Court did not transcribe oral arguments at the time, the only record of the *Korematsu* argument was the handwritten notes of Colonel Archibald King, the judge advocate general's observer. King's record shows that the advocates stuck hard to their positions while the justices tried to pin down whether confinement was part of the case. Under pressure, Fahy acknowledged that temporary detention was necessary to facilitate evacuation. But a temporary hold would open the door to "permanent detention," Justice Jackson observed. And, Justice Rutledge interjected, "[a]ssuming all that you say, . . . should not the order have given some assurance of the temporary character of the detention?" All Fahy could reply was that this suggested limitation would impose "too strict a rule" on needed military flexibility.[38]

In conference, according to notes preserved by Douglas and Murphy, the Chief Justice pressed the government's view. Only violation of the order to leave the area was at issue, Stone argued; General DeWitt's relocation order had not yet been invoked. Applying the traditional understanding that a court decides only issues squarely presented, Stone was saying that the most severe deprivation, relocation, was not before the Court and would have to await the next case. Stone was wrong here. The exclusion order itself not only required evacuation from the area but also authorized transfer to a relocation center. Moreover, Stone's distinction between failure to leave and relocation ignored the intermediate step of temporary detention for weeks or even months at an assembly center, usually a racetrack or fairground that housed people in "converted horse stalls." In any event, Black, Reed, and Frankfurter joined their chief at conference, while Roberts, Douglas, Murphy, and Jackson called his hair splitting disingenuous; they perceived a case, fundamentally, of unconstitutional confinement. There must have been more than a little tension—indeed, a moment of high drama on the nation's highest court—when the most junior justice, after the others had divided 4 to 4, was ready to speak. Announced Rutledge: "I had to swallow Hirabayashi. I didn't like it. At that time I knew if I went along with that order I had to go along with detention for [a] reasonably necessary time. Nothing but necessity would justify it." Because of Hirabayashi, he concluded, "I vote to affirm."[39]

Straightaway, Stone assigned the opinion to Black as the justice most likely to keep the majority intact. Initially, Justice Black made the task easier by proceeding from Stone's suspect premise—that only exclusion from the area was at issue. Then, relying on *Hirabayashi*, though acknowledging that exclusion was "a far greater deprivation" than a curfew, Black circulated an opinion sustaining the conviction for "remaining in a prohibited area," without reaching, as he put it, the "constitutional validity of the detention orders." The truth was, however, as Black soon recognized, the detention issue could not be rejected out of hand, because the exclusion order itself required everyone affected to gather at assembly centers as way stations intended "'to insure orderly evacuation and resettlement'" of Japanese-Americans. No one affected could leave the area to live instead with a cousin in Ohio or New Jersey.[40]

In subsequent drafts, therefore, Justice Black expressly acknowledged Korematsu's argument that the exclusion order embraced temporary, then indefinite, detention, and that these related deprivations should be treated as inextricable subsets of one unlawful order.[41] But Black himself continued to treat the three subsets as legally distinct and severable requirements, with only exclusion before the Court, untainted by any detention and thus justified by a modest extension of *Hirabayashi*.

Justice Black had circulated his first draft in early November. Almost immediately, Wiley Rutledge and Stanley Reed signed on without comment. In other chambers, however, Black's handiwork caused explosions. Justice Roberts saw the exclusion orders and war relocation program not as a sequence of legally severable steps of increasing severity but as a "single and indivisible" effort to convict and punish an American citizen "for not submitting to imprisonment in a concentration camp, based on his ancestry, and solely because of his ancestry, without evidence or inquiry concerning his loyalty and good disposition towards the United States"—a "clear violation of Constitutional rights." [42]

Justice Murphy saw the situation in similar terms, calling the exclusion a "fall[] into the ugly abyss of racism." But unlike Justice Roberts, who focused mainly on the majority's unwillingness to deal with internment, Murphy reviewed the use of the war power itself and concluded that the government had overreached. "The judicial test" under the war power, Murphy wrote, citing precedent more stringent than Stone's rather relaxed test in *Hirabayashi*, is "whether the deprivation is reasonably related to a public danger that is so 'immediate, imminent, and impending' as not to admit of delay and not to permit the intervention of ordinary constitutional processes to alleviate the danger." Murphy saw no such danger here that would preclude evaluation of Japanese-Americans "on an individual basis," since "nearly four months elapsed after Pearl Harbor before the first exclusion order was issued; nearly eight months went by until the last order was issued; and the last of these 'subversive' persons was not actually removed until almost eleven months had elapsed." He noted that the British had required only six months to examine the loyalty of 74,000 Germans and Austrians before "alien tribunals or hearing boards." [43]

Justice Jackson, who at conference had proclaimed, "'I stop with Hirabayashi,'" circulated a curious dissent. On the one hand, Jackson acknowledged the evils that Roberts and Murphy had cited, adding his own complaint that the record gave the Court insufficient information for reviewing the military order. But courts, he added, "never have any real alternative to accepting the mere declaration of the authority that issued the order that it was reasonably necessary from a military viewpoint." And if a court were to sustain a racially discriminatory military order under the due process clause, he wrote, that would be "a far more subtle blow to liberty than the promulgation of the order itself." Why? Because a military order, he said, "is not apt to last longer than the military emergency," whereas an approving court order "for all time" would validate the "principle of racial discrimination in criminal procedure" that would "lie[] about like a loaded weapon ready for the hand of any authority that can bring forward a plausible claim of an urgent need." Accordingly, Jackson seemed to be saying, the very likelihood of approving a military order that "may overstep the bounds" of the constitution is reason enough for the courts to forbear from passing in review. Rather than take the chance of legitimating an unconstitutional order that they are in no position to scrutinize, Jackson implied, the courts—for lack of information and expertise—should simply back off and permit the military to do its job.⁴⁴

That sounds like the doctrine of abstention, which would have left Korematsu to his plight. In his last paragraph, however, striking a Janus-like posture, Jackson did a right about-face and announced that he "would reverse the judgment and discharge the prisoner."⁴⁵ While he believed that he could not review the merits of a military judgment, he would not have the Court be a party to enforcing an order that facially violated constitutional principles. Therefore, because the military had sought a court's help by initiating the criminal proceeding, Jackson in effect would remove that proceeding from the criminal court's docket and, as a consequence, free Korematsu.

As a matter of law, of course, Justice Jackson did review a military judgment, for he voted to "reverse" Korematsu's conviction. Probably the only way he could have invoked an abstention rationale would have been by saying that the case presented a nonjusticiable political question, a result that would have left the young man entirely without protection aside from the military itself. But Jackson, in the end, was not going to tolerate what he believed would be a perverse outcome; he concluded that courts should not "execute a military expedient that has no place in law under the Constitution." In answer to Jackson, Justice Frankfurter filed a concurrence reminding that the war power is as much a provision of the Constitution as any other, and that "dialectic subtleties" should not be employed to avoid judicial review of its use.⁴⁶

Justice Douglas, in the meantime, was having second thoughts. He too had circulated a dissent emphasizing the inevitability of indefinite relocation once someone, like Korematsu, had been excluded from a military area and detained at an assembly center. To Douglas, therefore, Justice Black's opinion was deficient, first of all, in failing even to accept that temporary assembly, and thus at least some period of detention, was inherent in the exclusion order. Douglas recognized that Fred Korematsu had no lawful way of leaving the area without remaining for awhile against his will in an assembly center. Nor did Korematsu fall within one of the categories, such as the elderly, the infirm, or certain agricultural workers, who might qualify during the assembly period for exemption from relocation. But possibly because there was an escape route from assembly centers, at least for a few, leaving a theoretical break between assembly and relocation, Douglas offered Black a bargain: Douglas would withdraw his dissent if Black agreed to add a sentence. That sentence, while not acknowledging an inevitable link between steps one and three—exclusion and relocation—at least recognized, and justified, the tight link between steps one and two—exclusion and temporary detention. Douglas believed that the majority opinion would be disingenuous without accepting at least that reality, and he was prepared to retreat from his own view that relocation also was at issue if Black would cure the defect that Douglas had identified.[47]

Black agreed. "Some of the members of the Court," he wrote in words supplied by Douglas, "are of the view that evacuation and detention in an Assembly Center were inseparable." But, Black continued, quoting Douglas, even if that assembly process "was conceived as a part of the machinery for group evacuation[,] . . . any forcible measure" justified by "military imperative," such as the evacuation here, "must necessarily entail some degree of detention or restraint." This military necessity coupling evacuation with temporary detention was constitutional, as Douglas had indicated earlier in *Hirabayashi*, and approval of that coupling supplied for Douglas the missing legal piece required for candid approval of the exclusion order.[48]

But now the Chief Justice was not satisfied. He was troubled by Black's failure to state expressly that Korematsu's violation of the exclusion order did not necessarily expose him to indefinite detention under a relocation order. Stone was insistent here because Justice Roberts was now arguing forcefully in dissent the inevitability of relocation—the very point that Douglas had abandoned. Black recognized that Stone was still misreading the record. Exclusion and relocation were not legally separable any more than exclusion and assembly were; the exclusion order embraced all three. Black compromised nonetheless. Douglas did not object. And in the end Black wrote: "[Had Korematsu] left the prohibited area and gone to an assembly center we cannot say either as a matter of fact or law that his presence in that center would have resulted in his detention in a relocation center. . . . It will be time enough to decide the serious constitutional issues which petitioner seeks to raise when an assembly or relocation order is applied *or is certain to be applied to him*, and we have its terms before us." (Emphasis added.)[49]

At that point the coherency of Black's opinion unraveled. The terms of an assembly and relocation order *were* before the Court; the exclusion order that Korematsu violated inexorably triggered both kinds of detention, absent an identified, applicable exemption. Indeed, once Black compromised with Douglas by accepting that for some court members temporary detention was in the case, there was no credible way to ignore that indefinite relocation was also. Perhaps one could try to distinguish temporary assembly from indefinite relocation as meaningfully different in degree for constitutional purposes, but compulsory assembly for weeks or months in a horse stable, although temporary, hardly seems an insignificant detention. Possibly for this reason, therefore, Justice Black personally continued to avoid that kind of distinction. In fact, he began the majority opinion by stressing that any discrimination against "a single racial group" is "immediately suspect," requiring "the most rigid scrutiny." As a result, *Korematsu* can be cited today as seminal authority for holding racial classifications of any kind inherently suspect.[50] But despite requiring "rigid scrutiny," Justice Black did not apply his own test to determine the result here. Instead, he adopted a formalistic analysis that defined the problem away by shifting the focus from the terms of the DeWitt order to the terms of the charge against Korematsu.

Thus, for his own rationale in the majority opinion—in contrast with the alternative added to satisfy Douglas—Black steadfastly employed the fiction that no detention whatsoever was at issue, simply because the prosecutor, in charging Korematsu with failure to evacuate, had not added a count charging failure to assemble. Unlike Douglas, therefore, Black was never willing to confront the constitutional implications of Korematsu's failure to leave the area through the only legally available door marked, in practical effect, "detention exit." Black accordingly was willing to achieve the government's purpose by deciding a "hypothetical case," without legitimating what really had been going on.[51] Technically, therefore, one can say that the Supreme Court never upheld relocation and internment. But by acknowledging the finding by "some members of the Court" that "evacuation and detention in an Assembly Center were inseparable," the majority opinion effectively sustained major racial discrimination tantamount to imprisonment under the war power and—to use Justice Jackson's analogy—left a loaded weapon ready for use in the next case.

The decision to affirm the Court of Appeals came down 6 to 3 on December 18, 1944. The majority's unwillingness to deal with the reality that Fred Korematsu and thousands like him faced indefinite confinement was one of the saddest episodes in the Court's history. Because Korematsu was arrested and jailed immediately upon violating the evacuation order, there was no way under the majority's theory for him to test the relocation provision short of leaving home voluntarily for a relocation center. Furthermore, even without regard to relocation, the evacuation and assembly requirements were obviously much more intrusive than the curfew order in *Hirabayashi*. It was disingenuous for the majority to conclude, without elaboration, that the degree of deprivation was legally insignificant.

Finally, the Supreme Court, in accepting the "military necessity" of the internment program, failed to apply the high standard—"most rigid scrutiny"—that Justice Black announced for reviewing all government action based on racial classification. Instead, all members of the Court majority, even those who shared the Douglas view that detention, not just evacuation, was at issue, adhered to the more relaxed standard, deferential to the military, applied in *Hirabayashi*. As a result, the Court majority threw away the only tool that might have penetrated the government's case. Rigid scrutiny would have highlighted, as Justice Murphy spelled out in dissent, that General DeWitt had told a House Naval Affairs subcommittee, "I don't want any [persons of Japanese ancestry] here. They are a dangerous element. There is no way to determine their loyalty." (DeWitt's most succinct condemnation—"A Jap is a Jap"—was edited out of the hearing transcript.) Furthermore, in his Final Report on Evacuation of Japanese from the West Coast, dated June 5, 1943, but released in January 1944, General DeWitt had called all persons of Japanese descent "subversive." Also in that report, DeWitt had labeled the Japanese an "enemy race," unaffected even by "United States citizenship," since their "racial strains are undiluted." In sum, he believed there was no way to avoid wholesale evacuation and internment, because there was no way of separating the loyal from the disloyal "with any degree of safety" and "time was of the essence." The general's final report, therefore, when coupled with his other racially charged statements, formed a solid basis for reversal; the strong evidence of racial stereotyping that underlay the evacuation program gave sound reason to hold that the government had failed to sustain its heavy burden of justifying such a severe deprivation of liberty. Indeed, Solicitor General Fahy conceded at oral argument that a commanding general's personal hostility toward Japanese-Americans would not have been a sustainable basis for "military necessity" under the war power.

But Fahy was not entirely locked into a racist interpretation. Language in DeWitt's report allowed him to represent that DeWitt had based military necessity for mass evacuation not on racial stereotyping but on lack of time during the emergency to check thousands of individuals for loyalty. The Supreme Court majority bought that argument. Thus, in accepting Fahy's representation and deferring to DeWitt's military judgment, the majority rejected any need for more detailed factual findings to assure that DeWitt's racial attitudes did not determine "military necessity." Absent a stricter standard of review, however, the majority's reliance on Fahy was not surprising. Traditionally, the Court accords great deference to the representations of the solicitor general, who is understood to have a special obligation to the Court (in addition to the client) that generates, in turn, considerable trust from the justices. Sadly, however, the Justice Department knew at the time but withheld from the Court (over protestations by various department officials) that General DeWitt had documented military necessity for the evacuation and internment program with demonstrably false claims that Japanese-Americans had been signaling enemy ships with illegal radio transmitters on shore and conducting other subversive activities. Had this falsity been disclosed, more justices than the three who dissented might have questioned DeWitt's real motivations.

Forty years later, after learning about the withheld information, a federal district judge reversed Fred Korematsu's conviction upon reviewing his petition for writ of error *coram nobis* (error of fact). The judge also relied on the findings of a congressionally established Commission on Wartime Relocation and Internment of Civilians, which unanimously concluded in 1982 that internment had been premised not on military necessity but on "race prejudice, war hysteria and a failure of political leadership." Then in 1988, federal legislation awarded every internment camp survivor $20,000 and a national apology. But the real point should not be lost: even without regard to disclosures and remedies that came long after the *Korematsu* decision, one must say, looking back, that the Supreme Court—in ignoring its announced obligation to apply "most rigid scrutiny" to an "immediately suspect" racial classification—slipped badly. Roberts's and Murphy's dissents in particular, based on evidence available at the time, made that default quite clear.[52]

Throughout the circulation of draft opinions, Wiley Rutledge had remained silent.[53] He had signed on with Black before Douglas added the gloss linking exclusion to detention, even though he was aware from chambers research that detention, then relocation, was inherent in the exclusion order. Nor, once the detention issue was in the opinion, did Rutledge address the majority's purported severance of relocation from the case. Why was Wiley Rutledge so quick to vote for affirmance? And why, during all that was going on, did he watch passively, in contrast to his active participation in *Hirabayashi*?

The short answer is to take Rutledge at his word: when he agreed to join in *Hirabayashi*, he knew that he was deciding *Korematsu*. *Hirabayashi* and the first *Korematsu* case were argued the same day, May 11, 1943, less than three months after Rutledge joined the Court.[54] Although *Korematsu* at the time presented only the threshold question whether the defendant's probation order was a final, appealable decision, it was clear to all the justices that soon after the curfew challenge was resolved, the Court would have to deal with General DeWitt's exclusion order. It was true, of course, that Fred Korematsu was challenging constraints far more severe than a curfew. It also was true that Rutledge himself, concurring in *Hirabayashi*, had written of the courts' "power to protect the civilian citizen" when a military officer—though entitled to "wide discretion"—oversteps "bounds beyond which he cannot go."[55] But how is a court to discern such bounds?

Remember Rutledge's exclamation to Victor Brudney while discussing *Hirabayashi*: "Pearl Harbor was attacked and more may happen. Who are we to question this?" There was no satisfactory way, in Rutledge's view, to weigh the constitutional demands of civil liberty against the constitutional authority—and responsibility—to wage war. The "generals have said this [curfew] is necessary for the preservation and security of the country," Rutledge had stressed to Brudney.[56] How then, the justice would later have asked himself, can judges question the military judgment of generals who say that evacuation and relocation too are necessary?

The answer, of course, should have been that judges are in the business of weighing competing demands and values—in setting the "bounds" —in virtually an infinite variety of difficult situations, including those in wartime. The Constitution, as Rutledge himself well recognized, does not exempt the generals entirely from court scrutiny. Judges are duty-bound to declare when the military strays too far from constitutional values antithetical to the war power. Indeed, judges did so in the Second World War. Federal district courts ruled against the military in at least three cases challenging the exclusion of Nazi sympathizers from designated areas near the East Coast. And the Supreme Court itself struck down the continued use of martial law in Hawaii after Admiral Nimitz had testified that it was still necessary. In this connection, however, it is important to note that Justice Rutledge had not served in the military, so he did not bring to judicial review of General DeWitt's orders the healthy skepticism of command judgments shared by many former officers and enlisted personnel who have seen the military mind at work from the inside. Deference to the military probably came more easily to Rutledge than to many judges.[57]

It is not a stretch, moreover, to understand how an external threat— indeed, a bombing of American territory—would push the justice's alarm button, allowing him with profound "anguish" to accept a temporary suspension of civil liberty, however racially discriminatory it turned out to be, to protect our very soil, not just our institutions and way of life.[58] He had to know that many American people in the days following Pearl Harbor, especially on the West Coast, were terrified.[59] More fundamentally, he had written earlier in the year, for a symposium on constitutional rights in wartime, not only that "war is autocratic" but that the present war was "different" in "total scope" from all others in our history, requiring that society be mobilized more pervasively—with greater "alterations of power and liberty"—than ever before.[60] Wiley Rutledge, the civil libertarian, "couldn't bear the thought of those cases coming down," according to his law clerk at the time;[61] but Wiley Rutledge, the judge, was not about to interfere with the judgment of John DeWitt, the general.

In reality, of course, the relocation program was a political, not merely a military, decision. In large measure it bowed to the racial prejudice reflected in demands for internment by western governors and by Attorney General Earl Warren of California, who were loudly opposed to mere evacuation and uncontrolled Japanese-American migration inland. Rutledge, therefore, was not deferring simply to military judgment. He was deferring, more significantly, to the president, who ultimately was responsible for that judgment. Wiley Rutledge had profound, even reverential, regard for Franklin Roosevelt. Beginning with the Depression, and then during the war, Rutledge saw Roosevelt as a national savior, without whom our institutions themselves might have collapsed and our territory been overtaken. Rutledge believed that Roosevelt had kept our national life whole for the common people, and now Roosevelt was leading the nation—after Wilson's failed peace at Versailles—toward a second chance at a safe world order, if only the Axis powers could be defeated. Roosevelt had appointed Rutledge to the Supreme Court. At some level of consciousness, Wiley Rutledge was not going to turn his back on his president.[62]

There were other human factors affecting Rutledge. The two justices he had come to respect most were Stone and Black. He had enormous regard for the Chief Justice, a man with strong impulses to protect civil liberties, who so unhesitatingly saw the need to support the government's position first in *Hirabayashi*, then in *Korematsu*. Rutledge had occasionally disagreed with Stone and did not shrink from taking a position contrary to the chief's. But *Korematsu* was not a patent or an admiralty case. Without doubt Stone, twenty-two years Rutledge's senior, was a judicial father figure to the much younger, and newest, justice, who must have felt that kinship, and the wisdom of that senior judgment, in this case.[63]

Then there was Hugo Black. In contrast with Stone—born in New Hampshire, graduate of the élite Amherst college, Columbia law dean, and Republican attorney general—Black came from Alabama, earned a law degree from the state university, and served in the U.S. Senate as a passionate New Dealer. Eight years older than Rutledge, Black was more a brother than the elder to his newest colleague. They both came from modest beginnings, and from their earliest years both were Democrats. Most significantly for *Kore-*

matsu, Wiley Rutledge knew Hugo Black as a committed civil libertarian and had unqualified respect for Black as a person and a judge. And they had become friends. Stone, therefore, had been shrewd indeed to charge Black with the writing assignment, after the initial 5-to-4 vote in conference made absolutely clear that the Chief had to hold an uncomfortable Justice Rutledge.[64]

Did Rutledge later have regrets? All who see an indelible national stain when looking back at the relocation program, and who know of Justice Rutledge's strong commitment to civil liberties, are likely to assume that he must have wished, at some point, that he had voted to reverse in *Korematsu*. Rutledge, many would like to believe, must have come to realize—as Korematsu's counsel argued to the Court—that by May 1942, when the relevant exclusion order was issued, "all danger of Japanese invasion of the West Coast had disappeared." And some people like to say that a reflective justice like Rutledge, looking back to December 1944 when the Court issued its opinion, would have seen the folly of the relocation effort and wished that he had used the lesson of hindsight to pitch the decision toward preventing another such travesty.[65]

Rutledge, to be sure, would never have wished that he had trifled with the date as of which the Court was obliged to decide the case. On the other hand, given the evidence of racism in General DeWitt's Final Report—evidence that gave three of his colleagues enough pause to dissent (even without having new information, later disclosed, making clear how predominant that racial prejudice was)—Rutledge at least could have demanded a clearer record of what more precisely had motivated the general's orders before accepting their military necessity substantially on faith. But he did not. We may conclude, therefore, that even if Rutledge—taking stock—were to have accepted the factors affecting his vote that we have ascribed to his psyche, there is little reason to believe that he would have voted differently in *Korematsu* if given a second opportunity. Rutledge freely corresponded, and chatted with friends, about his agony over deciding particular cases. His papers at the Library of Congress are full of such talk. But not a word of this sort about *Korematsu* can be found, either in writing or in the memories of those available for interviews who knew him. There is the possibility, of course, that a man who had been a justice for less than two years when the Court decided *Korematsu* might have come out differently had the case reached him later, when his confidence as a justice had increased—say in early 1946, when he dissented from the war crimes convictions of Generals Yamashita and Homma. But if so, would he not have told somebody and left a record of that? We should add that Justice Rutledge died in 1949; he had less than five years after *Korematsu* to reflect, in contrast with Justice

Douglas, who in his memoirs many years later expressed regret at with-holding his dissent.[66]

There can be no doubt that the anguish Rutledge felt over *Hirabayashi* was even more intense when voting in *Korematsu*. Both decisions went against the very core of who he was and what he believed. From that per-spective perhaps we can understand his silence during Court deliberations after the conference. His pain, his very awareness of what he believed he had to do, may have short-circuited any contribution he otherwise might have made. He may have felt a paralysis of sorts, caught between the mili-tary necessity that he accepted and the inability of the Court, including Rutledge himself, to come up with an entirely convincing opinion sustain-ing it. But he took a stand nonetheless, acknowledging no legal distinction under the war power between a curfew and an evacuation and internment program that even the conservative Roberts and Jackson could discern. The question remains: Did Wiley Rutledge abandon principle out of loyalty to his president, or did he act instead with a kind of courage by coming to grips intellectually and emotionally with facts that he reluctantly had to agree created a military necessity justifying a constitutionally sound exception to his deepest instincts and principles? Many who knew him best would not hesitate to choose the second answer, but that he accepted Black's first draft, then a draft embracing a second theory, without engaging in the de-bate may say something else to others.

Korematsu demonstrated, if anything, that a virtually intractable situa-tion can arise where coherent, satisfactory resolution will be impossible, leading to repercussions from a judicial decision that can last for decades. And yet the judges, as even Justice Jackson finally agreed, cannot walk away. The irony for Wiley Rutledge, when viewed in hindsight, is that he partici-pated in a ruling of the sort that he would have berated, in other contexts, as another "*Dred Scott* decision."

SIXTEEN

First Amendment Freedoms

When Justice Rutledge took the bench in early 1943, the Court was seriously divided over government authority to adopt legislation that curtailed civil liberties. Two Roosevelt justices—Byrnes and Felix Frankfurter—as well as Justice Owen Roberts, had commonly deferred to what they believed were reasonable state-imposed limitations on First Amendment freedoms, much in the way that they deferred to congressional authority to regulate property. But three other Roosevelt justices—Black, Douglas, and Murphy—were holding the government to a substantially higher standard for restricting freedom of speech, the press, assembly, and religion. This left Chief Justice Stone, as well as the FDR justices Stanley Reed and Robert Jackson, as swing voters in what often became 5-to-4 decisions on First Amendment issues.

In 1941, for example, the Court had used the First Amendment to set aside, on a 5-to-4 vote, convictions for contempt of court stemming from remarks by newspaper officials and a labor leader, all of whom, it was said, had attempted to intimidate state court judges in pending proceedings.[1] A year later, however, again dividing 5 to 4, the Court subordinated freedom of speech and assembly to uphold an injunction against union picketing of a restaurant in violation of state antitrust law.[2] In the same term, moreover, in *Jones v. City of Opelika*,[3] the Court voted 5 to 4 to sustain convictions of Jehovah's Witnesses who had invoked their right to free exercise of religion to justify selling religious books and pamphlets without obtaining a municipal peddler's license and paying a related tax.

In *Opelika*, Chief Justice Stone and Justices Black, Douglas, and Murphy had dissented on several First Amendment grounds: speech, press, and religion.[4] And the last three justices had also written a separate dissenting statement[5]—a gratuitous mea culpa—admitting that they had erred two years earlier by joining the majority in *Minersville School District v. Gobitis*,[6] where the Court had sustained, over Stone's lone dissent, a law that required school children, including protesting Jehovah's Witnesses, to salute the flag contrary to their religious beliefs. Some administration advisors, therefore, particularly Attorney General Biddle and his assistant, Herbert Wechsler, had been committed to replacing Justice Byrnes with a justice who not only would help continue the Court's support for Roosevelt's liberal economic program but also would share Black's, Douglas's, and Murphy's developing commitment to the First Amendment. According to Wechsler, however, there was no discernible evidence that the president himself felt this particular concern.[7]

Rutledge's arrival on the Court had immediate impact. Less than a month after his investiture, the Court reheard *Opelika*, along with several similar cases for which the justices had granted certiorari in early 1943.[8] Voting 5 to 4 with Rutledge in the majority, the Court reversed course. Both in *Opelika* on rehearing and in a companion case, *Murdock v. Pennsylvania*, the Court invalidated the local license tax ordinances, as applied.[9] In another Jehovah's Witness case argued the same week, *West Virginia Bd. of Education v. Barnette*,[10] Rutledge's vote helped a new, 6-to-3 majority overrule the recent decision in *Gobitis*.[11] In an opinion by Justice Jackson, the Court used the First Amendment to invalidate a state requirement that schoolchildren salute the American flag. The new justice accordingly established himself early as a concerned protector of religious freedom.

On the March weekend before these cases were argued, Justice Frankfurter wrote a curious entry in his diary:

> After Conference, Brother Reed said to me he felt very unhappy by the indications of the state of mind of the new member of the Court as revealed by his attitude at the first Conference. Reed said he seemed to vote wrong on all the important issues, and wrong because "He is another one of these fellows who wants to do what he calls justice in the particular case without heeding the consequences in other situations not immediately before the Court, or in the general administration of justice." . . . I told Reed that . . . he ought not to be disappointed in Rutledge, that that was to be expected from him, that he is one of these men who fails to remember what Holmes said it was the first duty of a civilized man not to forget, namely, that he is not God. Rutledge evidently is one of these evangelical lads who confuses his personal desire to do good in the world with the limits within which a wise and humble judge must move. I said "He will be very conscientious and very earnest and formula-ridden and perhaps too easily taken in by big, noble sounding words."[12]

This reported colloquy is odd, indeed disingenuous, for during the three weeks between Rutledge's joining the Court and Frankfurter's writing this entry, the brethren discussed and voted on only six cases in which Rutledge heard argument.[13] Of these, Reed (who participated only in five) differed from Rutledge on two: an admiralty case written by the Chief Justice for a 7-to-2 Court, where Reed joined Frankfurter in dissent;[14] and an administrative law decision, also written by the Chief, for a 5-to-4 majority applying the Interstate Commerce Act, with Reed joining Douglas, Roberts, and Black in dissent.[15] None of these cases concerned individual liberties or otherwise invoked principles of law generating high emotion. And the company that Rutledge kept in these cases hardly reflected fringe thinking. Thus, unless Reed and Frankfurter were referring to votes on certiorari petitions (unlikely given Reed's apparent reference to Rutledge's votes on the merits), or unless Rutledge was commenting on cases argued but held over (apparently none) or on cases Rutledge had not heard argued (highly unlikely), it is perplexing to say the least how Reed and Frankfurter could come up with their quick indictment.

Perhaps the two were referring to the positions they anticipated Rutledge would take, antithetical to their own, during the next round of Jehovah's Witness cases, which the Court had voted, during the weekend conference before Rutledge joined the Court, to hear forthwith.[16] They could assume that Rutledge would probably apply his dissenting view from the Court of Appeals in *Busey*[17] to oppose their own position in *Opelika*; and Frankfurter, as he was known to do, may have had a clerk summarize Rutledge's opinions from the circuit to get a better idea of his new colleague before his arrival. In any event, whatever underlay Reed's and Frankfurter's colloquy of first impression, the relationship that Rutledge developed with each was mutually accommodating and cordial,[18] and one can judge from the pages that follow whether the two more seasoned justices were prophetic or not about Rutledge as a justice.

If the newest justice disappointed Reed and Frankfurter in *Opelika* and *Murdock* and in *Barnette*, however, one must note a development in the next term: Justice Rutledge, writing for the Court—and joined by Reed as well as by Stone, Black, and Douglas—rejected a claim testing the reach of the First Amendment's "free exercise" clause while Frankfurter supported a First Amendment reversal in concert with Roberts, Murphy, and Jackson. In *Prince v. Massachusetts*, the Court upheld a state statute—as applied to the custodial aunt of a nine-year-old girl, both Jehovah's Witnesses—imposing criminal fines for compelling or permitting a girl under eighteen or a boy under twelve to offer for sale (among other things) any newspaper or periodical, in this case religious literature, "in any street or public place." Rutledge's concerns about child labor, in a virtual "toss of the coin," trumped his commitment to religious freedom here.[19]

Wiley Rutledge came from a generation of liberal academic lawyers who had writhed under the impact of Supreme Court decisions narrowly construing the government's police power—especially when preventing Congress, whether relying on the commerce or the taxing power, from regulating child labor. Even the Child Labor Amendment to the Constitution, which Rutledge himself had worked mightily to achieve, had failed. Not until 1941, in fact, had Harlan Fiske Stone, writing for a unanimous Court in *United States v. Darby*,[20] overruled those stifling decisions[21] by upholding child labor provisions in the Fair Labor Standards Act. It is hardly surprising, therefore, that only three years after *Darby*, Justice Rutledge should have been unwilling to recognize still another constitutional obstacle to protecting children abused in the workplace. Particularly important was the power to protect children from the perils of the urban streets. Not infrequently, the popular press reported horror stories of homeless newsboys morally corrupted and physically injured there at night.[22]

Prince was a case, of course, where the Court had to draw a constitutional line; the historic document itself did not provide one. In dissent, Justice Murphy did not perceive "convincing proof" that the young girl, accompanied by her aunt, had been exposed to "a grave and immediate danger" to her "health, morals, or welfare." Writing for the other three dissenters, Justice Jackson acknowledged that state law, operating consistently with the First Amendment, can impinge on religious activities whenever they "begin to affect or collide with liberties of others or of the public." But because the Court's new line of cases beginning with *Murdock* had rejected that test, he felt bound to apply the new teaching, which he believed would not tolerate the subset of cases protecting child labor that Justice Rutledge was creating in *Prince*. Jackson wrote: "if worship in the churches and the activity of Jehovah's Witnesses on the street 'occupy the same high estate' and have the 'same claim to protection'" announced in the Court's recent decision in *Murdock* (overruling the first *Opelika* decision), then "it would seem that child labor laws may be applied to both if to either." Accordingly, Jackson wrote, "[i]f the *Murdock* doctrine stands along with today's decision, a foundation is laid for any state intervention in the indoctrination and participation of children in religion"—*even inside a church itself*—"provided it is done in the name of their health or welfare."[23]

Jackson was prescient in suggesting that *Prince* signaled a limitation on free exercise rights that would carry over in ways affecting First Amendment freedoms. As recently as 1990, for example, in *Employment Div., Dep't. of Human Resources of Oregon v. Smith*,[24] the Supreme Court cited

Prince in rejecting a free exercise defense against Oregon's ban on the use of peyote, a controlled substance, in religious ceremonies. Because the state was free to regulate drug use generally under its police power, and had not done so intending to regulate religious beliefs, communication, or training, the Court held that the free exercise clause provided no exemption. Rutledge's opinion in *Prince*, however, was premised on a belief that the child selling Jehovah's Witnesses literature was not of an age for a court to be sure she was engaging freely and maturely in a religious exercise; thus, child labor protections should not be lifted. To Rutledge, *Prince* was not a free exercise case at all. *Smith* in 1990, therefore, was a considerable stretch of Rutledge's analysis, as Justice Blackmun's dissenting opinion demonstrated in finding no compelling state interest that would justify extending the peyote ban to religious ceremonies.[25]

THE 1946 Term brought a memorable dissent by Rutledge. In the Court's first decision in almost forty years[26] construing the First Amendment's establishment-of-religion clause, *Everson v. Board of Education*, Justice Black wrote for a 5-to-4 majority upholding a New Jersey township ordinance that authorized reimbursement of transportation expenses on public buses for children traveling to Catholic, as well as public, schools (though not to schools "operated for profit"). At the outset, in applying the First Amendment to the state through the Fourteenth, Justice Black acknowledged: "No tax in any amount, large or small, can be levied to support any religious activities or institutions, whatever they may be called, or whatever form they may adopt to teach or practice religion." But, he concluded, subsidized bus fares—while admittedly helping children (including some who might not otherwise attend) get to church schools which unquestionably taught religion—did not break the constitutional "'wall of separation between church and State.'" This subsidy, wrote Black, essentially reflected neutral "public welfare legislation" comparable to tax expenditures for policemen who protect parochial as well as public school-children against harm from traffic, and to the "fire protection," "sewage disposal," and "highways and sidewalks" that support church-related and other schools equally.[27]

Joined by an unusual alignment of colleagues—Frankfurter, Jackson, and Burton—Justice Rutledge wrote a telling First Amendment dissent (he also suggested that the legislation was "invalid on its face" as a denial of equal protection of the laws in excluding "children who attend private, profit-making schools").[28] After presenting the history of the constitutional prohibition against establishment of religion, confirming that the First Amendment "forbids any appropriation, large or small, from public funds to aid or support any and all religious exercises" (as Justice Black himself acknowledged), Rutledge explained why payments for transportation aided children "in a substantial way to get the very thing they are sent to the particular school to secure, namely, religious training and teaching." Given the "admixture of religious with secular teaching in all such institutions"—which "is the very reason for their being"—the appropriation of transportation costs did not differ from tax-supported bus fares for "transportation to Sunday school, to weekday special classes at the church or parish house, or the meetings of various young people's religious societies, such as the Y.M.C.A., the Y.W.C.A., the Y.M.H.A., [or] the [Methodist] Epworth League"—all of which, he noted, "could not withstand constitutional attack."[29]

Rutledge reinforced his point by showing that "transportation, where it is needed, is as essential to education as any other element." Its cost, he observed, "is as much a part of the total expense, except at times in amount, as the cost of textbooks, of school lunches, of athletic equipment, of writing and other materials; indeed of all other items comprising the total burden." To analogize bus fares for Catholic schools to highways, sidewalks, and police, fire, and sewage protection, Rutledge warned, was to ignore entirely "the religious factor"—the only reason why a "substantial federal question" was presented. These other facilities and protections "are matters of common right, part of the general need for safety," he pointed out. "Certainly the fire department must not stand idly by while the church burns." But unlike the bus fares, none of these public services is targeted, even partially, for a religious purpose.[30]

Furthermore, Rutledge pointed out, taxpayer subsidies for students in parochial schools, in addition to those for students in public schools, were not necessary (as the majority seemed to believe) for preserving the state's neutrality in religious matters. From Rutledge's perspective, any purported subsidy of religion's "free exercise" (here, the choice of attending parochial school) to achieve parity of treatment was an act not of "neutrality" but of "establishment." Rutledge noted, "'Religion' appears only once in the Amendment. But the word governs two prohibitions and governs them alike. It does not have two meanings, one narrow to forbid 'an establishment' and another, much broader, for securing 'the free exercise thereof.' . . . Congress and now the states are as broadly restricted concerning the one as they are regarding the other.'" But under the majority's theory, Rutledge observed, the state would have "a ready method"—a "'public welfare-public function'" rationale—for nullifying the Amendment's "establishment" clause in favor of supporting "free exercise" on any occasion deemed appropriate.[31]

This majority view, Rutledge stressed, reflected inherent inconsistency. Years earlier the Court, in order to protect religious rights under the free exercise clause, had held that parents were entitled to send their children to parochial schools that met state educational standards—a decision premised, he noted, on the "private character of the function of religious education." By declaring, however, that "appropriation of public funds to defray part of the cost of attending those schools is for a public purpose," Rutledge wrote, the Court expressed no principled limitation on "why the state cannot go farther." Suppose, for example, that subsidies for textbooks and school lunches were justified on the ground that these expenditures, like bus fares, were small relative to others for education. It would be wholly irrational, according to Rutledge, "to make a public function of the smaller items" while characterizing as "wholly private in character the larger things," such as buildings and teachers' salaries. The justice concluded: if the state could supply the "smaller items of educational expense" for religious teaching, "it is hard to see why the larger ones also may not be paid."[32]

"This is not therefore just a little case over bus fares," warned Justice Rutledge. "In paraphrase of Madison, distant as it may be in its present form from a complete establishment of religion, it differs from it only in degree; and is the first step in that direction. . . . Today as in his time 'the same authority which can force a citizen to contribute three pence only . . . for the support of any one [religious] establishment, may force him' to pay more; or 'to conform to any other establishment in all cases whatsoever.'"[33]

Praising Rutledge's "vigorous dissent"—and in a later editorial calling it "monumental"—the *St. Louis Post-Dispatch* warned that *Everson* lent "abrupt support to an increasing and subtle encroachment to separation of church and state." The *Washington Post*, citing Rutledge's "powerful dissent," called Justice Black's opinion "superficial." The Raleigh *News and Observer* declared, "Justice Rutledge does not leave the Black opinion a leg to stand on." And of the student law review editors who expressed a view of the merits, most found Rutledge's position persuasive.[34] Rutledge received more mail on *Everson* than on any opinion of his to date, much of it forwarding "resolutions of protest by various interested bodies."[35] Indeed, *Everson* fed an intensifying religious conflict in postwar America. From the perspective of Francis Cardinal Spellman of New York, Protestant preachers and journals were citing *Everson* to launch a bigoted "crusade" against the Roman Catholic church.[36] By 1949 the cardinal himself was embroiled in a public dispute with Eleanor Roosevelt over her opposition to government funds for religious schools.[37]

The exchange between Spellman and Roosevelt was relatively quiet, however, compared to the acrimony stirred by the diatribes of Paul Blanshard, a lawyer whose *American Freedom and Catholic Power*, generating twenty-six printings, claimed a Catholic conspiracy to take over the country.[38] Wiley Rutledge had no association with Blanchard or his sympathizers; nor did the justice exhibit any bias against the Catholic church. His dissent in *Everson* came entirely from his historical understanding of the First Amendment. And despite his expressed concern that *Everson* had set the Court on a slippery slope, he did not at all share Blanchard's worries. Rutledge had confidence that in subsidizing parochial school bus fares, the state—in Black's words for the majority—had approached "the verge" of its constitutional power. To his former student George Heidlcbaugh, Rutledge wrote incautiously: "I think fairly clearly" that the *Everson* majority has "gone about as far as they intend to go in stretching the matter. I should not be surprised," he added, "to see school lunches sustained if and when such question is presented." But despite the warning in his dissent that Black's opinion theoretically would justify other, larger expenditures benefiting parochial schools, Rutledge did not believe that his colleagues would take this possibility further. To Heidlebaugh he added: "[T]here is little basis for believing, as some have insisted, that the Everson case opens up the way for full support of religious schools in such matters as tuitions, teachers' salaries, etc."[39]

Rutledge correctly assessed the caution that his colleagues would apply to the next case implicating the establishment clause. In the following term the Court in *McCollum v. Board of Education*, in an opinion by Justice Black, with only Justice Reed dissenting, denied to an Illinois school board the authority to establish a voluntary program of religious instruction conducted during the school day on school premises by instructors paid by outside religious groups but subject to "approval and supervision of the superintendent of schools." Relying only on *Everson* and quoting liberally from Rutledge's dissent as well as from his own majority opinion, Justice Black found an establishment clause violation not only in the use of "tax-supported public school buildings" for "dissemination of religious doctrines," but also in "the invaluable aid" that the state afforded to sectarian groups by providing "pupils for their religious classes through use of the State's compulsory public school machinery."[40] Fifteen years after *Everson*, in the Court's first ruling on a state-required school prayer, *Engel v. Vitale*, Justice Douglas—in declaring the prayer requirement unconstitutional—acknowledged that Rutledge, not the majority that Douglas himself had joined, had been right in *Everson*. "My problem today would be uncomplicated but for *Everson*," wrote Douglas; "Mr. Justice Rutledge stated in dissent what I think is durable First Amendment philosophy."[41]

In the years ahead, establishment clause issues, and analyses, became increasingly complex. Even in Rutledge's time there were questions, not presented to the Court, about the constitutional validity of the G.I. Bill, the National School Lunch Act applicable to public and nonprofit private schools, and federal and state tax exemptions for religious institutions.[42] And as the ensuing decades have shown, the contexts and judicial analyses have multiplied, testing whether a rigid "wall of separation" is feasible.[43] Recent Supreme Court decisions have justified benefits to religious schools when they have been freely conferred by government-subsidized individuals or otherwise have reflected religious "neutrality," such as tax deductions for parochial and other private school tuitions;[44] extension to students at Bible colleges, as well as nonreligious institutions, of nondiscriminatory state-supported vocational rehabilitation for the visually impaired;[45] state-subsidized sign-language interpreters for deaf students at parochial, as well as public, schools;[46] the allocation of state university student activity fees to a student newspaper with a Christian perspective, in addition to publications with a secular bent;[47] funds for remedial education under Title I of the Elementary and Secondary Education Act of 1965 in both parochial and public schools;[48] federal funds for library and computer materials lent to private (including religious) as well as public schools for secular purposes;[49] and, most recently, taxpayer-supported vouchers for students who elect to attend state-approved private—in fact, primarily religious— schools.[50]

Wiley Rutledge's First Amendment outlook would have been entirely at odds with these developments, as the justices dissenting in the voucher case recognized when relying, among other authorities, on his opinion in *Everson*.[51] That dissent remains as powerful a statement as any Supreme Court justice has written defending the "wall of separation between church and State" as a central tenet of our constitutional democracy.

ASIDE FROM *Prince*, arguably more a child labor than a religion decision, Wiley Rutledge supported a First Amendment defense in every case in which it was raised during his tenure on the Court, whether for speech, press, assembly, petition, or religion. He joined the 5-to-4 majority that reversed the conviction of a notorious anti-Semitic Catholic priest, Father Arthur Terminiello, who had disturbed the peace by railing against communists and Jews from inside an auditorium filled with his followers while a large, turbulent crowd outside eventually rioted, throwing bricks, bottles, and stink bombs into the auditorium and at the police.[52] Rutledge was also with the majority in holding that the state cannot criminally prosecute someone for distributing religious literature on the sidewalk of a company-owned town,[53] and he joined dissents from two decisions that upheld Hatch Act bans on political activity by federal and state employees.[54] He even went out of his way on occasion to find a free speech violation when a Court majority would rule for the aggrieved party on lesser grounds.[55]

Two of Rutledge's free speech opinions, one for the majority, another in dissent, reflect the continuing 5-to-4 split on First Amendment issues during the 1940s and the justice's own nearly absolutist views. In *Thomas v. Collins*, a celebrated and controversial opinion during the 1944 Term, Rutledge used the First Amendment to reverse, 5 to 4, a conviction for criminal contempt.[56] The defendant had ignored a Texas court's temporary restraining order forbidding him to solicit union membership at a scheduled "mass meeting" without first obtaining an "organizer's card," as required by state statute. Rutledge held that the registration requirement, as applied, was an unconstitutional prior restraint on constitutionally protected speech and assembly.

The state had argued that the statute had a rational basis in regulating business practices; that for regulatory purposes organizing unions was no different from selling insurance or securities, which the state doubtless had authority to supervise; and that in any event the registration statute conferred only ministerial, not discretionary, powers on state officials, who could not refuse application for an organizer's card. To the contrary, Rutledge noted, "the indispensable democratic freedoms secured by the First Amendment" had a "preferred place" that required a "clear and present danger"—not a mere rational basis—before the state's police power could interfere with their exercise. And there was no danger here. No public disturbance. No solicitation of funds requiring public scrutiny. Furthermore, he emphasized, even automatic, "ministerial" issuance of an organizer's card would impose an undue burden, however slight, on the exercise of First Amendment rights—a burden that if allowed, could be extended to interfere with an effort not only to organize labor but also "to rally support for any social, business, religious or political cause."[57] Justice Roberts, speaking also for the Chief Justice, Reed, and Frankfurter, relied in dissent on his own dictum in *Cantwell v. Connecticut* suggesting that the state could require anyone soliciting the public at least to provide identification. Such protection, wrote Roberts, was justified because anyone "persuaded to join a union" would be exposed to "business and financial liability."[58]

The decision in *Thomas* received considerable comment in law journals, especially as to whether the Court was affording preferential treatment to labor unions.[59] Justice Jackson, in a separate concurrence, asked rhetorically why employers should have any less freedom than labor organizers in speaking to their employees. That caused Justice Douglas to concur specially, in reply, that the Wagner Act legitimately regulated direct contact by employers because of their coercive economic power over employees.[60]

Roberts's dissent was not without force if *Thomas* could be understood to permit direct solicitation of individuals for union membership, one to one, without the need to register the solicitor's identity with the state as required of other businesses to protect against overreaching. Fairly read, Rutledge's opinion reserved that question for another day, limiting its reach to protection of union speakers soliciting membership only at mass gatherings, where pressure from individual importuning was not at issue.[61] But *Thomas* has endured more broadly as protection for noncommercial solicitations one on one. As recently as June 2002 in a Jehovah's Witness case, Justice Stevens quoted Rutledge's opinion extensively as the Court struck down a municipal ordinance that criminalized door-to-door religious and other advocacy without a mayor's permit.[62]

Of especial significance, moreover, as Douglas Hedin has astutely observed, Rutledge's opinion in *Thomas* was the Court's first explication of what later became known as the "chilling effect" analysis. Acknowledging that the state had the power to regulate unions in the public interest, Rutledge rejected the argument that "solicitation," requiring an organizer's card, was a clear-cut activity easily distinguishable from the "discussion" and "general advocacy" concededly protected by the First Amendment. He pointed out that this claimed distinction would depend on the various understandings of the hearers, forcing the speaker as a precaution "to hedge and trim" the message—even well short of the regulatory limitation—to avoid any impression of an invitation to join a union that might lead to prosecution. This insight, as Hedin has noted, became central to the Warren Court's First Amendment jurisprudence beginning in 1958 with Justice Brennan's opinion striking down a loyalty oath in *Speiser v. Randall*.[63]

IN HIS OTHER major free speech opinion, Rutledge dissented during the 1948 Term from a 5-to-4 decision upholding an ordinance in Trenton, New Jersey, barring from the "public streets, alleys or thoroughfares" every "sound truck" that emits "loud and raucous noises." He noted that only a few of the justices understood the indictment to limit the charge to a "loud and raucous" truck; others in the majority construed the indictment to charge as a criminal offense the defendant's operation of a sound truck, as such, without regard to decibel level. Thus, observed Rutledge, the defendant stood convicted, "but of what it is impossible to tell." In any event, while agreeing that legislatures could regulate sound trucks for abuse, without violating the First Amendment, by drafting "narrowly drawn statutes," Rutledge emphasized that any limitation must reflect the legitimacy of this relatively recent form of communication. He was responding to Justice Frankfurter, who in a separate concurrence expressed aversion to "the aural aggressions implicit in the use of sound trucks"; doubted that the drivers of these trucks should have "the constitutional rights accorded to the un-aided human voice"; and announced his willingness to leave the matter entirely to "the legislative judgment controlled by public opinion."[64] Rutledge countered:

> [To say] that the First Amendment limited its protections of speech to the natural range of the human voice as it existed in 1790 would be, for me, like saying that the commerce power remains limited to navigation by sail and travel by the use of horses and oxen in accordance with the principal modes of carrying on commerce in 1789. The Constitution was not drawn with any such limited vision of time, space and mechanics.

To Rutledge, it was "one thing to hold that the states may regulate the use of sound trucks by appropriately limited measures." It was "entirely another to say"—as Frankfurter and Jackson (concurring separately) appeared to be saying—that "their use can be forbidden altogether."[65]

Frankfurter also used this occasion to repudiate those of his colleagues and others who found "freedom of speech" to have a "preferred position" among the rights entitled to constitutional protection. A "mischievous phrase," he called it—a "deceptive formula" erroneously implying that "any law touching communication is infected with presumptive invalidity." Tracing the history of the "preferred position" debate through more than a dozen Court decisions, Frankfurter blamed his colleague Rutledge for "perhaps the strongest language" supporting the idea in *Thomas v. Collins*, the union organizer case. Frankfurter's objection, however, was more syntactical than substantive. While condemning the phraseology as "mechanical jurisprudence," he was not far from it himself in concept. Frankfurter endorsed Justice Holmes's view that (in Frankfurter's words) the liberties indispensable to an open society, such as "free inquiry," came to the Court "with a momentum for respect lacking when appeal is made to liberties which derive merely from shifting economic arrangements." To which Justice Rutledge replied, in ending his dissent: "I think my brother Frankfurter demonstrates the conclusion opposite to that which he draws, namely, that the First Amendment guaranties of the freedoms of speech, press, assembly and religion occupy preferred position not only in the Bill of Rights but also in the repeated decisions of this Court."[66]

SEVENTEEN

Acrimony in the Court

A justice's value on the Supreme Court is measured substantially by reference to analytical and writing ability, plus the intangible called "judgment." But there is more. Inevitably an institution where political views, judicial philosophies, and personal styles are mixed, the Court is a collegial body requiring compromise as well as principle, interpersonal skill as well as intellectual power, and—there are no two sides to these coins—integrity, industry, independence. The Court of the 1940s had many strong personalities and differing visions of the law and the Court's role in it, and the 1943 Term brought all these tendencies to the fore. Indeed, the term was to be unusually acrimonious, both judicially and personally, revealing a divide on the Court that may well have been more bitter than the dissension that accompanied the Court-packing controversy seven years earlier.

The first eruption occurred just after New Year's Day on January 3, 1944. The Court issued fourteen decisions—only four unanimous in result—requiring twenty-nine opinions (including twelve dissents and three concurrences), plus three qualified concurring utterances.[1] A week later an anonymous "member of the Supreme Court Bar"—later identified as Charles C. Burlingham, a close friend of Justice Frankfurter and Judge Learned Hand —wrote to the *New York Herald Tribune* to bemoan the "unhappy state of the Court." Burlingham enumerated the dissents on January 3 of each justice and noted the "growing tendency to disagree." He suggested that "if this is not checked the effect on the public will be unfortunate," leading to "doubt and uncertainty and a lack of respect and a loss of confidence in the Court." Newspaper columnists and staff writers alike began to pick up this theme, with headlines calling the "Supreme Court Divided as Seldom in Its History."[2]

The division was noticeably personal. In two decisions on January 3 in which Douglas wrote for the Court while Frankfurter dissented, Black and

Murphy issued a new species of opinion concurring with Douglas for the sole purpose of scolding Frankfurter—in effect, a "counterdissent." In a patent case, *Mercoid Corporation v. Mid-Continent Investment Co.*, the two accused Frankfurter of interpreting congressional intent by reference to his own "preconceived views on 'morals' and 'ethics.'" And in a major rate-making case, *Federal Power Commission v. Hope Natural Gas*, Black and Murphy chastised their colleague for "patently a wholly gratuitous assertion" about a controversial constitutional doctrine that Frankfurter, they said, knew was not before the Court but had invoked nonetheless to mislead the public. Newspaper headlines trumpeted the personal edge in the Court's opinions. One proclaimed: "Sharp Language Used by Justices Is Indicative of Growing Discord." A reporter noted that "[f]eeling must be running high," with the Justices' criticism of one another in the Court's opinions "motivated by an unconcealed impatience or anger."[3]

Hope Natural Gas was particularly significant because it established by a vote of 5 to 3 (with Justice Roberts not participating) a new, exceedingly deferential standard for judicial review of regulation of public utility rates by the Federal Power Commission. According to Douglas's majority opinion sustaining the commission's action, joined by Stone, Black, Murphy, and Rutledge, any "just and reasonable" rate balancing the interests of investor and consumer, regardless of the method used to determine it, would now survive judicial scrutiny. In making new constitutional law, Douglas was essentially adopting the view he had expressed jointly with Black and Murphy when concurring in a rate case two years earlier. Then, the three had emphasized that the legislature—not the Court—had the authority to fix prices, and thus that judicial review was limited to the reasonableness of the legislative decision delegated (with appropriate standards) to the regulatory commission; there was no room for the Court, by invoking "due process," to impose its own, independent view of what a reasonable rate would be.[4]

Justices Reed, Frankfurter, and Jackson, each dissenting separately in *Hope*, would have required justification of the rate order by reference to explicit criteria. And Frankfurter went out of his way to emphasize that for fifty years, the Court had given the judiciary, not the legislature, "the final say" about the reasonableness of a utility rate, and that Congress, by its silence, had acquiesced in that proposition. This reference to the "silent acquiescence" doctrine was the "wholly gratuitous assertion" that triggered Black's and Murphy's "counterdissent."[5]

The *Hope* case had not proceeded routinely. On Sunday, January 2, the night before the Court was scheduled to announce its decision, Drew Pearson—whose radio audience always anticipated a prediction—broadcast that the Supreme Court was split 4 to 4 in *Hope*, with "the ninth Justice trying to

Justice Wiley Rutledge during the 1943 Supreme Court Term. (Photograph by John F. Costelloe; Library of Congress, Rutledge Collection, PR 13 CN 1981:351)

make up his mind by today."[6] Pearson's information was only partially true. There was an equivocator, Justice Rutledge, but because Justice Roberts had removed himself from the case, the question was whether the decision would come down 5 to 3 to reverse the Court of Appeals and uphold the commission, or be split 4 to 4, leaving intact the appeals court decision vacating the commission's order but doing so without precedential value. In any event, the courthouse was in an uproar the next morning.[7]

Before the Court convened to announce its decisions, the Chief agreed to Justice Roberts's demand for a meeting to discuss the leak. According to Justice Jackson's published recollection, Roberts came equipped with a "transcript" of Pearson's broadcast showing that "Mr. Justice Rutledge couldn't make up his mind,"[8] although Jackson also recalled Pearson's having announced over the air only that "one justice had not been able to make up his mind." Murphy's and Black's law clerks at the time agree that Pearson referred on the radio not to "Rutledge" but to an unnamed "justice" yet to vote.[9] It would appear that Roberts did bring in Pearson's original text, which specified Rutledge, but that Pearson, for whatever reason, had not named the justice over the air.[10]

In any event, at conference on January 3 Justice Frankfurter reportedly suggested Douglas and Murphy as the most likely suspects. Douglas had called in sick—perhaps wanting to avoid a confrontation that he sensed was coming—and could not respond.[11] (Two days later, in a detailed memo to Stone, Douglas denied he was the leaker and sent the Chief a second memo the next day calling the accusation a "contemptible lie.") Murphy, whose dislike of Frankfurter was palpable, also denied the charge.[12] The meeting was inconclusive, apart from Rutledge's confirmation that he would join Douglas's opinion for a 5-to-3 majority. Over the objection of Justice Roberts, who asked his colleagues to hold up *Hope* as a way of masquerading the leak to Pearson, the justices took the bench to announce the decision along with the other thirteen.[13]

The Chief considered calling in the law clerks in the hope of tracking down the leak, but apparently concluding that this would be fruitless, he abandoned the effort. Soon it appeared likely that Douglas, who was close to Pearson and had attended a New Year's party where Pearson was present, was the culprit.[14] Even though the situation more than hinted that Douglas had mentioned Rutledge's name to Pearson, Rutledge did not emote about the incident in chambers and apparently saw no purpose in pursuing the issue. He seemed to understand Douglas—self-important and occasionally outside judicial propriety, but friendly to Rutledge and not typically unethical.[15] And in any event the truth of the matter was not available.

Justice Roberts, on the other hand, was so upset that reportedly he never spoke to Douglas after January 3. In fact, Roberts took it even further than that; he stopped having lunch with the Court or even joining his colleagues in the robing room for the traditional handshake before taking the bench. He became petulant, limiting his discussion in conference to "'I affirm'" or "'reverse'" and at least once refusing to assign a case for which he had the responsibility as senior justice in the majority. Roberts declared, according to a report heard by one of Douglas's clerks the following year, that he "was serving with men without honor."[16]

By the end of January, moreover, Justice Roberts—joined by Frankfurter —was dissenting with a diatribe in an admiralty case written by Stone. Roberts accused the majority of deliberately misstating the case law—a most serious charge directed primarily at his Chief—as well as willy-nilly overturning judicial precedent. Roberts then added a bitter, gratuitous shot at Black, Douglas, and Murphy for using their dissent in *Opelika* to invite relitigation of the flag salute issue.[17]

Two months later Roberts was still at it in *Smith v. Allwright*, where eight justices held that the Texas Democratic primary limited to white voters violated the equal protection clause, overruling a decision that Roberts himself had written for a unanimous Court in 1935. Justice Roberts could not handle this. "In the present term the court has overruled three cases," he wrote in dissent. "It is regrettable," Roberts added, "that in an era marked by doubt and confusion, an era whose greatest need is steadfastness of thought and purpose, . . . this court should now itself become the breeder of fresh doubt and confusion . . . as to the stability of our institutions." (Justice Jackson inflamed the situation a few months later, when in addressing the annual meeting of the American Law Institute he implicitly criticized his colleagues for "the most intolerable kind of *ex post facto* judicial law making.") Angered irretrievably by the *Hope* leak and by the Court's ease with overruling precedent, Justice Roberts, according to Justice Black's most recent biographer, decided that all the justices but Frankfurter and Jackson—whose views he generally shared—were "'against him.'" He would speak now only to these two.[18]

The observation that Roberts broke relations with all on the Court but Frankfurter and Jackson does not account carefully, however, for Roberts's relationship with his newest colleague, Wiley Rutledge. For the year since Rutledge had been on the Court, he and Roberts had been most friendly to one another, and there is no evidence that Roberts had ever experienced an unpleasant interaction with Rutledge over a Court decision or anything else. Furthermore, although Roberts had increasingly come to criticize the views of Black, Douglas, and Murphy, the voting record of Wiley Rutledge, while surely more liberal than Roberts's own, had not by early 1944 put Rutledge solidly into the camp of the other three.[19] Rutledge may have learned of how Roberts had put his friendship with Black on the line by demanding, unsuccessfully, that Black disclose and repudiate the *Hope* leaker; but any awareness of that confrontation did not necessarily, and certainly did not reasonably, put Rutledge himself in Roberts's line of fire.[20] On the other hand, Justice Jackson has reported that Black, Douglas, and Murphy, "and later Rutledge"—Jackson did not say when—had an understanding that "if any three felt strongly" about granting a writ of certiorari, "the fourth would join them." And according to Justice Douglas, "Frankfurter got Roberts to believe that new judges were scheming behind his back." We do not know whether Jackson's information, if true, applied as early as 1944 and affected Roberts, or whether Frankfurter's alleged effort to poison Roberts's mind against junior colleagues extended to Justice Rutledge. We can be reasonably sure, however, that Rutledge himself showed no disrespect for his colleague Roberts. All things considered, to the extent that Roberts's withdrawal included avoidance of Wiley Rutledge along with others in 1944, it would have resulted not from the *Hope* fiasco, in which Rutledge had no culpability, or from any action toward him by Rutledge, but from Roberts's sense of intellectual isolation—which he converted to personal isolation—from a Court that was liberalizing doctrine by overruling precedent to a degree that Roberts found intolerable.[21]

THE VERY PUBLIC reaction of Black and Murphy to Frankfurter in the *Hope* and *Mercoid* cases was in part a manifestation of their anger at the former professor's unrelenting effort to teach all his colleagues how to decide every case. Justice Frankfurter wrote his colleagues countless memos—often pretentious or patronizing—trying to persuade them to change their minds. He often dominated oral argument, using his questions as much to direct the thinking of the other justices as to elicit responses from counsel. And he routinely lobbied the justices through their law clerks. According to one of Rutledge's clerks, Frankfurter once exclaimed, "You ought to talk to your judge; that's a crazy position he's taking!" A clerk to Frankfurter recalled that the justice "would talk to clerks rather than eat."[22]

All this was more tolerable to the justices than Frankfurter's never-let-go performances at the Saturday conferences. To the consternation of everyone who had to listen, Chief Justice Stone—unlike his predecessor, Hughes—would permit Frankfurter to go on and on. Rutledge's second law clerk, Harry Shniderman, saw his boss come out of conference "roaring mad" at Frankfurter more than once, although Rutledge's anger "blew over" pretty quickly. As proof of the problem, a former Douglas clerk reported that on a Saturday when Frankfurter had laryngitis, the conference adjourned at 4:00 P.M.[23]

It was not just memos, lobbying law clerks, and the conference. Regularly trying to influence Justice Reed, Frankfurter would come to Reed's office carrying a draft opinion that Reed had just circulated and exclaim, "You're on the wrong side! This is the stupidest thing I've ever read in my life; you've got to revise this, Stanley!" And Frankfurter would make fun of Reed behind Reed's back, once even calling him a "vegetable." Frankfurter could also be Janus-headed, praising Murphy to his face while telling Murphy's law clerk that his boss was "one of the stupidest characters who ever came on the Court."[24] Frankfurter thought Justice Douglas was a "skunk," an opportunist who believed in nothing but furthering his own ambitions. Douglas reciprocated the enmity, and the two came to hate each other and literally stopped speaking. Once when Douglas was in the hospital and his clerk, while visiting, mentioned an opinion of Frankfurter, Douglas interjected, "He's hoping I'll die." That, the clerk recalled, "was not a joke."[25]

278 Judge, 1939–1949

Frankfurter disagreed profoundly, and often emotionally, with Justice Black on the fundamentals of interpreting the Constitution, leading to considerable discord between them during the 1940s. In their opinions they would direct barbs at one another that seemed personal as well as principled, and they would speak harsh words about one another to their clerks. Underneath it all, nonetheless, Black and Frankfurter were developing a grudging mutual respect that evolved, years later, into friendship.[26]

Despite their jurisprudential differences, Rutledge and Frankfurter respected each other and became friends. When first on the Court, Rutledge understood that Frankfurter had vigorously supported Learned Hand to succeed Justice Byrnes, and Rutledge was perplexed, if not annoyed, at Frankfurter's so obviously trying to flatter him. But just as Rutledge could accept Douglas for what he was, he could soon accept the pontificating Frankfurter for what he was, too. Rutledge had always respected Frankfurter's intellect, and of course he had strongly supported his nomination to succeed Justice Cardozo. Rutledge especially enjoyed the give and take with his senior colleague, much as he enjoyed intellectual combat with his own law clerks, to sharpen his thinking. Neither Frankfurter nor Rutledge ever took their intellectual differences personally, and as the years proceeded, the warmth between the two former professors—antagonists at law—continued to grow.[27]

JUSTICE DOUGLAS was closest on the Court personally to Justice Black and had particularly warm relations with Rutledge and Murphy. At the other extreme, Douglas's relationship with Jackson was not much better than that with Frankfurter, for Jackson neither liked nor respected him. Rutledge, for his part, had enormous respect for Douglas's intellect and legal judgment and in making up his own mind about a case would occasionally ask his clerk, "Do you know where Bill is going on this?" Rutledge also liked Douglas despite the obvious personal flaws, and while their personal relationship was not close, they unquestionably got on well together.[28]

Douglas was often criticized for his healthy diet of activities—especially politicking—away from the Court. Before the election of 1944, there was public speculation that Douglas was a likely prospect for the presidential nomination if FDR chose not to run again, and he was high on the list of many Democrats for the vice presidency that year (indeed, four years later he turned down President Truman's offer of second place on the ticket). On one occasion, Douglas delivered a speech at a CIO convention that created "an enormous political row," not only because a Supreme Court justice was addressing a labor convention but also because many were calling the CIO a collection of communist "fellow travelers." His friend Justice Black disapproved entirely of Douglas's flirtation with national political office. When Douglas addressed the CIO Black was quoted as saying that no Supreme Court justice should speak out like that to anybody; a justice should live monastically, removed from the fray (an absolutist view that Black himself compromised in addressing a "Win-the-War Rally" in Alabama at FDR's request).[29]

Douglas took seriously the Court's announced—or hoped-for—adjournment date in June, and having finished his own opinions, would leave on that date for the mountains of the West even though the other justices had not completed their work and the Chief had extended the Court's term. Corralling Douglas's vote for approval or changes of opinions still in process was nearly impossible as a result, making other justices "awfully angry with him," according to Court law clerks.[30] In the end, Douglas was as much irritant as team player. And not a leader.

WILEY AND ANNABEL attended FDR's fourth-term Inaugural Dinner at the Mayflower Hotel in January 1945.[31] Three months later, on April 12, the President was dead from a cerebral hemorrhage in Warm Springs, Georgia. Rutledge was numb. "We will not see a leader like him soon," he wrote to Dean Gavit of Indiana, adding: "Washington is quieter than I have ever seen it. . . . [T]here is a kind of stunned silence that seems all-pervading." Rutledge immediately wrote to President Truman, who responded graciously, and also to Mrs. Roosevelt:

> You are brave. You understand, more than any one, what a void has been left for this nation and the world. For millions it is also as personal as if a father and a brother in one had gone. We, and the children, are among these. We want to say this. And [to] voice . . . the hope your great courage will be equal to bearing your own loss, beyond all others,' in the sure knowledge you have been part of all he has done for so many.

In reply, Eleanor Roosevelt, after expressing her gratitude, added: "I know you share with me the relief that when God in His wisdom saw fit to take my husband, he did not suffer."[32]

Wiley and Annabel Rutledge joined the train carrying Mrs. Roosevelt and the many dignitaries to Hyde Park, New York, for the burial. The justice then had to work out his feelings by writing to several friends:

> The most impressive thing was not the [funeral] ceremonies themselves or watching the nation's greatest figures gather in tribute. It was rather the faces of the hundreds of thousands of people along the

streets here in Washington as they silently watched the body of their leader borne to and from the White House. . . . That meant a man simply loved by his people.

[President Roosevelt] had built himself into the hearts of the average men and women of the country as probably not even Abraham Lincoln had done.

I am sure even now he will rank with the greatest of our leaders. He may take first place with time.[33]

The justice felt the impact mightily soon after he and Annabel returned from Hyde Park and he "started in again to try to work." To Louise Larrabee he wrote:

Something has gone out of this world that is irreplaceable. We depended on him perhaps too much. Nevertheless it was always a comfort to know he was there to depend on. Not for one instant after his inauguration in 1933 did I waver in my faith either in his ultimate integrity or in his basic direction. I knew he was with us even though at times he acted as if he might be wavering. . . . [H]e perhaps more than any of our statesmen combined the ability to tack with the ability always to head toward the goal.[34]

ON MAY 7, 1945, Germany surrendered unconditionally to the allies at General Eisenhower's headquarters in France. April had seen the Soviets take Vienna and capture Berlin while General Patton's American army swept through Czechoslovakia and British troops swarmed over northern Italy. Mussolini died at the hands of his own people; Hitler apparently took his own life in his bunker. And beginning immediately thereafter, three events rocked the U.S. Supreme Court.

First, even before Germany formally surrendered, President Truman asked Justice Jackson to serve as the chief American prosecutor of the Nazis at the first international criminal tribunal in history. Jackson accepted on April 29 without even notifying, let alone consulting, his colleagues in advance. By May 22 he was on his way to Europe to make preliminary plans with representatives of the Allied powers. Jackson's colleagues, including Rutledge, were offended and annoyed given the extra work that each would have to undertake, not to mention the delays in final dispositions caused by 4-to-4 votes. And the Chief was upset, outspokenly, for reasons of principle. Stone questioned whether judges should undertake assignments that thrust them into a political arena, inevitably appearing to compromise judicial independence—a concern directed not only at Jackson but also, earlier, at Justice Roberts, who at FDR's request had chaired the commission that investigated the vulnerability of Pearl Harbor. Stone, in fact, questioned the very legality of an ad hoc international tribunal that would inevitably be choosing laws to apply ex post facto, and he became so exercised that in a letter to a friend he referred to Jackson's "high-grade lynching party in Nuremberg." Within a year, Wiley Rutledge would be expressing similar opinions about war crimes prosecutions.[35]

JUSTICE JACKSON was also central to the next Court-rocking event. On June 18, 1945, the day he left for Nuremberg for the duration, the Court denied rehearing in a case which had generated greater acrimony than any to date among the Roosevelt justices.[36] On May 7, the Court had announced its 5-to-4 decision in *Jewell Ridge Coal Corp. v. Local No. 6167, United Mine Workers of America*, with an opinion by Justice Murphy, joined by Black, Reed, Douglas, and Rutledge, holding that under the Fair Labor Standards Act travel time to and from the mine was "included in the compensable workweek."[37] The result awarded the miners considerable overtime pay without violation of War Labor Board guidelines. The conference had been hard fought, with Justice Reed eventually switching from the Chief's side favoring management to that of Justice Black, who, as Douglas recalled it, gave "very, very strong and vocal" support to the miners' position. Justice Jackson circulated a dissent, extensively quoting legislative history supporting his position from the mouth of Black when as a senator and chairman of the Senate Labor and Education Committee he had steered the Fair Labor Standards Act to final passage (after Jackson himself had testified for the administration, which Jackson did not mention). Black was livid, arguing to the Court that he had been quoted out of context by reference to an earlier version of the bill. But Jackson and his compatriots—Stone, Roberts, and Frankfurter—would not back down.[38]

Matters got worse. The coal corporation immediately sought rehearing on the ground that because Black's former law partner had argued the miners' case before the Court, Black should have disqualified himself. Corporate counsel was referring to a short-lived partnership, which had ended eighteen years earlier. To Black, that was no basis for recusal. Jackson felt differently and pressed Black to get off the case, even though an equally divided Court would have left the result—affirmance of the appellate court—in place (though without precedential effect).[39]

Black would not recuse himself. Everyone recognized, in any event, that recusal was the individual decision of each justice, not covered by Court rule, so Black insisted that no explanation accompany the Court's denial of the recusal motion lest the Court imply authority to rule on it. Jackson and the other dissenters, however, demanded some word from the Court, lest silence imply that all justices approved Black's position. There was to be no compromise. The petition was denied without explanation, but Jackson wrote a concurrence, joined by Frankfurter, explaining the Court's lack of authority to act upon it.[40]

The controversy generated white heat within the Court. The initial conference had brought loud argument, including table pounding, between Black and Jackson, and the recusal petition had intensified what Justice Douglas perceived by then as a feud between Black and Jackson. Douglas, as Black's ally, saw the fault lying entirely with Jackson, surely the more outspoken and erratic personality of the two. Indeed, Justice Rutledge once told Irving Brant, "Bob's just too mercurial. You never know what he's going to do." But the quieter Black, with temper in close control, could be "a rough man in an argument" nonetheless, using words with "a terrible edge," reported a biographer. In this instance, according to Justice Murphy, Black had "'tried to silence Bob and to intimidate him.'" Each of these two fierce competitors was ready made to despise the other. Jackson, however, was the more vindictive—as matters a year hence would reveal.[41]

Rutledge was entirely in Black's corner, as he had been in Stone's a year earlier when Justice Roberts objected, unsuccessfully, to the Chief's refusal to recuse himself in another matter. Rutledge had told Stone at the time that judicial disqualification was purely a matter of "taste," not of "morals." When the *Jewell Ridge* controversy erupted publicly a year later, Rutledge explained to friends, including an inquiring journalist, that too strict a policy of recusal to achieve "sheer appearance of impartiality" would result too often in "disabling the Court to act." It would also deprive the Court of a particular justice's considerable expertise—a serious price paid, Rutledge added, for Justice Douglas's policy at the time of recusing himself from all SEC cases.[42]

Rutledge had confidence in the integrity of judges individually to decide recusal questions; he focused more on the reality than on the appearance of partiality. Rutledge noted that friends had told him "in semi-facetiousness that if they should have cases coming" to the Court they would prefer to have him "sit out for fear that" he "might lean over backwards against them." But Rutledge disagreed that personal relationships automatically dictated recusal: "[I]f a man isn't big enough to sit here and decide on the law and the facts for or against a former partner when he has been away from that association for twenty years or more, then should he be here at all?" To Rutledge the answer was obvious: Supreme Court justices had the integrity to act impartially, and the public would be served better by their sitting on cases, absent highly obvious or self-acknowledged signs of partiality.[43]

THE THIRD DIVISIVE event of the term unfolded when Justice Roberts announced in June his resignation from the Court, effective the end of July 1945. The Chief sent to Black for his signature and transmittal down the line a letter to Roberts on behalf of the Court expressing the justices' "profound sense of regret," lauding Roberts's "wide knowledge of the law," and noting his "fidelity to principle." This last phrase (among others) caused Justice Black to balk, so Stone suggested that Black redraft the letter. He did so and circulated the revision, implying in his transmittal that the Chief had written it. Frankfurter learned, however, that Stone had drafted an earlier version, and Stone, at Frankfurter's insistence, circulated both letters. Rutledge and Murphy replied that they would sign either version. Reed remained silent. The others were divided. Black, in the meantime, had taken such offense at Stone's dual circulation that Black withdrew his signature from his own letter as a way of blocking possible unanimity. Justice Roberts received no letter from the Court—a sad ending for the service of a justice who, dissenting in *Korematsu*, had stood tall as one looks back.[44]

TO REPLACE Justice Roberts, President Truman chose Senator Harold H. Burton of Ohio—age fifty-seven, Republican, a man proud of his Swiss ancestry, a graduate of Bowdoin College in Maine and Harvard Law School, a faithful member of the Unitarian Church, and a former mayor of Cleveland. As mayor, Burton had supported New Deal relief efforts, and as a senator elected in 1940, he had worked closely with the chairman of the Senate Committee on the Conduct of the War, Harry Truman of Missouri, to investigate fraudulent claims against the government. Truman had also sought Burton's help in planning for an international peace organization after the war; and, taking on the isolationists of his own party, Burton had worked toward the country's participation in the United Nations. On domestic policy, Burton was middle of the road, joining most Republicans in a pro-management labor policy and in opposing the confirmation of Henry Wallace—to Burton, a "prodigal" government borrower and spender —as secretary of commerce. On the other hand, he co-sponsored the Hill-Burton Act to underwrite hospital construction throughout the country and supported the anti–poll tax amendment and related legislation that among other provisions would have established a Fair Employment Practices Commission. In short, Harold Burton was politically more moderate, in both domestic and international affairs, than his fellow Ohio Republicans, Senator Robert Taft, and especially Governor John Bricker, both of whom Burton

Senator Harold H. Burton posing for photo after his nomination to the Supreme Court in 1945. (Photograph by Harris and Ewing; Collection of the Supreme Court of the United States, p945.6.1)

contested briefly for the Republican presidential nomination in 1944 before the convention nominated Governor Thomas Dewey of New York.[45]

The *Washington Post* spoke for many editorial writers in praising the nomination, not only because Burton was "one of the ablest and best loved men in the Senate," but also because Truman had acted "as a statesman" in naming a Republican to avoid a "deplorable lack of balance" politically on the Court. But although Burton was a liberal Republican, he was not to be confused with a New Dealer. Liberal editorial writers such as Willard Shelton of the *Chicago Sun* were skeptical, pointing out that despite Democratic Party affiliation, the "so-called New Deal appointees actually have sharply divided" on the Court, resulting at times in "a conservative majority." The president unfortunately, wrote Shelton, had failed "to strengthen the liberal wing of the court."[46]

In a letter to Judge Steele in Denver, Justice Rutledge—who had known Burton "fairly well but not intimately for the last three or four years"— wrote that the reactions around the Court seemed "to be very favorable." He added, "Just between us, I think it was about as good as could be done on that side of the fence."[47] Law clerks at the time came to experience Burton as a friendly, courteous man who was approachable though typically reserved, much like Reed. Even his sense of humor was "mild," according to one of Burton's clerks. Howard Mann, who clerked both for Rutledge (on the Court of Appeals) and for Burton, proffered that Burton did not like all kinds of people the way Rutledge did, and a clerk to Vinson observed that Burton offered far "less warmth" than one received from Wiley Rutledge. Nor was Burton at all scholarly. He was as hard-working as any justice on the Court, however, and despite minimal and painfully slow production he rarely relied on his clerks to draft opinions.[48]

In Rutledge's mind, "Truman's propensity to choose men with whom he has had rather close personal acquaintance" had been the clincher in selecting Burton.[49] Of real significance, too, was Truman's view of the Court itself. In offering the nomination to Burton, Truman told him bluntly, "'I want someone who will do a thoroughly judicial job & not legislate. I know that you will do that because we have talked about it.'"[50] Burton was faithful to his sponsor. Perhaps even more judicially conservative than Owen Roberts, Justice Harold Burton rarely lined up with his more liberal-minded colleagues in cases where the Court was divided—although on occasion he would surprise.

EIGHTEEN

The Selective Service, Price Control, and Agency Review

In 1942 the government indicted a Jehovah's Witness, Nick Falbo, for knowingly failing to obey his local draft board's order to report, as a conscientious objector, to a civilian public service camp for "work of national importance." In his defense, Falbo claimed that as a minister of his faith, he was entitled to a statutory exemption from all forms of national service and thus had "no 'duty' to comply with a mistaken order." The district court declined to recognize the defense, instructing the jury that Selective Service classification was a matter for the board. The jury convicted. On appeal, Falbo argued that he was entitled to a trial de novo—a court trial to supplant the board proceeding. In the alternative, he contended that at the very least he was entitled to a district court review of whether the board had acted arbitrarily in expressing antipathy toward his religion, in failing to admit certain evidence, and in acting against the overwhelming weight of the evidence that he was a minister. The Third Circuit affirmed.[1]

Writing for seven members of the Supreme Court, Justice Black held that even if the Constitution entitled Falbo to judicial review of the local board's decision (an issue that the Court did not resolve), that review would not have been required until Falbo had actually been accepted for national service—an acceptance that in light of the public service camp's history of many rejections was far from automatic. Nor had Congress provided for such an "intermediate challenge[]." In short, Falbo had not exhausted his administrative remedies before coming to court. His conviction was affirmed.[2]

Black's opinion identified a congressional concern that procedural obstacles not impede the steady flow of men into the military, or of conscientious objectors into alternative national service.[3] Although Black did not mention it, he had to know that habeas corpus relief was available for anyone inducted unlawfully, especially because the Selective Service Act provided no direct right of judicial review. He thus would have seen the procedural burden of a habeas petition as a small price to pay for anyone claiming improper classification, one that was preferable to allowing an aggrieved draftee to stay at home and forgo any challenge until defending, much later, against a criminal proceeding.

Justice Murphy dissented, stressing that contrary to Justice Black's analysis, the administrative process had come to an end (that is, the public service camp's decision whether to accept an inductee was not part of the legal process). Murphy added that the right to judicial review of claimed "arbitrary and illegal administrative action" did not depend on a statute authorizing that review and that Falbo's effort to prove he was a minister had been prejudiced by refusal to admit evidence of a statement by a member of the local board who had allegedly said, " 'I don't have any damned use for Jehovah's Witnesses.' " [4]

Wiley Rutledge later wrote to his half-brother, Ivan, that *Falbo* had been a particularly "hard case," that he had been "very much on the fence," and that he was not at all sure he "shouldn't have joined Murphy's dissent." But Murphy had ignored the fact that Selective Service regulations allowed Falbo to take his case to a board of appeal. Falbo had done so and lost—and had failed to contend in the Supreme Court that the appellate board's order had not cured the claimed defect. For all the Court could tell, the board of appeal had resolved against Falbo, in a fair way, his allegation of local board "antipathy" to his religion. Rutledge, therefore, could see no principled reason why the Court should revisit the issue by permitting a collateral attack in a later criminal proceeding. On that basis, he issued a one-paragraph opinion concurring in the result. [5]

While Justice Murphy was simply willing to follow his liberal instincts, Justice Rutledge, although tugged by the same sympathies, was not going to ignore an established legal rule. He obviously agreed with Murphy—and reasonably so—that the majority had stretched the law to include the public service camp as part of the administrative process which Falbo had failed to "exhaust"; camp officials applied only physical and mental—not legal— requirements. Rutledge could not ignore, however, that Falbo himself had skipped over the board of appeal proceeding in presenting his case in court, a procedural default that erased his claim. But for this default, Rutledge would have voted to hear Falbo's case; indeed, in subsequent Jehovah's Witness conscription cases, he either wrote or joined opinions supporting the draftee. [6]

FALBO "came down" (as lawyers say) among the fourteen cases announced on January 3, 1944. By late March, Chief Justice Stone was citing it in a decision that upset Rutledge to his very core. In *Yakus v. United States*, the Court sustained a conviction 6 to 3—resulting in a six-month prison sentence and a $1,000 fine—for the willful sale of wholesale cuts of beef above the maximum price allowed by regulations of the Office of Price Administration (OPA).[7] The Court through Stone noted, first, that the statute authorizing OPA to issue the regulations expressly provided an exclusive procedure for challenging their validity as applied. First came an appeal to the administrator, normally to be filed within sixty days after the date the regulation was issued; then judicial review by an Emergency Court of Appeals consisting of federal district or circuit court judges; and, finally, review upon grant of certiorari by the U.S. Supreme Court. Because this protest procedure was exclusive, wrote the chief, a defendant like Yakus, charged criminally with violating OPA regulations, could not attack the validity of the regulations in the criminal proceeding itself. His failure to protest the regulations initially—in a civil proceeding before the administrator within the required sixty days—forever barred him from testing their validity later in defending a separate, criminal charge.

Moreover, the chief added, this congressional enactment of a "single procedure" for questioning the legality of an OPA regulation—a procedure premised initially on the administrator's "specialized knowledge"—created a "reasonable opportunity to be heard" sufficient to satisfy due process. The procedure was constitutional even more clearly, said Stone, in light of the reasonable congressional finding that national harm from inflation would permit neither a delay in regulatory implementation nor the conflict in legal interpretation expected to result from decisions in diverse judicial forums adjudicating criminal prosecutions. Stone explained, more specifically, that publication of the regulations in the Federal Register had given "constructive notice of their contents"; the sixty-day protest period was not "unreasonably short in view of the urgency and exigencies of wartime price regulation"; and the case law applicable in these circumstances had established firmly that due process did not require the administrative hearing to take place, or even temporary injunctive relief to be available, before a person affected had to comply with the questioned regulations.[8]

Wiley Rutledge could not have disagreed more. He wrote a highly publicized, lengthy dissent joined by Justice Murphy. According to feedback from law clerks in Stone's chambers, the dissenter's handiwork left the chief muttering. Rutledge did not quarrel with individual components of the unique remedy—part administrative, part judicial—in *Yakus*. Furthermore, he had "no difficulty" with conferring exclusive jurisdiction on the Emergency Court of Appeals to determine the validity of price regulations, nor did he worry about the unavailability of temporary injunctive relief or the lack of a pre-compliance hearing. Nor did Rutledge object to the general rule—as applied, for example, in his *Falbo* concurrence—that foreclosed a party from raising an issue in court, even a constitutional issue, when that party had "failed to exercise an earlier opportunity" to do so. But the junior justice pointed out that the rule he had cited in *Falbo* presupposed an earlier opportunity to raise the issue in "the same proceeding." In a case like *Yakus*, however—and here was Rutledge's central point—the Constitution did not permit the division of a criminal trial into "two parts in two courts." A criminal defendant, he said, could not constitutionally be required to challenge the price regulation earlier, before indictment, failing which the criminal trial would take place in a proceeding where "only a portion of the issues material to guilt" could be addressed because the defendant had not taken the initiative to lodge a timely statutory protest.[9]

The situation was even worse, Rutledge added, because the administrative proceeding itself was so summary, "trimmed almost to the bone of due process, even for wholly civil purposes." Indeed, the administrative protest was limited to "written evidence and argument" submitted to the administrator, without right of cross-examination. And the process was "pared down even further by a short statute of limitations." Rutledge found the protest procedure so skimpy, in fact, that apparently he would have permitted a defense attack on a price regulation in the criminal trial even if the defendant had already challenged it unsuccessfully before the administrator, all the way to a denial of certiorari by the Supreme Court.[10]

As authority for his analysis, Rutledge cited Article III, section 2, of the Constitution, which provides that the federal judicial power "shall extend to all Cases, in Law and Equity, arising under this Constitution, the Laws of the United States, and Treaties," and requiring that trials "shall be held in the State where the said Crimes shall have been committed." He also invoked the Sixth Amendment "right to a speedy and public trial, by an impartial jury of the State and district wherein the crime shall have been committed." These constitutional requirements, he emphasized, by incorporating the traditional criminal trial at common law, inherently negated the authority of Congress to impose the bifurcated trial procedure approved by the Court's majority. This was a separation of powers issue. Citing his *Schneiderman* concurrence, Rutledge wrote that Congress had no authority to restrict the courts' power and duty—inherent, he said, under Article III of the Constitution—to conduct criminal trials pursuant to the "fundamental law" that recognizes the right to put on a defense.[11] The justice noted, in addition, that both Article III and the Sixth Amendment barred a criminal trial outside the state where the crime had been committed, whereas the administrative proceeding routinely would take place elsewhere. Nor, added Rutledge, did the criminal trial contemplated by Article III and the Sixth Amendment allow proof of material issues by written testimony, not subject to cross-examination.[12]

Rutledge's dissent had intuitive, emotional appeal. It did not seem right that someone charged with a crime could not challenge the legality, as applied, of the very regulation the defendant was indicted for violating. And as a constitutional proposition, there was force in simply emphasizing the obvious: the traditional criminal trial mentioned in Article III and the Sixth Amendment did not include a bifurcated process whereby the defense had to be anticipated and proved in a prior, civil proceeding. But Rutledge's analysis, as he himself recognized, begged some questions, for to state what is traditional does not necessarily determine what is constitutional. Was it really true that the constitutional requirement of trial in the state where a crime occurred necessarily meant that the validity of a national price regulation, central to a criminal defense, also had to be adjudicated in that same state? Would adjudication of a price regulation, typically resolving whether it was confiscatory in a particular case, raise issues of fact triable by a jury, or might those issues be resolved, in a manner consistent with the Constitution, by an individual, administrative fact-finder subject to judicial review? If the latter, would written testimony suffice? If not, but if the administrator offered to permit a hearing with oral, cross-examined testimony on the protest at a place convenient to the protesting party—statutory opportunities that the defendant Yakus never tested—would that enhanced procedure cure any constitutional infirmity?[13]

Rutledge conceded that there was a sound, constitutionally defensible reason—namely, the importance of national uniformity in the inflation emergency—to adjudicate all price regulation issues in one process, comprising the OPA administrator and one Emergency Court of Appeals. Implicitly, therefore, he appears to have conceded that factual issues inherent in a price regulation were not necessarily jury-triable. Furthermore, if national uniformity was essential, it is hard to imagine exactly how Rutledge would have envisioned meeting the geographical requirements of the Constitution that he cited. Finally, if, as Rutledge appears to have conceded, national uniformity here was constitutionally defensible; and if, in the absence of an alleged criminal violation, due process would not be offended by the administrative-judicial procedure created for testing the legality of a price regulation; then why should a seller of a controlled product not be expected to test the regulation *before* willfully violating it, thus acting at the seller's peril in declining to do so? After all, there was little, if any, possibility that someone affected by a price regulation would have lacked a fair opportunity to contest it, for the sixty-day protest period was not absolute;

the statute required an extension if the grounds for protest arose after the original sixty days expired.[14]

Justice Rutledge's central point, however—the lack of congressional authority to impose a fundamentally unfair waiver of a criminal defense for failure to establish it affirmatively through an earlier, civil action—resonated throughout the country. An editorial in the Portland *Oregonian* called his dissent "a sizzling minority opinion which is likely to make legal history." And legal writers, focusing on constitutional theory, applauded Rutledge's recognition of the difference between the authority of Congress to regulate the federal courts' "jurisdiction" and the want of congressional authority to interfere with the courts' inherent "judicial power" received directly from Article III of the Constitution itself.[15] Congress, too, was offended by the majority ruling. Alerted by Rutledge's dissent, Congress soon amended the statute to permit a court to stay criminal proceedings while a defendant, who had a "reasonable and substantial excuse" for failing to file a civil protest, filed a belated protest with the OPA administrator and thereafter, if desired, with the Emergency Court of Appeals.[16] This resolution met Justice Rutledge's fundamental objection and probably came as close as reasonably possible to reconciling important, inherently conflicting national and individual interests.

More than most, this case caused a collision of legal theories that virtually defied satisfactory resolution. Whatever defects there were in Rutledge's approach, there were failures at least as great in the majority's approach. Although the Chief Justice probably won more "debater points," much of his argument relied on Yakus's failure to test how fair the administrative procedure could be. But that emphasis never came to grips with the real possibility, envisioned by Justice Rutledge, that a defendant—even though charged criminally for an allegedly "knowing" violation of a price regulation—might never have heard of the regulation, despite being on "constructive" notice, and thus would be legally impotent to defend on what otherwise might be a winning ground: that the regulation in fact was confiscatory.

BECAUSE *Falbo* and *Yakus* were criminal cases focused on the defendant's failure to pursue administrative remedies, the Court never had to consider the particular agency decisions involved or the federal courts' standard for reviewing agency action. *Hope Natural Gas* had revealed how contentious judicial review of an agency decision could be, however, and thus it is important to explain how Justice Rutledge, in addition to agreeing with the majority in *Hope*, understood the courts' role vis-à-vis federal agencies generally.

Four Rutledge opinions during the 1943 Term—three for the majority, one in dissent—are important here. The first, *McLean Trucking Co. v. United States*,[17] in which Rutledge sustained approval by the Interstate Commerce Commission of the merger of seven large motor carriers, deferred to ICC expertise in administering national transportation policy, even though without ICC approval the merger would have violated the antitrust laws. Justices Black, Douglas, and Murphy dissented, with Douglas writing that the ICC, in lifting the federal antitrust ban, should have been required to explain more adequately why its decision did not thwart the Transportation Act of 1920.[18] Three weeks later, in another ICC case, *Eastern-Central Motor Carriers Ass'n v. United States*,[19] while recognizing the obligation to defer to agency expertise, Rutledge used Douglas's dissenting rationale in *McLean Trucking* to announce for a different 6-to-3 majority that the commission, by failing to provide adequate explanation, had erred in rejecting rate schedules that motor carriers had proposed for meeting rail competition. This time Justice Frankfurter, joined by Stone and Reed, dissented on a ground that paralleled Rutledge's position in *McLean Trucking*: the commission's competence obviated further explication.

Rutledge's outcomes—joined in both cases by Roberts and Jackson—were not necessarily inconsistent; depending on the issue, a statute may require an agency to provide more, or less, explanation of its rationale for decision, based on the reviewing court's need for detail in judging whether the agency was acting reasonably within its mandate. It seems clear, therefore, that Justice Rutledge, far from showing interest in driving the administrative law in a particular direction, was simply trying his best to interpret congressional intent. To his half-brother Ivan, Wiley wrote: "Just between you and me, I had to swallow pretty hard to write the McLean case the way I did. Had I been on the Commission I would have voted the other way, and I think if I had been in Congress I would have voted to make a separate provision applicable to the truck lines. But as I read the statute and what the Commission had done, I couldn't come out substituting my own judgment for the latter's."[20]

Rutledge's third majority opinion, in *NLRB v. Hearst Publications, Inc.*, had long-term significance in the labor field. For an 8-to-1 majority (Justice Roberts dissenting), Rutledge held that the National Labor Relations Board had not erred in ruling that newsboys who "sell full-time at established spots" are "employees" in an appropriate bargaining unit, within the meaning of the Wagner Act, and thus that the publisher could not refuse to bargain collectively with them. Of importance here was rejection of the employer's argument that "common-law standards determine the 'employee' relationship under the Act," and that the common law would characterize the newsboys not as "employees" but as "independent contractors" free from collective bargaining obligations.[21]

Rutledge wrote that the history and purposes of the legislation, directed at "underlying economic facts," informed the statutory definitions of terms, such as "employee." These considerations entirely outweighed reliance on "technical legal classifications" formulated at common law for "purposes unrelated to the statute's objectives." Equally important, Rutledge said, Congress had assigned primary responsibility for defining terms under the act not to the courts but to the NLRB, whose expertise in administering the statute should prevail in defining "employee" if, on the factual record, the board's definition had "a reasonable basis in law." Rutledge then found an "ample basis" for employee status here, since the newsboys "worked continuously and regularly," and the publisher effectively set wages by dictating prices, fixing the markets, controlling the supply of newspapers, and to some extent prescribing hours of work while supervising efforts on the job.[22] By addressing, comprehensively, the respective roles of agency and court, requiring judicial deference to the administrative body's interpretation and application of the statute it was charged to administer, Rutledge reinforced in *Hearst Publications* the jurisprudence that protected administrative agencies against judges who would substitute their own judgments for the expertise of agency administrators. While not the first statement of this approach to judicial review, Rutledge's opinion moved the deference doctrine forward significantly.

Rutledge was not, however, as we have seen in *Eastern-Central Motor Carriers*, a slave to agency expertise. Nor was he an automaton for organized labor. In *Medo Photo Supply Corp. v. NLRB*—in dissent—he opined against a union. Accompanied by Justice Roberts (who dissented without opinion), Rutledge rejected a decision, written by the Chief Justice, sustaining an NLRB ruling that an employer had committed an unfair labor practice by dealing directly with employees represented by a union.[23] Rutledge's scrutiny of the record and the law convinced him that the employer had not yet recognized the union; and that even if the employer had done so, the employee majority could—and did—lawfully revoke the union's representation and approach the employer directly for a raise, without notifying the union first. Finally, Rutledge concluded that even if the employer had acted the way the Court majority required for avoiding an unfair labor practice—namely, telling the employees that because they were represented by a union the employer could not deal with them directly—this response would have brought as much pressure on the employees to discharge the union as did the employer's offer to grant a raise whether the employees were represented or not.[24]

Rutledge's dissent in *Medo Photo* is perplexing because it was premised on a highly questionable legal view that an employee majority had validly revoked union representation. That the common law of agency, on which Rutledge relied, would permit members of a union to revoke its authority without notifying union officers did not necessarily mean that federal labor law evolving under the National Labor Relations ("Wagner") Act would permit union members to go, informally, behind the back of a union they had designated, by formal vote, to represent them. Surely the justice who had rejected common law definitions when interpreting the statute in *Hearst Publications*, issued the same month as *Medo Photo*, had to know that! Furthermore, one can question Rutledge's conclusion that an employer's refusal to deal directly with unionized employees would be as much an inducement for employees to abandon the union as an employer's willingness to grant a wage increase whether the employees were unionized or not. What was going on?

Wiley Rutledge acknowledged the NLRB's expertise in interpreting the Wagner Act, and he strongly believed in organized labor. But he also had a special sensitivity to the problems of small business—a Brandeis mentality—in an economic environment of increasing business concentration. Recall, for example, the suggestion in his article "Significant Trends" that even a state's corporation law should be reformulated to recognize three types of entities: the "corner peanut wagon," the "small local concern," and the "gigantic corporation[]." Medo Photo Supply Corp. fit within his second category: the entire company had seventy employees, the collective bargaining unit at issue fewer than thirty. Thus, although Rutledge recognized that a "small employer," as well as a larger one, could not lawfully induce its employees to abandon their union, he also believed that this limitation on employer action was highly fact-specific. There was not, in Rutledge's view, an irrebuttable presumption that an employer commits an unfair labor practice in all cases by discussing a wage increase with a majority of its employees who tell the employer, before any discussion of wages, that the union no longer represents them.[25]

Rutledge conceded that "in large units, where there are difficult problems of ascertaining whether a majority exists at a particular time, a reasonable degree of stability in employment relations" might require that "a majority designation be deemed to continue for a reasonable period" until the employees' wishes could be sorted out. On the other hand, Rutledge concluded that "the actual desires of the majority" of a small employer's work force usually could be "easily and readily ascertained"; that in Medo's case an employee majority had taken the initiative to abandon the union and bargain directly with the employer; and thus that the facts in *Medo Photo* belied any finding of overreaching by the employer. Rutledge wrote to his Chief Justice, "I regret again the necessity of dissenting from an opinion of yours," but "I feel that this case simply goes too far in giving unions as such power to dictate relations between employers and employees."[26]

The premium that Rutledge had always placed on individual liberty served as a warning that each labor union had a life—a legal personality— uniquely its own. On the one hand, the union's collective power facilitated equality of bargaining power between labor and management, and occasionally Rutledge would concur specially to make clear that a ruling in which he joined against organized labor had narrow application.[27] On the other hand a union, particularly in a small business with few employees, could overreach its own members. *Medo Photo* accordingly revealed that once Rutledge got into the facts of a dispute involving an employer, a union, and employees, his would not be a sure vote for organized labor. His dissent may have been a less-than-satisfactory application of the law, but it brought truth to Herbert Wechsler's words in recommending Rutledge to Attorney General Biddle: although the judge's Court of Appeals record, "especially in the labor field," left "no room for doubt" that "properly progressive" values would be "safe in his hands," there was "independence of mind within that framework."[28]

IN EARLY MAY 1944, with but a month to go before the Court adjourned for the summer (and D-Day unfolded on the Normandy beaches), Justice Wiley Rutledge carried out his duties as assistant air raid warden for his Spring Valley neighborhood, patrolling Rockwood Parkway from 8:50 to 9:30 P.M. He liked that. He also probably enjoyed his more public life—the occasional White House or diplomatic reception or concert allowing him to see who the players were in official Washington. And he probably even felt a measure of satisfaction in achieving a place there himself.[29] But Rutledge was still the man who had been uncomfortable years earlier with the pretension and pointless talk at a Washington University faculty cocktail party, and if ever he had to choose he would take the neighborhood—meaning friendships with down-to-earth people—over gatherings of the powerful.

Typical was his friendship with Sam Wagshal, owner of a delicatessen near the Rutledge home. One night, an hour after closing time, Rutledge saw someone in the delicatessen, walked in, and asked, "May I have a ham sandwich, Smithfield ham?" "No," replied Wagshal. "Too late. I'll sell you the bread. Take it home and you can make your own sandwiches." Rutledge dropped by late on other occasions; he was turned away. "I'm sorry. I forgot. All right," he would say.[30] Eventually, Wagshal's daughter saw the justice's picture in the paper and showed her father. In telling the story of "The Most

Unforgettable Character I've Met" to *Reader's Digest*, Wagshal asked rhetorically, "Well, what happened the next time he came in? . . . Keep him out, I didn't. Not after that. But believe me, he got used to coming in on time — and staying late. . . . [W]e got to having big talks. With the Smithfield ham, the sour cream, the herrings — we also discussed issues." Continued Wagshal: "I remember the time he said: 'Well, Sammy — so you're a Republican. What's the matter — you got it so bad under the New Deal? Look at Sammy, the New Deal did him dirt. It brought him a lot of customers. It sure is tough for you, Sammy, isn't it?' That's the way he used to kid me." And the relationship grew. The justice even took his newest Republican friend as his guest to the Truman inauguration. "We used to talk about friendship," recalled Wagshal. "He was interested in my friends. And he used to bring in his friends to meet me."[31]

Once, when Wagshal's son, Ben, was complaining about how hard he had to work at the delicatessen and how much more money others were making, "Justice heard him," Wagshal remembered, and "he and the boy sat down for an hour. He told my son how proud he should be of his father — and of what I'm doing — an independent man — a small business man. . . . That's what makes America great, Justice said to my boy. It will be a different America when men can't work and live independent." Years later, Benjamin Wagshal recalled the occasion fondly. "He believed this country could only survive with the small businessman. I heard him say that." Ben Wagshal remembered Rutledge as "a really fine gentleman in every sense of the word" and a "true friend of my late dad." He was "very outgoing"; you "could see he was a man who was enjoying life." And "even if you didn't know he was a judge, you'd know he's a special person; you could see that in his face."[32]

The delicatessen had difficulties with a bakery whose driver would make deliveries only during the lunch hour. When the Wagshals insisted on a more convenient delivery time, the bakery canceled the account and the delicatessen contracted with another bakery. Soon thereafter, the president of the union representing the driver for the first bakery told the Wagshals they owed the driver $150, payable to him personally. When they paid the bill directly to the bakery owner, the union president somehow obtained the check, returned it, and advised as before that the payment was due the driver. The next day, the second bakery stopped doing business with the Wagshals because the union had threatened "to pull out all its drivers" if the bakery continued with the delicatessen. And the union effectively launched a boycott, cutting off the Wagshals' bread supply. The Wagshals obtained a temporary restraining order against the union in federal court, and the case eventually reached the Supreme Court, presenting the question whether under the Norris-LaGuardia Act, the controversy was a "labor dispute," permitting the union's immediate appeal of the temporary order.[33] With Rutledge recusing himself, the Supreme Court held 5 to 3—Black, Douglas, and Murphy dissenting—that the case concerned a "business controversy," not a "labor dispute," and ruled accordingly that the temporary order in the Wagshals' favor was not appealable and thus the order stood.[34]

The decision came down on a Monday when the delicatessen was closed, and Sam Wagshal threw a party there to celebrate. Midway through the evening, he answered a knock at the door. The recused Supreme Court justice had stopped by to offer congratulations.[35] Especially when one remembers *Medo Photo*, it becomes interesting to speculate how Wiley Rutledge, the believer in organized labor and the small businessman, would have come out in *Wagshal* by any other name.

IMMEDIATELY AFTER the Court adjourned in June 1944, Rutledge headed for Cleveland, Tennessee, where he arranged with Ivan's help to move their father and Miss Tamsey to a sanatorium in Asheville for the summer. Miss Tamsey had contracted tuberculosis, and the reverend's heart had weakened considerably; he could "go at any time," wrote the justice to friends. Rutledge had been back in Washington little more than a week when his father died on July 6. Having so recently spent days with his father and other family members, Rutledge did not return for the funeral. A cousin filled him in fully, however, and in September, after receiving an LL.D. from the University of Chattanooga, the justice drove over to Cleveland for help with emotional closure. He found the grave that Ivan had selected, atop a hill overlooking "the Tennessee River valley directly toward Walden's Ridge," with Pikeville, the father's birthplace, immediately beyond. "It really is almost perfect for him," Rutledge wrote to a friend.[36]

MISS TAMSEY died in her sixty-second year in December 1944, five months after her husband, and Rutledge went south again to spend a few days with Ivan.[37] On his return, the justice attended a gathering of law professors from all over the country then serving in Washington. When he entered the large dining room at the Harrington Hotel, everyone "stood up and cheered with the wildest kind of enthusiasm." A former clerk to Justice Black, John Frank, recalled how it "was obvious that he'd made an enormous number of personal friends in the profession" who were "devoted to him." And, Frank added, for the many Midwestern professors there was a "one of our boys made good feeling." Over fifty years later, Frank could still feel the "sheer fervor" of the moment; "my skin prickles," he said, in telling about it.[38]

The dinner speakers were Landis and Leach of Harvard, whose visions for legal education in the future, in John Frank's hearing, reflected Harvard of the 1920s. "For me," according to Frank, that was "discouraging," a sentiment that he conveyed to Rutledge as they left the hotel together. Rutledge, Frank recalled, then "turned on me in genuine anger—the only time he ever was angry with me about anything—and said, 'You have no right to be discouraged. For those of us who have been carrying the burden of Harvard on our backs and around our necks for years and years, we've learned how to handle it, and how to survive it, and how to get around it, and it's up to you to do the same thing. Get in there and fight!'"[39]

Rutledge was not anti-Ivy. His son attended Yale Law School; Rutledge himself had recruited Willard Wirtz from Harvard; and the justice eagerly took clerks from Columbia, Harvard, and Yale. But he also took clerks from Iowa and Northwestern. And he was proud of the Midwestern law school heritage—Cooley, Hammond, Wigmore, Pound, Freund—and of the countless professional colleagues and students he knew from the heartland and further west. To so many at the schools and in the profession, Rutledge had become the paramount professional representative of "MidAmerica," to use a favorite expression of his.[40]

THROUGHOUT HIS years on the Court, Wiley Rutledge continued to say—and without question he meant it—that he enjoyed teaching more than judging. Knowing that, his friends continued their efforts to lure him back to the academy either as a university chancellor or as a law professor. But he always replied that he could accomplish more for what he believed in by remaining on the Court—a conclusion buttressed by a feeling that in good conscience, he could never leave a post in which Franklin Roosevelt had asked him to serve. He felt locked in by duty, but he was at peace with that.[41]

Nonetheless, he never got beyond the feeling that the Court's work was terribly hard. Rutledge easily convinced himself every June that the Court's docket in the term just ended had been the roughest, toughest that any justice had faced in the Court's history. Summers in Colorado—by way of Iowa City or St. Louis, or perhaps both—became the respite he longed for and thoroughly enjoyed. They almost always required time out for speeches, whether at judicial conferences or the local Rotary or Kiwanis—true labors of love—but the summers also left time for renewing friendships, loafing, reading. And fishing. He loved driving to the mountains and wading the streams with his law school classmate, Clay Apple, more for the outdoors and the friendship than the catch. And the summer of 1944 brought a special treat: a ten-day fishing trip on the headwaters of the South Fork of the White River in Colorado, organized by a state trial judge, Robert W. Steele, from Denver. "There were fifteen in all," Rutledge wrote the Fuchses, including sons of four of the men. (Neal could not join his father because Hollis Fuchs was visiting Neal in Boulder.) He "had a grand week," the justice added, "notwithstanding the trout continued to be shy" (he had caught only a measly two). Rutledge elaborated to another friend: "We lived outdoors in tents" at a spot reached "by hiking eight miles up the canyon from the point where we left our cars"—"no newspapers, no mail, no telephone and no radio."[42]

The group was a "grubby lot"—they never shaved—and an interesting mix. In addition to several lawyers there were men who owned or operated a chain of ten-cent stores, a paint company, and a grain business, as well as a school board president, a dentist, and even a psychiatrist. The day began with a long breakfast—pancakes, eggs, bacon, coffee—followed by Rutledge's washing the dishes, since he was no cook. The men fished, walked in the woods, played bridge and poker, and talked long into the night about the war, politics, philosophy, and the history of the mountains, including the Native American Utes and their artifacts. There was campfire singing—"Home on the Range," "Roundup Time in Texas," "Bicycle Built for Two"—as well as story telling laced with dirty jokes. Officially, no alcohol was allowed, but there at least was one night of many too many whiskey sours. All of which was protected by the trip motto: "Nothing goes [back] across the river." The justice returned from the trip with "a little dark hirsute adornment" on his upper lip, which Neal urged him to shave off because it suggested that his father supported Governor Dewey, while Jean Ann and Mary Lou encouraged him to keep it because he was "much more handsome" with that much of his face covered up. He shaved it off.[43]

On the White River trip the next year Judge Steele's son, Bill, joined the outing and recalled Rutledge as "a wonderful, wonderful human being" with a special smile who "wasn't impressed with himself" and had insisted that the young man call him "Wiley." As the men came out of the woods, Bill Steele remembered, they learned that "we'd dropped the Tommy bomb"— the meaning of which they did not understand until they arrived at a ranch for the night and heard about Hiroshima and Nagaski.[44]

That summer of 1945 the justice returned early to Washington around Labor Day, just as Japan was signing the terms of its defeat aboard the battleship *Missouri* in Tokyo Bay. His son Neal, who had finished a year at Haverford before joining the Marines, arrived in Washington at about the same time after completing the Marines' Japanese-language school. His father—invited to the White House to join the gathering to welcome home General Jonathan M. Wainright after long imprisonment following the Bataan Death March—picked up his son at the train station. Unshaved, and in a rumpled uniform from his all-night ride in coach, Neal protested his father's insistence that he come along. To no avail. An embarrassed Neal Rutledge called the incident an example of his father's "Tennessee brand of humor" with its "edge of cruelty." "My father enjoyed my discomfort immensely," Neal added, not yielding to the suggestion that the justice, most of all, may have wanted his son to witness a historic event.[45]

NINETEEN

War Crimes and Military Commissions

In an extraordinary summer session in 1942 before Rutledge joined the Supreme Court, the justices upheld 8 to 0 (with Murphy not participating) the jurisdiction of a military commission, established by presidential order, to try in a secret proceeding eight German saboteurs (including an American citizen) who had landed surreptitiously on New York and Florida beaches carrying explosives.[1] This decision, *Ex parte Quirin*, served as the underlying text for the Court's contentious decision in *In re Yamashita*[2]— in which Justice Rutledge filed his celebrated dissent—reviewing the military commission conviction of the Japanese general charged with command responsibility for atrocities in the Philippines at the end of World War II.

In his first draft opinion for the Court in *Yamashita*, Chief Justice Stone noted initially that the Constitution authorized Congress to create military commissions "for the trial and punishment of offenses against the law of war," and that federal court scrutiny of military commissions was limited to "habeas corpus" review. This meant that the courts had the authority to examine only whether the commission had "lawful power" to try the accused for the offense charged, leaving the military authorities alone with the power to review the legality of the charges, the commission's factual findings, and, as a result, the accused's guilt or innocence.[3]

Stone quickly rejected the first defense contentions by opining that General Styer, as the military commander of the area where the Manila atrocities occurred, had lawfully created the commission to try General Yamashita, and that its authority continued in the absence of a peace treaty after hostilities had ceased. The Chief Justice then turned to meatier issues: the substance of the charge and the commission's procedures. Stone had no difficulty demonstrating that the charge against Yamashita, buttressed by bills of particulars specifying 123 offenses, adequately identified violations of the law of war. Next, he asked, how detailed would the Court's inquiry have to be to determine whether the commission had "lawful power" to adjudicate Yamashita's "command responsibility" for those violations? Not very, concluded the chief. Citing the Fourth and Tenth Hague Conventions and the Geneva Red Cross Convention of 1929, Stone announced, first, that the law of war imposed "an affirmative duty to take such measures" as are within a commander's "power" and are "appropriate in the circumstances" for protecting "prisoners of war and the civilian population." The prosecution's charge, he said, satisfied that standard in alleging that General Yamashita had committed an "unlawful breach of duty" by "permitting" troops under his command—whom he had an obligation to "control"—to commit "the extensive and widespread atrocities specified."[4]

But this conclusion begged a fundamental question that the defense had raised before the commission and brought again to the Supreme Court. Should not the prosecution have to prove that the commander knew of the atrocities before he could be charged criminally with failing to prevent them? If not actual knowledge, should not the commander at least have had reason to know that the carnage was taking place? Stone never expressly addressed the "knowledge" issue, but then, confusingly, he injected it indirectly. After emphasizing that in sustaining the charge, the Court did "not weigh the evidence," he added inexplicably: "We . . . hold . . . that the commission, *upon the facts found*, could properly find petitioner guilty" of a command violation. To be sure, he was not evaluating the quality of the evidence against Yamashita; but he appeared to be saying that the very power of the commission to adjudicate the general's guilt depended not only on a correct legal formulation of the charge but also on the adequacy of the commission's factual findings in support of it. Was he using the "facts found" to amplify the ambiguous charge enough to cover and satisfy, albeit in conclusory fashion, the "knowledge" issue? Even if he was, Stone's failure to address that issue more clearly, by explaining the importance of the commission's factual findings in determining the commission's "lawful power" over General Yamashita, bred substantial confusion.[5]

Yamashita's next contention—that the commission lacked jurisdiction because its procedures permitted conviction on evidence not admissible under the Articles of War (enacted by Congress), the Geneva Convention (adopted by treaty), and Fifth Amendment due process (established by the Constitution)—gave the Court a most difficult issue. The commission, over defense objection, had admitted not only live testimony subject to cross-examination but also depositions, hearsay, and opinion evidence contrary to the plain language of the Articles of War and the Geneva Convention. Specifically, Article of War 25 prohibited deposition evidence in capital cases before military commissions; Article of War 38 limited the "procedure, including modes of proof," in cases before military commissions—to the extent that the president "shall deem practicable"—to the "rules of evidence" generally applicable in federal district court criminal trials, which excluded hearsay and lay opinion; and Article 63 of the Geneva Convention of 1929 limited sentencing of prisoners of war "to the same procedures" applicable to members of "the armed forces of the detaining power," that is, in military courts martial.[6]

Stone held for the Court majority, however, that because according to Article of War 2 the articles applied to "persons subject to military law," Articles 25 and 38 applied only to "members of our own Army" and to personnel who "accompany the army"—not to "[e]nemy combatants." Further, Stone concluded, Article 63 of the Geneva Convention, while applicable to enemy prisoners, pertained only to offenses committed while in captivity, not to war crimes before capture. Lastly, Stone summarily held the due process clause of the Fifth Amendment inapplicable, writing cryptically that for "reasons already stated" only the military authorities, not the courts, had authority to review the "commission's rulings on evidence" and "mode of conducting these proceedings."[7]

IN RESPONSE to Stone's draft, Rutledge suggested to Murphy, "You take the charge; I'll take the balance." Justice Murphy soon circulated a broadside against the majority. Proclaiming that "due process of law applies to 'any person,'" including "an enemy belligerent," Murphy perceived "no serious attempt" to charge Yamashita with "a recognized violation of the laws of war." The general had not been charged with "personally participating" in "acts of atrocity," whether by "ordering," "condoning," or even knowing about them. Rather, opined Murphy, he had been charged merely with failing to discharge a duty "to control" the troops under his command, a charge without the "slightest precedent" in international law, especially in the context of a defeated army in disarray from "constant and overwhelming assault." Murphy called "misplaced" Stone's reliance on "vague and indefinite references" in the Hague and Geneva Conventions to define violations of the law of war; the provisions cited were "devoid of relevance." Murphy reiterated: "In no recorded instance . . . has the mere inability to control troops under fire or attack by superior forces been made the basis of a charge of violating the laws of war." Fundamentally, Murphy was accusing the majority of applying an ex post facto law by permitting the "military commission to make the crime whatever it willed," depending on its "biased view" of Yamashita's "duties" and "disregard thereof."[8]

Murphy was preaching a sermon based on natural law, not just on the Constitution. "The *immutable rights* of the individual, *including* those secured by the due process clause of the Fifth Amendment, belong not alone to the members of those nations that excel on the battlefield or that subscribe to the democratic ideology" (emphasis added). Rather, "[t]hey belong to every person in the world, victor or vanquished, whatever may be his race, color or beliefs." And because prisoners of war lack direct access to the courts, the "judicial review available by habeas corpus must be wider than usual in order that proper standards of justice may be enforceable," Murphy added. "Indeed," he concluded, "an uncurbed spirit of revenge and retribution, masked in formal legal procedure for purposes of dealing with a fallen enemy commander, can do more lasting harm than all of the atrocities giving rise to that spirit."[9] Murphy overstated his case: the international conventions cited by Stone offered a substantial basis, albeit with little precedent, for charging criminal liability for breach of command responsibility. Some of Murphy's analysis, moreover, tended toward assertion rather than documentation.[10] It remained for Justice Rutledge to expose with intellectual precision the flaws in Stone's presentation.

Murphy had begun writing his dissent before the Court heard from Stone. Because Rutledge's task was more complex, he waited until he received Stone's "full opinion" on January 22, so that he would know his target precisely. Stone had seemed so determined to issue the Court's opinion on Monday, January 28, that one of the justices had even suggested having the majority honor that deadline by requiring the dissenters to file their opinions later. "I was not going to do that," Rutledge wrote to a friend. Not trusting that the majority would extend the usual courtesy of waiting to issue the Court's opinion until all who were writing had finished, the dissenting justice "worked night and day until Saturday noon [the 26th], finishing the first draft one minute before the conference bell." He had worked "one night until five o'clock" in the morning, and had collaborated on Friday night with law clerk and secretary "until after midnight."

> Then I went home and worked the rest of the night, not taking off my clothes, and coming back the next morning without either breakfast or shaving, to spend the next two hours driving here at my desk with all my might. . . . I notified the conference that my opinion would be circulated that afternoon. . . . [T]he brethren all at once realized that *they* might not be ready Monday morning. . . . Now that the tables were somewhat turned they agreed that we would meet on Monday morning at ten o'clock to discuss whether the case should be sent down at noon.

Stone and the majority decided that they needed another week.[11]

Rutledge later wrote to Victor Brudney: "I had not heretofore had an experience here, and hope never to have another one, of being forced to the gun as we were in that case." The justice added, "I didn't give the boys as much hell in Yamashita as I wanted to. I felt like turning loose with all the fire that Murphy poured on." Concerned about Murphy's vituperation, however, Rutledge believed that for maximum impact, he had to keep his own "tone within some bounds of restraint." So Rutledge's dissent began respectfully:

> Not with ease does one find his views at odds with the Court's in a matter of this character and gravity. Only the most deeply felt convictions could force one to differ. That reason alone leads me to do so now, against strong considerations for withholding dissent.

> More is at stake than General Yamashita's fate. There could be no possible sympathy for him if he is guilty of the atrocities for which his death is sought. But there can be and should be justice administered according to law. . . .

> With all deference to the opposing views of my brethren, whose attachment to . . . [our great constitutional] tradition needless to say is no less than my own, I cannot believe in the face of this record that the petitioner has had the fair trial our Constitution and laws command.[12]

In a dissent that scholars have called "masterful" and "penetrating," "undoubtedly a great opinion"—a "careful examination of detail" that exemplifies "the fairness" which the justice himself "commends as a precept" —Wiley Rutledge produced an exhaustive analysis that combined scholarship with eloquence. It is one of the Court's truly great, and influential, dissents. Wrote Charles Fairman, then of Stanford, later of the Harvard law faculty: "Whether one agrees with him or not on his several points—and individuals will vary greatly in their evaluation of the competing interests involved—one must respect the ideal of justice" for which Rutledge was striving.[13]

In apt summary of the disagreement, Rutledge observed in dissent:

> The difference between the Court's view of this proceeding and my own comes down in the end to the view, on the one hand, that there is no law restrictive upon these proceedings other than whatever rules and regulations may be prescribed for their government by the executive authority or the military and, on the other hand, that the provisions of the Articles of War, of the Geneva Convention and the Fifth Amendment apply.

In elaborating his position, Justice Rutledge first agreed, briefly, with the defense argument that *Ex parte Quirin* did not justify trial by military commission rather than a civilian court, since cessation of hostilities had removed all "military necessity" for such a commission. Rutledge accordingly disagreed with Justice Murphy's acknowledgment that the commission had been legally established. For that reason, in addition to his concern about his colleague's tone—Murphy even used the word "vengeance"—Justice Rutledge did not formally join Murphy's opinion (although Murphy joined his). Rutledge did, however, join unequivocally in Murphy's condemnation of the charge against General Yamashita.[14]

Specifically, in Rutledge's view, the law of war permitted conviction of a commander for failure to control his troops only if there was credible proof that the commander knew of the crimes his troops had committed in time to stop or at least punish them. According to Rutledge, however, Stone's opinion would uphold the general's conviction on the ambiguous charge that he had failed in his duty simply by "permitting" his troops "to commit brutal atrocities and other high crimes." Although some might read the word "permitting" to imply knowledge and acquiescence, Rutledge noted, others would say that it implied "mere failure to discover" through the institutional structure of command—at worst, negligence. Because the charge, fairly read, authorized conviction on the latter interpretation—which did not state a law-of-war violation—Rutledge concluded that it was fatally defective.[15]

But assuming that the charge adequately informed Yamashita of the conduct and "knowledge" that made him legally accountable, under the law of war, for what his troops were doing, Rutledge argued that the commission's findings were inadequate. As noted earlier, the only two witnesses who proclaimed Yamashita's direct knowledge of the brutality had been discredited so substantially that the prosecutor ignored them in closing argument. Years later, Major William H. Parks, in an exhaustive analysis of the record, identified circumstantial evidence that the commission might have specified to find that Yamashita had at least had reason to know of several alleged brutalities as they were going on. The commission made no such express finding, however.[16] At most, according to Rutledge (and to others who have studied the case), the commission—referring to no facts—proffered "inferential findings" that Yamashita had "had knowledge." In the commission's words, the prosecution had "presented evidence" tending to show the crimes to have been "so extensive and widespread" that the general must have "wilfully permitted" or "secretly ordered" them. On their face, these findings revealed no more than surmise, Rutledge thought.[17]

Furthermore, the "ultimate findings"—commonly called conclusions of law—on which the commission premised guilt did not mention the general's knowledge. As Rutledge noted, the commission based conviction

General Yamashita testifying at his trial.
(U.S. Army photograph; National Archives, III-SC-221263)

on no more than "(1) the fact of widespread atrocities and crimes" and (2) Yamashita's failure "to provide the effective control . . . required by the circumstances." In sum, Rutledge stressed, whatever findings the record may have supported, the commission—sustained by the Stone majority —found Yamashita guilty, and recommended death by hanging, without either specifying the level of knowledge, if any, legally required for culpability or attributing to the general any awareness of a particular atrocity. Because of its ambiguity, Rutledge concluded, the commission's ruling could be read as no more than a conviction for negligence.[18]

Moreover, Rutledge proposed, even assuming that these ultimate findings, ambiguous at best as to knowledge, would suffice nonetheless for conviction if supported by the evidence, the required proof was lacking, because the evidence was tainted by the "complete abrogation of customary safeguards" required for its admission. The commission's regulations allowed in evidence "[e]very conceivable kind of statement, rumor, report, at first, second, third or further hand, written, printed or oral, and one 'propaganda' film." The commission thus condemned the general to death, Rutledge observed, with findings based substantially on "untrustworthy, unverified, unauthenticated evidence" not questioned—or even effectively questionable—by "cross-examination or other means of testing credibility, probative value or authenticity." As a result, Rutledge reasoned, Yamashita had been convicted based on knowledge merely imputed to him from evidence that in fair part "would be inadmissible in any other capital case or proceeding under our system, civil or military." Nor, finally, had Yamashita received a real opportunity to prepare his defense, according to the justice, if only because the commission had denied a requested continuance after the prosecution—three days before trial—served on defense counsel "a supplemental bill of particulars" that contained "59 more specifications" in addition to the 64 originally charged.[19]

Critical to the dissent, of course, was Rutledge's legal analysis showing why these procedural shortcuts violated enforceable rights of a Japanese general tried for war crimes in the Philippines. Even the majority would have agreed that the Articles of War, the Geneva Convention of 1929, and the Fifth Amendment due process clause—if applicable—would have required reversal of Yamashita's conviction and a retrial, because the commission's loose charges and methods of proof had not conformed to the standards prescribed. Rutledge accordingly detailed the arguments refuting Stone's legal analysis.

In the first place, Rutledge noted, Article of War 25 (excluding, in capital cases, deposition evidence not cross-examined) and Article of War 38 (incorporating insofar as "practicable" the rules of evidence applicable to criminal trials in federal district courts) expressly applied to trials by "military commissions." Rutledge recognized, along with Stone, that Article 2 specified categories of military and related personnel who were "subject to these articles," namely members of the Regular Army, cadets, Marines attached to the army, "retainers to the camp" and other civilians "accompanying or serving with" the army, persons "under sentence adjudged by courts-martial," and residents of the "Regular Army Soldiers' Home." But he emphatically rejected Stone's conclusion that Article 2 should be read to delimit the entire universe of persons eligible for Article 25 and 38 protections.[20] Where, more specifically, was the conflict between Stone and Rutledge?

After Congress revised the Articles of War in 1916, the articles recognized, as they always had, the military "court martial" traditionally used to try U.S. military personnel for military crimes. In addition, as Justice Rutledge observed, the revised articles acknowledged, for the first time, the "military commission." Since the days of the Mexican War, the military had convened such commissions—without statutory authority—to try civilians for ordinary crimes committed in the "theater of hostilities," and to prosecute both civilians and enemy belligerents for offenses against the common law of war. Confusion developed, however, because the revised articles did not retain courts martial and military commissions as mutually exclusive tribunals; to some extent they became overlapping. Specifically, field commanders were given court-martial authority to try civilians and enemy belligerents who theretofore, when charged with violating the law of war, had been triable only by military commission. But that broadened authority was optional. To make clear, accordingly, that expanded court-martial jurisdiction did not contract the jurisdiction of military commissions, the revised articles expressly stated that the provisions expanding court-martial jurisdiction should not be interpreted to deprive "military commissions" of "concurrent jurisdiction" for trial of "offenders or offenses" under the "law of war."[21] The question for interpretation, then, was whether the procedural safeguards in the revised Articles of War—newly applicable in courts martial of civilians and enemy belligerents—also applied now to trials before military commissions. Stone answered no; Rutledge, yes.

Stone acknowledged that the revised articles did grant protection, for the first time, to U.S. military (and related) personnel if tried by military commission, but he perceived no congressional intent to extend that protection to others. Rutledge, on the other hand, found no such bifurcation of rights; to him, the revised articles' plain language and legislative history— both of which he addressed in detail—conferred rights, such as those in Articles 25 and 38, on trials before courts martial and military commissions alike, without differentiation among particular classes of defendants. After illustrating various anomalies revealed by Stone's interpretation—including the unavailability of the articles' procedural guarantees to American civilians tried before military commissions—Rutledge concluded that Congress could not have intended "two types of military commission" in the articles, the first conducting trials of American military personnel and civilian followers in one way, the second trying other American civilians and enemy belligerents in a different way.[22]

Through similar, meticulous textual analysis, Rutledge also countered Stone's conclusion that the Geneva Convention applied only to offenses committed by prisoners while prisoners. If, as Rutledge contended, Geneva Convention protections applied to the trial of war crimes committed before capture, then the Articles of War—court-martial protections—would have applied by way of that treaty. Finally, Justice Rutledge invoked Fifth

Amendment due process "[w]holly apart from the violation of the Articles of War and of the Geneva Convention," and rejected the majority's denial of "all such safeguards." To Rutledge, due process was "the great issue in the cause." "Not heretofore," according to the justice, "has it been held that any human being is beyond [the Fifth Amendment's] universally protecting spread in the guaranty of a fair trial in the most fundamental sense." Rutledge warned, "That door is dangerous to open. I will have no part in opening it. For once it is ajar, even for enemy belligerents, it can be pushed back wider for others, perhaps ultimately for all." [23]

Specifically, he added, "the heart of the security" of a fair trial, especially a trial on charges carrying the death penalty, lies in two elements of due process. "One is that conviction shall not rest in any essential part upon unchecked rumor, report, or the results of the prosecution's ex parte investigations, but shall stand on proven fact; the other, correlative, lies in a fair chance to defend," including a timely understanding of "the exact nature" of the charged offense, a "reasonable time for preparing to meet the charge," the "aid of counsel," and reasonable continuances to deal with "surprise." [24]

In conclusion, after forty printed pages (compared with Stone's twenty-one and Murphy's sixteen), Rutledge wrote: "What military agencies or authorities may do with our enemies in battle or invasion . . . is beside the point. Nor has any human being heretofore been held to be wholly beyond elementary procedural protection by the Fifth Amendment. I cannot consent to even implied departure from that great absolute." [25] (Rutledge did not address how due process, as applied to prisoners of war, might differ, if at all, from the protections guaranteed to our own military by the Articles of War.)

Upon receiving Rutledge's dissent, Stone over the weekend drafted a section on due process, concluding that the military commission—by analogy to an expert administrative agency—had used a procedure and applied an evidentiary standard high enough to satisfy the Fifth Amendment. His colleagues Reed, Frankfurter, and Douglas remained on board, and Burton for the first time joined. But Justice Black balked. He found Stone's analogy to an administrative agency too strained; the commission had conducted a judicial proceeding carrying criminal sanctions. If due process applied, Black said, the commission had failed. Black accordingly drafted a concurring opinion to explain why constitutional due process was unavailable for trials by military commission. In order to avoid a fractured majority, the chief withdrew all discussion of due process. Black withdrew his own draft and joined Stone. The others in the majority remained. The opinions came down on February 4, 1946. Four days later, President Truman denied executive clemency. By sunrise on February 23, 1946, General Tomoyuki Yamashita was dead.[26]

THE MAJORITY's refusal to address due process in *Yamashita*, according to Princeton's eminent constitutional historian Edward S. Corwin, reflected "a complete retreat, as well as a completely *silent* retreat," from the German saboteur case, *Ex parte Quirin*, on which Stone had relied to establish the commission's authority and the Court's standard of review. In *Quirin*, Stone himself had written that "the detention and trial" of enemy aliens, charged before a military commission with sabotage in the United States, were "not to be set aside by the courts without the clear conviction that they are in conflict with the Constitution or laws of Congress constitutionally enacted." But, the chief had emphasized, "Constitutional safeguards for the protection of all who are charged with offenses are not be disregarded in order to inflict merited punishment on some who are guilty." The *Quirin* Court accordingly had to evaluate, on habeas corpus, whether the Constitution permitted trial of "unlawful combatants"—in that case, spies without uniforms—before a military commission rather than a civilian court, and held the commission proceeding constitutional. In so ruling, the Court not only addressed the power of a military commission to try "unlawful combatants" for alleged violations of the law of war but also necessarily analyzed (before rejecting) the defendants' claimed Fifth Amendment right to presentment before a grand jury and Sixth Amendment right to a jury trial. Four years later, however, the *Yamashita* Court, in dealing with a uniformed prisoner of war—a "lawful combatant"—altogether avoided constitutional analysis in rejecting without discussion the general's Fifth Amendment due process claim.[27]

As to construing the Articles of War, Charles Fairman, a military and constitutional law expert, wrote at the time that "Mr. Justice Rutledge would seem to have the better of the argument."[28] Other scholars have agreed.[29] But this is not to say that the Chief Justice lacked a plausible interpretation. When Stone's statutory approach is compared with Rutledge's analysis, one must say that persons trained in the law could reasonably differ on this first-time case. Critical statutory language was ambiguous; some provisions, literally construed, conflicted with others; legislative history was confusing as witnesses before congressional committees, in focusing on one point, ignored the implications of their testimony for other issues perhaps not even visible at the time.

For difficult cases such as *Yamashita*, therefore, the interesting question is often not which judge is "correct" when interpreting a statute or treaty (especially since Congress, in drafting or approving the legislation, probably did not come to grips with the issue); in these situations, there is no "right" answer short of what a majority of the appellate bench says it is. The question is, rather, how a conscientious judge goes about marshaling the statutory language, committee reports, hearing testimony, and floor speeches in a way that leads to a particular, coherent result.

Initially, the judge will examine these data and, when the "answer" is not readily apparent, will try to find the most reasonable interpretation by applying time-honored canons of statutory construction and scrutinizing the legislation by reference to external sources, such as earlier versions of the statute that may suggest a change of congressional policy, and prior judicial decisions that give answers to analogous questions. But there is a deeper influence at work—the judge's own persona—that in the most complex and controversial cases is likely to channel the judge, at the threshold of the inquiry, in a particular direction if not toward a foreordained result.

Three members of the *Yamashita* majority—Stone, Black, and Douglas —had evidenced over the years profound concern for civil liberties. But they had joined Justices Reed and Frankfurter—and Rutledge—to make up the majority during the last Court term in *Korematsu*, upholding the military directive that ordered relocation and internment of all persons, even American citizens, of Japanese ancestry living in designated areas on the West Coast.[30] After Japan's attack on Pearl Harbor, the Constitution's war power had left these six justices unwilling to interfere with Congress, the president, and the military. Once hostilities ceased, however, with Japan's surrender in early September 1945, a different reality confronted the Court. Although the nation technically remained at war with Japan—there was no peace treaty until 1952—this defeated enemy posed no threat. And yet in the war's aftermath a new mix of anti-Japanese psychology took hold among the general public, including the judiciary. There was a powerful American feeling that the Philippine people, whom Japanese forces had brutalized, deserved to have those responsible for the carnage brought to justice as soon as possible. Manila, after all, had been "the second-most devastated city of World War II, after Warsaw." Thus, beginning with the trials of Generals Yamashita and Homma, already in captivity, the pursuit of justice in the Philippines was to proceed swiftly, beginning less than two months after the fighting stopped. Indeed, these first war crimes trials required expedition for another reason: 2,000 Japanese awaited prosecution before U.S. military commissions by November 1945.[31]

In addition to pressure for speed, other factors were to affect these initial prosecutions. The trials were to be held in Manila, not an emotionally stable venue. Furthermore, all members of the commissions appointed to try the two generals were affiliated with the American (and in Homma's case also the Philippine) military command. Neither of these commissions, therefore, had even the increment of detachment that might have been achieved by appointing a member or two from another allied country.[32] There surely was concern in the air, moreover, that unless the prosecution obtained convictions in these first "command responsibility" trials under international law, subsequent trials might go nowhere. This widely felt need for conviction surely affected commission procedure. MacArthur's headquarters knew that evidence gathering in war-torn areas was difficult, and particularly that arranging for testimony subject to cross-examination would often be impossible. Had General MacArthur prescribed for military commissions the evidentiary standards of the Constitution, or even of the Articles of War and the Geneva Convention, he would have imposed requirements that made the trial of war crimes more problematic. Finally, although the commission members had participated in military trials, none was a lawyer—not even the commission president designated the "law member" with final authority over legal rulings. Thus, there was serious risk that both in conducting the trials and in preparing their findings, the Yamashita and Homma commissions could stumble badly, or at least make a reviewing court's task far more difficult than it would have been if the commission members had legal training.[33]

For all these reasons, the first trials of Japanese generals before U.S. military commissions in the Philippines immediately after the war would inevitably deviate substantially from norms that governed criminal trials in federal and state courts on the American mainland. U.S. Supreme Court justices looking at what happened in those first commission proceedings, therefore, had to know that under the circumstances not much better could have been expected. Thus one can understand why a justice, recognizing the situation, would not have felt obliged to set the bar higher than the Stone majority placed it. In any event, were not the war crimes trials part of the war itself—a final reckoning—rather than severable accountings under a system of justice applicable only in peacetime? Rutledge and Murphy were taking standards of criminal procedure prevalent in a stable society and applying them to judgment of behavior in a chaotic, war-torn environment—not to mention behavior of the vilest sort.

This arguable disconnect between wartime evil and peacetime justice made for a powerful pressure to temporize. The Supreme Court justices could not have avoided thinking about the predictable impact of a decision to reverse the first conviction of a Japanese general. Other commission proceedings in progress would have had to be redone or even abandoned. Feelings in America, let alone the Philippines, would run high. And there was likely to be damage to the Court as an institution if publicly branded again—recall the "Court-packing" days less than a decade earlier[34]—as an obstructionist institution out of touch with the nation's idea of justice, particularly when coming out of a war with several brutal enemies. And what if the president, or even General MacArthur himself, decided to execute General Yamashita no matter what the Court said? These possibilities may not have been as far-fetched as modern Court observers may assume.[35] The justices' inevitable concern about the Court's reputation thus compounded the pressure not to interfere with military commission justice.

Undoubtedly aware—especially after reading Stone, Murphy, and Rutledge—that the *Yamashita* decision could reasonably go either way, each justice had to make a judgment that realistically would not be purely legal. Its content, unavoidably, would be intellectual, practical, and emotional. In deciding General Yamashita's fate, would it be more sound and responsible for a justice to invoke separation of powers doctrine, meaning deferral to the president and General MacArthur, or instead to extend rights specified in international treaties and the U.S. Constitution to enemy prisoners of war in trials of charges condemning belligerent acts before capture? Put another way, should the Court clear the way for the democratically elected branches of government to assume the moral and political responsibility for determining, ultimately, the rules for going forward against captured enemy commanders—subject only to the most limited scrutiny by a small cadre of lifetime judicial appointees in the Marble Palace on Capitol Hill? Or, for the sake of the very principles that the war was fought to defend, should the only branch of government established by the Founders to protect the individual against majority passions resist procedural shortcuts— which, upon reflection in less stressful moments, might be seen to suggest vengeance more than justice?

It is doubtful that any justice put questions to himself in quite this way. Any issue presented to a court, at least initially, is posed in a conscientious judge's mind as a purely legal one. And in most instances, it stays that way because the law has developed to a point where the result is indicated without serious doubt. Yet sometimes the issue is novel, the result far from clear, the consequences enormous, and the judge—after hard work and deep debate—honest enough to acknowledge, privately, that an opinion will "write"—that is, will reflect sufficient intellectual integrity—with more than one outcome. At that point, as Rutledge himself would have acknowledged,[36] the judge inevitably confronts a question of personal values that ultimately drive the judge's decision, however clothed in legal language. Once that inherently emotional "values" content is added to the mix, moreover, a decision on which reasonable minds can differ will often become transmuted in the particular judge's mind into a decision that could come out only one way. Merger of emotion with intellect becomes complete. The inquiry, initially laden with doubt, becomes a conviction, finally suffused with certainty—sometimes even permitting anger at a colleague who disagrees.

Armed with conviction by this process at once intellectual, practical, and emotional, the Court majority in *Yamashita*, led by Stone but influenced significantly by Black, opted for the war power over individual rights— indeed, for forbearance and deference to the executive over prerogative and engagement as a Court. Justice Black's desire to avoid compromising due process jurisprudence, as Stone's revisions in response to Rutledge would have required, achieved some damage control. And Justice Stone's desire, shared by others, for as nearly unanimous an opinion as possible accomplished an authoritative decision, without dilution by separate concurrence. But as we have seen, by skipping discussion of the Fifth Amendment, the *Yamashita* majority voted for constitutional avoidance.

To Justice Wiley Rutledge, as well as to Justice Frank Murphy, any rationale for compromising a constitutional protection of individual rights was suspect. There can be little doubt that the anguish Rutledge felt in joining the decisions in *Korematsu* and *Hirabayashi*—however justifiable he believed they were—must have fed his emotions while writing, in his *Yamashita* dissent, that "the Constitution follows the flag" to the Philippines.[37] Rutledge cared very much about the Court as an institution; he was not temperamentally a contrarian; and in war matters he had shown his respect for congressional and executive prerogatives. Furthermore, he tried conscientiously to discern and apply the law in every case with intellectual honesty, come what may. And there can be no doubt that he tried very hard to evaluate Stone's positions with an open mind. But Wiley Rutledge's highest personal, political, and judicial value was the worth — the dignity— of the individual. And by his lights, once the war was over, everything in his makeup encouraged a reading of the Constitution and our international treaties that would protect the due process rights of every individual within this country's jurisdiction.

But where, more precisely, did Rutledge get the idea that uniformed enemy combatants, taken as prisoners of war and tried overseas by military commissions for atrocities violating the law of war, were entitled to constitutional due process? At the time that was not established law. "We enter wholly untrodden ground," Rutledge acknowledged.[38] Squarely presented in *Yamashita*, however, the issue would be decided.

As a justice vigilant to protect constitutional rights in all criminal prosecutions, Rutledge proceeded from an inclination, call it a rebuttable presumption, that General Yamashita could rely on the Fifth Amendment. Rutledge was aware, as already noted, that the Court had never before "held that any human being is beyond its universally protecting spread in the guaranty of a fair trial." This perspective accordingly affected how he expressed the specific question presented: whether "our system of military justice" shall alone "among all our forms of judging" remain outside constitutional protection. He found no useful legal precedent in the Court's jurisprudence or in that of any other democratic nation. But, Rutledge observed, "[p]recedent is not all-controlling in law." He then outlined his approach to constitutional decision making. "There must be room for growth, since every precedent has an origin. But it is the essence of our tradition for judges, when they stand at the end of the marked way, to go forward with caution keeping sight, so far as they are able, upon the great landmarks left behind and the direction they point ahead." His eye was on a new world order, under law. "If, as may be hoped, we are now to enter upon a new era of law in the world, it becomes more important than ever before for the nations creating that system to observe their greatest traditions of administering justice. . . . The proceedings in this case veer so far from some of our time-tested road signs that I cannot take the large strides validating them would demand."[39]

In ratifying the Constitution, Rutledge emphasized, the American people had created a government with a "basic scheme," reflecting "basic concepts" and "elementary protection[s]" formulated into trial standards that incorporate "the fundamentals of fair play." Significantly, Rutledge found no indication in text or history that these protections did not apply to everyone within the reach of our government institutions. Particularly because our postwar government anticipated joining a world community—with enlightened legal protections reciprocally enforced, he hoped—it was important that this country, in its own interest, not fail to enforce norms that it would expect others to extend to its own nationals.[40]

By saying simply that the commission's evidentiary rulings and "mode" of procedure were "not reviewable by the courts,"[41] the *Yamashita* majority held cryptically but unequivocally that the Fifth Amendment was not available to the general. In the next term of Court, moreover, Justice Frankfurter—over the dissenting votes of Justices Black, Douglas, Murphy, and Rutledge—rejected due process for enemy aliens in greater detail than in Chief Justice Stone's *Yamashita* ruling. Frankfurter held for the Court that during a declared war, the president had authority under the Alien Enemy Act of 1798, unfettered by due process, to deport an enemy alien.[42] Later, in the 1950 Term, the Court in an opinion by Justice Jackson ruled that German enemies tried and held by the U.S. military on foreign soil were not entitled to habeas corpus review of their detention after convictions by military commission, expressly rejecting the petitioners' contention that they were protected by the Fifth Amendment. Justices Black, Douglas, and Burton dissented. Of determinative significance, Justices Tom Clark and Sherman Minton, who had taken the seats vacated in 1949 upon the deaths of Justices Murphy and Rutledge, were necessary for the majority. As this book goes to press, however, the Supreme Court is reviewing that ruling anew in the context of international terrorism.[43]

SCHOLARS HAVE DEBATED, in light of the Yamashita commission's conclusory findings, whether the decision held the general "strictly accountable" for his troops' criminal acts; or rather found implicitly, given the commission's reference to "extensive and widespread" crimes "both as to time and area," that General Yamashita either knew, or must have known, what was going on.[44] Justice Jackson's successor as chief prosecutor at Nuremberg, Telford Taylor, pressed for the stricter understanding at German war crimes trials two years after *Yamashita*, but he failed.[45] The military tribunals conducting multi-defendant trials known for short as the German *Hostage* and *High Command* cases took the knowledge issue seriously. The first applied a standard expressly limiting criminal responsibility to a commander who "knew or should have known" what the troops were doing. The second appeared to impose an even higher standard, requiring "personal dereliction" amounting to a "wanton, immoral disregard" of subordinates' actions and tantamount to "acquiescence."[46]

In the years after *Yamashita*, war crimes trials took place around the world, not only in Manila and Nuremberg and Tokyo but also in Britain, Australia, China, Russia, Canada, New Zealand, and the Netherlands. *Yamashita* established for use in these trials the doctrine of criminal liability under the international law of war for violating the duty of command responsibility, as refined case by case to resolve a variety of issues inherent in a chain of command. But the war crimes tribunals established after *Yamashita* and *Homma* to scrutinize conduct during the Second World War rejected strict accountability in favor of holding a commander criminally responsible only if he either had actual knowledge, or under all the circumstances should have had knowledge, of his troops' derelictions—and, with means at his disposal, failed to act. By 1956 this standard appeared in the U.S. Army Field Manual.[47]

Move ahead to the late 1990s. Under Article 7(3) governing individual criminal responsibility for war crimes tried at The Hague by the International Criminal Tribunal for the Former Yugoslavia, a commander will be adjudged criminally responsible for the acts of a subordinate only if the commander "knew or had reason to know" of those acts and "failed to take the necessary and reasonable measures" to "prevent" them or to "punish the perpetrators." In contrast, one panel of the International Criminal Tribunal for Rwanda required, for conviction, proof that the commander's "negligence was so serious as to be tantamount to acquiescence or even malicious intent." The point is, therefore, that in war crimes prosecutions after *Yamashita* and *Homma* to the present day, the "knowledge" deficiency identified by Justices Wiley Rutledge and Frank Murphy has been recognized the world over, beginning almost contemporaneously at Nuremberg and reaching the atrocities in Bosnia and Rwanda over a half-century later.[48]

Is *Yamashita*, nonetheless, still good law in the United States, with its "must have known" (or lesser) standard for imputing to commanders criminal responsibility for their subordinates' war crimes? And with its largely carte blanche deference to military commission trials of U.S. prisoners of war? Because *Yamashita* did not permit conviction of a commander expressly found to be *without* knowledge of a subordinate's atrocities—indeed, because the military commission probably should be understood to have found, however imprecisely, that the general must have had at least an inkling of what was going on in Manila—*Yamashita* does not foreclose an argument that an appreciable level of knowledge by a commander is required.[49]

Furthermore, important amendments in Geneva, which the United States has accepted, brought change to the treatment of prisoners of war by U.S. military commissions, effectively overruling *Yamashita*. Not long after the Second World War, tribunals in France, the Netherlands, and Italy, in line with *Yamashita*, rejected arguments that the Geneva Convention of 1929 applied to trials for war crimes allegedly committed before capture (although later the French Supreme Court of Appeal, taking the Rutledge view, reversed that position).[50] Then in 1949—a month before Justice Rutledge died—the International Committee of the Red Cross revised the Geneva Convention to conform to Rutledge's understanding of the 1929 provisions, applying the convention's protections to "prisoners of war" charged with offenses "prior to capture" as well as after.[51] The 1949 revisions, ratified by the U.S. Senate in 1955,[52] also assure that prisoners of war held by the United States for war crimes prosecution will receive the same procedural safeguards guaranteed to members of the U.S. military, beginning with notice of the charge "as soon as possible and at least three weeks before . . . trial"[53] and the right to "qualified" counsel and a "competent" interpreter.[54] Of greatest significance overall, in language virtually identical to that of the Geneva Convention of 1929, a "prisoner of war can be validly sentenced only . . . *by the same courts according to the same procedure*" applicable to the "armed forces of the Detaining Power" (emphasis added).[55] And a convicted war criminal is entitled to the same "right of appeal or petition from any sentence" available to the detaining power's armed forces.[56] As a result, by reflecting the obligation imposed on the United States by treaty to try prisoners of war in a forum, and with right of appeal, under rules equivalent to a military court martial, the Geneva Convention of 1949 has effectively satisfied, and thus substantially mooted, Justice Rutledge's procedural concerns about the Court's failure to apply the Articles of War either by their own terms or through the earlier Geneva Convention.[57] (It is unlikely that Fifth Amendment due process, if applicable to prisoners of war as Rutledge contended, would have afforded greater protections than those guaranteed by the Articles of War to the U.S. military.)[58]

The *Yamashita* dissents doubtless contributed to the eventual acceptance around the world of the rights that the dissenters espoused for prisoners of war charged with war crimes. By preventing a unanimous Court in the first postwar trial, and by articulating their legal views with precision — and passion — Justices Rutledge and Murphy offered to lawyers and judges in future war crimes trials, as well as international delegates soon to revisit the Geneva Convention itself, persuasive alternatives to the rules of law and procedure applied in *Yamashita*. Undoubtedly, lawyers in subsequent trials would have argued, without help from Rutledge and Murphy, that guilty knowledge is required before criminal liability can be imposed on a commander for atrocities committed by the troops. But with Rutledge and Murphy in powerful dissent, that effort was all the more credible. Their dissents also had a chastening impact on the press and the public. They made opinion leaders think, as editorials reflected nationwide — some praising them greatly.[59] These dissents energized the American liberal community in particular to monitor the increasing number of war crimes trials taking place around the world.[60] And the dissents stood out as expressions of national conscience at a time when feelings of hate and revenge might otherwise have overwhelmed the nation.

Near the beginning of his *Yamashita* dissent, Justice Rutledge wrote:

> In this stage of war's aftermath it is too early for Lincoln's great spirit, best lighted in the Second Inaugural, to have wide hold for the treatment of foes. It is not too early, it is never too early, for the nation steadfastly to follow its great constitutional traditions, none older or more universally protective against unbridled power than due process of law in the trial and punishment of men, that is, of all men, whether citizens, aliens, alien enemies or enemy belligerents. It can become too late.

He closed by quoting Thomas Paine: " 'He that would make his own liberty secure must guard even his enemy from oppression; for if he violates this duty he establishes a precedent that will reach to himself.' " [61]

TWO WEEKS before General Yamashita ascended the gallows in February 1946, another five-general military commission convicted Lieutenant General Masaharu Homma of crimes attributable to the Bataan Death March and prisoner-of-war abuses in the Philippines. The commission found Homma, like Yamashita, guilty of failing to "control the operations of the members of his command" and of "permitting them to commit brutal atrocities and other high crimes." A week after *Yamashita* came down, the Supreme Court summarily denied Homma's motions for leave to file petitions for writs of habeas corpus, prohibition, and certiorari. Rutledge and Murphy each dissented briefly, but powerfully. Rutledge relied for the most part on his *Yamashita* dissent but added that several "serious questions" not raised in the earlier case deserved Supreme Court review, including commission procedures that allowed "forced confessions" to be admitted in evidence; allowed in as well, as *"prima facie* evidence" against the accused, all evidence received against others convicted at an earlier trial of criminal action by a group that included the accused; and granted "full faith and credit" to prior findings and judgments of the "criminal character, purpose or activities" of a group that included the accused. [62]

To John Frank, Rutledge acknowledged: "A dissenter of course is apt to exaggerate in his view of what the majority do. Maybe I do so here." But Rutledge did not really believe that. He had been angry, indeed furious, since the *Yamashita* ordeal. "Just between you and me," he wrote to a friend at Harvard—stressing that "[t]his comment must be absolutely confidential"—"I think the [Yamashita] decision was the worst in the Court's history, not even barring Dred Scott." Rutledge had joined Murphy's dissent in *Homma* that referred to "revengeful blood purges" and "judicial lynchings," even though Rutledge had been concerned that Murphy might have been speaking "with too much vehemence for the most effective force." On balance, however, Rutledge supported Murphy's rhetoric because it "stirred up attention" to the unfair procedures in *Homma* that "otherwise would have gone altogether unnoticed." [63]

According to the editors of the *St. Louis Star-Times*: "If Justices Murphy and Rutledge have called attention to possible irregularities or a tendency to move with too great haste in trial of Japanese war criminals, their dissent should be welcome." A month later the same editorial page offered a reprise, concluding with reference to both *Yamashita* and *Homma*: "These brilliant dissents are being ignored now, but it is inevitable that, in the future, lawyers will turn to them time and time again." The *Chicago Tribune* cited Rutledge and Murphy: "Bad law is being made in these Japanese atrocity cases." And praising Rutledge, the *Washington Post* observed: "[T]he record of the case piles up volumes of evidence indicating, as we said at the time, that the trial was not conducted in the true spirit of American justice." The *Cincinnati Times-Star* added, "The vigorous minority opinions in the Yamashita case seem to us to do credit to our present not always impressive Supreme Court." Other editorial writers saw differently. The Abilene, Texas, *Reporter News*, for example, berated Murphy and Rutledge as "hair-splitting legal eagles," while the *Salt Lake Tribune* chided their "sentimental concern for the wishes of the red-handed leader of murderous mobs."[64]

For some, the very fact of a split on the Court, reflecting intense scrutiny, enhanced the impression that justice had been achieved. The *St. Louis Post-Dispatch* emphasized: "The Supreme Court's 6-to-2 decision against Yamashita proves that his case received every legal consideration." The government's war crimes prosecutor in Tokyo, however, Joseph B. Keenan, saw no virtue attributable to the dissents. Keenan issued a statement referring in particular to Murphy's dissent in *Homma* as "offensive," and assuring the American people that there would not be a "procession of judicial lynchings." An amused Rutledge, enjoying Keenan's protest that Murphy's rhetoric would not apply to the Tokyo proceedings, laughed that Keenan had taken the bait "hook, line and sinker."[65]

General MacArthur, Supreme Commander for the Allied Powers, furious with Murphy and Rutledge, issued his own statement: "No trial could have been fairer than this one, no accused was ever given a more complete opportunity of defense, no judicial process was ever freer from prejudice." Referring to the dissenters in *Homma*, he added from Japan: "Those who would oppose such honest method can only be a minority who either advocate arbitrariness of process above factual realism, or who inherently shrink from the stern rigidity of capital punishment."[66]

Mail flowed into Rutledge's chambers, some condemning the "shame" of "Jap coddlers," but more—from ordinary citizens, military men, and academics—conveying, in the words of one, "deepest respects" for "your courageous defense" of due process. Treasured as much as any expression he had received for work on the Court was a note handed to him within "three minutes" of reading his dissent in *Yamashita* in open court. It came from the taciturn clerk of the court, C. E. Cropley, who by tradition did not comment on the merits of the Court's or a justice's position. "Though you do not subscribe to the new law made in the heat of today—your contribution to the classics of American philosophy will be recognized in a cooler tomorrow, and, I hope, not too late." Even a judicial page remarked to Rutledge a day or so after the justice had read his dissent in *Yamashita*: "Justice, you surely spoke a fine piece Monday. I didn't know you could *preach* like that!" Counsel for Yamashita, Captain Frank Reel, had heard something more: a "bitter" tone as the deep-voiced dissenter glanced tellingly at the Chief Justice.[67]

THREE WEEKS after the Court decided *Yamashita* and *Homma*, the justices resolved a third major military tribunal case. Immediately after Pearl Harbor, Hawaii's governor had put the territory under martial law, and the civilian courts had been replaced by military provost courts and commissions guided but not limited by the penalties applicable to military courts-martial. Not long thereafter, the civilian courts began to resume some of their normal operations, but for nearly three years military tribunals exercised exclusive jurisdiction over wartime criminal prosecutions for violations of military orders and the laws of Hawaii. In *Duncan v. Kahanamoku*, the Court reversed the military convictions of two civilians, one charged with embezzling stock and the other with assaulting two Marines. With Justice Jackson not participating and only Justices Frankfurter and Burton in dissent, the Supreme Court ruled that the governor's authority to declare martial law under Hawaii's Organic Act did not extend to "supplanting of courts by military tribunals," absent imminent military danger. Justice Black's opinion for the majority thus purported to rely on a statute, but his conclusion that legislative authority to impose "martial law" did not include a shutdown of civilian courts was a constitutional ruling in disguise. Black relied not on statutory language or history but on our "principles and practices" and "political philosophy and institutions" to say that the Act's reference to martial law did not embrace military courts under the circumstances—surely an invocation of a constitutional limitation.[68]

Subjectively, it may feel hard to understand why military court convictions of civilians for embezzlement and assault should have been deemed more egregious, in law, than civilian court convictions of Japanese-Americans resisting internment. That the war was over by the time the Supreme Court ruled in *Kahanamoku* but not in *Korematsu* was legally irrelevant. Thus, on the facts established, the meaningful distinction between the two has to be that exclusion and internment—however abhorrent—had a demonstrable, if imprecise, connection to a legitimate end in wartime, namely prevention of sabotage and espionage, whereas the military's control of the justice system when the threat of immediate danger had passed, and without discernible relationship to offenses charged, exceeded the war power under the Constitution. In the words of *Hirabayashi*: there must be a "substantial basis for the conclusion" that the "protective measure" taken was "necessary" to meet a "threat" that "would substantially affect the war effort" and "might reasonably be expected" to aid the enemy.[69] The military regime still at work in *Kahanamoku* did not meet that test.

The question for today, of course—one not faced by Justice Rutledge and his colleagues in the 1940s—is how, after *Quirin*, *Korematsu*, *Yamashita*, *Kahanamoku*, and other cases,[70] the Supreme Court should rule when the president, joined by Congress or not, supplants civilian courts with "military commissions" to adjudicate prosecutions of terrorist acts. More specifically, is a demonstrable violation of the "law of war," coupled with a declaration of "war" by Congress, necessary to trigger the use of military commissions rather than civilian courts to try alien defendants—or American citizens—for acts of "terrorism"? Can one be tried lawfully before a military commission if the defendant is not an "alien enemy" sponsored by a foreign state? What preventive measures curtailing civil liberties in the United States would be justified in addressing international terrorism— whether state-sponsored or privately initiated—absent a congressional declaration of war? What procedural due process—including evidentiary protections and rights of appeal and habeas corpus—does the Constitution or a treaty guarantee to defendants before American military commissions? Is there a relevant distinction between "unlawful combatants," as in *Quirin*, and "prisoners of war," as in *Yamashita*? To what extent, if at all, does the location of a military commission trial—on foreign or American soil—have legal significance in prosecuting terrorist acts committed in the United States? In foreign territory? What if the federal authorities detain an "unlawful combatant" or "prisoner of war" indefinitely, without affording the right to counsel or bringing that individual before a military commission or court?

One can only speculate how Justice Rutledge, who concurred in *Hirabayashi* and *Korematsu*, would rule on particular civil liberty restraints demanded by intelligence agencies to deal with a clandestine, terrorist enemy. Even in an era of international terrorism, however, we can be reasonably sure that Justice Rutledge—concurring in *Kahanamoku*, dissenting in *Yamashita*—would insist on the right of all detainees, even "unlawful combatants," to legal representation and some manner of due process.

TWENTY

A New Chief, Jackson's
Blast from Nuremberg,
and the Striking Mine Workers

Not three months after the Court's struggle in *Yamashita* and *Homma*, the Chief Justice was announcing decisions in open court when Justice Rutledge saw him "fumbling through the pages" he was about to read, then heard him speak in a low voice. Whereupon Justice Black suddenly banged the gavel and, with Justice Reed, helped the collapsing chief off the bench. Later that day, April 22, 1946, Harlan Fiske Stone died. Calling Stone a "grand man" with whom it had been "a great privilege" to work, Rutledge told a friend that he had been saddened by their "increasing differences." Nonetheless, Rutledge added, Stone had always exhibited "a calm poise combined with firmness and tolerance which gave real balance to our discussions. . . . We shall miss him."[1]

The press, of course, began guessing about the next Chief Justice immediately, even in the news story announcing Stone's funeral. Jackson, Douglas, and Frankfurter were mentioned. A minor effort, supported by organized labor, unfolded in behalf of Justice Black with his unenthusiastic approval. And soon Justice Reed, who was known to be interested, reportedly "figured prominently" in Washington's "inner circle" speculation. By early May, Douglas's chances were said to be "diminishing" while "Justice Wiley Rutledge was being considered, according to informants," along with Secretary of State Byrnes and Secretary of the Treasury Fred M. Vinson. One reporter had heard that the president was looking for a "vigorous organizer, preferably from west of the Mississippi River."[2]

Before the end of April, at least one attorney in St. Louis had urged the president to nominate Rutledge as chief, and in May Rutledge's good friend Luther Ely Smith, also of St. Louis, asked Irving Brant to lead the charge. Brant replied that he had already written to Truman "suggesting Wiley as one of three men on the court qualified to succeed Stone." Rutledge would have none of it, however, citing his "physical" and "intellectual" limitations. According to Brant, Rutledge believed that the job had "killed Stone," and added, "I could not stand up under that duty for longer than three or four years." Brant soon discovered that a Rutledge candidacy, in any event, would be "futile." He reported to Smith: "H.S.T., who a year ago praised Rutledge all over the lot in talking with me, now damns him over the same terrain—presumably because of the way he scorched the Japanese trials."[3]

Rutledge hoped that the nominee would not come from inside the Court. Only a new personality, he believed, untainted by the pervasive acrimony, could take hold effectively. By this time Jackson and Black were feuding. Douglas and Frankfurter were ignoring each other. Frankfurter and Murphy exhibited mutual disdain and, with Black, were still smarting after the *Hope Natural Gas* and *Mercoid* decisions. Jackson and Murphy continued to feel a mutual antipathy from the days when Jackson, denigrating Murphy's legal competence and self-promotion, had opposed Murphy's nomination to the Supreme Court even though Jackson could anticipate succeeding Murphy as attorney general. And tempers were smoldering since the fiasco surrounding Roberts's resignation letter. Unless the president looked outside the Court, he risked a most unhealthy situation.[4]

Rutledge was apprehensive in the main about Jackson, who was the one colleague known to have coveted the position since the day Roosevelt had nominated Stone and virtually promised Jackson that he would succeed the new chief.[5] Jackson, as Rutledge saw him, was an unpredictable, difficult individual whose judgment was not worthy of his ambition—as ensuing events confirmed. Since his Senate days, President Truman had admired Jackson greatly—witness the appointment to Nuremberg. Truman was in fact so high on Jackson that early on he believed he should either name Jackson Chief Justice or endorse him for president if Truman himself chose not to run in 1948. On a personal level, however, Truman was closer to his former Senate colleague Hugo Black and thus naturally called Black for advice. Black told the president that Douglas would be a far better choice than Jackson. From that point on, Jackson—in Nuremberg with no promoter in Washington—had little chance, if any.[6]

The details have been repeated often and thus receive summary treatment here. Two days after Stone's death, Drew Pearson predicted that two justices (without mentioning their names, Black and Douglas) would resign if Jackson became chief. Truman invited the views of former Chief Justice Hughes and retired Justice Owen Roberts. Not long after Roberts spelled out the animosities on the Court, someone—the evidence points to Justice Black—fed to the Washington *Evening Star*'s Doris Fleeson the in-

side story of the *Jewell Ridge Coal* controversy, which reporters had missed
a year earlier. Fleeson revealed all on May 16. According to her column, the
president, in learning about the Court's acrimony, had confided to a senator: "'Black says he will resign if I make Jackson Chief Justice and tell the
reason why. Jackson says the same about Black.'" The day after Fleeson's
column, Justice Douglas called the president, apparently to reinforce the
threat of resignation—Black's as well as his own—although it is unclear
whether the two were serious or were merely trying to defeat Jackson's candidacy. Douglas reportedly took other steps as well to diminish Jackson—
and to advance his own campaign for chief, led by Tommy Corcoran.[7]

On June 6, 1946, in a choice that surprised many, the president named
as Chief Justice of the United States Rutledge's friend from Court of Appeals days, the fifty-six-year-old secretary of the treasury, Fred M. Vinson.
While reportedly suggesting others as well, both Charles Evans Hughes
and Owen Roberts had recommended Vinson. And both the president and
the attorney general, Tom Clark, easily agreed that Vinson—in their view,
the "best peacemaker" in Washington and coincidentally the president's
"favorite poker companion"—was the obvious choice. The nomination was
generally well received, although one newspaper analyst observed that as
"a member of the Court of Appeals, Judge Vinson did not write any single
decision which stands out as being of especial significance."[8]

Rutledge was delighted and told a friend that Vinson had been his personal choice. To another he wrote: "He is a fine man, an able lawyer, and
will do a fine job here." To his half-brother Ivan, he added: "I am as pleased
with Fred Vinson as with anyone who might have been appointed in the
present circumstances." Rutledge predicted to Victor Brudney that Vinson
would be a real asset: "He has administrative ability, poise, courage and get-
along ability, all of which we need here as much as strictly legal capacity."
Rutledge was particularly eager for a chief with greater administrative skill
than Stone, whom Rutledge had faulted for allowing the Saturday conferences to run on interminably.[9]

From the U.S. Court of Appeals Vinson had moved to the executive
branch with increasing responsibilities as director of the Economic Stabilization Board and then head of the Office of War Mobilization and Recon-
version before President Truman tapped him for Treasury. He was "a man
of action," not an intellectual or scholar, and although he no doubt made
his own judicial decisions, Vinson, like Murphy, relied on his clerks to write
the opinions, subject only to occasional revisions at his request.[10] Vinson
had great capacity for friendship. Court law clerks at the time experienced
him as "extremely likeable"—"homespun," "cordial," "decent." And law, to
Vinson, was not all-consuming. He loved baseball, always declaring a Court

*"All you have to do is to pull it together again, Fred"—cartoon by Jim Berryman.
(Washington, D.C.,* Evening Star, *June 12, 1946; Richard Westervelt Collection,
Ohio State University Cartoon Research Library)*

recess during the World Series. Vinson and Reed, in fact, talked baseball
so much in the lunchroom that Frankfurter—finding the conversation un-
congenial—reportedly absented himself and ate in chambers.[11]

The new chief's reviews as an administrator were mixed. Rutledge and
the others appreciated Vinson's control over the Saturday conferences, now
typically limited from noon to 5:00 o'clock. And Vinson's assignment of
opinions was generous, reserving few if any significant ones for himself.
Jackson considered this a sign of laziness, however, and Black, too, was
critical of the chief for the time he spent with the president and former
political cronies. Vinson's approach was often imperious. Some saw him
trying to run the Court, a collegial institution, the way he ran Treasury. On
one occasion, for example, when Vinson asked Jackson to do something, his
tone apparently set Jackson off: "You only make $500 more than I do; leave
me alone." And even Vinson's friend Rutledge could take umbrage. Vinson

328 <i>Judge, 1939–1949</i>

once sent his clerk next door to Rutledge's chambers, informing the justice that the chief would like to see him. Rutledge sent back a note: "Certainly." Vinson repeated his request and Rutledge conveyed the same answer. After the third Vinson overture, Rutledge replied through Vinson's clerk, "Please tell the Chief that my door is open to him at any time." Rutledge reportedly was "mad as hell"—a rare event—that Vinson would behave like a boss rather than simply walking next door.[12] As a justice, the chief would dishearten his friend Rutledge, who had predicted that Vinson would vote much like Stone although less on the side of civil liberties. The days ahead revealed that Rutledge was prophetic in this latter respect: Vinson was no friend of individual rights.[13]

WITHIN A WEEK after the president named Vinson, Justice Jackson issued a shocking statement from Nuremberg, addressed to the chairmen of the Senate and House Judiciary Committees, calling the new Chief Justice "upright, fearless and well qualified," then denying as "utterly false" a report that Jackson had threatened to resign if Justice Black had received the honor of heading the Court. Initially Jackson, still hopeful that Truman would nominate him for center chair, had prepared the statement as a memo to the president to correct distortions that Jackson saw in Fleeson's column on *Jewell Ridge*. Jackson held the memo, however, but after Vinson's nomination Jackson cabled a redraft to Truman, requesting permission to make it public. The president refused, so Jackson redirected it to Congress without the president's permission.[14]

Jackson may have rationalized that he should correct the record, but his statement came across as pure spleen. Jackson acknowledged that he and Black were engaged in a "feud." And it was serious, he reported—not a "mere personal vendetta" that a "tactful presiding officer" could soothe, but an irreconcilable divide that went to "the reputation of the court for nonpartisan and unbiased decision." Jackson then elaborated his allegations of Black's impropriety in *Jewell Ridge Coal* and threatened that if the practice of hiring a justice's former law partner to argue before the Court "is ever repeated" while he was on the bench, he would make his "Jewell Ridge opinion look like a letter of recommendation by comparison."[15] An editor of the *St. Louis Post-Dispatch* spoke for many in finding Jackson's angry outburst "impetuous and almost incoherent," full of "wild words" that "humiliated the country in the eyes of its enemies." An editorial in a paper in Macon, Georgia, called Jackson "an Unmitigated Ass." Some newspapers, however, including the *New York Times*, supported Jackson. But overall Jackson's reputation suffered the most.[16]

Rutledge was entirely sympathetic with Black on the merits of the disqualification issue and believed that Jackson had become a sad case. To his clerk, Rutledge sighed, "Too bad, but it's just like Bob. I'm not surprised." To others, however, Rutledge was far more guarded, referring merely to the "blast from overseas" that left the Court only one course: "to keep silent and let the winds blow."[17]

At least as a public matter, little further came of the incident, except as an excuse for a handful of Court haters to vent. Senator Styles Bridges, Republican of New Hampshire, publicly demanded that Black should resign from the Court, while Senator Scott Lucas, Democrat of Illinois, demanded the resignation of both Black and Jackson. Bridges even joined Senator James Eastland of Mississippi in proposing a bizarre constitutional amendment intended to stop the "bickering" and "petty factionalism," and especially the usurpation of congressional authority, by "unpacking" the Court. The amendment would have limited a president to appointing no more than three justices, and would have applied retroactively, forcing Justices Douglas, Murphy, Jackson, and Rutledge off the bench. It went nowhere. Chief Justice Vinson, in the meantime, trying to calm hurt feelings, invited the justices to Vinson's apartment for a social gathering and, playing the piano, tried to get everybody to sing along with him. "That was an utter disaster," according to Murphy.[18]

Jackson returned from Nuremberg for the fall term of 1946, and in October Justice Burton saw Jackson and Black at the regular Court conference engaging in perfunctory conversation, beginning with a handshake. The brethren all treated the explosion from Nuremberg as though it had never happened. Vinson, in the meantime, had taken his oath as chief at a festive ceremony at the White House on June 24 attended by ambassadors and the Cabinet, members of Congress and the electorate—entertained by a band.[19]

At no time had Wiley Rutledge been part of the brouhaha. In July, an assistant to the president of the New York *Herald Tribune*, while addressing a local Rotary Club, commented that there was "only one man on the Supreme Court Bench today who had the dignity and the background" that justified membership on the Court—meaning Rutledge. Another Court observer later wrote: "Throughout the bickering on the Court, Rutledge has kept out of the crossfire. Equally important," he added, Rutledge "has not been mentioned in the public argument about it. . . . His personal prestige is unsullied and he can go right on with his liberal law . . . without pulling punches."[20] And Wiley Rutledge did so.

ON APRIL FOOL'S DAY 1946, three weeks before Chief Justice Stone died, John L. Lewis and his United Mine Workers launched a nationwide coal strike. It fell within a progression of strikes—"the longest, most costly siege

John L. Lewis.
(Photograph by
Albert R. Miller;
Library of
Congress,
LCUSZ62-93291)

of labor trouble in the nation's history"—beginning in 1945 soon after V-J Day. A massive steelworkers strike had begun in January. Others had walked out, too—meatpackers, telephone workers, even glass workers and coffin makers—as organized labor, while the cost of living rose, tried to obtain for the forty-hour week at least the gains achieved from regular overtime and bonuses during the war. The coal strike affected every major industry. Although the steel strike had been settled by May, the steel plants, without coal, "were again banking their furnaces." Ford and Chrysler then shut down, while freight loadings and the use of electricity fell off dramatically. Desperate to preserve the national economy, President Truman issued an executive order on May 21 pursuant to the War Labor Disputes Act of 1943, directing the secretary of the interior to seize and operate the coal mines on behalf of the federal government.[21]

By month's end, Interior Secretary Julius Krug had negotiated an operating agreement with Lewis, but by October the scowling union chief was claiming that the government was violating the agreement. Lewis demanded a conference to renegotiate the arrangement, asserting that the agreement he had reached with Krug had carried forward a provision of the earlier National Bituminous Coal Wage Agreement authorizing either party to demand a "negotiating conference" at any time, and further had empowered each, after a failed negotiation, to terminate the agreement outright.[22] The government denied that the agreement between Krug and Lewis had incorporated the "negotiating conference" provision but agreed nonetheless to meet with Lewis. Discussions proved fruitless, and Lewis announced that the union was "exercising its option" to terminate the agreement effective midnight, November 20.[23] Because of the union's traditional "no contract, no work" policy, the government knew a strike was imminent. Government counsel rushed into federal court seeking declaratory and injunctive relief, beginning with a temporary restraining order, which the district judge granted immediately—and the union ignored.

By the time of the first hearing ten days later on the government's motion for preliminary injunction, the government had also filed a petition, which the judge granted, for Lewis and the union to show cause why they should not be held in contempt of court for willfully violating the restraining order. They defended on the ground that under the Norris-LaGuardia Act, the court lacked jurisdiction to grant injunctive relief in a labor dispute; that the court's order violated sundry constitutional rights; and that in any event the government had not satisfied the statutory requirements for a contempt order.

Calling the union's action "evil," "demonic," and "monstrous," the judge rejected the Norris-LaGuardia Act defense, finessed the union's other contentions, and found the defendants guilty of both criminal and civil contempt, fining Lewis $10,000 and the union $3.5 million. The judge also issued a preliminary injunction, pending final resolution of the government's petition for a permanent one. Citing the public interest, the Supreme Court accepted the case without requiring the usual intermediate ruling of a U.S. Court of Appeals. The Court scheduled argument for January 7.[24]

Congress had enacted the Norris-LaGuardia Act in 1932 to prevent employers from breaking strikes by going to court for injunctive relief, indeed even for a temporary stay of the strike, which typically was enough to wreck the union's effort. Specifically, the act withdrew federal court jurisdiction to grant injunctions in nine specified types of "labor dispute." In the mine workers' case, Chief Justice Vinson issued the decision in early March 1947 for a 5-to-4 majority, agreeing that the act would have barred injunctive relief "if the basic dispute had remained one between defendants and a private employer." But the new chief opined that the act did not extend to the government as employer. According to a traditional canon of statutory construction, he noted, legislation should not be interpreted to withdraw rights from the sovereign unless there is express language—absent here— to that effect.[25]

*Chief Justice
Fred M. Vinson.
(Photograph by
Harris and
Ewing; Collection
of the Supreme
Court of the
United States,
p946.7.2)*

The government, the chief stressed, did not—as the mine workers contended—simply stand in the shoes of the private employers. The reality was the other way around. The government was entirely in control, as though each mine were a "Government facility," as evidenced by provisions of the agreement between Krug and Lewis which the private operators had "vigorously opposed." That the mine workers were not government employees "for every purpose" was irrelevant. In any event, Vinson added, no "labor dispute" was involved, because—in the words of Norris-LaGuardia—a labor dispute takes place exclusively between "persons," and here one party, the sovereign, in "common usage" is not considered a person. Finally, Vinson concluded, the act's legislative history—evincing a purpose to regulate collective bargaining relationships in the private sector—did not undermine the government's right to injunctive relief against its own employees.[26]

If he was certain of anything, Justice Felix Frankfurter was confident that the anti-injunction provisions of the Norris-LaGuardia Act *did* prohibit the government from obtaining the injunctive relief that the district judge ordered. Frankfurter had been a drafter, interpreter, and promoter of the legislation in 1932. Thus, from his own perspective (which, of course, he did not cite), reinforced by congressional rejection of proposals to authorize injunctive relief for the government under the War Labor Disputes Act of 1943, Frankfurter wrote a powerful—one contemporary scholar said "unanswerable"—refutation of Vinson's analysis.[27] On this issue he carried the votes of Jackson, Murphy, and Rutledge.

The five votes holding the Norris-LaGuardia Act inapplicable did not end the matter, however. Justices Black and Douglas, who agreed with Vinson, Reed, and Burton on that issue, were unpersuaded that Lewis and his union were guilty of criminal contempt. According to Black and Douglas, defendants' good-faith belief that "they were acting within their legal rights" in ignoring the restraining order, though that belief was erroneous, justified no more than a conditional, civil sanction designed to coerce compliance. Specifically, that meant a fine payable only in the event that the mine workers failed to withdraw the contract termination notice and call off the strike by a court-ordered date certain.[28]

In the end, however, this limited defection by Black and Douglas did not restrict the sanction to civil relief for the government. Frankfurter and Jackson joined Vinson, Reed, and Burton in holding that both Lewis and his union were guilty of criminal contempt for willful failure to comply with the court's restraining order, even if it turned out on appeal that the order was premised—as two justices in this majority believed—on an unlawful injunction. Finally, after upholding the $10,000 fine against Lewis, the Court trimmed the union's criminal fine to $700,000 and characterized the balance of $2.8 million as a conditional, civil fine, payable only if the union failed to comply with the restraining order within five days of the Court's mandate.[29]

Justice Rutledge, it was clear, did not respect the compromise of intellect and principle that he saw in the majority result. In dissent, joined by Justice Murphy (who also wrote a brief dissent of his own), Rutledge began:

> This case became a cause celebre the moment it began. No good purpose can be served by ignoring that obvious fact. But it cannot affect our judgment save only perhaps to steel us, if that were necessary, to the essential and accustomed behavior of judges. In all cases great or small this must be to render judgment evenly and dispassionately according to law, as each is given understanding to ascertain and apply it.

The justice then, briefly, agreed with Frankfurter's analysis of the Norris-LaGuardia Act while adding his personal view that the War Labor Disputes Act of 1943, also applicable here, not only "confirm[ed] the applicability" of

Norris-LaGuardia but also, by its own terms, "excluded resort to injunctive relief for enforcement of its own provisions in situations of this sort."[30]

Rutledge then shifted to his second reason for dissent: Vinson's virtually unprecedented ruling that a defendant could be held in contempt for disobeying an order which the court—as finally decided on appeal—had no authority to issue. Vinson had acknowledged (but found inapplicable) an exception that would forbid a contempt conviction for willful disobedience of a court's order when the claimed basis for the court's jurisdiction was "frivolous and not substantial." Apparently crafted by Justice Frankfurter and conveyed to his chief to soften the harshness of the rule the Court was adopting, this excepted enforcement of a "frivolous" contempt order— an exception not held applicable in this case—did not impress Rutledge. With or without the exception, he said, the Court had "overthrown and subverted" the "long prior course of decisions" (summarized accurately in the dissent) holding that a court order "void for want of jurisdiction" may be "disobeyed with impunity pending but depending upon determination of its validity by appeal." The reason for this limitation on the contempt power—which of course permitted conviction, ultimately, if the defendant guessed wrong about the lawfulness of the disobeyed order—was obvious to Rutledge. He pointed out that unless one is free to disobey an order which the court has no power to issue, a lawless tribunal can enter an almost simultaneous contempt conviction that not only makes a criminal out of a defendant engaged in lawful activity but also, "in practical effect"—as with the fines imposed on Lewis and his union—terminates the litigation without resolution of the underlying dispute.[31]

The result would be particularly harsh, Rutledge explained, when "First Amendment liberties" were nullified by the "censorship established" through preliminary restraint potentially available in "every case presenting a substantial question concerning the exercise" of First Amendment rights. Two terms earlier, as we have seen, with Justice Rutledge writing for the majority, the Court held in *Thomas v. Collins* that the defendant "was within his rights" in refusing to obey a court order that enjoined him from soliciting union membership without an official organizer's card, because— as it turned out on appeal—the statute requiring the card was unconstitutional as applied. If one cannot be punished for violating a statute that turns out to be unconstitutional, Rutledge asked, why should one be penalized for refusing to honor a court order that is not merely erroneous but void for lack of the very power required to issue it? To make his point in another way, Rutledge postulated that John L. Lewis "had been imprisoned rather than fined." According to the majority's theory, he reasoned, Lewis "could not be released by habeas corpus" even though the Supreme Court would hold that "the restraining orders were beyond the District Court's jurisdiction to issue."[32]

The majority, to be sure, cited authority, a unique decision by Justice Holmes, *United States v. Shipp*.[33] But Rutledge demonstrated that Holmes himself, recognizing the uniqueness of *Shipp*, joined later in reaffirming the line of cases that declined to require compliance with a court order held void, ultimately, for lack of jurisdiction.[34] Specifically, in *Shipp*, the trial court had stayed all proceedings pending an appeal by the defendant, Johnson, who had been sentenced to death for rape. Aware of the order, Sheriff Shipp allegedly conspired with a mob that lynched Johnson while his appeal to the Supreme Court was pending. The sheriff and his collaborators, as a result, were charged with contempt of the Supreme Court. Accepting Holmes's reasoning, the Supreme Court rejected the defense argument that because Johnson's constitutional contentions were frivolous, the lower courts, as well as the Supreme Court itself, lacked jurisdiction over his appeal. The "necessity of the case," according to Holmes, gave the Supreme Court authority at least to determine its jurisdiction, which the Court could not do if the underlying case became moot because of Johnson's death. The sheriff and his cohorts, therefore, had a corresponding responsibility not to ignore the court's order to preserve the status quo—including, fundamentally, Johnson's life—without regard to the ultimate validity of that order, failing which they could be held liable for criminal contempt.[35]

In the United Mine Workers case, as Justice Rutledge pointed out, the disobedience of Lewis and the union—unlike the lynching in *Shipp*—did not end the underlying case on appeal. Necessity, in the *Shipp* sense of keeping the appeal alive, did not dictate compliance. Furthermore, in *Shipp* the court did not issue its stay order "directly in contravention of an act of Congress," as allegedly occurred in the mine workers case; rather, Rutledge observed, the order in *Shipp* was "in complete conformity with the statutes conferring authority" on the courts to take jurisdiction.[36]

Rutledge next identified a procedural defect in Vinson's analysis. Without much elaboration, the chief—ignoring "one of the great constitutional divides"—found no "substantial prejudice" to Lewis and the union from combining civil and criminal contempt proceedings. To the contrary, Rutledge wrote, by failing to detail the respective charges and to announce whether civil relief or criminal punishment was "the object in view," the district judge had made it impossible for the defendants to know "which set of procedural rights" applied and otherwise how to defend. In short, according to Justice Rutledge, in this "criminal-civil hodgepodge" the defendants were never on notice of exactly what they were up against.[37]

Finally, Rutledge dissented as to the sanction. Not only was the $3.5

million fine levied against the union constitutionally excessive, as the majority itself concluded, but according to Rutledge there were no trial court findings that could serve as a basis for the "allocation of specific portions" among "civil damages" (based on a "proven amount of injury") and "civil coercion" (subject to voidance upon compliance) and "criminal punishment" (subject to Eighth Amendment limitation). Without such findings, the Court's revisions of the lump-sum fine were wholly speculative, in Rutledge's view. They also usurped what the Supreme Court itself, in a labor union contempt proceeding, had said was a trial court function to remedy under proper instructions on remand. And in any event, Rutledge added, these revisions included a criminal portion of $700,000 that was constitutionally excessive in light of benchmark fines mandated by Congress, such as the $5,000 maximum under the War Labor Disputes Act.[38]

With some irony, Rutledge used as the text for his dissent a well-known quotation from the author of *Shipp*, Holmes himself: "Great cases like hard cases make bad law. For great cases are called great, not by reason of their real importance in shaping the law of the future, but because of some accident of immediate overwhelming interest which appeals to the feelings and distorts the judgment. These immediate interests exercise a kind of hydraulic pressure which makes what previously was clear seem doubtful, and before which even well settled principles of law will bend." To Howard Mann, Rutledge observed that "the Lewis decision had many of the earmarks which characterized the Yamashita performance here. . . . It begins to look as if once or perhaps twice a term we get cases of great emotional interest which have the inevitable tendency to strain all the law there is toward the breaking point."[39]

In an important respect Rutledge was correct: the Court majority declined to apply a well-established line of decisions from the previous century, choosing instead to rely on a unique case, *Shipp*, that did not readily fit the United Mine Workers situation. On the other hand, just as Justice Frankfurter conceded that there could be extreme situations in which defiance of a frivolous contempt order would be justified without penalty, Justice Rutledge acknowledged that there could be extreme situations, like that in *Shipp*, in which violation of an unlawful contempt order should not go unpunished. The question would always be: within the extremes, where does the next case fall? The view of Frankfurter and Jackson that the *Shipp* doctrine should be extended through exercise of the Court's equity power to meet an economic crisis, especially in wartime, was not as radical as Rutledge would have it. There is something to be said for the proposition, in a society based on law, that the Supreme Court should not encourage people subject to a restraining order to take the law into their own hands by guessing whether the trial court had jurisdiction to issue the order in the first place.

All things considered, however, the four-member minorities on the Norris-La Guardia Act issue and the civil-versus-criminal-sanction issue—with only Rutledge and Murphy common to both—had the more persuasive legal arguments. Ultimately, of course, the decision turned on contempt policy where again, it seems clear, the view of Rutledge and Murphy was stronger than the prevailing one of Frankfurter and Jackson *if* precedent alone, strictly applied, were to control. Nonetheless, as the various opinions demonstrated, the *United Mine Workers* decision would "write" with at least three coherent outcomes. Inevitably, therefore, none of the issues could be divorced entirely from a justice's personal values. The outcome favored by Rutledge would have been the most "conservative" legal position. Vinson's would have been the most "conservative" in terms of public policy. In both respects, Black and Douglas were the "moderates."

IN OCTOBER 1946, Rutledge took time to address the National Federation of Settlements honoring Eleanor Roosevelt at a gathering of over a thousand in New York City. That same fall, he felt "very much honored" when the law school at Duke University installed the Wiley Rutledge Chapter of the Phi Alpha Delta legal fraternity, although he attended the ceremony "with a little bit of the feeling of one who is about to die." Despite the honor, Justice Rutledge—an admittedly "natural joiner"—wrote to a friend that he had serious reservations about fraternities. Although he had joined two in college, he had not been "too comfortable," adding: "If I had my own way I would abolish all social fraternities, although I concede that in many instances individual chapters do a fine job for youngsters." On the whole, however, particularly because of their racial exclusions, "they stand for a selectivity which I consider essentially undemocratic in our collegiate life. I had hoped that the war might knock them out, but the hope turned out to be only a delusion." Undoubtedly adverting to his Iowa years, Rutledge recalled that he had expressed himself to Phi Alpha Delta "once or twice" about racial discrimination, knowing that he "would not get very far." In effect he had spoken softly without carrying a big stick.[40]

In the spring of 1947, the Rutledge chapter of Phi Alpha Delta at Duke invited the justice to a ceremony initiating new members, including one graduate of Duke's law school recently elected to the House of Representatives, Richard M. Nixon of California, who had come to Washington with the Republican takeover of the 80th Congress. Rutledge was unable to attend. There is irony here. The antithesis of Rutledge, Nixon the campaigner —berating Democratic leaders " 'who front for un-American elements, wittingly or otherwise'"—was contributing to a new "Red Scare" welling up in the country. The Republican national chairman claimed that radical Democrats were "'Sovietizing'" the nation. Senator Robert Taft of Ohio warned that the Democratic Party was "'divided between Communism and Americanism.'" And Wiley Rutledge was alarmed. To a professor at Colorado he wrote: "I think we are heading into one of the most repressive eras the country has ever known and I suspect we are going to have a repetition of our experience with the alien and sedition laws."[41]

Rutledge had been experiencing the Red Scare vicariously. In the fall of 1946, three of his close friends on the Indiana law faculty, Dean Bernard G. Gavit, Professor Fowler V. Harper, and a young associate professor, Howard Mann, a Rutledge clerk on the Court of Appeals and Justice Burton's first law clerk, had signed a petition to the governor supporting the Communist Party's request in late July—after gathering 11,000 supporting signatures—to appear on the state ballot in November. Responding to the American Legion, the governor ordered the university's Board of Trustees to investigate "the possibility of Communistic or any other subversive or un-American activity at Indiana University." The board reported in December that no Communist or other subversive activity had been found on campus; that the three law professors had presented testimony and corroborating evidence, accepted as true, that "they were not members of the Communist Party and detested its philosophy"; and, incidentally, that in the end the state election board had placed the Communist Party on the ballot, and that it had polled "over 800 votes."[42] The board's report also referred to Professor Harper's tendered resignation, which had been forced to a considerable extent (though not entirely) because of his political activities. Profoundly upset by Indiana's "witch hunt," Justice Rutledge wrote two letters on Harper's behalf to the Yale law faculty, where Harper was eventually invited to teach.[43]

IN MARCH 1947, a month after *Everson* and within days of *United Mine Workers*, Wiley Rutledge received a personal warning. He had high blood pressure, and his physician advised him "to take it more slowly for the remainder of this term." Reluctantly, the justice who thrived on southern fried cooking and no exercise canceled some, though not all, of his speaking engagements. His family pressed successfully for vacation time on the Maine coast at Ogunquit, rather than in Colorado with its demanding drive west, its inevitable stops in Iowa City or St. Louis, and the required public appearances. There were other reasons as well for the change. Annabel and Wiley, too, had always wanted "to see something of New England"; Jean Ann, who graduated from Indiana University in June, wanted time to look

Ensign John Paul Stevens, ca. 1942–45. (Photograph by Helen Webster; Collection of the Supreme Court of the United States, 1994.10.3)

over law schools in the East; and Neal, who had transferred to Harvard to be closer to his fiancée at Wellesley, Catherine Le Fevre, anticipated an August graduation in Cambridge. Rutledge spent two months "just lolling around on the beach and enjoying the seafoods," his first summer without speeches. At summer's end, he joined his colleagues Vinson and Reed at the University of Louisville for the awarding of honorary doctorates to the three sons of Kentucky on the Supreme Court.[44]

Before leaving for Ogunquit, Rutledge had sat for several days for a portrait commissioned by the University of Iowa, an experience he had "anticipated with horror" but found "very pleasant" while worrying about the number of pending cert petitions. There were "around 1600," he wrote to Ivan. This meant "trying to decide about four cases a day. It just can't be done if one tries to do it right." Fortunately, however, by the end of June a bill to add a second law clerk for each justice had passed the House and was on its way through the Senate for signature by the president in early July. As a result, having already given a position for the next term to Stanley Temko from Columbia, whom Chief Justice Stone had hired just before his death, Rutledge now was able to accept the recommendation from Willard Wirtz for a second clerk, John Paul Stevens of Northwestern, who one day would himself serve on the high bench.[45]

TWENTY-ONE

A More Seasoned Justice, Sharp Divides over Criminal Procedure

Most of the time, Wiley Rutledge came down on the liberal side of an issue; indeed, those who assessed voting patterns would have called Rutledge and Murphy the two most liberal justices on the Court. And yet the clerks of the conservative justices at the time, as well as those who served the more liberal-minded, have insisted, from the way they saw him work, that Rutledge was not a "knee-jerk liberal" willing "to let go of things on the basis of feelings." Rutledge was perceived rather as "a servant of the law." Wherever his predisposition may have led him, he initially resisted. He asked, first, What is the law? Given no clear answer, he would inquire, What do our constitutional, legislative, and common law histories suggest? Toward what policy has the law, from all these sources, been tending?[1]

Rutledge then would work doggedly toward the answer. His own law clerks, as well as those of other justices, saw him as "conscientious" and "hard-working"—almost to the point of "affliction"—late into the evening. He was seen as a "scholar" exploring every angle, remaining undecided until he worked the problem through in writing and could convince himself finally, by reading the analysis, what the best result was. As in Court of Appeals days, if a "hunch" controlled the tough decision, the written elaboration had to convince. According to his last clerk, the Hon. Louis H. Pollak—former dean of the law schools at Yale and Pennsylvania, now a federal district judge—for Rutledge "the writing was not an afterthought" but the "ultimate test" of whether he had "made the decision properly." His opinions showed the work; they did not cut corners. By laying out the struggle, they reflected intellectual integrity.[2]

Rutledge, moreover, showed great independence. He concurred separately on occasion, even when he agreed with the majority result, to make sure that his unique perspective was registered. He believed that a justice had an obligation to share individual insights when the majority took an approach that he found not quite convincing. His willingness to make this extra effort added to the intellectual respect he gained from justices and clerks alike. Colleagues may have been frustrated on occasion at the length of a draft opinion by Rutledge that they had to review, or at the length of time he took to get back to them on their own drafts—Justice Jackson was known to express frustration on this score. But these annoyances did not detract seriously from a fundamental respect for his intelligence, hard work, and overall contribution. Hugo Black Jr. recalled that "in a way" his father had had "more intellectual respect" for Rutledge than for Douglas, because in Black's view Rutledge "had more intellectual integrity."[3]

Rutledge did not have the intellectual firepower—the flash of brilliance, the encyclopedic recall, the genius of synthesis and exposition—that in different ways his colleagues Black, Frankfurter, Douglas, and Jackson could demonstrate. But no one familiar with Rutledge could reasonably doubt his ability—equal to that of any other justice—to understand and work through any problem to a coherent, well-reasoned conclusion reflecting carefully marshaled legal authority and, on occasion, creative insight. This justice, who for years had taught around the curriculum and then served as an appellate judge, was well grounded in the law. He was not known for an expertise comparable to Stone's in equity and patent law, or Douglas's in government regulation. But he was acquainted with the law as broadly as any of the justices—perhaps even more so than the others. He may not have survived Justice Jackson's basic criticism of colleagues who had little, if any, experience practicing law, but the clerks who saw the justices' work commonly characterized Rutledge, for his knowledge and practical reactions, as a very good lawyer. Rutledge, moreover, was a quick learner. Within a few years on the Court, as explained in chapters that follow, he had spelled out coherent theories of the commerce clause and of constitutional rights that he had not explored earlier. Finally, he was committed to articulating the Court's decisions with depth and precision—without slight or shortcut.[4] For all these reasons, Rutledge was seen as a very able and strong contributor to the Court's work.

But what about leadership? We have seen Rutledge acknowledge that making the decisions came hard,[5] just as writing the opinions came hard[6]— an understandable correlation because, for him, deciding and writing were largely the same process. This consuming preoccupation with "getting it right" left Rutledge no time to lobby his colleagues the way Frankfurter or Black did. If he felt strongly, Rutledge would have no difficulty getting his colleagues to listen, but for the most part he let his writing—draft opinions, as well as memoranda on drafts submitted by others—speak for him.[7]

Rutledge was less assertive than Black or Frankfurter for still other reasons. Although he had values as strongly held as those of any colleague, and recognized that the Court was a political, not a mere law-finding, institution, Rutledge did not approach his job as someone empowered by presidential appointment and Senate confirmation to press a personal agenda. Psychologically, he could not have proceeded from that posture of self-importance, and interpersonally he was not inclined toward lobbying a colleague. Surely his dissents in *Yamashita* and *Homma*, as well as in *Yakus*, *Everson*, and *United Mine Workers*, showed a passionate commitment to ideals and a bulldog's tenacity in advocating them. Overall, however, Rutledge was satisfied—by temperament as well as intellect—that in fairness to task and to colleagues, interchange in the proverbial marketplace of ideas, rather than arm twisting with a long-term goal in mind, was the way to arrive at decisions (as on the Iowa faculty). Perhaps in this outlook he was naïve, for he looked at colleagues only from their best side; he expected each to deal openly, to be constructive, to feel a common enterprise. He would not necessarily have perceived that on occasion, a colleague was "playing games."[8]

Finally, Wiley Rutledge found himself, along with Frank Murphy, in the minority on enough occasions, apart even from Black and Douglas, to experience a sense of futility that must have influenced his soft-sell approach. Rutledge had to perceive that his voice in large measure was speaking to future hearers, not to his colleagues of the day.

On a personal level, in the words of Court law clerks, Justice Rutledge was "warm" and "down to earth," "likeable," typically "smiling" and "outgoing." He was "gentle." The words "modest," "common touch," even "old shoe" described him. He was an "informal," "friendly," "big bear of a guy." There was "no arrogance"; "he seemed to have no ego." He showed no "meanness"; he was not "rude" or "inconsiderate." To the contrary, he was "gracious," "kindly," "decent." Some former clerks would generalize: "a wonderful human being"; "such a joy to talk to"; "one of the nicest persons I ever met." Unlike Frankfurter, Rutledge did not cultivate the clerks of other justices, who might have found that offensive, but he enjoyed lunch on occasion with clerks from around the Court, and after working late at night, he made a point of stopping by a clerk's office to offer a ride home.[9] The justice also came across as "highly ethical" beyond the integrity of his opinion writing. He refused to accept free books from a legal publisher. He would not even permit his law clerk to help him on public addresses or lectures; they were not the Court's work. And he was seen as clean cut. If ever he swore, one was surprised to the point of shock at hearing it. As for his personal life, others saw "a great deal of warmth" between Wiley and Annabel—a "gentle understanding" and "affection," recalled Victor Brudney.[10]

There was, overall, a "reserve" about Wiley Rutledge. He was "even-tempered." Unlike Frankfurter, Rutledge was rarely seen as an extrovert. Frankfurter, the former Harvard professor, in his high-pitched voice, would "cackle"; Rutledge, the former Midwestern dean, in his deep, husky voice would "chuckle." (He "sounded like a cowboy" his clerk Harry Shniderman recalled.) There was something reassuring about his demeanor. If one were looking at several justices standing together talking, a clerk observed, Rutledge would appear the most relaxed and least self-important. In the best sense, he seemed "an ordinary man." With his readiness to talk with people and his gentle touch, he conveyed an "abiding concern for the difficulties of life." A Douglas clerk recalled, "If he'd been my father, I'd have been proud of him." [11]

In addition to intellectual respect from his colleagues, Wiley Rutledge had their personal respect. He was on good terms with all the justices and never participated in the Court's acrimony, either intramurally or in published outbursts. Closest personally to Murphy, he was close as well to Black, and particularly friendly with Douglas, Frankfurter, and Reed—less so with Burton and Jackson and, over time, with Vinson. While his friendship with the chief carried over from Court of Appeals days, Vinson's imperial approach to administration, coupled with his judicially conservative views, left the two with little in common. Burton's conservatism and Jackson's unpredictable personality left these two as well less close to Rutledge than he felt toward others on the Court. These differences in relationships, however, were but differences in degree. Even Justice Jackson, who sometimes showed exasperation with Rutledge's slow pace, would speak to his clerks affectionately about "Felix" and "Wiley" while referring to his other colleagues only by last name (or to Vinson as "Chief"). While Rutledge's closest friends were off the Court—Fuchs, Wirtz, Apple, and others—his relationships with all his colleagues on the Court were cordial, indeed congenial. He thus tended to draw "the best out of everybody," "tempered some of that bitterness" on the Court, and helped take "the harder edges off." [12]

Rutledge, in fact, was the only Court member in those days about whom it could be said, with certainty, that he enjoyed the respect, both intellectual and personal, of all his colleagues. He brought integrity and civility, as well as ability. He showed character. He was not petulant. He was forgiving. He was forward-looking—a forerunner of the Warren Court—without acting judgmental toward those who thought differently. If he lost a battle, he knew another day would come. [13] He was the Court's most collegial member.

Here was a Court with a majority of the justices (Black, Jackson, Murphy, Frankfurter, Douglas, and earlier Roberts) in various combinations of acrimony; with a chief (Vinson) who had marginal respect from his colleagues; and with two justices (Reed and Burton) who—while unquestionably pleasant, hard-working colleagues—offered little creativity, let alone leadership. A former clerk to Vinson, recognizing that Rutledge also was not a leader in the conventional sense, saw him nonetheless—in this particular group of players—as vital, if not indispensable, to the Court's institutional well-being. Focusing on the strained personal relationships that when fueled by ideological divisions ignited centrifugal dynamics, this clerk aptly characterized Justice Rutledge, a calming influence, as the "balance wheel" of the Court.[14] Or, to use an electrician's metaphor, Rutledge was the Court's "ground."

This role not only encompassed legal ability and collegiality—a contribution to the Court's intellectual and functional well-being—but also enhanced the integrity of the Court's decision making itself. If Wiley Rutledge was not the Court's greatest "justice," in the sense of vision and leadership, he surely was, as one of Douglas's clerks put it, the Court's finest "judge." That is to say, he never got away from his Court of Appeals habit of deciding not just the great issues but the entire case. He kept the parties themselves in mind. As another Douglas clerk put it, "He didn't act as though the litigants were just providing him with a springboard for dogma and doctrine to build American law"; Rutledge saw them as "people who were part of a process and were personally involved as well as serving the public interest." That sensitivity, the clerk added, "was a rare quality." A Frankfurter clerk put the idea more succinctly: Rutledge "would not turn his back on the record." By steeping himself in the facts, Rutledge contributed substantially to making sure that the decision was faithful to the parties' respective cases, not distorted for the sake of retaining or establishing a doctrinal rule. Furthermore, because Rutledge had always been suspicious of "oversimplified rules in treating complex problems"—recall his letter to Professor Beale criticizing the Restatement of Contracts—the detailed facts in an opinion by Rutledge served also to distinguish future cases in the event that extension of his ruling would seem unjust.[15]

In addition, Wiley Rutledge added a progressive spirit. He was the "conscience of the Court."[16] Justice Murphy too has been called this,[17] with good reason, but there was a major difference. Within the Court itself, Murphy was seen not to offer the thoroughness, cogency, and force that Rutledge brought to bear on the precedent-breaking cases concerning individual rights. Frankfurter and Jackson, in particular, had no respect for Murphy.[18] Rutledge, on the other hand—through careful, powerful articulation of constitutional rights that others balked at recognizing—took stands that other justices, including his colleagues Black and Douglas, rejected at the time but respected nonetheless and eventually, in some cases, came to accept.[19] Hugo Black Jr. recognized this Rutledge influence. "I think he very well could have enlarged my father's heart."[20] Through his example, therefore, Wiley Rutledge too was a leader, with major impact on the institution during his brief tenure there.

Soon after Rutledge joined the Court, he and Frank Murphy became good friends, sharing a dominant value—an almost unyielding concern for the individual—combined with a shared sense of humor. Especially since *Yamashita*, they had also come to share a reputation as the Court's most reliable civil libertarians. Aside from *Korematsu*, the only civil liberties issue where they parted company was freedom of religion—to wit, in *Prince*, the case involving child labor and religious literature, and later *Everson*, the parochial school bus fare case.

The two often kidded each other about religion. After the term ended in June 1947 Murphy, a Catholic, wrote to Rutledge:

> My dear Baptist Brother:
> If you come to Harbor Beach, Michigan, this summer I promise you a real old fashioned baptism in the sweet waters of Lake Huron. In return, you can sprinkle a little holy water on me.
> I do not know how I would have gotten on this year unless you were in the corner next to me. Your kindness and congeniality made the burdens of the Court bearable. . . .[21]

Rutledge replied:

> Dear Frank:
> I intended to have another visit with you before you got away. Now I note you are relaxing by the waters of that little pond which you presume to call a lake. I wish there were some chance of my coming to Harbor Beach but since I last saw you all of our summer plans have been changed. . . .
> The place [in Ogunquit] . . . looks out over a real body of water, namely, the Atlantic Ocean. So, as for baptism, my suggestion is that, instead of fooling around with sprinkling from the water of Puddle Huron, you come over to Ogunquit and I will cleanse your soul not only with the waters but with the salt of the Atlantic Ocean. . . .
> I hardly need to reiterate the sentiment expressed in your letter, for it is indeed a mutual one. Without you here, I do not know how I could stand the grind. I do hope you will have a completely restful summer and that when you return in the fall you will be ready for another year of vigorous and unwavering defense of the rights of men.[22]

Although the bond between Rutledge and Murphy at its deepest undoubtedly depended on the shared values that the two justices came to
advocate on the Court, surely their friendship also reflected the attraction of
opposites in many ways beyond religious heritage. Murphy was a politically
ambitious, teetotaling bachelor who loved cocktail parties and the ladies,
drove a convertible, displayed an "earthy" brand of humor, and stood out
as a vain, insecure man who did not work particularly hard, was an inveter-
ate moralizer, and knew he enjoyed less than solid respect from his Court
colleagues. Rutledge, the devoted husband, profane only to the point of an
occasional "damn," had been ambitious only to be a good teacher and dean,
was a non-threatening, self-effacing — though self-understanding, secure —
man, who drove an old Buick, preferred dinner with friends to superficial party talk, worked late into the evening, and held the respect of the
full bench.[23]

The "Baptist Brother" was thrilled early in 1947 when the lifelong bachelor Murphy, at fifty-seven, became engaged to Joan Cuddihy, described by
a biographer of Murphy as "a young woman of gentle charm." Before year's
end, Rutledge was writing to Cuddihy: "As your attorney, I have been keeping a close eye on this man Murphy. He is very astute, as you know. But I
have the real goods on him — so much that whenever you may be ready to
take action he will have no way out but to walk the straight and narrow path,
for the first time in his life." To which Murphy dissented: "Your lawyer is a
professor and does not know the facts of life."[24]

THE JUSTICES had to share writing the unglamorous opinions for the Court,
but Rutledge seemed to receive an inordinate number of them. In 1947
his law clerk, Richard Wolfson from Yale, registered disappointment with
the types of cases Rutledge was writing. "The Chief doesn't seem to be
giving you very good assignments." And Neal Rutledge recalled, "My father
felt he wasn't getting the decisions he wanted to write," even when Justice
Black, the most senior of the liberal-minded justices, assigned the opinions.
Although Rutledge's junior status may have affected assignments during
his earlier years on the Court, the principal reason why both Stone and Vinson, as well as Black, were reluctant to direct major opinions to Rutledge
was his style. He wrote long opinions that not only took him considerable
time to produce and his colleagues extra time to review, but also commonly
included one or more thorough, scholarly discussions — as in Court of Appeals opinions — that went beyond the issues presented and thus might take
the justices further than they wished to commit themselves.[25]

In response to an exegesis by Rutledge on the commerce clause, for example, even his most deferential colleague, Justice Murphy, could balk:

"Sections II, III and IV—pages 8 to 22—should be eliminated. . . . I know you have done a great deal of work on this and I don't like to make such a suggestion. But I can't see how those sections add anything to the issue in the case and I frankly don't know whether I can subscribe to all the analyses and conclusions that you make therein." As to the same draft opinion, Justice Frankfurter added: "I do not disagree with anything that you say, but . . . I do not want to commit myself to all that you say *as an opinion*. . . . I do not know how some of these general observations will be made to appear— what use will be sought to be made of them—as concrete situations arise in the future." Well aware of such reactions, therefore, the chief or other senior member in the majority (usually Black) tended to assign to Rutledge the less controversial opinions as a way of avoiding protracted resolution of the more difficult cases. Over a quarter of the majority opinions that Rutledge wrote were for a unanimous Court, and almost half had no more than two in dissent.[26]

The other side of this assignment ritual, however, was the desire of the assigning member to influence as much as possible the approach that the opinion would take. That influence was much less likely through an assignment to Rutledge, whether by a conservative chief or by a liberal Justice Black. Black in particular took for himself the cases he wanted most to control, and, depending on his priorities for the other opinions that he assigned, Black was likely to find Douglas more efficient and Murphy more predictable than Wiley Rutledge.

How much did Rutledge agree with his various colleagues? That, of course, depended on the issue, but statistics show that he agreed with some of his colleagues far more often than with others:

Murphy	79%
Black	74%
Douglas	71%
Stone	57%
Reed	56%
Jackson	49%
Frankfurter	48%
Vinson	46%
Burton	45%
Roberts	34%

All told, Justice Rutledge wrote 169 opinions during his six and a half years on the Court—65 majority, 43 concurring, 61 dissenting.[27] After his first year and a half, Rutledge averaged 29 opinions a year, with a low of

20 in the 1944 Term and a high of 40 in the 1945 Term (when Jackson was absent and most justices wrote more than usual). On the whole, Rutledge's numerical production was above the average, usually behind Black, Frankfurter, Douglas, and Jackson, but typically ahead of one or the other for fourth place in most years and well ahead of his remaining colleagues. During the four terms beginning in 1945, for example, Rutledge averaged over 31 opinions, topped by Frankfurter (41), Douglas (37), Black (33), and Jackson (32) while substantially exceeding Reed and Murphy (22), Vinson (13 for his three terms during the period), and Burton (11).[28]

These numbers signify little in themselves, for some opinions, especially concurrences, can be perfunctory. Furthermore, numerical totals do not suggest the relative significance or quality of the opinions written. Nor do they reveal who commanded majorities. Justice Frankfurter, for example, wrote more opinions than any other justice during the four years 1945-49, but in each of those years either Black or Douglas wrote the most for a majority. Rutledge tied for third place in majority opinions with Reed and Murphy in the 1945 Term with 15, while Black wrote 31 and Douglas 28. Overall, however, beginning with the 1943 Term, Rutledge averaged only 10 majority opinions a year, usually ranking sixth to eighth depending on the year.

Writing for a majority, however, has its own limitations, sometimes reflecting adherence to retrograde tradition. Views that qualify instead only for minority concurrences or dissents may reflect high principle—or even portend the future—by exposing superficial reasoning, forcing deeper thinking, even causing the majority to hold something back on occasion, and for all these reasons commanding respect. For the most part these were the kinds of contributions that Wiley Rutledge made to the Court's product—as exemplified by his dissents in *Yakus*, *Yamashita* and *Homma*, *Everson*, *United Mine Workers*, and other cases discussed later.

Beginning with the 1945 Term, Rutledge became especially active writing separate concurrences, often short—perhaps two pages—but with serious purpose. The opinion could be crucial to outcome when necessary to create a majority by coupling it to a plurality decision.[29] Other concurrences were intended to emphasize how narrow[30]—or how broad[31]—the majority ruling was, or why the particular facts[32] or the rights[33] at issue made the majority view especially compelling. Still others were written to reveal a simpler, more direct route to the result,[34] or—in partial dissent—to concur in finding one statutory violation (such as an unfair labor practice) but not two.[35] Rutledge also added concurring opinions to make clear that particular, difficult issues lurking in the decision were reserved for another day, at least for him.[36] Finally, a number of Rutledge's concurrences were major statements with jurisprudential significance, some eventually commanding the vote of a Court majority.[37]

By the end of the term in June 1946, Wiley Rutledge had developed perspective enough to demonstrate a reasonably consistent approach to statutory and constitutional issues. As a result, he occasionally would express limitations on his willingness to join majority opinions that suggested directions in which he was unwilling to go. He had become well recognized as a strong voice for protecting the constitutional rights of the individual, even an enemy of the nation. And as many of his separate concurring and dissenting opinions revealed, Rutledge often expressed a unique approach, probably more so than anyone else on the Court save, perhaps, Robert Jackson.

The forty opinions that Justice Rutledge produced during the 1945 Term not only far exceeded the number in any previous year, or in any thereafter, but also came at a price. While typically warm and smiling when he passed a clerk in the corridor, Rutledge began to show a "haggard," "worried" look on his face, even a "frown" at times. His health was perceptibly changing. Justice Black told one of his former clerks, "Wiley's going to kill himself with the hours he keeps." Edna Lingreen believed that after *Yamashita*, the justice's health never quite recovered from the strain. He had become noticeably grayer, at fifty-two, than upon his arrival at the Court that cold February almost three and a half years earlier.[38]

THE STONE and early Vinson Courts addressed an increasing variety of criminal cases attributable to wartime regulation and to accelerating reliance on the Bill of Rights. While Justice Rutledge served, the Court considered 122 criminal cases of individual, non-corporate defendants. Of these, the majority ruled for the government in 58, from which Rutledge dissented in 36. Of the 64 decisions in which the Court ruled for the defendant, Rutledge joined the majority in 62. All told, Wiley Rutledge sided with the defendant 80 percent of the time compared to the Court's 52 percent. Only Justice Murphy voted more often—by a handful—for the defendant, and both justices sided against the government considerably more often than any colleague did.

Especially when the death penalty was available, Justice Rutledge would construe an ambiguous statute against the government and grant the defendant a generous interpretation of constitutional due process. When due process would seem too great a stretch, he would invoke the Court's inherent supervisory power over the administration of criminal justice in the federal courts to impose the treatment he deemed fair to the accused. The

Court in Rutledge's time never considered the constitutionality of capital punishment as such, and Rutledge himself is not known to have expressed an opinion on that. But his law clerk in the 1944 Term, Harry Shniderman, recalled that the justice was "awfully careful before he let a capital case go."[39]

In *Robinson v. United States*, for example, the Federal Kidnapping Act authorized the death sentence, but not "if, prior to its imposition, the kidnapped person has been liberated unharmed."[40] Construing that language, Justice Black wrote for the majority that the defendant, Robinson, could be executed because the victim, beaten with an iron bar, had not healed by the time she was freed after six days' captivity, although she had received no permanent injury and showed no evidence of injury at the time of sentencing.

Rutledge, joined by Murphy, dissented on the ground that the statutory language, unexplained by legislative history, was too vague to assure that Black's approval of the "extreme penalty" was correct. The law, Rutledge wrote, "should not rest on doubtful command or vague and uncertain conditions." For example, "what is 'unharmed'?" How would that word relate to a "scratch, a cut, abrasions left by removal of tape or rope, bruises, nervous shock, disturbance of digestion . . . ?" Does the statute allow the execution of a kidnapper who releases a victim with visible but impermanent injuries quickly, but not of a kidnapper who holds the victim much longer until an injury heals? Assuming that Congress intended the statute "to offer the maximum inducement to liberation," the best interpretation would be to date the evaluation of harm as of the date of sentence, Rutledge concluded, as an inducement for the kidnapper "once injury is inflicted, though serious, to surrender the victim in the hope that care after surrender might bring about cure" and thus foreclose the death penalty.[41]

In another capital case, *Malinski v. New York*, concerning the murder of a police officer, Rutledge joined the 5-to-4 majority reversing the state court conviction of the defendant, Malinski, on the ground that the police had violated due process by coercing his confession later received in evidence. However, a 7-to-2 majority, in opinions written by Douglas and Stone, affirmed the conviction of the co-defendant, Rudish, on the ground that Malinski's confession, redacted to call accomplices "X" and "Y," did not name Rudish and thus was not sufficiently prejudicial to warrant reversal. Rutledge, joined by Murphy, dissented on the ground that in the context of all the testimony, the coerced confession's disguised reference to the other criminal participants so obviously implicated Rudish that especially in this capital case, Rudish too was entitled to reversal.[42]

In still another capital case, Rutledge relied in dissent solely on the

Court's supervisory power over criminal justice in the federal courts.[43] In sustaining a death sentence for murder, the majority rejected an argument that even though the defendant Fisher's mental condition would not support a finding of insanity, the trial judge should have instructed the jury to consider Fisher's "psychopathic aggressive tendencies, low emotional response and borderline mental deficiency" in evaluating the deliberation and premeditation necessary for conviction—a kind of diminished capacity defense. Without constitutional justification, Justice Rutledge, joined by Frankfurter and Murphy, argued that in fairness Fisher was entitled to the instruction. In this case of "life or death," he wrote, the instructions the judge gave to the jury, while literally correct, were "wholly abstract." The judge had not related them to the evidence, even in "broad outline," in the way that Rutledge believed Congress had intended.[44]

Rutledge did not need the death penalty to justify use of the Court's supervisory power when a criminal conviction, not assuredly unconstitutional, "fractures the spirit" of due process nonetheless. In *Pinkerton v. United States*,[45] the Court held that Daniel Pinkerton, who conspired with his brother, Walter, to commit criminal acts of a general character—tax evasion in whiskey sales—was also guilty of the individual, substantive crimes committed by Walter Pinkerton, even though Daniel had not advised with respect to those particular crimes or even known about them. In a dissent joined only by Justice Frankfurter, Rutledge wrote that in the absence of evidence that Daniel Pinkerton had aided or abetted the particular crimes committed by his brother, the use of the conspiracy alone to justify imposition of criminal responsibility for the underlying offenses was taking "vicarious criminal responsibility" too far.[46]

Death cases were not the justice's only serious concern. Beginning in the 1945 Term, Rutledge began what eventually became a campaign to assure criminal defendants a truly effective right to counsel in state, as well as federal, courts. In *Canizio v. New York*, the Court in an opinion by Justice Black upheld the conviction of a defendant who had pleaded guilty in state court to armed robbery without the advice of a lawyer and without being informed of his right to one. Because the accused had received legal assistance at sentencing, the majority ruled that his deprivation had been cured, since his lawyer could have raised the error before sentencing and, presumably, obtained a trial with counsel. Rutledge dissented because under New York law, contrary to the federal rule, the prosecution could have introduced in evidence against the defendant his initial plea of guilty, which in Rutledge's view would have been unduly prejudicial—"a species of self-incrimination" (as he had ruled while on the Court of Appeals in *Wood v. United States*).[47]

If *Canizio* upset Rutledge, two opinions by Frankfurter for 5-to-4 majorities during the 1946 Term must have enraged him. In the first, *Foster v. Illinois*, eleven years after pleading guilty to burglary and larceny, Foster and other petitioners filed writs of error in an Illinois state court claiming violation of due process—the right to counsel—under the Fourteenth Amendment. Acknowledging that the Sixth Amendment guaranteed every indigent defendant the right to counsel in federal court, Justice Frankfurter noted that according to Supreme Court precedent, the states were "not subject to this fixed requirement." Not finding in the record a defense proffer claiming a miscarriage of justice in the way the plea hearing had been conducted without a lawyer for the accused, Frankfurter rejected petitioners' "bald claim." Frankfurter then volunteered that "probably most" guilty pleas "have been made without the felt need of counsel," and that the "abrupt innovation" asked for "would furnish opportunities hitherto uncontemplated for opening wide the prison doors of the land."[48]

Joined by Black, Douglas, and Murphy, Justice Rutledge dissented on the ground that even if the Sixth Amendment right to counsel did not apply automatically in the states, the Fourteenth Amendment due process clause "by its own force" prescribed a "partial similar guarantee" that on this record had been ignored. Under applicable Illinois law, Rutledge noted, indigent defendants in noncapital cases were assigned "competent counsel" if requested. Here, however, at no time were Foster and the others advised of their right to a free lawyer, let alone offered one. This deliberate refusal of state officials to inform the petitioners of these crucial rights, according to Rutledge, violated due process. But there was more. As to persons without means unaware of their rights, Rutledge also saw "a denial of the equal protection of the laws," since wealth or poverty would "make all the difference in securing the substance or only the shadow of constitutional protections"—one of the earliest statements from a Supreme Court justice premising denial of equal protection on poverty.[49]

The other ruling by Frankfurter, in *Gayes v. New York*, felt even more egregious to Rutledge. In that case young Gayes, a sixteen-year-old who answered "No" when asked if he "desired the aid of counsel" had been convicted of petit larceny—stealing a few cigarettes, two flashlights, and three dollars—and of third-degree burglary for breaking into a "building and garage." Upon release from custody three years later, he was arrested and charged with another third-degree burglary and pleaded guilty. The record did not show whether he had a lawyer. He was sentenced, severely, as a second offender. Later he brought a pro se petition to vacate his sentence as a second offender on the ground that his first conviction, without assistance of a lawyer, had violated his constitutional right to counsel. Justice Frankfurter rejected the claim on the ground that under the Court's opinion in *Canizio*, the young man's failure to challenge his first conviction at the time of his sentencing for the second offense effectively waived his right to proceed further.[50]

Justice Rutledge in dissent, joined again by Black, Douglas, and Murphy, observed that Gayes proffered (without contradiction) that he had answered no when asked whether he desired counsel in the first case only because he believed he would have to pay a fee; that New York law did not clearly permit an attack on the first conviction at the time of the second one; and that the record, in any event, did not disclose whether Gayes had received a lawyer's assistance at the second sentencing—surely a necessity for the *Canizio* challenge that the majority required of him. "I am unwilling," Rutledge concluded, "to subscribe to such a doctrine of forfeitures concerning constitutional rights, which in the extreme circumstances of this case seems to me shocking."[51] In the years ahead, Rutledge would issue two more dissents, join in a third, and announce his vote to reverse in still a fourth when the majority rejected the claimed right to counsel.[52]

Rutledge was particularly concerned about fair procedure at trial. There was a long-established rule: if—but only if—defense counsel attempts to create doubt in the jurors' minds of the defendant's guilt by presenting "character" evidence demonstrating the defendant's good general reputation in the community will the prosecutor be allowed to rebut with specific evidence of the defendant's prior "bad acts" that otherwise would be ruled irrelevant and prejudicial. In *Michelson v. United States*, Jackson for the majority and Rutledge for the dissent wrote classic opinions—tightly reasoned, beautifully expressed, often cited today when jurisdictions around the country review their policies on the admission of "character" evidence in criminal trials. Rutledge rejected Jackson's view that in such rebuttal, the prosecutor could inquire whether the witness had ever heard that decades earlier the defendant had been "arrested for receiving stolen goods." Joined in dissent only by Justice Murphy, Rutledge objected to the prosecutor's reference to an arrest, implying guilt without evidence of conviction. But his principal concern was the companion rule forbidding the defense to rebut the prosecutor's specifics. A fair rule, opined Rutledge, either would permit the defendant to reply to the particular accusations developed by the prosecutor during cross-examination, or would limit the prosecution's "counterproof" to general reputation in the same way the defendant's own evidence was limited.[53]

Another of Rutledge's dissents revealed how deeply divided the Court was over the role of the trial judge in monitoring lawyers' behavior. With Black, Douglas, and Murphy, Justice Rutledge would have overturned a trial judge's contempt conviction of a lawyer who, according to the judge, was attempting to give the jury irrelevant information. The dissenting four not only disagreed with the judge—and with the Court's majority—that the lawyer had violated the trial judge's rulings, but also believed that the judge's own behavior merited sanction. Rutledge concluded: "Whatever the provocation, there can be no due process in trial in the absence of calm judgment and action, untinged with anger, from the bench."[54]

On four occasions Rutledge wrote reversals of criminal convictions. In three, writing for a unanimous Court, he dismissed the charges through statutory interpretation.[55] In the fourth, *Kotteakos v. United States*, a complicated conspiracy case, he formulated the standard that still prevails for evaluating, in a criminal proceeding where no constitutional violation is found, whether a trial judge's "error"—for example, in admitting particular evidence—is "harmless" enough for the conviction to stand.[56] Appellate courts, state and federal, rely on *Kotteakos* so routinely that this is probably Rutledge's most frequently cited Supreme Court opinion.

As noted earlier, Rutledge voted in the government's favor only twice when the majority ruled for the defendant. In one, accepting a statutory interpretation that the majority rejected, he joined a dissent concluding that the defendant had committed fraud.[57] The other instance involved a civil rights prosecution in which Rutledge and Justice Murphy parted company with their colleagues. In *Screws v. United States*, a sheriff and his deputies arrested, brutalized, and murdered a young African American man. In the absence of a state murder prosecution, they were convicted in federal court of willfully violating the victim's civil rights. Three justices agreed with Sheriff Screws that the statute—creating a criminal offense for acting willfully, under "color of any law," to deprive someone "of any rights, privileges or immunities secured or protected by the Constitution and laws of the United States . . . by reason of . . . color, or race"—was too vague to give notice of any particular violation. For a plurality, however, Justice Douglas wrote that the willfulness requirement—meaning "intentional" and animated by a "bad purpose"—implied, if met, that the defendant had been aware of violating a protected right, whether established by statute, the Constitution itself, or a court decision. Thus, the defendant would not be "punished for violating an unknowable something." Because the trial judge had not instructed the jury properly on this meaning of "willfulness," however, the Court must remand for a new trial, Douglas wrote.[58]

Rutledge, like Murphy, would have affirmed the convictions, for he found substantial case law sustaining the civil rights statute against vagueness claims.[59] There could be "no clearer violation" of a statute implementing the Fourteenth Amendment's protection of the right to "life" than the violation of a murder statute, Rutledge wrote, and the defendant had not raised at trial, or even in the cert petition, any failure to instruct on willfulness. Nonetheless, because three justices (Roberts, Frankfurter, and Jackson) voted to reverse outright, and Murphy stuck by his vote to affirm while the other four justices voted to remand, Rutledge agreed to break the stalemate by voting to join the four who would award a new trial.[60]

There were, finally, five instances where Rutledge wrote for a majority to affirm criminal convictions. Three involved statutory interpretation, suffi-ciency of the evidence, and the constitutionality of an insurance regulation with criminal penalties.[61] The other two were more interesting: one re-flected pique at defense counsel's manipulation of jury selection; the other, which anticipated a development under the Warren Court, was an opinion that Rutledge reached more through instinct than reason.

Frazier v. United States was highly unusual. Twelve federal government employees ended up on a jury in a federal narcotics prosecution, largely be-cause defense counsel had used peremptory challenges to eliminate nine prospective jurors employed in the private sector. The defendant then at-tacked the traditional method of jury selection that allowed prospective jurors to opt out freely, often leaving mostly "government employees and housewives, and the unemployed" to serve. Perceiving that the attack was disingenuous since the defendant had himself been largely responsible for the composition of the jury, Rutledge wrote for a 5-to-4 majority that coun-sel's proffer was too vague, and without a sufficient factual foundation, to show the "systematic exclusion" of private-sector jurors which the case law required to justify a complaint. Justice Jackson, forming an unusual combi-nation in dissent with Frankfurter, Douglas, and Murphy, complained that "a jury, every member of which is in the hire of one of the litigants, lacks something of being an impartial jury," at least in appearance. He would have had the Court exercise "its supervisory power over federal courts" to disapprove the "system which has produced such an objectionable result."[62]

Rutledge worried that his opinion might be used some day to permit peremptory challenges that systematically excluded African Americans from jury panels. But given the factual record before him, he analyzed the case by the book, purely as an appellate judge would have done. Consis-tently with that approach, Jackson might have refuted Rutledge by arguing that defense counsel's proffer had been enough to shift to the prosecutor the burden of producing more detailed facts, to ascertain whether the trial court's practice had resulted in a distorted jury panel. The disposition, then, would have been a remand for further trial court proceedings to resolve that issue. Instead, Jackson automatically accepted the proffer as adequate, implicitly faulting the trial court itself for failing to perceive and correct a flawed system.

The last criminal opinion that Rutledge wrote for a Court majority, *Brinegar v. United States*,[63] was probably his least felicitous effort. Rutledge upheld the warrantless seizure of bootleg liquor from an automobile, finding "probable cause" to do so on facts similar to those in an earlier decision written by Chief Justice Taft (over the dissents of Justices McReynolds and Sutherland!).[64] By merely comparing the facts with those in the Taft opinion—itself an unsatisfactory analysis—and then piggybacking on the result, Rutledge did not sort the discussion into the steps logically required for the result he adopted. In particular, having found "probable cause" (a dubious ruling on the facts), he did not deal with the next question: why a lawful arrest inevitably justified a search of the car and seizure of its contents without, first, impoundment of the vehicle and the obtaining of a search warrant.

Rutledge had regularly honored Fourth Amendment protection, dissenting, for example, from a majority ruling that consent to the warrantless search of a room waived the defendant's constitutional claim, even though the police had threatened to break down the door if the accused had refused entry.[65] Rutledge had also joined majority opinions and dissents written by others refusing to accept warrantless searches.[66] Curiously, however, he rejected the Fourth Amendment claim in *Brinegar* because, in his view, a car was not a "place of privacy" like a home[67]—a surprising view that Justice Jackson, in dissent, repudiated in favor of an equally perplexing analysis.

Joined by Frankfurter and Murphy, Jackson conceded that "judicial exceptions to the Fourth Amendment" might be necessary when police officers confronted automobiles, since they frequently "aid in the escape of criminals." But Jackson would make exceptions "depend somewhat upon the gravity of the offense," permitting, for example, a pervasive roadblock and search of "every outgoing car" from a neighborhood where a "child is kidnaped," while refusing to "strain to sustain such a roadblock and universal search to salvage a few bottles of bourbon and catch a bootlegger." In the latter situation the automobile, for Jackson, would have the sanctity of a home. On the facts in *Brinegar*, where the defendant had been seen loading liquor into a vehicle days earlier, had the "reputation" for hauling liquor and had previously been arrested for doing so, and was seen driving a "heavily loaded" car from "wet" Missouri toward the "dry" Oklahoma line, Jackson saw facts adding up only to "mere suspicion," not "probable cause" to stop the car.[68]

The fundamental difficulty posed by a case such as *Brinegar* during the 1940s lay in the either-or dichotomy the Court had to apply ("mere suspicion" versus "probable cause"). It took almost another two decades for the Supreme Court in *Terry v. Ohio*,[69] an opinion by Chief Justice Earl Warren, to announce an intermediate category—"reasonable suspicion"—that permits police officers to stop someone and freeze the situation for allowable non-coercive questioning short of an arrest ("Hello, Brinegar, how much liquor have you got in the car this time?"). The information thus gained ("Not too much," Brinegar in fact replied) will count toward a finding of probable cause justifying an arrest, as well as a search and seizure—sometimes without a warrant—if, for example, contraband is in plain view inside the car (as it was, possibly, in *Brinegar*).[70]

TWENTY-TWO

State Courts, the Bill of Rights, and Access to Federal Courts

Inherent in many Supreme Court criminal cases of the 1940s was the question whether the federal Bill of Rights—or instead some lesser state protection—was available to defendants in state court trials. The Court had said from time to time, over occasional dissent, that the Bill of Rights applied only against the federal government, not against the states.[1] Beginning in the 1920s, however, individual justices began to indicate, and the Court itself eventually held, that Fourteenth Amendment due process safeguarded the freedoms of speech and press protected by the First Amendment.[2] And in 1937, in *Palko v. Connecticut*, Justice Benjamin Cardozo—squarely presented with the argument that the Fourteenth Amendment incorporated the first eight amendments in their entirety—rejected that proposition by formulating instead what soon became known as the doctrine of "selective incorporation."[3] Specifically, Cardozo perceived Fourteenth Amendment incorporation only of the particular Bill of Rights provisions found "implicit in the concept of ordered liberty," namely, those " 'so rooted in the traditions and conscience of our people as to be ranked as fundamental.' " How to tell? Evaluate, he wrote, whether in withholding the right "the hardship imposed will be so shocking that our polity will not endure it."[4]

That test did not invite easy incorporation, and the Court in the years immediately ahead was not shy about declaring a constitutional protection outside the realm of the "fundamental." In a capital case, for example, where the Sixth Amendment would have required a federal court to appoint counsel for the indigent defendant, the Supreme Court held that due process did not impose that same requirement on the states. Justice Black proclaimed in dissent that "the Fourteenth Amendment made the Sixth applicable to the states," hinting at his eventual view that *Palko* was wrong—

that the Fourteenth Amendment incorporated the Bill of Rights in full.[5] It took five more terms of Court, however, before the incorporation issue came to a head.

In *Louisiana v. Resweber*—the infamous "Willie Francis case"—a condemned prisoner was strapped into the electric chair when the first surge of electricity failed from "mechanical difficulty." The Louisiana courts approved a second effort to electrocute Francis for murder, and a 5-to-4 majority affirmed the state supreme court's order.[6] Assuming, without deciding, that violation of the Fifth Amendment prohibition against double jeopardy and the Eighth Amendment prohibition against cruel and unusual punishment would violate Fourteenth Amendment due process, Justice Reed wrote for a plurality that neither provision had been violated. As to the claimed cruelty of a second round of electric jolts, Reed opined that the Constitution protected only against the basic "method of punishment," not against the "suffering involved" in a normally humane means of execution.

Rutledge and Murphy immediately drafted dissents. Rutledge was succinct—and untroubled as to whether Bill of Rights incorporation or Fourteenth Amendment due process in itself was the vehicle for decision:

> No one would hold, I think, that Louisiana would be free deliberately to place a convicted man in the electric chair, turn on the current, cut it off before death, remove him and later reelectrocute him. That would be sheer torture. Due process outlaws this barbarism in our scheme, whether as contravening the most elementary standards of decency in dealing with persons charged with crime, or as incorporating the commands against cruel and unusual punishments and punishing a man twice for the same offense. . . . I do not think the element of torture is removed because the state acts carelessly rather than deliberately.[7]

Justice Harold Burton—who in the mid-1940s shared with Chief Justice Vinson the title of "most conservative justice" on the Supreme Court in cases concerning individual rights—took, for him, a bold step. He too circulated a dissent, opining without express reference to the incorporation issue that "death by installments" violated the cruel and unusual punishment standard inherent in Fourteenth Amendment due process.[8] At Burton's request, Rutledge and Murphy withdrew their drafts so that, with Douglas, the four could join under Burton's signature in united opposition.[9]

Justice Frankfurter was not content to join Reed. Because Reed had assumed applicability of the Eighth Amendment through due process, and Burton had used language that arguably implied approval of incorporation, Frankfurter decided to run the analysis through *Palko*. He emphasized that "the penological policy of a State is not to be tested by the scope of the Eighth Amendment." The "innocent misadventure" of failing to electrocute Francis the first time did not mean a second effort, in words from *Palko*, would be "'repugnant to the conscience of mankind.'"[10] Frankfurter still did not have his majority for a definitive rejection of full incorporation. It remained for Justice Black to force the issue in the weeks ahead — and for Justice Rutledge, as well as his friend Murphy, to find even greater protection in the Fourteenth Amendment than the Bill of Rights in full would offer.

WHEN CALIFORNIA tried a defendant named (really) Admiral Dewey Adamson for murder, state law permitted the prosecutor to ask the jury to draw inferences against Adamson from his failure to testify and deny or explain the evidence against him. Had Adamson testified, moreover, the law would have permitted the prosecutor to impeach his veracity by referring to his prior convictions. Adamson was convicted and sentenced to death. In *Adamson v. California*, the Court, with Justice Reed writing for the majority, affirmed the conviction 5 to 4, with Justice Black joined by Douglas dissenting in one opinion and Justice Murphy joined by Rutledge dissenting in another.[11]

Justice Reed accepted for the sake of argument that Fifth Amendment due process barred comment on a defendant's failure to testify in a federal prosecution. But he ruled that this level of protection was not constitutionally required of the states. The Fifth Amendment did not apply to the states, Reed wrote, and the protection sought was not "'implicit in the concept of ordered liberty.'" Ruling definitively on the issue that he had assumed away in *Francis*, Reed added: "The due process clause of the Fourteenth Amendment . . . does not draw all the rights of the federal Bill of Rights under its protection."[12] Here, finally, a Court majority was adopting the constitutional jurisprudence of Felix Frankfurter.

In a concurring opinion,[13] Frankfurter attacked at length the idea identified by Reed—and advocated by Justice Black in dissent—that the first section of the Fourteenth Amendment (in particular, the due process and the privileges and immunities clauses) incorporated the first eight amendments to the Constitution. Summarizing his understanding of due process by quoting almost verbatim from a concurring opinion he had written two years earlier anticipating the issue,[14] Frankfurter wrote that judicial review under the due process clause of the Fourteenth Amendment required an "exercise of judgment" to determine whether (in his own paraphrase of *Palko*) particular criminal proceedings "offend those canons of decency and fairness which express the notions of justice of English-speaking peoples."

Frankfurter added, "These standards of justice are not authoritatively formulated anywhere as though they were prescriptions in a pharmacopoeia." "But," he stressed, "neither does the application of the Due Process Clause imply that judges are wholly at large." Their judgment "must move within the limits of accepted notions of justice and is not to be based upon the idiosyncrasies of a merely personal judgment." Frankfurter concluded that an "added safeguard" against such individual judgment "is an alert deference to the judgment of the state court under review."[15]

This flexible standard gave Justice Black fits. Characterizing it as an invitation to apply "natural law," Black called it "an incongruous excrescence on our Constitution." Black based his scholarly dissent on meticulous historical research evidencing the intent of the Fourteenth Amendment drafters to incorporate the entire Bill of Rights, not just some of them selected by an ever-changing bench of justices.[16] (When Black's law clerk, Louis Oberdorfer, later a federal district judge, hand-carried a copy of Black's draft to Justice Frankfurter and stood by while Frankfurter read it, the former Harvard professor turned to Oberdorfer, a recent Yale law graduate, and—flinging the dissent across his desk onto the floor—asked sarcastically, "At Yale they call this scholarship?")[17]

Black had two problems with Frankfurter's approach. First, it degraded the Bill of Rights, and thus the Fourteenth Amendment, by withholding basic rights that Black believed the Constitution had guaranteed the people in relation to their state governments. Second, it gave judges mischievous powers "to roam at large in the broad expanses of policy and morals," trespassing "on the legislative domain," both federal and state, in the name of the Constitution. Frankfurter's judicial license to identify civil liberties, Black said, was dangerously akin to that of the discredited *Lochner* decision that used due process as an immutable principle of natural justice to protect property and contract rights against government regulation. Full incorporation, Black concluded, would provide for civil rights and liberties the higher minimum intended for the states by the Fourteenth Amendment. But of corresponding importance, he stressed, full incorporation would set a rights maximum (absent constitutional amendment). The fixed stars of the Bill of Rights not only would guide judges but restrain them against judicial overreaching.[18]

Wiley Rutledge and Frank Murphy, like Hugo Black, were not impressed by any argument that attempted to justify lesser rights in the state criminal courts than in federal ones. On the other hand, these two, like Frankfurter (though from a vastly different perspective), exemplified the second of Black's concerns: they believed in judicial lawmaking under the due process clause. While agreeing with the higher rights "floor" that Black's incorporation theory would achieve automatically, Rutledge and Murphy worried about the new rights "ceiling" that it would impose. Writing for them both in a separate dissent, Murphy was "not prepared to say" that the Fourteenth Amendment was "entirely and necessarily limited by the Bill of Rights." Murphy added, "occasions may arise where a proceeding falls so far short of conforming to fundamental standards of procedure as to warrant constitutional condemnation in terms of a lack of due process despite the absence of a specified provision in the Bill of Rights."[19]

Rutledge and Murphy concurred separately because of confusion over what "incorporation" meant for "due process," a requirement that appeared both in the Fifth Amendment (among the Bill of Rights) and in the Fourteenth Amendment. If the Fourteenth Amendment were to incorporate the complete Bill of Rights, then ostensibly the two clauses would merge. Why, then, would a dissent be necessary to reserve the possibility of due process protections in addition to those in the Bill of Rights? The answer was straightforward: in reality, Hugo Black proposed incorporation of every Bill of Rights protection *except* due process. That is why, even though the Bill of Rights contained a due process clause, the dissent by Murphy and Rutledge pointed to the possible need for due process protection in "the absence of a specified provision in the Bill of Rights."[20]

Black confirmed this understanding of incorporation—we can call it "incorporation minus"—in several ways. First, in writing to Murphy disputing the need for a second *Adamson* dissent, Black agreed that the right to due process was not limited to the other explicit guarantees of the Bill of Rights. But in doing so, he did not grant independent significance to due process as a constitutional elastic, stretchable to embrace new protections as needed. Rather, he acknowledged only that due process requires, in addition to compliance with specific Bill of Rights guarantees, the observation of "other Constitutional prohibitions relating to *procedure*."[21] (He may have meant, for example, that due process would apply to a state extradition proceeding governed by Article IV, Section 2.)[22] Black appeared to be saying, therefore, that express provisions of the Constitution, found in the Bill of Rights and in a few other places, made up the entire universe of "due process." That phrase was no more than a collective description of these other provisions taken together; it did not, in itself, have independent, rights-granting significance.

Black reinforced the point, explicitly, at lunch with the Court law clerks. He had said, according to Justice Rutledge's clerk at the time, Richard F. Wolfson, that the two due process clauses "had no meaning, except for emphasis," and thus that due process alone—apart from some other constitutional violation—could never be the basis for overturning a trial.[23] Finally, because of Black's very aversion to the Court's exploiting due process to impose on society the "natural law" views of a Court majority, it seemed almost self-evident that Black would not have found much if any meaning in due process incorporation. He had to be talking about incorporating only the specifically identifiable guarantees of the Bill of Rights—period.

Rutledge and Murphy disagreed profoundly with Black's impotent idea of due process. They might have joined his dissent without reservation, of course, since incorporation literally would add both due process clauses together, available for future justices to apply more creatively than Black himself would have permitted. But because Black's dissent could be read to incorporate only the explicit protections of the Bill of Rights, leaving due process from both amendments in a limbo of sorts, Murphy and Rutledge felt obliged to make clear that they saw an expanding role for due process, one that Black's inflexible incorporation would not accommodate.

In rejecting judicial application of "natural law" or "natural justice" to discern constitutional rights, Justice Black criticized implicitly—and not unfairly—the way Justice Murphy sometimes decided cases. Murphy, instinctively, would find answers in the natural order of things attributable, ultimately, to God. Not so Rutledge. Or Frankfurter. In identifying constitutional rights protected by due process—applying the idea of "liberty," for example, in new contexts—Rutledge and Frankfurter would look not to abstract principles of justice but to American history and tradition, much as judges decided the common law. But there similarities ended.

Paradoxically, as applied by Frankfurter himself, the flexible due process standard was problematic not because, as Black worried, it gave too much running room but because Frankfurter allowed it to give too little. To Frankfurter, the very freedom to wield judicial authority under his imprecise, arguably wide-open standard was too awesome, too powerful to permit broad exercise in good conscience. As a public trust it was thus confining, not emancipating. Power dictated restraint, not activism. As a result, Frankfurter was willing to identify the "accepted notions of justice" inherent in Fourteenth Amendment due process at least as much by deference to the opinions of high court judges in the states as by reference to the insights of the highest court justices of the nation.[24]

To Rutledge, Frankfurter's deference to state experimentation, as approved by state supreme court judges, was a clear abdication of responsibility. For example, in an egregious case, *In re Oliver*, the Court majority, with Frankfurter and Jackson dissenting, found a due process violation when a trial judge, acting as a "one-man grand jury" in Michigan, summarily held in contempt and sentenced to jail for sixty days a defendant who the judge believed had given false testimony. Likening the proceeding to one in the English Court of Star Chamber in the seventeenth century, Justice Black found a due process violation of the historic right to a public trial (without relying on his *Adamson* incorporation argument) and in the judge's failure to provide "a reasonable opportunity to defend."[25] Justice Rutledge concurred separately to identify double jeopardy and equal protection violations, but his most compelling reason for writing was his desire to attack the acceptance in *Adamson* of the states' "selective departure" from the "scheme of ordered personal liberty established by the Bill of Rights." The Court, he complained, was continuing to encourage the very kind of experimentation which had led to the disaster in *Oliver*: Michigan's one-member grand jury premised on the continental, not the English, system of civil justice. Rutledge concluded:

> So long as . . . the Bill of Rights is regarded here as a strait jacket of Eighteenth Century procedures rather than a basic charter of personal liberty, like experimentations may be expected from the states. And the only check against their effectiveness will be the agreement of a majority of this Court that the experiment violates fundamental notions of justice in civilized society.[26]

The Supreme Court eventually tired of state experimentation with procedures which, in the federal courts, would have violated constitutional rights. Increasingly, though selectively, the Court by the late 1960s had applied to the states through the Fourteenth Amendment virtually all the rights found in the first eight amendments to the Constitution.[27] To this extent Justice Black was prophetic. But Murphy and Rutledge were equally so. Substantive constitutional rights have emerged not found expressly in the Bill of Rights, such as the right to privacy,[28] the right to travel,[29] and, even before *Adamson*, the right "to marry, establish a home and bring up children"[30]—each justified, at least in part, as an interest in "liberty" guaranteed by "due process." By 1961 Justice Black's lone joiner in *Adamson*, Justice Douglas, was acknowledging: "Though I believe that 'due process' as used in the Fourteenth Amendment includes all of the first eight amendments, I do not think it is restricted and confined to them."[31]

There is something altogether unreal in suggesting that Justice Black was a strict constructionist, exercising great judicial restraint. Some two years after *Adamson*, and not long after Justice Rutledge had died, his last law clerk, Louis H. Pollak, was visiting with Justice Black. In remembering his colleague fondly, Black told Pollak how much he envied Rutledge. "Wiley didn't feel the same constraints that I feel to follow prior decisions." If the Court had been wrong before, forget about it and move on, Rutledge would say to Black. As Pollak recalled years later, "I was talking to somebody

*Louis H. Pollak.
(Courtesy of
Yale Law School
Archives)*

who sincerely believed what he was saying! I was talking to one of a half
dozen judges in our history who found his way around any precedent he
found inconvenient." Pollak added: "Clearly he saw Rutledge as a judicially
freer spirit." But Black was engaging in "Olympian self-deception."[32]

JUSTICE FRANKFURTER never lost his battle to maintain the ad hoc approach
set forth in *Palko* for identifying due process under the Fourteenth Amendment. But in the 1948 Term the conflict among the three approaches advanced in *Adamson* brought interesting results in *Wolf v. Colorado*, a major
due process case in which Wiley Rutledge supplied a significant dissent.[33]

A 6-to-3 majority, including Justice Black, held that the "core" of the
Fourth Amendment's protection against unreasonable search and seizure
was "implicit in the 'concept of ordered liberty.'" But the majority also held
that the federal sanction for violation—exclusion of the seized evidence
from the criminal trial—was not constitutionally required of the states.

Writing for the majority, Justice Frankfurter described the origin of the exclusionary rule "as a matter of judicial implication." This appeared to suggest that the exclusionary sanction was a requirement of the Fourth Amendment itself, not of the Court's supervisory power over the administration of criminal justice. Because reasonable persons could conclude, however, that other sanctions, such as a "private action" against the offending official or "internal discipline of the police," would be "equally effective," Frankfurter wrote, the exclusionary rule was not central enough to the Fourth Amendment's core protections to make it inherent in due process.[34]

Justice Black, concurring in the judgment, did not see the exclusionary rule in the Fourth Amendment at all, even implicitly. To Black, a former Alabama prosecutor and Senate investigator who was never a Fourth Amendment enthusiast, the exclusionary sanction was but "a judicially created rule of evidence which Congress might negate."[35] Thus, Black's belief that the Fourteenth Amendment incorporated the Fourth and no more—certainly not a supervisory, evidentiary gloss—brought him to the very result espoused by the Frankfurter majority.

In perhaps his most persuasive dissent ever, Justice Murphy (joined by Douglas and Rutledge) convincingly answered Frankfurter's argument that alternate sanctions such as civil actions and internal discipline against the police could be as effective as the exclusionary rule for enforcing the Fourth Amendment.[36] Among other things, Murphy noted that a typically judgment-proof police officer, employed by a sovereign not inevitably subject to suit—let alone to punitive damages—would not be likely to afford the defendant any meaningful relief.[37] And Murphy was far from convinced that prosecutors or police officials would discipline officers who carried out the officials' own commands.[38] He cemented his point by demonstrating from testimony in the trial record that in states which embraced the exclusionary rule, police training to observe Fourth Amendment requirements substantially exceeded the training in jurisdictions that rejected the rule.[39] Murphy accordingly opined that the exclusionary rule, in effect in the federal courts since 1914,[40] was inherent in the Fourth Amendment and thus in due process.

Joining Murphy while also dissenting separately, Justice Rutledge agreed that "the Amendment without the sanction is a dead letter." But he wrote primarily to repudiate Justice Black's premise that the exclusionary rule was but an evidentiary limitation that Congress could "negate." The rule not only was inherent in the Fourth Amendment, according to Rutledge, but also was part of the amendment's core protection. Consequently, Rutledge concluded, "state legislators and judges—if subject to the Amendment, as I believe them to be—may not lend their offices to the admission in state courts of evidence thus seized." Twelve years later, the Court overruled *Wolf*. Justice Black acknowledged that the "force" of Rutledge's dissent had "become compelling"; the exclusionary rule, Black reluctantly had come to believe, was not severable from the Fourth Amendment.[41]

FOUR CASES during the 1948 Term illustrate the view of Murphy and Rutledge (and Frankfurter) that a federal right guaranteed only by court rule, without regard to the Bill of Rights, could generate a constitutional right under the due process clause of the Fourteenth Amendment. In the first, *Upshaw v. United States*,[42] a 5-to-4 majority per Justice Black—with Reed, joined by Vinson, Jackson, and Burton dissenting—applied the Federal Rules of Criminal Procedure to overturn the conviction of a District of Columbia defendant who had confessed to grand larceny after thirty hours of interrogation but prior to arraignment before a magistrate. Local officials lost the opportunity to use the confession, the Court opined, because they had violated the federal rule requiring arraignment "without unnecessary delay." The states of Indiana, Pennsylvania, and South Carolina, however, did not enforce the rule. In three cases where defendants were held for interrogation in those states without access to counsel (for six days in Indiana, five in Pennsylvania, and five in South Carolina), five of the justices—including Frankfurter, who wrote for himself, Murphy, and Rutledge—found constitutional violations.[43] In the Indiana case, Frankfurter stressed several elements of abuse: a failure to arraign promptly, the coercive quality of the interrogation, and the absence of counsel. He then summarized: "To turn the detention of an accused into a process of wrenching from him evidence which could not be extorted in open court with all its safeguards, is so grave an abuse of the power of arrest as to offend the procedural standards of due process."[44] Justice Douglas concurred separately in each result, focusing on the delayed arraignment,[45] while Justice Black, also concurring in the judgments, relied on case law forbidding coerced confessions.[46]

In dissent, Justice Jackson asked rhetorically: if the "ultimate quest in a criminal trial is the truth and if the circumstances indicate no violence or threats of it, should society be deprived of the suspect's help in solving a crime merely because he was confined and questioned when uncounseled?"[47] Justice Reed, also in dissent, emoted: "Today's decision puts another weapon in the hand of the criminal world."[48] Jackson's and Reed's words undoubtedly caused Wiley Rutledge to cringe.

THERE ARE TWO channels for guaranteeing federal Bill of Rights protections in state courts: (1) certiorari from the Supreme Court to the state's highest court, and (2) collateral attack against the state's ruling by habeas corpus or some other writ filed initially in a federal district court, followed by Court of Appeals and (discretionary) Supreme Court review. Either route has often been highly limited and complicated, usually presenting the threshold question whether the applicant for federal relief has exhausted all state court remedies.

After twenty-two years in an Illinois penitentiary for murder, a prisoner named Marino asked a state trial court for a writ of habeas corpus ordering his release for violation of his constitutional rights. At the time of his conviction, Marino was eighteen, in the country two years, and unable to understand English. He heard the charge through an interpreter (the arresting officer), waived a jury trial, pleaded guilty, and received a life sentence. He had no lawyer. Habeas corpus was denied, and the U.S. Supreme Court granted certiorari. The Illinois attorney general admitted that the state had denied due process to Marino and consented to reversal, which the Supreme Court ordered.[49]

That did not satisfy Wiley Rutledge. Concurring separately (joined by Douglas and Murphy) during the 1947 Term in *Marino v. Ragen*, Rutledge noted that of the many similar cases coming from Illinois—accounting for over 50 percent of the indigent prisoner petitions from all jurisdictions during the previous three terms—the "only substantial difference" in Marino's case was the state's confession of error.[50] In the others, according to Rutledge, the Supreme Court had denied relief with "mechanical regularity" because almost invariably, the petitioner had failed to exhaust his state remedies. But, Rutledge noted, the rule requiring a petitioner to pursue all the relief the state can grant before seeking help in federal court presupposed that "an adequate state remedy" was "actually available." Experience had convinced Rutledge, however, that the state remedy in Illinois was "nothing but a procedural morass offering no substantial hope of relief."[51]

Specifically, a petitioner would have to seek a writ of "*habeas corpus*," or of "*coram nobis*," or of "error," depending, for example, on whether the critical facts were known to the judge at the time of trial, or on how many years had passed since the conviction. Failing to make the right choice in this "muddled" system would lead automatically to denial of relief. Justice Rutledge was convinced, accordingly, that but for the Illinois attorney general's confession of error, Marino would have been lost in an Illinois system "made up entirely of blind alleys," each "useful only as a means of convincing the federal courts that the state road which the petitioner ha[d] taken was the wrong one" and thus that state relief was still available. For the future, therefore, Rutledge proposed that the Court "no longer require exhaustion" of the "ineffective and inadequate remedies" in Illinois before permitting state prisoners to seek relief in federal court.[52]

A majority would not agree. Later in the term, in *Parker v. Illinois*, the Supreme Court, over Rutledge's dissent, continued its pattern of permitting Illinois procedure to defeat constitutional claims. A trial judge had ordered a party, Parker, to produce documents in a civil case. Upon reviewing them, the judge held Parker in contempt of court and sentenced him to ninety days in jail for filing "scurrilous" statements amounting to an "obstruction of justice" because they "reflected on the integrity of the court." Parker sought relief from the Illinois Supreme Court on due process and free speech grounds. Denied. Then the trial court, on its own, entered a revised contempt order and resentenced Parker, purportedly to cure a defect in the first order. This time, Parker appealed that second order to the state's intermediate appellate court, which found no state law ground for reversal and noted that it had no authority to consider constitutional questions. Parker then appealed the second order to the Illinois Supreme Court, which denied relief on the ground that by going first to the appellate court without jurisdiction over constitutional claims, Parker had waived all constitutional issues! Justice Douglas, writing for a 6-to-3 majority, noted that at "all critical stages" Parker had been "represented by counsel." And the majority "Affirmed."[53]

Counsel or no counsel, Rutledge was furious. "I cannot accept this hypertechnical procedural nullification of constitutional rights in a case involving the liberty of the individual," he wrote in dissent, joined by Black and Murphy. In the first place, noted Rutledge, both trial court orders were "in reality the same order"; the only difference was language in the second order adding that the allegedly scurrilous documents "incorporated by reference" in the first order were also "made a part" of the order as exhibits. (The trial judge had probably added this language, according to Rutledge, solely as a protection against an Illinois procedure that limited the record on appeal of a contempt order to the order itself; the judge apparently feared that his first order, by merely referring to the allegedly scurrilous documents, might be read not to include them in the order.) Rutledge therefore would have accepted *Parker* for review without parsing the order as though it were in two pieces.[54]

But even if the Illinois Supreme Court rulings embraced two separate orders, Justice Rutledge saw no waiver of constitutional rights. He was willing to assume that in the usual case, a decision to seek relief from an intermediate appellate court would waive constitutional claims that should have been brought first to the state supreme court; the U.S. Supreme Court had upheld that Illinois waiver rule years earlier.[55] But the present case was unusual, Rutledge wrote; there was no "well-settled Illinois law" that relief sought in the intermediate court *after* the state's highest court had ruled on a constitutional claim canceled that constitutional ruling, by then the "law of the case." An imputed waiver in that situation, he concluded, would be altogether unreasonable—a violation of due process.[56]

In summarizing, Justice Rutledge saw Parker as a victim, in today's parlance, of a "Catch-22," and he would have none of that.[57] Either the package before the nation's highest court constituted one final order, including the Illinois Supreme Court's original denial of Parker's constitutional claim, or it comprised two state supreme court orders, the second one defective for imputing a waiver of the constitutional claim, though correctable by adding to it the court's original constitutional ruling. Had he then reached the merits, Rutledge would have held the contempt order itself a violation of due process. The trial judge, he said, had compelled Parker "to publish the statements by filing them," and then sent him to jail "for obeying the court's order." The justice declared: "I know of no constitutional power which permits a state to force a citizen into such a dilemma, and I think the most elementary conception of due process under the Fourteenth Amendment forbids any such action."[58]

In addition to the "procedural labyrinth" erected by Illinois, its statutory right to counsel in noncapital cases was ephemeral. The state supreme court had ruled, as Justice Rutledge noted the previous term in *Foster*, that under state law the trial court had no duty to inform the accused of this right, and was obliged to provide a lawyer only upon the request of one who verified inability to pay.[59] When that Illinois approach came before the Court during the 1947 Term in *Bute v. Illinois*, Justice Burton wrote for a 6-to-3 majority that due process did not require the Illinois courts to inform the accused in a noncapital case of this right to counsel, and accordingly the Court sustained the petitioner's two consecutive twenty-year sentences imposed after guilty pleas.[60] Justice Rutledge, along with his colleagues Black and Murphy, joined Justice Douglas in dissent.

The Court extended Justice Burton's ruling later in the term in *Gryger v. Burke*. It upheld a Pennsylvania conviction of a defendant who had pleaded guilty without benefit of counsel and received a sentence as a fourth-time offender. This time Justice Rutledge wrote for the same four dissenters, finding a due process violation in light of the sentencing judge's misconception—unchallenged in the absence of defense counsel—that the life sentence he imposed was mandatory, not discretionary.[61] Rutledge could not distinguish the case from another decided the same term, *Townsend v. Burke*, in which the Court did find a violation of due process when the trial judge sentenced the "uncounseled defendant" based either on the "prosecution's submission of misinformation" at sentencing or on the "court's own misreading of the record."[62] Rutledge found it "difficult to comprehend" how the "court's misreading or misinformation concerning the facts" vital to sentencing deprived the defendant of due process in one case (*Townsend*), whereas the court's "misreading or misconception of the controlling statute" brought no constitutional violation in the other (*Gryger*). "Perhaps," he added in still another blast at *Adamson*, "the difference serves to illustrate how capricious are the results when the right to counsel is made to depend not upon the mandate of the Constitution"—through recognition that due process incorporated the Sixth Amendment—"but upon the vagaries of whether judges . . . will regard this incident or that in the course of particular criminal proceedings as prejudicial."[63]

Eventually, the full Court was fed up with Illinois. During the 1947 Term, in *Loftus v. Illinois*, the Court heard the Illinois attorney general explain that the state's high court had used state law grounds for rejecting an indigent prisoner's due process claim, based on denial of counsel, because the petitioner had erroneously sought a writ of "error," not "habeas corpus." Unwilling to rely on the attorney general's interpretation of what had happened below, the Supreme Court continued the case until the Illinois Supreme Court clarified the basis for its ruling. In September 1948, that court issued an "announcement" that it had denied the petition because the prisoner had sought a writ of error based on an inadequate record—an inadequacy which the "announcement" implied may have been as much the fault of the trial court as of the uncounseled defendant.[64]

To his previous year's clerk, John Paul Stevens, Justice Rutledge acknowledged that his colleagues had been waiting expectantly "for the Illinois Supreme Court to do something" after *Loftus*. When "it became obvious that nothing would be done" to simplify Illinois procedure, the Court took further action.[65] In early June 1949, over the chief's signature, the justices essentially did what Rutledge had recommended in his *Marino* concurrence two years earlier. Granting certiorari in eight Illinois prisoner cases, the Court remanded each for one last opportunity to guarantee a "post-trial procedure by which federal rights may be vindicated in Illinois." Otherwise, it was clear, the Court would review the cases on the merits without the Illinois high court's input.[66] In the meantime, already energized by Rutledge's harsh criticism in *Marino*, the Illinois State Bar had been demanding reform.[67] Aided by the latest pressure from the Court in *Loftus*, Bar leaders pushed through legislation in early July, signed by the state's new governor, Adlai Stevenson, guaranteeing an uncomplicated, single post-trial remedy.[68]

THE CONTINUING impatience of Wiley Rutledge with procedural rules barring access to the federal courts was evident from the civil, as well as the criminal, side of the Supreme Court's docket. In a deportation case, *Ahrens v. Clark*, he dissented from one of the weakest opinions William O. Douglas ever wrote. Some 120 German nationals were about to be deported under the Alien Enemy Act of 1798. They sought writs of habeas corpus from a federal court in the District of Columbia to stop that action on the ground that the government had issued deportation orders unlawfully after hostilities with Germany had ceased. Writing for a 6-to-3 majority, Douglas upheld the lower court's dismissals because, he said, the applicable statute limited a federal District Court's habeas authority to prisoners confined within the court's own territorial jurisdiction, whereas the petitioners were confined beyond the D.C. federal court's reach at Ellis Island in New York.[69]

In a powerful opinion joined by Black and Murphy, Justice Rutledge demonstrated that the statutory language, legislative history, and case law overwhelmingly supported a conclusion that the person whose location governed the court's jurisdiction was the jailer, namely, the individual who had lawful power over the prisoner and thus could carry out the court's order. In this case, that individual was the U.S. attorney general, wherever found — and the attorney general could always be found in the District of Columbia, where the petitions were filed. Rutledge's hypotheticals proved his point. What if a prisoner's location is unknown to his or her counsel? What if the prisoner is in one state, while the jailer can be served with process only in another? And what if the prisoner is wholly outside any federal jurisdiction but the jailer is within a court's reach? Douglas offered no satisfactory answers to these questions. *Ahrens* was eventually overruled.[70]

THE SUPREME COURT in the 1940s had no stronger (though usually unsuccessful) advocate for increased citizens' access to the federal courts than Wiley Rutledge. A number of cases tested the extent to which the federal courts, under the rule of *Erie R. Co. v. Tompkins*,[71] must defer to state procedural rules when federal jurisdiction is based on diversity of citizenship.[72] More specifically, *Erie* held that where federal jurisdiction was based on diversity, not on a federal claim, the federal court must apply the substantive law of the appropriate state, not some superseding federal common law that the court itself might develop. But that often left open the question whether a particular state rule of court was "substantive," and thus applicable through *Erie*, or merely "procedural," and thus trumped by a different federal court rule.

In the 1944 Term, joined only by Murphy, Justice Rutledge dissented from the Court's ruling in *Guaranty Trust Co.* that in a diversity case, a state statute of limitations barred, because of *Erie*, an equity suit that a federal court otherwise would have entertained.[73] Later, in the 1948 Term —

with a single dissent covering three *Erie* decisions—Rutledge expressed a minority view that would limit all federal court deference by narrowing it to state court rules that were "clearly substantive in nature."[74] He refused, accordingly, to join colleagues in the majority who would incorporate into federal procedure the New Jersey rule that a plaintiff who loses a stockholders' derivative action must pay the defendant's expenses, including attorney's fees;[75] or the Mississippi rule that barred from court any foreign corporation which had not qualified to do business in the state;[76] or the Kansas rule that would keep the statute of limitations period running until the date a summons was served, not "tolling" it as of the earlier date when the complaint was filed.[77] To Rutledge, these were all procedural rules of the forum, not "clearly substantive" rules requiring federal deference to state law.

Rutledge had always been skeptical about the "wisdom" of *Erie* itself and never accepted the majority's understanding that "a federal court is 'merely another court of the state in which it sits,'" such that "in every situation in which the doors of state courts are closed to a suitor" the federal courts also must remain shut. "[S]ound historical reason" convinced the justice that "one of the purposes of the diversity clause was to afford a federal court remedy when, for at least some reasons of state policy, none would be available in the state courts." Rutledge recognized that "in many situations procedure and substance are so interwoven that rational separation becomes well-nigh impossible." Nonetheless, he said, "this fact cannot dispense with the necessity of making a distinction," for under *Erie* doctrine "it is the Congress which has the power to govern the procedure of the federal courts in diversity cases, and the states which have that power over matters clearly substantive in nature." If rules of procedure are seen too easily as substantive law, he said, Congress's power is seriously impaired. Judges thus "cannot escape making the division," even when the constituent procedural and substantive elements of a rule of law are as linked together as "Siamese twins." "It is in these close cases, this borderland area," he observed, where "we are going too far" in allowing *Erie* to cut off a federal remedy.[78]

JUSTICE RUTLEDGE was also eager to narrow rules that obstructed access to the federal courts in situations unrelated to *Erie*. He dissented, for example, in cases where the majority upheld dismissal of an appeal for filing too late,[79] ordered dismissal of a suit on grounds of *res judicata* (preclusion of a claim previously adjudicated),[80] denied review of a criminal conviction by writ of habeas corpus,[81] and ruled that there was no final, appealable order.[82] In seeking to keep federal forums open, however, Rutledge was not interested (when *Erie* imposed no limitation) in creating federal common law to supplement federal legislation. On one occasion, for example, the federal government tried to recover from the Standard Oil Company the hospital costs and salary that it had paid for a soldier injured by a Standard Oil truck. Rutledge noted that under Supreme Court precedent, the government's claimed right of recovery presented a question of federal, not state, law. And because no federal statute granted a right of recovery, the more specific issue was whether the Court would create a federal common law right of recovery. For an 8-to-1 majority, Rutledge rejected the government's claim, ruling that the issue, fundamentally, was one of "federal fiscal policy" better left to Congress.[83]

The justice acknowledged that after the *Erie* decision, there was still the potential for "federal common law" development in a case, such as *Standard Oil*, where neither state common law nor a federal statute was at issue. Nor would he "deny the Government's basic premise" that the "law's capacity for growth" must include "the creative work of judges." Otherwise, he acknowledged, soon "all law would become antiquated strait jacket and then dead letter." "But in the federal scheme," Rutledge concluded, the federal courts' "part in that work" (aside from constitutional interpretation) is "more modest" than the state courts' "freedom to create new common-law liabilities." "Congress," he said, "not this Court or the other federal courts, is the custodian of the national purse" and "most often the exclusive arbiter of federal fiscal affairs." On numerous occasions, he wrote, Congress "has taken positive action" to "prevent interference with federal funds, property or relations" and, if necessary, could do so here.[84]

TWENTY-THREE

The Commerce Clause and Equal Protection

While awaiting oral argument in *United Mine Workers*, Justice Rutledge was preparing a series of three lectures on the commerce clause for the University of Kansas School of Law. They were delivered December 2–4, 1946, and eventually published in a small book, *A Declaration of Legal Faith*. In reference to this commitment, Rutledge wrote to Victor Brudney, "I have lost all sense of restraint about what I can get done," to which Edna Lingreen added in brackets as a note to the former clerk, "Don't you agree?"[1] Initially, however, the task did not seem as daunting to the justice as a lecture series suggests, because he planned to present the comprehensive understanding of the commerce clause that he had developed while preparing opinions in state tax cases the previous term and was elaborating further in a concurring opinion in process.[2] In retrospect, however, he found that he had been "foolish" to undertake the lectures, given the time they took away from opinion writing; but he acknowledged to Ralph Fuchs that he had "had a lot of fun doing the job and especially during the three days" he "spent in Lawrence."[3]

After an opening lecture elaborating the "legal faith" (summarized earlier) that informed his decision making as a judge, Justice Rutledge turned to the history of the commerce clause under Supreme Court rulings. He reminded his audience that "the generating source of the Constitution lay in the rising volume of restraints upon commerce" between the states which the new nation, operating under the Articles of Confederation, "could not check." But through adoption of the commerce clause—"The Congress shall have Power . . . To regulate Commerce . . . among the several States . . ."—the nation in time became "a continental area of free trade," resulting in "vast economic development." Without that clause, Rutledge suggested, it was doubtful whether the nation "could long have survived." To the commerce clause, he concluded, "may be credited largely the fact

376

we are an independent and democratic country today," powerful enough to have claimed "victory in the war just closed."[4]

"Deceptively simple in wording," however, the clause has "not been a simple one for execution." Over time, according to Rutledge, it had required "intricate adjustments for the states, the Congress, the courts, and the people" answering a host of questions in a variety of contexts. What is regulation? Does it include prohibition? Taxation? What is commerce? Does it "encompass manufacturing, mining, farming, and labor relations involved in those pursuits"? What is interstate? Is congressional power "exclusive or only paramount"?[5]

Justice Rutledge told the story of the commerce clause in orderly fashion, beginning with Chief Justice Marshall's view that "Commerce . . . among the several States"—a concept that Marshall defined broadly—was entrusted exclusively to Congress (although at least once he acknowledged an exception).[6] In the extreme, this meant that if Congress declined to regulate, no state could do so either, with potentially "devastating" consequences for "matters vitally affecting state interests arising out of interstate commerce" within a state's borders. Of necessity, he said, the Supreme Court eventually rejected Marshall's premise. In 1851, in *Cooley v. Board of Wardens*, the Court recognized the states' authority, in the absence of congressional action, to regulate interstate commerce at least in matters "of primarily local importance" until Congress affirmatively enacted overriding legislation. As a result, since Congress showed little interest in commercial regulation much before the last decade of the nineteenth century, the nation experienced a long period of state regulation, upheld under the "rule of permissible local diversity" though sometimes sustained, alternatively, as outside the meaning of "commerce."[7]

When Congress did begin taking initiatives by enacting the Interstate Commerce Act of 1887 and the Sherman Antitrust Act of 1890, however, the Supreme Court handed Congress a significant defeat, the justice noted. In 1895 the Court held the sugar trust immune from attack under the Sherman Act on the ground that only "manufacture," not "commerce," was involved.[8] Within ten years, however, the pendulum had begun to swing back in favor of Congress, Rutledge observed, with antitrust decisions effectively overruling the sugar trust case.[9] Indeed, the New Deal Court eventually extended congressional power under the commerce clause not only to manufacturing but also to labor relations, to child labor, and even to regulating farm products intended not for commerce but wholly for consumption by the farmers themselves.[10]

With Congress heavily in the field, therefore, its regulatory silence became more pregnant with possible meaning. According to Rutledge, the very existence of the commerce clause authorizing congressional regulation created a "negative inference" that "state power was limited to some extent." But rather than revert to Marshall's premise that the states could impose virtually no regulation when Congress was silent, or adopt at the other extreme a view once expressed by Justice Black that the states could regulate at will until Congress acted, the Court continued to follow the lead of Marshall's successor, Chief Justice Roger Taney, by interpreting the "silence of Congress" as a matter of intent by Congress either to reserve a particular field for itself or to allow the states to act. Indeed, rejection of Marshall's general approach became of "vital importance," Rutledge noted, once Congress began nullifying Court decisions barring state action. "If the commerce clause itself forbids state action 'by its own force,'" as the Court on occasion held, how could Congress by "expressly consenting" implement a national policy that incorporated forbidden state regulation?[11]

Rutledge answered that once both Congress and the states had become active in the regulation of commerce, the Court's trend had "been toward sustaining state regulation formerly regarded as inconsistent with Congress' unexercised power over commerce," so that "the states and the Congress largely may work together, concurrently regulating commerce" while "still the federal power is supreme."[12] But how did this work? In *Prudential Insurance Co. v. Benjamin*, which Rutledge wrote in the 1945 Term, South Carolina had levied an annual tax on an out-of-state insurance company for the privilege of doing business in the state—a tax not imposed on South Carolina corporations. Congress then passed the McCarran Act, expressly authorizing the states to tax and otherwise regulate insurance.[13] In a "more sustained consideration" of the issue than ever before given by a justice, according to one scholar, Rutledge assumed for purposes of analysis that but for the McCarran Act, the tax would fall as a discriminatory burden on interstate commerce. Rutledge then held the tax valid nonetheless, not because Congress could legitimate a forbidden state power but because Congress could use the states as vehicles for implementing *congressional* authority over interstate commerce—unfettered by any discriminatory impact which the Constitution forbids the states but not Congress to impose.[14]

The analysis worked for two reasons. First, congressional power under the commerce clause, constrained only by what is "commerce," is broader than the states' limited power to tax and regulate activities affecting interstate commerce. Second, Congress had neither "adopted" the state's tax as its own (imposing thereby a nonuniform excise tax in violation of Article I, Section 8, of the Constitution) nor delegated congressional power unlawfully to the states (violating Article I, Section 1). Rather, both sovereigns had acted. Legitimated, to be sure, by Congress's having taken part, the tax regulation resulted as much from action initiated by the states—a joint "exercise of all the power of government residing in our scheme."[15]

There may be conceptual difficulty with the idea that Congress, having plenary authority under the commerce clause, is dependent nonetheless on independent state action for this particular form of regulation to take place. But given that state governments are inherent in our federal system—and that Article I of the Constitution limits the taxing power of Congress—one can just as easily look at the situation as one in which Congress maximizes its reach under the commerce power by taking advantage of an option not otherwise available to the federal legislature. With the "coordinated action" theory of *Prudential Insurance*, Justice Rutledge not only made "congressional consent" an "assured doctrine" but, as one scholar has put it, legitimated a new "flexibility in the operations of the federal system."[16] Indeed, the Supreme Court accepts the *Prudential Insurance* rationale to this day.[17]

To his Kansas audience, Rutledge explained that such coordinated approaches have meant that greater "leeway and deference are given for legislative judgments, national and state"; that larger "emphasis is put on scrutiny of particular facts and concrete consequences"; and thus, more and more, that "the controlling considerations of policy implicit in thinking, judgment, and decision are brought into the open," while less and less (though "still too much") stress "is placed upon large generalizations and dogmatisms." In short, Justice Rutledge was embracing, and encouraging the Court to apply, a "realistic" jurisprudence of the commerce clause, fact based and policy driven. The "enduring quality" of the Constitution, he concluded, depended on making room for "the continuing adjustment and readjustment of federal-state relationships, without which no federal scheme could long survive." That, he made clear, at least in the "silence of Congress," was the work of discerning judges.[18]

To a friend, Rutledge wrote several months after the lectures: "When I got into the history of the silence doctrine I came to realize that the doctrine was really just a vacuum into which the Court could pour whatever ideas and consequences it wished until Congress came along and repudiated them."[19] The justice was a man of candor. And as his opinions in *Prudential Insurance* and other commerce clause cases demonstrated, Rutledge himself was thorough to a fault in articulating with precision, supported by case law authority, the "ideas and consequences" that he poured into his rulings.

WHILE JUSTICE RUTLEDGE was preparing his Kansas lectures on the powers of Congress and the states to act concurrently under the commerce clause, he was dealing at the Court with the power of the states themselves to tax interstate transactions when Congress was silent. To that end he concurred separately in *Freeman v. Hewitt*, writing a tour de force taking up twenty-five pages in the *United States Reports* and supplementing an analysis he had presented in a trilogy of cases—dissenting in one, concurring in two—during his first full term three years earlier.[20]

In the first of these earlier cases, Justice Frankfurter, writing for a 5-to-4 Court, upheld a ruling by the Arkansas Supreme Court that Arkansas had violated the commerce clause. The state had imposed a "sales tax" on a transaction in which a Tennessee salesman for a Tennessee company, without an office or license to do business in Arkansas, had solicited an order for goods in Arkansas, subject to acceptance in Tennessee by the company, which shipped them to the purchaser in Arkansas. Frankfurter held that because the sale—the transfer of ownership—had taken place in Tennessee, Arkansas could not constitutionally "project its powers beyond its boundaries" and, as a result, "tax an interstate transaction." Justice Frankfurter all but conceded, however, that if Arkansas had imposed a "use tax" on the same transaction, meaning a tax on the use or enjoyment of the goods in Arkansas, the tax would have avoided its extraterritorial reach and thus passed the constitutional test. The only difference, he said, was one of "conception."[21]

In a companion case from Iowa, with another opinion by Justice Frankfurter, the Court upheld such a "use tax" on goods shipped from Minnesota in situations similar to those in the Arkansas case.[22] And in the third case, written by Justice Douglas, the Court upheld Indiana's power to tax the "gross receipts" from a variety of "interstate transactions consummated within its borders."[23]

In the Arkansas case, Black, Douglas, Murphy, and Rutledge dissented from the conceptualism that Justice Frankfurter had used to distinguish "sales" from "use" taxes. The four thus voted to sustain the state taxes in all three cases. Writing for himself, Black, and Murphy, Justice Douglas—the former "legal realist" professor—pointed out that sales and use taxes had the "same economic incidence"; their effect on interstate commerce was "identical." Nor was there discrimination against interstate commerce, for every purchaser would pay the same tax whether the goods were generated within the state or shipped from without. Furthermore, the buyer's "receipt of goods within the State" was "as adequate a basis for the exercise of the taxing power as use within the State"—due process was satisfied. Accordingly, Douglas wrote, the state had the constitutional power to impose this basic tax, however labeled. Commerce clause issues, in sum, should "turn on practical considerations and business realities," not on "dialectics."[24]

Justice Rutledge, writing separately, agreed entirely with Douglas, but in Rutledge's view a broader look was required. By focusing only on the Arkansas case, he wrote, one would have to infer that only Tennessee could tax the transaction. But if that were true, how could Iowa impose a use tax, rather than leave the transaction's tax exclusively to Minnesota where the sale took place? Given that each of the two states had enough connection with the transaction for its tax to satisfy due process, and given further that under the Arkansas and Iowa decisions each state could impose a tax of one kind or another, what would happen, Rutledge asked, if *both* states— Arkansas and Tennessee, or Iowa and Minnesota—taxed the transaction?[25]

In an effort to discourage his newest colleague from taking the inquiry that far, Justice Frankfurter wrote a memo urging Rutledge to agree that "we should pursue the creep-crawl method of dealing with tax cases arising under the Commerce Clause decide no more and say no more than we inescapably can." But Rutledge was not persuaded; to him, the discussion lacked reality without at least flagging the problem of double taxation— which he unhesitatingly announced would violate the commerce clause.[26]

Rutledge proceeded from the premise, attributable to opinions by Stone beginning in 1938, that states in the absence of congressional prohibition were free to tax transactions in interstate commerce, provided that they did not result in "multiple" or "undue" burdens on interstate commerce.[27] Rutledge noted, accordingly, that the Iowa statute eliminated any undue burden problem by crediting the Iowa use tax with a sales tax paid elsewhere on the same transaction. (A system of apportionment would also be constitutional, though more complicated, he added.) Rutledge then concluded, tentatively, that in the event neither state would yield and the Court thus had to impose a credit, the tax at the "state of origin" (meaning shipment) should yield to the tax at the "state of market" (meaning consumption).[28] Why?

To avoid an undue burden on interstate commerce, presumably the tax burden on the seller from out of state should be no greater than the burden on the local sellers with which it competed. If the tax were imposed at the state of origin, that state might levy a heavier tax burden on the goods shipped interstate than the burden imposed on the local sellers with which the interstate shipper would compete in the consuming state. By contrast, if the consuming state imposed the tax, the burden on interstate and local sellers would be the same.[29] (Furthermore, a tax by the consuming state would guard against an undue benefit to the interstate seller in the event of a tax by the state of origin lighter than the one imposed by the consuming state.)

Three years later, in *Freeman v. Hewitt*, the Court faced a situation where two states taxed an interstate stock transaction and thus presented the question whether the Court should impose an apportionment mechanism, as Rutledge had suggested. Indiana taxed the gross receipts of an Indiana trustee's sale of stock through a New York broker. New York taxed the transfer.[30] For the majority Justice Frankfurter, rejecting the multiple burden approach, returned to an old test barring any "direct" tax on interstate commerce and struck down the Indiana tax issue.[31]

Justice Rutledge concurred in the result, though not in Frankfurter's opinion, because the Indiana tax on top of the New York tax imposed a "cumulative" burden that discriminated against an interstate transaction. But Rutledge rejected, as he put it, Frankfurter's "reversion" against the "trend of recent decisions" to the formalistic, discarded test barring taxation simply because of a "direct" impact on interstate commerce. Rutledge was unwilling "to give interstate commerce a haven of refuge from taxation," but he also would not accept a fact-based determination in each case that would inevitably incite "a volume of litigation." He thus proposed (as applied to the facts in *Freeman*) "vest[ing] the power to tax in the state of the market [New York], subject to power in the forwarding state [Indiana] also to tax by allowing credit to the full amount of any tax paid or due at the destination [New York]."[32] His approach, joined by no other justice, would have maximized state taxation while preventing a double sales (or equivalent) tax on items in interstate commerce.

As noted by several commentators, however—including Rutledge's friend Thomas Reed Powell, who twitted him for the length of his opinion—Rutledge's approach did not offer a complete solution to the multiple tax problem. In most kinds of interstate commerce, a resourceful forwarding state (or "state of origin" or, simply, "seller" state) could impose, in lieu of a sales tax, a levy on an earlier stage of the commercial process, such as manufacturing or processing, that might escape the demand for apportionment.[33] And another commentator opined that Rutledge's preference for taxation by the state of market (or, more simply, the "buyer" state) would favor the wealthier, consuming states over producing states.[34] Rutledge was applauded, nonetheless, for insisting on economic realism over Frankfurter's return to verbal formulae.[35] And while some law school experts were uncertain that his ideas represented a real advance, none would gainsay his important contribution to the dialogue about a nearly intractable constitutional problem. All recognized his creativity in proposing a new, seller state's "credit"—a modified form of apportionment—more likely than other approaches to achieve allocation of taxes on interstate transactions to all states involved.[36]

In proposing his "credit" approach among acknowledged alternatives,

Justice Rutledge, it would appear, was not merely interpreting the Constitution; he was using constitutional history and policy to formulate a rule of federal common law in aid of the Constitution.[37] He saw a need to make the commerce clause workable for the states, as well as for the federal government, and felt no obligation to shift the creative burden to Congress. At the same time, Rutledge was always careful to assure that the facts justified the tax a state would impose. In *Nippert v. City of Richmond*, for example, writing for the majority over the dissents of his usual supporters Black, Douglas, and Murphy, Rutledge held that the commerce clause barred a state license tax on an agent or "drummer" who solicited orders for interstate shipment of goods by an out-of-state corporation having no place of business in the taxing state. In *Nippert*, the tax applied—without regard to volume of business or regularity of solicitation—to an agent who had solicited in Richmond during only five days. In Rutledge's view, this brought an "exclusionary" impact "especially upon small out-of-state operators."[38] The justice was always attuned to the effect of a ruling on small business.

With his concurrence in *Freeman*, Justice Rutledge kept alive the cumulative burden analysis, for in the same term the Court decided two other cases acknowledging the relevance of apportionment.[39] Two years later in *Interstate Pipeline Co. v. Stone*, Rutledge wrote a plurality opinion, joined by Black, Douglas, and Murphy in a 5-to-4 decision, upholding a "privilege tax" on interstate commerce measured by gross receipts from oil pipeline operations, wholly within Mississippi, not subject to taxation elsewhere.[40] The four dissenters per Justice Reed, joined by Vinson, Frankfurter, and Jackson, adhered to the proposition that "the privilege of carrying on interstate commerce is immune from state taxation . . . with or without fair apportionment even if not discriminatory."[41] Justice Burton broke the tie, voting to uphold the tax on the ground that "intrastate commerce" alone was involved.[42] By the end of his service on the Court, therefore, Wiley Rutledge had achieved four votes in support of an opinion with its "essential premises" drawn from his views in *Freeman*.[43] But not five votes.

Thirty years after *Freeman*, however, and almost a generation after his death, Justice Rutledge prevailed. In *Complete Auto Transit, Inc. v. Brady*, the Supreme Court overruled Frankfurter's formalistic rationale in *Freeman* in favor of Rutledge's functional approach.[44] Rutledge had summarized his *Freeman* criteria in a short concurring opinion the next term: he would sustain a state tax affecting interstate commerce if it satisfied "due process," meaning that there was "'jurisdiction to tax'"; the tax was "nondiscriminatory," that is, it "place[d] no greater burden upon interstate commerce than the state place[d] upon competing intrastate commerce of like character"; it was "duly apportioned," meaning it did not "undertake to tax any interstate activities carried on outside the state's borders"; and it could not "be repeated by any other state."[45] In *Complete Auto*, Justice Blackmun expressly recognized Rutledge's contribution and announced for a unanimous Court a four-part test that virtually tracked Rutledge's criteria.[46] These have continued to define the law.[47]

THE COMMERCE CLAUSE required the accommodation of federal and state interests, but, as we have seen, it also invoked analysis protecting individuals against discriminatory tax levies. Thus the commerce clause has an aspect that invites, more broadly, a look at "equal protection" doctrine. Justice Rutledge had an instinct for equal protection of the laws; recall his reaction to withholding legal counsel from impoverished criminal defendants. Had he lived longer, Rutledge would have been out front against discrimination based on race and gender. He joined the majorities that relied on equal protection theories to strike down an all-white primary in Texas[48] and on commerce clause theories to nullify a Virginia statute separating the races on interstate buses.[49] And as we have seen, he would have joined with Murphy in affirming the convictions of Sheriff Screws and his cohorts— whom Georgia refused to prosecute for murder—for violating the federal civil rights of a young African American.[50]

The 1946 Term brought an unusual kind of discrimination. In *Kotch v. Board of River Port Pilot Commissioners*, Justice Black, writing for a 5-to-4 majority, upheld a Louisiana state-sponsored system permitting an association of river pilots—required by law to help navigate boats along the Mississippi River near New Orleans—to choose all its new pilots exclusively from among family members and friends. The majority found no constitutional basis for requiring state officials "to select state public servants by competitive tests or by any other method of selection." Rutledge's dissent was brief—three pages—and powerful. "The result of the decision," he concluded, "is to approve as constitutional state regulation which makes admission to the ranks of pilots turn finally on consanguinity. Blood is, in effect, made the crux of selection. That, in my opinion, is forbidden by the Fourteenth Amendment's guaranty against denial of the equal protection of the laws."[51]

In the next term, Rutledge extended his concern from "blood" line to racial discrimination in *Fisher v. Hurst*, in which he dissented alone. Earlier, the Court had ruled that Oklahoma must offer a young African American woman, Ada Lois Sipuel, a legal education "in conformity with the equal protection clause of the Fourteenth Amendment and provide it as soon as it does for applicants of any other group." In response to the mandate, the Oklahoma county court had ordered the University of Oklahoma either to admit Sipuel to its law school until "a separate law school for negroes," substantially equal to that attended by whites, was "established and ready to function," or "not to enroll any applicant of any group" in the first-year class until the separate school was available. When the university subsequently refused admission to Sipuel her attorney, Thurgood Marshall, sought leave from the Supreme Court to file a petition for writ of mandamus to compel compliance with the Court's earlier mandate. The Court responded in *Fisher* by denying leave to file.[52]

Justice Rutledge dissented. He saw a loophole in the Oklahoma court's interpretation of the mandate. By ordering the university—if it refused to admit Ms. Sipuel—not to enroll any other "applicant" (including any white applicant) in petitioner's entering "class" until a separate (but equal) school was available, the Oklahoma court was nonetheless keeping the law school open for white students in the second- and third-year classes. To Rutledge, that did not "comply with" the Court's "mandate." The Court had "plainly meant," he wrote, that unless the state could establish overnight a separate law school for petitioner equal "in fact, not in legal fiction"—clearly an impossibility—"Oklahoma should end the discrimination practiced against petitioner at once," either by admitting her to the state university or by shutting down the university's law school entirely so that no one could benefit.[53] Justice Murphy would have set the matter for a hearing. Otherwise, Rutledge was alone.

Justice Rutledge had another opportunity to condemn racial discrimination during the 1947 Term. Writing this time for a 7-to-2 majority (with Vinson and Jackson dissenting) in *Bob-Lo Excursion Co. v. Michigan*, Rutledge held that the commerce clause, standing alone, did not interfere with Michigan's prosecution of a charter boat company under the state's civil rights act. The company carried passengers to Bois Blanc Island, a part of Ontario known as the Coney Island of Detroit, located fifteen miles upriver from the city without established access from Canada. When company officials spied a young African American in a girls' high school class boarding a boat for the island, they ordered her off by explaining that as a "private concern," they could exclude anyone they pleased. A local court fined the company for unlawful discrimination, and the Supreme Court of Michigan affirmed.[54]

Addressing the only issue pursued on appeal, Justice Rutledge noted that it would be "hard to find" foreign commerce of a "more highly local concern." He discerned no adverse impact, foreign or domestic, on legitimate national interests protected by the commerce clause, such as immigration, customs, navigation—and certainly no impact that would override Michigan's interest in forbidding racial discrimination. Rutledge used the unique, localized facts to distinguish precedent that according to Jackson and Vinson, in dissent, would have barred Michigan from interfering with interstate commerce. (Although the parties had withdrawn all Fourteenth Amendment arguments, Justice Douglas concurred on equal protection grounds, saying that they "cut[] deeper" than commerce clause jurisprudence in barring racial discrimination.)[55]

Bob-Lo is an example of a colleague's reluctance to sign on to an opinion by Rutledge because of its lengthy details; but it also illustrates how Frankfurter and Rutledge differed on spelling out the facts of racial discrimination when not entirely necessary to decision. Rutledge initiated a draft elaborating the indignities which the excursion company officials had visited upon the young African American girl forced off the boat. Specifically, he recited the officials' getting "angry," "yell[ing]" at the girl, and conscripting "three white . . . waiters" to "'throw this woman off.'" Frankfurter objected because the severity of her treatment, while "relevant in a suit for false imprisonment or battery," had no bearing on a discrimination claim. Frankfurter wrote in response to the draft:

> Before coming down here, when I was of counsel for the Association for the Advancement of the Colored People, considerable practical experience with problems of race relations led me to the conclusion that the ugly practices of racial discrimination should be dealt with by the eloquence of action, but with austerity of speech. . . . It does not help toward harmonious race relations to stir our colored fellow citizens to resentment by even pertinent rhetoric or by a needless recital of details of mistreatment which are irrelevant to a legal issue before us. Nor do we thereby wean whites, both North and South, from what so often is merely the momentum of the past in them.
>
> Forgive this little sermon.

Rutledge replied that he was "glad" to have the "little sermon," adding:

> Perhaps the complete statement I have made is not entirely essential, but it is still true that this [is] a case which involves racial discrimination. Indeed, the racial angle sticks out of this as much or possibly more than it did in the *Fisher* case. I agreed with you there that the facts had to be stated to give the true picture and flavor of the situation. . . . I think this case would be very colorless without those facts or a somewhat shorter summary. And on reflection I hope you will agree with me both on the authority cited and in principle. If you do not, I should like to reserve final decision about the matter and discuss it with you in person.

Frankfurter rejoined: "[I]t does not make the slightest difference to our decision whether Miss Ray was asked to leave the ship with Chesterfieldian courtesy or with barroom roughness," whereas *Fisher*, according to Frankfurter, turned "on the very facts of conduct and the characteristics and psychological relationships of people."

Rutledge was not convinced.

> Felix:
> ... The case probably will not go down Monday, contrary to your hope, and I will consider further about the statement of facts.
> Wiley.
> P. S. Sermonette: All racial discrim. is relevant to Chesterfieldian courtesy and bar room roughness and, as they say, vice versa.

A month went by before the opinion issued—without the factual elaboration Rutledge had intended.[56]

RUTLEDGE WAS distressed by having to disqualify himself from the most important civil rights case of the 1947 Term, *Shelley v. Kramer*, challenging the constitutionality of covenants barring ownership, or even occupancy, of real estate by "any Negro or colored person" or anyone "not of the Caucasian race."[57] Rutledge, Jackson, and Reed had restrictive covenants in their own deeds and, for that reason, each decided not to sit.[58] Rutledge had looked for a way to participate, sending his clerks to the Recorder of Deeds office in search of a property law basis for finding his own covenants unenforceable so that he might participate.[59] But that surely would not have saved disqualification in any event. The justice was searching for a way to bend the rule because he truly worried about the outcome. (His views on the racial covenant issue, not to mention his lone dissent in the Oklahoma law school case, led his clerk for the following year, Louis Pollak, to believe that Rutledge "would have moved" on outlawing racial discrimination in the schools "if he'd had the chance.")[60]

Within days after argument in *Shelley*, Ralph Fuchs wrote, "Dear Wiley, ... I have had a vivid sense of the pain it must have caused you to leave the bench during the argument of the restrictive covenant cases. ... There has been a good deal of argument around here over whether judges should disqualify themselves in such situations. I stick to my point of view that you are right in doing so, and I only hope you have not been caused too much unhappiness by your step."[61] The recusing justices received a good deal of criticism from those who inferred that the disqualifications were attributable to "a huge property value in restrictive covenants" or, more simply, to the justices' racial prejudice. Irving Brant accordingly believed, as he wrote to Rutledge, that "the self-disqualification of three members of the court gave a hard and needless jolt, because of mistaken inferences from it." And Brant wrote a letter to Justice Reed (with copies to Jackson and Rutledge) encouraging Reed—who apparently had indicated to a reporter that he might issue a statement explaining his recusal when the Court handed down its opinion—to make known his "trifling personal interest" in a racial covenant in his property in Kentucky.[62]

Upon receiving his copy of the letter to Reed, Rutledge wrote to Brant: "About all I can say is that whatever one does here, whether to sit or not to sit, decide or not decide, and how he decides, inevitably brings criticism, very often entirely groundless, sometimes perhaps justified. The only way to survive it is to have a thick skin and move on to the next mistake." No public explanation from the recusing justices was forthcoming. Justice Rutledge welcomed the result, however: 6-to-0 opinions by Chief Justice Vinson holding that court enforcement of racial covenants was state action in violation of the equal protection clause of the Fourteenth Amendment and, in the District of Columbia, a violation of the Civil Rights Act of 1866.[63]

Before issuing his opinions in the restrictive covenant cases, the Chief Justice had written another on the side of civil rights. Carrying the votes of six justices (with Reed, Jackson, and Burton dissenting), Vinson declared unconstitutional under the equal protection clause, "as applied in this case," the California Alien Land Law that effectively barred from owning land children of Japanese aliens ineligible for naturalization—even children who were American citizens. Black, Douglas, Murphy, and Rutledge went further, however, concluding that the statute violated the equal protection clause on its face—meaning in all cases. While Douglas joined Black's brief concurrence to that effect, Rutledge—reflecting anguish over *Korematsu?*—joined Murphy's long opinion chronicling the history of discrimination against the Japanese and Chinese in this country.[64]

IN MARCH 1948, Wiley Rutledge appeared on a speaker's podium at Bryn Mawr College to address an audience honoring Eleanor Roosevelt and Anna Lord Strauss, national president of the League of Women Voters. Titling his remarks "Women's Rights—Barometer of Democracy," the justice observed that slavery had "put very largely out of sight other institutions antithetic to any conception of broad-scale freedom and democracy," especially "the universal disenfranchisement of women." Although women finally "came broadly to full citizenship in 1920" with ratification of the Nineteenth Amendment, Rutledge noted, their emancipation was not yet complete: legally so, perhaps, but not so in fact. "There still remain large areas in which unjustifiable discrimination is practiced on wide-spread scale."

The "learned professions" require of women "more in ability and energy" than demanded of men, Rutledge stressed; and, in the workplace generally, "it remains true that women cannot rely upon equal pay for equal work." Moreover, "after a quarter of a century of nationally secured suffrage, the occupancy of public office continues too largely male."[65]

The justice continued: "I am not one who believes that all of the remaining inequalities can be, or should be eradicated by law. Some no doubt can and should be thus eliminated. But law has its limits of accomplishment." This did not mean, however, that the law must always follow rather than lead social and economic change. In pursuing equal treatment for women, "[t]here is danger in seeking an absolute legal identity in disregard of basic physical differences." But, Rutledge emphasized, "there is equal danger in permitting specific social and economic discriminations, unjustified by such relevant differences and at war with the fundamental conception of equality in the status of freedom, to go unchallenged and unrectified."[66]

Despite gains, said Rutledge, there were still too many—both men and women—who would deny a woman "full exercise of the rights she had won." Thus there was "still reason," he regretted to admit, "for women to be on guard and in some respects to act politically as women." He did not mean there was "need for a woman's party." He meant, rather, that there was "need for groups to be watchful of continuing discriminations, to make their occurrence known, and to fight them by all lawful and effective methods."[67]

Bluntly, the justice then noted that "[h]alf of the political power of the country now rests ultimately in women's hands. . . . If therefore woman's freedom remains incompletely achieved, or if in any respect it comes under special threat, this will be due in no small part to her own indifference to its preservation and expansion." Confident, however, that women would protect their "special interest[s]," Justice Rutledge believed that a woman's "greatest influence" would be "exerted by acting as citizen rather than merely as woman."

> In doing so her special understanding will be made to work for the benefit of all, not merely of a group or segment of the population. And thereby her status as citizen will attain its most complete maturity. For so long as any group continues to act politically only as a group, not only is there evidence that it has not attained complete political equality. There is also, to some extent, evidence that it has not achieved full political maturity.[68]

There are women today who might find some of Rutledge's remarks patronizing. But in his time, a half-century ago, he was far out front, especially for a man, on equality for women. He had steadfastly supported his female students; had encouraged a daughter and his secretary to attend law school; and regularly offered counsel, encouragement, and strong employment recommendations for women he had taught.[69] Indeed within months of his Bryn Mawr speech, early in the next term, Wiley Rutledge—in dissent—wrote the first modern gender discrimination opinion. In *Goesaert v. Cleary*, joined by Douglas and Murphy, Rutledge found invidious discrimination in a Michigan statute, upheld in an opinion by Frankfurter, that forbade any "female" to tend bar in a licensed liquor establishment unless she was " 'the wife or daughter of the male owner.' " Said Rutledge, the statute "arbitrarily discriminates between male and female owners," since a "female owner may neither work as a barmaid herself nor employ her daughter in that position, even if a man is always present in the establishment to keep order."[70]

IN AN ILLINOIS voting rights case, *Colegrove v. Green*, Rutledge's vote was crucial to the outcome. Concurring only "in the result," however, Rutledge explained why he voted to help create a majority in a 4-to-3 decision—with Justices Black, Douglas, and Murphy in dissent—that declined to resolve whether the disparities in population among congressional districts in Illinois denied to the voters equal protection of the laws. With the dissenters, Rutledge acknowledged that the Court had the authority to declare invalid, and thus to enjoin, state apportionment legislation; he thus could not join in Justice Frankfurter's opinion holding that the case presented a nonjusticiable, "political" question that Congress had "exclusive authority" to resolve. But Rutledge concluded that the appeal should be dismissed nonetheless, in the Court's discretion, for "want of equity." The "shortness of the time" remaining before the election, he reasoned, realistically would leave the voters without a reapportionment remedy. Voting "at large"—the likely result if the Court declared the apportionment unconstitutional— "might bring greater equality of voting right," he acknowledged, but would deprive the voters of "representation by districts which the prevailing policy of Congress commands." Because of the "considerable latitude" inevitably vested in the governing bodies responsible for redistricting, moreover, there could be at best a "rough approximation" of equality in any event. In sum, "[t]he right here is not absolute. And the cure sought may be worse than the disease."[71]

In *Colegrove*, Justice Rutledge may have used a theory of discretionary, equitable power to deny relief, in contrast with Justice Frankfurter's view that the Court had no power to grant relief at all. But Rutledge's stated concern about avoiding decision "upon grave constitutional questions" when one could anticipate a "clash with the political departments of the Government" reflected the same deferential attitude toward Congress in matters of redistricting that Frankfurter and the others in majority expressed. This time the dissenters had the prophetic voice, as the Court ruled eighteen years later in striking down substantially unequal voting districts for elections to Congress and to state legislatures.[72]

Rutledge, it should be noted, had second thoughts about *Colegrove*, voting unsuccessfully in the next term to rehear the case while dissenting from the Court's refusal to review an equal protection challenge against the Georgia county unit system for selecting congressional and gubernatorial candidates.[73] That said, however, Rutledge maintained a reluctance for the federal courts to interfere with state election procedures. Illinois kept the Progressive Party off the November 1948 ballot because, in obtaining the required 25,000 signatures, the party had failed to gather at least 200 from at least 50 counties. Although this requirement clearly empowered the less populated areas to keep off the ballot political candidates whose party strength was confined to the larger counties, a five-member majority in *MacDougall v. Green* found no constitutional violation in the required "diffusion of political initiative." Douglas, Black, and Murphy, however—noting that "the electorate in 49 of the counties which contain 87% of the registered voters could not form a new political party"—perceived an unconstitutional "dilution of political rights," as they had done several years earlier in *Colegrove*.[74]

Justice Rutledge did not join the majority that found no violation of equal protection. But as in *Colegrove*, he voted to deny injunctive relief that would have ordered the Progressive Party onto the ballot. By the time the Court heard the case, the election was but twelve days away, and despite the Illinois attorney general's confession of "error," Rutledge was not convinced that effective relief could be granted. He acknowledged that the state had "not made an absolutely conclusive factual showing that new ballots, containing the names of appellants' candidates, could not possibly be printed and distributed for use at the election." But from the record of the case before the Court, he was "gravely doubtful that it could be accomplished." Even if it could, moreover, absentee voters would be disenfranchised, he noted. That certain disenfranchisement, coupled with the "gravest risk" of disrupting the electoral process completely, left Rutledge unwilling to order the Progressives onto the Illinois ballot.[75]

TWENTY-FOUR

The Justice's World View

When Wiley Rutledge addressed the Centennial Celebration of the New Orphan Asylum for Colored Children in Cincinnati in the summer of 1945, he disclosed that he would like to have lived in the Jacksonian era. "That was the day of individualistic democracy—men standing as individuals and not simply as elements or units in organizational structures. It was the time when corporate organization had not come to dominate industry, finance and transportation." But at mid-twentieth century, he continued, "most men find their freedoms and their means of full expression" through a group, whether it be "a religious institution, a business corporation, or a charitable organization." Taking that reality to its highest level, he stressed that after winning the war the United States must help establish, through an international organization, the "basic rights" of "men of all races, all colors, all creeds, all nationalities" to think and speak freely, to believe in God in one's own way, and to earn a "decent living."[1] He sounded like an international human rights advocate in 2004.

Rutledge often spoke on the same two themes: dependence on domestic organization to preserve freedom and creativity, dependence on international organization to preserve world peace. Two years earlier, focusing on the home front, Rutledge had reminded his audience of Iowa alumni that the postwar challenge in a "more tightly knit" world would be to find in group culture a way to preserve the "dignity, individuality, and independence of each citizen."[2] And after V-J Day, 1945, he became increasingly worried about civil rights and civil liberties as the pressures of war began to lift. Speaking at Maryville College on the occasion of receiving an honorary LL.D., Rutledge observed sadly: "Loyalties forged in combat and common cause loosen. Prejudices, hatred, special interests, strains and pullings apart, held in check or suppressed by war's overwhelming necessities, revive." The justice lamented, "Crosses burn again in Georgia."[3] By 1949, as the Cold War was intensifying, Rutledge had become even more alarmed. Upon receiving an honorary doctorate at Washington University, he warned against the national witch-hunts that he saw chilling free speech—an aggression from within, he called them, more threatening than communist infiltration from without.[4] The man who had worried angrily about fairness to defeated Japanese generals now felt emotions of similar intensity as he perceived the basic rights of his own compatriots coming under siege.

To Wiley Rutledge, moreover, domestic justice was never far removed from international justice. Thus, his second and principal theme near war's end on that summer day in Cincinnati—as it had been since 1941 in Court of Appeals days—was the necessity for an international organization with the power to enforce international law and, he hoped, prevent war. While on the Supreme Court Rutledge gave eleven formal addresses (not to mention countless luncheon talks) elaborating that idea, including five in 1943 alone.[5] Here was an American, then, who trusted that our government could negotiate with the Soviets and other nations a new world polity, one that through compromise hammered out much like the accommodation which produced our own Constitution could structure workable, endurable international relationships. He was with Henry Wallace, not the Cold Warriors; he abhorred Churchill's "Iron Curtain" speech for laying down a gauntlet that he feared could lead to war with the Russians; and he saw the Truman Doctrine, offering aid to Greece and Turkey, as an unnecessary, provocative step toward dangerous East-West confrontation. His understanding that the United States, realistically, could not withdraw troops from Europe, coupled with his support of the Marshall Plan to rebuild devastated economies, revealed a growing awareness that efforts for international peace could not be achieved easily through international negotiation. But he never lost the same vision of the world that Woodrow Wilson had worked so hard to achieve after the last war to end all wars.

Justice Rutledge expressed his ideas for a world order most comprehensively in his major address of 1943 before the American Bar Association. The context for his proposal—to create a powerful international organization as the only way of achieving a "durable peace"[6]—will illuminate its details. As early as 1940, the Roosevelt administration had begun to discuss establishing an international organization through which "four policemen"— the United States, Great Britain, the USSR, and China—would have charge of maintaining international peace and security. In the following year, in August 1941, Roosevelt and Churchill had framed an Atlantic Charter, soon signed as well by the Soviet Union (by then Hitler's enemy) and nine governments in exile, promising to create among other things a "permanent system of general security." Within a month after Pearl Harbor, Roosevelt and Churchill convened an international conference at the White House where twenty-six governments endorsed the Atlantic Charter, each pledging to cooperate in the war against the Axis powers and agreeing not to make a separate peace. Then, during 1943, Churchill's government and the Soviets negotiated a declaration, eventually signed in Moscow, agreeing to work toward establishing a comprehensive global organization. Also in 1943, international gatherings established a United Nations Relief and Rehabilitation Administration for emergency food relief and other assistance to liberated areas, and initiated plans for a permanent Food and Agriculture Organization.

Just how focused Rutledge was on each of these developments is unclear, but it is reasonable to infer that a man who followed the war as closely as he did, and had such strong views about the failure of the League of Nations to avert world war, would have been watching very carefully all discernible efforts to create a more effective, permanent international structure this time around. It is clear from his ABA address, moreover, that despite his disclaimer—"someone in my position can hardly go far"—he was willing to get amazingly specific for a Supreme Court justice in prescribing essentials for the new international order.[7]

The "permanent structure of law in the world" necessary for the "maintenance of peace," Rutledge declared to the nation's lawyers, must include "all nations capable of disrupting the peace and the law of the world," beginning with the United States, the British Commonwealth, Russia, and China. When the defeated nations recuperated "they, too, must be received" and "eventually accorded full and equal participation" after a "period of probation" that would "demonstrate their will to peace." Small nations, inherently "vulnerable to attack from aggressive larger ones," also must be included to assure their "general security." And, given disparities of size among the members, "some type of federated system," such as those in the British Commonwealth, or the USSR, or the United States, would have to be worked out. Then came his controversial premise for success: the "instruments for decision of conflicts" and the "effective sanctions for enforcement" would require each member to "*surrender a portion of its sovereignty*" (emphasis added). He saw this as a surrender of "limited authority, equal to the essential task and no more."[8] But to this extent a world government would supersede the authority of the United States government in dealing with other nations.

Rutledge added other requirements: the charter must bar "any single, victorious nation" from asserting any "'mandate'" over a "conquered area," and—to rectify the most destructive injustice after the First World War— "the defeated nations must be given adequate access to materials of others for supplying their essential civilian and peaceful needs." Rutledge also stressed the importance of getting started right away, of creating the new structure before the "pressures which now unite us" in war abated to the point of disunity and thus failure. After the first war "we waited too long," he reminded his audience.[9] It must not happen again.

Soon after the ABA address, Rutledge received a letter full of praise from William B. Lloyd Jr., national director of the Campaign for World Government, whom the justice had met in Chicago. Rutledge replied that he wished he could be more helpful, but that as a Supreme Court justice he was "at all times conscious of the limitations" under which he must speak.[10] It is not clear, however, how he defined those limitations. No published formulation of judicial ethics applied to the Supreme Court. Since 1924, American Bar Association Canons of Judicial Ethics had found their way into state law, requiring judges to "avoid making political speeches" while encouraging them to use their "observation and experience" to advise legislators how "to remedy defects of procedure" in the courts.[11] Not until the early 1970s did the ABA—followed by the Judicial Conference of the United States, having administrative authority over the federal courts—fill in the middle ground, permitting judges to "speak, write, lecture, teach, and participate in . . . activities concerning the law, the legal system, and the administration of justice."[12] This ground rule for public speaking undoubtedly reflected an understanding which had developed over the nearly half-century between adoption of the two sets of canons. Presumably, therefore, a U.S. Supreme Court justice in the 1940s, while governed by no rule on speaking out, instinctively would—or at least should—have felt constrained against commenting publicly on proposals in the political arena not strictly limited to the administration of justice. Wartime, however, had arguably created an imperative for every citizen at least to consider alternatives for the ultimate administration of justice, including an international law enforceable by a tribunal empowered to rein in outlaw nations and enforce world peace. It probably did not appear to many, therefore, that Wiley Rutledge was speaking out beyond perceived limitations on what a Supreme Court justice should and should not discuss in public.

But how did Rutledge contemplate dealing with the Soviets? He began with considerable respect for their role and power. The "greatest single effect of the first World War," according to Rutledge, was creation of the Soviet Union—without which "in all probability" the world "would now be a Nazi empire or one divided between the Nazis and the Japs." But if the Soviets' intervention saved us, he warned, we now must face an undeniable fact: "Russia today is the earth's strongest military power."[13] An enduring peace, he said, must account for that reality. The Potsdam agreement in July 1945 had conferred responsibility on the foreign ministers of Britain, France, the United States, and the Soviet Union to initiate drafts of peace agreements, but the initial ministers' conference in London two months later dissolved into wrangling over procedure. This particularly disheartened Rutledge, for whom the atomic bomb made all the more urgent the establishment of "some workable institutions for world government."[14] And this meant "compromise or adjustment"—whatever was required—to achieve a representative international authority with no nation having "controlling or imperialistic power." He thought this was possible without imposing democratic institutions on nations that did not want them. He believed that "different systems"—he particularly had in mind the Soviet Union—could "live together and adjust their differences," failing which democracy could not "survive anywhere on the face of the earth."[15] In short, he trusted the Soviets' good faith desire for peaceful international order and rejoiced at the United Nations' founding in late 1945.

Rutledge accordingly deplored the partition of Germany into "separate areas" controlled by individual world powers; the process was moving in the wrong direction. His consternation increased exponentially when Winston Churchill visited Westminster College at Fulton, Missouri, in March 1946 and gave, in the justice's words to a friend, a "grossly unfortunate" speech. In describing the "iron curtain" which had "descended across the Continent," and then calling for an Anglo-American alliance against Soviet power, Churchill frightened many a congressman and editorial writer—not just Wiley Rutledge—into worrying that a confrontational stance by the West might undo the United Nations and provoke the Soviets into war.[16]

Henry Wallace, by then secretary of commerce, shared that view. Concerned that the administration's attitude toward the Soviet Union was becoming too stiff, Wallace began speaking out against Churchill's thesis, acknowledging the "undying debt of gratitude" the United States owed the Soviet Union, and proclaiming that the "American people do not want an English-speaking alliance." His speeches reflected his advice to the president: stress a policy of supporting the United Nations, not of ganging up with Britain against Russia.[17]

Even before Churchill's address at Westminster College, George F. Kennan, the State Department's chargé d'affaires in Moscow, had advocated a policy of Soviet "containment," supported enthusiastically by an array of high government officials such as James Forrestal, Dean Acheson, Averell Harriman, and Charles Bohlen. On the Wallace side were other opinion leaders and former government officials, including Walter Lippmann, Harold Ickes, and Henry Morgenthau Jr. Truman was in the middle, offering "no comment" on Churchill's speech and remaining noncommittal while plunging into a domestic mess in mid-1946: strikes followed by government seizures of the coal mines and railroads; battles over price controls in a period of escalating inflation; and farmers discontented over black markets in meat and other commodities.[18] In the fall, however, the president had to make up his mind.

Wallace scheduled a speech before a left-leaning political rally at Madison Square Garden on September 12, 1946, where he added a few extemporaneous remarks to the text he had cleared with President Truman, including an improvised warning that "the danger of war is much less from Communism than it is from imperialism." His most controversial comment was an admonition: "[W]e should recognize that we have no more business in the political affairs of Eastern Europe than Russia has in the political affairs of Latin America, Western Europe and the United States." Eight days later, after bitter complaint from Secretary of State Byrnes and public controversy over how much of Wallace's speech Truman had approved, the president fired Wallace.[19]

Justice Rutledge followed these developments from his family's summer retreat in Colorado. Scheduled to speak in Oregon and Michigan in September, he prepared one speech for both occasions preaching the Wallace line in a "much more guarded way," as he wrote to a former law clerk. He analogized the times to the years 1785–86 in American history, "just before the Constitutional Convention," noting that our own constitutional development had been "almost entirely a record of compromise," sometimes "absurd ones"—even on "issues of the greatest consequence"—when necessary to "forming a more perfect union." He rejected the "fatal talk" that war, again, was inevitable.[20] An international community based, ultimately, on compromise and friendship—even affection—was achievable, as in the poem of Walt Whitman that he recited:

Were you looking to be held together by lawyers?
Or by an agreement on a paper? Or by arms?
—Nay—nor the world, nor any living thing, will so cohere.

Over the carnage rose a prophetic voice,
Be not dishearten'd—
Affection shall solve the problems of
Freedom yet;

One from Massachusetts shall be a Missourian's comrade;
From Maine and from hot Carolina, and another, an Oregonese,
Shall be friends triune,
More precious to each other than all the riches of the earth.[21]

Former Justice James F. Byrnes, President Harry S. Truman, and Secretary of Commerce Henry A. Wallace at the funeral ceremony for President Franklin D. Roosevelt, April 14, 1945. The photograph was taken seventeen months before Truman fired Wallace from the cabinet under pressure from Byrnes, then secretary of state, and other cold warriors aligned against Wallace's softer stance toward the Soviet Union. (Harry S. Truman Library, Independence, Missouri, ARC 199072)

Few were prepared to believe, however, that someone from Russia could be an American's "comrade," or that the British, the French, and the Soviets could be "friends triune." The vision shared by Henry Wallace and Wiley Rutledge was widely dismissed as naïve.

Rutledge continued to believe, as he wrote to a friend, that the United States was doing its best "to set up a situation which may make war almost inevitable." "[T]here can be no consistency whatever," he added, in calling Wallace a traitor, as some were doing, while "giving great acclaim" to Churchill. As Rutledge saw the situation, "Churchill's Fulton speech set the direction of our foreign policy from that moment to this. It was an audacious thing to do and we were cat's-paws to fall for it."[22] A major example

of Churchill's influence, as Rutledge perceived it, was the president's proposal, signed into law in May 1947, for massive financial aid to Greece and
Turkey, to forestall the creation of Soviet puppet states there. Just before
the Senate was to take up the measure, Rutledge observed to a Colorado
friend: "Unless we are willing to back up what we do with force whenever
occasion may demand, we are taking awfully long chances in getting ourselves involved in the Greek and Turkish situations. I see no end in sight to
that policy."[23] Still perceiving the Soviets as having a good faith desire for
peace and being uninterested in world domination, Rutledge evaluated the
world situation from the Soviets' own perspective, as he saw it, and thus saw
his own country as the provocateur without the military strength necessary
to act if the Soviets decided to strike back with force.

To Louise Larrabee he explained:

> I do not believe that the Russians want war, and I doubt that they will
> make it unless we force it on them. In that fact lies my reason for
> hope. . . . I do not by any means believe in just letting the Russians
> have their way on everything they want. . . . On the other hand, I don't
> believe in bawling them out for doing substantially the same things
> we do ourselves. Nor do I think that the way to achieve democracy
> is to go in to support a rotten semi-fascist regime, such as had con-
> trol in Greece and also in Spain. I think also there are some limits to
> what the United States can do, I mean by virtue of the fact that we
> are now a nearly completely demobilized nation. While we can pretty
> well look out after this hemisphere and exercise our influence both
> in Europe and in Asia, I don't think we ought to do anything that runs
> a real risk of plunging the world into another war either immediately
> or at any near time in the future. . . . I am quite sure that if Russia
> were to come over and stick her nose into Cuba or Brazil or Mexico
> we would be on the warpath about it pretty quickly.

Rutledge made clear that he was not calling for a return to isolationism. The
solution, rather, was "to find the means of working out such problems as
Greece and Turkey present and also all other European problems through
the United Nations." According to Rutledge, "If that organization is to have
any strength and is eventually to become a structure to maintain peace and
law in the world, we have to begin to use it for those purposes now."[24]

Rutledge did not limit his support for the United Nations to merely a
political solution. In obvious reference to Secretary of State Marshall's plan
for European recovery announced at Harvard's commencement in June
1947, the justice wrote to Louise Larrabee that it was "not too late" to "set

up a scheme" in Europe with an "economic" as well as a "legal" frame-work that "while supporting the people, will at the same time, take strong measures to prevent" the outbreak of war.[25]

WILEY RUTLEDGE had still other complaints in the summer of 1947. Ever since *Yamashita* if not before, he had worried about the international war crimes trials scheduled for Tokyo and Nuremberg, as well as the trials by military commission to be held elsewhere. Even Chief Justice Stone had referred to Nuremberg's "false facade of legality"; and Rutledge, too, came quickly to the conclusion after *Yamashita*—described to a friend as a "pseudo-trial"—that all the war crimes trials were "perversions of the legal process." He wrote to Louise Larrabee that he had known "hundreds of lawyers throughout the country who were totally opposed to the whole busi-ness," but he had heard of only one, in Denver, "who lifted up his voice in public against the proceedings." Rutledge had written to that lawyer, Mor-rison Shafroth, congratulating him for his courage and expressing concern that other "[v]oices of protest" from the bar—from "the men whose very business it is to see that the most basic traditions of our judicial institutions are preserved"—had not been heard. To Larrabee he continued: "I think the Nuremberg and other proceedings like it and the subsequent adminis-tration by the [allied military government] in Germany have done more to destroy any conception of democracy among the German and other Euro-pean peoples than almost any course we could have pursued."[26]

IN THE SPRING of 1948, Harold J. Laski, the British economist and Labor Party leader, addressed an audience in St. Louis. He denigrated the Ameri-can "wave of hysteria" that was calling war with Russia "only a matter of time." According to a press report, "Laski admitted that Russia is 'very dif-ficult to deal with. . . . But Russia wants international security more than anything else.'" Laski's solution? "'If I were an American, I would send the greatest living American today—Gen. Eisenhower—on a plane to Rus-sia to frame an agenda of peace. You could find terms the Russians would accept.'" Upon receiving a clipping about Laski's speech from a friend, Rutledge replied enthusiastically: "I think Laski is giving a message which should be shouted from every housetop in the country. . . . It is too bad that Laski didn't speak at Fulton, Missouri, rather than Winston. The story might have been considerably different."[27]

IN HIS LAST major public address urging a new world order under law, Jus-tice Rutledge spoke "before an audience of 1,000" on the Washington Uni-versity quadrangle on a hot July evening in 1948. Evidencing a pessimism not expressed in earlier speeches, he said he had come to realize that creation of an enduring world peace would be more difficult than it would have been after the First World War if our nation had backed the League of Nations. The difference? After the last war "distance had not yet become annihilated nor had forces of destruction attained their present speed and proportions. . . . [T]here was still time to find the way for creating the political and legal institutions essential for controlling international lawlessness and for avoiding international anarchy." By adhering to "the illusion of escape through withdrawal and retreat," however, America lost the chance for a world order of law and of peace. Now, Rutledge warned, that task had "become vastly more difficult." The recent war had destroyed "governments and peoples and their vital means of living. . . . No institutions of the conquered are left with which peace can be concluded and life can be carried on." As a result, the victor "cannot pull out and go home, free of the shackles of occupation. . . . He must in conscience remain; he must pay and pay and pay, if only to ward off mass hunger and death." Nor could the victor leave "when the minimum of economic rehabilitation necessary" has been achieved, for the vanquished might then launch an even more violent attack unless a change in thinking had been accomplished. But changing a nation's thinking is problematic, Rutledge observed, and to make matters worse, no conqueror can "impose democratic ideas and institutions over so vast a space and diversified populations."[28] (He obviously was thinking of Europe, not Japan.)

If democracy therefore cannot live securely "by conquest," how "is it to survive?" The justice responded, "As long as the world was divided in many camps there was a degree of safety in the division." But if the world "should become divided into two and they unable to find a way to live in peace"— he now had the West and the Soviet Union in mind—"then a final conflict would become inevitable and from it would flow destruction for their institutions, their wealth and their peoples hitherto not imagined." "There is only one way out," Rutledge concluded: the United Nations. For the first time, however, he recognized publicly that the Cold War did not permit military relaxation, even the withdrawal of military occupation, in the absence of an acceptable international accord. Sadly, he noted that "within the short space of three years after the end of active hostilities in a great war[,] . . . even the school boy in his teens knows that he may be called almost at any instant from his books to arms."[29]

The homecoming for Wiley Rutledge at Washington University brought for his listeners an occasion of high emotion. One friend wrote, "You have the rare quality of being able to create a close bond among all who know you and hear you speak. You literally articulate humility, and one could not help but leave a meeting such as the one the other night without feeling richer for the experience." Another felt much the same:

> [Y]ou have the unique ability of not only creating a close and intimate relationship with those to whom you speak, but also of making each member of your audience feel closer to all others in the group—a sort of feeling of kinship, if not brotherhood. It is a quality I have always attributed to Abraham Lincoln, and I suppose you will have to forgive me when I say that your qualities of simplicity, sincerity and deep concern for your fellow-men bring this example to mind.
>
> I could say more, but shall not for fear that you may think I exaggerate. I assure you that I do not, for I am really understating what is virtually a spiritual exaltation—and there are others who have already today indicated the same mood. So you will simply have to put up with the devotion and respect and admiration of those who know you, even if our feelings about you verge on the point of idolatry.

Added his first correspondent: "I only hope that you will be spared for many years to serve as a great public servant."[30]

IN FEBRUARY 1948, Wiley Rutledge had celebrated his fifth anniversary on the Supreme Court with "good-hearted roasting" at a gathering of judges, lawyers, and law clerks who had served Rutledge on the Supreme Court and the Court of Appeals. The following month, Drew Pearson reported an incident that the justice later said he had found amusing. At the annual dinner of University of Wisconsin alumni in Washington, the chapter president "veered from a nostalgic speech about his alma mater" and began to praise General MacArthur. Thereupon another alumnus offered a resolution to ban the alumni association "as a political platform for any presidential candidate," after which bedlam erupted. "Finally," Pearson reported, "scholarly Justice Rutledge, sitting next to the pro-MacArthur toastmaster, tried to restore order. 'This is most unfortunate,' declared the jurist. He didn't explain whether he was referring to the MacArthur speech or the resolution condemning it." Eventually the resolution was "tabled, amid boos," whereupon the president again began to tout MacArthur. Hecklers took over. Rutledge ruled them "'out of order.'" Finally, Senator Alexander Wiley of Wisconsin "gave a soothing sermon on brotherly love, quoting at length from scripture."[31]

THE RUTLEDGE FAMILY'S biggest news in 1948 was Neal's and Cathy Le Fevre's wedding on June 22. For the groom's father, a highlight was his half-brother, Dwight, sharing duties with the organist at All Saints Episcopal Church. To a friend and former student, Rutledge wrote effusively that the "wedding went off beautifully, although there were the inevitable last-minute hitches and surprises. Cathy's little brother, who was ringbearer, lost the pillow and had her frantic for the last two hours before the ceremony. Apparently they discovered it within fifteen minutes of the time they were to appear at the church." [32]

A few days after the wedding, while Annabel remained in Washington, Rutledge flew to Colorado for a month of loafing, visiting with friends, and "looking over that grand scenery." He took time out to attend the Tenth Circuit Judicial Conference in Denver and, in mid-July, to address the summer session lecture series at Washington University. Then he flew back to Washington, packed up the family, and drove to Ogunquit, Maine, for another "grand period of relaxation." [33]

As WILEY RUTLEDGE was ready to begin his seventh term on the Supreme Court, the upcoming election dominated family discussion. Rutledge had been upset when FDR dropped Henry Wallace from the ticket in 1944 and, at that time, had written to the vice president, "We of Iowa, and liberals everywhere, are prouder of you today than ever before. Take courage, and carry on." The justice did not care for Truman, whose connection with the Pendergast political machine in Kansas City had soured Rutledge on him long ago. Rutledge was also bothered by the president's propensity to limit his appointments to close political friends. And as we have seen, the justice was not impressed by the administration's Cold War foreign policy. There was of course no question of supporting the Republican candidate, Governor Thomas Dewey of New York, let alone the Dixiecrat, Strom Thurmond of South Carolina. The choice was between Truman and Wallace, the Progressive Party nominee, whom the justice supported as a man of "principle" in debates with Neal and Cathy, both of whom objected to a vote that might help Dewey.

In July, Rutledge had written to George Heidlebaugh: "I will say frankly that [the] outlook for me at the moment is a pretty dark and disappointing one. I am not quite sure just where I will be when fall comes along, but I recall that in 1920 [Harding versus Cox] and also in 1924 [Coolidge versus Davis] I didn't care very much whether I cast a ballot or not. It may work out for me that way this year." [34] Although he had worked for the Henry Wallace campaign in Connecticut, Neal Rutledge cast his vote for Truman in 1948. After the president's reelection, the justice asked his son whom he had voted for. Hearing Neal's answer, his father "just clammed up; he didn't say a thing," Neal recalled. "I couldn't get out of him whom he'd voted for." [35]

In mid-October, a Republican friend of Rutledge had predicted that the election was "going to be a great deal closer" than the Republicans expected. Rutledge agreed, "greatly surprised" by the president's "apparent partial comeback" on the campaign trail against "all the odds." Rutledge had noticed the "warmth" of Truman's personality—his "extremely effective" presentations—when speaking extemporaneously, rather than using a manuscript. Added Rutledge, "he finally woke up, or was awakened, to the realization that he could talk even if he can't read." The justice believed, nonetheless, that the president would probably not pull off the "political miracle" required to defeat Dewey, in part because of the Dixiecrat threat in the South. Rutledge did believe, however, that Truman's efforts would make a "horse race" for the Senate and, very likely, bring about Democratic control.[36]

After the election, the justice was in "a gloating mood." He had planned to "turn on the radio for ten minutes" on election night and turn in early "for a full night's sleep." The returns transfixed him. Returning from a movie, Rutledge stayed up until 6:30 in the morning. "It was about the most exciting night I remember spending," he wrote to Ralph Fuchs—a great victory for "the common people of the country."[37] Rutledge had been "as much surprised by the results of the election as Dr. Gallup," he wrote to Carl Wheaton. "For once in my life I was a darn fool in swallowing all the dope which the press, the pollsters and the radio were dishing out." To Willard Wirtz, he was more condemnatory. Rutledge now perceived "a general newspaper conspiracy, including the radio and the pollsters as well, to read down the President's chances and the effect he has having on the people." Rutledge "drew this conclusion not only from the obvious slant of all these so-called authorities on public affairs and opinion, but also because throughout the campaign" he "received rumors from other sources concerning events favorable to the President, no word of which was whispered in any of the press reports" that he saw. "In short," he concluded, "the wise boys just decided they would throw this election and do it by keeping from the people the facts that might tend in a contrary direction. I think the performance of the press and the radio, as well as the pollsters, . . . was about as despicable as anything I have seen in politics." Rutledge reiterated to Wirtz that "until the campaign," Truman "had not given the country the kind of leadership which was demanded." But now his "direction on domestic affairs is pretty straight and right," Rutledge concluded. "I am hoping he will come through. . . . I think his biggest accomplishment to date has been the effect of his campaign in itself, namely in preventing the return of a highly reactionary Congress to power. I can forgive the man many mistakes for that highly constructive achievement."[38]

Rutledge saw as the election's "big gain" the "infusion of fine new blood in the Democratic Party, both at the state level and at the congressional one" (Mayor Hubert Humphrey of Minneapolis, for example, was elected to the Senate). At the "national level," he wrote to Bill Bartley, the "surprising outcome" was "probably worth as much for what it prevented (that is, by way of keeping the Old Guard out of office) as anything which could be characterized as a real step forward." With the "hysteria that is now sweeping the country," he added, "it is not difficult to imagine how much worse things might have been, had the result been the other way." Rutledge was referring to the accelerating national perception of a threat from communism, as evidenced by President Truman's Loyalty Order of March 1947, implemented by procedures to ferret out security risks in government, and by the increasingly active agenda of the House Un-American Activities Committee (Whittaker Chambers had testified in August 1948).[39] Truman was involved in the witch hunts, Rutledge realized, but the Republican zealots worried him more.

Neal and Cathy Rutledge have always believed that in 1948, the justice supported Wallace, whereas his daughters heard enough, indirectly, to remain confident that their father voted for Truman. Without doubt, Rutledge was tempted to vote Progressive out of admiration for Henry Wallace, but immediately after the election he wrote to Ralph Fuchs, "I did not desert what I considered the sinking ship."[40]

TWENTY-FIVE

Last Term

After the first round of arguments in October during the 1948 Term, Rutledge incurred an additional responsibility as the justice assigned to oversee the Tenth Circuit. Every circuit court judge had refused to overrule the district court's denial of bail for a "Denver group of Communists." Rutledge worked for eight days on the applications for reversal, then ordered bail for every applicant.[1]

JUSTICE MURPHY missed the opening of Court in 1948 because of an "attack of sciatic neuralgia." After joining his colleagues briefly, "[b]outs of shingles forced him in and out of the hospital all year." Murphy kept up with the Court's calendar by reading briefs in the hospital while using his clerks, as always—now guided by his friend, Rutledge—to draft his opinions. Rutledge cast Murphy's vote in conference and on cert petitions, as well as on argued cases. Just before Thanksgiving, Murphy wrote to thank Rutledge "for carrying the load" for him in conference. "You have been so generous and thoughtful about it but you could not be otherwise. I shall be so happy when I am at your side again." Murphy had indicated that he would be returning to Court by month's end, to which Rutledge replied:

> That will be a happy occasion for all of us. It has been a pleasure to have two votes to cast in conference. It will be a greater pleasure to sit by you again and see you follow the lead when I give it to you—more especially when you go wrong in the first place and have to back up to do it!
>
> I heard something today from Bill [Douglas] about the lineup of nurses reaching from the hospital to General Motors. I cannot say that I am glad they are all so happy to see you go, but we will make up here in warmth of welcome for their unanimous concurrence in bidding you good-by.

Murphy, unfortunately, did not remain at the Court long; "he was hospital-ized again for short spells in February, April, and June." From the perspec-tive of one of Rutledge's clerks, in the 1948 term Justice Murphy "didn't exist."[2]

DURING THE 1948 Term a case challenging access to federal courts in the District of Columbia grappled with the very structure of the Constitution. According to Rutledge's clerk Louis H. Pollak, *National Mutual Insurance Co. v. Tidewater Transfer Co.* produced real "passion" within the Court that brought the justices to "swords point." Congress in 1940 had enacted legis-lation expanding the federal courts' "diversity" jurisdiction beyond suits between citizens of different "states"—as expressly authorized by Article III of the Constitution—to suits between citizens of "the District of Colum-bia, the Territory of Hawaii, or Alaska, and any State or Territory."[3] The question, then, was whether Congress had violated the Constitution by per-mitting a citizen of the District of Columbia to sue a citizen of Virginia in federal court.

The tension developed because in *Tidewater*, the Court voted 5 to 4 to sustain the enlarged diversity jurisdiction, even though seven justices agreed that the District of Columbia was not a "state" within the meaning of Article III. Early on, Chief Justice John Marshall had held in the *Hepburn* case that the District of Columbia was not a "state" within the meaning of the Judiciary Act of 1789, which limited federal court diversity jurisdiction, in the words of Article III, to suits between citizens of different "states." Justice Jackson, joined by his colleagues Black and Burton, accepted Mar-shall's interpretation but found an alternate route to the congressional goal. They relied on Article I, section 8, clause 17, the so-called District clause, which granted Congress authority to "exercise exclusive Legislation in all Cases whatsoever over such District (not exceeding ten Miles square) as may, by Cession of particular States, and the Acceptance of Congress, be-come the Seat of the Government of the United States." Jackson found authority here for Congress to exercise power over the District of Colum-bia on matters not limited to its geographic area, and thus the authority to confer federal diversity jurisdiction over lawsuits between citizens of the District and elsewhere who otherwise would have had no federal forum for resolving disputes with one another.[4]

Justice Rutledge and his five other colleagues dissented vigorously from this view, all concluding that the judicial power under Article III was lim-ited expressly in nonfederal cases to suits between citizens of different "states." Writing separately, Rutledge explained that the "Constitution is not so self-contradictory" as to prescribe a limitation on the jurisdiction that Congress may confer on the federal courts, only to impose "no limitation when Congress decides to cast it off under some other Article, even one relating to its authority over the District of Columbia." Not many years earlier in *O'Donoghue*, he noted, the Court had made clear that "Congress derives from the District clause distinct powers in respect of the constitutional [Article III] courts of the District *which Congress does not possess in respect of such courts outside the District*" (emphasis added).[5]

There was a practical concern as well, Rutledge observed. For years, Congress had created "legislative courts" under Article I, including the local court system of the District of Columbia and some specialty courts, such as the federal Court of Claims. These did not enjoy all the protections, such as lifetime tenure and irreducible salaries, guaranteed to judges serving on "constitutional courts" under Article III. The question whether a court fell within Article I or Article III had generated a good deal of litigation, Rutledge noted, and thus to justify diversity jurisdiction now under Article I "would entangle every district court of the United States . . . in all of the contradictions, complexities and subtleties" inherent in the " 'legislative court–constitutional court' controversy."[6]

For Vinson, Reed, Frankfurter, and Douglas that was the end of the matter. Because the District of Columbia was not a "state," they concluded, the Constitution allowed no diversity jurisdiction over claims involving its citizens. Justice Rutledge rejected that literal analysis, however. Taking Chief Justice Marshall head on — saying that in *Hepburn*, "the master hand which later made his work immortal faltered" — Rutledge, joined by Murphy, concluded that for purposes of federal diversity jurisdiction the District of Columbia was a "state."[7] Five justices, therefore, knitting together two clashing theories, sustained the congressional purpose.

The premise underlying Rutledge's analysis was the "apparent fact that the Framers gave no deliberate consideration one way or another to the diversity litigation of citizens of the District of Columbia." Especially, he observed, "since the District was not in existence when the Constitution was drafted, it seems in no way surprising that the Framers, after conferring on Congress plenary power over the future federal capital, made no express provision for litigating outside the boundaries of a hypothetical city conjectured controversies between unborn citizens and their unknown neighbors." Under these circumstances, he concluded, he could not "accept the proposition that absence of affirmative inclusion is, here, tantamount to deliberate exclusion."[8] Nor, added Rutledge, could one infer from the "historic purposes" of Article III's "diversity clause" any reason why suits by and against District citizens should not have the protection of a federal forum.

Significantly, Rutledge pointed out that in *Hepburn*, Chief Justice Marshall had defined "State" in Article III exclusively by reference to the constitutional provisions that allocated representatives, senators, and presidential electors by "state," namely, the provisions governing "the organization and structure of the political departments of the government." Marshall did not advert to other provisions conferring "civil rights" in the states, such as the Sixth Amendment rights to a speedy, public criminal trial before an impartial jury—rights that the Supreme Court later extended to District residents even though limited literally to defendants brought to trial in a "State." Other key words in the Constitution conferring individual rights, Rutledge observed, had received broadened meanings to fit constitutional purposes, as in the Court's ruling that "Citizens" in Article III included corporations.[9] To Rutledge, therefore, the distinction between provisions governing structure and those conferring rights was determinative, for over the years since *Hepburn*, he stressed, the Court had expanded individual rights under the Constitution beyond the narrow literalism of constitutional language.[10] Rutledge concluded:

> Reasonable men may differ perhaps over whether or, more appropriately, to what extent citizens of the District should have political status and equality with their fellow citizens. But with reference to their civil rights, especially in such a matter as equal access to the federal courts, none now can be found to defend discrimination against them save strictly on the ground of precedent.
>
> I cannot believe that the Framers intended to impose so purposeless and indefensible a discrimination, although they may have been guilty of understandable oversight in not providing explicitly against it. Despite its great age and subsequent acceptance, I think the *Hepburn* decision was ill-considered and wrongly decided.[11]

In a rare dissent of his own, Chief Justice Vinson, joined by Justice Douglas, agreed with Rutledge's repudiation of Jackson's Article I analysis while rejecting Rutledge's imputation of nominal statehood to the District of Columbia under Article III. But Vinson did accept Rutledge's distinction (in Vinson's words) between inflexible, constitutional provisions "concerned solely with the mechanics of government" and the malleable provisions to which "time and experience were intended to give content." Vinson simply disagreed with his colleague as to which category could better be said to encompass access to the federal courts. The chief had "little doubt" that only mechanics, not civil rights, were involved.[12]

Writing for himself and Justice Reed, Justice Frankfurter took a more historical approach in dissent, noting that Chief Justice Marshall had "had no mean share in securing adoption of the Constitution and took special interest in the Judiciary Article." Thus, Frankfurter opined, Marshall "merely gave expression to the common understanding—the best test of the meaning of words—when he rejected summarily" the notion that in Article III the citizens of "States" included residents of the District. Furthermore, Frankfurter could find no instance where the District was treated as a state under a constitutional provision expressly "limited to 'States.'" And, like Vinson, Frankfurter put federal court jurisdiction on the untouchable "mechanics of government" side of the line: "The very subject matter of sections 1 and 2 of Article III," he wrote, "is technical in the esteemed sense of that term. These sections do not deal with generalities expanding with experience."[13]

Of the nine justices, therefore, only Rutledge and Murphy saw the availability of federal diversity jurisdiction as an access-to-justice—a civil rights —issue, not as a mechanics-of-government issue. It is interesting to note, moreover, that in 1996 the Supreme Court ruled that Congress could not employ Article I to "expand the jurisdiction of the federal courts beyond the bounds of Article III."[14] Only Rutledge's theory, therefore, remains available to sustain access to the federal courts for District of Columbia citizens in diversity cases.

IN THE 1947 Term and again in 1948, four justices, Vinson, Reed, Frankfurter, and Burton, voted to deny petition after petition for writ of habeas corpus by German war criminals convicted by American military courts (under authority of the Allied Control Council) at Nuremberg, Dachau, and elsewhere.[15] These courts had sentenced most of the petitioners to death for executing American prisoners of war, or for torturing and killing Jews and others interned at Hitler's concentration camps. The four justices denying habeas—undoubtedly aware that some of these cases, if the Geneva Convention or constitutional due process applied, were vulnerable to reversal for coerced confessions, witness tampering, and too little time allowed for defense preparation—had premised their votes to deny on "want of jurisdiction." Sixty years earlier, the Supreme Court had ruled that in cases not involving an ambassador or a state, the Court had authority to grant habeas relief only in the exercise of its appellate jurisdiction—that is, only when reviewing a lower court's denial of the writ—which had not occurred in these cases.[16] Furthermore, precedent equally old appeared to withhold from the Court jurisdiction over military courts.[17] Skeptical of this precedent in view of the Court's recent willingness to review military commission judgments in *Quirin*, *Yamashita*, and *Homma*, Justice Rutledge felt strongly that the German cases deserved a hearing. Joined by Black, Douglas, and Murphy, he voted routinely to set each case "for argument forthwith," leaving the

Court evenly divided since Justice Jackson, a Nuremberg prosecutor, took no part.[18]

In considering the first habeas petition, *Milch v. United States*, Rutledge had assumed that four votes, the number required to grant a cert petition, would be enough to order a habeas hearing. To his surprise, the chief entered an order denying the petition. Swiftly, with the help of Edna Lingreen, who struck gold consulting with Justice Reed's secretary next door, Rutledge discovered from Reed's private records a precedent from 1939 that proved the Court had not limited to cert petitions its practice of granting a hearing with four votes. Complimenting Lingreen ("Some sleuthing and good work!"), he asked her to be sure that she and Reed's secretary kept "mum" about where he had found the precedent, lest they all get "in Dutch with S.R." He assured Lingreen, however, that if "the thing gets hot," he would "come forward to take the heat."[19]

Rutledge confirmed the 1939 precedent with Douglas, then sent his colleagues a memo requesting the chief to call a meeting "at 4:30"—failing which he proposed to issue a brief dissent (copy attached) protesting the Court's deviation from an "invariable practice." The chief mooted the threatened dissent by gathering the brethren. Rutledge moved to withdraw the *Milch* order. With Jackson recusing, all save Rutledge voted no, accepting the futility of granting even one hearing when four colleagues of the eight who would vote were resolved unalterably against finding jurisdiction.[20]

When similar petitions came in during December 1948 from high officials of the Japanese government sentenced to death by the International Military Tribunal for the Far East sitting in Tokyo, the vote was the same, 4 to 4. Convinced after the conference that this vote would end the matter summarily, as in the German cases, Rutledge drafted a dissent in two of the cases styled *Hirota v. MacArthur*. He acknowledged that if the tribunal were "a validly constituted international one," then presumably its rulings would fall "beyond our reach." The Court would also lack jurisdiction, Rutledge wrote, if the tribunal were "a political body, exercising power under forms of legal procedure strange to our institutions and traditions, established wholly or in part by the political departments of our Government by action our judicial institutions have no authority or power to check." But neither proposition was "self-evident" from the record.[21]

In the first place, Rutledge observed, the tribunal was enough a General MacArthur enterprise to raise "grave questions" whether it was truly an international court. On the other hand, the justice noted, if the tribunal should be considered an American military undertaking, *Yamashita* and *Homma* did not control the Court's jurisdiction, let alone the merits. Those cases concerned enemy combatants, whereas Hirota's service to Japan, in civilian posts only, had terminated before Pearl Harbor. Furthermore, Yamashita and Homma had been able "to invoke the jurisdiction of an inferior court"—the Supreme Court of the Philippines—"subject to our review," whereas Hirota and related petitioners had had "no such forum available." Although *Yamashita* and *Homma* determined "that enemy belligerents have none of our constitutional protections," it did not follow, Rutledge concluded, that those decisions "held enemy civilians to occupy the same denuded status," with "no remedy for reviewing action by an American military tribunal in disregard of all constitutional limitations."[22]

Justice Jackson mooted Rutledge's dissent, however, by deciding to break the tie in favor of hearing *Hirota.* Expressing concern that the *Hirota* executions would appear to lack legitimacy if "half of this Court tells the world" that the sentences "are on so doubtful a legal foundation" that they warrant "fuller review," Jackson voted to grant argument in the hope of "even a faint chance of avoiding dissents in this matter." At the December 4 conference, Jackson, in voting to "pass," had not revealed an intention to participate, let alone write.[23] Nor is it clear whether Jackson was aware that Rutledge would be writing. The two justices' opinions, both dated December 6, apparently crossed in the intra-Court mail.

During the week before Christmas 1948, three days after oral argument, the Supreme Court, in an unsigned opinion and without the participation of Justice Jackson, denied the motions for leave to file petitions for writs of habeas corpus. Because the sentencing court "is not a tribunal of the United States," the justices ruled, "the courts of the United States have no power or authority to review" the sentences. Justice Douglas concurred in the result "for reasons to be stated in an opinion." Justice Murphy "dissent[ed]" without opinion. Justice Rutledge "reserve[d] decision and the announcement of his vote until a later time."[24]

Douglas issued his concurring opinion when the Court printed its decision on the last day of the term, June 27, 1949. In *Ahrens v. Clark,* limiting habeas jurisdiction to prisoners held within the district served by the court, Douglas had reserved the question whether a federal district court could issue a writ of habeas corpus to inquire into the restraint on the liberty of a petitioner held on foreign soil. *Ahrens,* according to Douglas, had merely resolved a "problem of judicial administration" by allocating jurisdiction among the federal courts throughout the country; *Ahrens* had not announced "a method of contracting the authority of the courts so as to delimit their power to issue the historic writ." For prisoners held by American officials abroad, Douglas accepted Rutledge's view that the court having jurisdiction over someone "who is responsible for the custody of petitioners" was the tribunal to resolve the questions presented. In *Hirota*, Douglas concluded, that tribunal was located in the District of Columbia, where officials of the War Department were responsible, ultimately, for the American officials in charge of the petitioners in Tokyo.[25] According to Douglas, however, federal court power over General MacArthur and other Americans connected with the international tribunal in Tokyo ultimately offered no appellate forum for the convicted Japanese. He conceded an American court's power to compel an American jailer abroad not to surrender a prisoner to an international tribunal over which the American court itself had no review jurisdiction; but he concurred with the Court's majority in withholding that power in *Hirota*. In Douglas's view, the international tribunal and all American involvement with it was the work of the executive branch—the president—who used not a conventional military tribunal (as in *Yamashita*) but an international forum created under his authority to conduct the war and govern foreign relations. In short, because the president acted "in a political role on a military matter," his "discretion cannot be reviewed by the judiciary."[26]

Because of illness, Murphy registered his dissent without opinion.[27] He left no paper trail revealing his rationale for a vote, an omission all the more perplexing because both his clerks, after thorough research, saw no way around denial of the petitions.[28] A Murphy biographer may have had the answer, however: by "the end of World War II" Murphy had come to conceive of the Court "as a vehicle of ideological protest" in "race and war power cases," without worrying about a sound basis for decision.[29]

Rutledge, on the other hand, never voted in *Hirota*. He "passed" in conference after remarking (according to Murphy's notes): "This is an international tribunal but if I get over that hump I would act."[30] Since his vote would make no difference, Rutledge elected to take his time in arriving at a position, hoping to find his way to a satisfactory conclusion before Douglas's opinion, and thus the Court's opinion package itself, was ready for publication. From indications in his draft dissent, mooted once the case was heard, Rutledge must have thought that he could find broad habeas jurisdiction akin to the jurisdiction he and Murphy had invoked to review the military commissions in *Yamashita* and *Homma*. But Rutledge had also recognized that a truly "international" tribunal, or even a purely "political body" created by our government to function as a military court, likely would escape Supreme Court jurisdiction. Later, after argument, Rutledge could not conjure up a plausible theory for issuing the writ. He had to realize that the month of June, when the Court adjourned, would bring a deadline he should honor. And by then, especially after reading Douglas's persuasive concurrence, Rutledge should have recognized that no sound basis for dissent remained. Even if Rutledge could have found a way around the "appellate" jurisdictional prerequisite for habeas relief (present in *Yamashita* but not in *Hirota*), Douglas had demonstrated the "purely political" nature of the tribunal that Rutledge himself knew the Court accordingly should not review. And yet even in July, upon inquiry from the office of the Court's reporter, Rutledge replied that "he had not yet made up his mind how he would vote."[31]

Why Justice Rutledge could not face up to the decision and at least join Douglas remains a mystery—unless we accept the likelihood that in *Hirota*, Rutledge had finally come upon a decision where his head and his gut were so irreconcilable that his decision-making ability became paralyzed.

BY THE SECOND WEEK of July 1949, Wiley, Annabel, and Mary Lou were in Ogunquit. Jean Ann, in the meantime, had sailed with a friend to Europe, while Neal and Cathy remained in New Haven hoping for occasional weekends in Maine. The senior Rutledges had opted again for "real relaxation, instead of the more active type of re-creation the West affords." Barely a week after arriving in Ogunquit, Rutledge received word on his birthday, July 20, that Justice Murphy had died the previous day. Murphy's secretary wrote Rutledge immediately:

> . . . He seemed quite well and in good spirits and at six o'clock this morning had a heart attack and died at seven-thirty am.
>
> You, Ed Kemp and myself were his closest Washington friends and you will never know how he loved you.
>
> He was mindful of your birthday and I cannot resist sending on the following as he dictated it to me—it was to be sent to you today:
>
> DEAR BROTHER WILEY
> ON YOUR BIRTHDAY I SHALL DRINK ONE FOR YOU AND ON THAT HAPPY
> OCCASION I TRUST YOU WILL DRINK TWO FOR YOUR GOOD SELF. FOR MY
> PART I HOPE YOU WILL LIVE ONE HUNDRED YEARS. AFFECTIONATELY
>   FRANK MURPHY
>
> He truly wouldn't want you to interrupt your holiday in Maine and I trust you won't make the effort to do so. The chief Justice, Justice Black and the Marshall will represent the Court. . . .

Weeks later Murphy's clerk wrote to Rutledge: "You know, I am sure, of his deep affection for you, but I wonder whether you ever realized how constantly that affection manifested itself. Hardly an opinion of yours was circulated without some talk from my boss about his Baptist Brother—'heart of a lion.'"[32]

Rutledge was devastated. And nothing would keep him from the funeral on July 22 in Harbor Beach, Michigan, miles and miles north of Detroit on Lake Huron. According to his daughter Mary Lou, Rutledge had not been feeling well, and she begged him not to leave, but he looked at her sternly and said, "Mary Lou, I have to go." The justice had difficulty getting there, sitting on train and bus overnight to make it on time. His daughter Jean Ann has observed, in apt description, that "when you look at the photo of dad at that funeral it breaks your heart." And Mary Lou has recalled, "He wasn't well from the moment he returned from the funeral." "Dear Judge," Victor Brudney wrote, the "burden now remaining on you is not light—and by that fact alone underscores an *obligation* to take it easy this summer."[33] Rutledge did so.

TWENTY-SIX

Last Days

The Man and the Justice Remembered

On Sunday evening, August 27, not five weeks after he returned from Michigan, Wiley was driving Annabel to a potluck supper at a Baptist church in Ogunquit when he suddenly slumped over the steering wheel. Annabel managed to reach the brakes and stop the car. She flagged down someone, who called an ambulance. Mary Lou, at home in the cottage waiting for Jean Ann's scheduled arrival from Europe, received a call from the hospital in York Harbor that her father appeared to have suffered a stroke. She telephoned Neal and Cathy. A friend drove Mary Lou to her father.[1]

The family sent for the justice's Washington physician, and the vigil began. The press at first reported a "circulatory condition" but followed with information that one side of Rutledge's body was paralyzed. According to Mary Lou, her father came in and out of consciousness, generally unable to speak, although once she heard him whisper the word "water" to his nurse. To prevent choking, the nurse offered him ice, and, according to Mary Lou, "he actually smiled." Once, when several of the family were in the hospital room, they saw the justice bringing his hand to his mouth repeatedly, as though he were smoking. Their conversation about this caused reporters, overhearing imperfectly, to print that the justice was doing fine, sitting up in bed smoking. The United Press was more accurate, however, reporting that Rutledge had suffered a relapse on August 31, rallied, then suffered another setback on September 2, leaving him in a coma reportedly based on a cardiac condition. He rallied again a week later; then came another coma, called "cyanotic," meaning a "morbid condition in which the surface of the body becomes blue because of insufficient aeration of the blood." His temperature reached 106. On the evening of September 10, Justice Wiley Rutledge was gone. He was fifty-five years old.[2]

That night, President Truman wrote to Annabel Rutledge that a "tower of strength has been lost to our national life."[3] The funeral took place at

Pallbearers carrying Justice Rutledge's casket from All Souls Unitarian Church in Washington, D.C. (AP/Wide World Photos)

All Souls' Unitarian Church on September 12. The Rev. A. Powell Davies reminded all:

> The natural kindness of Wiley Rutledge, his gentleness, his ready comprehension, his flashes of humor, his quick sympathy, his warm humanity, his directness of thought and purity of motive: these, like his humility and the friendly dignity of his bearing, we shall not soon forget. But most of all, I think, we shall remember how faithfully he followed the guiding precepts of the greatest of all Americans, Abraham Lincoln, his exemplar, whom he loved: "to do right as God gives us to see the right," and thus guided, to "finish the work we are in."[4]

Edna Lingreen was conscious of the "staff people, char people, elevator operators, shoe shine people coming to the service." "I regret to say," she added, "that the help was sent up to the balcony."[5]

WILEY RUTLEDGE had come to the Supreme Court with three discernible characteristics. First, nurtured in his early life by a loving family and sustained over the years by faith in a benign universe, he was emotionally secure. Whether relating to other people, expressing ideas, managing work, or otherwise confronting daily life, he had no need for self-promotion, pretense, or dissimulation, or desire to put down others. Nor was he influenced by money (at his death his personal estate, in addition to a modest insurance policy and his joint interest in the family home, was valued at $473, represented by an old Buick).[6] Happy for years as a professor and dean, he found the Court of Appeals personally worthwhile, though less satisfying than the classroom. In 1943 he was thinking wistfully about a return some day to teaching. He was at peace within himself and with his place in the world. By that time he had no ambition whatsoever for the Supreme Court.

Second, as the son of a gregarious, caring pastor and an especially warm family on his mother's side, Rutledge really liked people. Beyond that, as a struggler with tuberculosis bound together with other sufferers at the "San," he was empathic, feeling genuine regard for people of all stations. He thus extended himself naturally not only to students, colleagues, and legions of other friends, but also to strangers on a train, or in the hospital, or at a gas pump.[7] For the times, too, he was unusually sensitive to the aspirations of women, of Jews, and—helped along by Annabel—of African Americans. He had become a federal appellate judge, but to his very core he remained a man for others, especially the unpretentious. He was a teacher and mentor, a law school association regular, a Midwestern Rotarian, a luncheon speaker for all occasions, a small-towner comfortable in a large city, an admirer of the small businessman and the ordinary worker, and a champion of legal aid for the poor.

Finally, taught by the progressive Herbert Hadley and further influenced by Roscoe Pound, Woodrow Wilson, Louis Brandeis, and above all Franklin Roosevelt, Wiley Rutledge arrived at the Supreme Court believing in the creative power of law to forge equitable and workable relationships in the public interest, while protecting individuals against an overreaching government. And he was comfortable with the idea that judges routinely make law through common law adjudication, statutory construction, and constitutional interpretation. As to the Constitution, he saw judges as custodians of a living document, adaptable to needs in a changing society much in the way that the common law itself evolved. While express language had to be honored, Rutledge rejected any idea that the framers' "original intent" could apply when the nation's founders would have had little if any inkling of the context presented. In 1943, therefore, the Supreme Court received a new member who felt free to deal with clashing values in concrete cases by applying his own vision of how constitutional principles best resolved the claims of everyone affected. But that vision did not mean rule by fiat. To be constitutionally legitimate, according to Rutledge, the opinion elaborating the decision had to satisfy a test of coherence in addressing text and precedent that would lead even detractors to acknowledge that the ruling, if not on balance persuasive, had integrity.

Rutledge served on the Court for only six and a half terms, leaving him relatively unknown among long-tenured colleagues: Stone, Black, Frankfurter, Douglas, Jackson. But he had real significance in that environment nonetheless. Aside from the internment case (*Korematsu*), in which his silent behavior, if not his vote, is highly questionable, Wiley Rutledge stood against the tide, in dissent, in the most controversial Supreme Court cases of his day, whether concerning war crimes (*Yamashita*; *Homma*), labor unrest (*United Mine Workers*), establishment of religion (*Everson*), criminal violation of price controls (*Yakus*), or revocation of naturalized citizenship (*Knauer*). In other contexts, he led the way in pressing for an expanded right to counsel in criminal cases. He was out in front of all colleagues but Murphy in advocating doctrinal broadening of criminal due process in state as well as federal courts. And he worked harder than any at achieving federal court review of state criminal convictions, provoking along the way a reform of the byzantine appellate system in Illinois.

The Court of the 1940s had no stronger advocate for free speech and other First Amendment rights than Wiley Rutledge; no more thoughtful student of the commerce clause; no more consistent supporter of access to the federal courts; and, but for reluctance about remedy as to voting rights, no more expansive thinker about equal protection—including virtually the earliest expression of a Court member's concerns about discrimination based on gender and poverty in addition to race. In all these endeavors, Rutledge had limited success in his time, although beginning with the Warren Court his views received considerable acceptance years later.[8]

Rutledge's decisions were coherent, rarely ad hoc, and by the 1945 Term, at least on constitutional issues, substantially predictable. If an opinion by Rutledge seemed uncharacteristic, as in *Medo Photo* (where he would have allowed the employer to deal directly with employees represented by a union), or in *Brinegar* (where he found probable cause to search an automobile without a warrant), the answer lay in his willingness to permit the facts, rather than a legal rule, to drive the result. Rutledge was not one to bend a factual record to support a general view. And he would concur specially, or dissent, to make clear what facts, for him, were critical to a decision. Rutledge thus came to have a discernible jurisprudence held as tenaciously as by any colleague; but inside the Court his advocacy was largely limited to the written word in memoranda and circulated opinions, rarely augmented by oral combat in Court conference or a colleague's office. As we have seen, by temperament and plodding work style this justice, unlike Frankfurter and Black, had neither inclination nor time to work his colleagues like a Court politician pressing an agenda.

Rutledge's influence within the Court might have been formidable nonetheless had he been a more felicitous writer, but the justice's prose—often powerful but also typically long, even convoluted, as well as slow in the writing—must have fueled his colleagues' exasperation as much as informed their intellect from time to time. When we have seen Douglas or Black write years later that Rutledge had been right after all about the First or the Fourth Amendment, for example, we can wonder whether impatience may have affected the other justice's receptor at the time decision was aborning. All this said, however, the other justices' respect for Rutledge as highly principled, of keen mind, and hard working—a producer of thoughtful, serious products—meant that a position by Rutledge on the edge of precedent or beyond was taken seriously, even if ultimately rejected. Typically, he forced his colleagues to think. And at the personal level, if he caused irritation on occasion from delay or prolixity, his manifest integrity and industry, coupled with his decency and collegiality, more than compensated.

During his time on the Supreme Court, Wiley Rutledge was showing growth—becoming increasingly self-confident, learned and coherent in more and more areas, and passionately committed to expanding due process and equal protection for the individual. Beginning with *Yamashita* and continuing through the right-to-counsel cases (*Foster*; *Marino*), followed by *United Mine Workers* and then the habeas petitions from war crimes tribunals in German and Japanese venues (*Milch*; *Hirota*), one can sense a zeal in Rutledge that might well have made him a more assertive actor, and thus perhaps a more effective justice in later years, had he lived. That might well have depended, however, on attaining an efficiency, if not a fluency, that Rutledge never showed signs of achieving.

Although constrained by his judicial role to forswear political activism, Justice Rutledge could not resist offering suggestions to local groups for establishing political rights in the District of Columbia, a sympathy reflected as well in his *Tidewater* opinion deeming the District a "state" for purposes of federal court diversity jurisdiction. Rutledge was also a thoroughgoing internationalist. He spoke out on issues pertaining to postwar arrangements for the world order, strongly advocating a role for the United Nations that would make up for the failed League of Nations. His faith in people generally—and thus in the willingness of governments the world around, including the Soviet Union, to make accommodations for peace—led him to trust in possibilities for limited world government. That, he believed, would offer greater protection against future wars than a

A JUSTICE IN THE GREAT TRADITION

"A Justice in the Great Tradition"— cartoon by Fitzpatrick, September 12, 1949. (Reprinted with permission of the St. Louis Post-Dispatch, *2003)*

balance-of-powers regime. Such views, of course, left him in the company of a small minority of idealists. For Wiley Rutledge, however, there was no disconnect between the potential for accommodation of interests within the United States, enforceable by just laws, and the potential for similar accommodation within the world at large.

After Rutledge died, the editors of the *Iowa Law Review* and the *Indiana Law Journal* published jointly a symposium in Rutledge's honor, with former colleagues detailing his contributions as a justice, a teacher, and a human being. The Supreme Court Bar and the Supreme Court itself also held memorial proceedings, with remarks by many who knew him well. And in later years two of Rutledge's former law clerks wrote chapters about Rutledge: Justice John Paul Stevens in *Mr. Justice* and Judge Louis H. Pollak in *Six Justices on Civil Rights*.[9] All these contributions offer perceptive insight into the man and his work from many who knew him well, and they are well worthy of attention from all who seek further understanding.

One comment from the Supreme Court Bar proceedings, by Willard Wirtz, offers fitting closure. "Wiley Rutledge, above almost all others, loved and respected his fellow men. This was the quality of his great personal attraction and it was the core of his reputed liberalism."[10] The source of these remarks was a close friend. What is remarkable, however, is the virtual universality of the sentiment among those who knew the justice. His love of people governed his personal relationships, underlay his optimistic view of the world, and generated his unswerving faith that law could deliver justice. Not one to cut corners, he would explore all the possibilities of a case before him, with all the parties in mind—to the point of intellectual and physical exhaustion. Then he would speak with a principled voice.

Notes

ABBREVIATIONS USED IN THE NOTES

A. Rutledge Papers	Early letters between Wiley Rutledge, Annabel Person Rutledge, and other family members, Collection of Dr. Theodore S. Needels and Mary Lou (Rutledge) Needels, Washington, D.C.
Bates Papers	Henry Moore Bates Papers, Bentley Historical Library, University of Michigan, Ann Arbor
Biddle Diary	Francis Biddle Diary, Franklin D. Roosevelt Library, Hyde Park, N.Y.
Biddle Papers	Francis Biddle Attorney General File, Franklin D. Roosevelt Library, Hyde Park, N.Y.
Black Papers	Hugo Black Papers, Library of Congress
Borah Papers	William E. Borah Papers, Library of Congress
Brant Papers	Irving Newton Brant Papers, Library of Congress
Burton Papers	Harold H. Burton Papers, Library of Congress
Chancellor's Papers	Chancellor, Archives, John M. Olin Library, Washington University, St. Louis, Mo.
Douglas Appt. File	William O. Douglas, Appointment Files of Supreme Court Justices, 1930–71, National Archives
Douglas Papers	William O. Douglas Papers, Library of Congress
FDR Official File	Franklin D. Roosevelt Official File, Franklin D. Roosevelt Library, Hyde Park, N.Y.
FDR Personal File	Franklin D. Roosevelt Personal File, Franklin D. Roosevelt Library, Hyde Park, N.Y.
Frankfurter Appt. File	Felix Frankfurter, Appointment Files of Supreme Court Justices, 1930–71, National Archives
Frankfurter Papers	Felix Frankfurter Papers, Library of Congress
Fuchs Papers	Ralph Fuchs Papers, Lilly Library, Indiana University, Bloomington
Gilmore Papers	Eugene A. Gilmore Papers, University Libraries, State University of Iowa, Iowa City
Gressman Diary	Eugene Gressman Diary, Bentley Historical Library, University of Michigan, Ann Arbor
H. F. Stone Papers	Harlan Fiske Stone Papers, Library of Congress
Hadley Missouri	Herbert S. Hadley Papers, Ellis Library, University of Missouri, Columbia
Hadley Northwestern	Herbert S. Hadley Student Records, Northwestern University Library, Evanston

Iowa Dean Reports	Reports of the Dean, 1935-39, Law Library, State University of Iowa, Iowa City
Iowa Faculty Minutes	Faculty Minutes, 1935-39, Law Library, State University of Iowa
Jackson Papers	Robert H. Jackson Papers, Library of Congress
K. Stone Papers	Kimbrough Stone Papers, Ellis Library, University of Missouri, Columbia
Murphy Papers	Frank Murphy Papers, Bentley Historical Library, University of Michigan, Ann Arbor
Nagel Papers	Charles Nagel Papers, Yale University Library, New Haven, Conn.
PQ Club Records	Public Question Club Records, Missouri Historical Society, St. Louis
Reed Papers	Stanley Reed Papers, Margaret I. King Library, University of Kentucky, Lexington
Rosenwald Papers	Robert E. Rosenwald Papers, John M. Olin Library, Washington University, St. Louis, Mo.
Rutledge Appt. File	Wiley Blount Rutledge, Appointment Files of Supreme Court Justices, 1930-71, National Archives
Rutledge Nom. File	Wiley Rutledge Nomination Papers, National Archives
Rutledge Papers	Wiley Blount Rutledge Jr. Papers, Library of Congress
Smith Missouri	Luther Ely Smith File, Missouri Historical Society, St. Louis
Stephens Papers	Harold M. Stephens Papers, Library of Congress
Vinson Papers	Fred M. Vinson Papers, Margaret I. King Library, University of Kentucky, Lexington
WCL Archives	Washington College of Law Archives, American University, Washington, D.C.
WR Colorado	Wiley Blount Rutledge Jr. Student Records, University of Colorado Archives, Boulder
WR Iowa	Wiley Blount Rutledge Jr. Papers, University Libraries, Special Collections, State University of Iowa, Iowa City
WR Maryville	Wiley Blount Rutledge Jr. Student Record, Lamar Memorial Library, Maryville College, Maryville, Tenn.
WR Mercantile	Wiley Blount Rutledge Jr. File, Mercantile Library, St. Louis, Mo.
WR Missouri	Wiley Blount Rutledge Jr. File, Missouri Historical Society, St. Louis
WR Wisconsin	Wiley Blount Rutledge Jr. Student Record, Office of the Registrar/Certification, University of Wisconsin, Madison
WU Faculty Minutes	Faculty Minutes, 1924-35, School of Law, Washington University, St. Louis, Mo.
Wyatt Papers	Walter Wyatt Papers, Alderman Library, University of Virginia, Charlottesville

INTRODUCTION

1. Lawrence Taylor, *A Trial of Generals*, 1-7, 111.

2. Daly, "The Yamashita Case and Martial Courts," part I; Lawrence Taylor, *A Trial of Generals*, 103-13; *In re Yamashita*, 327 U.S. 1, 16 (1946); Lael, *The Yamashita Precedent*, 7-9.

3. Lael, *The Yamashita Precedent*, 9-13, 16, 21-23, 26, 28, 30-31; Lawrence Taylor, *A Trial of Generals*, 116, 120, 122-23.

4. Lael, *The Yamashita Precedent*, 31-32; Lawrence Taylor, *A Trial of Generals*, 124-26.

5. Lael, *The Yamashita Precedent*, 14, 18, 33-37; Piccigallo, *The Japanese on Trial*, 50.

6. Lael, *The Yamashita Precedent*, 59-65.

7. Lael, *The Yamashita Precedent*, xi, 2, 56, 58-59, 66-69, 72; Piccigallo, *The Japanese on Trial*, 51, 63, *see* 49, 57, 214.

8. Lael, *The Yamashita Precedent*, 71-73; Lawrence Taylor, *A Trial of Generals*, 131-35; *see* Reel, *The Case of General Yamashita*, 35-39.

9. Lawrence Taylor, *A Trial of Generals*, 135-36; Piccigallo, *The Japanese on Trial*, 51; Lael, *The Yamashita Precedent*, 80-81; Reel, *The Case of General Yamashita*, 40-41; Whitney, "The Case of General Yamashita," 19 (refuting Reel's claim that no commission member "was a combat man").

10. Lael, *The Yamashita Precedent*, 81-83; Lawrence Taylor, *A Trial of Generals*, 131, 208, 223. For scholars who have cited *Yamashita* to argue for imputing criminal responsibility to high commanders for atrocities in Vietnam see Telford Taylor, *Nuremberg and Vietnam*, 181-82; Falk, "The Circle of Responsibility," 224-26; *see* Falk, *A Global Approach to National Policy* 146; Lael, *The Yamashita Precedent*, 129 & n. 16; Piccigallo, *The Japanese on Trial*, 59; Parks, "Command Responsibility for War Crimes."

11. *In re Yamashita*, 327 U.S. 1, 5 (1946); Lael, *The Yamashita Precedent*, 81, 83-87, 89-90; Lawrence Taylor, *A Trial of Generals*, 137, 161-62; Parks, "Command Responsibility for War Crimes," 29-30; Whitney, "The Case of General Yamashita," 18-19.

12. Lawrence Taylor, *A Trial of Generals*, 166-67; Reel, *The Case of General Yamashita*, 165-66, 174; Lael, *The Yamashita Precedent*, 94-95.

13. Lael, *The Yamashita Precedent*, 82, 95 (citing trial transcript at 4061-63); Reel, *The Case of General Yamashita*, 171-74.

14. Lael, *The Yamashita Precedent*, 92-94, 99; Piccigallo, *The Japanese on Trial*, 57; *Chicago Sunday Tribune*, Dec. 9, 1945, part 1, p. 14, col. 6.

15. Wiley Rutledge (hereafter WR) to Victor Brudney, April 1, 1946; typewritten draft memorandum denying petitions in No. 61, *In re Yamashita* (for writs of habeas corpus and prohibition), and No. 672, *Yamashita v. Styer* (for writ of certiorari), case file *In re Yamashita*, box 137, Rutledge Papers; Justice Wiley Rutledge, handwritten draft dissent from denial of petitions in Nos. 61 and 672, case file *In re Yamashita*, box 137, Rutledge Papers; Lael, *The Yamashita Precedent*, 100, 105 & n. 28, 106 & n. 32; Fine, *Frank Murphy*, 453; *see* WR to John L. [*sic*] Frank, Feb. 22, 1946; draft letter from WR to John Frank, Feb. 13, 1946 (apparently not sent in view of shorter, similar — and less revealing — letter to Frank of Feb. 22, 1946); Harper, *Justice Rutledge and the Bright Constellation*, 185; Diary of Harold H. Burton, Dec. 18-20, 1945, Burton Papers.

16. Piccigallo, *The Japanese on Trial*, 54-55; Lael, *The Yamashita Precedent*, 105-6, 118 (Yamashita had filed a petition for writ of certiorari and requested leave to file writs of habeas corpus and prohibition); Fine, *Frank Murphy*, 454-55; *see* Mason, *Harlan Fiske Stone*, 667; Howard, *Mr. Justice Murphy*, 368-70; *see* draft letter from WR to John Frank, Feb. 13, 1946; WR to John L. [*sic*] Frank, Feb. 22, 1946.

17. *See* notes 15, 16.

CHAPTER ONE

1. Heilprin and Heilprin, eds., *A Complete Pronouncing Gazetteer or Geographical Dictionary of the World*, 432; Israel, "Wiley Rutledge"; Pollak, "Wiley B. Rutledge"; Thompson, *History and Legend of Breckinridge County, Kentucky*, 27; Margarete G. Smith, "Cloverport Looking Backward," *Cloverport Gazette*, May 3, 1979, p. 10, col. 1, June 28,

1979, p. 6, cols. 1–3, and untitled, undated, unnumbered page with photo of "Main Street Cloverport 1956" (all found in Margarete G. Smith, *Cloverport*); *see* Sulzer, "Kentucky's Abandoned Railroads, No. 18," 52.

2. WR to J. L. Wigginton, March 8, 1939; WR to Fred A. Sweet, Feb. 18, 1943; Edward Gregory, "The Tar Springs," in "Memories of the Past" (1932), in Margarete G. Smith, *Cloverport*; unidentified flyer, "The Waters," in "Beautiful Tar Springs," in Margarete G. Smith, *Cloverport*; *see* Frank L. Moorman to WR, Feb. 9, 1943; WR to T. M. Ingersoll, May 19, 1943; Sulzer, "Kentucky's Abandoned Railroads, No. 18," 52; Potter, *A History of Owensboro and Daviess County, Kentucky*, 146; unidentified newspaper clipping, "The Healing Waters Flow" (1898), in "Beautiful Tar Springs," in Margarete G. Smith, *Cloverport*; Thompson, *History and Legend of Breckinridge County, Kentucky*, 27–28; unidentified newspaper clipping, "Notes on the Fire," Rutledge Papers.

3. WR to Rev. J. E. Spring, April 22, 1943; WR to Mrs. Charles R. Hyde, June 19, June 29, and Sept. 30, 1946; Mrs. Charles R. Hyde to WR, July 9, 1946; WR to A. G. Ewing, July 5, 1947; WR to John Granville Sims, Feb. 11, 1939; WR to Samuel B. Whitaker, Nov. 12, 1940; WR to Thomas W. Child, Oct. 10, 1947; "Early Family Information," Rutledge Papers; Donald Grant, *Des Moines Register*, Feb. 25, 1939, sec. 6, p. 1, col. 2.

4. *Compare* WR to A. G. Ewing, July 5, 1947, *and* WR to S. A. Rutledge, March 2, 1939, *with* WR to Fred A. Sweet, Feb. 18, 1943; Schwartz, *A History of the Supreme Court*, 17, 28, 381.

5. Bryan C. Collier, *Courier-Journal* (Louisville), March 5, 1939, sec. 3, p. 1, cols. 1–6; WR to Bessie B. Ross, Feb. 27, 1939.

6. Unidentified newspaper clippings, Rutledge Papers ("A Frightening Storm"; "Baby Rutledge to Santa Claus"; "Mob Attacks the Parsonage at Cloverport"; "Notes on the Fire"); "Early Family Information," Rutledge Papers, 2; WR to T. M. Ingersoll, May 19, 1943; WR to Bruce Dana McDowell, March 7, 1949; WR to Fred A. Sweet, Feb. 18, 1943; Elizabeth L. Sheffield to WR, Jan. 15, 1943; Frank L. Moorman to WR, Feb. 9, 1943; interviews, M. L. (Rutledge) Needels, I. Rutledge, N. Rutledge.

7. "Early Family Information," Rutledge Papers, 1; WR to Fred A. Sweet, Feb. 18, 1943; WR to Rev. J. E. Spring, April 22, 1943; WR to Mrs. Charles R. Hyde, Sept. 30, 1946; WR to Bruce Dana McDowell, March 7, 1949; William Thurman to WR, June 7, 1943; Mrs. J. B. Randall to WR, March 2, 1943; William Thurman to WR, June 7, 1943; WR to Annabel Rutledge, Aug. 9, 1920.

8. WR to T. M. Ingersoll, May 19, 1943.

9. WR to Annabel Rutledge, undated [Nov. 1917].

10. Family information provided by May Wood Wigginton according to handwritten notation by "W.R.," Aug. 31, 1945; "Early Family Information," Rutledge Papers, 2; interview, M. L. (Rutledge) Needels; WR to Wallace A. McKay, Feb. 24, 1945; WR to "Aunt Bess" Wigginton, March 9, 1939; Collier, *Courier-Journal* (Louisville), March 5, 1939, sec. 3, p. 3, col. 6.

11. Collier, *Courier-Journal* (Louisville), sec. 3, p. 1, cols. 1–6, sec. 3, p. 4, col. 5.

12. WR to Annabel Rutledge, Aug. 9, 1920 (identifying photograph), A. Rutledge Papers; WR to F. W. Kent, July 9, 1948 (same), WR Iowa; George Pennell to WR, Feb. 6, 1943.

13. "Early Family Information," Rutledge Papers, 1–2, and accompanying family trees and related notes; WR to James W. Wigginton, May 4, 1939; Harper, *Justice Rutledge and the Bright Constellation*, 1–3 (containing more detailed recitation of Wigginton and Lovell family genealogies than appears herein).

14. "Early Family Information," Rutledge Papers, family trees; WR to Annabel Rutledge, Aug. 9 and 14, 1920 (concerning John Ludwell Wigginton), A. Rutledge Papers; WR to "Aunt Bess" Wigginton, March 9, 1939; WR to Mrs. O. H. McGrain, June 24, 1946; Wiley Rutledge, untitled, undated handwritten essay written during first half of 1916 at the North Carolina Sanatorium for the Treatment of Tuberculosis, 7, A. Rutledge Papers.

15. WR to Wallace A. McKay, Feb. 24, 1945; WR to Bruce Dana McDowell, March 7, 1949; WR to "Aunt Bess" Wigginton, March 9, 1939.

16. "Justice Rutledge Visits Bradley, Thinks Outlook on War Healthy," *Chattanooga Times*, June 21, 1944, Rutledge Papers; *Asheville* (N.C.) *Citizen*, July 7, 1944, p. 1, col. 4, p. 2, col. 7; "Early Family Information," Rutledge Papers, 1; WR to Lon T. Williams, March 1, 1939; Collier, *Courier-Journal* (Louisville), March 5, 1939, sec. 3, p. 1, cols. 1–6, p. 3, col. 6, p. 4, col. 5.

17. Interviews, M. L. (Rutledge) Needels, J. A. (Rutledge) Pollitt, I. Rutledge; "Early Family Information," Rutledge Papers, 2; *see* WR to Wayne C. Williams, undated [1945]; Harper, *Justice Rutledge and the Bright Constellation*, 4.

18. Interviews, M. L. (Rutledge) Needels, J. A. (Rutledge) Pollitt, I. Rutledge.

19. Interview, I. Rutledge; George Pennell to WR, Feb. 6, 1943; Elizabeth L. Sheffield to WR, Jan. 15, 1943; George W. King to WR, Feb. 16, 1943; John E. Kincheloe to WR, undated; E. L. Robertson to WR, April 15, 1939.

20. WR to Hon. Samuel E. Whitaker, Nov. 12; 1940; WR to Bruce Dana McDowell, March 7, 1949; O. T. Ault to WR, May 8, 1943; WR to Ralph [S.] Carson, March 3, 1939; interview, I. Rutledge; D. M. Brown, *Educational, Economic and Community Survey*, 9, 27–28; report card of Mr. Wiley Rutledge, fall term, Pikeville Training School, Sept. 3–Dec. 21 (year not given); Wiley Rutledge, "Looking over Ancient Days in Tennessee," address before "Atlantic Highlanders," April 19, 1941, speech notes in outline form.

21. WR to Bruce Dana McDowell, March 7, 1949; WR to Samuel E. Whitaker, Nov. 12, 1940; Andriot, *Population Abstract of the United States*, 772; U.S. Historical Census Data, Blount County, Tennessee, 1910; *see generally* Blair and Walker, *By Faith Endowed*.

22. WR to Wayne C. Williams, May 21, 1945; WR to Wayne C. Williams, Nov. 3, 1941.

23. Ralph Waldo Lloyd to WR, March 13, 1939; Wiley Blount Rutledge Jr., grade report, Maryville College, 1910–13; *see* WR to Lon T. Williams, March 1, 1939; Robert W. Wright to WR, Jan. 11, 1943; H. M. Wyrick to WR, Jan. 14, 1943; C. Hodge Mathes to WR, Feb. 13, 1943; WR to Addison S. Moore, June 24, 1946; Christine Nugent to author, Dec. 19, 2000.

24. Blair and Walker, *By Faith Endowed*, 1–2, 10–11, 32–33, 48, 53, 67–69, 87–88, 96–97, 111–12.

25. Interviews, I. Rutledge, N. Rutledge.

26. WR to Ralph [S.] Carson, March 3, 1939; WR to John Granville Sims, Feb. 25, 1939; WR to Ralph W. Lloyd, March 13, 1939; WR to Bruce Dana McDowell, March 7, 1949; WR to Lon T. Williams, March 1, 1939; Lon T. Williams to WR, Feb. 5, 1944; H. M. Wyrick to WR, Jan. 14, 1943; Robert W. Wright to WR, Jan. 11, 1943; Wiley Blount Rutledge Jr., grade report, Maryville College, 1910–13, WR Maryville; Dr. James R. Smith, *Knoxville News-Sentinel*, Jan. 17, 1943, p. A7, cols. 2, 4; Ralph Waldo Lloyd, "Wiley Blount Rutledge, Citation for the Honorary Degree of Doctor of Laws (LL.D.)," Oct. 27, 1945, 1, Rutledge Papers; interviews, M. L. (Rutledge) Needels, N. Rutledge; letterhead of "Wilson and Marshall Club of Maryville College, Maryville, Tennessee," 1912, showing "W. B. Rutledge, Jr., President" and containing text of Rutledge's statement supporting Woodrow Wilson for president; *Maryville College Monthly*, undated, 22.

27. Program for "Freshman-Sophomore Debate, Elizabeth R. Voorhees Chapel, Maryville College, Friday Evening, May 3, 1912."

28. Debate flyer, "Wilson-Roosevelt Campaign Issues . . . Voorhees Chapel. Saturday Night November 2nd at 7:30."

29. Wiley Rutledge, text of second speaker for affirmative case supporting a responsible form of cabinet government, undated; *see* R. Webb to WR, Feb. 17, 1913; [undecipherable handwritten name] to WR, Feb. 21, 1913.

30. "Commencement Exercises of the Polytechnic School, Friday Evening, May 17, 1912, 8:00 o'clock"; "Oration, 'The Problem of the Present,' May 17, 1912," 4, 5.

31. Wiley Rutledge, text of third speaker for Democratic Party, "Wilson-Roosevelt Campaign Issues, . . . Voorhees Chapel, Saturday Night November 2nd at 7:30," Rutledge Papers.

32. *See* Wiley Blount Rutledge [Jr.], grade report, Maryville College Preparatory [School], 1908-10, WR Maryville; "Athenian–Alpha Sigma Debate, Elizabeth R. Voorhees Chapel, April 29, 1910, Maryville College, Maryville, Tenn."

33. "Athenian–Alpha Sigma Debate, Elizabeth R. Voorhees Chapel, April 29, 1910, Maryville College, Maryville, Tenn." 1-3.

34. "Athenian–Alpha Sigma Debate," 3, 4.

35. "Athenian–Alpha Sigma Debate," 5.

36. "Athenian–Alpha Sigma Debate," 6-7.

37. "Athenian–Alpha Sigma Debate" (results typed at bottom of manuscript); N. Behar to WR, April 19, 1910.

38. WR to Bruce Dana McDowell, March 7, 1949.

39. Smith, *Knoxville News-Sentinel*, Jan. 17, 1943, p. A7, col. 4; interview, M. L. (Rutledge) Needels.

40. Smith, *Knoxville News-Sentinel*, Jan. 17, 1943, p. A7, col. 5.

41. Interview, N. Rutledge; D. J. Brittain, "New Supreme Court Justice Rutledge Once Played Practical Joke in Knoxville," *Knoxville News-Sentinel*, ca. Jan. 14, 1943, p. 12, col. 2, Rutledge Papers.

42. Interviews, M. L. (Rutledge) Needels, N. Rutledge; WR to Fred A. Sweet, Feb. 18, 1943; Harper, *Justice Rutledge and the Bright Constellation*, 9.

43. Interviews, M. L. (Rutledge) Needels, J. A. (Rutledge) Pollitt, N. Rutledge; Ralph S. Carson to WR, March 6, 1939; Robert W. Wright to WR, Jan. 11, 1943; Wiley Blount Rutledge Jr., grade report, Maryville College, 1910-13, WR Maryville.

44. Interviews, M. L. (Rutledge) Needels, N. Rutledge; *see* W. B. Rutledge grade report, University of Wisconsin, Feb. 7, 1914, WR Wisconsin; Wiley Blount Rutledge Jr., Official Transcript, University of Wisconsin, Madison, WR Wisconsin.

45. Samuel T. Wilson to WR, Aug. 7, 1913; WR to Ralph [S.] Carson, March 3, 1939; WR to Malcolm Scott Hallman, April 9, 1939; WR to Rev. & Mrs. Addison S. Moore, June 24, 1946; WR to Fred A. Sweet, Feb. 18, 1943; interview, N. Rutledge; W. B. Rutledge grade report, University of Wisconsin, Feb. 7, 1914, WR Wisconsin; Donald Grant, *Des Moines Register*, Feb. 25, 1939, sec. 6, p. 4, col. 4.

46. WR to Ralph Waldo Lloyd, March 15, 1939; H. M. Wyrick to WR, Jan. 14, 1943; Robert W. Wright to WR, Jan. 11, 1943; WR to Lucille B. Zeller, Aug. 6, 1942; Wiley Rutledge, "Looking over Ancient Days in Tennessee."

47. Wiley B. Rutledge Jr., "Abstract of Qualifications," 1, attached letter from John B. Hamilton to WR, July 9, 1914; Wiley B. Rutledge Jr., grade report, Maryville College, 1910-13 ("Entrance blank U. T. filled 8/8/13"), WR Maryville; 2 *Who's Who In America*

3748 (1998) (entry for Rutledge, Ivan Cate, Dec. 24, 1915, son of "Wiley Blount and Tamsey (Cate)"); WR to Mrs. W. E. Logan, Feb. 6, 1943; WR to Mrs. L. G. Thompson, Nov. 12, 1941; WR to John B. White, Oct. 5, 1943; WR to Lon T. Williams, March 1, 1939.

CHAPTER TWO

1. U.S. Bureau of the Census, *Fourteenth Census of the U.S.*; Workers of the Federal Writers' Project of the Works Progress Administration in the State of Wisconsin, *Wisconsin*, 217.

2. Cronon and Jenkins, *The University of Wisconsin*, 4; Carrington and King, "Law and the Wisconsin Idea," 299–302; Carrington, "Law as 'The Common Thoughts of Men,'" 507–12.

3. Carrington and King, "Law and the Wisconsin Idea," 300–304, 313–14; Curti and Carstensen, *The University of Wisconsin*, 32–33; Hofstadter, Preface to "Lincoln Steffens Reports La Follette's Reforms."

4. Cronon and Jenkins, *The University of Wisconsin*, 9, 11; Carrington and King, "Law and the Wisconsin Idea," 297, 299, 314–16; Woodrow Wilson, "Woodrow Wilson on the Meaning of the New Freedom"; Hofstadter, "The Meaning of the Progressive Movement," 12–13.

5. W. B. Rutledge grade report, University of Wisconsin, Feb. 7, 1914, WR Wisconsin; Wiley Blount Rutledge Jr., Official Transcript, University of Wisconsin, Madison ("Graduated 1914 (S[ummer]. S[chool].) With degree of B. A."), WR Wisconsin; WR to George E. Worthington, April 15, 1940; WR to Harry C. Thoma, Dec. 12, 1939.

6. Rutledge, "Two Centuries of the Wisconsin Idea"; Bryan C. Collier, *Courier-Journal* (Louisville), March 5, 1939, sec. 3, p. 3, col. 6; *see* WR to Harry C. Thoma, Dec. 12, 1939; WR to George E. Worthington, April 15, 1940.

7. WR to Annabel Person, Dec. 14, 1915, A. Rutledge Papers; WR to J. L. Harman, July 11, 1939; WR to J. L. Harman, July 11, 1939; J. Murray Hill to WR, July 8, 1939; A. J. Sym to Whom It May Concern, Sept. 10, 1917.

8. Ralph Gaebler to author, Nov. 2 and Dec. 18, 2000; WR to J. L. Harman, July 11, 1939; *see* Donald Grant, *Des Moines Register*, Feb. 25, 1939, sec. 6, p. 4, col. 5; *see generally* Tuchman, *The Guns of August*.

9. [Undecipherable] to WR, Aug. 7, 1915; unidentified application for teaching position showing Connersville annual salary of $1,036; W. W. Ernest to WR, May 18, 1916; A. J. Lynn to W. W. Earnest, July 16, 1917; WR to Rev. Ralph [S.] Carson, March 3, 1939; WR to J. L. Harman, July 11, 1939; Editha Feigert to WR, Jan. 14, 1943; WR to James J. Laughlin, March 12, 1941; *see* J. Murray Hill to WR, July 8, 1939; Ruth Pohlman to WR, Feb. 17 and March 7, 1939; Edwin L. Rickert to WR, March 24, 1939; WR to Edward L. Rickert, April 18, 1939; WR to Rosella Martin Roberts, Oct. 9, 1940; WR to Gladys Riddle, July 22, 1941.

10. *See, e.g.*, Annabel Rutledge to WR, Nov. 29, 1917, A. Rutledge Papers; WR to Annabel Rutledge, Aug. 18, 1920, A. Rutledge Papers; WR to Annabel Rutledge, Aug. 21, 1920, A. Rutledge Papers; interviews, M. L. (Rutledge) Needels, J. A. (Rutledge) Pollitt, N. Rutledge.

11. WR to Annabel Person, Dec. 14, 1915, A. Rutledge Papers; W. W. Ernest to WR, May 18, 1916; *see* WR to J. L. Harman, July 11, 1939; WR to Rosella Martin Roberts, Oct. 9, 1940; interview, N. Rutledge; Wiley Rutledge, "Adventures in the Land of T.B.", 1–3; Wiley Rutledge, typed addendum to unidentified employment application.

12. Rutledge, "Adventures in the Land of T.B.," 3, 4, 5, 6, 9; Wiley Rutledge, first handwritten draft of p. 4, "Adventures in the Land of T.B.," A. Rutledge Papers; L. B. McBrayer, M.D., superintendent and director, Bureau of Tuberculosis, North Carolina Sanatorium for the Treatment of Tuberculosis, Sanatorium, North Carolina, "To Whom It May Concern," certifying "that W. B. Rutledge was a patient in this Sanatorium from July 8, 1916 to March 7, 1917" (Oct. 15, 1917); Wiley Rutledge, undated handwritten description of trip on "eastbound local" to sanatorium for treatment of tuberculosis, A. Rutledge Papers; Thomas K. Squier to Sara W. Smith, Nov. 16, 2000 (letter in author's possession confirming location of former state sanatorium, with mailing address of Sanatorium, North Carolina, in Hoke County, now the McCain Correctional Hospital in McCain, North Carolina).

13. Rutledge, first handwritten draft of p. 4, "Adventures in the Land of T.B."; Rutledge, "Adventures in the Land of T.B.," 12, 15, 16, 17, 18; L. B. McBrayer, M.D., to Whom It May Concern, Oct. 15, 1917; WR to Ralph [S.] Carson, March 3, 1939.

14. Rutledge, "Adventures in the Land of T.B.," 5; Wiley Rutledge, untitled, undated handwritten essay written during first half of 1916 at the North Carolina Sanatorium for the Treatment of Tuberculosis, 1, 2, 3, A. Rutledge Papers.

15. Wiley Rutledge, untitled, undated handwritten essay written during first half of 1916 at the North Carolina Sanatorium for the Treatment of Tuberculosis, 3–8, A. Rutledge Papers.

16. Rutledge, "Adventures in the Land of T.B.," 1, 7, 8, 10, 11, 18.

17. WR to Ralph [S.] Carson, March 3, 1939; WR to Albert C. Ayres, March 9, 1939; John Milne to WR, Aug. 23, 1917 (letter and telegram); *see* WR to Ralph [S.] Carson, March 3, 1939; WR to Rosella Martin Roberts, Oct. 9, 1940; Wiley Rutledge, untitled, undated essay handwritten during first half of 1916, 5, A. Rutledge Papers.

18. Annabel Person to Mrs. O. S. Person, undated [ca. Aug. 23, 1917], A. Rutledge Papers; Annabel Rutledge to Mrs. O. S. Person, undated [ca. Aug. 28, 1917], A. Rutledge Papers; WR to Rev. Ralph [S.] Carson, March 3, 1939; WR to Rosella Martin Roberts, Oct. 9, 1940; announcement of wedding of Annabel Person to Wiley Blount Rutledge Jr., Aug. 28, 1917; interviews, J. A. (Rutledge) Pollitt, N. Rutledge.

19. Annabel Person to Mrs. O. S. Person, Aug. 25, 1917, A. Rutledge Papers; Annabel Rutledge to Mrs. O. S. Person, undated [ca. Aug. 28, 1917], A. Rutledge Papers.

20. Poster, "Public Debate: The Initiative and Referendum, Freshmen v. Sophomore on Friday Eve., May 3, In Voorhees Chapel, 7:30"; Robert W. Wright to WR, Jan. 11, 1943.

21. Balcomb, *A Boy's Albuquerque*, 61, 65, 94; Crans, *The Book of Albuquerque*, 6; Byron A. Johnson, *Early Albuquerque*, 54, 74–75; Luckingham, *The Urban Southwest*, 46.

22. John Milne to WR, Aug. 23, 1917 (telegram and letter); WR to Annabel Rutledge, Oct. 13 and Nov. 22, 1917, A. Rutledge Papers; Rutledge, "Adventures in the Land of T.B.," 19–20; interview, I. Rutledge.

23. Annabel Rutledge to WR, late Nov. 1917, A. Rutledge Papers; WR to Annabel Rutledge, undated [Nov. 1917], A. Rutledge Papers; interviews, T. Needels, N. Rutledge; Wiley Rutledge, "Adventures in the Land of T.B.," 20.

24. *See* Thomas F. Harvey to WR, Sept. 26, 1922; Addison S. Moore to WR, Feb. 20, 1923; WR to Annabel Rutledge, Aug. 10, 1920; Wiley Rutledge, memorandum "To the Members of the Board of Education," Albuquerque, New Mexico, undated [spring 1920]; interviews, M. L. (Rutledge) Needels, T. Needels, N. Rutledge; Wiley Rutledge, "Adventures in the Land of T.B.," 21.

25. Wiley Rutledge, memorandum "To the Members of the Board of Education"; Rut-

ledge, "Adventures in the Land of T.B.," 21; interview, N. Rutledge; WR to Emmet Ray Feighner, March 14, 1939; WR to R. J. Bretnall, June 1, 1920; R. J. Bretnall to WR, June 10, 1920; WR to R. J. Bretnall, June 12, 1920; *see* WR to Ralph [S.] Carson, March 3, 1939; WR to Rosella Martin Roberts, Oct. 9, 1940.

26. "Mother" [Martha] Person to WR, March 11, 1918, A. Rutledge Papers; "Momma" Person to Myrtie Person, March 12, 1918, A. Rutledge Papers; "Momma" Person to WR, Annabel Rutledge, & Myrtie Person, April 8, 1918, A. Rutledge Papers; "Momma" Person to Myrtie Person, May 7, 1918, A. Rutledge Papers; WR to Annabel Rutledge, Aug. 13 and 14, 1920, A. Rutledge Papers; WR to Emmet Ray Feighner, March 14, 1939; WR to R. J. Bretnall, June 1, 1920; R. J. Bretnall to WR, June 10, 1920; WR to R. J. Bretnall, June 12, 1920; *see* WR to Ralph [S.] Carson, March 3, 1939; WR to Rosella Martin Roberts, Oct. 9, 1940; WR to Annabel Rutledge, Aug. 6, 1920, A. Rutledge Papers; interview, N. Rutledge.

27. WR to Annabel Rutledge, Aug. 14, 1920, A. Rutledge Papers; WR to Annabel Rutledge, Aug. 15, 1920 (undated "Sun. Night" letter datable from context and relation to subsequent letters; postmarked Aug. 17, 1920), A. Rutledge Papers; WR to Annabel Rutledge, Aug. 16, 1920 (undated "Mon. Night" letter datable by reference to preceding and subsequent letters), A. Rutledge Papers.

28. WR to Annabel Rutledge, Aug. 18 and 21, 1920, A. Rutledge Papers; Annabel Rutledge to WR (undated "Monday p.m." in Aug. 1920), A. Rutledge Papers; WR to Annabel Rutledge, Aug. 24, 1920, A. Rutledge Papers.

29. WR to Annabel Rutledge, Aug. 7, 9, 21, 24, 26, 31, Sept. 1, 2, 1920, A. Rutledge Papers; WR to Annabel Rutledge, Aug. 16, 1920 (undated "Mon. Night" letter datable by reference to preceding and subsequent letters), A. Rutledge Papers; Annabel Rutledge to WR, Aug. 18, 20, 1920, undated "Sunday" in Aug. 1920, A. Rutledge Papers; Annabel Rutledge to WR, unidentified "Monday p.m.," Aug. 1920, A. Rutledge Papers; Annabel Rutledge to WR, undated "Friday," Aug. 1920, A. Rutledge Papers; Annabel Rutledge to WR, undated "Wednesday," Sept. 1920, probably Sept. 1, A. Rutledge Papers.

CHAPTER THREE

1. WR to Annabel Rutledge, Sept. 1, 2, 3, 5, 18, 1920, A. Rutledge Papers; Annabel Rutledge to WR, Sept. 8, 13, 1920, A. Rutledge Papers.

2. WR to Annabel Rutledge, Sept. 3, 5, 6, 7, 11, 1920, A. Rutledge Papers; WR to Annabel Rutledge, undated Sept. 1920 (datable as Sept. 13 by reference to previous and subsequent letters), A. Rutledge Papers; WR to Annabel Rutledge, undated Sept. 1920 (datable as Sept. 14 by reference to previous and subsequent letters), A. Rutledge Papers.

3. WR to Annabel Rutledge, Sept. 7, 11, 1920, A. Rutledge Papers; WR to Annabel Rutledge, undated Sept. 1920 (datable as Sept. 13 by reference to previous and subsequent letters), A. Rutledge Papers; Annabel Rutledge to WR, Sept. 13, 1920, A. Rutledge Papers.

4. William E. Davis, *Glory Colorado!*, 1, 6, 14, 19, 24, 301; Allen, Foster, Andrade, Mitterling, and Scamehorn, *The University of Colorado*, 57; *see* University of Colorado, *Bulletins, School of Law*, 1919-20, 303-4, 1920-21, 258-59, 262-66, 1921-22, 273, 277-80; University of Colorado, Commencement Exercises, Macky Auditorium, June 12, 1922, and Summer Quarter, September 2, 1922, WR Colorado; class photograph, "University of Colorado, School of Law, 1922."

5. University of Colorado, *Bulletins, School of Law*, 1920-21, 260, 1921-22, 275; Carrington, "Hail! Langdell!," 739.

6. Corwin, "The 'Higher Law' Background of American Constitutional Law," part 1,

152–58, 171–72, 177, 183, part 2, 365, 367 & nn. 5–6, 368, 375 (quoting *Dr. Bonham's Case*); Trevelyan, *The Shortened History of England*, 119–24, 137–38, 270; Sayles, *The Medieval Foundations of England*, 340–43; Jollife, *The Constitutional History of Medieval England from the English Settlement to 1485*, 208–16; Holland, *The Elements of Jurisprudence*, 32; Meyers, "Parliament, 1422–1509," 182–83; A. L. Brown, "Parliament, c. 1377–1422."

7. Corwin, "The 'Higher Law' Background of American Constitutional Law," part 2, 379–80, 394, 405, 407; Locke, *Second Treatise on Civil Government*, §§ 124–26, 143–44, 159, in Barker, ed., *Social Contract*, 105–6, 122–23, 136; *see* Ernest Barker, Introduction, in Barker, ed., *Social Contract*, xxvi–xxvii (referring to Charles Louis de Secondat, Baron de Montesquieu, *Spirit of the Laws*); Blackstone, *Commentaries on the Laws of England*, 1:51–55, 69–70, 155–56 (original emphasis omitted).

8. Horwitz, *The Transformation of American Law, 1780–1860*, 4 & n. 18 (Rhode Island adopted a receiving provision in 1798, followed by Connecticut in 1818); Tucker, "Of the Unwritten, or Common Law of England," 326, 341–45.

9. Tucker, "Of the Unwritten, or Common Law of England," 329–37, 338–40; Tucker, "On the Study of Law," 4, 9–10; Clyde N. Wilson, Foreword, vii, ix; Brainerd Currie, "The Materials of Law Study," 360.

10. Tucker, "Of the Unwritten, or Common Law of England," 339–40.

11. Horwitz, *The Transformation of American Law, 1780–1860*, 19–20 (quoting James Wilson).

12. Horwitz, *The Transformation of American Law, 1780–1860*, 23 & n. 60 (quoting H. Brackenridge, *Law Miscellanies*, 84, and Whittlesey, "Reeve and Gould's Lectures," I, 1).

13. Horwitz, *The Transformation of American Law, 1780–1860*, 1, 7–9, 30; *accord* Howe, "The Creative Period of the Law of Massachusetts," *quoted in* Horwitz, *The Transformation of American Law, 1780–1860*, 2 (before the Civil War, judicial activism had transmuted "questions of private law" into "questions of social policy").

14. Robert Stevens, "Two Cheers for 1870," 412–14; *accord* Stolz, "Clinical Experience in American Legal Education," 59; Boyd, *The ABA's First Section*, 1; Carrington, "Hail! Langdell!," 695 & n. 20; Carrington, "Legal Education for the People," 5; *see* Carrington, "The Missionary Diocese of Chicago," 470, 471; Brainerd Currie, "The Materials of Law Study," 331, 350–51 & n. 41.

15. Sutherland, *The Law at Harvard*, 99, 107–8, 134–35; Horwitz, *The Transformation of American Law, 1780–1860*, 255; Woodard, "The Limits of Legal Realism," 697 & n. 20; Carrington, "Law as 'The Common Thoughts of Men,'" 516; Carrington, "William Gardiner Hammond and the Lieber Revival," 2136 n. 7; Carrington, "Hail! Langdell!," 733; Twining, "Pericles and the Plumber," 401–2; *see* Robert Stevens, "Two Cheers for 1870," 423. For a comprehensive treatment of legal education in this country see Robert Stevens, *Law School: Legal Education in America from the 1850s to the 1980s* (Chapel Hill: U. of North Carolina Press, 1983).

16. Horwitz, *The Transformation of American Law, 1780–1860*, 253; *see* Horwitz, *The Transformation of American Law, 1780–1860*, 35–41, 44–47, 74–76, 88, 98, 127–39, 212–23, 226–37; Carrington, "Law as 'The Common Thoughts of Men,'" 509 & n. 96.

17. Carrington, "Hail! Langdell!," 698–700 & n. 53; Carrington, "Law as 'The Common Thoughts of Men,'" 496, 510–11, 515, 518; Robert Stevens, "Two Cheers for 1870," 416–19, 425 n. 3, 426; Goebel, ed., *A History of the School of Law, Columbia University*, 36–38, 41–42; Carrington, "Law and Economics in the Creation of Federal Administrative Law," 364; Elizabeth Gaspar Brown, *Legal Education at Michigan*, 181–95.

18. Robert Stevens, "Two Cheers for 1870," 426-27, 432, 434-35, 436 & n. 50; Carrington, "Law as 'The Common Thoughts of Men,'" 517-18 (citing Seligman, *The High Citadel*, 22); Carrington, "Hail! Langdell!," 740; Sutherland, *The Law at Harvard*, 165, *see generally* 162-246; Williston, *Life and Law*, 200; Stolz, "Clinical Experience in American Legal Education," 58; La Piana, *Logic and Experience*, 55, 70, 78; Grey, "Langdell's Orthodoxy," 5, 16-20, 36 (interpreting Langdell's law-as-science as akin to geometry).

19. La Piana, *Logic and Experience*, 77, 122-24; Carrington, "Hail! Langdell!," 710; Grey, "Langdell's Orthodoxy," 34 & n. 131.

20. Robert Stevens, "Two Cheers for 1870," 426, 432-33 nn. 32-34, 436 n. 49, 437; Woodard, "The Limits of Legal Realism," 699-703; Carrington, "Hail! Langdell!," 712; *see* Carrington, "Law as 'The Common Thoughts of Men,'" 520.

21. Robert Stevens, "Two Cheers for 1870," 437-38; Elizabeth Gaspar Brown, *Legal Education at Michigan*, 200-212; Carrington, "Hail! Langdell!," 739.

22. Wiley Blount Rutledge Jr., final grade report, School of Law, University of Colorado, Sept. 1922, WR Colorado; Chas. H. Utley to WR, Jan. 12, 1943; WR to Tyrrell Williams, Nov. 27, 1940; Worner, "The Public Career of Herbert Spencer Hadley," 66, 74 75, 146-47, 225, 289-90, 297-99, 311, 315; Kevin B. Leonard to author, Oct. 6, 2000 (citing Northwestern University School of Law records listing senior class members, including Herbert S. Hadley, taking examinations in evidence Dec. 18, 1893, and torts March 16, 1894, both taught by Wigmore, and dating Hadley's graduation to June 14, 1894); Northwestern University School of Law, Student Records, series 17/9, box 57, folders 6 (evidence) and 7 (torts), Hadley Northwestern; Tyrrell Williams, "Herbert Hadley and Legal Education," 137; Rahl and Schwerin, "Northwestern University School of Law," 146.

23. WR to Edward R. Schauffler, April 9, 1940; WR to Tyrrell Williams, Nov. 27, 1940; Tyrrell Williams to President Franklin D. Roosevelt, Jan. 4, 1939, Frankfurter Appt. File; Tyrrell Williams to the Attorney General, Nov. 7, 1942, Rutledge Appt. File; Tyrrell Williams, "Seventy-Five Years of Legal Education at Washington University," 482.

24. Wiley Blount Rutledge Jr., final grade report, School of Law, University of Colorado, Sept. 1922; WR to J. Perry Reynolds, Feb. 7, 1945; WR to Roy McCaskill, Jan. 21, 1947; Kenneth E. Grant to WR, Feb. 20, 1939; Thomas F. Harvey to WR, Sept. 26, 1922.

25. WR to Annabel Rutledge, undated Thurs. 1922 (text indicates date before July 1); John H. Fry to WR, Sept. 7, 1922; John H. Fry to WR, Sept. 28, 1922; Fred A. Sabin to WR, Sept. 23, 1922; WR to Annabel Rutledge, Sept. 22, 1922; WR to Annabel Rutledge, Oct. 22, 1922; WR to Ralph [S.] Carson, March 3, 1939; WR to Rosella Martin Roberts, Oct. 9, 1940; WR to E. Charles Eichenbaum, March 1, 1939; WR to Myrtie Person, Nov. 6, 1922 (telegram); Wiley Rutledge, "Adventures in the Land of T.B.," 21.

26. William E. Davis, *Glory Colorado!*, 1, 3; Workers of the Federal Writers' Project of the Works Progress Administration in the State of Colorado, *Colorado*, 105-6; Frink, *The Boulder Story*, 14; Robert G. Athearn, *The Coloradans*, 234-35; Caughey and Winstanley, *The Colorado Guide*, 212; *compare* Wright, "The Politics of Populism," 262, *with* Judah, *Governor Richard C. Dillon*, 10.

27. Allen, Foster, Andrade, Mitterling, and Scamehorn, *The University of Colorado*, 78-81.

28. William E. Davis, *Glory Colorado!*, 332-35; Athearn, *The Coloradans*, 167; Harper, *Justice Rutledge and the Bright Constellation*, 16.

29. "Industrialism Is Still Not Solved, . . . W. B. Rutledge Tells Lions New Way Must Be Found out of Many Disputes," unidentified newspaper (presumably in Boulder, Colo.),

Dec. 6, 1922, Rutledge Papers; "Lions Heard Music and Address by Rutledge," unidentified newspaper (presumably in Boulder, Colo.), Dec. 6, 1922, Rutledge Papers.

30. WR to J. L. Wigginton, March 6, 1939; WR to Edward A. Krueger, Feb. 23, 1939; *see* WR to Ralph [S.] Carson, March 3, 1939 ("I have not been active politically since leaving Colorado in 1926.").

31. "Boulder Democracy Host to Mr. Daniels," unidentified newspaper (presumably in Boulder, Colo.), July 10, 1923; Rutledge Papers; "Harding World Court Plan Is Assailed by Daniels in Address," unidentified newspaper (presumably in Boulder, Colo.), July 10, 1923, Rutledge Papers; Josephus Daniels to WR, June 15, 1923; Josephus Daniels to WR, Sept. 5, 1923.

32. Wiley Rutledge, undated handwritten description of trip on "eastbound local" to sanatorium, Rutledge Papers; WR to Annabel Rutledge, Aug. 21, 1920, A. Rutledge Papers; *see, e.g.,* Thomas H. Harvey to WR, Sept. 26, 1922; WR to Annabel Rutledge, undated [Nov. 1923], A. Rutledge Papers; WR to Annabel Rutledge, second undated [Nov. 1923], A. Rutledge Papers; interviews, M. L. (Rutledge) Needels, J. A. (Rutledge) Pollitt.

33. Wiley Rutledge, "Cycles," "Impotence," "Beauty," "Summer," "Western Autumn Evening," "Fortitude," "What's the Use o' Frownin'?," "When Your Plans Don't Pan," "Unknown," all undated. Rutledge also wrote the words to a song, "Fortitude," with music by Gustave Barto and the notation "For Sale by the National Literary and Publishers' Service Bureau, Hannibal, Mo.," A. Rutledge Papers.

34. Wiley Rutledge, "A Piece of Broken Machinery (February 6, 1924)," A. Rutledge Papers

35. Wiley Rutledge, "Turn Out the Light," undated, A. Rutledge Papers.

36. Wiley Rutledge, "To A—," "Perfect Love," undated, A. Rutledge Papers.

37. Wiley Rutledge, "121st," "123d" [*sic*], "130th," A. Rutledge Papers.

38. Worner, "The Public Career of Herbert Spencer Hadley," 326, 337–42; WR to Ralph [S.] Carson, March 3, 1939; WR to Rosella Martin Roberts, Oct. 9, 1940; WR to E. Charles Eichenbaum, March 1, 1939; *see* H. S. Hadley to WR, April 6, 1926; WR to H. S. Hadley, April 26, 1926; 17 *Colorado Alumnus* 8 (Sept. 1926); Fuchs, "Law School in Transition."

39. University of Colorado, *Bulletin, School of Law,* 1924–25, 241–43. The bulletin does not indicate that Rutledge taught conflict of laws, but he must have done so as a pinch-hitter, because the Rutledge Papers contain an examination he offered in conflict of laws on Dec. 17, 1924; University of Colorado, *Bulletin, School of Law,* 1925–26, 257–59; Herbert S. Hadley to WR, April 6, 1926.

40. Interview, J. A. (Rutledge) Pollitt; Sutherland, *The Law at Harvard,* 275–76; *see* Manley O. Hudson to WR, Jan. 21, 1926.

41. Herbert S. Hadley to WR, April 6, 1926; WR to H. S. Hadley, Aug. 21, 1926; WR to Herbert S. Hadley, April 26, 1926, Hadley Missouri; *see* WR to Annabel Rutledge, undated "Saturday p.m." in fall 1926; Herbert Hadley to WR, Aug. 22, 1926 (telegram); 17 *Colorado Alumnus* 8 (Sept. 1926); WR to H. S. Hadley, Aug. 21, 1926; Herbert Hadley to WR, Aug. 22, 1926 (telegram).

CHAPTER FOUR

1. Workers of the Federal Writers' Project of the Works Progress Administration in the State of Missouri, *The WPA Guide to 1930s Missouri,* 295, 298, 305; Barry, *Rising Tide,* 23, 56, 65.

2. Morrow, *Washington University in St. Louis*, 1-4.

3. *Id*. at 54-55; Hansen, "The Early History of the College of Law, State University of Iowa," 42-43; Perkins, "The Story of the Iowa Law School," 262 & n. 32; Carrington, "William Gardiner Hammond and the Lieber Revival," 2135 & n. 3, 2137, 2140-41, 2144 (citing Lieber, *Legal and Political Hermeneutics*); Tyrrell Williams, "Seventy-Five Years of Legal Education at Washington University," 480; Carrington, "Hail! Langdell!," 697; Brainerd Currie, "The Materials of Law Study," 378; Goebel, ed., *A History of the School of Law, Columbia University*, 46-47.

4. Carrington, "William Gardiner Hammond and the Lieber Revival," 2135-39, 2144; Brainerd Currie, "The Materials of Law Study," 379.

5. Carrington, "William Gardiner Hammond and the Lieber Revival," 2144; Morrow, *Washington University in St. Louis*, 56-57; Robert Stevens, "Two Cheers for 1870," 456. Initially, AALS was open for membership to law schools that required of applicants a high school education or its equivalent, offered two years of acceptable legal study, and provided a law library with an adequate collection of state and U.S. reports of decided cases. Boyd, *The ABA's First Section*, 15, 37; Tyrrell Williams, "Herbert Hadley and Legal Education," 483.

6. Morello, *The Invisible Bar*, 3, 12, 37-38 (Margaret Brent); Drachman, *Sisters in Law*, 16, 37, appendix 1, 251; Hayes, "A Pioneer Iowa Law School," 108; Pettus, "The Legal Education of Women," 239, *cited in* Carrington, "William Gardiner Hammond and the Lieber Revival," 2142 & n. 36; Morrow, *Washington University in St. Louis*, 57.

7. Morrow, *Washington University in St. Louis*, 351 (William S. Curtis (1894-1915) and Judge Richard Goode (1915-26)); Carrington, "Hail! Langdell!," 739; *see also* Fuchs, "Law School in Transition"; Herbert S. Hadley to Tyrrell Williams, Sept. 25, 1926.

8. Interviews, J. A. (Rutledge) Pollitt, N. Rutledge; WR to Annabel Rutledge, "Saturday p.m." [Sept. 11, 1926]. This letter and all but one thereafter from Wiley to Annabel during the period September-November 1926 are undated, referring only to the day of the week written, as quoted. Because one letter was dated September 21, however, and the School of Law opened on Thursday, September 23, 1926, Wiley's letters, easily sequenced, have made it possible to identify the dates for the days used to head his correspondence.

9. WR to Annabel Rutledge, "Saturday p.m." [Sept. 11, 1926], "Sunday night" [Sept. 12, 1926], "Monday night" [Sept. 13, 1926].

10. WR to Annabel Rutledge, "Monday night" [Sept. 13, 1926], Sept. 21, 1926, "Friday p.m." [Sept. 24, 1926].

11. WR to Annabel Rutledge, "Sunday night" [Sept. 13, 1926].

12. WR to Annabel Rutledge, "Monday a.m." [Oct. 11, 1926].

13. WR to Annabel Rutledge, "Sunday night" [Sept. 12, 1926], "Sunday night" [Sept. 13, 1926], "Friday p.m." [Sept. 24, 1926], "Sunday night" [Oct. 10, 1926], "Monday a.m." [Oct. 11, 1926], "Monday night" [Oct. 18, 1926], "Thurs. night" [Oct. 28, 1926], "Monday night" [Nov. 2, 1926], "Tues. night" [Nov. 3, 1926].

14. WR to Annabel Rutledge, "Saturday p.m." [Sept. 11, 1926], "Monday night" [Sept. 13, 1926], "Saturday night" [Oct. 2, 1926], "Monday night" [Oct. 18, 1926], "Thursday a.m." [Oct. 21, 1926], "Saturday night" [Oct. 23, 1926]; WR to Mary Lou Rutledge, "Wed. Night" [Nov. 4, 1926], "Monday night" [Nov. 9, 1926].

15. WR to Annabel Rutledge, "Thurs. night" [Oct. 28, 1926]; John D. Fleming to WR, Jan. 24, 1927; Milo G. Durham to WR, Dec. 20, 1929, Jan. 7, 1932, Jan. 7, 1936; WR to Emmett Ray Feighner, Feb. 2, 1939; interviews, M. L. (Rutledge) Needels, N. Rutledge.

16. WR to Annabel Rutledge, "Saturday night" [Oct. 2, 1926], "Thursday a.m." [Oct. 21,

1926]; notation on page 357 between handwritten minutes of meetings of June 11, 1926, and Sept. 28, 1926, WU Faculty Minutes; Herbert Hadley to WR, Aug. 22, 1926 (telegram); WR to Annabel Rutledge, "Wed. night" [Oct. 6, 1926]; Bulletins of Washington University, St. Louis, *Catalogue of the School of Law*, March 10, 1927, 13-17, April 20, 1928, 16-22, April 20, 1929, 20-26, April 20, 1930, 21-28, March 10, 1931, 22-26, March 20, 1932, 22-24, April 1, 1933, 20-22, April 1, 1934, 22-24; Herbert H. Hadley to William Green Hale, March 8, 1927 (telegram); Fuchs, "Law School in Transition," 12; WR to Edward R. Schauffler, April 9, 1940; WR to Ernst W. Puttkammer, Oct. 23, 1936; interview, Greensfelder.

17. WR to Edward R. Schauffler, April 9, 1940; WR to Emmett Ray Feighner, March 14, 1939; interview, Margolin; *see* Fuchs, "Law School in Transition," 12; "Washington U. Truce after Campus Fracas: Engineers Apologize for Almost Hanging Law Student in General Melee," *St. Louis Star*, April 2, 1931, Rutledge Papers; Marshall D. Hier, "Justice Wiley B. Rutledge's St. Louis Years," *St. Louis B.J.*, fall 1993, 37, 38 (quoting *St. Louis Globe-Democrat*, Nov. 10, 1949).

18. WR to Mrs. R. H. Sanford, July 1, 1941[8?]; interviews, Greensfelder, Gross, Hanke.

19. Interviews, Bridell, Hocker; "Washington U. Truce," *St. Louis Star*, April 2, 1931, Rutledge Papers.

20. Karen Baker, manager, faculty records, Office of Human Resources, Washington University, to author, Oct. 2, 1996; interviews, Blair, Greensfelder, Gross, Hanke, Margolin, Strauss. *But compare* Beisman, Margolin, Muldoon, Vogt (Conant a good teacher).

21. Interviews, Blair, Greensfelder, Hanke, Margolin, Peper, Vogt.

22. Bulletin of Washington University, St. Louis, Missouri, *Catalogue of the School of Law*, April 1, 1933, 20; interviews with Beisman, Blair, Greensfelder, Gross, Hanke, Margolin, Peper, Vogt. *But compare* Beisman, Greensfelder, Strauss (concerning Cullen as a good teacher).

23. Interviews, Beisman, Greensfelder, Hanke, Margolin.

24. Bulletin of Washington University, St. Louis, *Catalogue of the School of Law*, April 29, 1929, 21, 22, 23, 24, 28; Bulletin of Washington University, St. Louis, *Catalogue of the School of Law*, March 10, 1931, at 22, 23, 24, 26, 27; Ralph Fuchs to WR, June 28, 1934; interviews, Beisman, Blair, Gross, Hanke, Hocker, Margolin, Peper, Vogt; Cathay, *Recollections*.

25. Interviews, Blair, Greensfelder, Gross, Hanke, Hocker, Margolin, Peper; *see* Ralph Fuchs to WR, June 25, 1933.

26. "Lawyers' Day Celebration Now in Full Swing on Campus," *Washington University Student Life*, April 24, 1931, Rutledge Papers; interviews, Broderick, M. A. Brown, Chused, Freeze, Gross, Hanke, Kenton, Margolin, Shampaine, Vogt, Wussler.

27. Interview, Gross.

28. Graf A. Boepple (1931) to WR, Feb. 18, 1939; interviews, Beisman, Blair, Broderick, Chused, Crawley, Freedman, Greensfelder, Hanke, Margolin, Muldoon, Newman, Shampaine, Vogt, Waltuch.

29. Interviews, Campbell, Crawley, Kenton, Lewin, Waltuch. *Contra* Muldoon, Wolf.

30. Walter G. Stillwell to WR, May 7, 1930; interviews, Arbetman, Beisman, Blair, Broderick, Campbell, Crawley, Freedman, Gross, Hanke, Hocker, Lewin, Margolin, Peper, Strauss, Vogt, Waltuch, Wussler. *Contra* Muldoon.

31. Harry Jones to WR, Feb. 13, 1943; interviews, Bridell, Campbell, Gross, Hanke, Kenton, Newman, Shampaine, Vogt.

32. Interviews, Campbell, Freeze, Shampaine, Waltuch.

33. Interviews, Arbetman, Beisman, Blair, Broderick, Campbell, Chused, Freedman, Freeze, Greensfelder, Gross, Hanke, Hocker, Kenton, Klene, Lewin, Newman, Peper, Shampaine, Vogt, Waltuch, Wolf, Wussler.

34. Graf A. Boepple (1931) to WR, Feb. 18, 1939; interviews, Crawley, Hocker, Margolin, Shampaine, Strauss.

35. Morrow, *Washington University in St. Louis*, 146–48, 151, 308–9, 354; Fuchs, "Law School in Transition," 11.

36. Brookings, *Education for Political Leadership*; Morrow, *Washington University in St. Louis*, 354–55 (citing Robert S. Brookings to Ralph Fuchs, June 18, 1927 (emphasis in original)); Worner, "The Public Career of Herbert Spencer Hadley," 344–47 (quoting *Gazette* (Emporia, Kan.), Dec. 3, 1927); Carrington, "Hail! Langdell!," 695.

37. WR to Edward R. Schauffler, April 9, 1940; WR to Emmet Ray Feighner, March 14, 1939; Fuchs, "Law School in Transition," 12; Morrow, *Washington University in St. Louis*, 267; interviews, Chused, Gross, Hanke, Margolin; two typewritten listings included with WU Faculty Minutes, one titled "Deans in the Law School" (from the "Office of the Chancellor," dated "December 6, 1938") and the other titled "Law School Deans" (undated), both showing William G. Hale having resigned as dean as of "June 30, 1930"; unidentified newspaper clipping, "Dean of Law School, Washington U., Quits, William G. Hale Said to Have Been Disappointed in Budget Allotment," April 16, 1930, Rutledge Papers; William G. Hale to George R. Throop, March 15, 1930; George R. Throop to William G. Hale, March 18, 1930. All letters to and from George R. Throop in this chapter are found in the Chancellor's Papers, Archives, John M. Olin Library, Washington University, unless otherwise indicated.

38. Worner, "Hadley," 345; Morrow, *Washington University in St. Louis*, 144, 267; Fuchs, "Law School in Transition," 12–13; interview, Morrow; George R. Throop to William G. Hale, Feb. 25, 1930; George R. Throop to WR, May 1, 1930; WR to George R. Throop, May 2, 1930; handwritten listing, "Law School Deans"; *see, e.g.*, Norman Bierman to WR, May 1, 1930, Julian K. Glasgow to WR, May 1, 1930, W. A. Kelly to WR, May 4, 1930; George R. Throop to WR, May 25, 1931; George R. Throop to WR, May 31, 1931; WR to George R. Throop, June 5, 1931; Alberta Lawrence, *Who Was Who among English and European Authors*, 1:425. Professor Philip Mechem also left at this time for Iowa but was replaced by Assistant Professor Israel Treiman. *Compare* Bulletin of Washington University, St. Louis, *Catalogue of the School of Law*, April 20, 1930, 7 (Mechem), *with* Bulletin of Washington University, St. Louis, *Catalogue of the School of Law*, March 10, 1931, 7 (Treiman).

39. Fuchs, "Law School in Transition," 10; Karen Baker to author, Oct. 2, 1996; Tyrrell Williams to George R. Throop, April 23, 1930; C.J. Hilkey to Tyrrell Williams, Dec. 12, 1930; Tyrrell Williams to George R. Throop, Dec. 15, 1930; WR to Willard Pedrick, Oct. 7, 1940; WR to Phil Mechem, March 10, 1931; Philip von Frech to WR, June 5, 1931; Sept. 30, 1931.

40. Petition of senior class of 1931 to board of directors of Washington University, April 24, 1931 (showing thirty-four signatures from a class of forty-two listed in Bulletin of Washington University, St. Louis, *Catalogue of the School of Law*, March 10, 1931, 38); interviews, Blair, Gross, Hanke, Margolin, Strauss; Law School Faculty Minutes, May 31, 1927; Fuchs, "Law School in Transition," 12–13; Karen Baker to author, Oct. 2, 1996.

41. Washington University, the School of Law, Assembly Lectures, Fall Semester Series, "The Law, the Sciences and Society" (nine programs on subjects including scientific method, sociology, psychiatry, 1930), Spring Semester Series, "The Law and Modern

Business" (thirteen programs on "the borderland between law and economics," 1931); WU Faculty Minutes, Sept. 18, 1930; Bulletin of Washington University, St. Louis, *Catalogue of the School of Law*, March 10, 1931, 6-7, 38-40; *see* Bulletin of Washington University, St. Louis, *Catalogue of the School of Law*, April 20, 1930, 6-7; unidentified newspaper clipping, "Law Class Meets, Draws up Petition to Administration, No Real Choice of Courses, Middle Lawyers Aver, Four Courses Dropped, Second Year Class Asks for More Professors in Petition," undated; George R. Throop to WR, May 25, 1931; Herbert S. Hadley to William G. Hale, March 8, 1927 (telegram), Chancellor's Papers; William G. Hale to Herbert S. Hadley, March 9, 1927 (telegram), Chancellor's Papers.

42. Unidentified newspaper clipping, "Person Triumphs despite Dry Bolt," undated [1930]; WR to Philip Mechem, March 10, 1931; interview, N. Rutledge.

43. Dr. Mary C. Mackin to WR, April 18, 1927; Dr. R. A. Morter to WR, July 15, 20, 23, and 27, 1935; Mrs. William H. Knapp to WR, July 25, 1935; Dr. R. A. Master to WR, July 15, 20, 1935; WR to Robert L. Stearns, June 30, 1936; interview, Neal Rutledge.

44. Fuchs, "Law School in Transition," 15; WU Faculty Minutes, Feb. 11, 1929, March 27, 1934; WR to Edward R. Schauffler, April 9, 1940.

45. In 1928-29 legal ethics was a "course of five lectures in alternate years" required of second- and third-year students. Bulletin of Washington University, St. Louis, *Catalogue of the School of Law*, April 20, 1928, 24. Legal ethics was omitted from the curriculum until the 1933-34 school year, when Rutledge offered a required course in the first year, for two hours a week in the second semester, entitled "Organization and Ethics of the Bench and Bar." Bulletin of Washington University, St. Louis, *Catalogue of the School of Law*, April 1, 1933, 20. Thereafter, that course was renamed "Introduction to Law" and expanded to three hours a week in the first semester, taught by Rutledge and other professors. Bulletin of Washington University, St. Louis, *Catalogue of the School of Law*, April 1, 1934, 22. One student who described his views at the time initially believed that learning legal ethics in the first year put "the cart . . . before the horse," but later, in his "rear view mirror," saw "that it was the most important class of the entire three years." Interview, Freeze; WU Faculty Minutes, Jan. 9, 1933.

46. Law School Faculty Minutes, Sept. 28, 1932, April 19, May 17, and June 3, 1933, May 27, 1935; George R. Throop to WR, June 16, 1931; *see* William G. Hale to WR, July 25, 1930, Sept. 3, 1930; William G. Hale to E. M. Grossman, Sept. 3, 1930; Frank J. Bruno to WR, July 16, 1935.

CHAPTER FIVE

1. Interview, N. Rutledge; Public Question Club Collection, box 3, Record Book, 1928-29, 57, PQ Club Records; Emily Ann O'Neil, *Globe-Democrat* (St. Louis), Tempo Roto Magazine, Jan. 21, 1951, p. 5; Stadler, "Manuscripts"; statement of purpose, Public Question Club, undated, *quoted in* Public Question Club, *Program: 50th Anniversary Celebration & Reunion*, April 3, 1953, box 4 (unpaginated), PQ Club Records.

2. Statement of purpose, Public Question Club; Public Question Club, Secretary's Reports for 1930-31, 1931-32, 1932-33, box 3, scrapbook 3, PQ Club Records; Wiley Rutledge, Notes, "Intercollegiate Athletics—Inimical to Higher Education and Should Be Abolished," undated; O'Neil, *Globe-Democrat* (St. Louis), Tempo Roto Magazine, Jan. 21, 1951, 5; interviews, Peper, Martin.

3. WR to Annabel Rutledge, "Sunday night" [Sept. 12, 1926]; Ryland Knight to WR, Nov. 16, 1928; Ryland Knight to WR, May 2 and 8, 1930.

4. Carlos F. Hurd, "Agnostic in Forum on Religion with Catholic, Protestant, Jew; Dar-

row Says There Is No Evidence of Order in World," *St. Louis Post Dispatch*, May 21, 1931, Rutledge Papers; Albert Einstein, "Cosmic Religion," unidentified newspaper clipping, Rutledge Papers; "Urges World Creeds to Debunk Religion; Maharajah Gaekwar of Baroda Is Opening Speaker at Chicago Conference," Associated Press, Aug. 23, 1933, unidentified newspaper, Rutledge Papers; *St. Louis Post-Dispatch*, Jan. 23, 1933, part 1, p. 8A, col. 2; WR notes on Harry Elmer Barnes, *Science vs. Religion*; WR notes on Whitehead, *Science and the Modern World*; Wiley Rutledge, "What Is Left of Religion? Science Offers No Evidence of Immortality or God," Jan. 30, 1929, box 3, record book, 1929–30, pp. 21, 34, PQ Club Records. At the same meeting, Branch Rickey gave a speech entitled "The Faith of Our Fathers" and Frank Bruno addressed the question "Is there a Reconciliation?" *Id. See also* Wiley Rutledge, "Modern Scientific Theory: A Triumph of Rationalism," March 26, 1931, box 3, record book, 1930–31, pp. 24, 58, PQ Club Records; Wiley Rutledge, undated, unidentified notes of speech, "Religion & Social Progress."

5. "Has Man a Free Will?," Public Question Club Subjects Discussed during 1928–29; "What Makes Right and Wrong?," Public Question Club Subjects Discussed during 1928–29; "Christian Science," Public Question Club Secretary's Report for 1929–30; "What Is Left of Religion?," Public Question Club Secretary's Report for 1929–30; "Were You There When They Crucified My Lord?," Public Question Club Secretary's Report for 1930–31; "Is Philosophy a Substitute for Religion?," Public Question Club Secretary's Report for 1930–31; "The Essence of Religion," Public Question Club Secretary's Report for 1931–32; "The Golden Rule," Public Question Club Secretary's Report for 1932–33; "The Future of the Church," Public Question Club Secretary's Report for 1933–34; "Is there a Supreme Being?," Public Question Club Secretary's Report for 1933–34; "Christianity," Public Question Club Secretary's Report for 1934–35 (all in box 3, scrapbook 3, PQ Club Records).

6. *See* note 5.

7. *See* note 5.

8. *See* note 4.

9. Rutledge, undated, unidentified notes of speech, "Religion & Social Progress."

10. Lyttle, *Freedom Moves West*, 243–58.

11. Lyttle, *Freedom Moves West*, 255–56.

12. Interview, N. Rutledge; David Robinson, *The Unitarians and the Universalists*, 244–45.

13. Interviews, J. K. Mann, M. L. (Rutledge) Needels, J. A. (Rutledge) Pollitt, N. Rutledge; David W. Brown, *When Strangers Cooperate* 85; Charles Reagan Wilson, "Manners"; Harper, *Justice Rutledge and the Bright Constellation*, 11; record book, 1929–30, box 3, 53, PQ Club Records; Secretary's Report for 1929–30, box 3, scrapbook 3, PQ Club Records.

14. Interview, N. Rutledge; *Dred Scott v. Sandford*, 60 U.S. (19 How.) 393 (1857).

15. Interview, N. Rutledge; Morrow, *Washington University in St. Louis*, 463–71; *see* "Gift of $15,000.00 Given Up," *Kansas City Times*, Oct. 31, 1947, Rutledge Papers; "St. Louis U. Gets Sum Washington Refused," unidentified newspaper article, Rutledge Papers; Robert E. Rosenwald (class of 1930) to Arthur Compton, Oct. 31, 1947, Rosenwald Papers; WR to Robert E. Rosenwald, Nov. 26, 1947, Rosenwald Papers.

16. Rutledge, "The Varied Carols I Hear," 77 (address delivered Oct. 18, 1940); WR to Merle Miller, Sept. 22, 1941; WR to Frank F. Messer, Nov. 27, 1943; WR to Joseph Klamon, April 24, 1944; WR to Henry Weihofen, March 14, 1940; WR to Clarence Morris, Oct. 29, 1935; WR to Ralph R. Neuhoff, Nov. 24, 1937; WR to Mason Ladd, Oct. 3, 1939.

17. Wm. Draper Lewis to WR, April 20, 1928; Henry S. Caulfield to WR, Sept. 26,

1930; WR to Mrs. E. M. Grossman, June 12, 1935; Mrs. E. M. Grossman to WR, Aug. 27, 1936; Richard C. Bland to WR, May 13, 1932; *see* WR to Jacob Billikopf, Oct. 18, 1948 (WR Missouri); interview, Wechsler; "Criminal Code Reform in Missouri 'Black,' Dean Rutledge of Washington U. So Characterizes Legislature's Failure to Correct Abuses; Draws Lesson from Hauptmann Trial; In Address Suggests Means for Elimination of the 'Unconscionable Lawyer,'" undated article [ca. 1934], *St. Louis Post-Dispatch*, Rutledge Papers; "Favors Letting Bar Pass on Admissions, Dean Rutledge Says "18th Century Legislatures" Block Judicial Reform," undated, unidentified newspaper article [ca. 1935], Rutledge Papers; Brant, "Mr. Justice Rutledge," 25 *Ind. L. J.* 429 (1950), 35 *Iowa L. Rev.* 550 (1950).

18. "Law Dean Has Plan to Fight Racketeer Evil," *St. Louis Star*, Nov. 29, 1930, 1, Rutledge Papers; draft text of WR proposal for dealing with "public enemies," 4, 7.

19. Draft text of WR proposal for dealing with "public enemies," 6, 8, 9; "Law Dean Has Plan," *St. Louis Star*, Nov. 29, 1930, 1.

20. Wiley Rutledge, "Child Labor and the Supreme Court," *St. Louis Post-Dispatch*, Nov. 20, 1933, part 2, p. 2B, col. 4; editorial, *St. Louis Post-Dispatch*, May 2, 1933, part 3, p. 2C, col. 2.

21. Clyde C. Beck to WR, May 18, 1933; Ralph Coglan to WR, May 16, 1933; Courtenay Dinwiddie to WR, Nov. 13, 1933; WR to Courtenay Dinwiddie, Nov. 16, 1933; Anna Day (Mrs. D. C.) Chastain to WR, Jan. 3, 1935; WR to Mrs. D. C. Chastain, Jan. 8, 1935; Wiley Rutledge, "The Child Labor Amendment," radio address over station KWK, St. Louis, Jan. 25, 1935; "Dean Rutledge on Child Labor," *St. Louis Post-Dispatch*, May 17, 1933, part 3, p. 2C, col. 3.

22. Rutledge, "The Federal Government and Child Labor."

23. Rutledge, "The Federal Government and Child Labor," 556; "U.S. Child Labor Law Opposition Scored by Dean Rutledge; Attack Centered on Clarence Martin, American Bar Association Head," unidentified newspaper article, May 17, 1933, Rutledge Papers; *St. Louis Post-Dispatch*, May 17, 1933, part 3, p. 2C, col. 3; *Hammer v. Dagenhart*, 247 U.S. 251 (1918) (commerce power); *Bailey v. Drexel Furniture Co.*, 259 U.S. 20 (1922) (taxing power).

24. "Child-Labor Amendment to the Constitution of the United States," Report [and Minority Report] (Washington: U.S. Gov't. Printing Office, 1924); National Child Labor Committee pamphlet, "Ratify the Child Labor Amendment."

25. Arizona, Arkansas, California, Colorado, Montana, Wisconsin. *Id.*

26. Rutledge, "Child Labor and the Supreme Court"; WR and Alphonse G. Eberle to "The Honorable . . . ," Nov. 27, 1933 (form letter to Missouri state senators at Jefferson City, Mo.); Rutledge, "The Federal Government and Child Labor," 556, 567.

27. Illinois, Michigan, New Hampshire, New Jersey, North Dakota, Ohio, Oklahoma, Oregon, Washington. National Child Labor Committee pamphlet.

28. North Dakota, Ohio, Oregon, Washington. "Status of Child Labor Amendment," *Literary Digest* (date and author unknown), Rutledge Papers; National Child Labor Committee pamphlet.

29. *Id.*

30. Rutledge, "The Federal Government and Child Labor," 555 n. 1.

31. Wiley Rutledge, "Child Labor and the Supreme Court"; Rutledge, "The Federal Government and Child Labor," 555 n. 1; *Panama Refining Co. v. Ryan*, 293 U.S. 388 (1935); *Schechter Poultry Corp. v. United States*, 295 U.S. 495 (1935).

32. *See* Nicholas Murray Butler to editor of *New York Times*, Dec. 27, 1933 (quoting ABA resolution of August 30, 1933, opposing child labor amendment); Rutledge, "The Federal Government and Child Labor," 556.

33. *See, e.g.*, WR to Michael Kinney, Dec. 20, 1933; WR and Alphonse G. Eberle to "The Honorable . . . ," Nov. 27, 1933 (form letter to Missouri state senators at Jefferson City, Mo.).

34. Wiley Rutledge, "Memorandum in Re Child Labor Amendment," undated (transmitted by WR to Sen. Michael Kinney, Dec. 20, 1933).

35. Rutledge, "Child Labor and the Supreme Court"; League Bulletin, Nov. 11, 1933; W. W. Burke to WR, Dec. 12, 1933; undated "Tentative List of Speakers at Child Labor Hearing."

36. Rutledge, "The Federal Government and Child Labor," 556–57.

37. Rutledge, "The Federal Government and Child Labor," 557–58.

38. Rutledge, "The Federal Government and Child Labor," 567; Rutledge, "The Child Labor Amendment," 3.

39. Rutledge, "The Federal Government and Child Labor," 568; WR and Alphonse G. Eberle to "The Honorable . . ." (Nov. 27, 1933) (form letter to Missouri state senators at Jefferson City, Mo.); editorial, *St. Louis Post-Dispatch*, May 2, 1933, Part 3, p. 2C, col. 2; Rutledge, "The Child Labor Amendment," 3

40. Rutledge, "The Federal Government and Child Labor," 561–62, 570; U.S. Const., Art. I, Sec. 8, cl. 1.

41. Bernard C. Gavit to WR, Dec. 5, 1933; *see* WR and Alphonse G. Eberle to "The Honorable . . . ," Nov. 27, 1933 (form letter to Missouri state senators at Jefferson City, Mo.); Nicholas Murray Butler to Rabbi Ferdinand M. Isserman, Dec. 29, 1933.

42. WR to Michael Kinney, Dec. 20, 1933; Rutledge, "The Child Labor Amendment," 1–3.

43. WR to Mrs. D. C. Chastain, Jan. 8, 1935.

44. *United States v. Darby Lumber Co.*, 312 U.S. 100 (1941); *Hammer v. Dagenhart*, 247 U.S. 251, 277 (1918) (Holmes, J., dissenting); *compare* Rutledge, "The Federal Government and Child Labor," 562–64, *with Darby*, 312 U.S. at 115–17 (Stone, J.).

45. Rutledge, "The Federal Government and Child Labor," 558, 562, 569–71; Rutledge, "The Child Labor Amendment," 1.

46. Robert Stevens, "Two Cheers for 1870," 431–32, 454–55.

47. Boyd, *The ABA's First Section*, 16–17 (quoting Walter George Smith, Esq.).

48. Robert Stevens, "Two Cheers for 1870," 461; Boyd, *The ABA's First Section*, 24.

49. Robert Stevens, "Two Cheers for 1870," 503; Boyd, *The ABA's First Section*, 33.

50. WR to Tyrrell Williams, April 1, 1940; WR to Jacob Lashly, April 8, 1940; *see* WR to Ralph R. Neuhoff, Sept. 19, 1938.

51. Wiley Rutledge, "The Future of the Interstate Power Holding Company," *St. Louis Post-Dispatch*, May 5, 1935, p. 1H, col. 3; WR to Edward G. Jennings, Nov. 22, 1938; WR to Charles Nagel, May 8, 1935, Nagel Papers.

52. "An Interesting Program to Be Given Wednesday Eve., October 21, 1931, Dean Wiley B. Rutledge, Jr., Auspices, United Hebrew Temple Man's Club."

53. "Seminar on Law In Contemporary Society, in Appreciation of the Distinguished Service of Associate Justice Oliver Wendell Holmes on the Occasion of His 91st Birthday, March 8, 1932, Arranged by the St. Louis Social Justice Commission."

54. "Criminal Code Reform in Missouri 'Black,'" *St. Louis Post-Dispatch*, ca. 1934, Rutledge Papers.

55. E. H. Sager to Dean Debatin, Oct. 22, 1934, Rutledge Papers; WR handwritten notes on "Workmen's Compensation."

56. WR handwritten notes on "'Are the Schools Preparing for Intelligent, Dynamic Citizenship?' (Before Phi Delta Kappa at Y.M.C.A. Jan. 19, 1935)."

57. WR typed notes on "'Present Foreign Policy & Peace.' Tuesday Club 4/16/35."

58. "Favors Bar Pass on Admissions," unidentified newspaper article [ca. 1935], Rutledge Papers.

59. Transcript of radio dialogue between Wiley Rutledge and Roland G. Usher, station KMOX, St. Louis, May 12, 1935, Rutledge Papers; *St. Louis Post-Dispatch*, March 28, 1935, sec. 2, p. 1B, col. 2; Wiley Rutledge, notes for "Present Foreign Policy & Peace," speech before the Tuesday Club, April 16, 1935, 9; WR to William H. Bartley, Oct. 17 and 24, 1940; WR to A. J. Freund, Feb. 23. 1939.

60. Morrow, *Washington University in St. Louis*, 361–62; WR to George R. Throop, Feb. 16, 1933; George R. Throop to WR, June 3, 1935; WR to Charles Nagel, undated [1935]; WR to Emmet Glore, March 14, 1939; WR to William G. Hale, Oct. 26, 1935.

61. Eugene A. Gilmore to WR, May 24, 1935.

62. Carrington and King, "Law and the Wisconsin Idea," 336–37; Eugene A. Gilmore to Herschel W. Arant, Dec. 29, 1934; Herschel W. Arant to Eugene A. Gilmore, Jan. 6, 1934 [*recte* 1935]; Herschel W. Arant to Eugene A. Gilmore, Feb. 14, 1935; Eugene A. Gilmore to E. Blythe Stason, May 24, 1935; E. Blythe Stason to Eugene A. Gilmore, May 30, 1935; Eugene A. Gilmore to Charles T. McCormick, July 13, 1934; Charles T. McCormick to Eugene A. Gilmore, March 5, 1935; Roscoe Pound to Eugene A. Gilmore, March 11, 1935; Harold M. Stephens to Eugene A. Gilmore, March 23, 1935; Eugene A. Gilmore to Roscoe Pound, April 11, 1935; Roscoe Pound to Eugene A. Gilmore, April 25, 1935; Harold M. Stephens to Eugene A. Gilmore, June 7, 1935 (all in Gilmore Papers).

63. List of "Applications and Recommendations," file 65, box 13, 1934–35, Gilmore Papers; Armstrong, *A Century of Service*, 193, 204; Eugene A. Gilmore to Philip Mechem, June 8, 1935 (telegram), Gilmore Papers; Philip Mechem to Eugene A. Gilmore, June 8, 1935 (telegram), Gilmore Papers; E. Blythe Stason to Eugene A. Gilmore, May 16, 1935, Gilmore Papers; Eugene A. Gilmore to E. Blythe Stason, May 25, 1935, Gilmore Papers; *The AALS Directory of Law Teachers* 116 (1942).

64. WR to Eugene A. Gilmore, June 10, 1935; WR to Eugene A. Gilmore, June 22, 1935 (telegram); George R. Throop to WR, June 25, 1935 (night letter).

65. WR to George R. Throop, June 24, 1935.

66. WR to Charles Nagel, undated [1935] (replying to Nagel's letter of July 3, 1935); WR to William G. Hale, Oct. 26, 1935; WR to Ralph R. Neuhoff, Nov. 20, 1935; WR to Emmett Ray Feighner, Feb. 25, 1939; *see* WR to J. A. Wigginton, March 8, 1939.

67. Carrington and King, "Law and the Wisconsin Idea," 317, 323, 325, 326, 328–29, 334–36 (quoting Gilmore, "Some Criticisms of Legal Education," 230); *see* Boyd, *The ABA's First Section*, 26.

68. *See* WR to Robert E. Rosenwald (class of 1930), Jan. 9, 1939.

69. WR to Ernst W. Puttkammer, Oct. 23, 1936; WR to William G. Hale, Oct. 26, 1935; interview, Morrow.

70. Therese M. Loeb to WR, July 1, 1935.

71. Sam Elson to WR, July 2, 1935.

72. Ralph F. Fuchs to WR, June 28, 1935.

CHAPTER SIX

1. Ryland Knight to WR and Annabel Rutledge, Nov. 16. 1928; W. B. Parsons to WR, Jan. 4, 1929; William Draper Lewis to WR, April 20, 1928; Joseph H. Beale to WR, April 24, 1928.

2. WR to Joseph H. Beale, June 4, 1928.

3. WR to Emmet Glore, Oct. 19, 1940.

4. Rutledge, "Legal Personality"; Warren, *Corporate Advantages without Incorporation*, 1, 11–13; Kalman, *Legal Realism at Yale*, 49; *see* Sutherland, *The Law at Harvard*, 217.

5. Warren, *Corporate Advantages without Incorporation*, 11, 13.

6. University of Colorado, *Bulletins, School of Law*, 1921–22, 280; 1925–26, 259; Bulletins of Washington University, St. Louis, *Catalogues of the School of Law*, March 10, 1927, 18, April 20, 1928, 22, April 20, 1929, 25, April 20, 1930, 28, March 10, 1931, 26, March 20, 1932, 24, April 1, 1933, 22, April 1, 1934, 24; Rutledge, "Legal Personality," 2, 31.

7. Warren, *Corporate Advantages without Incorporation*, 665–67.

8. *Id.*

9. Rutledge, "Legal Personality," 31.

10. Rutledge, "Legal Personality," 27 nn. 86, 88, 28 n. 89, 31 nn. 97, 99 (citing Pound, *The Spirit of the Common Law*).

11. Carrington, "Law as 'The Common Thoughts of Men,'" 523–25, 528, 532; Cooley, *Constitutional Limitations*, 371–79.

12. Horwitz, *The Transformation of American Law, 1870-1960*, 47–51, 109–10, 125, 127–28, 131–32, 138–39, 140–42; Holmes, "The Path of the Law"; White, *Social Thought in America*, 14.

13. Sutherland, *The Law at Harvard*, 200–204, 238; Carrington, "The Missionary Diocese of Chicago," 507, 509; Carrington, "Hail! Langdell!," 724 & n. 169, 726, 727; Carrington, "William Gardiner Hammond and the Lieber Revival," 2151 (citing Gray, *The Nature and Sources of the Law*, 222–34); Pound, *The Spirit of the Common Law*, 1, 95–96, 175–76; *see generally* Sayre, *The Life of Roscoe Pound*; Wigdor, *Roscoe Pound* 189–90 (judicial legislation), 199 (social engineering), 204 (dean), 231–32 (common law) (1974).

14. Pound, *The Spirit of the Common Law*, 129–30, 135–36, 185–89, 195, 205; Pound, "Mechanical Jurisprudence," 609–10.

15. Rutledge, "Legal Personality," 31 & n. 97.

16. W. B. Rutledge grade report, University of Wisconsin (1913–14), WR Wisconsin; Wiley Blount Rutledge Jr., grade report, Maryville College, 1910–13, WR Maryville; J. L. Harman to WR, June 29, 1939; J. Murray Hill to WR, July 8, 1939; WR to J. L. Harman, July 11, 1939; WR to Leon Henderson, Sept. 22, 1939; WR to Edward R. Schauffler, April 9, 1940.

17. The private corporations casebook covered offenses under the Sherman Act; there was no separate offering in trade regulation. Warren, *Select Cases on Private Corporations*, 514–97; *see* University of Colorado, *Bulletins, School of Law*, 1920–21, 262–66, 1921–22, 277–80, 1922–23, 314–17, 1924–25, 241–43, 1925–26, 257–59.

18. Latty and Frampton, *Basic Business Associations*, xvii; Bryant Smith, "Legal Personality," 288; W. Jethro Brown, "The Personality of the Corporation and the State," 370; Henry Winslow Williams, "An Inquiry into the Nature and Law of Corporations," 1, 2, 11; John P. Davis, "The Nature of Corporations," 287 & n. 5; *Dartmouth Coll. v. Woodward*, 17 (4 Wheat.) U.S. 518, 636 (1819) (Marshall, C.J.); *id.* at 666, 667 (opinion of Story, J.).

19. *Dartmouth Coll. v. Woodward*, 17 (4 Wheat.) U.S. at 636; Warren, *Corporate Advantages without Incorporation*, 10 (quoting Blackstone, *Commentaries on the Laws of England*, book I, 467 ("These artificial persons are called . . . corporations.")); Henry Winslow Williams, "An Inquiry into the Nature and Law of Corporations," 141 ("A corporation is an artificial person."); *Bank of Augusta v. Earle*, 38 U.S. (13 Pet.) 519, 588–89, 596 (1839). Others have called the corporation an "imaginary" or "fictitious" person. *See*

Dewey, "The Historic Background of Corporate Legal Personality," 665–66; Arthur W. Machen Jr., "Corporate Personality," 255–56. Something artificial, of course, is not necessarily imaginary or fictitious. But theorists variously have used all three adjectives in efforts to analogize corporate "persons" to individual human beings when that comparison was useful for analyzing legal duties and rights. *See* Arthur W. Machen Jr., "Corporate Personality," 255–56.

20. Horwitz, *The Transformation of American Law, 1870–1960*, 72–73; *Bank of Augusta v. Earle*; Berle and Means, *The Modern Corporation and Private Property*, 10, 73, 128; *Dartmouth Coll. v. Woodward*, 17 (4 Wheat.) U.S. at 638, 643–44, 650–54 (finding contract among state, Dartmouth's donors, and trustees).

21. Horwitz, *The Transformation of American Law, 1870–1960*, 76, 83; *see, e.g., People v. North River Sugar Refining Co.*, 3 N.Y. Supp. 401, 408 (1889); *State v. Standard Oil Co.*, 30 N.E. 279 (Ohio 1892).

22. *People v. North River Sugar Refining Co.*, 3 N.Y. Supp. at 408; *see State v. Standard Oil Co.*, 30 N.E. at 290 (holding that delegation of control and management to Standard Oil Trust subjected defendant "to a control inconsistent with its character as a corporation"); *Cent. R.R. Co. v. Collins*, 40 Ga. 582 (1869) (holding that corporate combination strayed beyond purposes authorized in charters of constituent companies); *Whittenton Mills v. Upton*, 10 Mass. (Gray) 582 (1858) (holding that authority delegated to joint enterprise unlawfully diluted shareholder authority in constituent companies).

23. Horwitz, *The Transformation of American Law, 1870–1960*, 83–84; Rutledge, "Significant Trends in Modern Incorporation Statutes," 22 *Wash. U. L. Q.* 307–8, 3 *U. Pitt. L. Rev.* 276–77.

24. *See* Rutledge, "Significant Trends in Modern Incorporation Statutes," 22 *Wash U. L. Q.* 308, 3 *U. Pitt L. Rev.* 277.

25. Horwitz, *The Transformation of American Law, 1870–1960*, 87–89; Glad, *McKinley, Bryan, and the People*, 39–40; Hofstadter, "The Meaning of the Progressive Movement," 12–14.

26. 118 U.S. 394 (1886). The Court's entire opinion read as follows: "The Court does not wish to hear argument on the question whether the provision in the Fourteenth Amendment to the Constitution, which forbids a State to deny to any person within its jurisdiction the equal protection of the laws, applies to these corporations. We are all of the opinion that it does." *Id.* at 396. Professor Morton J. Horwitz has noted from the briefs of counsel and the lower courts' opinions that the Supreme Court apparently premised *Santa Clara v. Southern Pacific Railroad* not on a perception that corporations had an intrinsically independent status as "person" but on the "veil-piercing" view that the corporation derived its constitutional rights from those of its individual shareholder "persons." Horwitz, *The Transformation of American Law, 1870–1960*, 67, 69–70, 105–6.

27. *Hale v. Henkel*, 201 U.S. 43, 76 (1906); *id.* at 78 (Harlan J., concurring). In the same case, however, the Court—after characterizing the corporation as "a creature of the state" subject to investigation into how its "franchise[] had been employed"—concluded that the corporation was not a "person" entitled under the Fifth Amendment to protection against self-incrimination. *Id.* at 74, 75. *See* Horwitz, *The Transformation of American Law, 1870–1960*, 73.

28. Derived from the German legal theorist Otto Gierke, and popularized in America—beginning around 1900—through writings of the English legal historian Frederic Maitland, Professor Ernst Freund of the University of Chicago, and others, this theory characterized the corporation not as an artificial creature of the state but as a natural entity—

a "living organism"—that typically existed *before* the state's permission to operate, not as a result of it. Horwitz, *The Transformation of American Law, 1870-1960,* 71-72, 75, 100-107; Machen, "Corporate Personality," 256, 260, 262; Dewey, "The Historic Background of Corporate Legal Personality," 658 (quoting Gierke, *Political Theories of the Middle Age,* xxvi (translated and prefaced by Maitland)); W. Jethro Brown, "The Personality of the Corporation and the State," 369-71; Raymond, "The Genesis of the Corporation," 363.

29. Horwitz, *The Transformation of American Law, 1870-1960,* 104-5.

30. Woodrow Wilson, Annual Address, American Bar Association, Chattanooga, Tenn., 1910, *quoted in* Ripley, *Main Street and Wall Street,* 5-6; Arthur Meier Schlesinger, *The Rise of Modern America 1865-1951,* 217.

31. Horwitz, *The Transformation of American Law, 1870-1960,* 66; *Louis K. Liggett Co. v. Lee,* 288 U.S. 517, 541, 564-67 (1933) (Brandeis, J., dissenting in part).

32. Rutledge, "Cases and Materials on Business Associations," 1109-12 (reviewing book by Laylin K. James); *see* Kalman, *Legal Realism at Yale,* 84-86.

33. Wiley Rutledge, *Private Corporations* (mimeographed typewritten draft), Rutledge Papers. From a student's notes of Wiley's courses at Iowa, from correspondence during Wiley's first fall at Iowa, and from the dates of the most recently cited cases and articles, we can reasonably infer that virtually all these materials had been available for several years of teaching at Washington University. *See* D. Berkeley Smith (State University of Iowa College of Law class of 1937), class notes in "Business Associations" and "Business Organization" (hereafter "Class Notes") (a complete set of these notes is in the author's possession); Clarence Morris to WR, Oct. 14, 1935; WR to Clarence Morris, Oct. 16, 1935. Aside from the citations to a Supreme Court case and to Senate hearing testimony from 1933, and to a newspaper article and a book from 1934, the casebook contains no citations after 1932.

34. Rutledge, *Private Corporations,* part I, 2 n. 1 (quoting hearing before the Senate Committee on Banking and Currency, June 9, 1933 (statement of R. C. Leffingwell)), part I, 3 (quoting Robert S. Brookings, *The Way Forward,* 12), part II, 177; *Louis K. Liggett Co. v. Lee,* 288 U.S. at 567, 580 (Brandeis, J., dissenting in part); *see Mueller v. Oregon,* 208 U.S. 412 (1908); Horwitz, *The Transformation of American Law, 1870-1960,* 188, 209.

35. Smith, Class Notes, 1-8; Warren, *Corporate Advantages without Incorporation,* 15; *accord* Rutledge, "Legal Personality," 7.

36. Gray, *The Nature and Sources of the Law,* 27; Holland, *The Elements of Jurisprudence*; Salmond, *Jurisprudence or the Theory of the Law,* 334, 335; Bryant Smith, "Legal Personality," 283-84.

37. Rutledge, *Private Corporations,* part II, 1 ("Legal Personality. Introductory. Legal Persons and Legal Relations."); *see, e.g.,* Rutledge, *Private Corporations,* part II, 9 ("Chapter II. The Individual Human Being as a Legal Person."), 13 ("Section 2. Differentiation of the Natural Person and the Legal Person."), 62a ("Chapter III. The Institution as a Legal Person"), 126 ("Historical Evolution of the Concept [of Corporate Individuality and Continuity]. Influence of Notions of 'Natural' Personality in the Formative Period."); *see also* Smith, Class Notes (reflecting first semester class organized by reference to issues of legal personality).

38. Rutledge, *Private Corporations,* part II, 12, 17-21, 25-31, 50-51.

39. Smith, Class Notes, part 1, 92.

40. Interview, Hellwege; Smith, Class Notes, part II, 20; Rutledge, *Private Corporations,* part II, 162.

41. Rutledge wrote, for example, about "Variety in Legal Status of Human Beings at

Common Law," Rutledge, *Private Corporations*, part II, 20; "the conception of the corporation sole" (single shareholder), part II, 44; "The Relation of Institutional to Individual Legal Personality," part II, 67; "The Institution as a Social Process," part II, 90; "Psychological Attitudes Created by the Institutional Process," part II, 93; limited liability, part II, 139; "Historical Evolution of the Concepts of 'Capital' and 'Share,'" part II, 139; proposals for federal incorporation statutes, part II, 162; and "completeness of incorporation" (de jure and de facto corporations), part II, 216. Other Rutledge essays included "The 'Concession Theory' of Institutional Legal Status," Rutledge, *Private Corporations*, part II, 96; "Continuity of the Associate Relation," part II, 111; "Historical Evolution of the Concept [of Incorporation]. Influence of Notions of 'Natural' Personality in the Formative Period," part II, 126; "The Relation of Control or Power of Representation to Interest," part II, 135; "Historical. Manifestation of Governmental Authority [Over Incorporation]," part II, 158; "General Incorporation Laws. Historical," part II, 177.

42. *E.g.*, Dowdall, *Estatification*, 18; McDougall, *The Group Mind*, 16, 31, 33, 95; Maciver, *Community*, 77; James, *Varieties of Religious Experience*, 334; Freund, *The Legal Nature of Corporations*, 20, 30, 141, 143; Meyer, "Fascism, Bolshevism and Socialism"; Underhill Moore, "The Rational Basis of Legal Institutions" (*all quoted in* Rutledge, *Private Corporations*, 90–95).

43. *E.g.*, Rutledge, *Private Corporations*, part II, 1, 21, 24, 32, 62a, 82, 86, 89, 129, 225.

44. Robert Stevens, "Two Cheers for 1870," 470–81; *see generally* Kalman, *Legal Realism at Yale*.

45. Kalman, *Legal Realism at Yale*, 74–75, 86–87; Murphy, *Wild Bill*, 75–80.

46. *Bulletin of Yale University, the School of Law, for the Academic Year 1938–1939* (July 15, 1938); Kalman, *Legal Realism at Yale*, 86; Douglas and Shanks with Cooper, *Cases and Materials on Business Units*; Douglas and Shanks, *Cases and Materials on the Law of Management of Business Units*; Douglas and Shanks, *Cases and Materials on the Law of Financing of Business Units*. Douglas and Shanks also prepared cases and materials for a fourth, advanced course on "Corporate Reorganization." Douglas and Shanks, *Cases and Materials on the Law of Corporate Reorganization*.

47. Douglas and Shanks with Cooper, *Cases and Materials on Business Units*, iii; Douglas and Shanks, *Cases and Materials on the Law of Management of Business Units*, iv.

48. Douglas and Shanks, *Cases and Materials on the Law of Management of Business Units*, iv; Kalman, *Legal Realism at Yale*, 9, 28–29 (citing Douglas, "A Functional Approach to the Law of Business Associations").

49. Dewey, "The Historic Background of Corporate Legal Personality," 669–73; Horwitz, *The Transformation of American Law, 1870–1960*, 67, 101.

50. Smith, Class Notes, part I, 17.

51. Rutledge, *Private Corporations*, part II, 95 ("in the disposition of problems affecting the institution, the necessity is unavoidable to apply now one attitude, now another, as determined by the nature of the immediate problem which concerns our action").

52. Rutledge, "Significant Trends in Modern Incorporation Statutes," 22 *Wash. U. L. Q.* 338–39, 3 *U. Pitt. L. Rev.* 304–5.

53. Rutledge, "Significant Trends in Modern Incorporation Statutes," 22 *Wash. U. L. Q.*, 339–40, 3 *U. Pitt. L. Rev.*, 305–6.

54. WR to Clarence Morris, Oct. 16, 1935; *see* WR to E. R. Campbell, May 10, 1939.

55. Clarence Morris to WR, Oct. 28, 1935.

56. Rutledge, "Cases and Materials on Business Associations," 1110–13.

57. *E.g.*, Brant, "Mr. Justice Rutledge," 35 *Iowa L. Rev.* 552 (1950), 25 *Ind. LJ.* 431–32 (1950).

58. *E.g.*, Rutledge, "Eighty-Six: Forty-Six."

59. Commencement address of June 4, 1936, by WR at Iowa City High School.

60. Rutledge, *A Declaration of Legal Faith*; Wiley B. Rutledge, "Appendix III, Addresses and Other Writings, 1927-1949," 25 *Ind. LJ.* 565 (1950), 35 *Iowa L. Rev.* 699 (1950).

CHAPTER SEVEN

1. Federal Writers' Project of the Works Progress Administration for the State of Iowa, *The WPA Guide to 1930s Iowa*, 264; interview, Pickett.

2. Stow Persons, *The University of Iowa in the Twentieth Century: An Institutional History*, 4 (1990); Reed, *Training for the Public Profession of the Law*, 380; Perkins, "The Story of the Iowa Law School," 261-62, 266-69; Hansen, "The Early History of the College of Law, State University of Iowa," 38, 42-43, 54, 61-62; Carrington, "William Gardiner Hammond and the Lieber Revival," 2142-43; Carrington, "Hail! Langdell!," 735-36; Carrington and King, "Law and the Wisconsin Idea," 336.

3. College of Law, Reports of the Dean for the Academic Years Ending June 30, 1936, 2 (101 freshmen), June 30, 1937, 1-2 (87 freshmen), and June 30, 1938, 1-2 (98 freshmen); WR to Tyrrell Williams, Nov. 23, 1937; interviews, Schweibert, Meyer, Remley.

4. Interviews, Barker, Birch, Hellwege, Morrison, Mosier, Reed.

5. Interview, Mosier.

6. Interviews, Barker, Galloway, Metcalf, Seaton. The practice was declared unconstitutional as a denial of equal protection of the laws in *Missouri ex rel. Gaines v. Canada*, 305 U.S. 337 (1938).

7. Morello, *The Invisible Bar*, 12; Drachman, *Sisters in Law*, 16, appendix 1, 251; Hayes, "A Pioneer Iowa Law School," 108; Pettus, "The Legal Education of Women," 239, *cited in* Carrington, "William Gardiner Hammond and the Lieber Revival," 2142 & n. 36; Frost, "On Women and the Law"; interviews, Barker, P. E. Brown, Fitzgibbons, Gleysteen, Gray, Jack, McPharlin, Moeller, Pasley, Ryan, Stohr.

8. Interviews, Ahlers, Barker, Buckingham, McPharlin, Remley.

9. Interview, Barker.

10. Interview, Grant.

11. Interview, Mosier.

12. *The State University of Iowa, Catalogue Number 1935-1936, College of Law*, 271; College of Law, Report of the Dean for the Academic Year Ending June 30, 1936, 16, Iowa Dean Reports; interview, Ryan.

13. Interviews, Adler, Barker, Gray, Metcalf, Reitz Jr., Remley.

14. Interview, Wirtz; *accord* interviews, Gray, Ryan.

15. WR to Clair S. Cullenbine, Oct. 16, 1935; WR to Chester K. Wentworth, Dec. 3, 1935; WR to Ralph R. Neuhoff, Nov. 20, 1935.

16. Interview, Schweibert.

17. Interviews, Fitzgibbons, Goodenow, Heartney Jr., Johnson, Lewis, Mayer, Mitchell, Reed, Schweibert, Seaton, Shepherd, Stohr, Wirtz.

18. Interviews, Adler, Fitzgibbons, Gibbs, Goodenow, Grosenbaugh, Heartney Jr., Lewis, Noel, Reitz Jr., Rosenberg, Schwilck, Seaton, Thomas; *The State University of Iowa, Catalogue Number 1935-1936*, 277, 278.

19. Interviews, Buckingham, Fitzgibbons, Gibbs, Goodenow, Jebens, Johnson, McDermott, Stohr; *The State University of Iowa, Catalogue Number 1936-1937*, 290, 292, 294.

20. Interviews, P. E. Brown, Fitzgibbons, Grant, Jack, Johnson, McPharlin, Metcalf, Schweibert, Seaton.

21. Interviews, Adler, P. E. Brown, Dodd, Fitzgibbons, Heartney Jr., Mayer.

22. *The State University of Iowa, Catalogues Number 1935-1936*, 276-77, 278-79, *1936-1937*, 291, 293-94; College of Law, Reports of the Dean for the Academic Years Ending June 30, 1936, 8-9, June 30, 1937, 19; WR to Herschel Arant, March 4, 1937; *Des Moines Register*, March 16, 1937, p. 11, col. 7.

23. WR to Joseph A. McClain, Feb. 11, 1939; WR to Leon Green, Feb. 17, 1937. Rutledge had addressed the same concern at Washington University by recommending the appointment of a politically conservative professor to balance the more liberal flavor of the faculty at the time. WR to Albert J. Harno, March 31, 1938.

24. WR to Ralph Fuchs, Nov. 23, 1937.

25. Interviews, Fitzgibbons, Remley.

26. WR to Ora C. Gayle, Feb. 21, 1938; Givens, *All Cats Are Gray*, 57.

27. University of Michigan, *Official Publication, Vol. 40, No. 22, Law School Announcement 1938-1939*, 5, 64; *Indiana University Bulletin*, vol. 36, no. 4, *School of Law 1938-39* (March 15, 1938), 4-5, 23-26; Ohio State University, *Annual Report of the Registrar and University Examiner: Enrollment for 1939-40 (Law)*; Faculty Rosters, Ohio State University College of Law (1935-37, 1938, 1940), supplied by Linda Poe, OSU College of Law Library, to author, Feb. 14, 2000; University of Illinois, *Bulletin Vol. 35, No. 92, College of Law Announcement for 1938-1939* (July 15, 1938), 5; University of Wisconsin, *Bulletin, the Law School Announcement of Courses 1938-39*, 6; University of Minnesota, *Bulletin Vol. 39, No. 35, the Law School Announcement for the Years 1936-1938*, 4; University of Chicago, *Announcements, the Law School for the Sessions of 1938-1939*, 2; *Northwestern University Bulletin, the School of Law for the Session 1935-36*, 14-28.

28. WR to Kenneth Field, March 10, 1937; WR to Leon Green, Feb. 17, 1937.

29. WR to Kenneth Field, March 10, 1937; Ralph Fuchs to WR, July 16, 1936; College of Law, Reports of the Dean for the Academic Year Ending June 30, 1937, 3; June 30, 1936, 7; *The State University of Iowa, Catalogue Number 1936-1937*, 291; interview, Grosenbaugh.

30. Interview, Wirtz; *see* WR to Joseph A. McClain, April 15, 1939.

31. *See* WR's outline for Judicial Process (1938-39); class notes for Judicial Process from Richard C. Reed (class of 1941) (in author's possession).

32. 5 U.S. (1 Cranch) 137 (1803).

33. Interview, Reed.

34. Interview, Metcalf; *accord* interviews, Barker, P. E. Brown, Dodd, Jack, Johnson, Kean, Mayer, Moeller, Reed, Reitz Jr., Rosenberg, Stohr, Thomas.

35. Interview, Metcalf.

36. Interview, Joiner.

37. Interview, Johnson.

38. Interviews, *compare* Birch, Meyer, Noel, Reed *with* Cameron, McCarthy.

39. Report of the Dean for the Academic Year Ending June 30, 1938, 2; WR to William G. Hale, Dec. 1, 1937.

40. Interview, Johnson; Mason Ladd to W. Willard Wirtz, April 15, 1996.

41. Interview, Johnson.

42. Interview, Metcalf.

43. Interview, Joiner.

44. Interview, Johnson. Rutledge occasionally would enlist his newest colleague, Willard Wirtz, to help him think through issues that Rutledge proposed for Judicial Process,

and he invited Wirtz to class on occasion. Wirtz recalled "feeling quite inadequate about it. . . . I would realize he was finding depths to something when my inclination was to get on to the next subject." Interview, Wirtz.

45. Interviews, Barker, Dalbey, Kean, Meyer, Ryan.

46. Interviews, Birch, P. E. Brown, Gibbs, Heartney Jr., Hellwege, Johnson, Metcalf, Meyer, Mosier, Smith, Stohr.

47. Interviews, Fitzgibbons, Heartney Jr.; Matthew J. Heartney Jr. to W. Willard Wirtz, April 6, 1950.

48. Interviews, Fitzgibbons, Mosier.

49. Interview, Fitzgibbons.

50. Interview, Hellwege.

51. Interviews, Beving, Morrison, Stohr.

52. Interview, Ryan.

53. Interview, Birch.

54. Interviews, Jebens, Ryan.

55. Interviews, Cray, Hunt.

56. Interviews, Goodenow, Morrison, Mosier.

57. Interview, Mosier.

58. Interview, Elderkin.

59. Interview, Dodd.

60. Interview, Goodenow.

61. Interviews, Hellwege, Jebens, Reed, Schindler.

62. Interviews, Cunningham, Galloway, Lewis, Moyer, Pickett, Schweibert, Smith, Stevens.

63. Interviews, P. E. Brown, Morrison, Thomas.

64. Interview, McCoy.

65. Interview, Noel.

66. Interview, Remley.

67. Interview, Pasley.

68. Interviews, Morrison, Ryan.

69. Examination of January 23, 1939, in the Judicial Process.

70. Interview, Johnson.

71. Interviews, Bruner, Cameron, Dodd, Galloway, Jebens, Johnson, Reed, Remley, Rosenberg, Ryan, Schweibert, Seaton.

72. Interviews, Barker, Birch, P. E. Brown, Browne, Cunningham, Fitzgibbons, Galloway, Gibbs, Goodenow, Heartney Jr., Johnson, Lewis, McCoy, Meyer, Moeller, Ryan, Vogel.

73. Interviews, Birch, Browne, Cameron Jr., Fitzgibbons, Galloway, Heartney Jr., Jack, Kean, Lewis, Pickett, Reed, Reitz Jr., Rosenberg, Thomas.

74. Interview, Schweibert.

75. Interviews, Birch, Metcalf, Reed, Schweibert.

76. Interview, Schweibert.

77. Interview, Cunningham.

78. Interview, Birch.

79. Interviews, Brady ("probably the weakest law professor I had. . . . He just never got anything across"), Dodd, Goodenow, Pickett, Vogel.

80. Interviews, Birch, P. E. Brown, Heartney Jr.

81. Interviews, Galloway, Hellwege, Moyer, Reitz Jr., Ryan, Schwilck, R. L. Stevens, Stohr.

82. Interviews, Browne, Bruner, Dodd, Gleysteen, Gray, Grosenbaugh, Hunt, Jebens, Lewis, McCarthy, McCoy, McPharlin, Moeller, Mosier, Schweibert, Smith, Thomas.

83. Interviews, Barker, Cunningham, Edson, Grosenbaugh, Hunt, Jack, Moeller, Morrison, Moyer, Reitz Jr., Rosenberg, Schweibert, Vogel; Wirtz. *Contra* Elderkin ("I didn't like him personally.").

84. Interview, Morrison.

85. Interview, Wirtz.

86. Interview, Wirtz.

87. Interview, Seaton; *accord* interviews, Galloway, Mayer; Stephen H. Bush to WR, March 23, 1939.

88. Interview, Morrison.

89. Interview, Hunt.

90. Interview, Adler.

91. Interview, Morrison.

92. Interview, Seaton.

93. Interviews, R. L. Stevens, Vogel.

94. Interview, R. L. Stevens.

95. Interviews, Brady (re another student), Jebens (re another student).

96. Interview, Schweibert (re another student).

97. Interview, Remley (re another student).

98. Interview, Rosenberg.

99. Interview, Lewis.

100. Interviews, Heartney Jr., Mayer.

101. Interview, Schweibert; *see* W Wirtz, "Mr. Justice Rutledge."

CHAPTER EIGHT

The document in the Rutledge Papers cited in Chapter 8 as the "Court-packing manuscript"—without identified authorship, though quoting freely from Irving Brant's *Storm over the Constitution* without attribution or even quotation marks—is so polemical that it cannot have been prepared as a draft for a Senate hearing in response to the scholarly opposition to the president's bill by Dean Leon Green of Northwestern and Dean Henry Bates of Michigan. *See* Hearings on S. 1392, "A Bill to Reorganize the Judicial Branch of the Government," Before the Committee on the Judiciary (hereafter Judicial Reorganization), 75th Cong., 1st Sess., 225 (testimony of Leon Green, March 18, 1937), and 885 (testimony of Henry M. Bates, April 1, 1937). Indeed, compared to the "Court-packing manuscript," Irving Brant's testimony before the senators in support of the plan was measured. *See* Judicial Reorganization, 379 (testimony of Irving Brant, March 20, 1937). On the other hand, this manuscript is not the typical draft Rutledge speech, which he would have written by hand for his secretary to type if he chose to abandon his usual practice of speaking extemporaneously from note cards. No handwritten draft is retained (he typically would have saved one). Furthermore, the manuscript is a triple-spaced, pica-size typed statement without an introduction or a conclusion. Thus, the document was prepared on a typewriter foreign to the dean's office, which—as Rutledge correspondence and reports make clear—invariably used an elite typeface (Rutledge was not known to type himself at home or elsewhere in those years). There is, in the Rutledge Papers, a separate sheet with a single-spaced, elite-size typed concluding paragraph prepared for testimony—not for a speech—supporting the Court-packing bill, using modes of expression unquestionably Rutledge's own. This sheet has been clipped onto a letter from Rutledge to the Iowa state representative Leo A. Hoegh of April 5, 1937 (see note 101, below), perhaps by the Library of Congress cataloguer. There is no indication that Rutledge himself had prepared this concluding paragraph to accompany the "Court-packing manuscript." There are no handwritten corrections on the manuscript, moreover, let alone a date or occasion marked on it, that would reflect the usual Rutledge practice when preparing a document for a speech or other use.

This evidence would indicate that someone else, perhaps a student research assistant, drafted a speech for the dean using *Storm over the Constitution* for ideas at Rutledge's suggestion, but left it for Rutledge to pen a more personal beginning and ending. Rutledge was speaking out informally on the subject, but undoubtedly there was demand for him to present a major statement in a local forum; so a draft speech more formal than usual could have been expected. Nonetheless, there is no evidence that Rutledge used assistants to help him write speeches on other occasions; indeed, later as a justice he would have found it unethical for a law clerk to provide such service. Furthermore, one must doubt whether a student assistant would take the risks for himself and his dean of apparently committing plagiarism. And what student would have characterized Supreme Court justices by quoting from Kipling, as the manuscript does, on the incompetency of aged English generals in the Boer War? (*see* Court-packing manuscript, 14-15)—unless, of course, Rutledge had handed his aide a copy of Kipling, whom Rutledge on occasion was known to quote. *E.g.*, Ruthann Hayes, "Justice Rutledge Has Busy Summer," *Silver and Gold* (U. of Colorado), Sept. 8, 1943, Rutledge Papers.

Instead, could Irving Brant himself have supplied the document? That might explain the free use of Brant's prose—improved here and there—without concern for quotation marks, in contrast with the manuscript's careful use of quotations from other sources. Under this theory, any issue of attribution could be cleaned up later if publication were indicated. But there is no direct evidence that Brant wrote the draft. Brant's papers at the Library of Congress, containing scores of draft speeches for others, do not include a copy of the "Court-packing manuscript." Nor do the Rutledge or the Brant Papers contain correspondence about it, which typically would have been produced had Brant contributed to the effort. And, in any event, why would Brant have drafted a speech for Rutledge, the consummate speech-maker on his own?

Of one thing we can be sure: Wiley Rutledge would not have presented a speech, let alone testimony before a Senate committee, stealing someone else's prose. For that reason alone we may conclude that Rutledge did not initiate the draft manuscript—or, if he did, that he was not about to use it as is. As between Brant and a student assistant, Brant seems the likelier suspect given the appropriation of Brant's own language and the level of discourse, including common Rutledge references such as concerns about "autocracy" and "another Dred Scott decision."

In any event, whoever drafted the manuscript, there can be no question that it reflects the thinking and style of Wiley Rutledge. By the time it was drafted, Brant and Rutledge both supported Roosevelt's plan (although Brant a year earlier in *Storm* had rejected Court packing). Irving Brant, *Storm over the Constitution*, 242 & n. And the two had remarkably similar modes of expression when presenting passionately held political views. If Rutledge himself did draft the manuscript, it was by no means in final form and thus was apparently never used. One can tell from other manuscripts in the Rutledge Papers when he used one; his telltale markings are always there—and none is here. All things considered, despite the mystery of the manuscript's derivation, it seems appropriate to quote from it as Rutledge material, for purposes of spreading his thinking on the record. This may have not been a final, Rutledge-endorsed statement. But anyone familiar with his views on the Supreme Court at the time and, in particular, his position on the Court-packing bill, could not doubt that this manuscript is vintage Rutledge if not unquestionably the work of his own hand.

1. Interview, Remley.
2. College of Law, Report of the Dean for the Academic Year Ending June 30, 1937, 34–37, Iowa Dean Reports; interviews, Fitzgibbons, Metcalf.
3. Interview, Fitzgibbons.
4. Interview, Moeller.
5. Interviews, Barker, Fitzgibbons, Jebens, Metcalf, Moeller, Schweibert, Seaton; see College of Law, Reports of the Dean for the Academic Years Ending June 30, 1937, 35, June 30, 1938, 58; *Daily Iowan*, March 13, 1937, p. 1, col. 7.
6. Interviews, Barker, Seaton.
7. *See, e.g.*, the program for "Supreme Court Day, The Iowa Law School Eleventh Annual Celebration, Thursday, April 15, 1937"; College of Law, Reports of the Dean for the Academic Years Ending June 30, 1937, 33, June 30, 1938, 51; WR to Mason Ladd, April 22, 1941; Matthew J. Heartney Jr. to W. Willard Wirtz, April 5, 1950; interviews, Pasley, Remley, Wirtz.
8. Ferdinand M. Isserman to WR, Oct. 14, 1935; WR to Ferdinand M. Isserman, Oct. 17, 1935.
9. Interviews, Gibbs, Johnson, Moyer, Schindler, Vogel.
10. Interview, Lewis.
11. Interviews, Jebens, Metcalf, Ryan, Wirtz.
12. Interview, Grant.
13. Interview, Jebens.
14. Interview, Hirsch.
15. Interview, Jebens.
16. Interviews, Birch, Gray, Pasley.
17. Interview, Ryan.
18. Interviews, Gibbs, Noel.
19. Interview, Metcalf.
20. Interview, Cunningham.
21. Interviews, Adler, Galloway, Gleysteen, Goodenow, Gray, Jack, Mayer, McPharlin, Moeller, Pasley, Smith, Stohr.
22. Interview, Gray, Kemler.
23. Interview, Galloway.
24. Interview, Adler.
25. Interview, Fitzgibbons.
26. Interviews, Jebens, Noel, Ryan.
27. Interview, Heartney Jr.
28. Iowa Faculty Minutes of Aug. 4, 1939, approved Dec. 7, 1939; interview, Schwilck.
29. Interview, Ryan.
30. Interview, Ryan.
31. WR to Robert E. Rosenwald, Oct. 7, 1936.
32. WR to Robert E. Rosenwald, May 22, 1936.
33. WR to Robert E. Rosenwald, Oct. 7, 1936.
34. College of Law, Report of the Dean for the Academic Year Ending June 30, 1936, 15.

35. George R. Gray to WR, Oct. 16, 1935.

36. George R. Gray to WR, Oct. 16, 1935; Wiley Rutledge, speech notes.

37. WR to George H. Ramsey, Nov. 13, 1935; Wiley Rutledge, speech notes.

38. WR to James P. Gaffney, June 2, 1936; Wiley Rutledge, speech notes.

39. Warner Fuller to WR, Oct. 6, 1936; Warner Fuller to WR, Dec. 3, 1936; Rutledge, "Significant Trends in Modern Incorporation Statutes," 22 *Wash. U. L. Q.* 305, 3 *U. Pitt. L. Rev.* 273.

40. Herschel W. Arant to WR, Feb. 10, 1937; WR to Herschel W. Arant, Feb. 16, 1937; Warner Fuller to WR, Aug. 23, 1938; WR to Warner Fuller, Sept. 20, 1938; Warner Fuller to WR, Sept. 23, 1938; WR to William O. Douglas, Oct. 13, 1938; WR to Joseph C. O'Mahoney, Oct. 14, 1938; WR to Leon Green, Oct. 29, 1938; WR to [members of the AALS committee on the Business Round Table], Oct. 29, 1938; WR to William O. Douglas, Nov. 2, 1938; William O. Douglas to WR, Nov. 17, 1938; WR to Warner Fuller, Nov. 17, 1938; Edward G. Jennings to WR, Nov. 21, 1938; WR to Edward G. Jennings, Nov. 22, 1938; WR to Joseph C. O'Mahoney, Jan. 3, 1939; WR to Edward G. Jennings, Jan. 3, 1939.

41. WR to Lloyd Garrison, March 3, 5, 1937; Herschel W. Arant to WR, March 9, 1937; WR to Albert J. Harno, April 17, 1937; Everett Fraser to WR, Nov. 4, 1937; Albert J. Harno to WR, Nov. 4, 1937; Lloyd K. Garrison to WR, Nov. 5, 1937; Charles E. Clark to WR, Nov. 6, 1937; Wayne L. Morse to WR, Nov. 8, 1937; K. N. Llewellyn to WR, undated [Feb. 1937]; M. T. Van Hecke to WR, Nov. 9, 1937; J. A. Wickes to WR, Nov. 13, 1937.

42. Draft AALS Report of the "Committee on Cooperation with the Bench and Bar" (Nov. 1, 1937), 10, 13 (hereafter AALS Draft Report); *compare* final AALS "Report of the Committee on Cooperation with the Bench and Bar," 49 (in Program and Reports of Committees for the 35th Annual Meeting, Dec. 29–31, 1937) (hereafter AALS Final Report).

43. AALS Draft Report, 14–15; AALS Final Report, 52.

44. AALS Draft Report, 15–19; AALS Final Report, 52–55.

45. Albert J. Harno to WR, Nov. 4, 1937; Charles E. Clark to WR, Nov. 6, 1937; M. T. Van Hecke to WR, Nov. 9, 1937; Everett Fraser to WR, Nov. 4, 1937; Wayne L. Morse to WR, Nov. 8, 1937; WR to Herschel W. Arant, Nov. 12, 1937; AALS Final Report, 49.

46. AALS Final Report, 52.

47. WR to Myron B. Bush, Nov. 28, 1940.

48. Nelson Kraschel to WR, June 8, 1937; WR to Nelson Kraschel, June 12, 1937.

49. Armstrong, *A Century of Service*, 11, 15 (quoting Graves, *Uniform State Action*).

50. Horwitz, *The Transformation of American Law, 1780–1860*, 18, 257–58; Horwitz, *The Transformation of American Law, 1870–1960*, 117; Schlesinger, *The Age of Jackson*, 118–21, 330–31.

51. WR to William C. Ramsey, Dec. 7, 1937; William C. Ramsey to WR, Jan. 4, 1938; WR to Alexander V. Armstrong, Jan. 12, 1938; WR to K. M. Klamon, Aug. 1, 1938.

52. N. E. H. Hull, "Restatement and Reform: A New Perspective on the Origins of the American Law Institute," in *The American Law Institute, Seventy-Fifth Anniversary 1923–1998* (1998), 49.

53. Burt J. Thompson, "Bar Integration: A Discussion of the Theory and Procedure and Purposes of an Integrated Bar," Oct. 1937, 6.

54. Buell McCash to WR, Dec. 16, 1937.

55. J. C. Pryor to WR, Dec. 24, 1937.

56. E. N. Farber to WR, Dec. 15, 1937.

57. WR to Ralph J. Neuhoff, Feb. 19, 1938; Mason Ladd to WR, Aug. 18, 1938.

58. WR to Ralph Fuchs, June 7, 1938, Fuchs Papers.

59. Wiley Rutledge, "Unauthorized Practice," address for the Iowa State Bar Association, June 10, 1938, Des Moines.

60. Leuchtenburg, *The Supreme Court Reborn*, 133–34; Lasser, *Benjamin V. Cohen*, 157, 162; interview, Gardner; *see* W. W. Gardner, Confidential Memorandum for the Solicitor General, "Congressional Control of Judicial Power to Invalidate Legislation," Dec. 10, 1936 (in author's possession).

61. *Panama Refining Co. v. Ryan*, 293 U.S. 388 (1935); *Schechter Poultry Corp. v. United States*, 295 U.S. 495 (1935).

62. *R.R. Ret. Bd. v. Alton R.R. Co.*, 295 U.S. 330 (1935).

63. *United States v. Butler*, 297 U.S. 1 (1936).

64. *Carter v. Carter Coal Co.*, 298 U.S. 238 (1936).

65. *Ashton v. Cameron County Water Improvement Dist. No. 1*, 298 U.S. 513 (1936).

66. *Louisville Bank v. Radford*, 295 U.S. 555 (1935).

67. Leuchtenburg, *The Supreme Court Reborn*, 137; Lasser, *Benjamin V. Cohen*, 164.

68. WR to Clay R. Apple, March 10, 1937.

69. Untitled, undated manuscript in Rutledge Papers, box 203, Judicial Reorganization—Court Packing Plan, reflecting either a draft speech or draft testimony on the Court-packing plan (hereafter Court-packing manuscript). *See* note on Court-packing manuscript preceding note 1, above; *Iowa City Press-Citizen*, July 22, 1936, p. 3, col. 2; WR to Irving Brant, July 18, 1936; Geraldine L. Dibb to WR, July 22, 1936; Irving Brant to WR, Aug. 5, 1936.

70. Court-packing manuscript, 4.

71. Court-packing manuscript, 3.

72. Court-packing manuscript, 4 (*compare* Brant, *Storm over the Constitution*, 249).

73. Court-packing manuscript, 5 (*compare* Brant, *Storm over the Constitution*, at 250).

74. Court-packing manuscript, 5 (*compare* Brant, *Storm over the Constitution*, 247).

75. WR to C. F. Murphy, Feb. 10, 1939.

76. WR to C. F. Murphy, Feb. 10, 1939 (referring to *Scott v. Sanford*, 60 U.S. 393 (1857)).

77. Court-packing manuscript, 2.

78. Court-packing manuscript, 2.

79. Court-packing manuscript, 16.

80. Court-packing manuscript, 16.

81. WR to Clay R. Apple, March 10, 1937.

82. Court-packing manuscript, 8 (*compare* Brant, *Storm over the Constitution*, 245–46); Kalman, *Legal Realism at Yale*, 40, 247 n. 157 (quoting Charles Evans Hughes, speech at Elmira, N.Y., May 3, 1907 ("We are in a constitution but the constitution means what the courts say it means.")).

83. Court-packing manuscript, 2.

84. Court-packing manuscript, 2.

85. *Morehead v. New York ex rel. Tipaldo*, 298 U.S. 587 (1936).

86. Court-packing manuscript, 8 (*compare* Brant, *Storm over the Constitution*, 246).

87. Court-packing manuscript, 9.

88. Court-packing manuscript, 10.

89. Court-packing manuscript, 12.

90. Court-packing manuscript, 11.

91. Undated, hand-corrected manuscript of question-and-answer interview of Dean Wiley Rutledge by the *Cedar Rapids Gazette* on the Supreme Court and President Roose-

velt's Court-packing plan; *see* Ray Anderson to WR, March 2, 1937; WR to Ray Anderson, March 10, 1937; Ray Anderson to WR, March 13, 1937.

92. Interviews, Metcalf, Morrison.

93. Court-packing manuscript, 12.

94. WR to Clay R. Apple, March 10, 1937; *see* Warren, *The Supreme Court in United States History*, 229–30 (quoting James Monroe).

95. *See* Court-packing manuscript, 11.

96. WR to Clay R. Apple, March 10, 1937.

97. WR to Clay R. Apple, March 10, 1937.

98. Interview, Vogel.

99. *United States v. Carolene Prods. Co.*, 304 U.S. 144, 152 n. 4 (1938).

100. *See* David P. Currie, "The Constitution in the Supreme Court"; *see, e.g., United States v. Carolene Prods. Co.*, 304 U.S. at 152 n. 4; *Bridges v. California*, 314 U.S. 252 (1941); *Jones v. Opelika*, 319 U.S. 103 (per curiam) (vacating judgments in 316 U.S. 584 (1942)); *Murdock v. Pennsylvania*, 319 U.S. 105 (1943); *West Virginia Bd. of Educ. v. Barnette*, 319 U.S. 524 (1943) (overruling *Minersville School Dist. v. Gobitis*, 315 U.S. 722 (1942)).

101. *Des Moines Register*, April 4, 1937, p. 1, col. 1; *see* Hon. Leo A. Hoegh to WR, Mon., April 5, 1937 (referring to the "Sunday Register"), box 25, Rutledge Papers; Hearings on S. 1392, "A Bill to Reorganize the Judicial Branch of the Government," Before the Committee on the Judiciary (hereafter Judicial Reorganization), 75th Cong., 1st Sess., 885 (testimony of Henry M. Bates on April 1, 1937); *see* Judicial Reorganization, 225 (testimony of Leon Green, March 18, 1937).

102. WR to Ray Anderson, March 10, 1937.

103. Interview, Ryan.

104. *See* note 91.

105. Hon. Leo A. Hoegh to WR, April 5, 1937; WR to Hon. Leo A. Hoegh, April 6, 1937.

106. WR to Irving Brant, Jan. 2, 1939; WR to Thomas W. Keenan, March 11, 1943.

107. WR to Thomas W. Keenan, March 11, 1943.

108. *West Coast Hotel Co. v. Parrish*, 300 U.S. 379 (1937); *see* Leuchtenburg, *The Supreme Court Reborn*, 142; Lasser, *Benjamin V. Cohen*, 171.

109. *NLRB v. Jones & Laughlin Steel Corp.*, 301 U.S. 1 (1937); *see* Leuchtenburg, *The Supreme Court Reborn*, 142.

110. *Steward Machine Co. v. Davis*, 301 U.S. 548 (1937); *Helvering v. Davis*, 301 U.S. 619 (1937); *see* Leuchtenburg, *The Supreme Court Reborn*, 142.

111. *New York Times*, May 19, 1937, p. 1, cols. 7–8, p. 8, cols. 2, 3; *Des Moines Register*, May 19, 1937, p. 9, col. 2; *Washington Post*, May 20, 1937, p. 6, col. 1; *see* Leuchtenburg, *The Supreme Court Reborn*, 180, 188. Van Devanter's retirement became effective June 2, 1937, after Roosevelt signed the judicial retirement legislation into law. Pride, "Willis Van Devanter," 315.

112. *New York Times*, July 15, p. 1, col. 8; Leuchtenburg, *The Supreme Court Reborn*, 153, 181; Lasser, *Benjamin V. Cohen*, 176–77; Jackson, *That Man*, 54; *Washington Post*, July 23, 1937, p. 1 (banner headline).

113. WR to Louise Larrabee, Feb. 14, 1938; *accord* WR to C. F. Murphy, Feb. 10, 1939.

CHAPTER NINE

1. *New York Times*, May 19, 1937, p. 1, col. 8.

2. Kaufman, "Cardozo's Appointment to the Supreme Court," 23.

3. *New York Times*, May 19, 1937, p. 1, col. 8, p. 18, col. 5.

4. *Washington Post*, May 19, p. 6, col. 1.

5. Leuchtenburg, *The Supreme Court Reborn*, 180-81; Newman, *Hugo Black*, 233; Jackson, *That Man*, 50, 53; *Washington Post*, May 21, 1937, p. 1, col. 8; *New York Times*, May 21, 1937, p. 1, col. 8, July 15, p. 1, col. 5.

6. *New York Times*, May 20, 1937, p. 1, cols. 6-8, p. 15, col. 5 (Sens. Alben W. Barkley (Ky.), James F. Byrnes (S.C.), Pat Harrison (Miss.), and Key Pittman (Nev.)).

7. *Washington Post*, May 21, 1937, p. 1, col. 8.

8. *New York Times*, May 22, 1937, p. 1, col. 2.

9. *See* Leuchtenburg, *The Supreme Court Reborn*, 182.

10. *New York Times*, July 15, 1937, p. 1, col. 8.

11. *New York Times*, July 15, 1937, p. 13, col. 8.

12. Leuchtenburg, *The Supreme Court Reborn*, 183, 210; Newman, *Hugo Black*, 234.

13. Leuchtenburg, *The Supreme Court Reborn*, 181.

14. Newman, *Hugo Black*, 233.

15. Leuchtenburg, *The Supreme Court Reborn*, 182. Contemporary reporters have counted sixty. Alsop and Catledge, *The 168 Days*, 297.

16. *See* Newman, *Hugo Black*, 234 (refers to "seven" finalists: Judges Sibley, Hutcheson, Bratton, and Stacy, as well as Reed, Minton, and Black, and reports that the "next Supreme Court Justice" would be one of the last three); Leuchtenburg, *The Supreme Court Reborn*, 183 (concludes that "[i]n the end, they got down to a group of four," including Dean Garrison and the federal circuit judge Parker, who were not mentioned among the seven finalists identified by Newman).

17. Newman, *Hugo Black*, 135; Goings, *"The NAACP Comes of Age,"* 19-36.

18. Leuchtenburg, *The Supreme Court Reborn*, 183, 211; Newman, *Hugo Black*, 236; Lasser, *Benjamin V. Cohen*, 187 (last three names "in play" were Reed, Minton, Black).

19. Newman, *Hugo Black*, 228, 234-36; Leuchtenburg, *The Supreme Court Reborn*, 148, 185; Alsop and Catledge, *The 168 Days*, 303-5; Hon. Hugo L. Black, "Reorganization of the Federal Judiciary," Radio Address on Station WOL, Washington, Feb. 23, 1937, 81 *Cong. Rec.* 1525-26, app. 305-7 (daily ed., Feb. 24, 1937).

20. Leuchtenburg, *The Supreme Court Reborn*, 182-83, 210-11; Newman, *Hugo Black*, 234, 236-37; Lasser, *Benjamin V. Cohen*, 187 (quoting Alsop and Catledge).

21. Leuchtenburg, *The Supreme Court Reborn*, 190-99; Newman, *Hugo Black*, 258-59; WR to Louise Laribbee [*recte* Larrabee], Feb. 14, 1938.

22. Fassett, *New Deal Justice*, 195, 197-98 (also reporting other names mentioned: Professor Felix Frankfurter, Donald Richberg, James M. Landis, Robert M. Hutchins, Sen. Robert F. Wagner, Rep. Hatton Sumners, Circuit Judges Learned Hand and Florence E. Allen, and Ferdinand Pecora and Samuel Rosenman of the New York State Supreme Court); Swindler, *Court and Constitution in the Twentieth Century*, 88; *see* Bybee, "George Sutherland," 350.

23. Fassett, *New Deal Justice*, 197 (quoting Swindler, *Court and Constitution in the Twentieth Century*, 88).

24. WR to Louise Laribbee [*recte* Larrabee], Feb. 14, 1938.

25. Kaufman, *Cardozo*, 456, 466-71, 567.

26. *E.g.*, Irving Brant to President Franklin D. Roosevelt, Dec. 28, 1938; Irving Brant to WR, Dec. 27, 1938.

27. "Puts Frankfurter Up for High Bench; Senator Norris Asks Harvard Law Authority Be Appointed to Supreme Court," *New York Times*, Aug. 9, 1938, p. 3, col. 3.

28. Freedman, ed., *Roosevelt and Frankfurter*, 481.

29. *See* Kahn, "The Politics of the Appointment Process," 277 n. 180 (and sources cited); Ickes, *The Secret Diary of Harold L. Ickes*, 539, 545-46; Parrish, *Felix Frankfurter and His Times*, 275; Lasser, *Benjamin V. Cohen*, 210.

30. *New York Times*, Sept. 23, 1938, p. 15, col. 2; *see* Kahn, "The Politics of the Appointment Process," 278 n. 181 (citing *New York Times* article of Sept. 23, 1938, discussed in Thomas, *Felix Frankfurter*, 33).

31. Schlesinger, *The Age of Roosevelt*, 455-56; Ickes, *The Secret Diary of Harold L. Ickes*, 539; Parrish, *Felix Frankfurter and His Times*, 274-75 (quoting Phillips, *Felix Frankfurter Reminisces*, 280-81, and Farley, *Jim Farley's Story*, 161-62); Baker, *Felix Frankfurter*, 202.

32. WR to Dr. George Norlin, Jan. 7, 1939; WR to Edward C. Eicher, Jan. 10, 1939.

33. Freedman, ed., *Roosevelt and Frankfurter*, 481; Parrish, *Felix Frankfurter and His Times*, 276.

34. *See* Parrish, *Felix Frankfurter and His Times*, 274-76 (quoting Henry Morgenthau Jr., Memorandum, May 24, 1937, Morgenthau Drawer, 16, Roosevelt Library, Hyde Park, N.Y.); Ickes, *The Secret Diary of Harold L. Ickes*, 539-40; Baker, *Felix Frankfurter*, 202. Irving Brant, in particular, was convinced that "Cummings and Farley talked geography" as a way of masking "a faint touch of anti-Semitism in both of them." Irving Brant to WR, Jan. 14, 1939; Lash, *Dealers and Dreamers*, 385-87 ("Frankfurter's Jewishness" did not concern Cummings, but Cummings's "anti-Semitic feelings" fed his opposition to Jerome Frank for federal appellate court nomination).

35. Interview, Lingreen. Brant wrote the Madison biography from 1938 to 1961. All six volumes are entitled *James Madison*, with the following subtitles: *The Virginia Revolutionist* (1941), *The Nationalist, 1780-1787* (1948), *Father of the Constitution, 1787-1800* (1950), *Secretary of State, 1800-1809* (1953), *The President, 1809-1812* (1956), *Commander in Chief, 1812-1816* (1961). *See* Scope and Content Note, 1, Brant Papers.

36. Brant was a director of the National Public Housing Conference, headquartered in New York City, from 1935 to 1944. Biographical Note, Brant Papers.

37. From 1938 to 1940 Brant served Secretary of the Interior Harold L. Ickes as a consultant on conservation. Biographical Note and Scope and Content Note, Brant Papers. He also wrote many papers and pamphlets over the years on conservation, from 1930 to 1962 was treasurer of the Emergency Conservation Committee headed by Rosalie Edge, and, on assignment from President Roosevelt, "selected the land for inclusion in the Olympic National Park." Scope and Content Note, 2, Brant Papers.

38. Brant was a member of the American Civil Liberties Union for thirty years. Scope and Content Note, 2, Brant Papers. In addition to writing the book *The Bill of Rights: Its Origin and Meaning* (1965), he wrote articles and gave testimony in issues such as the poll tax, the Senate filibuster, and suffrage in the District of Columbia. Scope and Content Note, 2, Brant Papers.

39. *See* Franklin D. Roosevelt to Irving Brant, Sept. 1, 1920 ("I greatly appreciate all that you say about my acceptance speech."), Brant Papers.

40. *E.g.*, from the Brant Papers: Franklin D. Roosevelt to Irving Brant, March 28, 1931 ("I might add that if you were in New York you would realize that I am doing everything within my power to eradicate crookedness and bad government in every part of the State."), March 30, 1932 ("Naturally I wish that you felt more cordial toward my policies here in New York but I recognize your right to form your own conclusions from my record as it stands."), May 27, 1932 ("It was good of you to write me such a friendly comment. . . .

Your editorials are right on point and most stimulating."), June 11, 1932 ("I was pleased to hear from you again and to have you send me your editorials with their friendly interpretation of the Pennsylvania and Massachusetts results, as well as their criticisms on the New York State political situation."), June 27, 1932 ("I am grateful for that fine editorial."), Sept. 8, 1932 ("Thanks for what you say about my Columbus speech. I value your kindly expressions.").

41. WR to Sen. Guy M. Gillette, Feb. 24, 1939; interview, Wechsler.

42. *New York Times*, Feb. 14, 1939, p. 3, col. 4; Morris, *Calmly to Poise the Scales of Justice*, 90; Baker, *Felix* Frankfurter, 204-5; Irving Brant to WR, Jan. 14, 1939; Irving Brant to Ralph Fuchs, Dec. 31, 1938; *see* Irving Brant to President Franklin D. Roosevelt, Nov. 12, 1938, Dec. 28, 1938, Brant Papers.

43. Brant, "Mr. Justice Rutledge," 35 *Iowa L. Rev.* 550-51 (1950), 25 *Ind. LJ.* 429-30 (1950); editorial, *St. Louis Star-Times*, July 1, 1935, p. 12, col. 1; WR to Irving Brant, July 10, 1935; Irving Brant to WR, Feb. 13, 1936; interview, Peper and Martin; PQ Club Records.

44. *United States v. Butler*, 297 U.S. 1 (1936).

45. Brant, "Mr. Justice Rutledge," 35 *Iowa L. Rev.* 552 (1950) (footnote omitted), 25 *Ind. LJ.* 431-32 (1950) (footnote omitted). The three-star edition of the *St. Louis Star-Times* for Jan. 6, 1936, carried only the majority opinion in *Butler*, p. 7, cols. 1-8, as did the later five-star edition, p. 7.

46. Irving Brant to President Franklin D. Roosevelt, Nov. 12, 1938; Brant, "Mr. Justice Rutledge," 35 *Iowa L. Rev.* 555 (1950), 25 *Ind. L. Rev.* 434 (1950).

47. Irving Brant to WR, Feb. 12, 1936; WR to Irving Brant, Feb. 21, 1936; Rutledge, "The Federal Government and Child Labor"; Rutledge, "Social Changes and the Law."

48. WR to Irving Brant, May 28, 1936, Brant Papers.

49. Leuchtenburg, *The Supreme Court Reborn*, 108; WR to Irving Brant, Nov. 25, 1936.

50. Irving Brant to President Franklin D. Roosevelt, Nov. 12, 1938, Brant Papers; Brant, "Mr. Justice Rutledge," 35 *Iowa L. Rev.* 555 (1950), 25 *Ind. LJ.* 434 (1950).

51. Irving Brant to President Franklin D. Roosevelt, Nov. 12, 1938, Brant Papers; *accord* Brant, "Mr. Justice Rutledge," 35 *Iowa L. Rev.* 552 (1950) ("In six months, according to Professor Root of the Department of History, Dean Rutledge broke a tradition of fear which made political progressives afraid to speak their thoughts even at small dinner parties."), 25 *Ind. LJ.* 431 (1950) (same).

52. Irving Brant to President Franklin D. Roosevelt, Nov. 12, 1938, Brant Papers.

53. Irving Brant to WR, Nov. 12, 1938; Irving Brant to WR, Nov. 26, 1938; WR to Irving Brant, Dec. 1, 1938; *e.g.*, *The State University of Iowa, Catalogue Number 1938-1939*, 287 ("Frankfurter and Davison, *Cases on Administrative Law* (2d ed.)" (1935)).

54. Homer S. Cummings to Seth Thomas, Dec. 2, 1938, Frankfurter Appt. File; Seth Thomas to Homer S. Cummings, Dec. 6, 1938, Frankfurter Appt. File; Attorney General Homer S. Cummings to Joseph B. Keenan, Dec. 2, 1938 (memorandum), Frankfurter Appt. File; Joseph B. Keenan to Attorney General Homer S. Cummings, Dec. 12 and 15, 1938 (memorandum), Frankfurter Appt. File; *e.g.*, *New York Times*, Feb. 18, 1939, p. 3, col. 7; *Washington Post*, Feb. 19, 1939, p. 9, col. 8; Edward A. Sager to WR, Dec. 26, 1938; Irving Brant to WR, Dec. 27, 1938; George Norlin to Irving Brant, Dec. 5, 1938; George Norlin to President Franklin D. Roosevelt, Dec. 5, 1938, Frankfurter Appt. File; Irving Brant to WR, Dec. 27, 1938.

55. Irving Brant to WR, Dec. 27, 1938.

56. Irving Brant to President Franklin D. Roosevelt, Dec. 28, 1938 (referring, implicitly,

to *Consol. Edison Co. v. NLRB*, 305 U.S. 197 [1938]; *Gen. Talking Pictures Corp. v. W. Elec. Co.*, 305 U.S. 124 [1938]), Brant Papers.

57. Roscoe Anderson to WR, Dec. 28, 1938; Roscoe Anderson to WR, Jan. 4, 1939; Clay Apple to Dr. Theodore J. Kreps, Jan. 3, 1939; Arthur J. Freund to President Franklin D. Roosevelt, Jan. 4, 1939, Frankfurter Appt. File; Sam Elson to President Franklin D. Roosevelt, Jan. 4, 1939, Frankfurter Appt. File; Luther Ely Smith to President Franklin D. Roosevelt, Jan. 4, 1939, Frankfurter Appt. File; Carl Wheaton to President Franklin D. Roosevelt, Dec. 29, 1939, Frankfurter Appt. File; Ralph Fuchs to Irving Brant, Jan. 4, 1939; Tyrrell Williams to President Franklin D. Roosevelt, Jan. 4, 1939, Frankfurter Appt. File; Ralph S. Fuchs to President Franklin D. Roosevelt, Jan. 4, 1939, Frankfurter Appt. File; Ralph S. Fuchs to the secretary to the president, Jan. 5, 1939, Frankfurter Appt. File; Ralph Fuchs to WR, Jan. 4, 1939; J. C. Pryor to President Franklin D. Roosevelt, Dec. 30, 1938, Frankfurter Appt. File; Evens A. Worthley to President Franklin D. Roosevelt, Dec. 28, 1938, Frankfurter Appt. File.

58. Mason, *Harlan Fiske Stone*, 482.

59. Lash, *From the Diaries of Felix Frankfurter*, 154; see Ickes, *The Secret Diary of Harold L. Ickes*, 539–40, 545–46.

60. Ickes, *The Secret Diary of Harold L. Ickes*, 540; William K. Hutchinson, *Nashville Banner*, Feb. 24, 1939, p. 26, col. 5; Fine, *Frank Murphy*, 1, 4. Murphy took the oath of office Jan. 2, and the Senate confirmed him Jan. 17, 1939. Fine, *Frank Murphy*, 6.

61. Ickes, *The Secret Diary of Harold L. Ickes*, 545–46; see Fine, *Frank Murphy*, 33.

62. *Washington Post*, July 16, 1937, p. 1, col. 8; *Boston Evening Globe*, Feb. 16, 1939, p. 1, col. 3; Joseph Alsop and Robert Kintner, *Boston Daily Globe*, Feb. 17, 1939, p. 1, col. 1, p. 17, cols. 1–2; Ickes, *The Secret Diary of Harold L. Ickes*, 539.

63. Freedman, ed., *Roosevelt and Frankfurter*, 482; Parrish, *Felix Frankfurter and His Times*, 274–75; Lief, *Democracy's Norris*, 519; WR to Irving Brant, Jan. 5, 1939; WR to Guy M. Gillette, Feb. 18, 1939; see generally Norris, *Fighting Liberal*.

64. Irving Brant to WR, Jan. 14, 1939; Irving Brant to Ralph Fuchs, Dec. 31, 1938; Brant, "Mr. Justice Rutledge," 25 *Ind. L. J.* 434 (1950), 35 *Iowa L. Rev.* 555 (1950); Freedman, ed., *Roosevelt and Frankfurter*, 482.

65. Edward C. Eicher to WR, Jan. 6, 1939; WR to Edward C. Eicher, Jan. 10, 1939.

66. Irving Brant to Felix Frankfurter, Jan. 14, 1939 (quoting letters from WR to Irving Brant, Nov. 22, 1938, Jan. 2 and 5, 1939), Brant Papers.

67. "F.D.R." to Felix Frankfurter, Jan. 16, 1939 (memorandum), Brant Papers, box 13.

68. "Memorandum on Mr. X" from Thomas Reed Powell to Felix Frankfurter, undated [last week of Dec. 1938], Rutledge Papers.

69. Thomas Reed Powell to WR, Jan. 13, 1943.

70. Thomas Reed Powell to WR, Feb. 14, 1939.

71. "Memorandum on Mr. X" from Thomas Reed Powell to Felix Frankfurter.

72. Guy M. Gillette to WR, Jan. 11, 1939.

CHAPTER TEN

1. *New York Times*, Feb. 14, 1939, p. 3, col. 4.

2. *New York Times*, Feb. 18, 1939, p. 3, col. 7.

3. *New York Times*, Feb. 14, 1939, p. 1, col. 8, p. 3, col. 5; FDR Official File, box 55 (correspondence re Judge Hutcheson, among others).

4. *Washington Post*, Feb. 15, 1939, p. 3, col. 5.

5. *Burlington* (Iowa) *Hawkeye-Gazette*, Feb. 14, 1939 (clipping in Rutledge Papers, page and column numbers unavailable); FDR Official File, box 55 (correspondence re Sen. Schwellenbach, among others)

6. Interview, Ginsburg.

7. Murphy, *Wild Bill*, 8–10, 29–37, 40, 43–52.

8. *New York Times*, Feb. 19, 1939, p. 13, col. 3.

9. *New York Times*, Feb. 15, 1939, p. 1, col. 3; *Los Angeles Times*, Feb. 16, 1939, p. 5, col. 4; *Washington Post*, Feb. 15, 1939, p. 3, col. 3.

10. *New York Times*, Feb. 18, 1939, p. 3, col. 7; *accord Washington Post*, Feb. 19, 1939, sec. I, p. I, col. 2; sec. III, p. 9, col. 8.

11. *New York Times*, Feb. 18, 1939, p. 3, col. 7; *accord Boston Evening Globe*, Feb. 16, 1939, p. I, col. 3; *Washington Post*, Feb. 18, 1939, p. 2, col. 6.

12. *New York Times*, Feb., 18, 1939, p. 3, col. 7.

13. Joseph B. Keenan to the attorney general, Feb. 15, 1939, Douglas Appt. File.

14. Homer S. Cummings to Joseph B. Keenan, Jan. 5, 1939, Douglas Appt. File.

15. Joseph B. Keenan to the attorney general, Feb. 14, 1939 (attachment), Douglas Appt. File.

16. File memorandum from Frank Murphy, Feb. 14, 1939 (reflecting telephone conversation with Henry M. Bates), Douglas Appt. File; *accord* Henry M. Bates to Frank Murphy, Feb. 21, 1939, Murphy Papers, reel 49 (Rutledge "would not be a bad appointment" but "would not add to the strength or range of the vision of the Court").

17. FDR Official File, box 56, file 41-A; *see* Joseph B. Keenan to the Attorney General, Feb. 15, 1939, Douglas Appt. File.

18. Seymour H. Person to WR, Feb. 14, 1939.

19. Roscoe Anderson to WR, Feb. 14, 1939; Jesse E. Marshall to WR, Feb. 15, 1939; Benjamin C. Hilliard to WR, Feb. 15, 1939; Henry C. Shull to President Franklin D. Roosevelt, Feb. 18, 1939; Edward Stimson to WR, Feb. 16, 1939; Ferdinand M. Isserman to President Franklin D. Roosevelt, Feb. 17, 1939; interview, Margolin.

20. Edward C. Eicher to WR, Feb. 14, 1939; Arthur J. Freund to WR, Feb. 15, 1939; WR to Arthur J. Freund, Feb. 23, 1939; Thomas Reed Powell to WR, Feb. 14, 1939; Graf A. Boepple to WR, Feb. 18, 1939; W. L. King to WR, Feb. 17, 1939.

21. WR to Roscoe Anderson, Feb. 15, 1939; Clay Apple to WR, Feb. 16, 1939; WR to Clay Apple, Feb. 23, 1939.

22. WR to Seymour Person, Feb. 18, 1939.

23. *New York Times*, Feb. 15, 1939, p. 1, col. 4.

24. *See* Irving Brant to WR, Feb. 19, 1939.

25. Joseph Alsop and Robert Kintner, *Boston Globe*, Feb. 17, 1939, p. 14, col. 3.

26. *New York Times*, Feb. 19, 1939, p. 13, col. 2.

27. Irving Brant to WR, Feb. 19, 1939; Ickes, *The Secret Diary of Harold L. Ickes*, 589 (March 12, 1939); Murphy, *Wild Bill*, 166. Had Brant and Fuchs also visited Justice Reed, they would have found a Rutledge supporter, because Rutledge had been "born in Kentucky," Reed "had known him from the Bar Association and various places, and had liked him," and Reed "didn't know Douglas very well." Reed, Reminiscences, 258.

28. "Third Term Forces First Primary Test in Voting Today," *Evening Star* (Washington), March 12, 1940, p. A-1, col. 2.

29. Irving Brant to Frank Murphy, March 3, 1939.

30. Schwartz, *A History of the Supreme Court*, 150–51, 383.

31. Farley, *Jim Farley's Story*, 138, 146, 148; Lasser, *Benjamin V. Cohen*, 200.

32. Guy M. Gillette to WR, Feb. 16, 1939; *Washington Times-Herald*, Feb. 7, 1939, p. 8, col. 4.

33. Richard Wilson to WR, Feb. 7, 1939 (telegram); WR to Richard Wilson, Feb. 7, 1939 (telegram); WR to Guy M. Gillette, Feb. 18, 1939; Guy M. Gillette to WR, Feb. 21, 1939.

34. Guy M. Gillette to WR, Feb. 23, 1939; WR to Guy M. Gillette, Feb. 27, 1939; E. Charles Eichenbaum to WR, Feb. 24, 1939.

35. George W. Norris to Frank Murphy, Feb. 21, 1939, Douglas Appt. File.

36. WR to Mr. and Mrs. Robert Y. Kerr, Feb. 24, 1939; *see* Edward C. Eicher to WR, Feb. 14 and 15, 1939; *St. Louis Post-Dispatch*, Feb. 22, 1939, p. 1C, col. 4.

37. Krock, *Memoirs*, 176–77; Murphy, *Wild Bill*, 165–67; Schwartz, *New Dealers*, 174.

38. William K. Hutchinson, *Nashville* (Tenn.) *Banner*, Feb. 24, 1939, p. 26, cols. 5–6.

39. Interview, Ginsburg.

40. Interview, Ginsburg; *see generally* Ashby, *The Spearless Leader*; Claudius O. Johnson, *Borah of Idaho*.

41. Douglas, *Go East, Young Man*, 406.

42. Interview, Ginsburg.

43. At least the *Congressional Record* reported none; nor is a draft found in the Borah Papers or in those of Corcoran or Cohen at the Library of Congress.

44. Interview, Ginsburg; *accord* Douglas, *Go East Young Man*, 406.

45. Joseph Alsop and Robert Kintner, *Evening Star* (Washington), Feb. 20, 1939, p. A-11, col. 2.

46. William E. Borah to Frank Murphy, Feb. 24 (2 letters), 1939; Frank Murphy to William E. Borah, Borah Papers.

47. *Washington Times-Herald*, March 6, 1939, p. 6, col. 3.

48. Irving Brant to Frank Murphy, Feb. 23, 1939.

49. WR to Irving Brant, Feb. 26, 1939; WR to Clay Apple, March 1, 1939; *see* letter from President Franklin D. Roosevelt to Lloyd K. Garrison, March 7, 1979, FDR Official File, box 54, file 41-A.

50. WR to Clay Apple, March 1, 1939; WR to Guy M. Gillette, Feb. 20, 1939; WR to Arthur J. Freund, Feb. 25, 1939; WR to Emmett Ray Feighner, Feb. 25, 1939; WR to Ethyl Oliphant Keeler, March 2, 1939; *see* WR to Lon T. Williams, March 1, 1939.

51. Douglas, *Go East, Young Man*, 317; WR to Lon T. Williams, March 1, 1939.

52. Ralph Fuchs to WR, March 10, 1939.

53. *New York Times*, March 5, 1939, p. 1, col. 7; Harper, *Justice Rutledge and the Bright Constellation*, 36–37 (quoting column by Pearson and Allen of March 6, 1939); WR to J. L. Wigginton, March 6, 1939; Thomas Reed Powell to WR, March 6, 1939; WR to Albert C. Ayres, March 9, 1939; WR to Samuel Walker, March 9, 1939.

54. Ickes, *The Secret Diary of Harold L. Ickes*, 588–89 (March 12, 1939).

55. George W. Norris to President Franklin D. Roosevelt, March 7, 1939, Douglas Appt. File; George W. Norris to Frank Murphy, March 8, 1939, Douglas Appt. File.

56. Murphy, *Wild Bill*, 168–71; *see* Howard, *Mr. Justice Murphy*, 192; Fine, *Frank Murphy*, 336; Schwartz, *New Dealers*, 174.

57. Ralph Fuchs to Irving Brant, March 10, 1939; Ralph Fuchs to WR, March 10, 1939.

58. Irving Brant to President Franklin D. Roosevelt, March 10, 1939, Douglas Appt. File.

59. Jerome Frank to William E. Borah, March 13, 1939, Borah Papers.

60. WR to Emmett Ray Feighner, March 14, 1939.

61. Joseph R. Hayden to Frank Murphy, March 14, 1939, Douglas Appt. File.

62. Murphy, *Wild Bill*, 168.

63. WR to Irving Brant, March 21, 1939.

64. Acheson, *Morning and Noon*, 162, 212–14; Morris, *Calmly to Poise the Scales of Justice*, 89.

65. WR to Clay Apple, March 20, 1939.

66. WR to Clay Apple, March 20, 1939; WR to Frank Murphy, March 17, 1939.

67. WR to Irving Brant, March 20, 1939.

68. WR to William O. Douglas, March 20, 1939.

69. WR to Clay Apple, March 20, 1939; WR to Irving Brant, March 20 and 21, 1939.

70. WR to Roscoe Anderson, March 20, 1939; WR to Irving Brant, March 21, 1939; Frank Murphy to President Franklin D. Roosevelt, March 21, 1939; Irving Brant to Ralph Fuchs, March 21, 1939.

71. *Washington Post*, March 21, 1939, p. 9, col. 3.

72. Hutchinson, *Nashville* (Tenn.) *Banner*, Feb. 24, 1939, p. 26, cols. 5–6; Jackson, *That Man*, 54. Douglas has claimed that Justice Brandeis told FDR Douglas "was his candidate for his seat." Douglas, *Go East, Young Man*, 463.

73. Simon, *The Antagonists*, 187.

CHAPTER ELEVEN

1. Schwartz, *A History of the Supreme Court*, 17–19, 30, 177; Morris, *Calmly to Poise the Scales of Justice*, 37, 59–60.

2. *O'Donoghue v. United States*, 289 U.S. 516 (1933); *FTC v. Klesner*, 274 U.S. 145 (1927); Morris, *Calmly to Poise the Scales of Justice*, 60 n. 1, 87, 89.

3. Morris, *Calmly to Poise the Scales of Justice*, 87–88; *M.A.P. v. Ryan*, 285 A.2d 310, 312 (D.C. 1971).

4. Morris, *Calmly to Poise the Scales of Justice*, 90; *see generally* Ernst, "Dicey's Disciple on the D.C. Circuit"; Shepherd, "Fierce Compromise." For evidence of Rutledge's and Stephens's consistently good personal relations with each other see the file of their correspondence in the Stephens Papers, box 132, "Rutledge, Wiley Blount, Jr."

5. Morris, *Calmly to Poise the Scales of Justice*, 89–92; "History of the Federal Judiciary" (<http://www.fjc.gov>, Web site of the Federal Judicial Center, Washington); Fassett, *New Deal Justice*, 412; *Washington Post*, June 7, 1946, p. 1, col. 7; Hatcher, "Fred M. Vinson," 422–23; Kirkendall, "Fred Vinson," 2639, 2640; Fish, *The Politics of Federal Judicial Administration*, 129, 144.

6. Arthur T. Vanderbilt to WR, March 24, 1939.

7. *Washington Times-Herald*, March 28, 1939, p. 2, col. 4; 1943 Congressional Record, Senate 719–20 (Feb. 8, 1943); *Evening Star* (Washington), March 28, 1939, p. A-2, col. 8; *New York Times*, April 4, 1939, p. A-14, col. 3; Ernst, "Dicey's Disciple on the D.C. Circuit," 795; Thomas E. Martin to WR, April 5, 1939; George F. DeVenney to WR, April 5, 1939; WR to Katherine Cannell, April 12, 1939; WR to Thomas E. Martin, April 15, 1939; *see* letter from WR to Irving Brant (April 2, 1939).

8. "Rutledge Is Noon Speaker, Talks on 'Democracies and Judiciary' to Women's Group," *Iowa City Press Citizen*, April 3, 1939, Rutledge Papers; WR to W. J. Hotz, April 11, 1939; list of "those present" for Luncheon for Dean Wiley Rutledge at Fontenelle Hotel, 12:30 p.m. April 5th, 1939"; Clark Clifford to WR, March 29, 1939; *St. Louis Globe-Democrat*, April 29, 1939, part 1, p. 7A, col. 5; program for "Supreme Court Day, The Iowa Law School Thirteenth Annual Celebration, Thursday, April 13, 1939," 2, 3.

9. WR to President Franklin D. Roosevelt, April 20, 1939; WR to Joseph W. Stewart, April 24, 1939; *Evening Star* (Washington), May 2, 1939, sec. B, p. B-1, col. 4; listing of guests at administration of oath of office on commission of Wiley Rutledge as justice of the U.S. Court of Appeals for the District of Columbia; Annabel Rutledge to WR, undated [between May 2 and 8, 1939]; WR to Cottrell and Leonard, April 21, 1939 (night letter).

10. Program entitled "Justice Wiley Rutledge, Installation Ceremony—May 8, 1939," Rutledge Papers; *compare* Docket dated April 27, 1939, for the U.S. Court of Appeals for the District of Columbia for the weeks of May 8 and May 15, 1939, by order of the court, Joseph W. Stewart, clerk, *with* cases officially reported, *e.g.*, *Ritholz v. March*, 105 F.2d 937 (App. D.C. 1939) (Groner, Miller, Rutledge), *Pedersen v. Pedersen*, 107 F.2d 227 (App. D.C. 1939) (Groner, Miller, Rutledge), *Nat'l Benefit Life Ins. Co. v. Shaw-Walker Co.*, 111 F.2d 497 (App. D.C. 1940) (Groner, Stephens, Rutledge), *Cobb v. Howard Univ.*, 106 F.2d 860 (App. D.C. 1939) (Edgerton, Vinson, Rutledge), *J.C. Eno (U.S.) Ltd. v. Coe*, 106 F.2d 858 (App. D.C. 1939) (Groner, Edgerton, Rutledge).

11. WR to Annabel Rutledge, May 23, 1939; WR to Emmet Glore, Oct. 19, 1940; WR to A. A. Zimmerman, April 1, 1939; WR to Ralph Fuchs, Aug. 22, 1939; Bernard C. Gavit to WR, March 22, 1939; WR to Bernard C. Gavit, March 23, 1939; WR to Bernard C. Gavit, April 15, 1939; WR to Jack Swaner, June 12, 1939; *Cobb v. Howard Univ.*

12. Hugh J. Fegan to WR, May 8, 1939; Herbert M. Bingham to WR, May 16, 1939; Wiley Rutledge, speech notes entitled "The Young Lawyer & The Future of Legal Service, the Spirit of Youth & the Future of Law, the Barristers June 2, 1939."

13. WR memorandum of "Conversation at White House, May 23, 1939 F.D.R. & W.B.R., Jr.—Confidential" (undated).

14. James Cameron to WR, June 17, 1939; WR to James Cameron, June 20, 1939; WR to Edward C. Eicher, June 20, 1939; WR to "Mother" and the "Tribe," June 15, 1939; WR to "All" [the Rutledge family], May 20, 1939; WR to Glen Harlan, May 15, 1939; WR to Annabel Rutledge, May 23, 1939; WR to Mary Lou Rutledge, May 30, 1939; WR to Clay Apple, June 12, 1939.

15. WR to Henry Rottschaefer, Aug. 4, 1939; WR to Annabel Rutledge, May 23, 1939; WR to Ralph Fuchs, July 11, 1939.

16. WR to Jack Swaner, June 12, 1939; WR to Mrs. L. G. Thompson, June 14, 1939; WR to Clarence Updegraff, June 20, 1939; WR to James Cameron, June 20, 1939; WR to Henry Rottschaefer, Aug. 4, 1939; WR to Mason Ladd, Aug. 4, 1939; WR to Mason Ladd, May 22, 1939; Mason Ladd to WR, Sept. 28, 1939; WR to Mason Ladd, Oct. 3, 1939; Mason Ladd to WR, Nov. 11, 1939.

17. WR to Clay Apple, Oct. 3, 1939; WR to L. A. Owen, Sept. 22, 1939; WR to Justin Miller, April 11, 1939; WR to Katherine Cannell, April 12, 1939; WR to Glen Harlan, Sept. 27, 1939; WR to Mason Ladd, Oct. 3, 1939; WR to Clarence M. Updegraff, Oct. 3, 1939; WR to Rollin N. Perkins, Oct. 10, 1939; Ralph Fuchs to Edna Lingreen, Oct. 27, 1949; interview, Lingreen.

18. WR to Mason Ladd, Oct. 3, 1939; WR to Clarence Updegraff, Oct. 3, 1939; WR to Rollin N. Perkins, Oct. 10, 1939; WR to Glen Harlan, Sept. 27, 1939; Clay Apple to WR, Sept. 28, 1939; WR to Clay Apple, Oct. 3, 1939.

19. WR to Clay Apple, Oct. 3, 1939; WR to Clarence Updegraff, Oct. 3, 1939; WR to Chief Justice Groner, Oct. 6, 1939 (re Case No. 7329); WR to Justice Miller, Oct. 31, 1939 (re Case No. 7258).

20. Louis L. Jaffe to WR, Feb. 19, 1942; WR to Albert Abel, Nov. 29, 1940; WR to Ralph Fuchs, Nov. 2, 1939; WR to C. M. Updegraff, Dec. 16, 1941; H. W. E. (Justice Edgerton)

to Judge Groner and Judge Rutledge (re Case No. 7269); Wiley Rutledge, draft dissent (Case No. 7258), Rutledge Papers; Walter Gellhorn to WR, Nov. 24, 1939 (re *Int'l Ass'n of Machinists, Tool and Die Makers v. NLRB*, 110 F.2d 29 (App. D.C. 1939), *aff'd*, 311 U.S. 72 (1940)); *see* WR to Walter Gellhorn, Nov. 29, 1939.

21. WR to Albert Abel, Nov. 29, 1940; WR to Clarence Updegraff, Jan. 15, 1941; *see* WR to Louise Laribbee [*recte* Larrabee], Feb. 14, 1938.

22. E. R. Campbell to WR, April 28 and May 17, 1939; WR to E. R. Campbell, May 24, 1939; WR to W. Ross Livingston, Jan. 17, 1940; Norman C. Meier to WR, Jan. 30, 1940.

23. Norman C. Meier to WR, Jan. 30, 1940; WR to Carl Wheaton, March 12, 1940; WR to William A. Schnader, May 28, 1940; WR to Fred W. Shipley, Dec. 12, 1940; WR to C. M. Updegraff, Jan. 15, 1941; WR to Ralph Neuhoff, Feb. 1, 1940; WR to Mason Ladd, Jan. 4, 1940.

24. WR to Willard H. Pedrick, Oct. 7, 1940; WR to Mason Ladd, Dec. 5, 1940; WR to Clay Apple, Jan. 13, 1941.

25. Interviews, Lingreen, M. L. (Rutledge) Needels, J. A. (Rutledge) Pollitt, N. Rutledge; WR to Joseph O'Meara, Feb. 10, 1941; WR to Seth Thomas, June 16, 1941; *see* WR to Clarence M. Updegraff, Oct. 3, 1940.

26. WR to C. M. Updegraff, Jan. 15, 1941.

27. WR to Emmett Ray Feighner, Jan. 6, 1942; WR to Charles H. Compton, Jan. 23, 1941; *see generally* Meador, *Mr. Justice Black and His Books*.

28. WR to Edwin Borchard, Dec. 4, 1941; WR to Emmett Ray Feighner, Jan. 6, 1942; Edwin Borchard to WR, Nov. 27, 1941 (re *Washington Terminal Co. v. Boswell*, 124 F.2d 235 (App. D.C. 1941); *id.* at 18, 124 F.2d at 253 (Stephens, J., dissenting)).

29. WR to Byron G. McCollough, Dec. 31, 1941; WR to William M. Leiserson, June 16, 1942; WR to Clay Apple, Dec. 17, 1942.

30. Mason Ladd to WR, Sept. 28, 1939; Mason Ladd to WR, Oct. 11, 1939; WR to Huber Croft, Oct. 23, 1939; WR to William H. Bartley, Oct. 17, 1940.

31. Jackson, *That Man*, 54. WR to William H. Bartley, Oct. 17, 1940; WR to William H. Bartley, Oct. 24, 1940; WR to George D. Haskell, Jan. 24, 1941.

32. WR to Clay Apple, Jan. 13, 1941; Ralph Fuchs to WR, Oct. 19, 1940; Huber Croft to WR, Dec. 23, 1940; Ralph Fuchs to WR, Jan. 23, 1941; WR to Ralph Fuchs, Jan. 23, 1941.

33. WR to Huber Croft, Dec. 31, 1940; WR to William H. Bartley, Oct. 17, 1940; WR to Leslie H. Fisher, Jan. 2, 1941; WR to George D. Haskell, Jan. 24, 1941.

34. WR to W. Ross Livingston, Jan. 17, 1940; WR to J. C. Pryor, March 12, 1940; WR to President Franklin D. Roosevelt, July 19, 1940; WR to Clay Apple, Nov. 9, 1940; WR to Albert Abel, Nov. 29, 1940; WR to J. C. Pryor, Sept. 27, 1940; WR to William H. Bartley, Oct. 24, 1940; WR to President Franklin D. Roosevelt, folder 6765, FDR Personal File.

35. WR to William H. Bartley, Oct. 24, 1940; WR to Ralph Fuchs, Oct. 21, 1940; WR to Clay Apple, Jan. 13, 1940; WR to Carl Wheaton, June 4, 1941.

36. Ralph Fuchs to WR, Jan. 23, 1941; WR to Ralph Fuchs, Jan. 28, 1941; WR to Carl Wheaton, Sept. 22, 1941; Berg, *Lindbergh*, 413–16, 425–27.

37. WR to Ralph Fuchs, Jan. 28, 1941.

38. WR to L. R. Gaiennie, June 13, 1941; WR to George Haskell, June 12, 1941; WR to Clay Apple, June 2, 1941; WR to Clay R. Apple, June 27, 1941; WR to Merle Miller, July 18, 1941; WR to Carl Wheaton, June 24, 1941.

39. WR to Grove Dow, July 31, 1941; WR to Ralph Fuchs, Aug. 2, 1941; WR to W. Willard Wirtz, Dec. 8, 1941; WR to Mason Ladd, Dec. 22, 1941.

40. Robert L. Stearns to WR, May 20, 1940; Robert L. Stearns to WR, May 24, 1940;

WR to Robert L. Stearns, May 27, 1940; *Minersville Sch. Dist. v. Gobitis*, 310 U.S. 586 (1940); "Judge Rutledge Raps Flag-Salute Rule in Schools," *Evening Star* (Washington), June 10, 1940, p. 19, col. 3.

41. Rutledge, "The Varied Carols I Hear," 77, 81–82 (address delivered Oct. 18, 1940); Wiley Rutledge, "Survey of the Conference Problems," 22 [ca. July 16, 1942].

42. W. Willard Wirtz to WR, July 28, 1941; WR to W. Willard Wirtz, Aug. 6, 1941.

43. WR to W. Willard Wirtz, Dec. 8, 1941; WR to George Dow, July 31, 1941; Wiley Rutledge, speech notes for "The Common Man & World Organization, Univ. of Colorado Summer Assembly, 8/5/42"; unidentified and undated newspaper, "Form World Order Before War Ends, Rutledge Urges; Visiting Justice Fears Selfishness May Dominate Treaty Otherwise," Rutledge Papers; *accord* second unidentified and undated newspaper, "Judge Rutledge Speaker at Lions Meet Wednesday, Said Allied Nations Must Begin to Plan The Peace to Follow Victory," Rutledge Papers; Rutledge, "What Is the War Doing to Law and Lawyers?," 426.

CHAPTER TWELVE

1. Of the thirty federal cases in which Rutledge wrote an opinion, thirteen concerned government departments and agencies, including Interior, the NLRB, SEC, and FCC. Another twelve were patent cases, leaving five to address federal taxes, customs, war risk insurance, and a contract dispute governed by ICC tariffs.

2. Although there was a municipal court system with jurisdiction over minor crimes and over civil cases with limited amounts in controversy, the U.S. District Court sat as the principal trial court for most crimes, as well as for the larger civil cases, in the District of Columbia. The District Court also had exclusive jurisdiction over certain civil law categories, such as domestic relations. *E.g., Brown v. Brown*, 134 F.2d 505 (D.C. Cir. 1942). Thus, while some civil appeals of local matters came to the U.S. Court of Appeals through its discretionary review of the District of Columbia Municipal Court of Appeals, most came from the U.S. District Court. A few of the local law appeals that Justice Rutledge heard from the District Court, however, may have concerned cases brought there because of its federal diversity jurisdiction, not because of its jurisdiction as a local trial court. To that extent, the cases included in the statistics for Rutledge's local law appeals could be said to reflect the kinds of cases any federal court of appeals would hear. It is interesting to note, however, that Rutledge did not identify any diversity case as such, and it does not appear from his opinions that many—if any—could fit into that category. Accordingly, the allocation of Rutledge's caseload—70 percent local, 30 percent federal—appears to be accurate.

3. In addition, Rutledge would have written his fair share of the court's brief, unpublished opinions on motions and in easily resolved appeals unanimously affirming the trial court.

4. Canon 19, Judicial Opinions, American Bar Association, *Canons of Judicial Ethics* (Sept. 30, 1937) ("Except in case of conscientious difference of opinion on fundamental principle, dissenting opinions should be discouraged in courts of last resort.").

5. 129 F.2d 24, 28, 38 (D.C. Cir. 1942) (Rutledge, J., dissenting).

6. 316 U.S. 584, 600 (1942) (Stone, J., dissenting); *id.* at 611, 614 n. 4 (Murphy, J., dissenting); *id.* at 623 (Black, Douglas, and Murphy, JJ., dissenting).

7. 128 F.2d 265, 267, 268, 271 (D.C. Cir. 1942); *see Canizio v. New York*, 327 U.S. 82, 91 (1946) (Rutledge, J., dissenting).

8. 121 F.2d 865, 872 n. 11 (App. D.C. 1941).

9. 132 F.2d 545, 546, 547, 548, 554 (D.C. Cir. 1942) (en banc), *aff'd, FCC v. NBC,* 319 U.S. 239 (1943).

10. 124 F.2d 235 (App. D.C. 1941), *aff'd,* 319 U.S. 732 (1943) (per curiam) (equally divided court; Rutledge, J., not participating).

11. *Georgetown Coll. v. Hughes,* 139 F.2d 810 (D.C. Cir. 1942) (en banc).

12. *McKenna v. Austin,* 134 F.2d 659 (D.C. Cir. 1943).

13. *Melvin v. Pence,* 130 F.2d 423 (D.C. Cir. 1942).

14. *Frene v. Louisville Cement Co.,* 134 F.2d 511, 516 (D.C. Cir. 1943); *see Int'l Shoe Co. v. Washington,* 326 U.S. 310 (1945).

15. *Pedersen v. Pedersen,* 107 F.2d 227 (App. D.C. 1939).

16. *Schlaefer v. Schlaefer,* 112 F.2d 177 (App. D.C. 1940).

17. Justice Rutledge dissented in the following cases in addition to those discussed: *Joerns v. Irvin,* 114 F.2d 458, 459 (App. D.C. 1940) (Rutledge, J., dissenting); *Amer. Secur. & Trust Co. v. Frost,* 117 F.2d. 283, 287 (App. D.C. 1940) (Rutledge, J., dissenting); *Loughlin v. Berens,* 128 F.2d 23, 26 (D.C. Cir. 1942) (Rutledge, J., dissenting); *Mancari v. Frank P. Smith, Inc.,* 114 F.2d 834, 837 (App. D.C. 1940) (Rutledge, J., dissenting).

18. *Press Co. v. NLRB,* 118 F.2d 937, 947 (App. D.C. 1940) (Rutledge, J., dissenting in part).

19. *Lebanon Steel Foundry v. NLRB,* 130 F.2d 404 (D.C. Cir. 1942); *Warehousemen's Union v. NLRB,* 121 F.2d 84 (App. D.C. 1941); *Int'l Ass'n of Machinists, Tool and Die Makers v. NLRB,* 110 F.2d 29 (App. D.C. 1939), *aff'd,* 311 U.S. 72 (1940).

20. *Switchmen's Union of N. Am. v. Nat'l Med. Bd.,* 135 F.2d 785, 796, 797 (D.C. Cir. 1943) (Rutledge, J., dissenting).

21. 133 F.2d 25, 28 (D.C. Cir. 1942); *id.* at 29, 30, 31 (D.C. Cir. 1942) (Rutledge, J., dissenting).

22. *Balinovic v. Evening Star Newspaper Co.,* 113 F.2d 505, 507 (App. D.C. 1940) (Rutledge, J., dissenting).

23. *In re Rosier,* 133 F.2d 316, 333, 336, 337, 338 (D.C. Cir. 1942) (Rutledge, J., dissenting); D.C. Code sec. 24-501 (k)(5) (2001).

24. WR to Clarence M. Updegraff, Oct. 3, 1939; WR to Evan A. Evans, Feb. 5, 1938.

25. WR to Clarence Morris, March 15 and 21, 1940 (*Evening Star*); WR to W. Howard Mann, Dec. 31, 1940 (*Evening Star*); WR to Ralph F. Fuchs, Aug. 2, 1941 (*Washington Terminal*; referring to correspondence with Lloyd Garrison); WR to Frank E. Horack Jr., Nov. 18, 1941 (*Washington Terminal*); WR to Walter Gellhorn, Nov. 26, 1941 (*Washington Terminal*).

26. WR to Frank E. Horack Jr., Nov. 18, 1941; Walter Gellhorn, Nov. 26, 1941.

27. Canon 3A(4) (1973), Code of Conduct for United States Judges; WR to Mason Ladd, July 18, 1939; WR to Philip Mechem, Oct. 11, 1940; WR to Ralph Fuchs, Feb. 5, 1941; WR to Albert J. Harno, Oct. 27, 1941; WR to Edwin Borchard, Dec. 4, 1941.

28. *Balinovic v. Evening Star Newspaper Co.,* 113 F.2d at 507 (Rutledge, J., dissenting).

29. *Washington Terminal Co. v. Boswell,* 124 F.2d 235 (App. D.C. 1941), *aff'd,* 319 U.S. 732 (1943) (per curiam) (equally divided court; Rutledge, J., not participating).

30. WR to Clarence Morris, March 15 and 21, 1940; WR to Frank E. Horack Jr., Nov. 18, 1941; WR to Walter Gellhorn, Nov. 26, 1941; WR to W. Willard Wirtz, Dec. 8, 1941; *Washington Terminal Co. v. Boswell,* 124 F.2d 235 (App. D.C. 1941), *aff'd,* 319 U.S. 732 (1943) (per curiam) (equally divided court; Rutledge, J., not participating).

31. WR to Justice Miller, June 3, 1942 (memorandum); WR to Joseph O'Meara Jr., Feb. 6, 1940; WR to Karl N. Llewellyn, Oct. 29, 1940.

32. WR to Irving Brant, Dec. 1, 1938.

33. George M. Hopkins to President Franklin D. Roosevelt, Nov. 25, 1939; Albert Thomas to President Franklin D. Roosevelt, Jan. 2, 1940; A. F. Whitney to President Franklin D. Roosevelt, Jan. 4, 1940, FDR Official File, file 41a, box 55; Hutcheson, "The Judgment Intuitive," 276 & nn. 4, 6, 277 & n. 11, 279, 284–85 & nn. 27–28 (citing *S. Pac. v. Jensen*, 244 U.S. 205, 221 (1917) (Holmes, J., dissenting); Cardozo, *The Nature of the Judicial Process* and *Paradoxes of Legal Science*; and *Washington v. Dawson*, 264 U.S. 219, 236 (1924) (Brandeis, J., dissenting)).

34. WR to Clarence Morris, March 21, 1940; WR to Joseph O'Meara Jr., Feb. 6, 1940; WR to Ralph F. Fuchs, Aug. 2, 1941.

35. WR to Joseph O'Meara Jr., Feb. 6, 1940; *Washington v. Dawson, quoted in* Hutcheson, "The Judgment Intuitive," 276.

36. *E.g., Fox v. Johnson & Wimsatt, Inc.*, 127 F.2d 729 (D.C. Cir. 1942); *Int'l Ass'n of Machinists, Tool and Die Makers v. NLRB*, 110 F.2d 29 (App. D.C. 1939), *aff'd*, 311 U.S. 72 (1940).

37. *E.g., Acker v. Herfurth*, 110 F.2d 241 (App. D.C. 1939); *W.C. & A.N. Miller Dev. Co. v. Emig Properties Corp.*, 134 F.2d 36 (D.C. Cir. 1943); *Hohenthal v. Smith*, 114 F.2d 494 (App. D.C. 1940); *McKenna v. Austin*, 134 F.2d 659 (D.C. Cir. 1943); *Frene v. Louisville Cement Co.*, 134 F.2d 511, 516 (D.C. Cir. 1943); *Georgetown Coll. v. Hughes*, 139 F.2d 810 (D.C. Cir. 1942) (en banc); *Schlaefer v. Schlaefer*, 107 F.2d 227 (App. D.C. 1939); *Busey v. District of Columbia*, 129 F. 2d 24, 28 (D.C. Cir. 1942); *Amer. Nat'l Bank & Trust Co. v. United States*, 134 F.2d 674 (D.C. Cir. 1943); *Hartford Accident Co. v. Cardillo*, 112 F.2d 11 (App. D.C. 1940); *Jordan v. Group Health Ass'n*, 107 F.2d 239 (App. D.C. 1939); *Pederson v. Pederson*, 107 F.2d at 229, 232–34.

38. *Int'l Ass'n of Machinists, Tool and Die Makers v. NLRB*; *Press Co. v. NLRB*, 118 F.2d 937 (App. D.C. 1940).

39. *Christie v. Callahan*, 124 F.2d 825 (App. D.C. 1941).

40. *Fairclaw v. Forrest*, 130 F.2d 829 (D.C. Cir. 1942).

41. *Fox v. Johnson & Wimsatt, Inc.*

42. WR to Judges Stephens and Miller, July 9, 1940 (re *Jordon v. Bondy*, 114 F.2d 599 (App. D.C. 1940)).

43. *Fox v. Johnson & Wimsatt, Inc.*; *Burke v. Canfield*, 121 F.2d 877 (App. D.C. 1941); Fuchs, "The Judicial Art of Wiley B. Rutledge," 115, 119.

44. *E.g., Howard v. Overholzer*, 130 F.2d 429 (D.C. Cir. 1942); *Acker v. Herfurth*, 110 F.2d 241 (App. D.C. 1939); *see generally* Israel Treiman, "Mr. Justice Rutledge: An Appraisal Based upon His Opinions While on the United States Court of Appeals," 14 *Mo. B.J.* 4 (1943).

45. WR to Peter N. Chumbris, July 12, 1940; Peter N. Chumbris to WR, July 11, 1940; program, "The Cincinnati Conference on Law and Lawyers in the Modern World . . . Saturday, March 1, 1941"; "Discuss Legal Service For Low Income Group," *Cincinnati Times Star*, March 1941, Rutledge Papers; untitled address by Justice Wiley Rutledge to ABA Committee on Legal Aid, exact date unknown, September 1941, Indianapolis, at 1a, 2, 3 (hereafter "Legal Aid Address"). *See also* WR to Lester A. Royal, Nov. 5, 1941.

46. Legal Aid Address, 6–8, 11; WR to Lester A. Royal, Nov. 5, 1941.

47. Legal Aid Address, 13–16.

48. "Justice Rutledge Says Judges Have Too Much Sentence Power," unidentified newspaper, June 7, 1941, Rutledge Papers; *Evening Star* (Washington), June 7, 1941, sec. A, p. A-20, col. 5; *Times-Herald* (Washington), June 7, 1941, p. 16, col. 2.

49. William A. Schnader to WR, June 18, 1940; WR to W. Willard Wirtz, June 26, 1940;

W. Willard Wirtz to WR, July 1, 1940; WR to Farwell Knapp, Aug. 2, 1940; WR to Barton H. Kuhns, Oct. 9, 1941; WR to Henry S. Fraser, June 4, 1942; Henry S. Fraser to WR, July 14, 1942; John H. Wigmore to John C. Pryor, Aug. 29, 1941; John H. Wigmore to WR, Oct. 13, 1941; WR to John H. Wigmore, Oct. 17, 1941; WR to William A Schnader, Oct. 18, 1941; John H. Wigmore to WR, Oct. 23, 1941; WR to N. W. MacChesney, Nov. 24, 1941; WR to J. C. Pryor, Oct. 19, 1940; Jesse E. Marshall to WR, Oct. 25, 1940; WR to Ralph Fuchs, Oct. 29, 1940; Karl N. Llewellyn to WR, Oct. 25, 1940; WR to Karl N. Llewellyn, Oct. 29, 1940; Ralph Fuchs to WR, Nov. 9, 1940.

50. Grace Hays Riley to WR, Jan. 30, 1940; unidentified newspaper clipping, "A College Banquet, Wherein the Washington College of Law Celebrates Its 4th Anniversary with Turkey and Trimmin's and a Spot of Dancing at the Mayflower Hotel," Feb. 12, 1940, Rutledge Papers; Washington College of Law, American University, *Alumni Directory*, vi, WCL Archives.

51. WR to Grace Hays Riley, May 31, 1941; Grace Hays Riley to WR, June 4, 1941; WR to Carl C. Wheaton, June 4, 1941; WR to Lawrence W. DeMuth, Aug. 1, 1941; WR to Russell N. Sullivan, Nov. 27 and Dec. 23, 1942; Russell N. Sullivan to WR, Jan. 6, 1943; minutes of Meeting of the Board of Trustees, Washington College of Law, Jan. 15, 1943, WCL Archives; Russell N. Sullivan to Dr. Edwin C. Dutton, April 9, 1943 (cc: WR), WCL Archives.

52. WR to Dr. Paul Douglas[s], June 26, 1942; memorandum "To the Members of the Board of Trustees" (unsigned, Feb. 6, 1942), Rutledge Papers; "Report to the Board of Trustees of Washington College of Law" (unsigned and undated), Rutledge Papers; Dr. Edwin C. Dutton to WR, April 10, 1942; WR to Dr. Paul Douglas[s], June 26, 1942; Arthur T. Vanderbilt to WR, July 14, 1942; WR to Dr. Edwin C. Dutton, July 15, 1942, Rutledge Papers; memorandum from President [Paul] Douglass to Committee on Academic Standards, American University, March 24, 1949 (confirming "complete organic merger" of the Washington College of Law with the American University), WCL Archives.

53. WR to Grace Hays Riley, Nov. 14, 1941; WR to Jacob M. Lashly, March 16, 1942; WR to Merle D. Miller, July 7, 1942.

54. Ralph Fuchs to WR, Aug. 7, 1941; WR to Edward S. Stimson, Nov. 13, 1941; WR to Herbert Wechsler, Oct. 20, 1941; interview, Wechsler.

55. L. A. Moyer to WR, Dec. 31, 1941; WR to Clay R. Apple, Jan. 19, 1942; memorandum, "Board of Legal Examiners, State Examining Committee Members Cleared by the Board September 12, 1942."

56. President Franklin D. Roosevelt to WR, June 6, 1942; WR to President Franklin D. Roosevelt, June 6, 1942, folder 4991, FDR Official File; WR to President Franklin D. Roosevelt, June 10, 1942; White House press release, listing nine members whom the president appointed to the National Railway Labor Panel created by Executive Order No. 9172 on May 22, 1942 (including "Judge Wiley Rutledge, Associate Justice, U.S. Court of Appeals, District of Columbia"), folder 4991, FDR Official File; White House press release, May 22, 1942, summarizing Executive Order No. 9172, "Establishing a Panel for the Creation of Emergency Boards for the Adjustment of Railway Labor Disputes," folder 4991, FDR Official File.

57. WR to W. Willard Wirtz, May 31, 1939; WR to Will J. Jackson, Oct. 14, 1940; WR to assessor of taxes, April 15, 1942 (referring to letter of April 13, 1940, to D.C. assessor); 72 App. D.C. 30, 113 F.2d 25 (1940).

58. *Washington Post*, March 12, 1940, p. 10, col. 1; *Sweeney v. District of Columbia*, 113 F.2d 25, 26, 32, 33 (App. D.C. 1940); partial handwritten draft, *Sweeney v. District of Columbia*, 7.

59. WR to Clay R. Apple, March 7, 1940.

60. WR to Henry F. Long, March 15, 1940.

61. WR to Mrs. Eugene Callaghan, June 10, 1942.

62. H.R. 7339, 77th Cong., 2d sess. (July 1, 1942); WR to E. Barrett Prettyman, Oct. 8, 1942.

63. WR to Clay Apple, March 7, 1940; WR to J. C. Pryor, April 23, 1940; WR to J. C. Pryor, Feb. 1, 1941.

64. WR to Ralph Fuchs, March 7, 1940; WR to J. C. Pryor, April 23, 1940; WR to J. C. Pryor, Feb. 1, 1941; WR to J. C. Pryor, Feb. 6, 1941; WR to Joseph O'Meara, Feb. 10, 1941; WR to Seth Thomas, June 16, 1941; WR to J. C. Pryor, Oct. 3, 1941; WR to Clay R. Apple, March 8, 1940; WR to J. C. Pryor, April 25, 1940; WR to J. C. Pryor, May 1, 1940; WR to Robert H. Jackson, May 2, 1940; WR to Carl [J. C.] Pryor, May 10, 1940; WR to Oscar L. Chapman, May 22, 1940; WR to Clay R. Apple, May 22, 1940; WR to Aubrey Williams, May 29, 1940; WR to Robert H. Jackson, Dec. 18, 1940.

65. WR to Glenn Metcalf, Oct. 19, 1940; WR to Jerome A. Gross, Jan. 23, 1941; WR to Clarence Morris, Dec. 8, 1941; WR to Morton S. Adler, Dec. 17, 1941; WR to Charles A. Dewey, Dec. 17, 1941; WR to Clay R. Apple, April 2, 1941; WR to George D. Haskell, Jan. 24, 1941; Rutledge, "What Is the War Doing to Law and Lawyers?," 421–24; WR to Ronald J. Foulis, Jan. 19, 1942; WR to Clarence Morris, Dec. 9, 1941; WR to Leslie Hawes Fisher, March 5, 1942.

66. Edward Stimson to WR, Oct. 29, 1941; WR to Edward Stimson, Nov. 13, 1941; Louise Larrabee to WR, undated "Tuesday," Dec. 1941; W. Willard Wirtz to WR, Dec. 1, 1941; WR to W. Willard Wirtz, Dec. 8, 1941; W. Willard Wirtz to WR, Dec. 17, 1941; interview, Wirtz.

67. WR to George D. Haskell, Jan. 27, 1941; WR to William H. Bartley, Oct. 17, 1940.

68. WR to W. Willard Wirtz, June 26, 1940; *see* Clay R. Apple to WR, June 14, 1940.

69. K. E. Grant to WR, July 8, 1940; WR to Huber Croft, July 23, 1940; newspaper listings for 4928 Indian Lane, N.W., Rutledge Papers; M. A. Hess to WR, June 22, 1940; WR to M. A. Hess, June 26, 1940; WR to Ralph F. Fuchs, Sept. 19, 1940; WR to Carl C. Wheaton, April 11, 1939; Carl C. Wheaton to WR, July 3, 1940.

70. *Evening Star* (Washington), Jan. 22, 1941, p. 1, cols. 1–4; WR to Clay R. Apple, Jan. 29, 1941; WR to Jacob M. Lashly, Feb. 3, 1941; WR to W. Willard Wirtz, June 18, 1941; WR to Ralph F. Fuchs, Aug. 2, 1941.

71. WR to Joseph O'Meara, Jan. 25, 1941; *Washington Post*, June 3, 1941, p. 1, col. 6; William V. Nessly, "Roosevelt Accepts [Hughes'] Resignation Out of Consideration for Health and Age," *Washington Post*, June 3, 1941, p. 1, col. 8; Winfred B. Moore Jr., "James F. Byrnes," 403; Marsh, "Robert H. Jackson," 408.

72. Joseph O'Meara to WR, Jan. 23, 1941; WR to Joseph O'Meara, Jan. 25, 1941.

73. Interview, N. Rutledge; WR to J. C. Pryor, Feb. 6, 1941.

74. Clay R. Apple to WR, Aug. 13, 1941. A notation on Clay Apple's letter of August 13, 1941, indicates that Rutledge replied on August 16, presumably by hand because the Rutledge Papers do not contain a copy. No other correspondent, even the redoubtable Ralph Fuchs, mentions the rumor, so it apparently had no substance.

75. WR to Carl Wheaton, Sept. 22, 1941; WR to Albert Abel, Oct. 10, 1941; WR to Merle Miller, Sept. 22, 1941.

76. WR to Harold M. Stephens, Sept. 25, 1942; WR to W. Howard Mann, Aug. 20, 1942; WR to William H. Bartley, Sept. 21, 1942; *see* "Mr. Rutledge," examination in "Administrative Law, School of Law, University of Colorado, August 19, 1942."

CHAPTER THIRTEEN

1. Wilfred B. Moore Jr., "James F. Byrnes, 1941–1942," in Cushman, ed., *The Supreme Court Justices*, 401, 404–5; Newman, *Hugo Black*, 321; Biddle, *In Brief Authority*, 192–93.

2. J. Carl Pryor to WR, Oct. 7, 1942; WR to J. Carl Pryor, Oct. 16, 1942.

3. J. Carl Pryor to WR, Oct. 21, 1942; WR to J. Carl Pryor, Oct. 26, 1942; *see generally* Goings, *"The NAACP Comes of Age,"* 19–36.

4. Drew Pearson, *Washington Post*, Nov. 6, 1942, p. 12, cols. 7–8; *accord* Francis Biddle, Diary, Nov. 14, 1942, Barton Kuhns to WR, Nov. 6, 1942; Clay Apple to WR, Nov. 9, 1942; Paul P. Eagleton to WR, Nov. 9, 1942; WR to Joseph A. McClain Jr., Nov. 7, 1942; WR to Barton Kuhns, Nov. 10, 1942; WR to Clay Apple, Nov. 14, 1942; WR to Leon W. Powers, Nov. 19, 1942; WR to William B. Hart, Nov. 13, 1942; WR to David Rosner, Nov. 13, 1942; WR to Sen. George W. Norris, Dec. 12, 1942.

5. WR to Hon. Francis Biddle, Nov. 7, 1942.

6. Irving Brant to Luther Ely Smith, Oct. 31, 1942, Brant Papers; Luther Ely Smith to Hon. Francis Biddle, Nov. 3, 1942, Brant Papers; Luther Ely Smith to Irving Brant, Nov. 4, 1942, Brant Papers; Louise Larrabee to President Franklin D. Roosevelt, Nov. 8, 1942; Irving Brant to Hon. Francis Biddle, Nov. 10, 1942, Brant Papers; Roscoe Anderson to *St. Louis Post-Dispatch*, Nov. 8, 1942, part 4, p. 2D, col. 1; *see* Luther Ely Smith to Irving Brant, Nov. 10, 1941; James Rowe Jr. to Luther Ely Smith, Nov. 7, 1942, Smith Missouri.

7. Irving Brant to Virgil Hancher, Nov. 7, 1942, box 8, Brant Papers; Virgil M. Hancher to Irving Brant, Nov. 9, 1942, box 8, Brant Papers; Irving Brant to Hon. Francis Biddle, Nov. 10, 1942, Brant Papers; Roscoe Anderson to *St. Louis Post-Dispatch*, Nov. 8, 1942, part 4, p. 2D, col. 1; *see* Luther Ely Smith to Irving Brant, Nov. 10, 1942, Brant Papers; Libbey, *Dear Alben* (especially ch. 5); Polly Ann Davis, *Alben W. Barkley*; Harper, *Justice Rutledge and the Bright Constellation*, 39–40; Wallace, Reminiscences, 1975.

8. *Washington Post*, Nov. 5, 1942, p. 1, col. 1; WR to Hon. Francis Biddle, Nov. 7, 1942; WR to Joseph A. McClain Jr., Nov. 7, 1942; WR to Leon Powers, Nov. 19, 1942; WR to Joseph O'Meara, Nov. 19, 1942; WR to Clay Apple, Nov. 14, 1942; WR to Sen. George Norris, Dec. 12, 1942.

9. Irving Brant to Luther Ely Smith, Dec. 19, 1942; Biddle Diary, Oct. 28, 1942; Herbert Wechsler, "Memorandum for the Attorney General," Nov. 12, 1942 (authorship confirmed by Wechsler interview; hereafter "Wechsler memorandum"), Judicial Folder, Biddle Papers; Biddle, *In Brief Authority*, 196.

10. Biddle Diary, Nov. 14, 1942; Biddle, *In Brief Authority*, 193; Mason, *Harlan Fiske Stone*, 592 (quoting Harlan Fiske Stone to C. C. Burlingham, Nov. 14, 1942).

11. Biddle Diary, Nov. 14, 1942; Biddle, *In Brief Authority*, 193; *see* Gunther, *Learned Hand*, 281.

12. Biddle, *In Brief Authority*, 193; Biddle Diary, Oct. 28 and Nov. 19, 1942; interview, Wechsler; *see* Biddle Papers, box 41-A (correspondence re Justice Traynor, among others).

13. Wechsler memorandum, Nov. 12, 1942.

14. Wechsler memorandum, Nov. 12, 1942; John A. Garraty and Mark C. Carnes, eds., 17 *American National Biography* 34, 21 *American National Biography* 812 (1999).

15. Interview, Wechsler.

16. Gunther, *Learned Hand*, 3, 553–70 (citing Max Freedman, ed., *Roosevelt and Frankfurter*, 673); Hirsch, *The Enigma of Felix Frankfurter*, 166; Biddle Diary, Nov. 17, 1942; Burlingham, Reminiscences, 22–23; interview, Wechsler; WR to Mason Ladd, Oct. 3, 1939; Murphy, *The Brandeis/Frankfurter Connection*, 318–20.

17. Gunther, *Learned Hand*, 559 (quoting Freedman, ed., *Roosevelt and Frankfurter*, 673–74); Gunther, *Learned Hand*, 562 (quoting Douglas, *Go East, Young Man*, 331–32). Had the president selected Hand in 1943, the Court would have received a member whose jurisprudence and personality differed markedly from those of Wiley Rutledge. *See generally* Gunther, *Learned Hand*. Years later Hand reminisced: "He was a very good man, Rutledge, but I think he was a disastrous judge, myself. Yes, I think his trouble was the same as Black's. Rutledge had the notion that he was there to do right, and see that right was done. Hand, Reminiscences, 94.

18. Biddle Diary, Nov. 17, 1942; Biddle, *In Brief Authority*, 196–97.

19. Gunther, *Learned Hand*, 568; Douglas, *Go East Young Man*, 332 ("[sic]" flags Brant as *St. Louis Star-Times* editor); Kahn, "The Politics of the Appointment Process," 280 n. 199, 282; Felix Frankfurter to WR, Jan. 10, 1943; Nomination Reference and Report, in Executive Session, Senate of the United States, Jan. 11, 1943, Rutledge Nom. File.

20. Interviews, Folsom, J. K. Mann, Temko, Wechsler.

21. Felix Frankfurter to WR, Jan. 10, 1943; Harlan F. Stone to WR, Jan. 11, 1943; Stanley Reed to WR, Jan. 11, 1943; Robert H. Jackson to WR, Jan 11, 1943; Frank Murphy to WR, Jan. 11, 1943; Owen J. Roberts to WR, Jan. 12, 1943; William O. Douglas to WR, Jan. 16, 1943; John J. Parker to WR, Jan. 11, 1943; Ben V. Cohen to WR, Jan. 12, 1943; Thomas Reed Powell to WR, Jan. 13, 1943. Justice Black conveyed his congratulations by telephone to the Rutledges' daughter, Mary Lou, on Jan. 18. WR to Hugo Black, Jan. 18, 1943, Black Papers, box 62, "Rutledge, Wiley B., 1935–50."

22. WR to Thomas Reed Powell, Jan. 18, 1943.

23. *New York Times*, Feb. 2, 1943, p. 26, col. 5; *Evening Star* (Washington), Feb. 1, 1943, p. 1, col. 7; *Washington Post*, Feb. 2, 1943, p. 1B, col. 4; Homer Ferguson to WR, Feb. 2, 1943; Edna Lingreen to W. Howard Mann, Feb. 6, 1943; 89 *Cong. Rec.* S719-20 (daily ed., Feb. 8, 1943); *Washington Post*, Feb. 9, 1943, p. 7, cols. 7–8; Francis Biddle to WR, Feb. 10, 1943, Rutledge Appt. File; Commission of "Wiley Blount Rutledge to Be an Associate Justice of the Supreme Court of the United States," signed by the president, Feb. 11, 1943, Rutledge Appt. File.

24. WR to President Franklin D. Roosevelt, Feb. 15, 1943; *see* Schwartz, *A History of the Supreme Court*, 381–84.

CHAPTER FOURTEEN

1. *Washington Post*, Feb. 15, 1943, sec. 1, p. 1, cols. 5–8; WR to Arthur K. Shipe, Feb. 19, 1943.

2. Mason, *Harlan Fiske Stone*, 3, 181, 568; Urofsky, *Division and Discord*, 13, 300; interviews, Birdzell Jr., Boskey, Brudney, Elman, Gressman, Kabot, Lomen, Pickering, Shniderman.

3. Simon, *The Antagonists*, 117, 127, 158–59, 188; Yarbrough, *Mr. Justice Black and His Critics*, 184; interviews, Allan, Coleman Jr., Elman, Frank, Gartner, Groner, Haber, Joslin, Kabot, Kurland, Lake, Loman, Morrison, Nickerson, Oberdorfer, Weiss, von Mehren, Wollenberg.

4. Interviews, Allan, Allen, Birdzell Jr., Ebb, Gardner, Gartner, Haber, Helman, Joslin, Kabot, Kurland, Lomen, Luce, Marsh, Morrison, Nickerson, Oberdorfer, Pollak, Rosenthal, Seder Jr., Spitzer, Tone, Torre, von Mehren, Weiss, Wollenberg; *see* Fassett, *New Deal Justice*, 372, 648.

5. Simon, *The Antagonists*, 117, 127, 188; interviews, Allan, Allen, Brudney, Cole-

man Jr., Ebb, Elman, Frank, Gartner, Gressman, Groner, Joslin, Kurland, Lake, Lomen, Mann, Marsh, Neal, Nickerson, Oberdorfer, Rosenthal, Seder Jr., Shniderman, Spitzer, J. P. Stevens, Temko, von Mehren, Weiss, Weston, Wollenberg.

6. Interviews, Allen, Beyer Jr., Coleman Jr., Ebb, Gartner, Gressman, Groner, Haber, Henkin, Hobbs, Joslin, Kabot, Lake, Lomen, Luce, Neal, Nickerson, Oberdorfer, Pickering, Rosenthal, Seder Jr., Shniderman, Temko, Torre, von Mehren, Wollenberg; David J. Danelski, "Lucile T. Lomen," 47–48 (unlike other clerks, invited to six or so dinner parties by the Douglases); Urofsky, "Getting the Job Done," 37–44 (discussing Douglas's relationships with his law clerks primarily in the 1950s and later); Urofsky, "William O. Douglas and His Clerks"; Murphy, *Wild Bill*, 408–15.

7. Howard, *Mr. Justice Murphy*, 214; Gressman, "The Controversial Image of Mr. Justice Murphy"; Kurland, "Judicial Biography," 491; interviews, Allan, Allen, Birdzell Jr., Boskey, Coleman Jr., Elman, Gartner, Gressman, Haber, Helman, Henkin, Kurland, Lake, Lomen, Luce, Marsh, Morrison, Nickerson, Pickering, Seder Jr., Shniderman, Temko, Torre, von Mehren, Weston; Sheridan L. Hill-Ellis to author, Oct. 26, 1995 (enclosure).

8. *E.g.*, *Thornhill v. Alabama*, 310 U.S. 88 (1940) (reversing conviction for violating state anti-picketing statute as facially invalid under freedom of speech protection of Fourteenth Amendment); *Korematsu v. United States*, 323 U.S. 214, 233 (1944) (Murphy, J., dissenting from decision upholding exclusion of all persons of Japanese ancestry from designated military area on West Coast and related requirement to report to specified assembly centers); *Oyama v. California*, 332 U.S. 633, 650 (1948) (Murphy, J., concurring, on grounds of Fourteenth Amendment equal protection clause violation, in judgment striking down California Alien Land Law barring persons of Japanese ancestry from owning real property); *Wolf v. Colorado*, 338 U.S. 25, 41 (1949) (dissenting from majority's refusal to extend to state courts federal "exclusionary rule" barring admission in criminal trial of evidence seized in violation of Fourth Amendment).

9. Marsh, "Robert H. Jackson"; Mason, *Harlan Fiske Stone*, 566–67 & n.*; Gerhart, *America's Advocate*, 230; Jackson, *That Man*, 107; interviews, Allen, Birdzell Jr., Boskey, Coleman Jr., Ebb, Feller, Gardner, Gartner, Gressman, Groner, Helman, Hobbs, Joslin, Kabot, Lomen, Luce, Marsh, Morrison, Nickerson, Oberdorfer, Pickering, Seder Jr., Shniderman, Spitzer, Tone, Torre, Weston, Wollenberg.

10. Interviews, J. K. Mann, M. L. (Rutledge) Needels, J. A. (Rutledge) Pollitt, N. Rutledge.

11. WR to President Franklin D. Roosevelt, Feb. 15, 1943; WR to the attorney general, Feb. 15, 1943; WR to Sen. George Norris, Feb. 15, 1943; WR to Virginia Morsey, Dec. 14, 1942; WR to Virginia Morsey, Jan. 6, 1943; Virginia Morsey to WR, March 8, 1943; WR to the Chief Justice, June 21, 1943 (memorandum); *see* John Frank to Ralph Fuchs, Jan. 11, 1943; interview, Brudney.

12. Interview, Lingreen; *see* WR to Philip Mechem, March 8 and April 6, 1949.

13. Interview, Brudney; WR to Philip Mechem, March 8, 1949; WR to Philip Mechem, April 6, 1949. The decision, 6 to 3, was *Lyons v. Oklahoma*, 322 U.S. 596 (1944) (voluntary confession twelve hours after coerced confession held admissible against defendant where judge and jury found that effects of coercion had been dissipated before second confession); *id* at 605 (Rutledge, J., "dissents" without opinion); *id.* at 605 (Murphy, J., joined by Black, J., dissenting).

14. Interview, Brudney.

15. *Id.*; *accord* interviews, Pollak, Shniderman, J. P. Stevens.

16. Interview, Brudney.

17. Interviews, Brudney, Pollak, Shniderman, J. P. Stevens, Temko, Tone; "Statement Showing the Number of Cases Filed, Disposed of, and Remaining on Dockets, at Conclusion of October Terms—1940, 1941 and 1942," 320 U.S. 217 (1943); "Statement Showing the Number of Cases Filed, Disposed of, and Remaining on Dockets, at Conclusion of October Term—1943, 1944 and 1945," 328 U.S. 883 (1946).

18. Interviews, Pollak, Stevens, Temko; *see* Brudney and Wolfson, "Mr. Justice Rutledge," 35 *Iowa L. Rev.* 579 (1950), 25 *Ind. L.J.* 456 (1950).

19. Interviews, Brudney, Pollak, Shniderman, J. P. Stevens, Temko; Brudney and Wolfson, "Mr. Justice Rutledge," 35 *Iowa L. Rev.* 579 (1950), 25 *Ind. L.J.* 456 (1950).

20. Interviews, Brudney, Lingreen, Pollak, Shniderman, J. P. Stevens, Tone; Brudney and Wolfson, "Mr. Justice Rutledge," 35 *Iowa L. Rev.* 581 (1950), 25 *Ind. L.J.* 457-58 (1950).

21. Interviews, Lingreen, Pollak, Shniderman, J. P. Stevens, Temko, Tone.

22. Interviews, Brudney, Pollak, Shniderman, Stevens, Temko, Tone; WR to Henry W. Edgerton, Dec. 27, 1946.

23. Interviews, Brudney, Byse.

24. "Life Has Lighter Moments on Federal Judiciary," *University Daily Kansan*, Dec. 7, 1946, Rutledge Papers (quoting Rutledge); interviews, Brudney, Lingreen, J. K. Mann, Nickerson, Pollak, J. A. (Rutledge) Pollitt, Shniderman (arrived "not early"), J. P. Stevens (recalled "9:30"), Temko, Tone; WR to Ralph R. Neuhoff, Jan. 10, 1947.

25. 318 U.S. 724, 733-34 (1943) (Chief Justice Stone dissenting in one case; Justice Roberts not participating); Irving Dilliard, "Justice Rutledge's First Opinion on Supreme Court Holds Owners Liable for Seamen Hurt Ashore," *St. Louis Post-Dispatch*, April 20, 1943, part 2, p. 1B, cols. 1-2; *see also* Dilliard, "Mr. Justice Rutledge's First Opinion."

26. *Galloway v. United States*, 319 U.S. 372 (1943); *Direct Sales Co. v. United States*, 319 U.S. 703 (1943) (sustaining conspiracy conviction under Harrison Narcotics Act); *Owens v. Union Pac. R.R. Co.*, 319 U.S. 715 (1943) (reversing denial of railroad's liability under Federal Employers' Liability Act for death of switching crew foreman).

27. *Hirabayashi v. United States*, 320 U.S. 81, 114 (1943) (Rutledge, J., concurring); *Schneiderman v. United States*, 320 U.S. 118, 165 (1943) (Rutledge, J., concurring); *Bd. of County Comm'rs v. Seber*, 318 U.S. 705, 719 (1943) (Rutledge, J., concurring in result).

28. *Marconi Wireless Tel. Co. of Am. v. United States*, 320 U.S. 1, 64 (1943) (Rutledge J., dissenting in part).

29. 319 U.S. 372 (1943); *id.* at 396 (Black, J., dissenting).

30. Felix Frankfurter to WR, May 20, 1943; WR to Felix Frankfurter, May 21, 1943 (draft; not sent).

31. Handwritten note from Harlan Fiske Stone to WR on transmittal note from WR to the Chief Justice, May 19, 1943; Robert H. Jackson to WR, March 29, 1943.

32. WR to George W. Norris, June 1, 1943.

33. 320 U.S. 1 (1943); *id.* at 60, 61, 63 (Frankfurter, J., dissenting in part); *id.* at 64 (Rutledge J., dissenting in part).

34. *See* Mason, *Harlan Fiske Stone*, 248-49, 603-4; *Hydraulic Press Corp. v. Coe*, 134 F.2d 49 (D.C. Cir. 1943); *Abbott v. Shepherd*, 135 F.2d 769 (D.C. Cir. 1942); *Boucher Inventions, Ltd. v. Sola Elec. Co.*, 131 F.2d 225 (D.C. Cir. 1942); *Leighton v. Coe*, 130 F.2d 841, 842 (D.C. Cir. 1942) (Rutledge, J., concurring); *Seyfarth v. Coe*, 129 F.2d 58 (D.C. Cir. 1942); *Morrison v. Coe*, 127 F.2d 737 (App. D.C. 1941); *Frick-Gallagher Mfg. Co. v. RoTray Corp.*, 122 F.2d 81 (App. D.C. 1941); *Sloane v. Coe*, 122 F.2d 37 (App. D.C. 1941); *Hemphill Co. v. Coe*, 121 F.2d 897 (App. D.C. 1941); *Identification Devices v. United States*, 121 F.2d 895 (App. D.C. 1941); *Levine v. Coe*, 119 F.2d 185 (App. D.C. 1941); *Minnesota Mining &*

Mfg. Co. v. Coe, 113 F.2d 512 (App. D.C. 1940); WR to Harlan Fiske Stone, June 12, 1943, H. F. Stone Papers; *Marconi Wireless Tel. Co. of Am. v. United States*, 320 U.S. at 64–66 (Rutledge, J., dissenting in part).

35. WR to the Chief Justice, June 21, 1943; *see* Harlan F. Stone to WR, June 24, 1943; interview, Boskey.

36. Interviews, Bennett, Brudney, Cameron, Fitzgibbons, Lingreen, Pollak, Stevens, Temko; Lingreen, "The Greatest Gift," 2; Brudney and Wolfson, "Mr. Justice Rutledge," 35 *Iowa L. Rev.* 582 (1950), 25 *Ind. L.J.* 459 (1950).

37. March 21, 1943 (Colorado State Society), April 3, 8, 13 (Felix Frankfurter address on Thomas Jefferson), 21 (Catholic University), 29 (Federal Bar Ass'n), 1943, typewritten list of "Engagements," 1943; Stephen Early to WR, Feb. 25, 1943; "Reception Honors Justice and Mrs. Wiley B. Rutledge, Denver Bar Assisted C.U. Alumni Body in Entertaining," *Daily Camera* (U. of Colorado), Aug. 5, 1943, Rutledge Papers; Brudney and Wolfson, "Mr. Justice Rutledge," 35 *Iowa L. Rev.* 583 (1950), 25 *Ind. L. J.* 459–60 (1950); interview, Brudney.

38. "Jeffersonian Ideals May Be Challenged, Rutledge Predicts; Says Postwar Society Must Preserve Dignity of the Individual," *Evening Star* (Washington), Feb. 26, 1943, p. A-2, cols. 3, 5; Wiley Rutledge, "Three in One," remarks before the Third Judicial Circuit Conference of the District of Columbia Circuit, Feb. 26, 1943; *Evening Star* (Washington), March 19, 1943, p. B-14, col. 3; "Engagements," April 6, 1943; "Address of Mr. Justice Wiley B. Rutledge"; "Bind on World Outlaws Urged by Judge Rutledge," *St. Louis Globe-Democrat*, April 28, 1943, part 1, p. 2-A, col. 3; "Justice Rutledge Revisits St. Louis, Guest of Professional and Civic Groups; To Address Bar Tonight," *St. Louis Post-Dispatch*, April 27, 1943, part 2, p. 3B. col. 3; printed excerpt from "Address of Honorable Wiley Blount Rutledge" at "Special Luncheon" of Federal Bar Association, April 29, 1993; Rutledge, "This Is Armageddon"; "Says We Can Lead to Stable Freedom; Justice Rutledge Asserts Error of Aloofness After Last War Must Not Be Repeated, Urges World Federation," *New York Times*, May 11 or 12, 1943, Rutledge Papers.

39. WR to Harlan Fiske Stone, June 21, 1943; Edna Lingreen to William H. Bartley, June 7, 1943; WR to W. Howard Mann, Oct. 28, 1943; WR to Annabel Rutledge, July 3, 1943; program, "Forty-third Annual Meeting, Minnesota State Bar Association, Annual Banquet," June 24, 1943, Rutledge Papers; 24 *Chicago B. Rev.* 437 (1943); "U.S. to Decide World's Fate, Justice Says; Rutledge Heard at Bar Association Dinner," *Chicago Daily Tribune*, June 30, 1943, sec. A, p. 3, col. 3; program, "Divertisement given each year by the Chairman of the Entertainment Committee of the Chicago Bar Association, . . . June 29, 1943"; Rutledge, "Peace—Or Another Treaty?"; Barbara Selby, *Houston Post*, July 3, 1943, sec. 1, p. 1, col. 1; "Associate Justice Rutledge Visits City," *Iowa City Press Citizen*, July 8, 1943, Rutledge Papers; "'Law Is a Trust'—Rutledge; Peace Officers Hear Associate Justice Speak Today," *Iowa City Press Citizen*, July 12, 1943, Rutledge Papers.

40. *Rocky Mountain News*, July 22, 1943, p. 13A, col. 1; Rutledge, "Some Premises of Peace"; WR to "Momie dear & all," "Tues. p.m." [July 6, 1943]; WR to Annabel Rutledge, Sept. 29, 1943; John E. Corsuch to WR, Aug. 19, 1943; WR to Louise Larrabee, Sept. 25, 1943; WR to R. G. Gustavson [June 29, 1944]; program, "Conference of the District Judges Association," with "General Information" showing "State Bar Meeting . . . Annual Address By Mr. Justice Wiley B. Rutledge, . . . September 17, 1943."

41. "'Law Is a Trust,'" *Iowa City Press Citizen*, July 12, 1943, Rutledge Papers; "Uniform Code to Check Crime Is Urged by Justice Rutledge; Supreme Court Jurist Tells Conference of Federal Attorneys in Denver That Laws of Sentencing Have Grown Like Topsy in This Country," unidentified newspaper, July 22, 1943, Rutledge Papers.

CHAPTER FIFTEEN

1. *See generally* David P. Currie, "The Constitution in the Supreme Court: The New Deal, 1930-1941."

2. *In re Yamashita*, 327 U.S. 1 (1946).

3. Rutledge, *A Declaration of Legal Faith*, 4-6, 11; *see* Hebrews 1:11 (King James).

4. Rutledge, *Legal Faith*, 6-7.

5. Rutledge, *Legal Faith*, 8-9, 14, 16.

6. Rutledge, *Legal Faith*, 6-10, 17; *In re Yamashita*, 327 U.S. at 41, 43.

7. Rutledge, *Legal Faith*, 17.

8. *Bowles v. Willingham*, 321 U.S. 503, 521, 525 (1944) (Rutledge, J., concurring).

9. Wiecek, "The Legal Foundation of Domestic Anticommunism," 379-82, 386-87 & n. 44, 404-5 (citing *Schenk v. United States*, 249 U.S. 47 (1919); *Frohwerk v. United States*, 249 U.S. 204 (1919); *Debs v. United States*, 249 U.S. 211 (1919); *Abrams v. United States*, 250 U.S. 616 (1919); *Pierce v. United States*, 252 U.S. 239 (1920); *Bridges v. California*, 314 U.S. 252 (1941); and *Bridges v. Wixon*, 326 U.S. 135 (1945)).

10. 320 U.S. 118, 121 & n. 2 (1943).

11. *Id*. at 121, 127, 135, 136, 157, 158.

12. *Id*. at 161, 162, 163, 165 (Douglas, J., concurring).

13. *Id*. at 165, 166-67 (Rutledge, J., concurring) (footnote omitted); *see* Urofsky, *Felix Frankfurter*, 72.

14. E.g., *Baumgartner v. United States*, 322 U.S. 665 (1944).

15. *Knauer v. United States*, 328 U.S. 654 (1946); *id*. at 675, 677-79 (Rutledge, J., dissenting); *Klapprott v. United States*, 335 U.S. 601 (1949) (opinion of Black, J.), *modified* 336 U.S. 942 (1949); *id*. at 616, 617 (Rutledge, J., concurring in result).

16. 320 U.S. 81, 83-87 (1943); Exec. Order No. 9066, 7 Fed. Reg. 1407 (1942); Irons, *Justice at War*, 88; Fine, "Mr. Justice Murphy and the Hirabayashi Case," 196; Urofsky, *Felix Frankfurter*, 74; Grossman, "The Japanese American Cases," 651-52. For a detailed history of the relocation decision, coupled with related documents, see Daniels, *The Decision to Relocate the Japanese Americans*.

17. *Hirabayashi v. United States*, 320 U.S. 81, 89, 92 (1943).

18. *Id*. at 93-95.

19. *Id*. at 93, 96-99, 100, 101; *see* Rehnquist, *All the Laws but One*, 207.

20. *Hirabayashi*, 320 U.S. at 105.

21. *See Benton v. Maryland*, 395 U.S. 784 (1969) (eviscerating *Hirabayashi*'s "concurrent sentence doctrine"); Rehnquist, *All the Laws but One*, 205.

22. *Hirabayashi*, 320 U.S. at 105, 107, 109 (Douglas, J., concurring); *id*. at 109.

23. William O. Douglas, draft concurring opinion in *Hirabayashi*, June 7, 1943, box 79, *Hirabayashi* and *Yasui* folders, Douglas Papers, *quoted in* Irons, *Justice at War*, 244-45, 390 nn. 44, 52, 391 n. 69.

24. Irons, *Justice at War*, 234, 242, 244-47; *compare* Irons, *Justice at War*, 246, *with* Howard, *Mr. Justice Murphy*, 308, *and* Ball and Cooper, *Of Power and Right*, 112; Fine, "Mr. Justice Murphy and the Hirabayashi Case," 202-6. Felix Frankfurter to Frank Murphy, June 10, 1943, reel 127, Murphy Papers; *Hirabayashi*, 320 U.S. at 109, 110, 111, 113 (Murphy, J., concurring).

25. Irons, *Justice at War*, 247; *see* WR to the Chief Justice [Harlan Fiske Stone], Aug. [*recte* June] 12, 1943, box 68, *Hirabayashi* folder, H. F. Stone Papers.

26. *See* WR to the Chief Justice [Harlan Fiske Stone], Aug. [*recte* June] 12, 1943, box 68, *Hirabayashi* folder, H. F. Stone Papers.

27. Irons, *Justice at War*, 247; *see* WR to the Chief Justice [Harlan Fiske Stone], Aug. [*recte* June] 12, 1943, box 68, *Hirabayashi* folder, H. F. Stone Papers; *Hirabayashi*, 320 U.S. at 93; Yarbrough, *Mr. Justice Black and His Critics*, 234.

28. *Hirabayashi*, 320 U.S. at 114 (Rutledge, J., concurring).

29. Draft concurrence in *Hirabayashi*, Rutledge, J., in box 93, *Hirabayashi* folder, Rutledge Papers.

30. 320 U.S. 115 (1943); WR to the Chief Justice [Harlan Fiske Stone], Aug. [*recte* June] 12, 1943, box 68, *Hirabayashi* folder, H. F. Stone Papers; WR to W. Willard Wirtz, Aug. 6, 1941; *cf*. WR to Virgil Hancher, June 19, 1945 ("I recognize only one limitation on free expression, so far as preventing it is concerned. That is military security in time of war.").

31. Interview, Brudney; Greg Robinson, *By Order of the President*, 104, 114; Grossman, "The Japanese American Cases," 656–58, 665.

32. *Washington Post*, Oct. 11, 1944, p. 1, cols. 1–8; *Korematsu v. United States*, 323 U.S. 214, 221 (1944); *id*. at 233, 242 (Murphy, J., dissenting); Irons, *Justice at War*, vii, 73; Dembitz, "Racial Discrimination and the Military Judgment," 175.

33. Even today, on the highway on Mt. Lemmon outside Tucson, Arizona, there is a sign for the "Gordon Hirabayashi Recreation Area" at the "Prison Camp." E-mail from Stephen L. Wasby to the Law and Courts Discussion List, March 11, 2001. In his dissent, Justice Roberts called an "Assembly Center" a "euphemism for a prison," and characterized "Relocation Centers" as a "euphemism for concentration camps." *Korematsu*, 323 U.S. at 225, 230 (Roberts, J., dissenting).

34. 323 U.S. 283, 294 (1944). Years later, Solicitor General Fahy recorded that he had tried to get responsible government officials to "clear this [*Endo*] matter up" without "bothering" the Supreme Court about it. Fahy, Reminiscences, 179.

35. Irons, *Justice at War*, 93–94, 153–54; *Korematsu*, 323 U.S. at 216–17; *Korematsu v. United States*, 319 U.S. 432, 432–33 (1943).

36. Irons, *Justice at War*, 227; *Korematsu*, 319 U.S. at 433, 436; *Korematsu v. United States*, 140 F.2d 289 (9th Cir. 1943); *Yasui v. United States*, 320 U.S. 115 (1943).

37. Irons, *Justice at War*, 302–4, 312–16.

38. Irons, *Justice at War*, 312, 316–17.

39. Irons, *Justice at War*, 320–23, 338; Greg Robinson, *By Order of the President*, 129; Kennedy, *Freedom from Fear*, 753; conference notes of Justice Murphy, "No. 20, O.T. 1944," reel 129, Murphy Papers.

40. Irons, *Justice at War*, 323; draft opinion of the Court by Justice Black, Nov. 11, 1944, box 116, *Korematsu* and *Endo* file, Rutledge Papers; *Korematsu*, 323 U.S. at 221. The first exclusion order authorized affected persons to migrate to approved destinations of their choice, but that procedure was soon discontinued because, according to General DeWitt's final report, "the interior states would not accept an uncontrolled Japanese migration." Dembitz, "Racial Discrimination and the Military Judgment," 201.

41. *Korematsu*, 323 U.S. at 221.

42. Irons, *Justice at War*, 327. *Korematsu*, 323 U.S. at 225, 226 (Roberts J., dissenting).

43. *Korematsu*, 323 U.S. at 233, 234, 241, 242 n. 16 (Murphy, J. dissenting).

44. Irons, *Justice at War*, 322; *Korematsu*, 323 U.S. at 242, 245–48 (Jackson, J., dissenting); *see* undated law clerk's memorandum praising but indicating illogic of Jackson's dissenting opinion, Jackson Papers, box 132, "Supreme Court—O.T. 1944, Korematsu v. United States."

45. *Korematsu*, 323 U.S. at 248 (Jackson, J., dissenting); Murphy, *Wild Bill*, 234.

46. *Korematsu*, 323 U.S. at 248 (Jackson, J., dissenting); *id*. at 224, 225 (Frankfurter, J.,

concurring). For a thorough analysis of Justice Jackson's position see Hutchinson, "'The Achilles Heel' of the Constitution," 455. *See also* Rostow, "The Japanese American Cases," 510-12.

47. Irons, *Justice at War*, 329, 333-34; Ball and Cooper, *Of Power and Right*, 114-15; Dembitz, "Racial Discrimination and the Military Judgment," 199 n. 92.

48. William O. Douglas to Hugo Black, Dec. 6, 1944, box 113, *Korematsu* folder, Douglas Papers; *Korematsu*, 323 U.S. at 219, 222, 223.

49. *Id*. at 221-22.

50. *Id*. at 216; *see* Greg Robinson, *By Order of the President*, 229.

51. *See Korematsu*, 323 U.S. at 216, 222; *id*. at 231 (Roberts, J., dissenting).

52. *Korematsu*, 323 U.S. at 216, 218, 224; *Adarand Constructors, Inc., v. Pena*, 315 U.S. 200, 214-16 (1995) (opinion of O'Connor, J.) ("rigid scrutiny" standard announced in *Korematsu* "inexplicably" ignored there in favor of applying lesser standard of *Hirabayashi*); *id.*, 315 U.S. 271, 274 (Ginsburg, J., dissenting) ("most rigid" scrutiny standard of *Korematsu* ignored there as Court upheld "odious, gravely injurious racial classification"); *Korematsu*, 323 U.S. at 236 & nn. 1-2 (Murphy, J., dissenting); DeWitt, *Final Report*, vii, 8-9, 18-19, 33-35; *Hirabayashi v. United States*, 627 F. Supp. 1445, 1452 (W.D. Wash. 1986), *aff'd* in part, *rev'd* in part, *Hirabayashi v. United States*, 828 F.2d 591 (9th Cir. 1987); *Hirabayashi*, 828 F.2d at 600-602 & nn. 10, 12; *Korematsu v. United States*, 584 F. Supp. 1406, 1416-17, 1421-24 (N.D. Cal. 1984); Dembitz, "Racial Discrimination and the Military Judgment," 192; Rostow, "The Japanese American Cases," 503-4; Grodzins, *Americans Betrayed*, 281-83 & n. 25; Kennedy, *Freedom from Fear*, 757-58; Grossman, "The Japanese American Cases," 663-68; Commission on Wartime Relocation, *Personal Justice Denied*, 18; Yamamoto, "Korematsu Revisited," 10-30; Civil Liberties Act of 1988, Pub. L. 100-383, 102 Stat. 903 (codified at 50 app. U.S.C. secs. 1989a(a), 1989b-4 (2000)). Gordon Hirabayashi also successfully challenged his convictions, relying on still other newly discovered evidence. A researcher had uncovered an original version of General DeWitt's Final Report, suppressed by the War Department (and withheld even from the Justice Department), in which DeWitt expressly stated that the curfew and exclusion orders had been premised not on "insufficient time" to separate the loyal from the disloyal but, more fundamentally, on his personal belief that loyalty determinations would be "impossible." Why impossible? Because, to DeWitt, everyone of Japanese descent was inherently disloyal. For example, in addition to the language in his final report and his testimony before the House Naval Affairs subcommittee quoted in the text, transcribed telephone conversations revealed that DeWitt had warned another general, "There isn't such a thing as a loyal Japanese." Confronted by a racist rationale that was not likely to withstand constitutional scrutiny, Assistant Secretary of War John J. McCloy persuaded DeWitt to change his justification from "impossible" to determine loyalty to "insufficient time" to do so, the language in DeWitt's published Final Report that gave the solicitor general the hook he needed to argue for "military necessity" based on practical, not racist, grounds. Virtually all copies of the original version, dated April 15, 1943, were destroyed. *Hirabayashi*, 828 F.2d at 598-99, 601; *Hirabayashi*, 627 F. Supp. at 1449-54; Grodzins, *Americans Betrayed*, 283 n. 25. *See generally* Yamamoto et al., *Race, Rights and Reparation*, 277-388 (coram nobis cases), 390-408 (reparations).

53. Irons, *Justice at War*, 333.

54. *Hirabayashi v. United States*, 320 U.S. 81, 81 (1943); *Korematsu*, 319 U.S. at 432.

55. *Hirabayashi*, 320 U.S. at 114 (Rutledge, J., concurring). Professor Hutchinson has noted that the Court granted certiorari in *Korematsu* in March 1944 when the war was

turning in the Allies' favor and there were indications that the relocation program would soon end. Although the Court thus might have found reason to deny certiorari and avoid the detention issue, Hutchinson persuasively suggests that the justices did not want the Ninth Circuit's *Korematsu* opinion, indiscriminately applying *Hirabayashi*, to stand unscrutinized. Hutchinson, "The 'Achilles Heel' of the Constitution," 477–78.

56. Interview, Brudney.

57. *Duncan v. Kahanamoku*, 327 U.S. 304 (1946); *Scherzberg v. Maderia*, 57 F. Supp. 42 (E.D. Pa. 1944); *Ebel v. Drum*, 52 F. Supp. 189 (D. Mass. 1943); *Scheuller v. Drum*, 51 F. Supp. 383 (E.D. Pa. 1943); Dembitz, "Racial Discrimination and the Military Judgment," 226 n. 23, 232; interview, N. Rutledge.

58. Interview, N. Rutledge; *accord* interview, Shniderman; WR to W. Willard Wirtz (Aug. 6, 1941) ("undemocratic controls" necessary when "danger becomes too great" for "the democratic institution" otherwise "to survive").

59. *E.g.*, interviews, Kurland, N. Rutledge, Stevens; *see* Rehnquist, *All the Laws but One*, 188.

60. Rutledge, Foreword, 380, 381.

61. Interview, Shniderman.

62. Kennedy, *Freedom from Fear*, 753; Greg Robinson, *By Order of the President*, 96, 101–2, 117; Rehnquist, *All the Laws but One*, 188, 204; Dembitz, "Racial Discrimination and the Military Judgment," 201; Grossman, "The Japanese American Cases," 657; interview, D. Pollitt (son-in-law).

63. Interviews, Frank, N. Rutledge.

64. Mason, *Harlan Fiske Stone*, 18, 42–48, 81–84, 143–47; Newman, *Hugo Black*, 3, 6, 17–20, 117, 125–230; interviews, M. L. (Rutledge) Needels, D. Pollitt (son-in-law), J. A. (Rutledge) Pollitt, N. Rutledge; *see* Frank. It is interesting to note that Justice Rutledge's friends Herbert Wechsler and Ralph Fuchs were on the government's brief in *Korematsu*. That advocacy, however, reflecting assigned roles, would not have influenced Rutledge's decision to join the majority.

65. Interview, Frank; *Korematsu*, 323 U.S. at 218; *see* Rostow, "Our Worst Wartime Mistake," 197.

66. Douglas, *The Court Years*, 279–80.

CHAPTER SIXTEEN

1. *Bridges v. California*, 314 U.S. 252 (1941).

2. *Carpenters & Joiners Union v. Ritter's Café*, 315 U.S. 722 (1942).

3. 316 U.S. 584 (1942).

4. *Id.* at 600 (Stone, J., dissenting); *id.* at 611 (Murphy, J., dissenting).

5. *Id.* at 623 (Black, Douglas, and Murphy, JJ., dissenting).

6. 310 U.S. 586 (1940).

7. Interview, Wechsler; *see also* Jackson, *That Man*, 68–69.

8. *See Jones v. City of Opelika*, 318 U.S. 796 (1943); *Murdock v. Pennsylvania*, 318 U.S. 748 (1943).

9. *Jones v. City of Opelika*, 319 U.S. 103 (1943) (per curiam) (vacating judgments in 316 U.S. 584 (1942)); *Murdock v. Pennsylvania*, 319 U.S. 105 (1943); *see also Martin v Struthers*, 319 U.S. 141 (1943) (striking down 6 to 3, as applied to Jehovah's Witnesses, ordinance prohibiting door-to-door distribution of circulars).

10. 319 U.S. 624 (1943).

11. *Minersville School Dist. v. Gobitis*, 310 U.S. 586 (1940).

12. Lash, *From the Diaries of Felix Frankfurter*, 205.

13. *Ex parte Peru*, 318 U.S. 578 (1943); *Myers v. Matley*, 318 U.S. 622 (1943); *Aguilar v. Standard Oil Co.*, 318 U.S. 724 (1943); *Bd. of County Comm'rs v. Seber*, 318 U.S. 705 (1943) (Reed, J., not participating); *Barringer & Co. v. United States*, 319 U.S. 1 (1943); *Jersey Cent. Power & Light Co. v. FPC*, 319 U.S. 61 (1943).

14. *Ex parte Peru*.

15. *Barringer & Co. v. United States*.

16. *See Murdock v. Pennsylvania*, 318 U.S. 748, *cert. granted* Feb. 15, 1943; *Jones v. City of Opelika*, 318 U.S. 796, *cert. granted* Feb. 15, 1943).

17. *Busey v. District of Columbia*, 129 F.2d 24, 28, (D.C. Cir. 1942) (Rutledge, J., dissenting).

18. *E.g.*, case correspondence between WR and Stanley Reed, Reed Papers; case correspondence between WR and Felix Frankfurter, containers 95, 109, 121, 141, 155, 166, 177, Rutledge Papers.

19. *Prince v. Massachusetts*, 321 U.S. 158, 160 (1944); WR to Thomas Reed Powell, March 17, 1944.

20. 312 U.S. 100 (1941).

21. *Hammer v. Dagenhart*, 274 U.S. 251 (1918); *Bailey v. Drexel Furniture Co.*, 259 U.S. 20 (1922).

22. Interview, Brudney.

23. *Prince*, 321 U.S at 171, 174 (Murphy, J., dissenting); *id.* at 176, 177 (opinion of Jackson, J.).

24. 494 U.S. 872 (1990).

25. *Employment Div., Dep't of Human Res. v. Smith*, 494 U.S. at 907 (Blackmun, J., joined by Brennan and Marshall, JJ., dissenting).

26. *See Quick Bear v. Leupp*, 210 U.S. 50 (1908) (government ban on appropriations for sectarian schools not applicable to Indian treaty and trust funds nor barred by Constitution). The only earlier significant establishment clause decision in the Court's history was *Bradfield v. Roberts*, 175 U.S. 291 (1899) (appropriation for Roman Catholic hospital in District of Columbia not barred by First Amendment). *See generally* Choper, "Symposium on Law in the Twentieth Century," 1716-17; Westbrook, Comment, "Constitutional Law," 1003.

27. *Everson v. Bd. of Educ.*, 330 U.S. 1, 3 & n. 1, 8, 16-18 (1947); Justice Black cited for a limited purpose, *id.* at 7, but did not rely on for his analysis, an earlier decision in *Cochran v. State Bd. of Educ.*, 281 U.S. 370 (1930), in which the Supreme Court upheld— solely against a due process attack—a Louisiana statute authorizing distribution of the same textbooks, at state expense, to public and parochial students alike. *See Everson*, 330 U.S. at 28, 29 & n. 3 (Rutledge, J., dissenting).

28. *Everson*, 330 U.S. at 61-62 (Rutledge, J., dissenting). Jackson also penned a dissent of his own. *Id.* at 18 (Jackson, J., dissenting).

29. *Everson*, 330 U.S. at 41, 45, 47 (Rutledge, J., dissenting).

30. *Id.* at 47-48, 50, 60-61.

31. *Id.* at 32, 56-57.

32. *Pierce v. Society of Sisters*, 268 U.S. 510 (1925); *Everson*, 330 U.S. at 50 n. 42, 51 (Rutledge, J., dissenting).

33. *Everson*, 330 U.S. at 57.

34. *E.g.*, Westbrook, Comment, "Constitutional Law"; Mason and Schule, "Trans-

portation for Children Attending Parochial School"; Stark, "Constitutional Law"; Dowst and Sullivan, "Constitutional Law"; Humer, "Constitutional Law"; Prather, "Constitutional Law"; Gibson, "Constitutional Law"; Recent Case, "Constitutional Law: Religion"; Recent Decision, "Constitutional Law: Aid to Religion"; Note, "Public Aid to Establishment of Religion." *Contra* Hopkins, "State Transportation of Students to Parochial Schools."

35. WR to Irving Brant, March 18, 1947.

36. *New York Times*, June 12, 1947, p. 1, col. 2, p. 22, cols. 4–5.

37. Paul Blanshard, "Eleanor Roosevelt," in Blanshard, ed., *Classics of Free Thought*, 143; "The Spellman-Roosevelt Exchange," in Blanshard, ed., *Classics of Free Thought*, 144.

38. Blanshard, *American Freedom and Catholic Power*, vol. 2.

39. *Everson v. Bd. of Education*, 330 U.S. 1, 16 (1947); WR to George Heidlebaugh, March 18, 1947.

40. 333 U.S. 203, 208, 212 (1948). For a diatribe against Justice Rutledge's dissent in *Everson* and the Court's decision in *McCollum*, see O'Neill, *Religion and Education under the Constitution*, arguing that the First Amendment does not require "complete" separation of church and state and, in any event, does not apply to the states.

41. 370 U.S. 421, 437, 443 (1962) (Douglas, J., concurring); *see* Murphy, *Wild Bill*, 357.

42. Note, "Funds for Sectarian Schools"; Note, "Constitutionality of Tax Benefits Accorded Religion."

43. *See generally* Choper, "Symposium on Law in the Twentieth Century."

44. *Mueller v. Allen*, 463 U.S. 388 (1983).

45. *Witters v. Dep't of Servs. for the Blind*, 474 U.S. 481 (1986).

46. *Zobrest v. Catalina Foothills School Dist.*, 509 U.S. 1 (1993).

47. *Rosenberger v. Rector & Visitors of Univ. of Va.*, 515 U.S. 819 (1995).

48. *Agostini v. Felton*, 521 U.S. 203 (1997).

49. *Mitchell v. Helms*, 530 U.S. 793 (2000).

50. *Zelman v. Simmons-Harris*, 536 U.S. 639 (2002).

51. *E.g.*, *Zelman v. Simmons-Harris*, 536 U.S. 686, 689–90 & n. 3, 715 (Souter, J., dissenting); *id.* at 717, 722 (Breyer, J., dissenting); *Mitchell v. Helms*, 530 U.S. at 867, 874, 875 (Souter, J., dissenting).

52. *Terminiello v. Chicago*, 337 U.S. 1, 3 (1949); *id.* at 13, 15–21 (Jackson, J., dissenting). The case had focused in the Illinois courts exclusively on whether Terminiello had been using the kind of "fighting words" that under the "clear and present danger test" failed of First Amendment protection. *Chaplinsky v. New Hampshire*, 315 U.S. 568, 572 (1942); *Terminiello*, 337 U.S. at 3; *id.* at 6, 7 (Vinson, C.J., dissenting); *id.* at 8, 9 (Frankfurter, J., dissenting). Without reaching that question, the Court majority resolved the case in Terminiello's favor on a "preliminary" ground. The trial court's instructions had permitted the jury to convict for misbehavior that not only "molests the inhabitants in the enjoyment of peace and quiet" but also "stirs public anger, invites dispute, brings about a condition of unrest, or creates a disturbance." These grounds were unduly broad, according to the majority, since many reflected the very "function of free speech under our system of government," and any one could have served as the basis for the jury's general verdict of guilt. *Terminiello*, 337 U.S. at 3, 4, 6.

53. *Marsh v. Alabama*, 326 U.S. 501 (1946).

54. *United Pub. Workers v. Mitchell*, 330 U.S. 75, 104, 105 (1947) (Black, J., joined in

part by Rutledge, J., dissenting); *Oklahoma v. United States Civil Service Comm'n*, 330 U.S. 127, 146 (1947) (Black, J., and Rutledge, J., "dissent"). Justice Rutledge declined to pass on constitutional questions presented by particular federal appellants who he did not believe were properly before the Court. *Mitchell*, 330 U.S. at 104 (statement of Rutledge, J.). Justice Douglas separately dissented in part in the federal case. *Mitchell*, 330 U.S. at 115 (Douglas, J., dissenting in part). Neither Murphy nor Jackson participated in either decision.

55. *Musser v. Utah*, 333 U.S. 95, 98 (1948) (Rutledge, J., dissenting) (rejecting majority's remand of prosecution for conspiracy to advocate polygamy, in order to reconsider possible vagueness of statute, since "crucial question" brought to Court for review was First Amendment challenge to charge and jury instructions, both of which failed to distinguish between "specific incitations," subject to prosecution, and "more generalized discussions," constitutionally protected); *United States v. CIO*, 335 U.S. 106, 129 (1948) (Rutledge, J., concurring in result) (rejecting majority's construction of Federal Corrupt Practices Act that barred indictment for publication of political endorsement in union newspaper, since language prohibiting "expenditure in connection with any election" so clearly forbade political endorsement that "the Court in effect abdicate[d] its function" in avoiding constitutional ruling).

56. 323 U.S. 516 (1945).

57. *Id.* at 530, 540 (citing *Schneider v. State*, 308 U.S. 147 (1939); *Cantwell v. Connecticut*, 310 U.S. 296 (1940); *Prince v. Massachusetts*, 321 U.S. 158 (1944); *United States v. Carolene Prods. Co.*, 304 U.S. 144, 152-53 (1938).

58. 310 U.S. 296 (1940); *Thomas v. Collins*, 323 U.S. at 548, 556 (Roberts, J., dissenting).

59. Comment, "Employer Freedom of Speech in Labor Relations"; Note, "Organizer's Right to Speak"; Recent Decision, "Constitutional Law: Validity of Statute Requiring Registration of Labor Organizers as Applied to Speaker at Peaceable Public Meeting"; O'Neill, Recent Decision, "Constitutional Law"; Recent Case, "Labor"; Recent Case, "Constitutional Law: Freedom of Speech"; "Decision, Labor Law: Free Speech: Requirement of Registration before Solicitation of Members"; Feldman, Recent Decision, "Constitutional Law"; Hassett, Comment, "Constitutional Law"; Powers, Comment, "Constitutional Law."

60. *Thomas v. Collins*, 323 U.S. at 544, 547-48 (Jackson, J., concurring); *id.* at 543 (Douglas, J., concurring).

61. Actually, at the mass gathering Thomas solicited one individual by name in addition to urging the others, in general, to join the union. But because the Texas Supreme Court had approved the card requirement as to both forms of solicitation, Rutledge invoked the rule that reversal was required if either ground was invalid and, as a result, did not deal with the individual solicitation. *Thomas v. Collins*, 323 U.S. at 522-23, 528.

62. *Watchtower Bible & Tract Soc'y of New York, Inc. v. Village of Stratton*, 536 U.S. 150, 163-64 (2002).

63. *Thomas v. Collins*, 323 U.S. at 532, 535; Douglas A. Hedin, "The Union Organizer as First Amendment Litigant," 2 *Employee Rights Quarterly* 11, 15-16 (2002) (citing *Speiser v. Randall*, 357 U.S. 513, 526 (1958); and *New York Times Co. v. Sullivan*, 376 U.S. 254 (1964)). In *Speiser*, Justice Rutledge's reasoning in *Thomas v. Collins* was used to strike down a loyalty oath required for a California tax exemption. The Court held that the taxpayer's burden to prove that he or she did not advocate violent overthrow of the gov-

ernment violated due process, because the taxpayer would feel constrained to "steer far wider of the unlawful zone" of forbidden speech than necessary out of fear of government reprisal—later called an unconstitutional chilling effect on the right of free speech.

64. *Kovacs v. Cooper*, 336 U.S. 77 (1949) (opinion of Reed, J.); *id.* at 104, 105 (1949) (Rutledge, J., dissenting); *id.* at 89, 96, 97 (Frankfurter, J., concurring).

65. *Id.* at 105-6 (Rutledge, J., dissenting); *see id.* at 97, 98 (Jackson, J., concurring in result).

66. *Id.* at 90-96 (Frankfurter, J., concurring) (citing *Thomas v. Collins*, 323 U.S. at 530); *id.* at 106 (Rutledge, J., dissenting). For early analyses of Justice Rutledge's opinions on civil liberties and civil rights see Levitan, "Mr. Justice Rutledge," part 2; Rockwell, "Justice Rutledge on Civil Liberties"; Mosher, "Mr. Justice Rutledge's Philosophy of Civil Rights"; Mann, "Justice Rutledge on Civil Liberties."

CHAPTER SEVENTEEN

1. *See* 320 U.S. 508-698 (1944); Mason, *Harlan Fiske Stone*, 606.

2. *Id.* at 607, 609; *see* Freedman, ed., *Roosevelt and Frankfurter*, 4; editorial, *New York Herald Tribune*, Jan. 10, 1944, p. 16, col. 3; *New York Herald Tribune*, Jan. 10, 1944, p. 16, col. 4; Carroll Kilpatrick, *Chicago Sun*, Jan. 10, 1944, p. 5, col. 1; interview, Boskey.

3. Dunne, *Hugo Black and the Judicial Revolution*, 227; Fine, *Frank Murphy*, 264; Fassett, *New Deal Justice*, 367; *Mercoid Corp. v. Mid-Continent Inv. Co.*, 320 U.S. 661, 672 (1944) (opinion of Black, J., joined by Murphy, J.); *FPC v. Hope Natural Gas*, 320 U.S. 591 (1944); *id.* at 619-20 (opinion of Black and Murphy, JJ.); Lewis Wood, *New York Times*, Feb. 13, 1944, sec. B, p. 6B, cols. 1-4.

4. *Hope Natural Gas*, 320 U.S. at 602-3; *FPC v. Natural Gas Pipeline Co.*, 315 U.S. 575, 599 (1942) (Black, Douglas, and Murphy, JJ., concurring). Several years earlier, Justice Black expressed essentially the same view—that federal courts should uphold state rate making unless "palpably and grossly unreasonable"—when dissenting in *McCart v. Indianapolis Water Co.*, 302 U.S. 419 (1938). *See* Dunne, *Hugo Black and the Judicial Revolution*, 227.

5. *FPC v. Hope Natural Gas Co*, 320 U.S. at 620 (Reed, J., dissenting); *id.* at 624, 625 (Frankfurter, J., dissenting); *id.* at 628 (opinion of Jackson, J.); *id.* at 619, 620 (opinion of Black and Murphy, JJ.).

6. According to Professor Fowler Harper, who has not supplied a citation, Pearson stated over the air: "Tomorrow the Supreme Court will split wide open on one of the most important economic questions of the country—the fixing of gas and electric rates. The case involves a Standard Oil of New Jersey subsidiary, which supplies natural gas to Cleveland and Akron, but the issue of rate-fixing affects gas and electric consumers of the entire country. Yesterday the Court was split four to four, with the ninth Justice trying to make up his mind by today." Harper, *Justice Rutledge and the Bright Constellation*, 321-22; *accord* Newman, *Hugo Black*, 322; interviews, Brudney, Gressman, Lomen, Luce.

7. Interviews, Brudney, Gressman, Lomen, Luce. Because New Year's day fell on a Saturday, the day of the Court's regular conference, the justices met instead on Friday, December 31. According to Douglas, Rutledge had told him to "go ahead and print for release on January 3," and that it "was not likely he would change his mind," although "there was a chance he might do so." William O. Douglas to the Chief Justice, Jan. 5, 1944, box 74, "Douglas, William O. 1944" folder, H. F. Stone Papers. Thus, Rutledge cre-

ated the possibility that the vote would be 4 to 4, canceling release of the *Hope* opinions, since no opinion issues with an equally divided Court. A split would have left in place the Fourth Circuit's reversal of the Commission, although the Court's action would have had no precedential effect. *Curant v. Essex Co.*, 74 U.S. (7 Wall.) 107 (1868).

8. Newman, *Hugo Black*, 322; communications from Robert H. Jackson to Eugene C. Gerhart, May 7 and Oct. 25, 1949, *quoted in* Gerhart, *America's Advocate*, 493 n. 82 ("'When [Roberts] came to get the transcript of what [Pearson] said, the transcript showed that Mr. Justice Rutledge couldn't make up his mind.'") (quoting Jackson).

9. Eugene Gressman, Diary, Jan. 3, 1944 ("Drew Pearson's script had Rutledge named as the undecided man—but he didn't mention him by name on the radio.") (Gressman Diary quoted throughout with permission); interviews, Gressman, Luce; *see* Gerhart, *America's Advocate*, 493 n. 82.

10. Black's law clerk heard later that the network had pressed Pearson not to reveal the name. Interview, Luce. It is not apparent, however, why the network would have intervened to prevent disclosure of the justice or why Drew Pearson would have acceded to such pressure.

11. Fine, *Frank Murphy*, 264; Gressman Diary, Jan. 3, 1944; interview, Gressman. *But see* Newman, *Hugo Black*, 322 (implying that Douglas attended meeting).

12. William O. Douglas to the Chief Justice, Jan. 5 and 6, 1944, box 74, "Douglas, William O. 1944" folder, H. F. Stone Papers; interview, Gressman; Fine, *Frank Murphy*, 257, 264; *see* Newman, *Hugo Black*, 322.

13. Gressman Diary, Jan. 3, 1944 ("Rutledge did spend all day Sunday deciding which way he would vote—he didn't make his final decision until 11 o'clock this morning."); *see* 320 U.S. at 508-698 (1944).

14. Interviews, Brudney, Gressman, Lomen, Luce; Gerhart, *America's Advocate*, 258, 493 n. 82; Hutchinson, "The Black-Jackson Feud," 206; Gressman Diary, Jan. 3, 1944.

15. Interview, Brudney.

16. Interviews, Brudney, Gressman, Lomen, Luce, Neal, Shniderman; Gressman Diary, Jan. 11, 1944; Newman, *Hugo Black*, 322-23.

17. *Mahnich v. S. S.S. Co.*, 321 U.S. 96, 105, 112, 113 (1944) (Roberts, J., joined by Frankfurter, J., dissenting).

18. 321 U.S. 649 (1944); *id.* at 666, 669, 670 (statement of Mr. Justice Roberts); *Grovey v. Townsend*, 295 U.S. 45 (1935); Robert H. Jackson, "Decisional Law and *Stare Decisis*," address at Annual Meeting of American Law Institute, May 9, 1944, published in 30 *A.B.A. J.* 344 (1944), *quoted in* Mason, *Harlan Fiske Stone*, 626; Dunne, *Hugo Black and the Judicial Revolution*, 229; Newman, *Hugo Black*, 323; interview, Neal.

19. To the contrary, Roberts had joined in a Rutledge opinion separately concurring in the result of a tax case during the previous term. *Bd. of County Comm'rs v. Seber*, 318 U.S. 702, 719, 723 (1943) (Rutledge, J., concurring in result); interview, Nickerson; *see* Murphy, *Wild Bill*, 236.

20. Newman, *Hugo Black*, 322. Black's biographer cites evidence that Roberts considered Murphy the leaker and asked Black to stand up for Roberts by repudiating Murphy. Newman, *Hugo Black*, 678 n. 3. It is difficult to accept—given the evidence of Douglas's relationship with Pearson, the increasing antipathy between Roberts and Douglas, the collective perception of the Court's insiders at the time, and perhaps above all Murphy's close relationship with Rutledge—that Roberts would have suspected Murphy, not Douglas, of having committed the offense. *See* Murphy, *Wild Bill*, 210.

21. Jackson, Reminiscences, 1580-81; Newman, *Hugo Black*, 323 n.* (quoting Wil-

liam O. Douglas to Fred Rodell, May 9, 1949); interview, Gressman; *see* Murphy, *Wild Bill*, 238.

22. Interviews, Allan, Birdzell Jr., Boskey, Elman, Gartner, Gressman, Groner, Helman, Hobbs, Joslin, Kurland, Lomen, Mann, Rosenthal, Shniderman, Spitzer, Temko, Weiss, White, Wollenberg; Newman, *Hugo Black*, 322; Urofsky, *Felix Frankfurter*, 55.

23. Simon, *The Antagonists*, 259; Newman, *Hugo Black*, 320; Urofsky, *Felix Frankfurter*, 55; Ball and Cooper, *Of Power and Right*, 87; interviews, Elman, Gressman, Kurland, Lomen, Luce, Morrison, N. Rutledge, Shniderman.

24. Interviews, Boskey, Gressman, Rosenthal, Spitzer; Simon, *The Antagonists*, 116.

25. Interviews, Coleman Jr., Elman, Groner, Henkin, Hobbs, Joslin, Kurland, Luce, Rosenthal, Wollenberg; Ball and Cooper, *Of Power and Right*, 90-93; Hirsch, *The Enigma of Felix Frankfurter*, 178-79; Urofsky, "Getting the Job Done," 33; Murphy, *The Brandeis/Frankfurter Connection*, 264.

26. Interviews, Coleman Jr., Elman, Haber, Henkin, Joslin, Mansfield, Nickerson, Rosenthal; Simon, *The Antagonists*, 192; *see* Urofsky, *Division and Discord*, 36-39.

27. Interviews, Brudney, Kurland, Lingreen; Lingreen, "The Greatest Gift," 2; Felix Frankfurter to Harold Laski, Nov. 12, 1949, Frankfurter Papers.

28. Interviews, Coleman Jr., Gressman, Haber, Hobbs, Joslin, Lomen, Luce, Mann, Marsh, Neal, Oberdorfer, J. A. (Rutledge) Pollitt, N. Rutledge, Shniderman, Stevens, Temko, Tone; Howard, *Mr. Justice Murphy*, 269-70, 279-81, 459n; Ball and Cooper, *Of Power and Right*, 77; Urofsky, "Getting the Job Done," 33.

29. Interviews, Gartner, Joslin, Lake, Rosenthal, Torre; *see* Simon, *The Antagonists*, 191; Newman, *Hugo Black*, 313, 328-29; Culver and Hyde, *American Dreamer*, 348-53, 479; Murphy, *Wild Bill*, 212-32; Wiecek, "The Legal Foundation of Domestic Anticommunism," 403; Grossman, "The Japanese American Cases," 672.

30. Interviews, Rosenthal, Seder Jr., Torre; Urofsky, "Getting the Job Done," 34-35.

31. Invitation to the "Inaugural Dinner in honor of Franklin Delano Roosevelt[,] President of the United States[,] and Harry S. Truman[,] Vice President of the United States[,] Friday evening, January nineteenth[,] nineteen hundred and forty five . . . ," with notation "accepted 1/8/45," Rutledge Papers.

32. WR to Bernard C. Gavit, April 14, 1945; WR to President Harry S Truman, April 13, 1945; President Harry Truman to WR, May 2, 1945; Eleanor Roosevelt to WR, April 19, 1945.

33. Mrs. J. M. Helm to WR, April 13, 1945; WR to Mrs. P. P. (Sadie) McCain, April 21, 1945; WR to L. M. Campbell, April 21, 1945; WR to Bernard C. Gavit, April 14, 1945; WR to Ivan Rutledge, April 21, 1945; WR to Louise Larrabee, April 21, 1945.

34. WR to Mrs. P. P. (Sadie) McCain, April 21, 1945; WR to Louise Larrabee, April 21, 1945.

35. Gerhart, *America's Advocate*, 308, 311-12; Mason, *Harlan Fiske Stone*, 518-82, 707, 714-17; Dunne, *Hugo Black and the Judicial Revolution*, 243; Newman, *Hugo Black*, 340; Hutchinson, "The Black-Jackson Feud," 209-10; Doris Fleeson, *Evening Star* (Washington), May 16, 1946, sec. A, p. 1, cols. 4-7; interviews, Gressman, Shniderman, Stevens; WR to Henry S. Fraser, May 2, 1946; WR to Ivan Rutledge, June 22, 1946; WR to Dwight Rutledge, June 24, 1946; WR to F. Lander Moorman, June 22, 1946.

36. Mason, *Harlan Fiske Stone*, 640-46; Newman, *Hugo Black*, 333-37.

37. 325 U.S. 161, 163 (1945).

38. Newman, *Hugo Black*, 334-35; Mason, *Harlan Fiske Stone*, 642; *Jewell Ridge Coal Corp. v. Local No. 6167, United Mineworkers of Am.*, 325 U.S. 161, 170, 177-78 & n. 5 (1945) (Jackson, J., dissenting).

39. Mason, *Harlan Fiske Stone*, 642; Newman, *Hugo Black*, 335-36; Fine, *Frank Murphy*, 327; Gerhart, *America's Advocate*, 252.

40. Mason, *Harlan Fiske Stone*, 643-44; *Jewell Ridge Coal Corp. v. Local 6167, United Mine Workers of America*, 325 U.S. 897 (1945) (reh'g denied).

41. Newman, *Hugo Black*, 336, 680 n. 3; Frank, *Mr. Justice Black*, 134-35; Fine, *Frank Murphy*, 328; Ball and Cooper, *Of Power and Right*, 93-98; Hirsch, *The Enigma of Felix Frankfurter*, 185n.

42. Mason, *Harlan Fiske Stone*, 640-42; WR to Ernest Kirschten, June 19, 1946; WR to William F. Buchanan, June 22, 1946.

43. WR to William F. Buchanan, June 22, 1946; WR to Ernest Kirschten, June 19, 1946.

44. Mason, *Harlan Fiske Stone*, 765-69, 870 n. 7 (citing WR to the Chief Justice, Sept. 24, 1945); *see* Newman, *Hugo Black*, 338; Fine, *Frank Murphy*, 267; Fassett, *New Deal Justice*, 387; Gerhart, *America's Advocate*, 255-56; Jackson, Reminiscences, 1586-88 (as of Sept. 18, 1945, Rutledge had not replied).

45. Berry, *Stability, Security and Continuity*, 4, 7-13, 18-19, 21, 24-25. After obtaining the support of Chief Justice Stone, who believed that Burton's legislative experience as a senator from Ohio would help the Court, Truman nominated Burton on September 18, 1945. Diary of Harold H. Burton, Sept. 17, 1945, Burton Papers. Burton's Senate colleagues confirmed by unanimous consent two days later. *New York Times*, Sept. 20, 1945, sec. 1, p. 44, col. 2. In addition to Burton, Truman considered Under Secretary of War Robert Patterson, whom he promoted instead to secretary of war; Sen. Warren Austin, internationalist Republican from Vermont, whom he later appointed ambassador to the United Nations; and the judicially moderate circuit judges Orrie Phillips and John J. Parker. Diary of Harold H. Burton, Sept. 17, 1945, Burton Papers; *St. Louis Post-Dispatch*, Sept. 18, 1945, sec. 1, p. 1, cols. 6-7; Truman, *Memoirs by Harry S. Truman*, 145; Press Research, Inc., *Warren Robinson Austin*, 1; Mazuzan, *Warren R. Austin at the U.N.*, 1; Lowe, "Harold H. Burton," 416-18.

46. *Washington Post*, Sept. 19, 1945, sec. A, p. 10, cols. 2-3; *New York Times*, Sept. 19, 1945, sec. 1, p. 24, col. 3; Lewis Wood, *New York Times*, Sept. 19, 1945, sec. 1, p. 1, cols. 4-5; Ernest Lindley, *Washington Post*, Sept. 21, 1945, sec. A, p. 16, col. 4; *Chicago Sun*, Sept. 20, 1945, p. 12, col. 1; Willard Shelton to WR, Sept. 25, 1945.

47. WR to Hon. Robert W. Steele, Sept. 27, 1945.

48. Interviews, Allen, Coleman Jr., Feller, Gartner, Groner, Haber, Henkin, Lake, Mann, Marsh, Oberdorfer, Pollak, Seder Jr., Spitzer, Temko, Tone, Torre, Weiss, Weston, Wollenberg.

49. WR to Hon. Robert W. Steele, Sept. 27, 1945.

50. Diary of Harold H. Burton, Sept. 17, 1945, Burton Papers.

CHAPTER EIGHTEEN

1. *Falbo v. United States*, 320 U.S. 549, 550 & n. 2, 551 (1944), *aff'g United States v. Falbo*, 135 F.2d 464 (3d Cir. 1943).

2. *Id.* at 553 & n. 7, 554.

3. *See id.* at 551-52.

4. *Id.* at 555-57 (Murphy, J., dissenting).

5. WR to Ivan Rutledge, March 13, 1944; *Falbo*, 320 U.S. at 552; *id.* at 555 (Rutledge, J., concurring).

6. *Estep v. United States*, 327 U.S. 114, 132 (1946) (Rutledge, J., concurring); *Sunal v.*

Large, 332 U.S. 174, 184 (1947) (Rutledge, J., dissenting); *Cox v. United States*, 332 U.S. 442 (1947) (Murphy, J., joined by Rutledge, J., dissenting).

7. 321 U.S. 414 (1944); *Rottenberg v. United States*, 137 F.2d 850, 852 (1st Cir. 1943) (combining *Rottenberg* and *Yakus* cases).

8. *Yakus v. United States*, 321 U.S. at 433, 435-38.

9. *Id.* at 460, 465-66, 471, 472, 478 (Rutledge, J., dissenting). Justice Roberts dissented on entirely different grounds, concluding that Congress had unconstitutionally delegated legislative power to the OPA administrator, *id.* at 448, 452 (Roberts, J., dissenting) (citing *Schechter Poultry Corp. v. United States*, 295 U.S. 495 (1935)); interview, Brudney.

10. *Yakus*, 321 U.S. at 474, 475, 478 (Rutledge, J., dissenting).

11. *Id.* at 467-68, 479, 482; *Schneiderman v. United States*, 320 U.S. 118, 165, 169 (1943) (Rutledge, J., concurring).

12. *Yakus*, 321 U.S. at 479 & n. 34 (Rutledge, J., dissenting); *see id.* at 437 n. 5. (majority opinion).

13. *Id.* at 486-87 n. 40 (Rutledge, J., dissenting); *id.* at 436-37 & n. 5 (majority opinion).

14. *Id.* at 465, 475 n. 29 (Rutledge, J., dissenting); *id.* at 428 (majority opinion).

15. *Yakus*; *Oregonian* (Portland), April 26, 1944, p. 8, col. 1; Corwin, *Total War and the Constitution*, 178-79; *accord* McLauren, "Can a Trial Court of the United States Be Completely Deprived of the Power to Determine Constitutional Questions? (discussing *Rottenberg v. United States*, 137 F.2d 850 (1943), heard with *Yakus* before the Supreme Court), both *quoted in* Mason, *Harlan Fiske Stone*, 697.

16. Amendment to Section 204 of Emergency Price Control Act of 1942, sec. 107(b), 58 Stat. 639, 78th Cong., 2d Sess., June 30, 1944 (amending sec. 204 by adding new subsec. (3)(1)); *see* Mansfield, *A Short History of OPA*, 277, *quoted in* Mason, *Harlan Fiske Stone*, 696 n.*.

17. 321 U.S. 67 (1944).

18. *Id.* at 92 (Douglas, J., joined by Black, J., dissenting).

19. *E.-Cent. Motor Carriers Ass'n v. United States*, 321 U.S. 194, 210-12 (1944).

20. WR to Ivan Rutledge, March 13, 1944.

21. 322 U.S. 111, 120 (1944); *id.* at 135 (Roberts, J., dissenting).

22. *Id.* at 128, 129, 131-32.

23. 321 U.S. 678, 688 (1944) (Rutledge, J., dissenting).

24. *See id.* at 699. The language shown in quotation marks in the text is the author's more neutral-sounding statement reflecting the majority view rather than Justice Rutledge's own paraphrasing, as follows: "The union is your exclusive agent and we cannot deal with you while it is such." *Id.*

25. Rutledge, "Significant Trends in Modern Incorporation Statutes," 22 *Wash. U. L.Q.* 338-39, 3 *U. Pitt. L. Rev.* 303-5; *Medo Photo Supply Corp. v. NLRB*, 321 U.S. 678, 689, 697 (1944) (Rutledge, J., dissenting).

26. *Medo Photo Supply Corp.*, 321 U.S. at 697, 698-701 (Rutledge, J., dissenting); WR to the Chief Justice, March 30, 1944.

27. *AFL v. Am. Sash & Door Co.*, 335 U.S. 538, 557, 559 (1949) (Rutledge, J., concurring) (decision upholding Arizona's constitutional ban against employment discrimination based on "non-membership in a labor organization"—a "right to work" amendment —because case presented no question of right to strike against employer who hires nonunion members, a right possibly protected by Thirteenth Amendment bar against "involuntary servitude").

28. Herbert Wechsler, "Memorandum for the Attorney General," Nov. 12, 1942 (author-

ship confirmed by Wechsler interview), judicial folder, attorney general file, Biddle Papers.

29. A. M. Houghton to WR, May 4, 1944; "The White House Program of Receptions and Dinners, Season of 1946-1947"; invitation "To Celebrate the Birthday of His Majesty the King . . . at a Garden Party on Thursday, June 9th"; invitation to "a reception in celebration of the Thirty-Fifth Anniversary of The Founding of the Chinese Republic on Thursday, the tenth of October"; *see also* the invitation to "Justice and Mrs. Wiley Rutledge to attend the Global Premier of 'The Beginning or the End[,]' . . . the story of the Atom Bomb . . . Wednesday, February Nineteenth," with handwritten note reading "accepted 2/13/47."

30. Wagshal and Herling, "The Most Unforgettable Character I've Met," 12.

31. Wagshal and Herling, "The Most Unforgettable Character I've Met," 11-13.

32. Wagshal and Herling, "The Most Unforgettable Character I've Met," 14; interview, Wagshal.

33. *Bakery Sales Drivers Local Union No. 33 v. Wagshal*, 333 U.S. 437, 439-42 (1948).

34. *Id.* at 444-45.

35. Interview, Wagshal.

36. WR to Mayme Edens, July 1, 1944; WR to John J. Parker, July 4, 1944; WR to Mr. and Mrs. Frank Manly, June 26, 1944; Grace [Thompson] to WR, undated [July 1944]; WR to Edgar S. Vaught, Sept. 25, 1944; *Chattanooga Times*, July 7, 1944, p. 9, col. 2.

37. Karl Schaffle to WR, Dec. 11, 1944; WR to Ivan Rutledge, Dec. 11, 1944; WR to Karl Schaffle, Dec. 13, 1944; WR to George Pennell, Dec. 19, 1944; *Asheville* (N.C.) *Citizen*, p. 11, col. 3; "Step-Mother of Justice Dies Here Suddenly; Rites for Mrs. W. B. Rutledge, 61, Are Planned in Cleveland, Tenn.," unidentified newspaper clipping, Dec. 12, 1944, Rutledge Papers.

38. Interview, Frank.

39. Interview, Frank; *accord* Harper, *Justice Rutledge and the Bright Constellation*, 16.

40. Interview, Shniderman.

41. Jacob Lashly to WR, May 22, 1944; William L. Prosser to WR, Jan. 12, 1949; WR to Jacob M. Lashly, June 3, 1944; WR to Henry M. Bates, May 4, 1948, Bates Papers.

42. WR to Benjamin S. Galland, Sept. 27, 1944; Max L. Weiker to WR, Aug. 23, 1945; "We Must Hold Our Faith in Future, Rutledge Says; Justice of Supreme Court, Ex-Boulderite, Addresses Rotarians," unidentified newspaper clipping, summer 1945, Rutledge Papers; WR to Hollis Fuchs, Aug. 21, 1945; WR to Rudolph E. Bolts, July 31, 1944 (Dickens's *A Tale of Two Cities*); WR to A. E. Cunliff, Sept. 1, 1944; WR to Albert S. Abel, Sept. 25, 1944; Lowell White to WR, July 13, 1944; WR to Roscoe Taylor, Aug. 10, 1944; Ralph Fuchs to WR, Aug. 2, 1944; WR to Mr. and Mrs. Ralph F. Fuchs, Aug. 23, 1944.

43. Interview, Steele; WR to Roscoe Taylor, Aug. 10, 1944.

44. Interview, Steele; WR to Ivan C. Rutledge, Aug. 21, 1945; WR to Frederic Higbee, Aug. 21, 1945.

45. WR to Hollis Fuchs, Aug. 21, 1945; WR to Mrs. Herbert S. Baily, Sept. 29, 1944; WR to Ivan Rutledge, Sept. 29, 1944; WR to Dwight Rutledge, June 23, 1945; WR to Henrietta Hough, June 25, 1945; interview, N. Rutledge.

CHAPTER NINETEEN

1. *Ex Parte Quirin*, 317 U.S. 1, 47 (1942).

2. *In re Yamashita*, 327 U.S. 1 (1946).

3. U.S. Const. art. I, sec. 8, cl. 10; *In re Yamashita*, 327 U.S. at 7–9; *see id.* (courts have "no power to review" military commission "determinations" save only power to inquire, on habeas corpus, whether detention is "within the authority of those detaining the petitioner"); *see also* Bittker, "The World War II German Saboteurs' Case and Writs of Certiorari before Judgment by the Court of Appeals"; David J. Danelski, "The Saboteurs' Case."

4. *In re Yamashita*, 327 U.S. at 7–18.

5. *Id*. at 17 n. 4 (italics added). The Chief Justice acknowledged that even with knowledge, "an officer could not be found guilty for failure to prevent a murder unless it appeared that the accused had 'the power to prevent it.'" *Id*. at 16 n. 3. Defense counsel had argued before the commission that Yamashita had lacked power to control his troops. Reel, *The Case of General Yamashita*, 163. The commission itself, moreover, while concluding that the general had not taken the measures "required by the circumstances," had acknowledged Yamashita's difficulties of command attributable "to the swift and overpowering advance of American forces," as well as to "weaknesses in organization, equipment, supply . . . , training, communication, discipline and morale of his troops." Reel, *The Case of General Yamashita*, 17 n. 4. Before the Supreme Court defense counsel renewed the argument. Yamashita Brief in Support of Motion for Leave to File Petition for Writs of Habeas Corpus and Prohibition and of Petition for Writ of Certiorari (Jan. 7, 1946), 20, 26. Nonetheless, the Chief Justice in his opinion referred—inaccurately—to Yamashita's failure to contend before the Supreme Court that the commission had erroneously held him "responsible for failing to take measures that were beyond his control." *In re Yamashita*, 327 U.S. at 16. But Stone covered the point by noting that the commission had taken account of Yamashita's difficulties and had found he did not employ measures "required by the circumstances." *Id*. at 17 n. 4. One scholar who has reviewed the record in detail faults the commission for failing "to consider sufficiently" the mitigating factors that raised serious question whether the general had had control of Japanese forces sufficient to prevent the butchery. Lael, *The Yamashita Precedent*, 139–41.

6. Articles of War, 39 Stat. 650, 655, 656 (1916); Geneva Red Cross Convention of 1929, 47 Stat. 2021, 2052 (1932); U.S. Const. amend. V; *In re Yamashita*, 327 U.S. at 6, 18 nn. 5 & 6, 21.

7. Articles of War, 39 Stat. 650, 651 (1916); *In re Yamashita*, 327 U.S. at 19–23. Accordingly, Stone also ruled inapplicable the commission's alleged violation of article 60 of the Geneva Red Cross Convention of 1929: failure to notify Japan's "protecting power," Switzerland, before the trial. *Id*. at 24.

8. WR to Frank Murphy (undated), file 61, box 136, Murphy Papers, *quoted in* Howard, *Mr. Justice Murphy*, 370; *In re Yamashita*, 327 U.S. at 26, 28, 35–37, 39 (Murphy, J., dissenting).

9. WR to Frank Murphy (undated), file 61, box 136, Murphy Papers, *quoted in* Howard, *Mr. Justice Murphy*, 370; *In re Yamashita*, 327 U.S. at 26, 28 (Murphy, J., dissenting).

10. Parks, "Command Responsibility for War Crimes," 2–20; Fairman, "The Supreme Court on Military Jurisdiction," 869–70.

11. Draft letter from WR to John Frank, Feb. 13, 1946; WR to John L. [*sic*] Frank, Feb. 22, 1946.

12. WR to Victor Brudney, April 1, 1946; draft letter from WR to John Frank, Feb. 13, 1946; letter from WR to John L. [*sic*] Frank, Feb. 22, 1946; *In re Yamashita*, 327 U.S. at 41, 42 (Rutledge, J., dissenting).

13. Ganoe, "The Yamashita Case and the Constitution"; Howard, *Mr. Justice Murphy*, 369, 374; Fairman, "The Supreme Court on Military Jurisdiction," 870.

14. *In re Yamashita*, 327 U.S. at 46–47, 81 (Rutledge, J., dissenting); *id.* at 29 (Murphy, J., dissenting); *compare id.* at 47–56 (Rutledge, J., dissenting) *with In re Yamashita*, 327 U.S. at 31 (Murphy, J., dissenting).

15. *In re Yamashita*, 327 U.S. at 14; *id.* at 50–51, 52 & n. 17, 53–55 (Rutledge, J., dissenting); draft letter from WR to John Frank, Feb. 13, 1946. Justice Rutledge elaborated his own view later: "I would have no trouble in saying, if it were shown by clear proof of an admissible sort under our Constitution that an enemy general had known of criminal action on the part of his troops and had failed to take whatever measures he could to stop the conduct, that a charge valid under the laws of war would be stated. I doubt that I could go beyond that, for I still believe that it would be in essence ex post facto law to subject to hanging or shooting an enemy general for merely having failed to discover that his troops were misbehaving. Perhaps a person so negligent as not to know of widespread atrocities going on around him by his own troops should be dealt with capitally, but if so I think that rule should be framed in advance of the act, clearly announced, and supported by incontrovertible evidence of a legal sort." Draft letter from WR to John Frank, Feb. 13, 1946; Parks, "Command Responsibility for War Crimes," 87.

16. *In re Yamashita*, 327 U.S. at 53 (Rutledge, J., dissenting); Parks, "Command Responsibility for War Crimes," 24–30; Whitney, "The Case of General Yamashita," 18–19.

17. Rovine, "The Air War and International Law," 124, 139–41; Parks, "Command Responsibility for War Crimes," 87–88 (quoting Rovine); Landrum, "The Yamashita War Crimes Trial," 297–98; *In re Yamashita*, 327 U.S. at 50–51 (Rutledge, J., dissenting).

18. *In re Yamashita*, 327 U.S. at 51–53 (Rutledge, J., dissenting).

19. *Id.* at 49, 53, 57–58 (Rutledge, J., dissenting).

20. Articles of War, 39 Stat. 650, 651, 655, 666; *In re Yamashita*, 327 U.S. at 61 n. 29, 63–64 (Rutledge, J., dissenting); Daly, "The Yamashita Case and Martial Courts," part I, 158, part II, 233.

21. Daly, "The Yamashita Case and Martial Courts," part II, 221–25; *In re Yamashita*, 327 U.S. at 64 & nn. 30 & 31 (Rutledge, J., dissenting).

22. *In re Yamashita*, 327 U.S. at 20; *id.* at 62–63, 68–69, 71 (Rutledge, J., dissenting).

23. *Id.* at 72–79 (Rutledge, J., dissenting).

24. *Id.* at 79, 80 (Rutledge, J., dissenting).

25. *Id.* at 81 (Rutledge, J., dissenting).

26. Lael, *The Yamashita Precedent*, 115–19; Hugo L. Black to Harlan F. Stone, Jan. 28, 1946, box 283, Black Papers; *see* draft letter from WR to John Frank, Feb. 13, 1946; *In re Yamashita*, 327 U.S. at 1.

27. Corwin, *Total War and the Constitution*, 121; *In re Yamashita*, 327 U.S. at 7–9; *Ex parte Quirin*, 317 U.S. at 25, 31, 38–40, 44–45. The Court in *Quirin* also found no right to a jury trial under article III, section 2, of the Constitution. *Id.* at 44.

28. Fairman, "The Supreme Court on Military Jurisdiction," 872.

29. *See* Ganoe, "The Yamashita Case and the Constitution," 155; Daly, "The Yamashita Case and Martial Courts," part II, 225; Brody, Recent Decision.

30. *Korematsu v. United States*, 323 U.S. 214 (1944).

31. Lael, *The Yamashita Precedent*, 66–73, 137–39; *see* Piccigallo, *The Japanese on Trial*, 56, 61–62; *Homma v. Patterson*, 327 U.S. 759 (1946).

32. Piccigallo, *The Japanese on Trial*, 56, 60–61; Lawrence Taylor, *A Trial of Generals*, 171.

33. Fairman, "The Supreme Court on Military Jurisdiction," 878–82; Parks, "Command Responsibility for War Crimes," 130; Piccigallo, *The Japanese on Trial*, 37, 51; Whitney, "The Case of General Yamashita," 19.

34. *See, e.g.*, William E. Leuchtenburg, "FDR's 'Court-packing' Plan," in *The Supreme Court Reborn*, 132.

35. *See* Ganoe, "The Yamashita Case and the Constitution," 155.

36. *See* letter from WR to Clarence Morris, March 21, 1940 ("subconscious process" and "feeling" have role in judicial decision-making).

37. *Korematsu v. United States*, 323 U.S. 214 (1944); *Hirabayashi v. United States*, 320 U.S. 81, 114 (1943) (Rutledge, J., concurring); *In re Yamashita*, 327 U.S. 1, 47 (1946) (Rutledge, J., dissenting).

38. Brody, Recent Decision, 860 n. 20; *In re Yamashita*, 327 U.S. at 79 (Rutledge, J., dissenting); *see Johnson v. Eisentrager*, 339 U.S. 763, 783 (1950).

39. *In re Yamashita*, 327 U.S. at 42, 43, 45, 79 (Rutledge, J., dissenting).

40. *Id.* at 42–44, 46, 49, 56, 79, 80 (Rutledge, J., dissenting).

41. *In re Yamashita*, 327 U.S. at 23.

42. *Ludecke v. Watkins*, 335 U.S. 160 (1948).

43. *Johnson v. Eisentrager*, 339 U.S. at 783, 785; *Rasu v. Bush* and *Al Odah v. United States*, 321 F.3d 1124 (D.C. Cir. 2003), *cert. granted*, 72 U.S.L.W. 3323 (U.S. Nov. 10, 2003) (Nos. 03-334 and 03-343).

44. *E.g.*, Landrum, "The Yamashita War Crimes Trial," 297–98; Parks, "Command Responsibility for War Crimes," 37, 87–88; Rovine, "The Air War and International Law," 139–41; *see* Maga, *Judgment at Tokyo*, 25–27; Schabas, *Genocide in International Law*, 312.

45. Parks, "Command Responsibility for War Crimes," 1 n. 2, 24 n. 76.

46. Some scholars have perceived no material difference in *High Command* from the "knew or should have known" standard in *Hostage*. But others have found in *High Command*'s formulation a mere "fragment of should have known logic," permitting citation of that decision for an "actual knowledge" standard—the one used in the acquittal of Captain Ernest Medina for the 1969 massacre of civilians by his immediate subordinate, Lieutenant William L. Calley Jr., at My Lai in South Vietnam. Lael, *The Yamashita Precedent*, 124–25, 131–32; Bassiouni, *The Law of the International Criminal Tribunal for the Former Yugoslavia*, 362; Landrum, "The Yamashita War Crimes Trial," 298–99; Parks, "Command Responsibility for War Crimes," 38–64; McCarthy, *Medina*, 3; *see* Rovine, "The Air War and International Law," 141–42.

47. Parks, "Command Responsibility for War Crimes," 40–41 (intermediate commanders), 83–84 (command responsibility divided between "operational" and "administrative" control), 95; U.S. Department of the Army, *United States Army Field Manual*, ch. 8, sec. II, cl. 501, pp. 178–79; Bassiouni, *The Law of the International Criminal Tribunal for the Former Yugoslavia*, 363; Lael, *The Yamashita Precedent*, 127–28; Brackman, *The Other Nuremberg*, 52; *see generally* Piccigallo, *The Japanese on Trial*.

48. Bassuioni, *Criminal Tribunal for Former Yugoslavia*, 340. The Yugoslav tribunal standard itself contains ambiguities—failing to resolve, for example, whether imputed knowledge ("reason to know") is objective (based on a "reasonable person" analysis) or subjective (based on "actual personal knowledge"). Bassiouni, *Criminal Tribunal for Former Yugoslavia*, 345; Schabas, *Genocide in International Law*, 309.

49. On June 8, 1977, international delegates at Geneva adopted Protocol Additional to the Geneva Convention of 12 August 1949, and relating to the Protection of Victims of International Armed Conflicts (Protocol I). Article 86 incorporated a new, imputed knowledge standard: commanding officers must have "had information which should have enabled them to conclude in the circumstances at the time, that [a subordinate] was

committing or was going to commit" a war crime. This largely subjective standard, premised on receipt of "information," required a higher, more specific level of knowledge than a defeated proposal by the United States for a more objective standard holding a commander criminally responsible for a subordinate's war crime if the commander "knew or should *reasonably* have known in the circumstances at the time that [the subordinate] was committing or was going to commit such a breach" (emphasis added). Lael, *The Yamashita Precedent*, 134. Although most nations, including China, France, Germany, Great Britain, and the Russian Federation, have adopted Protocol 1 (many with "reservations"), the United States has not done so. <http://www.icrc.org/eng/party_gc> (Mar. 5, 2004).

50. Pictet, ed., *Commentary on III Geneva Convention Relative to the Treatment of Prisoners of War*, 413-14.

51. Art. 85, Convention (III) relative to the Treatment of Prisoners of War (Geneva, Aug. 12, 1949) (hereafter "Geneva Convention 1949"); Pictet, ed., *Commentary on III Geneva Convention Relative to the Treatment of Prisoners of War*, 413-27; Lael, *The Yamashita Precedent*, 121.

52. Lael, *The Yamashita Precedent*, 122.

53. Art. 104, Geneva Convention 1949; Pictet, ed., *Commentary on III Geneva Convention Relative to the Treatment of Prisoners of War*, 480-84.

54. Art. 105, Geneva Convention 1949, Pictet, ed., *Commentary on III Geneva Convention Relative to the Treatment of Prisoners of War*, 484-92; Lael, *The Yamashita Precedent*, 121.

55. Art. 102, Geneva Convention 1949; Pictet, ed., *Commentary on III Geneva Convention Relative to the Treatment of Prisoners of War*, 476.

56. Art. 106, Geneva Convention 1949; Lael, *The Yamashita Precedent*, 121; Pictet, ed., *Commentary on III Geneva Convention Relative to the Treatment of Prisoners of War*, 492-95. Curiously, Pictet adds: "It would not seem . . . that the drafters of the Convention intended by this wording to give prisoners of war access to certain means of appeal which are available only to nationals of the country concerned." Pictet, ed., *Commentary on III Geneva Convention Relative to the Treatment of Prisoners of War*, 493.

57. Parks, "Command Responsibility for War Crimes," 38 n. 119.

58. *See Reid v. Covert*, 354 U.S. 1, 19 & n. 36 (1957); *Johnson v. Eisentrager*, 339 U.S. at 783.

59. *E.g., Washington Post*, Feb. 6, 1946, sec. A, p. 6, col. 2; *Chicago Daily Tribune*, March 9, 1946, p. 8, col. 1; Editorial, *St. Louis Star-Times*, March 22, 1946, p. 22, cols. 1-2.

60. Howard, *Mr. Justice Murphy*, 377.

61. *In re Yamashita*, 327 U.S. 1, 41-42, 81 (1946) (Rutledge, J., dissenting) (quoting 2 *The Complete Writings of Thomas Paine* 588 (Foner, ed., 1945)).

62. Piccigallo, *The Japanese on Trial*, 63, 66; Lawrence Taylor, *A Trial of Generals*, 171; *Homma v. Patterson*, 327 U.S. 759 (Murphy, J., dissenting); *id.* at 761 & nn. 1-2 (Rutledge, J., dissenting).

63. Draft letter from WR to John Frank, Feb. 13, 1946; WR to John L. [*sic*] Frank (Feb. 22, 1946); WR to John M. Maguire, March 13, 1946; *Homma v. Patterson*, 327 U.S. at 760.

64. "General Homma's Conviction," *St. Louis Star-Times*, Feb. 14, 1946, Rutledge Papers; Editorial, *St. Louis Star-Times*, March 22, 1946, p. 22, cols. 1-2; *Chicago Daily Tribune*, March 9, 1946, p. 8, col. 1; *Washington Post*, Feb. 6, 1946, sec. A, p. 6, col. 2; "The Supreme Court and the Yamashita Case," *Cincinnati Times-Star*, Feb. 6, 1946, Rutledge

Papers; *Had They No Protector?*, *Reporter News* (Abilene, Texas), Feb. 13, 1946, Rutledge Papers; *Salt Lake City Tribune*, Feb. 6, 1946, p. 5., col. 1.

65. *St. Louis Post-Dispatch*, Feb. 6, 1946, sec. C, p. 2, col. 2; *Evening Star* (Washington), Feb. 13, 1946, sec. A, p. A-5, cols. 2–5; Draft Letter from WR to John Frank, Feb. 13, 1946.

66. *Washington Post*, March 21, 1946, p. 1, cols. 2–3; Lawrence Taylor, *A Trial of Generals*, 219–20; Whitney, "The Case of General Yamashita," 3.

67. Mrs. D. C. Cowles to WR, Feb. 5, 1946 (telegram); Clarence Streit to WR, Feb. 6, 1946; Paul R. Grabiel to WR, Feb. 13, 1946; Harrison Loesch to WR, April 2, 1946; Dayton M. Harrington to WR, undated [Feb. 1947]; Hans J. Morgenthau to WR, March 1, 1946; John M. McGuire to WR, March 6, 1946. Fred A. Dewey to WR, Feb. 13, 1946. WR to Victor Brudney, April 1, 1946; Victor Brudney to WR, April 12, 1946; C. E. C[ropley] to WR, Feb. 4, 1946; undated memorandum re "Robert the Rober" in WR's handwriting in *Yamashita* file, Rutledge Papers; Reel, *The Case of General Yamashita*, 216.

68. *Duncan v. Kahanamoku*, 327 U.S. 304, 307–9, 310, 319, 324 (1946); *id.* 327 U.S. at 337, 353 n. 6 (Burton, J., dissenting); Fairman, "The Supreme Court on Military Jurisdiction," 834–36, 855; Rehnquist, *All the Laws but One*, 212–17.

69. Fairman, "The Supreme Court on Military Jurisdiction," 855–58; *Hirabayashi v. United States*, 320 U.S. 81, 95 (1943).

70. *E.g.*, *Ex parte Milligan*, 71 U.S. (2 Wall.) 2 (1866); *Johnson v. Eisentrager*, 339 U.S. 763 (1950).

CHAPTER TWENTY

1. WR to Luther Ely Smith, April 23, 1946; Mason, *Harlan Fiske Stone*, 806.

2. *Evening Star* (Washington), April 23, 1946, p. 1, col. 1; Robert C. Albright, *Washington Post*, April 24, 1946, p. 1, cols. 6–7; *Oregonian* (Portland), May 4, 1946, p. 1, col. 3; Jack Bell, *St. Louis Globe-Democrat*, May 20, 1946 sec. A, p. 2A, col. 6.; Newman, *Hugo Black*, 341–43; Fassett, "The Buddha and the Bumblebee," 182, 184.

3. A. B. Frey to Hon. Harry S. Truman, April 30, 1946; Luther Ely Smith to Irving Brant, May 15 and 22, 1946, Brant Papers; WR to Abe Frey, May 1, 1946; Irving Brant to Luther Ely Smith, June 5, 1946, Brant Papers.

4. Irving Brant to Luther Ely Smith, June 5, 1946, Brant Papers; WR to Henry S. Fraser, May 2, 1946; WR to Abe Frey, May 1, 1946; WR to Luther Ely Smith, April 23, 1946; Howard, *Mr. Justice Murphy*, 219–25; Fassett, "The Buddha and the Bumblebee," 174 (citing Fine, *Frank Murphy*, 257); Jackson, *That Man*, 24–26.

5. Newman, *Hugo Black*, 344; Hutchinson, "The Black-Jackson Feud," 202, 205; *see* Jackson, *That Man*, 107.

6. Newman, *Hugo Black*, 339, 341, 344; Dunne, *Hugo Black and the Judicial Revolution*, 242; Ball and Cooper, *Of Power and Right*, 94, 97. One reporter disclosed "gossip" that the two threatening to resign were Black and Murphy. Gerhart, *America's Advocate*, 265; Hutchinson, "The Black-Jackson Feud," 214–19.

7. Newman, *Hugo Black*, 342–44; Ball and Cooper, *Of Power and Right*, 94–98; Murphy, *Wild Bill*, 243–46; Hutchinson, "The Black-Jackson Feud," 215, 226–27; Doris Fleeson, *Evening Star* (Washington), May 16, 1946, sec. A, p. A-15, cols. 4–5.

8. *Washington Post*, June 7, 1946, sec. 1, p. 1, cols. 1–8. There is controversy over whether Hughes recommended Vinson ahead of Jackson. Dunne, *Hugo Black and the Judicial Revolution*, 242; Gerhart, *America's Advocate*, 277–87; *see* Newman, *Hugo Black*,

341, 344 (reporting that Hughes recommended Jackson and Arthur T. Vanderbilt, then dean of the law school at New York University, and that Roberts recommended Vinson and Secretary of War—and former federal appellate judge—Robert Patterson); John H. Cline, *Evening Star* (Washington), June 9, 1946, sec. C, p. 1, cols. 3-5.

9. Harper, *Justice Rutledge and the Bright Constellation*, 316; WR to Mrs. Paul P. McCain, June 29, 1946; WR to Ivan Rutledge, June 22, 1946; WR to F. Lander Moorman, June 22, 1946; WR to Victor Brudney, June 11, 1946; WR to Ernest Kirschten, May 10, 1946; WR to George Heidlebaugh, June 22, 1946; *see* Ball and Cooper, *Of Power and Right*, 101-2. According to another friend of Rutledge, the justice had "strongly desired" the appointment as chief justice of Wisconsin's former dean Lloyd K. Garrison (then of the New York Bar). Frank, *The Marble Palace*, 59.

10. Hatcher, "Fred M. Vinson," 423; Kirkendall, "Fred Vinson," 2639, 2640; Urofsky, *Division and Discord*, 149; Allen, "Chief Justice Vinson and the Theory of Constitutional Government," 4; interviews, Allen, Coleman Jr., Ebb, Feller, Helman, Joslin, Marsh, Seder Jr., Spitzer, Temko, Tone, Torre, von Mehren.

11. Interviews, Allen, Groner, Helman, Tone, Weston, White; John P. Frank, "Fred Vinson and the Chief Justiceship," 212.

12. WR to Luther Ely Smith, Oct. 31, 1946; Walter Wyatt, Diary, Nov. 6, 1946, box 1, Wyatt Papers; interviews, Allan, Gressman, Hobbs, Kurland (reporting incident learned from Rutledge's clerk Richard F. Wolfson, now deceased), N. Rutledge, Temko, Tone, Weston, Wollenberg; Urofsky, *Division and Discord*, 149, 151; Frank, "Fred Vinson and the Chief Justiceship," 212-13.

13. WR to George Heidlebaugh, June 22, 1946; WR to Ivan Rutledge, June 22, 1946; WR to Victor Brudney, June 11, 1946; WR to F. Lander Moorman, June 22, 1946; *see* Allen, "Chief Justice Vinson and the Theory of Constitutional Government," 6-8; Frank, "Fred Vinson and the Chief Justiceship," 228.

14. *Evening Star* (Washington), June 11, 1946, p. A-5, cols. 2-5; Newman, *Hugo Black*, 345; Hutchinson, "The Black-Jackson Feud," 219-21; Gerhart, *Robert H. Jackson*, 264.

15. *Evening Star* (Washington), June 11, 1946, p. A-5, cols. 2-5.

16. Dunne, *Hugo Black and the Judicial Revolution*, 245, 247; Newman, *Hugo Black*, 348 (quoting *Macon* (Ga.) *Telegraph*); Harper, *Justice Rutledge and the Bright Constellation*, 311-12; Gerhart, *America's Advocate*, 265 (Jackson "committed an error in taste" whereas Black "committed the worse offense of lowering judicial standards"); Hutchinson, "The Black-Jackson Feud," 203; "Tirade of a Justice," *St. Louis Post-Dispatch*, June 12, 1940, Rutledge Papers. For Justice Jackson's own view of the controversy see his Reminiscences, ch. 56, "Controversy within the Court," 1577-99.

17. Dunne, *Hugo Black and the Judicial Revolution*, 247; Harper, *Justice Rutledge and the Bright Constellation*, 315; WR to Dwight Rutledge, June 24, 1946; WR to George Heidlebaugh, June 22, 1946. For competing analyses of the merits of the Jackson-Black controversy see Frank, "Disqualification of Judges" (supports Black), and Gerhart, *America's Advocate*, 265-77 (supports Jackson).

18. Dunne, *Hugo Black and the Judicial Revolution*, 248; Gerhart, *America's Advocate*, 265; Harper, *Justice Rutledge and the Bright Constellation*, 311, 314; Merle D. Vincent to WR, June 17, 1946; Merle D. Vincent to Hon. Claude Pepper, June 17, 1946; Robert C. Albright, *Washington Post*, June 19, 1946, p. 1, col. 7; interview, Gressman.

19. Diary of Harold H. Burton, Oct. 10, 1946, *quoted in* Dunne, *Hugo Black and the Judicial Revolution*, 241; Newman, *Hugo Black*, 347-48; Hutchinson, "The Black-Jackson Feud," 223; 329 U.S. iii n. 1 (1946) (listing the justices of the Supreme Court

and detailing the nomination, confirmation, commissioning, and oath of office of Chief Justice Fred M. Vinson).

20. Lester A. Royal to WR, July 15, 1946; McCune, *The Nine Young Men*, 211, *quoted in* Harper, *Justice Rutledge and the Bright Constellation*, 315.

21. McCullough, *Truman*, 481, 492, 493; Schlesinger, *The Rise of Modern America*, 461; *United States v. United Mine Workers*, 330 U.S. 258, 262-63 & n. 1 (1947); Watt, "The Divine Right of Government by Judiciary," 412.

22. *United Mine Workers*, 330 U.S. at 264; Watt, "The Divine Right of Government by Judiciary," 412.

23. *United Mine Workers*, 330 U.S. at 265; Watt, "The Divine Right of Government by Judiciary," 414.

24. Watt, "The Divine Right of Government by Judiciary," 416; *United Mine Workers*, 330 U.S. at 268-69.

25. Watt, "The Divine Right of Government by Judiciary," 443; *United Mine Workers*, 330 U.S. at 271, 272-73; *id.* at 342, 352-53 & n. 14 (Rutledge, J., dissenting) (quoting Frankfurter and Greene, *The Labor Injunction*, 200-201 (1930)).

26. *United Mine Workers*, 330 U.S. at 274-86.

27. Watt, "The Divine Right of Government by Judiciary," 423, 436; Baker, *Felix Frankfurter*, 202; *United Mine Workers*, 330 U.S. 307 (Frankfurter, J., concurring in the judgment).

28. *Id.* at 328, 330-35 (Black, J., and Douglas, J., concurring in part and dissenting in part).

29. *Id.* at 289-95, 304-5; *id.* at 309-12 (Frankfurter, J., concurring in judgment).

30. *Id.* at 342, 343 (footnote omitted) (Rutledge, J., dissenting).

31. *Id.* at 351-52, 355, 360 (Rutledge, J., dissenting) (citing, among others, *Ex parte Rowland*, 104 U.S. 604 (1881); *Ex parte Fisk*, 113 U.S. 713 (1885); *In re Sawyer*, 124 U.S. 200 (1888)); *id.* at 293 (opinion of Court); *accord id.* at 309-10 (Frankfurter, J. concurring in judgment).

32. *Id.* at 352-54 (Rutledge, J., dissenting); Watt, "The Divine Right of Government by Judiciary," 446-47.

33. 203 U.S. 563 (1906).

34. *United States v. United Mine Workers*, 330 U.S. 258, 357 (1948) (Rutledge, J., dissenting); *accord* Watt, "The Divine Right of Government by Judiciary," 441.

35. *See United Mine Workers*, 330 U.S. at 291.

36. *Id.* at 357-58 (Rutledge, J., dissenting).

37. *Id.* at 363, 368-76 (Rutledge, J., dissenting); *id.* at 298, 300, 301 (opinion of Court).

38. *Id.* at 376, 377 & n. 53, 379, 382, 384 (Rutledge, J., dissenting) (citing *Gompers v. United States*, 233 U.S. 604, 612 (1914)).

39. *Id.* at 342 n. 1 (Rutledge, J., dissenting) (quoting *N. Sec. Co. v. United States*, 193 U.S. 197, 400-401 (1904) (Holmes, J., dissenting)); WR to W. Howard Mann, April 7, 1947.

40. "Settlement Tribute Paid Mrs. Roosevelt," *New York Times*, Oct. 29, 1946, Rutledge Papers; "Justice Rutledge of Supreme Court at Duke Today," *Durham* (N.C.) *Sun*, Oct. 2, 1946, Rutledge Papers; *News and Observer* (Raleigh), Sept. 30, 1946, p. 7, col. 4; WR to Merritt W. Oldaker, April 4, 1947; WR to Lon T. Williams, April 16, 1947.

41. Matthew S. Rae Jr. to WR, Feb. 25, 1947; WR to Matthew S. Rae Jr., April 8, 1947; WR to Benjamin S. Galland, April 16, 1947.

42. Sheridan L. Hill-Ellis to author, Oct. 26, 1995 (enclosure); Fowler V. Harper to WR, Sept. 20, 1946; WR to Walton Hamilton, Sept. 30, 1946 (two letters); Ralph Fuchs to WR,

Oct. 6, 1946; W. Howard Mann to WR, Dec. 18, 1946; *New York Times*, Sept. 6, 1946, p. 6, cols. 2–3; Report to the Honorable Ralph F. Gates, governor of Indiana, from the Board of Trustees of Indiana University, Dec. 15, 1946.

43. Report to the Honorable Ralph F. Gates, governor of Indiana, from the Board of Trustees of Indiana University, Dec. 15, 1946; Fowler V. Harper to WR, Sept. 20, 1946; Ralph Fuchs to WR, Oct. 6, 1947; W. Howard Mann to WR, Dec. 18, 1947; WR to Walton Hamilton, Sept. 30, 1947; WR to Walton Hamilton, Sept. 30, 1947 (marked "Personal").

44. Interviews, M. L. (Rutledge) Needels, J. A. (Rutledge) Pollitt, C. Rutledge, N. Rutledge; WR to Huber O. Croft, March 12, 1947; John Caskie Collett to WR, April 7, 1947; WR to Hon. J. C. Collett, May 12, 1947; WR to Terrence M. O'Brien, May 12, 1947; Thomas H. Stewart to WR, May 12, 1947 (with handwritten notation); WR to Carl Wheaton, July 3, 1947; WR to Clay Apple, July 2, 1947; WR to Frank Messer, Oct. 27, 1947; John W. Taylor to WR, Aug. 28, 1947; "A Beloved Judge; Justice Rutledge of the Supreme Court Praises Kimbrough Stone; In a Glowing Tribute," *Kansas City Times*, May 23, 1947, Rutledge Papers; "University of Louisville Program Commemorating the One Hundredth Anniversary of the Founding of the School of Law 1846–1946[,] Friday Evening[,] September 19, 1947"; *Louisville Courier-Journal*, Sept. 19, 1947, sec. 2, p. 1, col. 5.

45. WR to Ivan C. Rutledge, June 24, 1947; WR to J. A. Rutledge, July 5, 1947; W. Willard Wirtz to WR, May 23, 1947; WR to W. Willard Wirtz, June 3 and 25, July 9, 1947; John Paul Stevens to WR, July 14 and 24, 1947.

CHAPTER TWENTY-ONE

1. Interviews, Allan, Ebb, Gartner, Kabot, Kurland, Seder Jr., J. P. Stevens, Temko.

2. Interviews, Allan, Allen, Brudney, Ebb, Feller, Frank, Gartner, Haber, Joslin, Kabot, Kurland, Lake, Lomen, Luce, W. H. Mann, Oberdorfer, Pollak, Seder Jr., Shniderman, Spitzer, J. P. Stevens, Tone, Wollenberg; *see generally* Pollak, "Wiley Blount Rutledge"; John Paul Stevens, "Mr. Justice Rutledge."

3. Interviews, Allan, Allen, Birdzell Jr., Black Jr., Coleman Jr., Elman, Feller, Haber, Hobbs, Kurland, Lake, Luce, Marsh, Nickerson, Pollak, Rosenthal, Shniderman, J. P. Stevens, Tone, Weston; Walter Wyatt, Diary, July 11, 1949, box 3, Wyatt Papers.

4. Interviews, Allan, Allen, Brudney, Coleman Jr., Elman, Gressman, Haber, Henkin, Hobbs, Frank, Joslin, Kurland, Luce, Pollak, J. P. Stevens, Temko, Tone.

5. Interviews, Elman, Feller, Kabot, Lake, Marsh, Neal, Nickerson, Pollak, Shniderman, Spitzer, J. P. Stevens, White. *But see* Tone ("I don't think he found deciding hard.").

6. Interview, Brudney. *But see* Shniderman ("I don't think he had trouble getting it down"; the "harder part of the job was making the decision."); Tone ("Opinion-writing did not come easily for Rutledge, but I don't think it came hard, either.").

7. Interviews, Coleman Jr., Luce, Seder Jr.

8. Interviews, Allen, Brudney, Haber, Pollak, Tone.

9. Interviews, Brudney, Coleman Jr., Ebb, Elman, Frank, Gressman, Groner, Haber, Hobbs, Joslin, Kabot, Kurland, Lomen, Luce, W. H. Mann, Nickerson, Oberdorfer, Pickering, Pollak, Seder Jr., Shniderman, J. P. Stevens, Temko, Tone, von Mehren, Weston, Wollenberg.

10. Interviews, Brudney, Frank, Pollak, Shniderman, J. P. Stevens, Temko.

11. Interviews, Coleman Jr., Ebb, Kabot, Kurland, Lomen, Luce, Pollak, Seder Jr., Shniderman.

12. Interviews, Allen, Brudney, Elman, Feller, Frank, Groner, Hobbs, Kurland, Lomen, Luce, J. K. Mann, W. H. Mann, Marsh, N. Rutledge, M. L. (Rutledge) Needels, Oberdorfer, J. A. (Rutledge) Pollitt, Rosenthal, N. Rutledge, Seder Jr., Shniderman, J. P. Stevens, Temko, Tone, Torre.

13. Interview, Temko.

14. Interview, Seder Jr.

15. Interviews, Coleman Jr., Torre; WR to Jack Bronston, Feb. 17, 1948.

16. Interview, Allen.

17. Howard, *Mr. Justice Murphy*, 491.

18. Urofsky, *Division and Discord*, 34 (Frankfurter); Howard, *Mr. Justice Murphy*, 268 (Jackson), 396 (Frankfurter); Simon, *The Antagonists*, 116 (Frankfurter); Ball and Cooper, *Of Power and Right*, 98 (Frankfurter and Jackson; the authors also add Stone and Reed); interview, Gardner (Jackson).

19. Yarbrough, *Mr. Justice Black and His Critics*, 227–228 (re *Kotch v. Bd. of River Port Pilot Comm'rs*, 330 U.S. 564 (1947) (Rutledge, J., dissenting)); *Mapp v. Ohio*, 367 U.S. 643, 661, 662 (Black, J., concurring); *Engel v. Vitale*, 370 U.S. 421, 437, 443 (1962) (Douglas, J., concurring).

20. Interview, Black Jr.

21. Frank Murphy to WR, June 29, 1947.

22. WR to Hon. Frank Murphy, July 3, 1947.

23. WR to Hon. Frank Murphy, July 3, 1947; Walter Wyatt, Diary, Nov. 26, 1947, box 1, Wyatt Papers; Howard, *Mr. Justice Murphy*, 166–67, 199, 216, 425, 495; WR to Morrison Shafroth, June 24, 1946; interview, Neal Rutledge.

24. Howard, *Mr. Justice Murphy*, 425 (quoting WR to Joan Cuddihy, Nov. 19, 1947).

25. Richard F. Wolfson to WR, May 13, 1948; interview, Neal Rutledge. In 1947 newspapers in Washington reported that during the 1946 Term Justice Douglas used 368 printed pages, the most of any justice, for his 37 opinions while Justice Rutledge required 335 pages—second-highest on the Court—for his 32 opinions. The colleague closest to Rutledge in number of opinions, Justice Jackson with 31, wrote only 226 pages. The average per justice was 273 printed pages. Frank, "The United States Supreme Court," 38 n. 65.

26. Frank Murphy to WR, May 25, 1946; Felix Frankfurter to WR, May 25, 1946 (emphasis added). Of Justice Rutledge's 65 majority (including plurality) opinions, 17 (or 26 percent) spoke for a unanimous Court while an additional 14 had two or fewer dissenters, for a total of 31 (or 48 percent) with no more than two in dissent.

27. Minor liberties are taken with the statistics to correspond to reality. For example, one opinion covering three similar cases, dissenting in one and concurring in two, is counted as a dissent. Where an opinion concurs in part and dissents in part, Rutledge's own label—concurrence or dissent—is used. Concurring statements of no more than a few lines are excluded.

28. Subject to the author's adjustments explained in the previous footnote, statistics for the 1940s relied on here—and other subsets of information comparing the justices' respective outputs—can be found in three law review articles by John P. Frank, each entitled "The United States Supreme Court" and found in 15 *U. Chi. L. Rev.* 1 (1947) (for 1946–47), 16 *U. Chi. L. Rev.* 1 (1948) (for 1947–48), and 17 *U. Chi. L. Rev.* 1 (1949) (for 1948–49). A major work applying a statistical method for analyzing Supreme Court decisions is Pritchett, *The Roosevelt Court*.

29. *E.g.*, *Colegrove v. Green*, 328 U.S. 549, 564 (1946) (Rutledge, J., concurring in result); *Screws v. United States*, 325 U.S. 91, 113 (1945) (Rutledge, J., concurring in result).

30. *New York v. United States*, 326 U.S. 572, 584 (1946) (Rutledge, J., concurring) (state not immune from federal tax on state-owned mineral waters).

31. *Comm'r v. Tower*, 327 U.S. 289, 292 (1946) (Rutledge, J., concurring) (sustaining tax deficiency assessed against husband on income transferred to alleged family partnership).

32. *Pennekamp v. Florida*, 328 U.S. 331, 370 (1946) (Rutledge, J., concurring) (reversing trial court order of contempt against newspaper that had criticized non-jury trials for being too soft on criminals and gambling establishments); *Heiser v. Woodruff*, 327 U.S. 726, 740 (1946) (Rutledge, J., concurring) (ruling bankruptcy court cannot disregard previous adjudication that claim was not procured by fraud).

33. *Estep v. United States*, 327 U.S. 114, 132 (1946) (Rutledge, J., concurring) (permitting habeas corpus review of draft classification after registrant has reported and been accepted for induction).

34. *Kraus & Bros., Inc. v. United States*, 327 U.S. 614, 628 (1946) (Rutledge, J., concurring) (remanding for new trial of charge that petitioner violated Emergency Price Control Act of 1942 by forcing chicken purchasers to buy skin and feet as condition of buying poultry).

35. *May Dep't Stores Co. v. NLRB*, 326 U.S. 376, 393 (1945) (Rutledge, J., concurring in part) (sustaining NLRB finding of unfair labor practices by employer that sought War Labor Board approval of wage increases without bargaining collectively with certified representative).

36. *Am. Tobacco Co. v. United States*, 328 U.S. 781, 815 (1946) (Rutledge, J., concurring) (sustaining conviction for monopolization in violation of Sherman Antitrust Act); *Holmberg v. Armbrecht*, 327 U.S. 392, 398 (1946) (Rutledge, J., concurring) (holding state statute of limitations does not bar federal court action based on federally created equity right); *United States v. Petty Motor Co.*, 327 U.S. 372, 381 (1946) (Rutledge, J., concurring) (ruling on measure of damages applicable to federal condemnation of leasehold during war).

37. *Compare Freeman v. Hewitt*, 329 U.S. 249, 259 (1946) (Rutledge, J., concurring) *with Complete Auto Transit, Inc. v. Brady*, 430 U.S. 274 (1977); *compare Marino v. Ragen*, 332 U.S. 561, 563 (1947) (Rutledge, J., concurring) *with Young v. Ragen*, 337 U.S. 235 (1949).

38. Interviews, Allen, Ebb, Frank, Haber, Joslin, Kurland, Lingreen, Luce, Oberdorfer, Pickering, Pollak, Seder Jr., J. P. Stevens, Tone.

39. Interview, Shniderman.

40. 324 U.S. 282, 283 (1945).

41. *Id.* at 286, 287–89, 290–91, 292 (Rutledge, J., dissenting).

42. 324 U.S. 401 (1945); *id.* at 420 (Rutledge, J., dissenting in part).

43. *E.g., McNabb v. United States*, 318 U.S. 332, 340 (1943).

44. *Fisher v. United States*, 328 U.S. 463 (1946); id. at 494, 495 (Rutledge, J., dissenting).

45. 328 U.S. 640 (1946).

46. 328 U.S. 640 (1946); *id.* at 648, 651 (Rutledge, J., dissenting in part).

47. 327 U.S. 82 (1946); *id.* at 91, 91 (Rutledge, J., dissenting); *Wood v. United States*, 128 F.2d 265, 267, 268, 271 (1942).

48. 332 U.S. 134, 137, 138, 139 (1947).

49. *Id.* at 141, 142 (Rutledge, J., dissenting).

50. 332 U.S. 145, 146 (1947); *id.* at 149, 150 & n. 2 (Rutledge, J., dissenting).

51. *Id.* at 150 n. 1, 151, 152–53, 154 (Rutledge, J., dissenting).

52. *Parker v. Illinois*, 333 U.S. 571, 577 (1948) (Rutledge, J., dissenting); *Gryger v. Burke*, 334 U.S. 728, 732 (1948) (Rutledge, J., dissenting); *Bute v. Illinois*, 333 U.S. 640, 677 (1948) (Douglas, J., dissenting); *Hedgebeth v. North Carolina*, 334 U.S. 806 (1948) (announcing Douglas and Rutledge, JJ., would reverse).

53. 335 U.S. 469, 472 (1948); *id.* at 488, 492-93, 494-95 (Rutledge, J., dissenting).

54. *Fisher v. Pace*, 336 U.S. 155 (1949); *id.* at 163 (Douglas, J., dissenting); *id.* at 166 (Murphy, J., dissenting); *id.* at 168, 169 (Rutledge, J., dissenting).

55. *United States v. Evans*, 333 U.S. 483 (1948) (Immigration Act); *Gibson v. United States*, 329 U.S. 338 (1946) (Selective Training and Service Act); *United States v. Anderson*, 328 U.S. 699 (1946) (Selective Training and Service Act).

56. 328 U.S. 750 (1946). Rutledge announced a reversible error standard, noteworthy as much for its convoluted language as for its substance: "If, when all is said and done, the conviction is sure that the error did not influence the jury, or had but very slight effect, the verdict and the judgment should stand, except perhaps where the departure is from a constitutional norm or a specific command of Congress. But if one cannot say, with fair assurance, after pondering all that happened without stripping the erroneous action from the whole, that the judgment was not substantially swayed by the error, it is impossible to conclude that substantial rights were not affected. The inquiry cannot be merely whether there was enough to support the result, apart from the phase affected by the error. It is rather, even so, whether the error itself had substantial influence. If so, or if one is left in grave doubt, the conviction cannot stand." *Id.* at 764-65 (citation omitted).

57. *Kann v. United States*, 323 U.S. 88, 95 (1944) (Douglas, J., dissenting).

58. 325 U.S. 91 (1945); Criminal Code sec. 20, 18 U.S.C. secs. 52, 88 (1940); *Screws v. United States*, 325 U.S. 91, 93, 101, 105 (1945).

59. *E.g., United States v. Classic*, 313 U.S. 299 (1941).

60. *Screws v. United States*, 325 U.S. at 113, 117, 118, 134 (Rutledge, J., concurring).

61. *United States v. Sheridan*, 329 U.S. 379 (1946); *Blumenthal v. United States*, 332 U.S. 539 (1947); *Robertson v. California*, 328 U.S. 440 (1946).

62. 335 U.S. 497, 501 n. 6., 504, 505 (1948) (citing *Thiel v. S. Pac. Co.*, 328 U.S. 217 (1946)); *id.* at 514, 515-16 (Jackson, J., dissenting); Walter Wyatt, Diary, Jan. 19, 1949, box 2, Wyatt Papers.

63. 338 U.S. 160 (1949).

64. *Carroll v. United States*, 267 U.S. 132 (1925).

65. *Davis v. United States*, 328 U.S. 582, 623 (1946) (Rutledge, J., dissenting).

66. *United States v. Di Re*, 332 U.S. 581 (1948) (majority opinion); *Johnson v. United States*, 333 U.S. 10 (1948) (majority opinion); *Lustig v. United States*, 338 U.S. 74 (1949) (majority opinion); *Trupiano v. United States*, 334 U.S. 699 (1948) (majority opinion); *Harris v. United States*, 331 U.S. 145 (1947); *id.* at 155 (Frankfurter, J., dissenting); *id.* at 183 (Murphy, J., dissenting); *id.* at 196 (Jackson, J., dissenting); *accord McDonald v. United States*, 335 U.S. 451, 456 (1948) (statement by Rutledge, J.).

67. *Brinegar v. United States*, 338 U.S. 160, 166 (1949).

68. *Id.* at 180, 182, 183, 188 (Jackson, J., dissenting); *id.* at 162-63.

69. 392 U.S. 1 (1968).

70. *Brinegar*, 338 U.S. at 163.

CHAPTER TWENTY-TWO

1. *O'Neil v. Vermont*, 144 U.S. 323, 361 (1892) (Field, J., dissenting); *id.* at 370 (Harlan, J., dissenting); *Maxwell v. Dow*, 176 U.S. 581, 605 (1900) (Harlan, J., dissenting);

Prudential Ins. Co. v. Cheek, 259 U.S. 530 (1922) (First Amendment speech clause); *Hurtado v. California*, 110 U.S. 516 (1884) (Fifth Amendment grand jury requirement); *West v. Louisiana*, 194 U.S. 258 (1904) (Sixth Amendment confrontation clause); *Twining v. New Jersey*, 211 U.S. 78 (1908) (Fifth Amendment privilege against self-incrimination); *see Barron v. Baltimore*, 32 U.S. (7 Pet.) 243 (1833) (Marshall, C.J.) (Fifth Amendment takings clause (pre-Fourteenth Amendment)).

2. *Gilbert v. Minnesota*, 254 U.S. 325, 343 (1920) (Brandeis, J., dissenting); *Gitlow v. New York*, 268 U.S. 562, 566 (1925); *Near v. Minnesota*, 283 U.S. (1931); *De Jonge v. Oregon*, 299 U.S. 353 (1937).

3. 302 U.S. 319 (1937); Urofsky, *Division and Discord*, 86.

4. *Palko v. Connecticut*, 302 U.S. at 325, 327 (quoting *Snyder v. Massachusetts*, 291 U.S. 97, 105 (1934)).

5. *Betts v. Brady*, 316 U.S. 455 (1942); *id.* at 474, 474 (Black, J., dissenting).

6. 329 U.S. 459, 460 (1947); *id.* at 472 (Burton, J., dissenting).

7. *Louisiana v. Resweber*, No. 142, Oct. Term, 1946 (Rutledge draft dissent), 1 (citations omitted), Rutledge Papers.

8. *Id.* at 329 U.S. at 474, 477, 481 (Burton, J., dissenting).

9. Wiecek, "Felix Frankfurter, Incorporation, and the Willie Francis Case," 57 (discussing *Francis* as prelude to *Adamson v. California*, 332 U.S. 46 (1947)).

10. *Louisiana v. Resweber*, 329 U.S. 466, 470, 471 (Frankfurter, J., concurring).

11. *Adamson v. California*, 332 U.S. 46, 48, 55-56, 57 (1947); *id.* at 68 (Black, J., dissenting); *id.* at 123 (Murphy, J., dissenting).

12. *Id.* at 50, 53, 54 (quoting *Palko v. Connecticut*, 302 U.S. 319, 325 (1937)).

13. *Id.* at 59 (Frankfurter, J., concurring).

14. *Compare id.* at 67-68 *with Malinski v. New York*, 324 U.S. at 412, 416-17 (Opinion of Frankfurter, J.).

15. *Adamson v. California*, 324 U.S. at 67-68 (Frankfurter, J., concurring).

16. *Id.* at 69, 70, 74-75, 77, 80, 89, 90, 91 (Black, J., dissenting). Scholars have debated the historical evidence of incorporation (or its absence), without consensus resolution. *E.g.*, Fairman, "Does the Fourteenth Amendment Incorporate the Bill of Rights?"; Stanley Morrison, "Does the Fourteenth Amendment Incorporate the Bill of Rights?"; William Winslow Crosskey, *Politics and the Constitution*, part v, 1049-1161; Charles Fairman, "The Supreme Court and the Constitutional Limitations on State Governmental Authority"; William Winslow Crosskey, "Charles Fairman, 'Legislative History,' and the Constitutional Limitations on State Authority"; Charles Fairman, "A Reply to Professor Crosskey"; Curtis, *No State Shall Abridge*.

17. Newman, *Hugo Black*, 354; *accord* interview, Oberdorfer.

18. *Adamson v. California*, 332 U.S. at 70, 90 (Black, J., dissenting); *Lochner v. New York*, 198 U.S. 45 (1905). *See also Chicago, M. & St. P. R.R. Co. v. Minnesota*, 134 U.S. 418 (1890); *Allgeyer v. Louisiana*, 165 U.S. 578 (1897).

19. *Adamson v. California*, 332 U.S. 123, 124 (Murphy, J., dissenting).

20. *Id.*

21. William M. Wiecek, untitled manuscript study of the Supreme Court, 1941-53 (hereafter "Supreme Court study"), 91 (2001) (ch. 5, *Adamson v. California*, quoting Black, J.; emphasis added).

22. *See* Wiecek, Supreme Court study, 92.

23. Richard F. Wolfson to WR, May 28, 1947, *quoted in* Tinsley E. Yarborough, *Mr. Justice Black and His Critics*, 100 & n. 100, and in Wiecek, Supreme Court study, 89.

24. Wiecek, Supreme Court study, 93-94.

25. 333 U.S. 257, 266–73, 278 (1948).

26. *Id*. at 278, 279, 280 (Rutledge, J., concurring); *see* Henry M. Bates to WR, March 22, 1948 (congratulations on *Oliver* concurrence), Bates Papers; WR to Henry M. Bates, April 13, 1948, Bates Papers.

27. Newman, *Hugo Black*, 530; Fish, *The Politics of Judicial Administration*, 101–6; *Duncan v. Louisiana*, 391 U.S. 145 (1968) (jury trial); *id*. at 162 (Black, J., concurring); *In re Oliver*, 333 U.S. 257 (1948) (notice of charge and public trial); *Gideon v. Wainwright*, 372 U.S. 335 (1963) (counsel); *Pointer v. Texas*, 380 U.S. 400 (1965) (confrontation and cross-examination); *Robinson v. California*, 370 U.S. 660 (1962) (cruel and unusual punishment); *Malloy v. Hogan*, 378 U.S. 1 (1964) (privilege against self-incrimination); *Griffin v. California*, 380 U.S. 609 (1965) (privilege against self-incrimination); *Washington v. Texas*, 388 U.S. 14 (1967) (compulsory process to obtain witnesses); *Klopfer v. North Carolina*, 386 U.S. 213 (1967) (speedy trial); *Benton v. Maryland*, 395 U.S. 784 (1969) (double jeopardy).

28. *Griswold v. Connecticut*, 381 U.S. 479 (1965).

29. *Shapiro v. Thompson*, 394 U.S. 618 (1959); *Kent v. Dulles*, 357 U.S. 116 (1958).

30. *Meyer v. Nebraska*, 262 U.S. 390, 399 (1923).

31. *Poe v. Ullman*, 367 U.S. 497, 509, 516 (1961) (Douglas, J., dissenting).

32. Interview, Pollak.

33. 338 U.S. 25 (1949).

34. *Id*. at 27, 28, 31, 33.

35. Newman, *Hugo Black*, 371, 555–56; Dunne, *Hugo Black and the Judicial Revolution*, 271; *Wolf v. Colorado*, 338 U.S. at 39, 40 (Black, J., concurring in judgment).

36. *Wolf*, 338 U.S. at 41, 42–43 (Murphy, J., dissenting).

37. *Id*. at 42–43 (Murphy, J., dissenting).

38. *Id*. at 42 (Murphy, J., dissenting).

39. *Id*. at 41, 42–43, 44–46 (Murphy, J., dissenting).

40. *Weeks v. United States*, 232 U.S. 383 (1914).

41. *Wolf*, 338 U.S. 25, 47, 48 (Rutledge, J., dissenting); *Mapp v. Ohio*, 367 U.S. 643 (1961); *id*. at 661, 662 (Black, J., concurring); Newman, *Hugo Black*, 555–56.

42. *Upshaw v. United States*, 335 U.S. 410 (1948).

43. *Watts v. Indiana*, 338 U.S. 49 (1949); *Turner v. Pennsylvania*, 338 U.S. 62 (1949); *Harris v. South Carolina*, 338 U.S. 68 (1949).

44. *Watts v. Indiana*, 338 U.S. at 54.

45. *Id*. at 56 (Douglas, J., concurring); *Turner*, 338 U.S. at 66 (Douglas, J., concurring); *Harris*, 338 U.S. at 71 (Douglas, J., concurring).

46. *Watts*, 338 U.S. at 55 (Black, J., concurring in judgment); *Turner*, 338 U.S. at 66 (Black, J., concurring in judgment); *Harris*, 338 U.S. at 71 (Black, J., concurring in judgment).

47. *Watts*, 338 U.S. at 57, 60 (Jackson, J., concurring in result); *Turner*, 338 U.S. at 66 (Jackson, J., dissenting); *Harris*, 338 U.S. at 71 (Jackson, J., dissenting).

48. *Upshaw v. United States*, 335 U.S. 410, 414, 436 (1948) (Reed, J., dissenting).

49. *Marino v. Ragen*, 332 U.S. 561, 562–63 (1947).

50. *Id*. at 563 (1947) (Rutledge, J., dissenting).

51. *Id*. at 563, 564 (1947) (Rutledge, J., dissenting).

52. *Id*. at 566–67, 570.

53. 333 U.S. 571, 572, 575, 577 (1948).

54. *Id*. at 577, 579, 580–81 (Rutledge, J., dissenting).

55. *Cent. Union Co. v. Edwardsville*, 269 U.S. 190 (1925).

56. *Parker v. Illinois*, 333 U.S. at 578, 582 (Rutledge, J., dissenting).

57. Parker had to go to the state supreme court first, to avoid waiving his constitutional claim. After losing there, however, he could not seek U.S. Supreme Court review, since there was no "final order" — state law issues remained — so he next sought relief as to those in the appellate court. He lost there, too. To be doubly sure of exhausting state remedies, he went again to the Illinois Supreme Court, which affirmed the appellate court's state law judgment but declined to reconsider his constitutional claims. Parker thus assuredly obtained a final order, ready for U.S. Supreme Court review, but by then, under Illinois law — applied only to the second state supreme court ruling as though its first order was a nullity — Parker was deemed to have waived his constitutional claims.

58. *Parker*, 333 U.S. at 578 (Rutledge, J., dissenting).

59. *Marino v. Ragen*, 332 U.S. at 567 (Rutledge, J., concurring); *Foster v. Illinois*, 332 U.S. 134, 141, 143-44 (1947) (Rutledge, J., dissenting).

60. 333 U.S. 640, 643-44 (1948).

61. 334 U.S. 728 (1948); *id.* at 732, 734-35 (Rutledge, J., dissenting); *id.* at 734-35.

62. 334 U.S. 736, 740 (1948), *cited in Gryger v. Burke*, 334 U.S. at 735-36 (Rutledge, J., dissenting).

63. *Gryger v. Burke*, 334 U.S. at 736 (Rutledge, J., dissenting).

64. *Loftus v. Illinois*, 334 U.S. 804, 805-6 (1948); *People v. Loftus*, 81 N.E.2d 495 (Ill. 1948).

65. WR to John Paul Stevens, July 5, 1949.

66. *Young v. Ragen*, 337 U.S. 235, 239 (1949).

67. Frank, "The United States Supreme Court: 1948-1949," 29-30 & n. 118; Katz, "An Open Letter to the Attorney General of Illinois"; *see also* Note, "Power to Appoint Counsel in Illinois Habeas Corpus Proceedings."

68. Frank, "The United States Supreme Court: 1948-1949," 30 n. 118; letter from John Paul Stevens to WR, July 11, 1949; *St. Louis Post-Dispatch*, June 6, 1949, part A, p. 1, cols. 6-8; *St. Louis Post-Dispatch*, July 3, 1949, part 1, p. 8A, cols. 5-8.

69. 335 U.S. 188, 189-93 (1948); *see* Frank, "United States Supreme Court: 1947-48."

70. *Ahrens v. Clark*, 335 U.S. 193, 195, 199 (Rutledge, J., dissenting); *Braden v. 30th Jud. Cir. of Ky.*, 410 U.S. 484 (1973).

71. 304 U.S. 64 (1938) (requiring federal courts, in exercising "diversity" jurisdiction over cases between citizens of different states, to apply appropriate state common law rather than creating and imposing a federal common law).

72. *Guaranty Trust Co. v. York*, 326 U.S. 99 (1945); *Cohen v. Beneficial Indus. Loan Corp.*, 337 U.S. 541 (1949); *Woods v. Interstate Realty Co.*, 337 U.S. 535 (1949); *Ragan v. Merchants Transfer & Warehouse Co.*, 337 U.S. 530 (1949).

73. *Guaranty Trust Co.*, 326 U.S. 112 (Rutledge, J., dissenting).

74. *Cohen*, 337 U.S. 557 (Rutledge, J., dissenting).

75. *Id.* at 561 (Rutledge, J., dissenting).

76. *Woods v. Interstate Realty Co.*, 337 U.S. 538 (Rutledge, J., dissenting).

77. *Ragan v. Merchants Transfer & Warehouse Co.*, 337 U.S. 534 (Rutledge, J., dissenting).

78. WR to John J. Parker, Oct. 28, 1948; *Cohen*, 337 U.S. 557, 558-59 (Rutledge, J., dissenting) (citing *Guaranty Trust Co.*, 326 U.S. 99 (1945)).

79. *Anderson v. Yungkau*, 329 U.S. 482, 486 (1947) (Rutledge, J., dissenting).

80. *Angel v. Bullington*, 330 U.S. 183, 201 (1947) (Rutledge, J., dissenting).

81. *Sunal v. Large*, 332 U.S. 174, 187 (1947) (Rutledge, J., dissenting).

82. *Republic Natural Gas Co. v. Oklahoma*, 334 U.S. 62, 74, 87 (1948) (Rutledge, J., dissenting).

83. *United States v. Standard Oil Co. of California*, 332 U.S. 301, 305, 311, 314 & n. 21. (1947).

84. *Id.* at 308, 313, 314, 315.

CHAPTER TWENTY-THREE

1. Rutledge, *A Declaration of Legal Faith*; WR to Victor Brudney, June 11, 1946.

2. WR to Frank E. Horak Jr., March 24, 1947; *Freeman v. Hewitt*, 329 U.S. 249, 259 (1946) (Rutledge, J., concurring).

3. WR to Ralph Fuchs, April 4, 1947.

4. Rutledge, *Legal Faith*, 21, 25, 27, 28-29; U.S. Const. Art I, sec. 8, cl. 3.

5. Rutledge, *Legal Faith*, 27-28, 29, 30.

6. Rutledge, *Legal Faith*, 36-37 (citing *Gibbons v. Ogden*, 22 U.S. (9 Wheat.) 1 (1824)). *But see Willson v. Black Bird Creek Marsh Co.*, 27 U.S. (2 Pet.) 245 (1829) (Marshall, C.J.) (sustaining state statute authorizing erection of dam across navigable creek).

7. Rutledge, *Legal Faith*, 37-38, 41 (citing *Cooley v. Bd. of Wardens*, 53 U.S. (12 How.) 299 (1851)).

8. Rutledge, *Legal Faith*, 41 (citing *United States v. E.C. Knight Co.*, 156 U.S. 1 (1895)).

9. Rutledge, *Legal Faith*, 42 (citing, among others, *N. Sec. Co. v. United States*, 193 U.S. 197 (1904); *Standard Oil Co. v. United States*, 221 U.S. 1 (1911); *United States v. Am. Tobacco Co.*, 221 U.S. 106 (1911)).

10. Rutledge, *Legal Faith*, 42 (citing *NLRB v. Jones & Laughlin Steel Corp.*, 301 U.S. 1 (1937) (manufacturing); *Associated Press v. NLRB*, 301 U.S. 103 (1937) (labor relations); *United States v. Darby Lumber Co.*, 312 U.S. 100 (1941) (child labor); *Wickard v. Filburn*, 317 U.S. 111 (1942) (farm products)).

11. Rutledge, *Legal Faith*, 45, 56-57 & n. 12, 58, 61 n. 21, 63-64 (citing *Gwin, White & Prince, Inc. v. Henneford*, 305 U.S. 434, 442, 446 (1939) (Black, J., dissenting)); *accord* Dowling, "Interstate Commerce and State Power," 548 (quoting *The License Cases*, 46 U.S. (5 How.) 504, 579 (1847)); Abel, "The Commerce Power," 25 *Ind. L.J.* 514 (1950), 35 *Iowa L. Rev.* 642-43 (1950).

12. Rutledge, *Legal Faith*, 67-68.

13. 328 U.S. 408, 410-11, 412, 429 (1946).

14. Dowling, "Interstate Commerce and State Power," 555; Rutledge, *Legal Faith*, 423-27, 429, 434.

15. Rutledge, *Legal Faith*, 423, 438-40 & n. 51; *see* Abel, "The Commerce Power," 25 *Ind. L.J.* 515 (1950), 35 *Iowa L. Rev.* 643-44 (1950); *Prudential Ins. Co. v. Benjamin*, 328 U.S. at 435, 436.

16. *See* Dowling, "Interstate Commerce and State Power," 556-57, 560; *Prudential Insurance Co.*, 328 U.S. at 434.

17. *See Gen. Motors Corp. v. Tracy*, 519 U.S. 278, 292 (1997); *U.S. Dep't of the Treasury v. Fabe*, 508 U.S. 491, 500 (1993); *New York v. United States*, 505 U.S. 144, 171 (1992); *Quill Corp. v. North Dakota*, 504 U.S. 298, 318 (1992).

18. Rutledge, *Legal Faith*, 70, 72.

19. WR to Frank E. Horak Jr., March 24, 1947.

20. 329 U.S. 249, 259 (1946) (Rutledge, J., concurring); *McLeod v. J.E. Dilworth Co.*,

322 U.S. 327, 349 (1944) (Rutledge, J., dissenting); *Gen. Trading Co. v. State Tax Comm'n of Iowa*, 322 U.S. 335, 349 (Rutledge, J., concurring); *Int'l Harvester Co. v. Dep't of Treasury*, 322 U.S. 340, 349 (1944) (Rutledge, J., concurring).

21. *McLeod v. J.E. Dilworth Co.*, 322 U.S. 327, 330 (1944).

22. *General Trading Co. v. State Tax Comm'n of Iowa*, 322 U.S. 335 (1944).

23. *Int'l Harvester Co.*, 322 U.S. 340, 349 (1944).

24. *McLeod v. J.E. Dilworth Co.*, 322 U.S. 332, 333, 334, 335 (Douglas, J., joined by Black, J., and Murphy, J., dissenting).

25. *McLeod v. J.E. Dilworth Co.*, 322 U.S. 349 (Rutledge, J., dissenting); *Gen. Trading Co.*, 322 U.S. 349 (Rutledge, J., concurring); *Int'l Harvester Co.*, 322 U.S. 349 (Rutledge, J., concurring).

26. Felix Frankfurter to WR, May 2, 1944; *Int'l Harvester Co.*, 322 U.S. at 358–60 (Rutledge, J. concurring). If asked, Rutledge would have had to admit he allowed his personal curiosity to influence his decision to write. "[F]or the first time," he told a former student, he was "forced to dig" into "problems of state taxation of interstate business." The newest justice's eagerness showed: "I had to take quite a little time to find the general direction that I wanted to follow and I think I found that, though there are still a good many details that I shall need to iron out." WR to Lowell C. Kindig, June 16, 1944.

27. *W. Livestock v. Bureau of Internal Revenue*, 303 U.S. 250, 255 (1938); *Adams Mfg. Co. v. Storen*, 304 U.S. 307, 311 (1938); *Gwin, White & Prince v. Henneford*, 305 U.S. 434 (1939); *McGoldrick v. Berwin-White Coal Mining Co.*, 309 U.S. 33 (1940). Rutledge accordingly had joined a Stone dissent rejecting the majority's approval of a Minnesota property tax on Northwest Airlines' entire fleet of planes, without apportionment based on the relatively small number of miles the planes flew in Minnesota. *Northwest Airlines v. Minnesota*, 322 U.S. 292, 308 (1944) (Stone, C.J., dissenting).

28. *Int'l Harvester Co. v. Dep't of Treasury*, 322 U.S. at 359, 360–61 (Rutledge, J., concurring).

29. *Id.* at 361.

30. *Freeman v. Hewitt*, 329 U.S. 249, 274 n. 34 (1946) (Rutledge, J., concurring).

31. *See* Dunham, "Gross Receipts Taxes on Interstate Transactions," 216–18, 226.

32. *Freeman v. Hewitt*, 329 U.S. at 277, 278, 279, 282, 283 (Rutledge, J., concurring).

33. Powell, "More Ado about Gross Receipts Taxes," 723, 38, 730–31; Dunham, "Gross Receipts Taxes on Interstate Transactions," 226.

34. Abel, "The Commerce Power," 25 *Ind. L. J.* 527 n. 187 (1950); 35 *Iowa L. Rev.* 658 (1950).

35. Dunham, "Gross Receipts Taxes on Interstate Transactions," 226; Abel, "The Commerce Power," 25 *Ind. L.J.* 530–31 (1950), 35 *Iowa L. Rev.* 660–61 (1950); *see* Note, "Gross Receipts Taxes."

36. *See* Abel, "The Commerce Power," 25 *Ind. L. J.* 530 (1950); 35 *Iowa L. Rev.* 660 (1950); Dunham, "Gross Receipts Taxes on Interstate Transactions," 219, 226; Frank, "The United States Supreme Court: 1946–47," 11, 12 n. 62 ("The concurrence is the clearest and best thought-out statement of the multiple-burden theory."). *But see* Powell, "More Ado about Gross Receipts Taxes," 733–41.

37. *See D'oench, Duhme & Co. v. FDIC*, 315 U.S. 447, 465, 470–72 (1942) (Jackson, J., concurring) ("Federal common law implements the federal Constitution and statutes, and is conditioned by them"); Dunham, "Gross Receipts Taxes on Interstate Transactions," 219 ("credit" idea a "legislative conclusion"); Dowling, "Interstate Commerce and State Power," 559 (federal common law analysis for *Prudential Ins. Co. v. Benjamin*).

38. 327 U.S. 416 (1946).

39. *Int'l Harvester Co. v. Evatt*, 329 U.S. 416, 423 (1947) (Rutledge, J., concurring); *Joseph v. Carter & Weekes Stevedoring Co.*, 330 U.S. 422 (1947).

40. *Interstate Pipeline Co. v. Stone*, 337 U.S. 662 (1949) (plurality opinion of Rutledge, J.).

41. *Id.* at 669, 677, 680 (Reed, J., dissenting).

42. *Id.* at 668 (Burton, J., concurring in judgment).

43. Abel, "The Commerce Power," 25 *Ind. L.J.* 531 (1950), 35 *Iowa L. Rev.* 662 (1950). For an earlier contemporary analysis of Justice Rutledge's opinions under the commerce clause see Levitan, "Mr. Justice Rutledge," part 1.

44. 430 U.S. 274 (1977).

45. *Memphis Natural Gas Co. v. Stone*, 335 U.S. 80, 96 (1948) (Rutledge, J., concurring).

46. *Complete Auto Transit, Inc. v. Brady*, 430 U.S. at 280–82, 287.

47. *See, e.g., Quill Corp. v. North Dakota*, 504 U.S. 298, 311 (1992); *id.* at 321, 326–27 (White, J., dissenting).

48. *Smith v. Allwright*, 321 U.S. 649 (1944).

49. *Morgan v. Virginia*, 328 U.S. 373 (1946).

50. *Screws v. United States*, 325 U.S. 91 (1945).

51. 330 U.S. 552, 564 (1947); *id.* at 564 (1947) (Rutledge, J., dissenting).

52. *Fisher v. Hurst*, 333 U.S. 147, 149 (1948) (Rutledge, J., dissenting); *Sipuel v. Bd. of Regents*, 332 U.S. 631, 633 (1948).

53. *Fisher v. Hurst*, 333 U.S. at 151, 152 (Rutledge, J., dissenting).

54. 333 U.S. 28, 31 (1948).

55. *Id.* at 34 n. 12, 35, 40; *Hall v. DeCuir*, 95 U.S. 485 (1878); *Morgan v. Virginia*, 328 U.S. 373 (1946); *Bob-Lo Excursion Co. v. Michigan*, 333 U.S. 28, 40 (1948) (Douglas, J., concurring).

56. *Bob-Lo Excursion Co. v. Michigan*, No. 374, Oct. Term 1947 (draft opinion), at 3; Felix Frankfurter to WR (Jan. 2, 1948) (second memorandum); Felix Frankfurter to WR (Jan. 2, 1948) (first memorandum); *Fisher v. United States*, 328 U.S. 463, 477 (Frankfurter, J., dissenting); *id.* at 490 (Murphy, J., dissenting); *id.* at 494 (Rutledge, J., dissenting); *compare* draft opinion with *Bob-Lo Excursion Co. v. Michigan*, 333 U.S. 28 (1948).

57. Interviews, Pollak, N. Rutledge, J. P. Stevens, Temko; 334 U.S. 1 (1948); *see Hurd v. Hodge*, 334 U.S. 24 (1948).

58. Interview, N. Rutledge.

59. Interview, J. P. Stevens.

60. Interviews, Pollak, N. Rutledge, J. P. Stevens, Temko; 334 U.S. 1 (1948); *see Hurd v. Hodge*, 334 U.S. 24 (1948).

61. Ralph Fuchs to WR, Jan. 18, 1948.

62. Irving Brant to Justice Stanley Reed, Jan. 26, 1948; Clyde M. Allison to WR, Jan. 16, 1948; Irving Brant to WR, Jan. 26, 1948; John D. Fassett, *New Deal Justice*, 447.

63. WR to Irving Brant, Feb. 10, 1948; *Shelley v. Kramer*, 334 U.S. 1 (1948); *Hurd v. Hodge*, 334 U.S. 24 (1948).

64. *Oyama v. California*, 332 U.S. 633, 640 (1948); *id.* at 647 (Black, J., concurring); *id.* at 650 (Murphy, J., concurring).

65. Invitation to attend the "fifth Presentation" of the "M. Carey Thomas Prize" in "Goodhart Hall, Bryn Mawr College on Thursday, March 11th, 1948 at 8:30 o'clock[,] Address by the Honorable Wiley Blount Rutledge"; Katherine McBeide to WR, March 31,

1948; Wiley Rutledge, "Women's Rights: Barometer of Democracy," Bryn Mawr College, March 11, 1948, 2, 5, 6, 11.

66. Rutledge, "Women's Rights," 2, 5, 6, 11.

67. Rutledge, "Women's Rights," 5, 6, 9–10.

68. Rutledge, "Women's Rights," 10–11.

69. *E.g.*, WR to Agnes Mae Wilson, May 13, 1936; WR to Louise Larrabee, June 10, 1936; Feb. 14, 1938; WR to Margaret I. Cunningham, Sept. 26, 1940; WR to C. E. Cooper, May 5, 1941; WR to E. R. Campbell, Oct. 19, 1944.

70. 335 U.S. 464, 465 (1948); *id.* at 467, 468 (Rutledge, J., dissenting).

71. 328 U.S. 549, 554, 556 (1946); *id.* at 564, 565, 566 (Rutledge, J., concurring in result). Rutledge also worried about the stability of a 4–3 order for an at-large election. Brant, "Mr. Justice Rutledge," 35 *Iowa L. Rev.* 564 (1950); 25 *Ind. L. J.* 442 (1950).

72. *Id.* at 564 (Rutledge, J. concurring in result); *Wesberry v. Sanders*, 376 U.S. 1 (1964) (congressional districts); *Reynolds v. Sims*, 377 U.S. 533 (1964) (state legislative districts).

73. *Colegrove v. Green*, 329 U.S. 828 (1947); *Cook v. Fortson*, 329 U.S. 675 (1947) (Rutledge, J., dissenting).

74. 335 U.S. 281 (1948) (per curiam); *id.* at 287, 288, 289 (Douglas, J., dissenting) (citing *Colegrove v. Green*, 328 U.S. 549 (1946)).

75. *Id.* at 284, 285–86, 287 (opinion of Rutledge, J.).

CHAPTER TWENTY-FOUR

1. Program, "Salmon P. Chase Day, . . . July 1, 1945, . . . Taft Auditorium[,] Centennial Celebration[,] The New Orphan Asylum for Colored Children"; *Cincinnati Enquirer*, July 2, 1945, p. 8, col. 5; Wiley Rutledge, text of speech at Centennial Celebration, New Orphan Asylum for Colored Children, Cincinnati, July 1, 1945, 4, 5, 7.

2. *Evening Star* (Washington), Feb. 26, 1943, p. A-2, col. 3.

3. Rutledge, "Who Has Won the War?," 103.

4. Arthur H. Compton to WR, May 6, 1949; WR to Arthur H. Compton, May 10, 1949; Arthur H. Compton to WR, May 19, 1949; WR to Arthur H. Compton, May 30, 1949; Sam Elson to WR, June 8, 1949; J. Sydney Salkey to WR, June 10, 1949; WR to Ralph Fuchs, July 2, 1949.

5. Rutledge, "Address of Mr. Justice Wiley B. Rutledge," 97; Rutledge, "Two Heroes of the Law"; Rutledge, "Peace—Or Another Treaty?," 256; Rutledge, "This Is Armageddon," 15; Rutledge, "Some Premises of Peace," 626; Rutledge, "Centennial Celebration" (July 1, 1945); Rutledge, "Who Has Won the War?," 103; Rutledge, "Eighty-Six, Forty-Six"; Rutledge, "Looking Forward in Law" (Sept. 26, 1947); Rutledge, "World at Unrest" (July 15, 1948).

6. Rutledge, "Looking Forward in Law," 9.

7. Rutledge, *Premises of Peace*, 625.

8. Rutledge, *Premises of Peace*, 625, 626, 627.

9. Rutledge, *Premises of Peace*, 625, 626, 627.

10. William B. Lloyd Jr. to WR, Aug. 26, 1943; WR to William B. Lloyd Jr., Sept. 6, 1943.

11. American Bar Association, *Canons of Professional Ethics[,] Canons of Judicial Ethics*, 26, 27 n.*, 34, 36 (Sept. 30, 1937) (indicating ABA adoption of canons on July 9, 1924, as amended Sept. 30, 1937).

12. American Bar Association, canon 4 A., *The Code of Judicial Conduct*, 64 (Aug. 16, 1972); Judicial Conference of the United States, canon 4 A., *Code of Judicial Conduct for United States Judges* (Sept. 1973).

13. Rutledge, "Who Has Won the War?," 102.

14. WR to Lowell C. Kindig, Oct. 29, 1945. WR to Frederic Higbee, Aug. 21, 1945; WR to R. G. Gustavson, Oct. 25, 1945; WR to Clarence Streit, Feb. 12, 1946. Rutledge, *A Declaration of Legal Faith*, 5–6.

15. WR to Margaret Cunningham, Sept. 21, 1946.

16. WR to Margaret Cunningham, Sept. 21, 1946; WR to Bryant Smith, Oct. 31, 1946; WR to Victor Brudney, March 9, 1946; McCullough, *Truman*, 489; Goldman, *The Crucial Decade*, 38; Culver and Hyde, *American Dreamer*, 412.

17. Culver and Hyde, *American Dreamer*, 414–15.

18. McCullough, *Truman*, 490–91, 493–506; Culver and Hyde, *American Dreamer*, 412–16.

19. Goldman, *The Crucial Decade*, 39; McCullough, *Truman*, 513–15, 517; Culver and Hyde, *American Dreamer*, 421–22, 426; Byrnes, *All in One Lifetime*, 371–76.

20. WR to [W.] Howard Mann, Sept. 21, 1946; WR to [W.] Howard Mann, Sept. 21, 1946; Rutledge, "Eighty-Six, Forty-Six," 71, 72, 75, 76, 77; *accord* Rutledge, *Legal Faith*, 20–21.

21. Rutledge, "Eighty-Six, Forty-Six," 69, 77 (quoting from Whitman, "Over the Carnage Rose Prophetic a Voice").

22. WR to Benjamin S. Galland, April 16, 1947.

23. WR to Ralph Fuchs, April 4, 1947; WR to Ernest Kirschten, April 5, 1947; WR to Benjamin S. Galland, April 16, 1947.

24. WR to Louise Larrabee, July 5, 1947.

25. WR to Louise Larrabee, July 5, 1947.

26. WR to Ernest Kirschten, May 10, 1946; WR to Louise Larrabee, July 5, 1946; WR to Morrison Shafroth, June 24, 1946; Mason, *Harlan Fiske Stone*, 715.

27. *St. Louis Globe-Democrat*, April 19, 1948, part 1, p. 6A, col. 4; WR to Luther Ely Smith, April 24, 1948.

28. *St. Louis Globe-Democrat*, July 16, 1948, sec. A, p. 4A, col. 1; Rutledge, "World at Unrest," at 4–8.

29. Rutledge, "World at Unrest," 3, 8, 9.

30. J. Sydney Salkey to WR, June 10, 1949; Sam Elson to WR, June 8, 1949.

31. WR to O. L. McCaskill, Feb. 17, 1948; WR to Ralph Fuchs, Feb. 17, 1948; George E. Worthington to WR, April 14, 1948; Drew Pearson, *Washington Post*, March 26, 1948, sec. C, p. 9C, cols. 6–8.

32. Ralph Fuchs to WR and Annabel Rutledge, June 11, 1948; WR to Ralph F. Fuchs, June 15, 1948; WR to William G. Hale, June 29, 1948; WR to Ivan C. Rutledge, July 7, 1948; WR to George E. Heidlebaugh, July 7, 1948.

33. WR to Ivan C. Rutledge, July 7, 1948; WR to George E. Heidlebaugh, July 7, 1948.

34. WR to Henry Wallace, July 22, 1944; WR to George E. Heidlebaugh, July 7, 1948; WR to W. Willard Wirtz, Nov. 9, 1948; interview, N. Rutledge.

35. Interview, N. Rutledge.

36. Lael R. Abbott to WR, Oct. 14, 1948; WR to Lael R. Abbott, Oct. 26, 1948; WR to W. Willard Wirtz, Nov. 9, 1948; WR to Lael R. Abbott, Nov. 9, 1948.

37. WR to Luther Ely Smith, Nov. 8, 1948; WR to Ralph F. Fuchs, Nov. 8, 1948; WR to Henry J. Haskell, Nov. 23, 1948.

38. WR to Carl Wheaton, Nov. 8, 1948; WR to W. Willard Wirtz, Nov. 9, 1948; WR to Henry J. Haskell, Nov. 23, 1948.

39. WR to William H. Bartley, July 5, 1949; *see* O'Brien, "Loyalty Tests and Guilt by

Association," 596; Emerson and Helfeld, "Loyalty among Government Employees," 2, 20–22; *see generally* Wiecek, "The Legal Foundation of Domestic Anticommunism."

40. WR to Ralph F. Fuchs, Nov. 8, 1948; interviews, M. L. (Rutledge) Needels, J. A. (Rutledge) Pollitt ("thinks" father voted for Truman but does not "know" that), C. Rutledge, N. Rutledge.

CHAPTER TWENTY-FIVE

1. WR to W. Howard Mann, March 1, 1949.

2. Howard, *Mr. Justice Murphy*, 458–59; Frank Murphy to WR, Nov. 21, 1949; Frank Murphy to William O. Douglas and WR, Nov. 20, 1948; WR to Frank Murphy, Dec. 2, 1948; interview, Pollak.

3. 337 U.S. 582, 584–85 (1949) (opinion of Jackson, J.); interview, Pollak.

4. *Hepburn & Dundas v. Ellzey*, 6 U.S. (2 Cranch) 445 (1805); *Nat'l Mut. Ins. Co. v. Tidewater Transfer Co., Inc.*, 337 U.S. 582, 584 (1949) (opinion of Jackson, J.).

5. *Nat'l Mut. Ins. Co.*, 337 U.S. at 604, 605, 609 (Rutledge, J., concurring) (quoting *O'Donoghue v. United States*, 289 U.S. 516, 551 (1933)).

6. *Id.* at 605, 608–11 (Rutledge, J., concurring).

7. *Id.* at 618 (Rutledge, J., concurring).

8. *Id.* at 621–22 (Rutledge, J., concurring).

9. *Id.* at 620–22 (Rutledge, J., concurring) (citing *Bank of the United States v. Deveaux*, 9 U.S. (5 Cranch) 61 (1809)).

10. *Id.* at 619, 620, 623 (Rutledge, J., concurring).

11. *Id.* at 625 (Rutledge, J., concurring).

12. *Id.* at 626, 645 (Vinson, C.J., dissenting).

13. *Id.* at 646, 653, 654 (Frankfurter, J., dissenting).

14. *Seminole Tribe of Florida v. Florida*, 517 U.S. 44, 65 (1996) (barring Indian tribe's suit in federal court to enforce federal gaming act since Congress lacked power under Indian Commerce Clause to abrogate state's sovereign immunity under Eleventh Amendment).

15. *Everett v. Truman*, 334 U.S. 824 (1948); *In re Ehlen*, 334 U.S. 836 (1948); *In re Gronwald*, 334 U.S. 857 (1949); *In re Stattmann*, 335 U.S. 805 (1948); *In re Vetter*, 335 U.S. 841 (1948); *In re Eckstein*, 335 U.S. 851 (1948); *In re Heim*, 335 U.S. 856 (1948); *accord Milch v. United States*, 332 U.S. 789 (1947); *Brandt v. United States*, 333 U.S. 836 (1948).

16. *Ex parte Hung Hang*, 108 U.S. 552 (1883).

17. *Wales v. Whitney*, 114 U.S. 564, 570 (1885) ("neither the Supreme Court of the District [of Columbia] nor this court has any appellate jurisdiction over the naval court martial nor over offenses which such a court has power to try").

18. *See Hirota v. MacArthur*, 335 U.S. 876, 877 (1948) (statement of Jackson, J.).

19. 332 U.S. 789 (1947); WR to Fred Vinson, Oct. 20, 1947, box 216, Vinson Papers; WR to the Members of the Conference (undated); *Milch v. United States*, No. 50, Misc., Oct. Term, 1947; WR to Edna [Lingreen] (undated, handwritten); E[dna] L[ingreen] to WR (undated, handwritten), container 159, Rutledge Papers; *Oklahoma v. Woodring*, 308 U.S. 508 (1939); *id.* at 526; *Oklahoma v. Woodring*, 309 U.S. 623 (1940).

20. WR to William O. Douglas, Oct. 20, 1947 (showing Douglas's handwritten response), container 159, Rutledge Papers; WR to the Members of the Conference (undated); *Milch v. United States*, No. 50 Misc., 1947 Term (Oct. 20, 1947) (Rutledge, J., draft dissent); WR handwritten note, container 159, Rutledge Papers.

21. *Hirota v. MacArthur*, 338 U.S. 197 (1949); *id.* at 199 (Douglas, J., concurring in result); *Hirota v. MacArthur*, Nos. 239 Misc., 240 Misc., 1948 Term (Dec. 6, 1948), at 4 (Rutledge, J., draft dissent), container 168, Rutledge Papers.

22. *Hirota v. MacArthur*, Nos. 239 Misc., 240 Misc., 1948 Term (Dec. 6, 1948), at 1–4.

23. *Hirota v. MacArthur*, 335 U.S. at 878, 880 (statement of Jackson, J.). WR conference notes, "Nos. 239, 240, 248 *Misc. Hirota, etc.*, 12/18/48," container 168, Rutledge Papers.

24. *Hirota v. MacArthur*, 338 U.S. at 198; *id.* at 199 n.* (Douglas, J., concurring in result); *id.* at 198 (Murphy, J., "dissents"); *id.* at 198 (Rutledge, J., reserving).

25. *Ahrens v. Clark*, 335 U.S. 188, 192 n. 4 (1948); *Hirota v. MacArthur*, 338 U.S. 199, 202–3 (Douglas, J., concurring in result).

26. *Id.* at 208–9 (Douglas, J., concurring in result).

27. Howard, *Mr. Justice Murphy*, 379.

28. Nos. 239, 240, 248, *Hirota v. MacArthur*, box 74, reel 141, Murphy Papers.

29. Howard, *Mr. Justice Murphy*, 379.

30. Nos. 239, 240, 248 Misc., *Hirota v. MacArthur*, container 168, Rutledge Papers; Nos. 239, 240, 248 Misc., *Hirota v. MacArthur*, box 74, reel 141, Murphy Papers (conference notes). A footnote to the statement in the officially reported opinion that Justice Rutledge had reserved decision added: "Mr. Justice Rutledge died September 10, 1949, without having announced his vote on this case." *Hirota v. MacArthur*, 338 U.S. at 198 n.*.

31. Walter Wyatt to William O. Douglas, April 18, 1950, box 186, Douglas Papers; Walter Wyatt, Diary, June 27, 1949, July 1, 1949, Aug. 9, 1949, box 3, Wyatt Papers.

32. Edna Lingreen to Mrs. F. H. McCrillis, July 7, 1949; WR to Benjamin S. Galland, July 5, 1949; WR to Clay Apple, June 30, 1949; WR to Ralph Fuchs, July 2, 1949; Thos. E. Waggaman to WR, July 19, 1949 (telegram marked "Rec. July 20, '49"); Eleanor Bumgardner to WR, July 19, 1949 (marked "Received July 20 at noon"); Larry Tolan to WR, Aug. 12, 1949; interviews, M. L. (Rutledge) Needels, J. A. (Rutledge) Pollitt; Howard, *Mr. Justice Murphy*, 467.

33. Interviews, M. L. (Rutledge) Needels, J. A. (Rutledge) Pollitt; Thos. E. Waggaman to WR, July 19, 1949 (telegram marked "Rec. July 20, '49"); Victor Brudney to WR, July 24, 1949.

CHAPTER TWENTY-SIX

1. Interview, M. L. (Rutledge) Needels.

2. "Rutledge Dies at 55, His Family at Bedside; Death Follows Jurist's Lapse into Second Coma at Maine Resort," unidentified newspaper, Sept. 11, 1949, Rutledge Papers; interviews, M. L. (Rutledge) Needels, Wald.

3. Pres. Harry S. Truman to Annabel Rutledge, Sept. 10, 1949.

4. The Rev. A. Powell Davies, "Spoken at the Memorial Service for Wiley Blount Rutledge, All Souls' Unitarian Church, Washington, D.C., Wednesday, September 14, 1949, at 3:00 p.m." The remains of Justice Rutledge are held at Cedar Hill Cemetery, Suitland, Maryland, near Washington, D.C., pending a family decision on his final resting place. Annabel Rutledge placed a headstone in his memory at Mountain View Cemetery in Boulder, Colorado. Interview, T. Needels.

5. Interview, Lingreen.

6. AP dispatch, Sept. 21, 1949 (unidentified newspaper clipping), WR Mercantile; interview, D. Pollitt (son-in-law).

7. Interviews, W. H. Mann ("If we stopped for gas, he'd want to talk with the attendant for a half hour."), Shapar, J. P. Stevens (Rutledge "traveled coach . . . because of conversations he'd have with ordinary people"), Wald.

8. *See generally* Renstrom, *The Stone Court*, 78–82.

9. Proceedings in the Supreme Court of the United States in Memory of Mr. Justice Rutledge, Tuesday April 10, 1951, 341 U.S. v (1951); A Symposium to the Memory of Wiley B. Rutledge (1894-1949), 25 *Ind. L.J.* (1950), 35 *Iowa L. Rev.* (1950); John Paul Stevens, "Mr. Justice Rutledge"; Pollak, "Wiley Blount Rutledge."

10. W. Willard Wirtz, Remarks.

Sources

The text is drawn from five general sources: (1) manuscript collections, principally the papers of Wiley Blount Rutledge Jr. at the Library of Congress; (2) approximately 160 interviews of the Rutledge family, the justice's former law students and law clerks, the law clerks of other justices during the period when Rutledge served on the Supreme Court, and other friends and acquaintances of Rutledge; (3) oral histories lodged at the Oral History Research Office, Rare Book and Manuscript Library, Columbia University; (4) the decisions of the U.S. Court of Appeals for the District of Columbia and of the U.S. Supreme Court in which Justice Rutledge participated (including drafts and memoranda prepared in connection with these decisions), as well as other court decisions; and (5) a variety of secondary sources—books, articles, newspapers.

All cited correspondence and other unpublished material will be found in the Rutledge Papers unless otherwise indicated. (Thus, if an item can be found in both the Rutledge Papers and another collection, namely an original and a carbon copy, no indication of second source appears.) Because the Rutledge Papers and other cited collections have been indexed so clearly, moreover, little purpose would be served by adding container or folder references to the notes, except for clarity in a few instances, and thus such references are usually omitted. One particular unpublished source should be explained. May Wood Wigginton, a distant cousin of Justice Rutledge on his mother's side, prepared "Early Family Information" to accompany family trees for both the Wigginton and Lovell families (the justice's forebears on his mother's side), as well as to supplement another document, "Rutledge Family Information," found in the Rutledge Papers. *See* May Wood Wigginton to Neal Rutledge, Dec. 22, 1969. Correspondence in the Rutledge papers adds to this information, as do several letters detailing the Rutledge side of the family. Little information is available about the family of Jane Hall, the justice's paternal grandmother.

As to the author interviews, many who responded sent letters before or after being interviewed, as indicated in the listing. This correspondence supplements the interviews and is cited in the endnotes as part of the "interview" itself. (A few persons acquainted with Justice Rutledge exchanged letters with the author but were not interviewed. Because these correspondents fit well within the groups of individuals sought for interviews, they, too, are listed with the interviewees and are cited as such.) Almost all the former Rutledge students were interviewed by telephone, as were approximately 60 percent of the Supreme Court clerks, although all former Rutledge Supreme Court clerks were interviewed in person. All Rutledge family interviews (except for those with the justice's half-brother, Ivan) took place in person, as did virtually all the interviews with the other Rutledge friends and acquaintances. All interviews were tape-recorded except for occasional follow-up questions and answers recorded in the author's notes. To avoid an overabundance of endnotes, interviewees are often grouped together as authority for a particular paragraph. Some interviewees may have supplied or confirmed most of the information in the paragraph, while others have provided only one item. No one is cited as authority for information in a paragraph that also contains a statement with which that person is known to disagree. Also, if a former student or law clerk is known to disagree with a particular point attributed to other students or clerks, that disagreement is noted. As to perceptions about Justice Rutledge and other members of the Supreme Court during the period 1943–49, interviews with law clerks tend to reflect a consensus among clerks serving justices from all sides of the Court and thus justify a reliance on clerks' perceptions that otherwise might not be indicated.

General background information is taken from Harry J. Carman and Harold C. Syrett, *A History of the American People*, vol. 1 (1956); John C. Culver and John Hyde, *American Dreamer: A Life of Henry Wallace* (2000); Frank Freidel and Alan Brinkley, *America in the Twentieth Century* (5th ed. 1982); Eric F. Goldman, *The Crucial Decade* (1956); Ernest R. May, *Strange Victory: Hitler's Conquest of France* (2000); David McCullough, *Truman* (1992); Mary Beth Norton et al., *A People and a Nation: A History of the United States* (6th ed. 2001); and Arthur Meier Schlesinger, *The Rise of Modern America, 1865–1951* (1951). These are cited in the notes only when quoted directly or the context otherwise requires. Newspaper clippings for which complete identification is unavailable are cited by reference to headline or other indicia and to the manuscript collection, usually the Rutledge Papers, in which they are found. Headlines are omitted for newspaper articles identifiable by reference to section, page, and column.

MANUSCRIPT COLLECTIONS

Ann Arbor, Michigan
Bentley Historical Library, University of Michigan
  Henry Moore Bates Papers
  Eugene Gressman Diary
  Frank Murphy Papers

Bloomington, Indiana
Lilly Library, Indiana University
  Ralph Fuchs Papers

Boulder, Colorado
University of Colorado Archives
  Wiley Blount Rutledge Jr. Student Records

Charlottesville, Virginia
Alderman Library, University of Virginia
  Walter Wyatt Papers

Columbia, Missouri
Ellis Library, Western Historical Manuscript Collection, University of Missouri
  Herbert S. Hadley Papers
  Kimbrough Stone Papers

Evanston, Illinois
Northwestern University Library, University Archives
  Herbert S. Hadley Student Records

Hyde Park, New York
Franklin D. Roosevelt Library
    Francis Biddle Attorney General File
    Francis Biddle Diary
    Franklin D. Roosevelt Official File
    Franklin D. Roosevelt Personal File

Iowa City, Iowa
Law Library, College of Law, State University of Iowa
    Faculty Minutes, 1935–39
    Reports of the Dean, 1935–39
University Libraries, Special Collections, State University of Iowa
    Eugene A. Gilmore Papers
    Wiley Blount Rutledge Jr. File

Lexington, Kentucky
Margaret I. King Library, Division of Special Collections, University of Kentucky
    Stanley Reed Papers
    Fred M. Vinson Papers

Madison, Wisconsin
Office of the Registrar/Certification, Transcript Department, University of Wisconsin
    Wiley Blount Rutledge Jr. Student Record

Maryville, Tennessee
Lamar Memorial Library, Information Resources and Services, Maryville College
    Wiley Blount Rutledge Jr. Student Record

New Haven, Connecticut
Yale University Library, Manuscripts and Archives
    Charles Nagel Papers

Norfolk, Virginia
General Douglas MacArthur Memorial
    Brigadier General Courtney Whitney, Memorandum, "The Case of General Yama-shita"

St. Louis, Missouri
John M. Olin Library, Washington University
    Chancellor, Archives
    Robert E. Rosenwald Papers
Mercantile Library
    Wiley Blount Rutledge Jr. File
Missouri Historical Society
    Public Question Club Records
    Wiley Blount Rutledge Jr. File
    Luther Ely Smith File
School of Law, Washington University
    Faculty Minutes, 1924–35

Washington, D.C.
Library of Congress, Manuscript Division

Hugo Black Papers
William E. Borah Papers
Irving Newton Brant Papers
Harold H. Burton Papers
William O. Douglas Papers
Felix Frankfurter Papers
Robert H. Jackson Papers
Wiley Blount Rutledge Jr. Papers
Harold M. Stephens Papers
Harlan Fiske Stone Papers

National Archives

Appointment Files of Supreme Court Justices 1930–1971, RG 60, Case Files for Wiley Rutledge for positions filled by:

William O. Douglas
Felix Frankfurter
Wiley Blount Rutledge

Wiley Rutledge Nomination Papers, NSCA Branch, RG 46, SEN 78B.A3, "Royal-Smith"

Dr. Theodore S. Needels and Mary Lou (Rutledge) Needels

Early letters between Wiley Rutledge, Annabel Person Rutledge, and other family members

Washington College of Law, American University, Archives

AUTHOR INTERVIEWS

Washington University School of Law (Showing Graduating Class)

Altman, C. William (1936), April 9, 2000 (letter)
Arbetman, Evelyn H. (1935), April 25, 2000
Beisman, Louise (1932), July 11, 1996
Bennett, Marian T. (1938), Dec. 5, 1995
Blair, Newell (1933), Oct. 6, 1995; April 24, 1996
Bridell, Albert M. (1933), June 14, 2000 (letter)
Broderick, Robert L. (1935), May 8, 2000
Brown, Marcus A. (1937), April 2, 2000 (letter)
Campbell, Galen M. (1932), April 4, 2000 (letter); April 14, 2000 (letter); April 24, 2000 (letter)
Chused, Joseph (1930), March 16, 2000
Crawley, J. Charles (1935), May 5, 2000
Freedman, Walter (1937), Oct. 3, 1995
Freeze, John S. (1937), April 10, 2000 (letter)
Greensfelder, Edward B. (1928), Nov. 22, 1995; May 2, 1996
Gross, Jerome A. (1931), Nov. 21, 1995; April 30, 1996; July 11, 1996
Hanke, Harold C. (1931), Nov. 21, 1995; April 30, 1996
Hocker, Lon (1934), Oct. 2, 1995; April 24, 1996
Kenton, Agnes Eilers (1936), April 25, 2000; April 19, 2000 (letter)
Klene, Benjamin C. (1927), April 27, 2000 (letter)
Lewin, Tobias (1932), April 10, 2000
Margolin, Abraham E. (1929), Nov. 25, 1995; April 30, 1996

Muldoon, Charles P. (1928), Oct. 2, 1995; May 24, 1996
Newman, Eric P. (1935), June 13, 2000
Peper, Christian B. (1935), Nov. 22, 1995; May 2, 1996; Sept. 18, 2000
Shampaine, H. Robert (1932), April 4, 2000
Strauss, David W. (1927), May 2, 1996
Vogt, William G. (1933), Oct. 13, 1995; April 24, 1996
Waltuch, Hy A. (1934), April 6, 2000 (letter)
Wolf, James (1935), March 31, 2000
Wussler, Edgar (1935), April 4, 2000 (quoted by daughter Rita Thornhill)

State University of Iowa College of Law (Showing Graduating Class)

Adler, Morton S. (1936), April 16, 1996; May 1, 1996 (letter)
Ahlers, Paul F. (1936), April 1, 1996
Barker, Don W. (1941), April 9, 1996; April 1, 28, 1996 (letters); July 28, 1999 (letter)
Beving, Don (1940), March 23, 1996
Birch, Thomas H. (1940), April 16, 1996; April 8, 1996 (letter); May 8, 1996 (letter)
Brady, James M. (1939), March 15, 1996; March 7, 1996 (letter)
Brown, Paul E. (1941), April 17, 1996; April 6, 1996 (letter)
Browne, John E. (1936), March 28, 1996 (letter)
Bruner, Robert S. (1936), March 29, 1996
Buckingham, Ben C. (1938), May 22, 1996
Cameron, James L. (1939), Nov. 9, 1995
Cunningham, Abishi C. (1941), April 15, 1996
Dalbey, Robert T. (1938), June 5, 1996
Dodd, Fred D. (1939), March 23, 1996; March 14, 1996 (letter)
Edson, Wendell T. (1936), April 8, 1996; March 28, 1996 (letter)
Elderkin, David M. (1937), March 12, 1996; May 24, 1996 (letter); June 17, 1996 (letter);
    December 16, 1996 (letter); June 3, 1997 (letter)
Fitzgibbons, Leo E. (1939), May 23, 1996; May 8, 1996 (letter)
Galloway, Donald F. (1941), April 15, 1996
Gibbs, Richard S. (1940), June 18, 1996; June 5, 1996 (letter)
Gleysteen, Carl (1937), March 14, 1996
Goodenow, John E. (1939), April 25, 1996; April 16, 1996 (letter)
Grant, Herman (1936), June 18, 1996
Gray, Lawrence H. (1938), March 15, 1996; May 2, 1996 (letter)
Grosenbaugh, Downey (1939), March 15, 1996
Heartney, Matthew J., Jr. (1940), April 22, 1996
Hellwege, Paul E. (1938), April 25, 1996; April 18, 1996 (letter)
Hirsch, Henry L. (1939); Sept. 8, 1999
Hunt, Robert T. (1940), April 3, 1996
Jack, Darold J. (1941), April 8, 1996; April 1, 1996 (letter)
Jebens, Arthur B. (1939), April 9, 1996; March 27, 1996 (letter); May 23, 1996 (letter)
Johnson, Corwin W. (1941), April 17, 1996; April 8, 1996 (letter)
Joiner, Charles W. (1939), Nov. 21, 1995
Kean, Joseph A. (1941), Sept. 14, 1999
Kemler, R. W. (1939), March 23, 1996; March 15, 1996 (letter)
Lewis, Irving (1939), April 25, 1996; April 22, 1996 (letter)

Mayer, Alan H. (1940), April 23, 1996
McCarthy, James T. (1940), April 15, 1996
McCoy, Hugh B. (1941), April 9, 1996
McDermott, Edward A. (1942), April 17, 1996
McPharlin, Eldon V. (1937), March 15, 1996
Metcalf, Glenn C. (1940), July 12, 1996; June 11, 1996 (letter)
Meyer, Isadore (1940), April 5, 1996; March 27, 1996 (letter)
Mitchell, Lyman (1936), April 23, 1996
Moeller, Armand D. (1938), April 9, 1996
Morrison, William F. (1937), April 8, 1996; March 29, 1996 (letter)
Mosier, Craig H. (1937), March 15, 1996; March 7, 1996 (letter)
Moyer, Clinton D. (1939), April 4, 1996 (letter)
Noel, Robert O. (1940), July 22, 1996
Pasley, Robert G. (1939), April 8, 1996; April 1, 1996 (letter)
Pickett, Charles J. (1937), April 4, 1996; March 26, 1996 (letter)
Reed, Richard C. (1941), May, 20, 1996; April 8, 1996 (letter)
Reitz, Walter L., Jr. (1941), July 18, 1996; June 17, 1996 (letter)
Remley, Howard M. (1938), March 18, 1996; March 4, 1996 (letter)
Rosenberg, Herbert (1939), March 14, 1996; March 4, 1996 (letter)
Ryan, Helen B. (1939), May 22, 1996; March 9, April 12, 1996 (letters)
Seaton, J. Everett (1941), April 9, 1996; April 3, 1996 (letter)
Schindler, Ralph J. (1938), March 25, 1996
Schweibert, Lloyd A. (1937), June 6, 1996; May 29, 1996 (letter)
Schwilck, Louise (1939), March 5, 1996 (letter)
Shepherd, Virgil E. (1936), July 19, 1996
Smith, D. Berkeley (1937), May 13, 1996
Stevens, Richard L. (1939), April 8, 1996
Stohr, Robert K. (1937), April 15, 1996
Thomas, Reynolds B. (1939), April 15, 1996
Vogel, Raymond H. (1940), April 2, 1996; March 26, 1996 (letter)

U.S. Court of Appeals Clerks (for Rutledge)

Gibbs, Richard S., June 18, 1996; June 5, 1996 (letter)
Mann, W. Howard, Oct. 11, 1995; March 11, 1996

U.S. Supreme Court Clerks (Showing Justice and Term(s) of Court)

Allan, F. Aley (Reed, 1946), Aug. 13, 1996
Allen, Francis A. (Vinson, 1946), April 8, 1996
Beyer, Eugene A., Jr. (Douglas, 1943); March 13, 2001
Birdzell, Luther E., Jr. (Reed, 1943), April 30, 1996
Boskey, Bennett (Stone, 1941-42), Nov. 20, 1995
Brudney, Victor (Rutledge, 1942-43), Oct. 3, 1995; March 7, 2001; March 13, 2001; April 2,
    2001; May 21, 2001; July 18, 2001; March 14, 2001 (letter)
Coleman, William T., Jr. (Frankfurter, 1948), Nov. 16, 1995
Ebb, Lawrence F. (Vinson, 1947), May 8, 1996
Elman, Philip (Frankfurter, 1941-41), April 10, 1996

Feller, David E. (Vinson, 1948), April 30, 1996
Frank, John P. (Black, 1942), Dec. 12, 1995; April 2, 2001 (letter); Sept. 25, 2001 (letter)
Gartner, Murray (Jackson, 1945–46), Feb. 28, 1996
Gressman, Eugene (Murphy, 1943–47), Oct. 10, 1995; March 13, 2001; April 9, 2001; July 16, 2001 (letter)
Groner, Isaac (Vinson, 1948–49), Nov. 8, 1995
Haber, David (Black, 1945), June 4, 1996
Helman, Irving (Frankfurter, 1947), July 9, 1996
Henkin, Louis (Frankfurter, 1946), April 2, 1996
Hobbs, Truman (Black, 1948), March 25, 1996
Joslin, William (Black, 1947), April 11, 1996
Kabot, Byron (Reed, 1944), May 7, 1996
Kurland, Philip (Frankfurter, 1945), Jan. 29, 1996
Lake, James (Burton, 1947–48), March 14, 1996
Lomen, Lucile (Douglas, 1944), March 28, 1996
Luce, Charles F. (Black, 1943), April 3, 1996; March 28, 2001 (letter)
Mann, W. Howard (Burton, 1945), Oct. 11, 1995; March 11, 1996
Mansfield, Harry K. (Frankfurter, 1944), March 12, 1996
Marsh, James (Jackson, 1947–48), Jan. 5, 1996; Aug. 2, 2003
Morrison, James L. (Stone, 1942–43), June 21, 1996
Neal, Phil C. (Jackson, 1943–44), Jan. 29, 1996
Nickerson, Eugene (Stone, 1944–45), Feb. 27, 1996
Oberdorfer, Louis F. (Black, 1946), Oct. 27, 1995
Pickering, John H. (Murphy, 1941–42), Oct. 31, 1995
Pollak, Louis H. (Rutledge 1948), Dec. 21, 1995
Rosenthal, Albert J. (Frankfurter, 1947), March 7, 1996
Seder, Arthur R., Jr. (Vinson, 1948), March 15, 1996
Shniderman, Harry L. (Rutledge, 1944), Nov. 29, 1995
Spitzer, John (Reed, 1947), May 1, 1996
Stevens, John Paul (Rutledge, 1947), Sept. 28, 1995; Oct. 10, 1996
Temko, Stanley L. (Rutledge, 1947), Sept. 27, 1995; July 11, 2001
Tone, Philip W. (Rutledge, 1948), Oct. 29, 1996
Torre, Gary J. (Douglas, 1948), June 21, 1996
von Mehren, Robert (Reed, 1947), March 14, 1996
Weiss, Emanuel G. (Reed, 1945), April 1, 1996
Weston, Harris K. (Burton, 1946), April 9, 1996
White, Byron R. (Vinson, 1946), Nov. 7, 1995
Wollenberg, J. Roger (Douglas, 1946), Nov. 16, 1995

Rutledge Family

Needels, Mary Lou (Rutledge), May 19, 1996; May 30, 1996
Needels, Dr. Theodore S. (son-in-law), March 17, 1996; May 19, 1996
Pollitt, Daniel (son-in-law), Sept. 22, 1995; July 9, 1996
Pollitt, Jean Ann (Rutledge), July 9, 1996
Rutledge, Catherine Le Fevre (daughter-in-law), May 30, 2000
Rutledge, Ivan C., October 25, 1995; June 5, 1996; Sept. 29, 1995 (letter); Oct. 29, 1995

(letter); Nov. 11, 1995 (letter); Dec. 3, 1995 (letter); Jan. 7, 1996 (letter); March 1, 1996
(letter)
Rutledge, Neal, Sept. 22, 1995; Feb. 5, 1997; May 30, 2000; Dec. 20, 2001

Rutledge Friends and Acquaintances

Black, Hugo, Jr., Sept. 10, 1996
Byse, Clark, Oct. 13, 1995
Folsom, Fred, Sept. 19, 1995
Lingreen, Edna, Oct. 19, 1995; Sept. 13, 1996; March 10, 1997; April 9, 2001; May 19, 2003
Mann, J. Keith, Feb. 23, 1997; Sept. 20, 1995 (letter)
Shapar, Howard, June 25, 1997
Steele, Walter A. ("Bill"), Dec. 1, 1995
Wagshal, Benjamin, Oct. 9, 1996
Wald, Robert L., March 27, 1997
Wechsler, Herbert, Oct. 3, 1995; March 7, 1997; July 30, 1997
Wirtz, W. Willard, Sept. 12, 1995; June 12, 1996; July 16, 1999 (letter)

Others

Gardner, Warner W., July 3, 1996
Ginsburg, C. David, May 27, 1997
Martin, Malcolm, Sept. 18, 2000
Morrow, Ralph E., Oct. 2, 1995
Rhyne, Charles S., Oct. 20, 1995

ORAL HISTORIES

The following entries are found in the Oral History Collection of Columbia University at
the Rare Book and Manuscript Library, Butler Library, New York, New York, and are
quoted or cited with permission.

Reminiscences of Charles Culp Burlingham, April 1961
Reminiscences of Charles Fahy, December 1958
Reminiscences of Learned Hand, April 1958
Reminiscences of Robert Houghwout Jackson, June 1955
Reminiscences of Stanley Reed, May 1960
Reminiscences of Henry Agard Wallace, June 1951

JUDICIAL OPINIONS OF JUSTICE WILEY RUTLEDGE
U.S. Supreme Court, Cited in Text or Notes

Aguilar v. Standard Oil Co. of New Jersey, 318 U.S. 724 (1943)
Ahrens v. Clark, 335 U.S. 188, 193 (1948) (Rutledge, J., dissenting)
AFL v. Am. Sash & Door Co., 335 U.S. 538, 557 (1949) (Rutledge, J., concurring)
Am. Tobacco Co. v. United States, 328 U.S. 781, 815 (1946) (Rutledge, J., concurring)
Anderson v. Yungkau, 329 U.S. 482, 486 (1947) (Rutledge, J., dissenting)
Angel v. Bullington, 330 U.S. 183, 201 (1947) (Rutledge, J., dissenting)

Blumenthal v. United States, 332 U.S. 539 (1947)

Bd. of County Comm'rs v. Seber, 318 U.S. 705, 719 (1943) (Rutledge, J., concurring in result)

Bob-Lo Excursion Co. v. Michigan, 333 U.S. 28 (1948)

Bowles v. Willingham, 321 U.S. 503, 521 (1944) (Rutledge, J., concurring)

Brinegar v. United States, 338 U.S. 160 (1949)

Canizio v. New York, 327 U.S. 82, 91 (1946) (Rutledge, J., dissenting)

Cohen v. Beneficial Indus. Loan Corp., 337 U.S. 541, 557 (1949) (Rutledge, J., dissenting)

Colegrove v. Green, 328 U.S. 549, 564 (1946) (Rutledge, J., concurring in result)

Comm'r v. Tower, 327 U.S. 289, 292 (1946) (Rutledge, J., concurring)

Cook v. Fortson, 329 U.S. 675, 675 (1947) (Rutledge, J., dissenting)

Davis v. United States, 328 U.S. 582, 623 (1946) (Rutledge, J., dissenting)

Direct Sales Co. v. United States, 319 U.S. 703 (1943)

E.-Cent. Motor Carriers Ass'n v. United States, 321 U.S. 194 (1944)

Estep v. United States, 327 U S 114, 132 (1946) (Rutledge, J., concurring)

Everson v. Bd. of Educ., 330 U.S. 1, 28 (1947) (Rutledge, J., dissenting)

Falbo v. United States, 320 U.S. 549, 555 (1944), *aff'g United States v. Falbo* , 135 F.2d 464 (3d Cir. 1943) (Rutledge, J., concurring)

Fisher v. Hurst, 333 U.S. 147, 149 (1948) (Rutledge, J., dissenting)

Fisher v. Pace, 336 U.S. 155, 168 (1949) (Rutledge, J., dissenting)

Fisher v. United States, 328 U.S. 463, 494 (1946) (Rutledge, J., dissenting)

Foster v. Illinois, 332 U.S. 134, 141 (1947) (Rutledge, J., dissenting)

Frazier v. United States, 335 U.S. 497 (1948) (Rutledge, J., dissenting)

Freeman v. Hewitt, 329 U.S. 249, 259 (1946) (Rutledge, J., concurring)

Galloway v. United States, 319 U.S. 372 (1943)

Gayes v. New York, 332 U.S. 145, 149 (1947) (Rutledge, J., dissenting)

Gen. Trading Co. v. State Tax Comm'n of Iowa, 322 U.S. 335, 349 (1944) (Rutledge, J., concurring)

Gibson v. United States, 329 U.S. 338 (1946)

Goesaert v. Cleary, 335 U.S. 464, 467 (1948) (Rutledge, J., dissenting)

Gryger v. Burke, 334 U.S. 728, 732 (1948) (Rutledge, J., dissenting)

Guaranty Trust Co. v. York, 326 U.S. 99, 112 (1945) (Rutledge, J., dissenting)

Heiser v. Woodruff, 327 U.S. 726, 740 (1946) (Rutledge, J., concurring)

Hirabayashi v. United States, 320 U.S. 81, 114 (1943) (Rutledge, J., concurring)

Holmberg v. Armbrecht, 327 U.S. 392, 398 (1946) (Rutledge, J., concurring)

Homma v. Patterson, 327 U.S. 759, 761 (1946) (Rutledge, J., dissenting)

In re Yamashita, 327 U.S. 1, 41 (1946) (Rutledge, J., dissenting)

Int'l Harvester Co. v. Dep't of Treasury, 322 U.S. 340, 349 (1944) (Rutledge, J., concurring)

Int'l Harvester Co. v. Evatt, 329 U.S. 416, 423 (1947) (Rutledge, J., concurring)

Interstate Pipeline Co. v. Stone, 337 U.S. 662 (1949) (plurality opinion of Rutledge, J.)

Klapprott v. United States, 335 U.S. 601, 616 (1949) (Rutledge, J., concurring in result)

Knauer v. United States, 328 U.S. 654, 675 (1946) (Rutledge, J., dissenting)

Kotch v. Bd. of River Port Pilot Comm'rs, 330 U.S. 552, 564 (1947) (Rutledge, J., dissenting)

Kotteakos v. United States, 328 U.S. 750 (1946)

Kovacs v. Cooper, 336 U.S. 77, 104 (1949) (Rutledge, J., dissenting)

Kraus & Bros., Inc. v. United States, 327 U.S. 614, 628 (1946) (Rutledge, J., concurring)

Lyons v. Oklahoma, 322 U.S. 596, 605 (1944) (Rutledge, J., "dissents")

MacDougall v. Green, 335 U.S. 281, 284 (1948) (opinion of Rutledge, J., concurring in result)

Malinski v. New York, 324 U.S. 401, 420 (1945) (Rutledge, J., dissenting)

Marconi Wireless Tel. Co. of Am. v. United States, 320 U.S. 1, 64 (1943) (Rutledge J., dissenting in part)

Marino v. Ragen, 332 U.S. 561, 563 (1947) (Rutledge, J., dissenting)

May Dep't Stores Co. v. NLRB, 326 U.S. 376, 393 (1945) (Rutledge, J., concurring in part)

McDonald v. United States, 335 U.S. 451, 456 (1948) (statement by Rutledge, J.)

McLean Trucking Co. v. United States, 321 U.S. 67 (1944)

McLeod v. J.E. Dilworth Co., 322 U.S. 327, 349 (1944) (Rutledge, J., dissenting)

Medo Photo Supply Corp. v. NLRB, 321 U.S. 678, 688 (1944) (Rutledge, J., dissenting)

Memphis Natural Gas Co. v. Stone, 335 U.S. 80, 96 (1948) (Rutledge, J., concurring)

Michelson v. United States, 335 U.S. 469, 488 (1948) (Rutledge, J., dissenting)

Musser v. Utah, 333 U.S. 95, 98 (1948) (Rutledge, J., dissenting)

Nat'l Mut. Ins. Co. v. Tidewater Transfer Co., 337 U.S. 582, 604 (1949) (Rutledge, J., concurring)

New York v. United States, 326 U.S. 572, 584 (1946) (Rutledge, J., concurring)

Nippert v. City of Richmond, 327 U.S. 416 (1946)

Owens v. Union Pac. R.R. Co., 319 U.S. 715 (1943)

Parker v. Illinois, 333 U.S. 571, 577 (1948) (Rutledge, J., dissenting)

Pennekamp v. Florida, 328 U.S. 331, 370 (1946) (Rutledge, J., concurring)

Pinkerton v. United States, 328 U.S. 640, 648 (1946) (Rutledge, J., dissenting in part)

Prince v. Massachusetts, 321 U.S. 158 (1944)

Prudential Ins. Co. v. Benjamin, 328 U.S. 408 (1946)

Ragan v. Merchants Transfer & Warehouse Co., 337 U.S. 530, 534 (1949) (Rutledge, J., dissenting)

Republic Natural Gas Co. v. Oklahoma, 334 U.S. 62, 74, 87 (1948) (Rutledge, J., dissenting)

Robertson v. California, 328 U.S. 440 (1946)

Robinson v. United States, 324 U.S. 282, 286 (1945) (Rutledge, J., dissenting)

Schneiderman v. United States, 320 U.S. 118, 165 (1943) (Rutledge, J., concurring)

Screws v. United States, 325 U.S. 91, 113 (1945) (Rutledge, J., concurring in result)

Sunal v. Large, 332 U.S. 174, 187 (1947) (Rutledge, J., dissenting)

Thomas v. Collins, 323 U.S. 516 (1945)

United States v. Anderson, 328 U.S. 699 (1946)

United States v. CIO, 335 U.S. 106, 129 (1948) (Rutledge, J., concurring in result)

United States v. Evans, 333 U.S. 483 (1948)

United States v. Petty Motor Co., 327 U.S. 372, 381 (1946) (Rutledge, J., concurring)

United States v. Sheridan, 329 U.S. 379 (1946)

United States v. Standard Oil Co. of California, 332 U.S. 301 (1947)

United States v. United Mine Workers, 330 U.S. 258, 342 (1947) (Rutledge, J., dissenting)

Wolf v. Colorado, 338 U.S. 25, 47 (1949) (Rutledge, J., dissenting)

Woods v. Interstate Realty Co., 337 U.S. 535, 538 (1949) (Rutledge, J., dissenting)

Yakus v. United States, 321 U.S. 414, 460 (1944) (Rutledge, J., dissenting)

U.S. Court of Appeals, Cited in Text or Notes

Abbott v. Shepherd, 135 F.2d 769 (D.C. Cir. 1942)

Acker v. Herfurth, 110 F.2d 241 (App. D.C. 1939)

Amer. Nat'l Bank & Trust Co. v. United States, 134 F.2d 674 (D.C. Cir. 1943)

Amer. Secur. & Trust Co. v. Frost, 117 F.2d 283, 287 (App. D.C. 1940) (Rutledge, J., dissenting)

Balinovic v. Evening Star Newspaper Co., 113 F.2d 505, 507 (App. D.C. 1940) (Rutledge, J., dissenting)

Boucher Inventions, Ltd. v. Sola Elec. Co., 131 F.2d 225 (D.C. Cir. 1942)

Boykin v. Huff, 121 F.2d 865 (App. D.C. 1941)

Brown v. Brown, 134 F.2d 505 (D.C. Cir. 1942)

Burke v. Canfield, 121 F.2d 877 (App. D.C. 1941)

Busey v. District of Columbia, 129 F.2d 24, 28 (D.C. Cir. 1942) (Rutledge, J., dissenting)

Christie v. Callahan, 124 F.2d 825 (App. D.C. 1941)

Cobb v. Howard Univ., 106 F.2d 860 (App. D.C. 1939)

Fairclaw v. Forrest, 130 F.2d 829 (D.C. Cir. 1942)

Fox v. Johnson & Wimsatt, Inc., 127 F.2d 729 (D.C. Cir. 1942)

Frene v. Louisville Cement Co., 134 F.2d 511 (D.C. Cir. 1943)

Frick-Gallagher Mfg. Co. v. RoTray Corp., 122 F.2d 81 (App. D.C. 1941)

Georgetown Coll. v. Hughes, 139 F.2d 810 (D.C. Cir. 1942) (en banc)

Geracy, Inc. v. Hoover, 133 F.2d 25, 29 (D.C. Cir. 1942) (Rutledge, J., dissenting)

Hartford Accident Co. v. Cardillo, 112 F.2d 11 (App. D.C. 1940)

Hemphill Co. v. Coe, 121 F.2d 897 (App. D.C. 1941)

Hohenthal v. Smith, 114 F.2d 494 (App. D.C. 1940)

Howard v. Overholzer, 130 F.2d 429 (D.C. Cir. 1942)

Hydraulic Press Corp. v. Coe, 134 F.2d 49 (1943)

Identification Devices v. United States, 121 F.2d 895 (App. D.C. 1941)

In re Rosier, 133 F.2d 316, 333 (D.C. Cir. 1942) (Rutledge, J., dissenting)

Int'l Ass'n of Machinists, Tool and Die Makers v. NLRB, 110 F.2d 29 (App. D.C. 1939), aff'd, 311 U.S. 72 (1940)

Joerns v. Irvin, 114 F.2d 458, 459 (App. D.C. 1940) (Rutledge, J., dissenting)

Jordan v. Group Health Ass'n, 107 F.2d 239 (App. D.C. 1939)

Jordon v. Bondy, 114 F.2d 599 (App. D.C. 1940)

Lebanon Steel Foundry v. NLRB, 130 F.2d 404 (D.C. Cir. 1942)

Leighton v. Coe, 130 F.2d 841, 842 (D.C. Cir. 1942) (Rutledge, J., concurring)

Levine v. Coe, 119 F.2d 185 (App. D.C. 1941)

Loughlin v. Berens, 128 F.2d 23, 26 (D.C. Cir. 1942) (Rutledge, J., dissenting)

Mancari v. Frank P. Smith, Inc., 114 F.2d 834, 837 (App. D.C. 1940) (Rutledge, J., dissenting)

McKenna v. Austin, 134 F.2d 659 (D.C. Cir. 1943)

Melvin v. Pence, 130 F.2d 423 (D.C. Cir. 1942)

Minnesota Mining & Mfg. Co. v. Coe, 113 F.2d 512 (App. D.C. 1940)

Morrison v. Coe, 127 F.2d 737 (D.C. Cir. 1942)

Nat'l Benefit Life Ins. Co. v. Shaw-Walker Co., 111 F.2d 497 (App. D.C. 1940)

NBC v. FCC, 132 F.2d 545 (D.C. Cir. 1942) (en banc), aff'd, 319 U.S. 239 (1943)

Morrison v. Coe, 127 F.2d 737 (D.C. Cir. 1942)

Pedersen v. Pedersen, 107 F.2d 227 (App. D.C. 1939)

Press Co. v. NLRB, 118 F.2d 937, 947 (App. D.C. 1940) (Rutledge, J., dissenting in part)

Schlaefer v. Schlaefer, 112 F.2d 177 (App. D.C. 1940)

Seyfarth v. Coe, 129 F.2d 58 (D.C. Cir. 1942)

Sloane v. Coe, 122 F.2d 37 (App. D.C. 1941)

Sweeney v. District of Columbia, 113 F.2d 25 (App. D.C. 1940)

Switchmen's Union of N. Am. v. Nat'l Med. Bd., 135 F.2d 785, 796 (D.C. Cir. 1943) (Rutledge, J., dissenting)

W.C. & A.N. Miller Dev. Co. v. Emig Properties Corp., 134 F.2d 36 (D.C. Cir. 1943)

Warehousemen's Union v. NLRB, 121 F.2d 84 (App. D.C. 1941)

Washington Terminal Co. v. Boswell, 124 F.2d 235 (App. D.C. 1941), *aff'd*, 319 U.S. 732 (1943) (per curiam) (equally divided court; Rutledge, J., not participating)

Wood v. United States, 128 F.2d 265 (D.C. Cir. 1942)

Supreme Court and Court of Appeals opinions of Justice Rutledge in addition to those discussed and cited herein are compiled, respectively, in appendices I and II of two symposium issues dedicated "to the memory of Wiley B. Rutledge (1894–1949)": 25 *Ind. L. J.* 559, 562 (1950), and 35 *Iowa L. Rev.* 693, 696 (1950).

OTHER JUDICIAL DECISIONS, CITED IN TEXT OR NOTES

Abrams v. United States, 250 U.S. 616 (1919)

Adams Mfg. Co. v. Storen, 304 U.S. 307 (1938)

Adamson v. California, 332 U.S. 46 (1947)

Adarand Constructors, Inc. v. Pena, 515 U.S. 200 (1995)

Agostini v. Felton, 521 U.S. 203 (1997)

Allgeyer v. Louisiana, 165 U.S. 578 (1897)

Al Odah v. United States, 321 F.3d 1134 (D.C. Cir. 2003), *cert. granted*, 72 U.S.L.W. 3223 (U.S. Nov. 10, 2003) (No. 03-343)

Ashton v. Cameron County Water Improvement Dist. No. 1, 298 U.S. 513 (1936)

Associated Press v. NLRB, 301 U.S. 103 (1937)

Bailey v. Drexel Furniture Co., 259 U.S. 20 (1922)

Bakery Sales Drivers Local Union No. 33 v. Wagshal, 333 U.S. 437 (1948)

Bank of Augusta v. Earle, 38 U.S. (13 Pet.) 519 (1839)

Bank of the United States v. Deveaux, 9 U.S. (5 Cranch) 61 (1809)

Barringer & Co. v. United States, 319 U.S. 1 (1943)

Barron v. Baltimore, 32 U.S. (7 Pet.) 243 (1833)

Baumgartner v. United States, 322 U.S. 665 (1944)

Benton v. Maryland, 395 U.S. 784 (1969)

Betts v. Brady, 316 U.S. 455 (1942)

Braden v. 30th Jud. Cir. of Ky., 410 U.S. 484 (1973)

Bradfield v. Roberts, 175 U.S. 291 (1899)

Brandt v. United States, 333 U.S. 836 (1948)

Bridges v. California, 314 U.S. 252 (1941)

Bridges v. Wixon, 326 U.S. 135 (1945)

Bute v. Illinois, 333 U.S. 640 (1948)

Cantwell v. Connecticut, 310 U.S. 296 (1940)

Carpenters & Joiners Union v. Ritter's Café, 315 U.S. 722 (1942)

Carroll v. United States, 267 U.S. 132 (1925)

Carter v. Carter Coal Co., 298 U.S. 238 (1936)

Cent. R.R. Co. v. Collins, 40 Ga. 582 (1869)

Cent. Union Co. v. Edwardsville, 269 U.S. 190 (1925)

Chaplinsky v. New Hampshire, 315 U.S. 568 (1942)

Chicago, M. & St. P. R.R. Co. v. Minnesota, 134 U.S. 418 (1890)
Complete Auto Transit, Inc. v. Brady, 30 U.S. 274 (1977)
Cochran v. State Bd. of Educ., 281 U.S. 370 (1930)
Consol. Edison Co. v. NLRB, 305 U.S. 197 (1938)
Cooley v. Bd. of Wardens, 53 U.S. (12 How.) 299 (1851)
Cox v. United States, 332 U.S. 442 (1947)
Curant v. Essex Co., 74 U.S. (7 Wall.) 107 (1868)
Dartmouth Coll. v. Woodward, 17 (4 Wheat.) U.S. 518 (1819)
D'oench, Duhme & Co. v. FDIC, 315 U.S. 447 (1942)
De Jonge v. Oregon, 299 U.S. 353 (1937)
Debs v. United States, 249 U.S. 211 (1919)
Dred Scott v. Sandford, 60 U.S. (19 How.) 393 (1857)
Duncan v. Kahanamoku, 327 U.S. 304 (1946)
Duncan v. Louisiana, 391 U.S. 145 (1968)
Ebel v. Drum, 52 F. Supp. 189 (D. Mass. 1943)
Employment Div., Dep't Of Human Res. v. Smith, 494 U.S. 879 (1990)
Engel v. Vitale, 370 U.S. 421 (1962)
Erie R.R. Co. v. Tompkins, 304 U.S. 64 (1938)
Everett v. Truman, 334 U.S. 824 (1948)
Ex parte Endo, 323 U.S. 283 (1944)
Ex parte Fisk, 113 U.S. 713 (1885)
Ex parte Hung Hang, 108 U.S. 552 (1883)
Ex parte Milligan, 71 U.S. (2 Wall.) 2 (1866)
Ex parte Peru, 318 U.S. 578 (1943)
Ex parte Quirin, 317 U.S. 1 (1942)
Ex parte Rowland, 104 U.S. 604 (1881)
FPC v. Hope Natural Gas, 320 U.S. 591 (1944)
FPC v. Natural Gas Pipeline Co., 315 U.S. 575 (1942)
Frohwerk v. United States, 249 U.S. 204 (1919)
FTC v. Klesner, 274 U.S. 145 (1927)
Gen. Motors Corp. v. Tracy, 519 U.S. 278 (1997)
Gen. Talking Pictures Corp. v. W. Elec. Co., 305 U.S. 124 (1938)
Gibbons v. Ogden, 22 U.S. (9 Wheat.) 1 (1824)
Gideon v. Wainwright, 372 U.S. 335 (1963)
Gilbert v. Minnesota, 254 U.S. 325 (1920)
Gitlow v. New York, 268 U.S. 562 (1925)
Gompers v. United States, 233 U.S. 604 (1914)
Griffin v. California, 380 U.S. 609 (1965)
Griswold v. Connecticut, 381 U.S. 479 (1965)
Grovey v. Townsend, 295 U.S. 45 (1935)
Gwin, White & Prince, Inc. v. Henneford, 305 U.S. 434 (1939)
Hale v. Henkel, 201 U.S. 43 (1906)
Hall v. DeCuir, 95 U.S. 485 (1878)
Hammer v. Dagenhart, 247 U.S. 251 (1918)
Harris v. South Carolina, 338 U.S. 68 (1949)
Harris v. United States, 331 U.S. 145 (1947)
Hedgebeth v. North Carolina, 334 U.S. 806 (1948)
Helvering v. Davis, 301 U.S. 619 (1937)

Hepburn & Dundas v. Ellzey, 6 U.S. (2 Cranch) 445 (1805)

"High Command" case (*United States v. Wilhelm von Leeb*), X and XI *Trials of War Criminals before the Nuremberg Military Tribunals under Control Council Law No. 10* ("TWC") (1948–49)

Hirabayashi v. United States, 627 F. Supp. 1445 (W.D. Wash. 1986), *aff'd* in part, *rev'd* in part, 828 F.2d 591 (9th Cir. 1987)

Hirota v. MacArthur, 335 U.S. 876 (1948); 338 U.S. 197 (1948 and 1949 (concurring opinion))

"Hostage" case (*United States v. Wilhelm List*), XI "TWC" (1949)

Hurd v. Hodge, 334 U.S. 24 (1948)

Hurtado v. California, 110 U.S. 516 (1884)

In re Eckstein, 335 U.S. 851 (1948)

In re Ehlen, 334 U.S. 836 (1948)

In re Gronwald, 334 U.S. 857 (1949)

In re Heim, 335 U.S. 856 (1948)

In re Oliver, 333 U.S. 257 (1948)

In re Sawyer, 124 U.S. 200 (1888)

In re Stattmann, 335 U.S. 805 (1948)

In re Vetter, 335 U.S. 841 (1948)

Int'l Shoe Co. v. Washington, 326 U.S. 310 (1945)

J.C. Eno (U.S.) Ltd. v. Coe, 106 F.2d 858 (App. D.C. 1939)

Jersey Cent. Power & Light Co. v. FPC, 319 U.S. 61 (1943)

Jewell Ridge Coal Corp. v. Local No. 6167, United Mineworkers of Am., 325 U.S. 161 (1945), *reh'g denied*, 325 U.S. 897 (1945)

Johnson v. Eisentrager, 339 U.S. 763, 783 (1950)

Johnson v. United States, 333 U.S. 10 (1948)

Jones v. Opelika, 316 U.S. 584 (1942); *reh'g granted, Jones v. City of Opelika*, 318 U.S. 796 (1943); *vacated, Jones v. Opelika*, 319 U.S. 103 (1943) (per curiam)

Joseph v. Carter & Weekes Stevedoring Co., 330 U.S. 422 (1947)

Kann v. United States, 323 U.S. 88 (1944)

Kent v. Dulles, 357 U.S. 116 (1958)

Klopfer v. North Carolina, 386 U.S. 213 (1967)

Korematsu v. United States, 319 U.S. 432 (1943)

Korematsu v. United States, 140 F.2d 289 (9th Cir. 1943)

Korematsu v. United States, 323 U.S. 214 (1944)

Korematsu v. United States, 584 F. Supp. 1406 (N.D. Cal. 1984)

The License Cases, 46 U.S. (5 How.) 504 (1847)

Lochner v. New York, 198 U.S. 45 (1905)

Loftus v. Illinois, 334 U.S. 804 (1948)

Louisiana v. Resweber, 329 U.S. 459 (1947)

Louis K. Liggett Co. v. Lee, 288 U.S. 517 (1933)

Louisville Bank v. Radford, 295 U.S. 555 (1935)

Ludecke v. Watkins, 335 U.S. 160 (1948)

Lustig v. United States, 338 U.S. 74 (1949)

M.A.P. v. Ryan, 285 A.2d 310 (D.C. 1971)

Mahnich v. S. S.S. Co., 321 U.S. 96 (1944)

Malloy v. Hogan, 378 U.S. 1 (1964)

Mapp v. Ohio, 367 U.S. 643 (1961)

Marbury v. Madison, 5 U.S. (1 Cranch) 137 (1803)

Marsh v. Alabama, 326 U.S. 501 (1946)

Martin v. Struthers, 319 U.S. 141 (1943)

Maxwell v. Dow, 176 U.S. 581 (1900)

McCart v. Indianapolis Water Co., 302 U.S. 419 (1938)

McCollum v. Bd. of Educ., 333 U.S. 203 (1948)

McGoldrick v. Berwin-White Coal Mining Co., 309 U.S. 33 (1940)

McNabb v. United States, 318 U.S. 332 (1943)

Mercoid Corp. v. Mid-Continent Inv. Co., 320 U.S. 661 (1944)

Meyer v. Nebraska, 262 U.S. 390 (1923)

Milch v. United States, 332 U.S. 789 (1947)

Minersville Sch. Dist. v. Gobitis, 310 U.S. 586 (1940); 315 U.S. 722 (1942)

Missouri ex rel. Gaines v. Canada, 305 U.S. 337 (1938)

Mitchell v. Helms, 530 U.S. 793 (2000)

Morehead v. New York ex rel. Tipaldo, 298 U.S. 587 (1936)

Morgan v. Virginia, 328 U.S. 373 (1946)

Mueller v. Allen, 463 U.S. 388 (1983)

Mueller v. Oregon, 208 U.S. 412 (1908)

Murdock v. Pennsylvania, 318 U.S. 748 (1943); 319 U.S. 105 (1943)

Myers v. Matley, 318 U.S. 622 (1943)

NLRB v. Jones & Laughlin Steel Corp., 301 U.S. 1 (1937)

Near v. Minnesota, 283 U.S. (1931)

New York Times Co. v. Sullivan, 376 U.S. 254 (1964)

New York v. United States, 505 U.S. 144 (1992)

N. Sec. Co. v. United States, 193 U.S. 197 (1904)

Northwest Airlines v. Minnesota, 322 U.S. 292 (1944)

O'Donoghue v. United States, 289 U.S. 516 (1933)

O'Neil v. Vermont, 144 U.S. 323 (1892)

Oklahoma v. United States Civil Serv. Comm'n, 330 U.S. 127 (1947)

Oklahoma v. Woodring, 308 U.S. 508 (1939); 308 U.S. 526 (1939)

Oyama v. California, 332 U.S. 633 (1948)

Palko v. Connecticut, 302 U.S. 319 (1937)

Panama Refining Co. v. Ryan, 293 U.S. 388 (1935)

People v. Loftus, 81 N.E. 2d 495 (Ill. 1948)

People v. North River Sugar Refining Co., 3 N.Y. Supp. 401 (1889)

Pierce v. Society of Sisters, 268 U.S. 510 (1925)

Pierce v. United States, 252 U.S. 239 (1920)

Poe v. Ullman, 367 U.S. 497 (1961)

Pointer v. Texas, 380 U.S. 400 (1965)

Prudential Ins. Co. v. Cheek, 259 U.S. 530 (1922)

Quick Bear v. Leupp, 210 U.S. 50 (1908)

Quill Corp. v. North Dakota, 504 U.S. 298 (1992)

R.R. Ret. Bd. v. Alton R.R. Co., 295 U.S. 330 (1935)

Rasu v. Bush, 321 F.3d 1134 (D.C. Cir. 2003), *cert. granted*, 72 U.S.L.W. 3323 (U.S. Nov. 10, 2003) (No. 03-334)

Reid v. Covert, 354 U.S. 1 (1957)

Reynolds v. Sims, 377 U.S. 533 (1964)

Ritholz v. March, 105 F.2d 937 (App. D.C. 1939)

Robinson v. California, 370 U.S. 660 (1962)

Rosenberger v. Rector & Visitors of Univ. of Va., 515 U.S. 819 (1995)

Rottenberg v. United States, 137 F.2d 850 (1st Cir. 1943)

Santa Clara v. S. Pac. R.R., 118 U.S. 394 (1886)

Schechter Poultry Corp. v. United States, 295 U.S. 495 (1935)

Schenk v. United States, 249 U.S. 47 (1919)

Scherzberg v. Maderia, 57 F. Supp. 42 (E.D. Pa. 1944)

Scheuller v. Drum, 51 F. Supp. 383 (E.D. Pa. 1943)

Schneider v. State, 308 U.S. 147 (1939)

Scott v. Sanford, 60 U.S. 393 (1857)

Seminole Tribe of Florida v. Florida, 517 U.S. 44 (1996)

Shapiro v. Thompson, 394 U.S. 618 (1959)

Shelley v. Kramer, 334 U.S. 1 (1948)

Sipuel v. Bd. of Regents, 332 U.S. 631 (1948)

Smith v. Allwright, 321 U.S. 649 (1944)

Snyder v. Massachusetts, 291 U.S. 97 (1934)

S. Pac. v. Jensen, 244 U.S. 205 (1917)

Speiser v. Randall, 357 U.S. 513, 526 (1958)

Standard Oil Co. v. United States, 221 U.S. 1 (1911)

State v. Standard Oil Co., 30 N.E. 279 (Ohio 1892)

Steward Machine Co. v. Davis, 301 U.S. 548 (1937)

Terminiello v. Chicago, 337 U.S. 1 (1949)

Terry v. Ohio, 392 U.S. 1 (1968)

Thiel v. S. Pac. Co., 328 U.S. 217 (1946)

Thornhill v. Alabama, 310 U.S. 88 (1940)

Townsend v. Burke, 334 U.S. 736 (1948)

Trupiano v. United States, 334 U.S. 699 (1948)

Turner v. Pennsylvania, 338 U.S. 62 (1949)

Twining v. New Jersey, 211 U.S. 78 (1908)

United Pub. Workers v. Mitchell, 330 U.S. 75 (1947)

United States v. Am. Tobacco Co., 221 U.S. 106 (1911)

United States v. Butler, 297 U.S. 1 (1936)

United States v. Carolene Prods. Co., 304 U.S. 144 (1938)

United States v. Classic, 313 U.S. 299 (1941)

United States v. Darby Lumber Co., 312 U.S. 100 (1941)

United States v. Di Re, 332 U.S. 581 (1948)

United States v. E.C. Knight Co., 156 U.S. 1 (1895)

United States v. Shipp, 203 U.S. 563 (1906)

U.S. Dep't of the Treasury v. Fabe, 508 U.S. 491 (1993)

Upshaw v. United States, 335 U.S. 410 (1948)

Wales v. Whitney, 114 U.S. 564, 570 (1885)

Washington v. Dawson, 264 U.S. 219 (1924)

Washington v. Texas, 388 U.S. 14 (1967)

Watchtower Bible & Tract Soc'y of New York, Inc. v. Village of Stratton, 536 U.S. 150 (2002)

Watts v. Indiana, 338 U.S. 49 (1949)

Weeks v. United States, 232 U.S. 383 (1914)

Wesberry v. Sanders, 376 U.S. 1 (1964)

West v. Louisiana, 194 U.S. 258 (1904)
West Coast Hotel Co. v. Parrish, 300 U.S. 379 (1937)
West Virginia Bd. of Educ. v. Barnette, 319 U.S. 524 (1943)
W. Livestock v. Bureau of Internal Revenue, 303 U.S. 250 (1938)
Whittenton Mills v. Upton, 10 Mass. (Gray) 582 (1858)
Wickard v. Filburn, 317 U.S. 111 (1942)
Willson v. Black Bird Creek Marsh Co., 27 U.S. (2 Pet.) 245 (1829)
Witters v. Dep't of Servs. for the Blind, 474 U.S. 481 (1986)
Yasui v. United States, 320 U.S. 115 (1943)
Young v. Ragen, 337 U.S. 235 (1949)
Zelman v. Simmons-Harris, 536 U.S. 639 (2002)
Zobrest v. Catalina Foothills School Dist., 509 U.S. 1 (1993)

PUBLISHED SOURCES

Abel, Albert S. "The Commerce Power: An Instrument of Federalism," 25 *Ind. L. J.* 498 (1950); 35 *Iowa L. Rev.* 625 (1950).
Acheson, Dean. *Morning and Noon*. Boston: Houghton Mifflin, 1965.
Allen, Francis A. "Chief Justice Vinson and the Theory of Constitutional Government: A Tentative Appraisal," 49 *Nw. U. L. Rev.* 3 (1954).
Allen, Frederick S., Mark S. Foster, Ernest Andrade Jr., Philip Mitterling, and H. Lee Scamehorn. *The University of Colorado, 1876-1976*. New York: Harcourt Brace Jovanovich, 1976.
Alsop, Joseph, and Turner Catledge. *The 168 Days*. New York: Da Capo, 1973.
American Bar Association. *The Code of Judicial Conduct* (1972).
———. *Canons of Professional Ethics, Canons of Judicial Ethics* (1937).
Andriot, John L. *Population Abstract of the United States*. McLean, Va.: Andriot Associates, 1980.
Armstrong, Walter P., Jr. *A Century of Service: A Centennial History of The National Conference of Commissioners on Uniform State Laws*. St. Paul: West, 1991.
Ashby, Le Roy. *The Spearless Leader: Senator Borah and the Progressive Movement in the 1920's*. Urbana: U. of Illinois Press, 1972.
Association of American Law Schools. *Directory of Law Teachers* (1942).
Athearn, Robert G. *The Coloradans*. Albuquerque: U. of New Mexico Press, 1976.
Baker, Liva. *Felix Frankfurter*. New York: Coward-McCann, 1969.
Balcomb, Kenneth C. *A Boy's Albuquerque, 1898-1912*. Albuquerque: U. of New Mexico Press, 1980.
Ball, Howard, and Phillip J. Cooper. *Of Power and Right: Hugo Black, William O. Douglas, and America's Constitutional Revolution*. New York: Oxford U. Press, 1992.
Barker, Ernest, ed. *Social Contract*. London: Oxford U. Press, 1953.
Barry, John M. *Rising Tide: The Great Mississippi Flood of 1927 and How It Changed America*. New York: Simon and Schuster, 1997.
Bassiouni, M. Cherif. *The Law of the International Criminal Tribunal for the Former Yugoslavia*. Irvington-on-Hudson: Transnational, 1996.
Berg, A. Scott. *Lindbergh*. New York: Putnam, 1998.
Berle, Adolph A., Jr., and Gardiner C. Means. *The Modern Corporation and Private Property*. New York: Commerce Clearing House, 1932.

Berry, Mary Frances. *Stability, Security and Continuity: Mr. Justice Burton and Decision-Making in the Supreme Court 1945-1958*. Westport: Greenwood, 1978.

Biddle, Francis. *In Brief Authority*. Garden City: Doubleday, 1962.

Bittker, Boris I. "The World War II German Saboteurs' Case and Writs of Certiorari before Judgment by the Court of Appeals: A Tale of Nunc Pro Tunc Jurisdiction," 14 *Const. Commentary* 431 (1997).

Blackstone, Sir William. *Commentaries on the Laws of England*. Chicago: U. of Chicago Press, 1979.

Blair, Carolyn L., and Arda S. Walker. *By Faith Endowed: The Story of Maryville College, 1819-1994*. Maryville, Tenn.: Maryville College Press, 1994.

Blanshard, Paul. *American Freedom and Catholic Power*. 2d ed. Boston: Beacon, 1958.

———, ed. *Classics of Free Thought*. Buffalo: Prometheus, 1977.

Boyd, Susan K. *The ABA's First Section: Assuring a Qualified Bar*. St. Paul: West, 1993.

Brackenridge, Hugh Henry. *Law Miscellanies*. Philadelphia: P. Byrne, 1814.

Brackman, Arnold C. *The Other Nuremberg: The Untold Story of the Tokyo War Crimes Trials*. New York: William Morrow, 1987.

Brant, Irving. *The Bill of Rights: Its Origin and Meaning*. Indianapolis: Bobbs-Merrill, 1965.

———. *James Madison*. 6 vol. Indianapolis: Bobbs-Merrill, 1941, 1948, 1950, 1953, 1956, 1961.

———. "Mr. Justice Rutledge—The Man," 25 *Ind. L. J.* 424 (1950); 35 *Iowa L. Rev.* 544 (1950).

———. *Storm over the Constitution*. Indianapolis: Bobbs-Merrill, 1936.

Brody, L. B. "Recent Decision," 44 *Mich. L. Rev.* 855 (1946).

Brookings, Robert S. *Education for Political Leadership*. Garden City: Country Life, 1927.

Brown, A. L. "Parliament, c. 1377-1422," in R. G. Davies and J. H. Denton, eds., *The English Parliament in the Middle Ages*, 124. Manchester: Manchester U. Press, 1981.

Brown, D. M. *Educational, Economic and Community Survey: Bledsoe County*. Knoxville: U. of Tennessee Press, 1927.

Brown, David W. *When Strangers Cooperate: Using Social Conventions to Govern Ourselves*. New York: Free Press, 1995.

Brown, Elizabeth Gaspar. *Legal Education at Michigan, 1859-1959*. Ann Arbor: U. of Michigan Law School, 1959.

Brown, W. Jethro. "The Personality of the Corporation and the State," 21 *L.Q. Rev.* 365 (1905).

Brudney, Victor, and Richard F. Wolfson. "Mr. Justice Rutledge: Law Clerks' Reflections," 25 *Ind. L. J.* 455 (1950); 35 *Iowa L. Rev.* 578 (1950).

Bulletins of Washington University, St. Louis. *Catalogues of the School of Law, 1927-1934*.

Bybee, Jay S. "George Sutherland, 1922-1938," in Clare Cushman, ed., *The Supreme Court Justices, Illustrated Biographies, 1789-1993*, 346. Washington: Congressional Quarterly, 1993.

Byrnes, James Francis. *All in One Lifetime*. New York: Harper and Brothers, 1958.

Cardozo, Benjamin. *The Nature of the Judicial Process*. New Haven: Yale U. Press, 1921.

———. *Paradoxes of Legal Science*. New York: Columbia U. Press, 1928.

Carman, Harry J., and Harold C. Syrett. *A History of the American People*. Vol. 1. New York: Alfred A. Knopf, 1956.

Carrington, Paul D. "Hail! Langdell!," 20 *J. Law & Soc. Inquiry* 691 (1995).

————. "Law and Economics in the Creation of Federal Administrative Law: Thomas Cooley, Elder to the Republic," 83 *Iowa L. Rev.* 363 (1998).

————. "Law as 'The Common Thoughts of Men': The Law-Teaching and Judging of Thomas McIntyre Cooley," 49 *Stan. L. Rev.* 495 (1997).

————. "Legal Education for the People: Populism and Civic Virtue," 43 *Kan. L. Rev.* 1 (1994).

————. "The Missionary Diocese of Chicago," 44 *J. Legal Educ.* 467 (1994).

————. "William Gardiner Hammond and the Lieber Revival," 16 *Cardozo L. Rev.* 2135 (1995).

Carrington, Paul D., and Erica King. "Law and the Wisconsin Idea," 48 *J. Legal Ed.* 297 (1997).

Cathay, Maurice. *Recollections: School of Law, 1928-1931.* St. Louis: Washington University School of Law, undated.

Caughey, Bruce, and Dean Winstanley. *The Colorado Guide.* Golden, Colo.: Fulcrum, 1991.

Choper, Jesse H. "Symposium on Law in the Twentieth Century: A Century of Religious Freedom," 88 *Calif. L. Rev.* 1709 (2000).

Comment, "Employer Freedom of Speech in Labor Relations," 14 *Ford. L. Rev.* 59 (1945).

Commission on Wartime Relocation and Internment of Civilians. *Personal Justice Denied.* Washington: U.S. Government Printing Office, 1982.

Cooley, Thomas M. *A Treatise on the Constitutional Limitations Which Rest upon the Legislative Power of the States of the American Union* (1868). 8th ed. Vol. 1. Boston: Little, Brown, 1927.

Corwin, Edward S. "The 'Higher Law' Background of American Constitutional Law," 42 *Harv. L. Rev.* 149 (part 1), 365 (part 2) (1928).

————. *Total War and the Constitution.* New York: Alfred A. Knopf, 1947.

Crans, Eleanor G. *The Book of Albuquerque: Albuquerque Guide and Book of Information.* Albuquerque: published privately, 1928.

Cronon, E. David, and John W. Jenkins. *The University of Wisconsin: A History, 1925-1945.* Vol. 3. Madison: U. of Wisconsin Press, 1994.

Crosskey, William Winslow. "Charles Fairman, 'Legislative History,' and the Constitutional Limitations on State Authority," 22 *U. Chi. L. Rev.* 1 (1954).

————. *Politics and the Constitution in the History of the United States.* Vol. 2. Chicago: U. of Chicago Press, 1953.

Culver, John C., and John Hyde. *American Dreamer: A Life of Henry Wallace.* New York: W. W. Norton, 2000.

Currie, Brainerd. "The Materials of Law Study," 3 *J. Legal Educ.* 331 (1951)(part 1).

Currie, David P. "The Constitution in the Supreme Court: The New Deal, 1930-1941," 54 *U. Chi. L. Rev.* 504 (1987).

————. "The Constitution in the Supreme Court: The Preferred-Position Debate, 1941-1946," 37 *Cath. U. L. Rev.* 39 (1987).

Curti, Merle, and Vernon Carstensen. *The University of Wisconsin: A History, 1848-1925.* Vol. 1. Madison: U. of Wisconsin Press, 1949.

Curtis, Michael Kent. *No State Shall Abridge: The Fourteenth Amendment and the Bill of Rights.* Durham: Duke U. Press, 1986.

Cushman, Clare, ed., *The Supreme Court Justices, Illustrated Biographies, 1789-1993.* Washington: Congressional Quarterly, 1993.

Daly, James J. A. "The Yamashita Case and Martial Courts," 21 *Conn. B. J.* 137 (part I), 210 (part II) (1947).

Danelski, David J. "Lucile T. Lomen: The First Woman to Clerk at the Supreme Court," 24 *J. of S. Ct. Hist.* 43 (1999).

———. "The Saboteurs' Case," 1 *J. of S. Ct. Hist.* 61 (1996).

Daniels, Roger. *The Decision to Relocate the Japanese Americans.* Philadelphia: J. B. Lippincott, 1975.

Davis, John P. "The Nature of Corporations," 12 *Pol. Sci. Q.* 273, (1897).

Davis, Polly Ann. *Alben W. Barkley: Senate Majority Leader and Vice President.* New York: Garland, 1979.

Davis, William E. *Glory Colorado! A History of the University of Colorado, 1858-1963.* Boulder: Pruett, 1965.

Decision, "Labor Law: Free Speech: Requirement of Registration before Solicitation of Members," 45 *Colum. L. Rev.* 465 (1945).

Dembitz, Nanette. "Racial Discrimination and the Military Judgment: The Supreme Court's Korematsu and Endo Decisions," 45 *Colum. L. Rev.* 175 (1945).

Dewey, John. "The Historic Background of Corporate Legal Personality," 35 *Yale L. J.* 655 (1926).

DeWitt, J. L. *Final Report: Japanese Evacuation from the West Coast 1942.* New York: Arno, 1978 (originally published by the U.S. Government Printing Office, 1943)

Dilliard, Irving. "Mr. Justice Rutledge's First Opinion," 108 *New Republic* 633-34 (May 10, 1943).

Douglas, William O. *The Court Years, 1939-1975: The Autobiography of William O. Douglas.* New York: Random House, 1980.

———. "A Functional Approach to the Law of Business Associations," 23 *Ill. L. Rev.* 675 (1929).

———. *Go East, Young Man: The Early Years.* New York: Dell, 1974.

Douglas, William O., and Carrol M. Shanks. *Cases and Materials on the Law of Corporate Reorganization.* Chicago: Callaghan, 1931.

———. *Cases and Materials on the Law of Financing of Business Units.* Chicago: Callaghan, 1931.

———. *Cases and Materials on the Law of Management of Business Units.* Chicago: Callaghan, 1931.

Douglas, William O., and Carrol M. Shanks, with James W. Cooper. *Cases and Materials on Business Units: Losses, Liabilities, and Assets.* Chicago: Callaghan, 1932.

Dowdall, Harold Chaloner. *Estatification.* Oxford: Clarendon, 1930.

Dowling, Noel T. "Interstate Commerce and State Power—Revised Version," 47 *Colum. L. Rev.* 547 (1948).

Dowst, Henry, Jr., and John F. Sullivan. "Constitutional Law: Establishment of Religion: Aid to Parochial School Students," 21 *B. U. L. Rev.* 281 (1947).

Drachman, Virginia G. *Sisters in Law: Women Lawyers in Modern American History.* Cambridge: Harvard U. Press, 1998.

Dunham, Allison. "Gross Receipts Taxes on Interstate Transactions (Ain't God Tough on Indiana)," 47 *Colum. L. Rev.* 211 (1947).

Dunne, Gerald T. *Hugo Black and the Judicial Revolution.* New York: Simon and Schuster, 1977.

Emerson, Thomas I., and David M. Helfeld. "Loyalty among Government Employees," 58 *Yale L. J.* 1 (1948).

Ernst, Daniel R. "Dicey's Disciple on the D.C. Circuit: Judge Harold M. Stephens and Administrative Law Reform, 1933-1940," 90 *Geo. L. J.* 787 (2002).

Fairman, Charles. "Does the Fourteenth Amendment Incorporate the Bill of Rights? The Original Understanding," 2 *Stan. L. Rev.* 5 (1949).

———. "A Reply to Professor Crosskey," 22 *U. Chi. L. Rev.* 144 (1954).

———. "The Supreme Court and the Constitutional Limitations on State Governmental Authority," 21 *U. Chi. L. Rev.* 40 (1953).

———. "The Supreme Court on Military Jurisdiction: Martial Rule in Hawaii and the Yamashita Case," 59 *Harv. L. Rev.* 833 (1946).

Falk, Richard A. "The Circle of Responsibility," in Richard A. Falk, Gabriel Kolko, and Robert J. Lifton, eds., *Crimes of War*, 222. New York: Random House, 1971.

———. *A Global Approach to National Policy*. Cambridge: Harvard U. Press, 1975.

Farley, James. *Jim Farley's Story: The Roosevelt Years*. Westport: Greenwood, 1948.

Fassett, John D. "The Buddha and the Bumblebee: The Saga of Stanley Reed and Felix Frankfurter," 28 *J. Sup. Ct. Hist.* 165 (2003).

———. *New Deal Justice: The Life of Stanley Reed of Kentucky*. New York: Vantage, 1994.

Federal Writers' Project of the Works Progress Administration for the State of Iowa. *The WPA Guide to 1930s Iowa*. Ames: Iowa State U. Press, 1986.

Feldman, Philip. Recent Decision, "Constitutional Law: State Statute Requiring Paid Labor Organizers to Apply to the Secretary of State for Organizers' Cards [Etc.]," 33 *Geo. Law J.* 227 (1945).

Fine, Sidney. *Frank Murphy: The Washington Years*. Vol. 3. Ann Arbor: U. of Michigan Press, 1984.

———. "Mr. Justice Murphy and the Hirabayashi Case," 33 *Pac. Hist. Rev.* 195 (1964).

Fish, Peter Graham. *The Politics of Judicial Administration*. Princeton: Princeton U. Press, 1973.

Frank, John P. "Disqualification of Judges," 56 *Yale L.J.* 605 (1947).

———. "Fred Vinson and the Chief Justiceship," 21 *U. Chi L. Rev.* 212 (1954).

———. *Marble Palace: The Supreme Court in American Life*. New York: Alfred A. Knopf, 1958.

———. *Mr. Justice Black: The Man and His Opinions*. New York: Alfred A. Knopf, 1949.

———. "The United States Supreme Court: 1946-47," 15 *U. Chi. L. Rev.* 1 (1947).

———. "The United States Supreme Court: 1947-48," 16 *U. Chi. L. Rev.* 1 (1948).

———. "The United States Supreme Court: 1948-49," 17 *U. Chi. L. Rev.* 1 (1949).

Frankfurter, Felix, and Nathan Greene. *The Labor Injunction*. New York: Macmillan, 1930.

Freedman, Max, ed. *Roosevelt and Frankfurter: Their Correspondence, 1928-1945*. Boston: Little, Brown, 1967.

Freidel, Frank, and Alan Brinkley. *America in the Twentieth Century*. 5th ed. New York: Alfred A. Knopf, 1982.

Freund, Ernst. *The Legal Nature of Corporations*. Chicago: U. of Chicago Press, 1897.

Frink, Maurice. *The Boulder Story: Historical Portrait of a Colorado Town*. Boulder: Pruett, 1965.

Frost, Iris. "On Women and the Law," *Iowa Advocate* 19 (Fall–Winter 1998).

Fuchs, Ralph F. "The Judicial Art of Wiley B. Rutledge," 28 *Wash. U. L.Q.* 115 (1943).

———. "Law School in Transition, 1926-1941," 3 *Wash. U. L. Sch. Mag.* 10 (Winter 1981-82).

Ganoe, John T. "The Yamashita Case and the Constitution," 25 *Or. L. Rev.* 143 (1946).

Gerhart, Eugene C. *America's Advocate: Robert H. Jackson*. Indianapolis: Bobbs-Merrill, 1958.

Gibson, J. Keith. "Constitutional Law: State Aid to Sectarian Schools under the Fourteenth Amendment," 12 *Mo. L. Rev.* 465 (1947).

Gierke, Otto. *Political Theories of the Middle Ages*. Trans. and with a preface by F. Maitland. Cambridge: Cambridge U. Press, 1902.

Gilmore, Eugene. "Some Criticisms of Legal Education," 7 *A.B.A. J.* 227 (1921).

Givens, Charles G. *All Cats Are Gray*. Indianapolis: Bobbs-Merrill, 1937.

Glad, Paul W. *McKinley, Bryan, and the People*. Philadelphia: J. B. Lippincott, 1964.

Goebel, Julius, Jr., ed. *A History of the School of Law, Columbia University*. New York: Columbia U. Press, 1955.

Goings, Kenneth W. *"The NAACP Comes of Age": The Defeat of Judge John J. Parker*. Bloomington: U. of Indiana Press, 1990.

Goldman, Eric F. *The Crucial Decade*. New York: Alfred A. Knopf, 1956.

Graves, W. Brooke. *Uniform State Action: A Possible Substitute for Centralization*. Chapel Hill: U. of North Carolina Press, 1934.

Gray, John Chipman. *The Nature and Sources of the Law*. 2d ed. New York: Macmillan, 1927.

Gressman, Eugene. "The Controversial Image of Mr. Justice Murphy," 47 *Geo. L. J.* 631 (1959).

Grey, Thomas C. "Langdell's Orthodoxy," 45 *U. Pitt. L. Rev.* 1 (1983).

Grodzins, Morton. *Americans Betrayed: Politics and the Japanese Evacuations*. Chicago: U. of Chicago Press, 1949.

Grossman, Joel B. "The Japanese American Cases and the Vagaries of Constitutional Adjudication in Wartime: An Institutional Perspective," 19 *U. Haw. L. Rev.* 649 (1997).

Gunther, Gerald. *Learned Hand: The Man and the Judge*. New York: Alfred A. Knopf, 1994.

Hansen, Millard Winchester. "The Early History of the College of Law, State University of Iowa: 1865-1884," 30 *Iowa L. Rev.* 31 (1944).

Harper, Fowler V. *Justice Rutledge and the Bright Constellation*. Indianapolis: Bobbs-Merrill, 1965.

Hassett, Arlyne F. Comment, "Constitutional Law: Freedom of Speech: Labor Unions," 25 *B.U. L. Rev.* 141 (1945).

Hatcher, John Henry. "Fred M. Vinson, 1946-1953," in Clare Cushman, ed., *The Supreme Court Justices, Illustrated Biographies, 1789-1993*, 421. Washington: Congressional Quarterly, 1993.

Hayes, Edward R. "A Pioneer Iowa Law School: Iowa Wesleyan University," 10 *Drake L. Rev.* 105 (1961).

Hayes, Ruthann. "Justice Rutledge Has Busy Summer," *Silver and Gold* (U. of Colorado), Sept. 8, 1943.

Heilprin, Angelo, and Louis Heilprin, eds. *A Complete Pronouncing Gazetteer or Geographical Dictionary of the World*. Philadelphia: J. B. Lippincott, 1905.

Hier, Marshall D. "Justice Wiley B. Rutledge's St. Louis Years," *St. Louis B. J.* 37 (Fall 1993).

Hirsch, H. N. *The Enigma of Felix Frankfurter*. New York: Basic Books, 1981.

Hofstadter, Richard. "The Meaning of the Progressive Movement," in Hofstadter, ed., *The Progressive Movement, 1900-1915*, 1. New York: Simon and Schuster, 1963.

———. Preface to "Lincoln Steffens Reports La Follette's Reforms, 1906," in Hofstadter, ed., *The Progressive Movement, 1900-1915*, 113. New York: Simon and Schuster, 1963.

Holland, Thomas Erskine. *The Elements of Jurisprudence*. 10th ed. Oxford: Clarendon, 1906.

Holmes, Oliver Wendell, Jr. "The Path of the Law," in *Collected Legal Papers*, 186. New York: Harcourt, Brace and Howe, 1920.

Hopkins, John J. "State Transportation of Students to Parochial Schools: The Everson Case," 36 *Ky. L. J.* 328 (1947).

Horwitz, Morton J. *The Transformation of American Law, 1780-1860*. Cambridge: Harvard U. Press, 1977.

———. *The Transformation of American Law, 1870-1960*. New York: Oxford U. Press, 1992.

Howard, J. Woodford, Jr. *Mr. Justice Murphy: A Political Biography*. Princeton: Princeton U. Press, 1968.

Howe, Mark DeWolfe. "The Creative Period of the Law of Massachusetts," 69 *Proceedings of the Massachusetts Historical Society* 237 (1947-50).

Humer, James R. "Constitutional Law: Due Process: Freedom of Religion: Use of Public Funds for Transportation of Parochial School Students," 51 *Dick. L. Rev.* 276 (1947).

Hutcheson, Joseph C., Jr. "The Judgment Intuitive: The Function of the 'Hunch' in Judicial Decision," 14 *Corn. L. Q.* 274 (1929).

Hutchinson, Dennis J. "The Black-Jackson Feud," 1988 *Sup. Ct. Rev.* 203 (1989).

———. "'The Achilles Heel' of the Constitution: Justice Jackson and the Japanese Exclusion cases," 2002 *Sup. Ct. Rev.* 455 (2003).

Ickes, Harold L. *The Secret Diary of Harold L. Ickes*. Vol. 2, *1936-39: The Inside Struggle*. New York: Simon and Schuster, 1954.

Indiana University. *Bulletin*, Vol. 36, No. 4, *School of Law, 1938-39* (March 15, 1938).

Irons, Peter. *Justice at War: The Story of the Japanese American Internment Cases*. New York: Oxford U. Press, 1983.

Israel, Fred L. "Wiley Rutledge," in Leo Friedman and Fred L. Israel, eds., *The Justices of the United States Supreme Court: Their Lives and Major Opinions*, vol. 4, p. 1313. New York: Chelsea House, 1969.

Jackson, Robert H. *That Man: An Insider's Portrait of Franklin D. Roosevelt*, ed. John Q. Barrett. New York: Oxford U. Press, 2003.

James, William. *Varieties of Religious Experience* (1904). New York: Penguin, 1985.

Johnson, Byron A. *Early Albuquerque: A Photographic History, 1870-1918*. Albuquerque: Albuquerque Museum, 1981.

Johnson, Claudius O. *Borah of Idaho*. Seattle: U. of Washington Press, 1967.

Jollife, J. E. A. *The Constitutional History of Medieval England from the English Settlement to 1485*. London: Adam and Charles Black, 1954.

Judah, Charles B. *Governor Richard C. Dillon: A Study in New Mexico Politics*. Albuquerque: U. of New Mexico Press, 1948.

Judicial Conference of the United States. *Code of Judicial Conduct for United States Judges* (1973).

Kahn, Michael A. "The Politics of the Appointment Process: An Analysis of Why Learned Hand Was Never Appointed to the Supreme Court," 25 *Stan. L. Rev.* 251 (1973).

Kalman, Laura. *Legal Realism at Yale, 1927-1960*. Chapel Hill: U. of North Carolina Press, 1986.

Katz, Wilbur G. "An Open Letter to the Attorney General of Illinois," 15 *U. Chi. L. Rev.* 251 (1948).

Kaufman, Andrew L. *Cardozo*. Cambridge: Harvard U. Press, 1998.

———. "Cardozo's Appointment to the Supreme Court," 1 *Cardozo L. Rev.* 23 (1979).

Kennedy, David M. *Freedom from Fear: The American People in Depression and War, 1929-1945*. New York: Oxford U. Press, 1999.

Kirkendall, Richard. "Fred M. Vinson," in Leon Friedman and Fred L. Israel, eds., *The Justices of the United States Supreme Court 1789-1969, Their Lives and their Opinions*, vol. 4, p. 2369. New York: Chelsea House, 1969.

Krock, Arthur. *Memoirs: Sixty Years on the Firing Line*. New York: Funk and Wagnalls, 1968.

Kurland, Philip C. "Judicial Biography: History, Myth, Literature, Fiction, Potpourri," 70 *N.Y.U. L. Rev.* 489 (1995).

Lael, Richard L. *The Yamashita Precedent: War Crimes and Command Responsibility*. Wilmington, Del.: Scholarly Resources, 1982.

Landrum, Bruce D. "The Yamashita War Crimes Trial: Command Responsibility Then and Now," 149 *Mil. L. Rev.* 293 (1995).

La Piana, William P. *Logic and Experience: The Origin of Modern American Legal Education*. New York: Oxford U. Press, 1994.

Lash, Joseph P. *Dealers and Dreamers: A New Look at the New Deal*. New York: Doubleday, 1988.

———. *From the Diaries of Felix Frankfurter*. New York: W. W. Norton, 1975.

Lasser, William. *Benjamin V. Cohen: Architect of the New Deal*. New Haven: Yale U. Press, 2002.

Latty, Elvin R., and George T. Frampton. *Basic Business Associations: Cases, Text and Problems*. Boston: Little, Brown, 1963.

Lawrence, Alberta. *Who Was Who among English and European Authors, 1931-1949*. Vol. 1. Detroit: Gale Research, 1978.

Leuchtenburg, William E. *The Supreme Court Reborn: The Constitutional Revolution in the Age of Roosevelt*. New York: Oxford U. Press, 1995.

Levitan, David M. "Mr. Justice Rutledge," 34 *Va. L. Rev.* 393 (part 1), 526 (part 2) (1948).

Libbey, James K. *Dear Alben: Mr. Barkley of Kentucky*. Lexington: U. Press of Kentucky, 1979.

Lieber, Francis. *Legal and Political Hermeneutics, or Principles of Interpretation and Construction in Law and Politics* (1837). 3d ed., ed. William G. Hammond. St. Louis: F. H. Thomas, 1880; republished in 16 *Cardozo L. Rev.* 1883 (1990).

Lief, Alfred. *Democracy's Norris: The Biography of a Lonely Crusader*. New York: Octagon, 1977.

Lingreen, Edna. "The Greatest Gift." Unpublished manuscript, 1998.

Locke, John. *Second Treatise on Civil Government, an Essay Concerning the True, Original Extent and End of Government*, in Ernest Barker, ed., *Social Contract*. London: Oxford U. Press, 1953.

Lowe, Jennifer M. "Harold H. Burton, 1945-1895," in Clare Cushman, ed., *Supreme Court Justices, Illustrated Biographies, 1789-1993*, 416. Washington: Congressional Quarterly, 1993.

Luckingham, Bradford. *The Urban Southwest: A Profile History of Albuquerque, El Paso, Phoenix, Tucson*. El Paso: Texas Western, 1982.

Lyttle, Charles H. *Freedom Moves West: A History of the Western Unitarian Conference, 1852-1952*. Boston: Beacon, 1952.

Machen, Arthur W., Jr. "Corporate Personality," 24 *Harv. L. Rev.* 253 (1911).

Maciver, R. M. *Community*. London: Macmillan, 1917.

Maga, Tim. *Judgment at Tokyo: The Japanese War Crimes Trials*. Lexington: U. Press of Kentucky, 2001.

Mann, W. Howard. "Mr. Justice Rutledge and Civil Liberties," 25 *Ind. L. J.* 532 (1950); 35 *Iowa L. Rev.* 663 (1950).

Mansfield, Harvey C. *A Short History of OPA*. Washington: Office of Temporary Controls, Office of Price Administration, 1948.

Marsh, James M. "Robert H. Jackson, 1941-1954," in Clare Cushman, ed., *The Supreme Court Justices, Illustrated Biographies, 1789-1993*, 406. Washington: Congressional Quarterly, 1993.

Mason, Alpheus Thomas. *Harlan Fiske Stone: Pillar of the Law*. New York: Viking, 1956.

Mason, George F., Jr., and James R. Schule. "Transportation for Children Attending Parochial School," 21 *St. John's L. Rev.* 176 (1947).

May, Ernest R. *Strange Victory: Hitler's Conquest of France*. New York: Hill and Wang, 2000.

Mazuzan, George T. *Warren R. Austin at the U.N., 1946-1953*. Kent, Ohio: Kent State U. Press, 1977.

McCarthy, Mary. *Medina*. New York: Harcourt Brace Jovanovich, 1972.

McCullough, David. *Truman*. New York: Simon and Schuster, 1992.

McCune, W. *The Nine Young Men*. New York: Harper and Brothers, 1947.

McDougall, William. *The Group Mind*. New York: G. P. Putnam's Sons, 1920.

McLauren, William G. "Can a Trial Court of the United States Be Completely Deprived of the Power to Determine Constitutional Questions?," 30 *A.B.A. J.* 17 (1944).

Meador, Daniel J. *Mr. Justice Black and His Books*. Charlottesville: U. Press of Virginia, 1974.

Meyer, Erwin F. "Fascism, Bolshevism and Socialism," 3 *Rocky Mt. L. Rev.* 85 (1931).

Meyers, A. R. "Parliament, 1422-1509," in R. G. Davies and J. H. Denton, eds., *The English Parliament in the Middle Ages*, 146. Manchester: U. of Manchester Press, 1981.

Moore, Underhill. "The Rational Basis of Legal Institutions," 23 *Colum. L. Rev.* 609 (1923).

Moore, Winfred B., Jr. "James F. Byrnes, 1941-1942," in Clare Cushman, ed., *The Supreme Court Justices, Illustrated Biographies, 1789-1993*, 401. Washington: Congressional Quarterly, 1993.

Morello, Karen Berger. *The Invisible Bar: The Woman Lawyer in America, 1638 to the Present*. New York: Random House, 1986.

Morris, Jeffrey Brandon. *Calmly to Poise the Scales of Justice: A History of the Courts of the District of Columbia Circuit*. Durham: Carolina Academic Press, 2001.

Morrison, Stanley. "Does the Fourteenth Amendment Incorporate the Bill of Rights? The Judicial Interpretation," 2 *Stan. L. Rev.* 140 (1949).

Morrow, Ralph E. *Washington University in St. Louis: A History*. St. Louis: Missouri Historical Society Press, 1996.

Mosher, Lester E. "Mr. Justice Rutledge's Philosophy of Civil Rights," 245 *N.Y.U. L. Q. Rev.* 661 (1949).

Murphy, Bruce Allen. *Wild Bill: The Legend and Life of William O. Douglas*. New York: Random House, 2003.

———. *The Brandeis/Frankfurter Connection: The Secret Political Activities of Two Supreme Court Justices*. New York: Oxford U. Press, 1982.

Newman, Roger K. *Hugo Black: A Biography*. New York: Pantheon, 1994.

Norris, George W. *Fighting Liberal*. New York: Macmillan, 1945.

Northwestern University. *Northwestern University Bulletin, the School of Law for the Session 1935-36.*

Norton, Mary Beth, David M. Katzman, David W. Blight, Howard P. Chudacoff, Thomas G. Paterson, William M. Tuttle Jr., and Paul D. Escott. *A People and a Nation: A Short History of the United States.* 6th ed. Boston: Houghton Mifflin, 2001.

Note, "Constitutionality of Tax Benefits Accorded Religion," 49 *Colum. L. Rev.* 968 (1949).

Note, "Funds for Sectarian Schools," 60 *Harv. L. Rev.* 793 (1947).

Note, "Gross Receipts Taxes: A Change in Doctrine," 56 *Yale L. J.* 898 (1947).

Note, "Organizer's Right to Speak," 21 *Ind. L. J.* 61 (1945).

Note, "Power to Appoint Counsel in Illinois Habeas Corpus Proceedings," 15 *U. Chi. L. Rev.* 945 (1948).

Note, "Public Aid to Establishment of Religion," 96 *U. Pa. L. Rev.* 230 (1947).

O'Brien, John Lord. "Loyalty Tests and Guilt by Association," 61 *Harv. L. Rev.* 592 (1948).

O'Neill, James Milton. *Religion and Education under the Constitution.* New York: Harper and Brothers, 1949.

O'Neill, John D. Recent Decision, "Constitutional Law: State Police Power Regulation of Labor Organizers under the 14th Amendment," 20 *Notre Dame Law.* 336 (1945).

Parks, William H. "Command Responsibility for War Crimes," 62 *Mil. L. Rev.* 1 (1973).

Parrish, Michael E. *Felix Frankfurter and His Times: The Reform Years.* New York: Free Press, 1982.

Perkins, Rollin. "The Story of the Iowa Law School," 15 *Iowa L. Rev.* 257 (1930).

Persons, Stow. *The University of Iowa in the Twentieth Century: An Institutional History.* Iowa City: U. of Iowa Press, 1990.

Pettus, Isabella M. "The Legal Education of Women," 38 *J. Soc. Sci.* 234 (1900).

Phillips, Harlan B. *Felix Frankfurter Reminisces: Recorded Talks with Dr. Harlan B. Phillips.* London: Secker and Warburg, 1960.

Piccigallo, Philip R. *The Japanese on Trial: Allied War Crimes Operations in the East, 1945-1951.* Austin: U. of Texas Press, 1979.

Pictet, Jean S., ed. *Commentary on III Geneva Convention Relative to the Treatment of Prisoners of War.* Geneva: International Committee of the Red Cross, 1960.

Pollak, Louis H. "Wiley Blount Rutledge: Profile of a Judge," in R. D. Rotunda, ed., *Six Justices on Civil Rights*, 177. London: Oceana, 1983.

———. "Wiley B. Rutledge, 1943-1949," in Clare Cushman, ed., *The Supreme Court Justices, Illustrated Biographies, 1789-1993*, 411. Washington: Congressional Quarterly, 1993.

Potter, Hugh O. *A History of Owensboro and Daviess County, Kentucky.* Daviess County, Kentucky Historical Society, 1974.

Pound, Roscoe. "Mechanical Jurisprudence," 8 *Colum. L. Rev.* 605 (1908).

———. *The Spirit of the Common Law.* Francetown, N.H.: Marshall Jones, 1921.

Powell, Thomas Reed. "More Ado about Gross Receipts Taxes," 60 *Harv. L. Rev.* 710 (1947) (part II).

Powers, Francis. Comment, "Constitutional Law: Freedom of Speech for Labor Organizers: Registration Requirement Invalid," 43 *Mich. L. Rev.* 1159 (1945).

Prather, John G. "Constitutional Law: Use of State Funds for Transportation of Children to Parochial Schools," 36 *Ky. L. J.* 324 (1947).

Press Research, Inc. *Warren Robinson Austin.* Washington: Press Research, July 24, 1945.

Pride, David T. "Willis Van Devanter, 1911-1937," in Clare Cushman, ed., *The Supreme*

Court Justices, Illustrated Biographies, 1789-1993, 311. Washington: Congressional Quarterly, 1993.

Pritchett, C. Herman. *The Roosevelt Court: A Study in Judicial Politics and Values, 1937-1946*. New York: Macmillan, 1948.

Rahl, James A., and Kurt Schwerin. "Northwestern University School of Law: A Short History," 55 *Nw. L. Rev.* 127 (1960).

Raymond, Robert L. "The Genesis of the Corporation," 19 *Harv. L. Rev.* 350 (1906).

Recent Case, "Constitutional Law: Freedom of Speech: Right of State to Require Union Organizers to Register," 30 *Minn. L. Rev.* 204 (1946).

Recent Case, "Constitutional Law: Religion: Laws Affecting the Establishment of Religion," 15 *Geo. Wash. L. Rev.* 361 (1947).

Recent Case, "Labor: Regulation of Union Agents," 19 *Tenn. L. Rev.* 494 (1946).

Recent Decision, "Constitutional Law: Aid to Religion: Taxation for Public Purpose," 22 *N.Y.U. L.Q.* 331 (1947).

Recent Decision, "Constitutional Law: Validity of Statute Requiring Registration of Labor Organizers as Applied to Speaker at Peaceable Public Meeting," 31 *Va. L. Rev.* 691 (1945).

Reed, Alfred Z. *Training for the Public Profession of the Law*. New York: Carnegie Foundation, 1921.

Reel, A. Frank. *The Case of General Yamashita*. Chicago: U. of Chicago Press, 1949.

Rehnquist, William H. *All the Laws but One: Civil Liberties in Wartime*. New York: Alfred A. Knopf, 1998.

Renstrom, Peter G. *The Stone Court: Justices, Rulings, and Legacy*. Santa Barbara: ABC-CLIO, 2001.

Ripley, William Z. *Main Street and Wall Street*. Boston: Little, Brown, 1927.

Robinson, David. *The Unitarians and the Universalists*. Westport: Greenwood, 1985.

Robinson, Greg. *By Order of the President*. Cambridge: Harvard U. Press, 2001.

Rockwell, Landon G. "Justice Rutledge on Civil Liberties," 59 *Yale L. J.* 27 (1949).

Rostow, Eugene V. "The Japanese American Cases: A Disaster," 54 *Yale L. J.* 489 (1945).

———. "Our Worst Wartime Mistake," 191 *Harper's Magazine* 193 (Sept. 1945).

Rovine, Arthur. "The Air War and International Law," in Raphael Littauer and Norman Uphoff, eds., *The Air War in Indochina*, 124. Boston: Beacon, 1972.

Rutledge, Wiley. "Address of Mr. Justice Wiley B. Rutledge," 14 *Mo. Bar J.* 96 (1943).

———. "Adventures in the Land of T.B." Unpublished manuscript, A. Rutledge Papers.

———. "Cases and Materials on Business Associations," 26 *Geo. L. J.* 1109 (1938) (book review).

———. *A Declaration of Legal Faith*. Lawrence: U. of Kansas Press, 1947.

———. "Eighty-Six, Forty-Six," 26 *Or. L. Rev.* 69 (1947).

———. "The Federal Government and Child Labor," 7 *Soc. Serv. Rev.* 555 (1933).

———. Foreword, 29 *Iowa L. Rev.* 379 (1944).

———. "Legal Personality: Legislative or Judicial Prerogative?," 14 *St. Louis L. Rev.* 1 (1929).

———. "Peace—Or Another Treaty?," 6 *Tex. B. J.* 255 (1943).

———. Private Corporations. Unpublished typewritten mimeographed draft, Rutledge Papers.

———. "Significant Trends in Modern Incorporation Statutes," 22 *Wash. U. L. Q.* 305 (1937); 3 *U. Pitt. L. Rev.* 273 (1937).

———. "Social Changes and the Law," *Proceedings, American Association of Collegiate Schools of Business* 88 (1934).

———. "Some Premises of Peace," 29 *A.B.A. J.* 623 (1943).

———. "This Is Armageddon," 15 *Pa. B. Q.* 14 (1943).

———. "Two Centuries of the Wisconsin Idea," 1949 *Wis. L. Rev.* 7 (1949).

———. "Two Heroes of the Law," 29 *A.B.A. J.* 425 (1943).

———. "The Varied Carols I Hear," 4 *Fed. B.A. J.* 75 (1946).

———. "What Is the War Doing to Law and Lawyers?," 15 *Ohio Bar* 419 (1942).

———. "Who Has Won the War?," 19 *Tenn. L. Rev.* 97 (1946).

Salmond, John W. *Jurisprudence or the Theory of the Law.* London: Stevens and Haynes, 1902.

Sayles, G. O. *The Medieval Foundations of England.* Philadelphia: U. of Pennsylvania Press, 1950.

Sayre, Paul Lombard. *The Life of Roscoe Pound.* Iowa City: College of Law Committee, State U. of Iowa, 1948.

Schabas, William A. *Genocide in International Law: The Crime of Crimes.* Cambridge: Cambridge U. Press, 2000.

Schlesinger, Arthur M. *The Rise of Modern America, 1865-1951* (1951).

Schlesinger, Arthur M., Jr. *The Age of Jackson.* New York: Macmillan, 1945.

———. *The Age of Roosevelt: The Politics of Upheaval.* Vol. 3. Boston: Little, Brown, 1960.

Schwartz, Bernard. *A History of the Supreme Court.* New York: Oxford U. Press, 1993.

Schwartz, Jordan A. *The New Dealers: Power Politics in the Age of Roosevelt.* New York: Knopf, 1993.

Seligman, Joel. *The High Citadel: The Influence of Harvard Law School.* Boston: Houghton Mifflin, 1978.

Shepherd, George B. "Fierce Compromise: The Administrative Procedure Act Emerges from New Deal Politics," 90 *Nw. U. L. Rev.* 1556 (1996).

Simon, James F. *The Antagonists: Hugo Black, Felix Frankfurter, and Civil Liberties In Modern America.* New York: Simon and Schuster, 1989.

Smith, Bryant. "Legal Personality," 37 *Yale L. J.* 283 (1928).

Smith, Margarete G. *Cloverport,* 1977. (unpaginated compilation in Breckinridge County Public Library, Hardinsburg, Kentucky)

Stadler, Mrs. Ernst A. "Manuscripts," in "New Acquisitions," 26 *Bulletin, the Missouri Historical Society* 166 (Jan. 1970).

Stark, Donald D. "Constitutional Law: Due Process: Establishment of Religion: Presumption of Constitutionality: Application of First Amendment to State Action through the Fourteenth Amendment," 21 *S. Cal. L. Rev.* 61 (1947).

Stevens, John Paul. "Mr. Justice Rutledge," in A. Dunham and P. Kurland, eds., *Mr. Justice,* 177. Chicago: U. of Chicago Press, 1958.

Stevens, Robert. *Law School: Legal Education in America from the 1850s to the 1980s.* Chapel Hill: U. of North Carolina Press, 1983.

———. "Two Cheers for 1870: The American Law School," in Donald Fleming and Bernard Bailyn, eds., 5 *Perspectives in American History* 405. Cambridge: Charles Warren Center, 1971.

Stolz, Preble. "Clinical Experience in American Legal Education: Why Has It Failed?," in Edmund W. Kitch, ed., *Clinical Education and the Law School of the Future,* 56. Chicago: U. of Chicago Law School, 1970.

Sulzer, Elmer G. "Kentucky's Abandoned Railroads, No. 18: 'In Breckinridge, Ohio, and Hancock,'" 15 *Kentucky Engineer* 17 (1953).

Sutherland, Arthur E. *The Law At Harvard: A History of Ideas and Men, 1817-1967*. Cambridge: Belknap, 1967.

Swindler, William F. *Court and Constitution in the Twentieth Century: The New Legality 1932-1968*. Indianapolis: Bobbs, Merrill, 1970.

Taylor, Lawrence. *A Trial of Generals: Homma, Yamashita, MacArthur*. South Bend: Icarus, 1981.

Taylor, Telford. *Nuremberg and Vietnam: An American Tragedy*. Chicago: Quadrangle, 1970.

Thomas, Helen S. *Felix Frankfurter: Scholar of the Bench*. Baltimore: Johns Hopkins U. Press, 1960.

Thompson, Bill. *History and Legend of Breckinridge County, Kentucky*. Privately published, 1976.

Treiman, Israel. "Mr. Justice Rutledge: An Appraisal Based upon His Opinions While on the United States Court of Appeals," 14 *Mo. B. J.* 4 (1943).

Trevelyan, George Macaulay. *The Shortened History of England*. New York: Longmans, Green, 1951.

Truman, Harry S. *Memoirs by Harry S. Truman: Year of Decisions*. Vol. 1. Garden City: Doubleday, 1955.

Tuchman, Barbara. *The Guns of August*. New York: Macmillan, 1962.

Tucker, St. George. "Of the Unwritten, or Common Law of England; and Its Introduction into, and Authority within the United American States," in Clyde N. Wilson, ed., *View of the Constitution of the United States with Selected Writings, St. George Tucker*, 313. Indianapolis: Liberty Fund, 1999.

————. "On the Study of Law," in Clyde N. Wilson, ed., *View of the Constitution of the United States with Selected Writings, St. George Tucker*, 1. Indianapolis: Liberty Fund, 1999.

Twining, William. "Pericles and the Plumber," 88 *L. Q. Rev.* 396 (1967).

U.S. Bureau of the Census. *Fourteenth Census of the U.S.* (1911).

U.S. Department of the Army. *United States Army Field Manual: The Law of Land Warfare (FM 27-10)* (1956).

United States Historical Census Data, Blount County, Tennessee, 1910 (Internet) << http://Fisher.lib.virginia.edu/census >>.

University of Chicago. *Announcements, the Law School for the Sessions of 1938-1939*.

University of Colorado. *Bulletins, School of Law*, 1919-22, 1924-26.

University of Illinois. *Bulletin*, Vol. 35, No. 92, *College of Law Announcement for 1938-1939* (July 15, 1938).

University of Michigan. *Official Publication*, Vol. 40, No. 22, *Law School Announcement, 1938-1939* (Sept. 14, 1938).

University of Minnesota. *Bulletin*, Vol. 39, No. 35, *The Law School Announcement for the Years 1936-1938* (July 6, 1936).

University of Wisconsin. *Bulletin, the Law School Announcement of Courses 1938-39* (Sept. 1938).

Urofsky, Melvin I. "Conflict among the Brethren: Felix Frankfurter, William O. Douglas, and the Clash of Personalities and Philosophies on the United States Supreme Court," 1988 *Duke L. J.* 71 (1988).

———. *Division and Discord: The Supreme Court under Stone and Vinson, 1941–1953*. Columbia: U. of South Carolina Press, 1997.

———. *Felix Frankfurter: Judicial Restraint and Individual Liberties*. Boston: Twayne, 1991.

———. "Getting the Job Done: William O. Douglas and Collegiality in the Supreme Court," in Stephen L. Wasby, ed., *"He Shall Not Pass This Way Again": The Legacy of Justice William O. Douglas*, 33. Pittsburgh: U. of Pittsburgh Press, 1990.

———. "William O. Douglas and His Clerks," 3 *W. Legal Hist.* 1 (1990).

Wagshal, Sam, and John Herling. "The Most Unforgettable Character I've Met," *Reader's Digest*, Jan. 1950, 12.

Warren, Charles. *The Supreme Court in United States History*. Vol. 1. Boston: Little, Brown, 1922.

Warren, Edward H. *Corporate Advantages without Incorporation*. New York: Baker, Voorhis, 1929.

———. *Select Cases on Private Corporations*. 2d ed. Cambridge: Published by author, 1916.

Washington College of Law, American University. *Alumni Directory* (1987).

Watt, Richard F. "The Divine Right of Government by Judiciary," 14 *U. Chi. L. Rev.* 409 (1947).

Westbrook, P. F., Jr. Comment, "Constitutional Law: Establishment of Religion, Due Process, and Equal Protection: Public Aid to Parochial Schools," 45 *Mich. L. Rev.* 1001 (1947).

White, Morton. *Social Thought in America: The Revolt against Formalism*. Boston: Beacon, 1957.

Whitehead, Alfred North. *Science and the Modern World*. New York: Macmillan, 1925.

Whitman, Walt. "Over the Carnage Rose Prophetic a Voice," in *Leaves of Grass*, repr. in *Walt Whitman: The Complete Poems*, 340. London: Penguin, 1986.

Whitney, Brig. Gen. Courtney. "The Case of General Yamashita: A Memorandum." Unpublished manuscript, Nov. 22, 1949. General Douglas MacArthur Memorial, R6-5: SCAP Papers, box 103, folder 6.

Whittlesey, E. *Reeve and Gould's Lectures*. Treasure Room, Harvard Law School Library, 1813.

Wiecek, William M. "Felix Frankfurter, Incorporation, and the Willie Francis Case," 26 *J. Sup. Ct. Hist.* 53 (2001).

———. "The Legal Foundation of Domestic Anticommunism: The Background of Dennis v. United States," 2001 *Sup. Ct. Rev.* 375 (2002).

———. "Untitled Manuscript Study of the Supreme Court, 1941–1953." Unpublished manuscript, 2001.

Wigdor, David. *Roscoe Pound: Philosopher of Law*. Westport: Greenwood, 1974.

Williams, Henry Winslow. "An Inquiry into the Nature and Law of Corporations," 38 *Am. L. Reg.* (n.s.) 1 (1899).

Williams, Tyrrell. "Herbert Hadley and Legal Education," 13 *St. Louis L. Rev.* 136 (1928).

———. "Seventy-Five Years of Legal Education at Washington University," 27 *Wash. U. L. Q.* 477 (1942).

Williston, Samuel. *Life and Law: An Autobiography*. Boston: Little, Brown, 1940.

Wilson, Charles Reagan. "Manners," in Charles Reagan Wilson and William Ferris, *Encyclopedia of Southern Culture*, 636. New York: Anchor, 1989.

Wilson, Clyde N., Foreword, in Wilson, ed., *View of the Constitution of the United States with Selected Writings, St. George Tucker*, vii. Indianapolis: Liberty Fund, 1999.

Wilson, Woodrow. "Woodrow Wilson on the Meaning of the New Freedom" (excerpts from *The New Freedom* (1913)), in Richard Hofstadter, ed., *The Progressive Movement, 1900-1915*, 169. New York: Simon and Schuster, 1963.

Wirtz, W. Willard. "Mr. Justice Rutledge—Teacher of Men," 25 *Ind. L. J.* 444 (1950); 35 *Iowa L. Rev.* 566 (1950).

———. Remarks, in *Proceedings of the Bar and Officers of the Supreme Court of the United States* 20 (April 10, 1951).

Woodard, Calvin. "The Limits of Legal Realism: An Historical Perspective," 54 *Va. L. Rev.* 689 (1968).

Worner, Lloyd Edson Jr. "The Public Career of Herbert Spencer Hadley" (1946) (Ph.D. dissertation, University of Missouri).

Wright, James E. *The Politics of Populism: Dissent in Colorado*. New Haven: Yale U. Press, 1974.

Workers of the Writers' Program of the Works Progress Administration in the State of Colorado. *Colorado: A Guide to the Highest State*. Lawrence: U. Press of Kansas, 1987.

Workers of the Writers' Program of the Works Progress Administration in the State of Missouri. *The WPA Guide to 1930s Missouri*. Lawrence: U. Press of Kansas, 1986.

Workers of the Writers' Program of the Works Progress Administration in the State of Wisconsin. *Wisconsin: A Guide to the Badger State*. New York: Duell, Sloan and Pearce, 1941 (repr. 1954 and 1973).

Yamamoto, Eric K. "Korematsu Revisited—Correcting the Injustice of Extraordinary Government Excess and Lax Judicial Review: Time for a Better Accommodation of National Security Concerns and Civil Liberties," 26 *Santa Clara L. Rev.* 1 (1986).

Yamamoto, Eric K., Margaret Chon, Carol L. Izumi, Jerry Kang, and Frank H. Wu. *Race, Rights and Reparation: Law and the Japanese American Internment*. Gaithersburg: Aspen Law and Business, 2001.

Yarbrough, Tinsley E. *Mr. Justice Black and His Critics*. Durham: Duke U. Press, 1988.

Acknowledgments

Ever since writing a college senior thesis on the life of Edward Mandell ("Colonel") House, Woodrow Wilson's advisor, I have wanted to write a complete biography of someone in our national political life. I explored various ideas with my friend Andrew L. Kaufman, a professor of law at Harvard and biographer of Justice Cardozo, who urged me to contact Dr. David Wigdor, assistant chief of the Manuscript Division at the Library of Congress, for additional suggestions. Dr. Wigdor immediately said, "Justice Wiley Rutledge," a prolific correspondent whose papers, he assured me, contained a book worth writing. I had always respected Justice Rutledge's jurisprudence; I noted with interest that he had been dean of law schools in Missouri and Iowa, states where I had roots; and, it was clear, the justice and his service on the Supreme Court during the 1940s had not received comprehensive study. Encouraged by Professor Kaufman, I decided to pursue Dr. Wigdor's suggestion.

Soon thereafter, upon examining the Rutledge Papers for the first time, I discovered that Victor Brudney, another Harvard professor who had chaired a law school committee on which I served years earlier, had been Justice Rutledge's first Supreme Court law clerk. I also learned that W. Willard Wirtz, a former U.S. secretary of labor whom I have long admired, had begun his teaching career as the first professor whom Wiley Rutledge hired after joining Iowa's College of Law as dean. Secretary Wirtz informed me that two of the Rutledge children, Mary Lou and Neal, lived with their spouses, Dr. Theodore S. Needels and Catherine Le Fevre Rutledge, in the Washington, D.C., area, and that the other Rutledge daughter, Jean Ann, lived in Chapel Hill, North Carolina, with her husband, UNC law professor Daniel Pollitt. All six Rutledge family members were enthusiastic about my project. They also urged me to get in touch with the justice's half-brother, Ivan C. Rutledge, and Ms. Edna Lingreen, secretary to Wiley Rutledge at the University of Iowa, the U.S. Court of Appeals, and the Supreme Court.

I want to underscore my special appreciation for the encouragement, time, and substantive help each of these individuals has given me. Professor Brudney read the entire manuscript, offering detailed, perceptive suggestions for every chapter. He also reviewed Wiley Rutledge's casebook on business organizations and file of law school examinations, guiding me to a deeper understanding of Rutledge as a teacher than I could have come to on my own. Professor Kaufman read the Supreme Court chapters, offering invaluable advice, including organizational recommendations. Secretary Wirtz was particularly helpful in my understanding Rutledge as teacher, dean, and person, and he also made important suggestions for a number of chapters. The family members and Ms. Lingreen, of course, offered recollections and insights that no others could have supplied.

I also wish to recognize, in particular, the special contribution of Dr. Needels. He had photocopied the entire Rutledge collection at the Library of Congress for the justice's family and organized the papers chronologically in notebooks. Usually every third weekend over many months I would borrow three volumes and return three—a time saver of incalculable value to the biographer. Dr. Needels and Mrs. Needels also made available correspondence between Annabel and Wiley Rutledge not found elsewhere, and they have been a major contributor of photographs for this book.

I am indebted as well to many, many others. In addition to Victor Brudney, five Rutledge Supreme Court clerks—the Hon. John Paul Stevens, the Hon. Louis H. Pollak, the Hon. Philip W. Tone, Harry L. Shniderman, and Stanley L. Temko—have given considerable assistance, including numerous interviews, for which I am especially grateful. It was a particular pleasure to participate with Justice Stevens at a retrospective on Justice Rutledge held at Iowa's College of Law in October 1999, and Mr. Temko gave a most useful critique of a chapter. I also appreciate very much the contributions of two Rutledge law clerks from the U.S. Court of Appeals, Professor W. Howard Mann and Richard S. Gibbs. Furthermore, the interviews I conducted with forty former law clerks of the other justices who served with Wiley Rutledge on the Supreme Court were crucial to reaching judgments about Court events and individual justices, including Justice Rutledge. I deeply appreciate their contributions, especially those of Eugene Gressman, Francis A. Allen, Arthur R. Seder Jr., James Marsh, John P. Frank, Charles F. Luce, Gary L. Torre, and Lucile Lomen.

The many interviews of former Rutledge law students at Washington University and at the University of Iowa were of special value, not only in explaining Midwestern law school life in the 1920s and '30s but also in revealing Wiley Rutledge as a person, and as a teacher and dean. I want to acknowledge, in particular, the major contributions of Rutledge's Washington University students Jerome A. Gross, Harold C. Hanke, Abraham E. Margolin, Christian B. Peper, Hy A. Waltuch, Edward B. Greensfelder, and H. Robert Shampaine, and of his Iowa College of Law students Helen B. Ryan, D. Berkeley Smith, Richard C. Reed, Louise Schwilck, Glenn C. Metcalf, Leo E. Fitzgibbons, William F. Morrison, Corwin W. Johnson, Don W. Barker, Thomas H. Birch, Howard M. Remley, Arthur B. Jebens, Irving Lewis, and David M. Elderkin. I also want to thank the other Rutledge friends, acquaintances, and observers who agreed to interviews. Each provided valuable new information or important corroboration, and some—in particular, Herbert Wechsler, Hugo Black Jr., Benjamin Wagshal, C. David Ginsburg, Warner W. Gardner, and Walter A. ("Bill") Steele—revealed hitherto untold tales and offered especially important insights.

Several others read the entire manuscript, namely Joseph F. Brinley Jr., director of the Woodrow Wilson Center Press; Kermit L. Hall, president and professor of history, Utah State University; Melvin I. Urofsky, professor of history at Virginia Commonwealth University; Lucas A. Powe Jr., professor of law and government at the University of Texas at Austin; and Mark V. Tushnet, professor of law at the Georgetown University Law Center. All made many important suggestions for which I am most grateful. Others, too, were kind enough to read chapters or background material that I prepared, offering helpful critiques, specifically Joel Seligman, dean of the Washington University School of Law; Paul D. Carrington, professor of law at Duke University School of Law; William Leuchtenburg, professor of history at the University of North Carolina at Chapel Hill; the Hon. Patricia M. Wald, formerly chief judge of the U.S. Court of Appeals for the District of Columbia Circuit and subsequently judge of the International Criminal Tribunal for the Former Yugoslavia; Christian B. Peper, Esquire, of St. Louis; and Nancy Padgett, librarian of the U.S. Court of Appeals for the District of Columbia Circuit. And Professor William M. Wiecek of the Syracuse University School of Law made available to me his splendid, yet-to-be published study of the *Adamson* decision. To them I am grateful indeed.

Indispensable to this book was the year I spent as a Fellow at the Woodrow Wilson International Center for Scholars in Washington. Led by its director, the Hon. Lee H. Hamilton, the Wilson Center offers a collegial setting in which the fellows become significant resources for one another. My fellows Jill Norgren and Sally Promey were particularly helpful. And the center's staff, especially Rosemary Lyon, Kimberly Conner, Arlyn Charles, Filipinas Naldo-Fontelo, Zdenek V. David, Janet Spikes, Dagne Gizaw, Susan Nugent, Lindsay Collins, Rositta Hickman, Sean McQuitty, and Renee Williams, provided assistance in many ways that helped make the year a delight, as well as a productive learning experience. I was fortunate as well to have outstanding support from four student interns recruited by Dr.

Benjamin Amini of the Wilson Center: Matthew Bongiorno, Adam Hunt, Tai Illig, and Sara W. Smith.

Still others offered assistance of various kinds, including source material, that contributed significantly to this study. They include the Hon. David H. Souter, the Hon. John A. Terry, the Hon. Michael W. Farrell, and the Hon. Avern Cohn; Deans Dorsey D. Ellis and N. William Hines; Professors Ralph E. Morrow, David J. Danelski, J. Woodford Howard Jr., Clark Byse, Morton J. Horwitz, Daniel R.Coquillette, James P. White, Daniel R. Ernst, Ronald D. Rotunda, James J. Tomkovicz, Michael F. Noone, Michael J. Glennon, John Q. Barrett, and Geoffrey C. Hazard Jr.; and Michael Greenwald, John M. McCabe, Peter A. Wonders, Marshall D. Hier, Malcolm Martin, Douglas A. Hedin, Zona F. Hostetler, Daniel M. Gribbon, Eugene R. Fidell, Daniel A. Rezneck, Laurie P. McManus, Lawrence J. Latto, Mark R. Wagshal, Julian Bond, Walter A. Smith Jr., Frank Cicero Jr., Doris Wechsler, Michael D. Eusdan, Thomas G. Yellin, Myra Moore, P. David Westbrook, Paul A. Hemsesath, Gail E. Ross, Roger K. Newman, Stephen Lynagh, and the Rev. Arthur E. Sundstrom.

I also wish to acknowledge with my deepest thanks the contributions of Harriet Rotter and Letty Limbach, librarians at the District of Columbia Court of Appeals, who volunteered to track down countless books and articles for me and provided cheerful encouragement along the way. Terri Santella, deputy librarian of the U.S. Court of Appeals for the District of Columbia Circuit, assisted in a variety of ways for which I am most grateful. Maja Kerch of the Prints and Photographs Division, as well as the staffs of the Manuscript Division, Microform Reading Room, and Law Library at the Library of Congress, were helpful, too, and unusually pleasant, an apt description of the National Archives reading room staff as well. And I am most appreciative of the support I received from Mary Marshall Clark, Jessica Wiederhorn, Jenny Gibson, and others at the Oral History Research Office in the Rare Book and Manuscript Library of Columbia University.

I received considerable assistance from other resourceful persons—assistant deans, librarians, archivists, and other officials: Christine Nugent and Angela Myatt Quick (Maryville College); Robert A. McCown, Earl M. Rogers, Eleanor M. Doling, Erin T. McCroskey, David McCartney, Thomas Eicher, and Jack Wertzberger (State University of Iowa); Philip C. Berwick, Karen Baker, Dorie Bertram, Carole Prietto, Rosemary Hahn, Ann Nicholson, Darryl Barker, and William L. Matthews (Washington University); Edward J. Reisner and Linda Struck (University of Wisconsin); David M. Hays, Marty Covey, Barbara Lichteig, Druet Klugh, and David Gosser (University of Colorado); Ralph Gaebler, Heather Munro, and Keith Buckley (Indiana University, Bloomington); Randy Roberts (University of Missouri–Columbia); Kathleen Franzoni and Kevin B. Leonard (Northwestern University); Kathryn Nilsen, Anne Frantilla, and Karen Jania (University of Michigan); Linda Poe, Bertha L. Ihnat, Sara Sampson, Katherine L. Hall, and Lucy Shelton Caswell (Ohio State University); Karen Blair (University of Chicago); Katherine Hedin (University of Minnesota); Adria P. Olmi, William H. Maher, and John Franch (University of Illinois); Michael Plunkett, Ann L. S. Southwell, Christina M. Deane, and Margaret Hrabe (University of Virginia); Barbara Amato, Kelly W. Waldron, and Janet Conroy (Yale University); David Read, Steven Smith, Lesley Schoenfeld, and David Ferris (Harvard University); Whitney S. Bagnall (Columbia University); Janet Sinda (Duke University); William Benemann (University of California, Berkeley); Susan Lyons (Rutgers University, Newark); Heather Bristow and Lesli Larson (University of Oregon); Audrey Ward (University of North Carolina); David Jaffe, Nathan Dimock, and Eric Johnson (American University); Jill Sayenga (U.S. Court of Appeals for the District of Columbia Circuit); Paul Wallace (U.S. Court of Appeals for the Fifth Circuit); Thomas Schrinel and Candace Cooper (U.S. Court of Appeals for the Fourth Circuit); Lynne Holton and Carmen Kissinger (Supreme Court of California); Fred J. Romanski, Robert M. Yahn, B. Whitten, and Rutha Beamon (National Archives and Records Administration); Karen Burtiss, Robert Parks, and Karen Anson (Franklin Delano Roosevelt Library); Pauline Testerman (Harry S. Truman Library); David Pride, Maeva Marcus, Clare Cushman, Brian Cullinane, and Jennifer Lowe (Supreme Court Historical Society); Gail Galloway, Sheridan L. Hill-Ellis, Catherine E. Fitts, Angela Frank, and Steve Petteway (Office of the Curator, U.S. Supreme Court); Nancy Strobeck (Eastern District of Washington Historical Society); Kirsten Hammerstrom and Martha Clevenger (Missouri Historical Society); Charles E. Brown (Mercantile Library of St. Louis); Roberta May (Breckinridge County, Kentucky, Public Library); Russell Rawlings (North Carolina Bar Center); James Zobel (General Douglas MacArthur Memorial, Norfolk); Jean J. Rickard (the Herb Block Foundation); David Hinshaw (*Charlotte Observer*); Greg Smith (*Iowa City Press-Citizen*); Russell James (*Washington Post*); Pam Scott (*Spokane Spokesman Review*); Hillary Levin and Janalyn Richardson (*St. Louis Post-Dispatch*); Rona Tuccelli and Dalton Zeruk (Getty Images); and Carolyn McMahon (AP/Wide World Photos).

I am indebted to Coralee Paull for research assistance in St. Louis, and to Karen Delaney Gifford for similar help in Boulder, Colorado. In addition, several friends—Aaron Hoag, Harold Feld, William Fennell, Richard Daley, Aaron Weiss, and Kacie Weston—volunteered significant legal and historical research. And I am particularly appreciative of the assistance from Linda Jackson, who has been indispensable in aiding a virtually helpless neophyte produce the kind of computer-generated manuscript that a publisher requires these days.

I am especially grateful to the University of North Carolina Press, in particular Kate Douglas Torrey, the director, who found significance in this biography and has given it high priority; Charles Grench, assistant director and senior editor, who wrote to me at the Wilson Center expressing interest in my project, read the initial manuscript, and has gone out of his way ever since to make publication a reality; Pamela Upton, assistant managing editor, and Kathleen Ketterman, assistant director and marketing manager, and their staffs, who have attended to the production and promotion of the book with great diligence and care; my editor, Fred Kameny, whose knowledge of language and style are awesome, and whose willingness— with great care—to purge the endnotes of their original law school bluebook complexity was an unmeasurable, very special gift; Vicky Wells, rights and contracts manager, Brian Frazelle, assistant editor, and Ellen C. Bush, chief copywriter and catalog coordinator, all of whom helped with other, very important details; and finally, assistant editor Amanda McMillan, who has facilitated virtually everything that goes on between an author and the Press, has helped relieve anxious moments, and has spread good cheer northward day by day.

The many photographs in the book are attributable to the generosity of the Supreme Court Historical Society, which made a significant financial contribution to the press to help the story come more alive in this way. I wish to thank the society—its chairman, Leon Silverman, its president, Frank C. Jones, its publications committee chairman, E. Barrett Prettyman Jr., and staff who took part—for enhancing the biography in a way that otherwise would not have been possible.

I am particularly grateful to five teachers who inspired my interest in history, biography, and the law: Bernard G. Mattson, Samuel H. Beer, Ernest R. May, Waldo H. Heinrichs Jr., and Erwin N. Griswold.

Finally, my wife, Linda, not only has given loving encouragement—even when the project reached the level of obsession—but also has assisted in research, offered sound ideas about organization of the manuscript, and, perhaps of greatest importance, insisted that much material I thought was exciting stuff had to go. Thank you, my dear!

Index of Subjects

Aberdeen, N.C., 33
Abrams, Creighton, 5
Acheson, Dean, 135, 154, 166–67, 211, 213, 396
Adams, John, 173
Adamson, Admiral Dewey, 361
African Americans: Rutledge's evolved view of, 17, 19, 23, 58, 71–72, 185, 418; as Maryville College students, 19, 71; as Iowa law students, 100, 116–17, 337; and equal protection, 237, 384–88; jury exclusions of, 356; and restrictive covenants, 387–88. *See also* Discrimination; Racism
Agricultural Adjustment Act (1933), 123, 141
Albuquerque, N.Mex., 34, 35–38, 48
Albuquerque High School, 34–35
Alien and Sedition Acts (1798), 338
Alien Enemy Act (1798), 316, 373
Aliens, 239, 311, 316, 323, 373, 388
Allen, Florence, 132
Allen, Robert S., 161, 163–64
Allied Control Council, 410
All Souls Unitarian Church (Wash., D.C.), 70–71, 417
Alsop, Joseph, 154, 161
American Bar Association (ABA), 72–73, 77–79, 92, 153, 202; conservatism of, 77, 141; Court appointment poll by, 137; Rutledge speeches to, 188, 393, 394; Committee on Legal Aid, 200; on judge's political activities, 395
American Civil Liberties Union (ACLU), 248, 457 (n. 38)
American Freedom and Catholic Power (Blanshard), 267
American Law Institute (ALI), 51, 73, 122, 144, 234, 276; "Restatements" of common law, 82, 84–85, 121; "Restatement of Contracts," 84, 345
American Legion, 338

American Social Science Association, 56
American University, 202
Anderson, Roscoe, 145, 211, 460 (nn. 19, 21)
Anti-Semitism, 49, 244, 268; and law schools, 78, 115–16, 118; as Supreme Court appointment factor, 138–39, 141, 457 (n. 34); of Lindbergh, 186
Antitrust, 30, 89–93, 292, 377
Appellate jurisdiction, 173–74, 181–82; direct review, 230; statutory interpretation, 311–12; habeas corpus, 411, 414. *See also specific courts*
Apple, Clay, 145, 153, 162–63, 166–67, 178, 181, 183, 185, 187, 206, 207, 211, 298, 344
Apportionment, 383, 390–91
Arant, Herschel, 80
Arnold, Thurman, 145, 154
Article I, 378, 379, 407–10; District clause, 407, 409–10; "legislative courts," 408
Article III, 173, 203, 241; judicial power, 141, 289–91; courts, 173, 203, 408, 410; diversity jurisdiction, 407–9, 410; "citizen" definition, 409
Article IV, 363
Articles of Confederation, 376
Articles of War, 302–3, 306–11, 313, 317–18
Assembly, right to, 260, 269, 271
Association of American Law Schools (AALS), 56, 64, 73, 77, 78, 100, 144, 202; Business Associations Round Table, 119; Committee on Co-operation with the Bench and Bar, 119–21
Atlantic Charter (1941), 393, 394
Atomic bomb, 299, 396
Austin, Warren, 485 (n. 45)
Automobile searches, 357–58, 419

Band of Bucks (Maryville College), 24
Baptist church, 13, 17–18, 35, 40, 69, 70, 71, 346
Barkley, Alben, 133, 135, 211

and Japanese-American cases, 242–43; and military commissions, 302, 303, 308–11, 314–19; and double jeopardy, 360, 365; Fourteenth Amendment incorporation of, 360, 361; and corporate "personhood," 444 (n. 27). *See also* Due process

"Fighting words," 480 (n. 52)

First Amendment, 127, 188–89, 191, 236, 260–71, 334, 419, 420; Fourteenth Amendment incorporation of, 264, 359; "clear and present danger" test, 269, 480 (n. 52); "preferred position," 271. *See also specific freedoms and rights (listed under key words)*

First World War. *See* World War I

Flag salute case, 188, 261, 275

Fleeson, Doris, 325 26, 328

Fleming, John D., 52, 58–59

Forrestal, James, 396

"Four Horsemen" (Supreme Court), 142, 206

Fourteenth Amendment: and corporate protection, 91, 444 (n. 26); Bill of Rights incorporation into, 264, 353, 359–68; and criminal cases, 353, 355–56, 359–61; and selective incorporation, 359; and privileges and immunities, 361. *See also* Due process; Equal protection

Fourth Amendment: and corporate protection, 91; and warrantless search, 357–58, 366–67, 419; and exclusionary rule, 367–68, 472 (n. 8)

France: fall of (1940), 183

Frank, Jerome, 151, 159–61, 165, 170, 457 (n. 34)

Frank, John, 297, 298, 320

Frankfurter, Felix: and Court vacancies, 135, 211–12; barriers to Court appointment of, 137–38, 141, 144–47; and Rutledge, 143, 148–49, 152–57, 162, 197, 219, 261–62, 278; appointment to Court of, 147, 148, 151, 156, 163, 165, 169; judicial philosophy of, 174, 364; and campaign for Learned Hand's Court appointment, 216–17, 219, 278; background and characterization of, 223–24, 327, 344; as Court's conservative wing leader, 223; and Rutledge's opinion-writing style, 232–33, 348, 386–87; and Japanese-American cases, 239, 244, 249, 251, 312; and First Amendment rights, 260, 262, 264, 269, 271; on "preferred position," 271; antagonism toward Douglas, 272–

73, 277, 325; and Court acrimony, 272–78, 281, 282, 344, 345; and Court cases, 273, 292, 310, 316, 322, 349, 386–87; attempted domination of Court by, 277–78; and Chief Justice appointment, 324; Norris-LaGuardia Act analysis by, 332–34; and "frivolous" contempt order, 334, 335, 336; Rutledge compared with, 342–43, 344; and criminal cases, 352–54, 356, 357; on Bill of Rights full incorporation, 360–62; on due process flexible standard, 361–67; on exclusionary rule, 367; on commerce clause, 380, 381, 384; on discretionary equitable power, 390–91; on equal protection, 390; on District of Columbia status, 408, 409–10; on diversity jurisdiction, 410

Fraser, Everett, 119, 121

Fraternities, 16, 115, 118

Frazier-Lemke Act (1934), 123

Freedoms. *See* First Amendment; *specific freedoms (under key words)*

Free enterprise, 91

Free exercise clause, 260–64, 265–66

French Indo-China, 187

Freund, Arthur J., 460 (n. 20)

Freund, Ernst, 96, 298, 444–45 (n. 28)

Fuchs, Hollis, 299

Fuchs, Ralph, 64, 66, 122, 156, 298, 376; Rutledge's friendship with, 61, 344; on Rutledge's Iowa law school deanship, 83; and Rutledge's Court candidacy, 145, 156, 163–66, 169; isolationism of, 184, 186–87; on Willkie candidacy, 185; and Brudney's clerkship, 227; on restrictive covenant cases, 387; and 1948 presidential election, 404, 405

Fujishige, Masatoshi, 2, 6

Fuller, Melville W., 164

Gallup, George, 404

Gallup poll, 187

Gambell, Mose, 19

Gangsterism, 73, 79–80, 153

Garner, John Nance, 152

Garrison, Lloyd K., 119, 127, 133, 150, 154, 162, 493 (n. 9)

Gavit, Bernard G., 279, 338

Gellhorn, Walter, 179

General welfare clause, 76, 123

Geneva Red Cross Convention of 1929, 302–4, 308–10, 313, 410

Geneva Red Cross Convention of 1949, 318–19

Index of Cases